D0848824

ENGLAND'S AMOROUS ANGELS,

1813–1823

Gayle Shadduck

UNIVERSITY
PRESS OF
AMERICA

Lanham • New York

Copyright © 1990 by

University Press of America®, Inc.

4720 Boston Way
Lanham, Maryland 20706

Library of Congress Cataloging-in-Publication Data

Shadduck, Gayle, 1949-
England's amorous angels, 1813-1823 / Gayle Shadduck.
p.   cm
Includes bibliographical references and index.
1. English poetry—19th century—History and criticism.   2. Angels in literature.
3. Bible in literature.   4. Romanticism—England.
I. Title.
PR585.A493S48   1990   821'.709382—dc20   90–39283 CIP

ISBN 0–8191–7856–X (cloth : alk. paper)

The paper used in this publication meets the minimum requirements of American National Standard for Information Sciences—Permanence of Paper for Printed Library Materials, ANSI Z39.48–1984.

Acknowledgements

ACKNOWLEDGEMENTS pages evoke as much derision as published books. Why? Only the Shadow knows for sure. (This, I realize, should have been quoted and attributed. I know not where to look.) True. Pages of this sort *are* places for self-aggrandizement. ("Look at the superstars *I* play with!") Should any of the highlighted luminaries respond in kind, however, one risks invitations to boring cocktail parties, at which one might actually have to speak to one's dream mentors. And hence I give overriding acknowledgement to the following: Thomas Hobbes, Dostoesvsky (in his *Notes from the Underground* period), Chuck Yeager, Dora Marsden (the late editor of the late *Egoist*), Stephen King, Moore (Thomas), a pair of Shelleys (Percy *and* Mary), Colin McEnroe (author of *Lose Weight Through Great Sex With Celebrities (the Elvis Way)*), Pope (Alexander), and Atilla the Hun. I know none of the above, admire all (for different reasons), and am glad to remain a distant admirer.

As for people who have actually helped me with this book, nearly all own titular adornments--and hence I omit all "*D*'s," "Ph.'s," "J.'s," "D.s," or other. I likewise omit admissions into the professoriate; most, if not there presently, have been there and have retired (with or without TIAA/CREF), or have defected; others are going there, in order to retire or to defect. This stuff will be of interest solely to the very few people looking at this book 100 years or more henceforth (presuming no nuclear bomb precludes this possibility), people wanting to know whether or not a human being was behind this book. Yes, one was. I speak *ex gravis*, and hence I speak the truth. Now, to this group, I leave the task of differentiating between the "*D*'s" and the "non-*D*'s" who have helped me, in various ways, with this project--some reading, some refusing to read; some engendering ideas, some sharpening; some keeping the faith; some tracking down hard-to-get materials; one indexing. I give you the following list: Barbara Bellus Upp, Gerald A. Larue, David Keeports, Ellen Caldwell, Laurel Balkema, Linda Goodrich-Giray, Phyllis Van Zant (hint: for laughing at the possibility of anyone's wanting to pursue such a venture), David Keeports, Mary Wright, Ruth Thompson, Lena Ksarjian, Emily Larue, Ruth O. Saxton, Roussel Sargent, Peter Thorslev, Robin Shadduck, Marvin Thompson, David Keeports, Eda Regan, Rachel Miller, Marilyn Shadduck, David Alexander, Jon Jellema (hint: for declining even a personal invitation to hear a public reading of the Preface; good work, Jon!), Penelope Alexander, Jane M. Townley (Thorslev and Townley both warranting full and public absolution, both early acquaintances, neither aware of his/her respective influences), Marjorie Worsdell, and David Keeports. *Gracias*.

And now, I present the legal acknowledgements for permissions to quote from the works listed below.

I wish to thank the following authors, editors, and publishers for their permission to quote extracts from the works here named: Associated University Presses, Cranbury, New Jersey, for portions from Wilfred S. Dowden's edition of *The Journal of Thomas Moore* © 1983-1987; The Belknap Press of Harvard University Press, Cambridge, Mass., for excerpts from *Byron's Letters and Journals*, ed. Leslie A. Marchand, © Editorial by Leslie A. Marchand, 1973, 1974, 1975, 1976, 1977, 1978, 1979, 1980, 1981, and 1982, © Byron, Copyright Material by John Murray 1973, 1974, 1975, 1976, 1977, 1978, 1979, 1980, 1981, and 1982; Columbia University Press, New York, for the extract from Frank Allen Patterson's edition of *The Works of John Milton* © 1931-38; Doubleday, a Division of Bantam, Doubleday, Dell Publishing Group, Inc., New York, for excerpts from James H. Charlesworth, *The Old Testament Pseudepigrapha* © 1983, 1985 by James Charlesworth; Encyclopædia Britannica, Inc., Chicago, for segments of Marcus Dod's translation of "The City of God" by St. Augustine, as printed in Vol. 18 of *Great Books of the Western World*, © 1952 Encyclopædia Britannica, Inc.; The Free Press, a Division of Macmillan, Inc., New York, for portions of Gustav Davidson's *A Dictionary of Angels*, © 1967 by Gustav Davidson; Greenwood Press, Inc., Westport, Connecticut, and Joel H. Wiener for excerpts from *Radicalism and Freethought in Nineteenth-Century Britain: The Life of Richard Carlile*, © 1983 by Joel H. Wiener; Ktav Publishing House, Inc., Hoboken, New Jersey, for excerpts from Leo Jung's *Fallen Angels in Jewish, Christian and Mohammedan Literature* © 1926, 1974; Macmillan Publishing Company, New York, for extracts from *John Milton: Complete Poems and Major Prose*, ed. Merritt Y. Hughes, © 1985; the Modern Language Association of America and Franklin E. Court for extracts from "The Social and Historical Significance of the First English Literature Professorship in England," *PMLA* 103 (1988): 796-807, © 1988; Pantheon Books, a Division of Random House, Inc., New York, for excerpts from *Eve and the New Jerusalem*, by Barbara Taylor, © 1983 by Barbara Taylor; the Soncino Press, New York, for selections from Maurice Simon's edition of *The Zohar* © 1934; Stanford University Press, Stanford, California, for an excerpt from Andrew Rutherford's *Byron: A Critical Study* © 1964; Twayne Publishers, a Division of G.K. Hall & Co., Boston, for portions from *Lamartine*, by Charles Lombard, © 1973; The University of New

Mexico Press, Albuquerque, for selections from *Shelley's Prose*, ed. David Lee Clark © 1964; The University of Pennsylvania Press, Philadelphia, for excerpts from Gerard S. Reedy, *The Bible and Reason* © 1984; The University of Texas Press, Austin, for excerpts from *Lord Byron's Cain*, by Truman Guy Steffan © 1968; and The University of Washington Press, Seattle, for passages from *A Reference Guide to the Literature of Travel*, by Edward Godfrey Cox © 1935, 1948.

England's Amorous Angels,
1813-1823

Contents

Preface

"CAIN WAS RIGHT to kill Abel that he might not have the bore of passing 200 years with him." The quip is Lord Byron's, made sometime shortly after Shelley's drowning in 1822, if Byron's friend Hobhouse reports accurately.[1] Accuracy is not at issue here. The sentiment is. Byron could well have articulated it, given his penchant for haltingly truthful utterances. The label "quip" perhaps unjustly devalues it. Much truth inheres. We think we strive for long life and even immortality, but few of us do, not really. *Cain* and Abel are indeed encumbered by a surplus of time; filial love--at its best a love of security and strength, based upon mutual respect and total acceptance--could well transform into filial contempt, a danger of overly prolonged association. Association throughout all time bodes even worse.

Thomas Moore's *The Loves of the Angels* (1822)--poem of crucial significance to this study and for the earlier nineteenth century--amplifies two sorts of malignancies endemic in immortality. The "Third Angel's Story" proposes what could well happen were lovers assured of the unending love--love literally enduring until time's end--so often longed for when love is new, passionate, and tender. Unending love breeds tedium, indifference, and impatience in Moore's tale--not always (for the lovers know joyous moments, as well as discordant ones), but frequently enough, and at sufficiently unpredictable intervals, to instill a chilling vision of the future as time, droning on, disrupted only by outbreaks of hostility. The specter of loss is an unfortunate, but necessary condition of love, which flourishes only when lovers are forced to attend to the specialness of the other, meditating upon the cherished facets of the other's being that, after death, will be markedly irreplaceable.

Tedium and discord, if unpleasant, may be borne. An even darker side of immortality is identified in the "Second Angel's Story." If we, but not our loved ones, were assured of immortality, "*le'chaim*" would be the most onerous of maledictions. Losing all who are dear to us, remaining alone, estranged, unwanted, horrifies more than death's kind oblivion. This the epic of *Gilgamesh* recognized some 5,000 years ago. At the opening, Gilgamesh, two-thirds' god and one third mortal, tyrannizes his subjects, because he does not know them. Ontogeny isolates him; his ignorance isolates him even further. He relinquishes the right to be a self, equating a role with a being. Rulers rule; they don't participate--or so he is led to believe. He rules, and keeps his distance. He mandates construction of walls that, upon completion, he orders dismantled.

Enkidu, part human, part beast, has had no Mesopotamian Castiglione to train him in decorous behavior; Enkidu does not know that one does not approach a king, or that, upon initial introduction to a king, one seldom ingratiates by aiming to beat the living daylights out of his majesty. In this case, however, Enkidu's unconsidered instincts prove apt; through hand-to-hand combat--and the magic of human touch--the two bond. Together they become wholly human. The man god learns to feel. The man beast learns to think. (Gilgamesh empathizes; Enkidu decides; in the latter case, decision leads to self-sacrifice, needless self-sacrifice, Enkidu unable to apprehend what Gilgamesh's immortality means.)[2] Enkidu dies, but the tragedy is Gilgamesh's--a tragedy ensured by that very immortality that humans often believe they would savor. Upon Enkidu's death, Gilgamesh experiences the despair of an estrangement far more profound than the mere isolation he has previously known. He cannot fight death. He cannot himself die. He can retell his tale of loss, but those who did not love Enkidu cannot care in the way that Gilgamesh cares. He comes to realize that even kings--and even kings engendered by deities--must reverberate with the "still, sad music of humanity." Being human requires participation; the species, to its great sadness, is interdependent. As the epic closes, the king walks about the walls of Erech, ready to be known by others, so that he may be known, ready to love, so that he may be loved. Through inference, this he will have to do time after time, as successive generations die.

I have indulged in this pause for a Mesopotamian reverie because *Gilgamesh* bears thematic pertinence both to the assertion with which this preface opens, and to the poems initiating this study. Byron's assertion obviously derives its wit from its abjectly one-sided perspective--Cain's perspective. Yet behind the wit is another truth--that Cain spares Abel the very malediction he would spare himself. Cain obviously gets the better bargain--or really, he does not. We leave unchallenged the claim that life is preferable to death. The claim is irrational. "Sometimes dead is better." Some want more standard philosophers than Stephen King. As an alternative, I offer Qoh'eleth, who sees life through the same prism shaping the world view of King's narrator in *Pet Sematary*. Neither accepts conventional wisdom or stock response. The preacher, as no one can forget, tells us that the dead are better off than the living, and that, better off still, are those who are never born. This is one of those legacies from Hebrew tradition that orthodoxy--Jewish and Christian alike--would not mind seeing excised.

Another least favorite Old Testament legacy intersects thematically with *Gilgamesh*, and inspired a literary vogue in England spanning the decade between 1813-1823, during which five long poems appeared exploring the subject of sexual union between "sons of God" (usually depicted as angels) and "daughters of men" (represented in most as Cain's female descendants). Some of these poems treat interspeciation as a means of perfecting humankind. (New Gilgameshes could be born to suffer.) Others look, with *Gilgamesh*, at the debilitation stemming from a bereaved immortality. Samuel C. Chew first notices this literary vogue; he identifies five poems derived from Genesis 6.1-4 (or from pseudepigraphic, New Testament, or Qur'anic equivalents)--namely, James Montgomery's *The World Before the Flood* (1813), George Croly's *The Angel of the World* (1820), Thomas Dale's *Irad and Adah, a Tale of the Flood* (1821), and Thomas Moore's *The Loves of the Angels* (1822)--as possible progenitors of the amorous angels populating Byron's *Heaven and Earth* (1823). When his quest for relationships among these poems ends in frustration, he quite rightly drops the matter. By doing so, however, he engendered in me frustrations of a slightly different sort, frustrations that impelled me to set forth on a complicated historical adventure; amusingly, his six pages of remarks in *The Dramas of Lord Byron* (135-40) have fostered the ten chapters I present here.

Ever since Chew introduced them to me, England's amorous angels have been after me. Their very being bewilders. Pope's *Rape of the Lock* offers whimsical angelology--as Moore well knew and appreciated. Cribbing from himself (a fact known only to his closest of associates), Moore's note to line 907 of his *Angels* refers to ". . . an article upon the Fathers, which appeared, some years since, in the Edinburgh Review (No. 47) . . . [in which] there is the following remark:

> --'The belief of an intercourse between angels and women, founded upon a false version of a text in Genesis, is one of those notions of St. Justin and the other Fathers, which show how little they had yet purified themselves from the grossness of heathen mythology, and in how many respects their heaven was but Olympus, with other names. Yet we can hardly be angry with them for this one error, when we recollect that possibly to their enamoured angels we owe the fanciful world of sylphs and gnomes, and that at this moment we might have wanted Pope's most exquisite poem, if the version of the LXX. had translated the Book of Genesis correctly.'"

Moore's lack of concern with the literal accuracy of this disputed passage--

his celebration of the poetic offspring the passage has recently engendered--reflects his freedom from the bondages of "verbal inspiration" and belief in inerrancy troubling a fair number even of his Anglican peers, not to mention masses of those touched by the "Wesleyan Presence." Angels had found serious use in poetry after Pope--but seldom as angels; Blake, for example, uses angels for their metaphoric conveniences. After over a century of retirement among chaemera, demigods, satyrs, nymphs, and, in short, the full complement of superannuated mythological trappings, angels were suddenly conscripted into active service to serious poetry, by poets who, save for Moore, expected that these embodied, male angels would be taken seriously.

Even more surprising is the fact that these angels were indeed taken seriously. For the orthodox, they posed serious theological threats--for highly irrational reasons, glimpsed at above. Objections to these poems are based upon indistinct angelological notions watered down, after being handed down, from Augustine and Aquinas. England's amorous angels--heralded abroad--met with a mixture of plaudits and disdain at home. Moore's poem, in fact, offended enough of the poet's friends and reviewers that Moore voluntarily revised it for its fifth edition, exchanging his pseudo-Judaeo-Christian mythological framework for a Qur'anic cosmology. Reactions to these poems--and particularly to Moore's--suggest a significant shift in sensibilities of the English readership. What was happening?

This book endeavors to answer. One observation warrants particular emphasis. I have suggested that this study leads us to the origins of popular culture as we have come to know it. We see a shift in sensibilities attendant upon an encroaching cost accountant's view of the world--a world of the apportionable self, the self comprised of hours, in a culture encouraging the individual to sell as many of each week's 168 hours of life as the market can find ways of obliviating. It little matters that the basic premise of this world makes absolutely no sense whatsoever--namely, that one must sell hours of life in order to ensure survival. In the earlier nineteenth century, this was coming to be a truth that would soon enough be held self evident. Literature began accommodating this view--readers making more efficient use of their unsold hours when combining entertainment with devotional ends (gone is the Horatian dual purpose of teaching through delighting), writers keeping managers happiest when literature kept workers from contemplating social injustices. While British literature did not yield to the new capitalist officialdom--the bourgeoisie, the factory owners and managers--and while literature and economics remained largely separate, many writers nonetheless capitulated to calls for literature devoid of thought, perhaps accounting for Byron's denial of the commonplace that his was a great age in English poetry.

Literature becomes a mass-market venture of the sort that has become epidemic; poetry and fiction were written for a less educated audience than formerly, an audience whose needs and tastes left poets insecure. (Strangely enough, Lockean epistemology taught poets nothing about measuring tastes and preferences; poets hypothesized, rather than asking.) Of the poems discussed here, many reflect this uneasiness about targeting--and writing for--an untested audience. Peculiarities in some of these poems may be attributed to this discomfort. Other of these works were aimed towards the "literary public," as the more educated audience was termed. Yet the "literary public" was yielding to the sensibilities of the less educated readership--including its readiness to take offense at anything conceivably offensive. These poems serve as an index to a radical change in audience.

In the present study, chapter titles designate their central concerns, Chapters 1-4 providing cultural, theological, and aesthetic backgrounds, Chapter 5 attempting to explain causes for the overwhelmingly warm approval Moore's and Byron's efforts met with on the Continent, Chapters 6 through 10 each exploring one of the English contributions to this vogue. Chapter 1 delineates the problem, or rather surveys the chance confluence of circumstances and events impelling the poets to chronicle concupiscent angels--events and circumstances in economics, theology, aesthetic theory, geology, antiquarian learning, publishing, Malthusian social thought, and, in short, arenas of concern and debate exhaustingly wide in their range.

Chapter 2 surveys the lapse into oblivion angelology had known by the end of the eighteenth century, and points to the threats to personal religious and political freedom inhering in the vaguely recollected notions about angels, honed from discarded ventures into Aquinas and Augustine, that reviewers and even many theologians took to be biblical. Chapter 3 explores a problem that should not have presented itself--namely, the problem and attendant controversies of embodying angels for poetic use in the earlier nineteenth century, a problem solved by/discarded before Milton's *Paradise Lost* first saw print. Chapter 4 surveys the reviewers' reactions to the angel/deluge narratives, contrasting the reviews to prevailing poetic theories of the age. Recipes for sublimity and genre ultimately left poets at odds with their readers--not to mention theorists' claims that poetry gives higher public service in legislating morality and tastes (very old claims, very recently forgotten). Unschooled audiences approached poetry just as they did the Bible--with an impoverished imagination, and with a rigid, literal-mindedness accounting for charges of licentiousness and blasphemy launched against sensual angels. Chapters 1-4, in short, outline reasons for the radical shift in England's readership, a product of what Antony E. Simpson calls "the first modern society."[3] Chapter 5 contrasts English outrage with the overwhelmingly warm approval Moore's and Byron's efforts met with on the Continent.

Each of Chapters 6 through 10 examines one of the English contributions to this vogue, in an attempt to understand why the angels of Genesis 6.1-4 engaged poetic imaginations and pens. As poems, the narratives share the theme of love--forbidden love, love that is either rightly or unjustly forbidden, depending upon the poets' attitudes towards divinely imposed barriers between species and against freedom in human conduct. Byron, as might be suspected, gives his angel/mortal lovers greatest sympathy. Croly and Dale prove merciless. Moore and Montgomery equivocate. All five poems raise the problem of theodicy. All five amplify the significance of the individual by asserting (or, in Byron's case, denying) that individual choices bear consequences touching the whole of the topocosm (Theodor Gaster's coinage from *topos*, for 'place,' *cosmos*, for 'universe,' suggesting a place-world, a world of distinct regions, realms, taxonomies, kinds, and subkinds).[4]

The earliest of these five poems, Montgomery's *The World Before the Flood*, the subject of Chapter 6, proved a boon for Longmans, who saw it through 4 separate editions in 1813. If *The World Before the Flood* shows no direct influence upon subsequent completed narratives based upon Genesis 6.1-4 (or its pseudepigraphic, New Testament, or Qur'anic counterparts), this diminishes nothing of Montgomery's inescapable influence as a critical force--bothered by the question of whether success in poetry may be measured by booksellers' receipts, or whether poetic 'genius' equates with 'success' that no clear gauge suits to measure; his predominance in his age is suggested by George Gilfillan's confession to awe upon seeing notice of an impending lecture by Montgomery, testimony quoted at length in Chapter 1, suggesting how unwarranted has been this poet's laspe into a hole in time. Neither diminished is the significance of Montgomery's ten-book epic on *The World Before the Flood* in allowing angels to proliferate in the 1820's. Montgomery reopened questions about the poet's--even Milton's--right to refashion Scripture into verse, questions settled by the end of Milton's age--settled, then, happily, forgotten.[5] Reviewers were as often outraged as pleased by Montgomery's reworking of Genesis 6.1-4; religious ignorance among even the more educated public reveals itself through the numerous singular condemnations printed in the reviews. (Readers were eager for this new production, as the Longmans were pleased to discover; that Montgomery emphasizes the secular love story informing his sacred poem alarmed those who feared poetry of even the higher kinds was degenerating into "popular literature" in the sense that the term has come to be used.)

Chapter 7 examines the best known of the five poems, Byron's "lyrical drama," *Heaven and Earth*. Still inviting critical comment, Byron's poem--crediting Genesis 6.1-2 as its source--bewilders in its purpose. Recent critics have found it pious, others blasphemous, the majority bewildering. Given the fact that *Heaven and Earth* appeared in the second number of Leigh Hunt's *The Liberal*, Byron's poem enjoyed more publicity--some of it positive--than would otherwise surround a product in an obscure (and, if known, usually maligned) publication, a likely obscurity heightened by the fact that Byron died just months after the poem's appearance, thus silencing those who would have used *Heaven and Earth* as a pretext to launch *ad* or *pro hominem* or partisan sallies. Moore, rather than Byron, proves accountable for the celebrity of his more generally celebrated friend's conceivably stillborn effort. Moore's dire financial straits--his liability (and possible imprisonment) for £6,000 stolen by his agent in Bermuda--made Moore compose unusually quickly, and compose for sales. Salability involved, in part, his fabrication of a literary rivalry with Byron--his apocryphal race to beat Byron to the presses upon learning that his friend was working on a poem on the same subject as *The Loves of the Angels* (this supposedly new confidence by Byron actually in Moore's possession for several years, as Chapter 1 documents). Moore's ploy worked. *Heaven and Earth* and *The Loves of the Angels* invited tandem reviews. Byron's poem drew notice, Moore's became a best seller.[6] In the case of *The Loves of the Angels*--the subject of Chapter 8--poetic success equated partly with success at the booksellers' stalls. Of the five angel/deluge poems, Moore's attracted by far the most attention, and, as Ward points out, received more reviews than any other single poem appearing during the period between 1821-1826.[7]

Despite its contemporary popularity, *The Loves of the Angels* seldom finds current readers--partly because it has been inaccessible for over 50 years, and partly because recent readers have been turned off by Moore's clear profit motive when, hearing objections to (and deaf to praises of) what still to many looked like a source in Genesis 6, Moore overhauled his poem for its fifth edition, ostensibly substituting a Qur'anic for a Biblical cosmology.[8] (While Moore claims Enoch 7.2 rather than Genesis 6.1-2 as his inspiration, the verse in Enoch draws directly from the passage in Genesis.) In part, too, Moore's gift for satire--including self-parody--may account for both contemporary and current difficulty in assessing how seriously Moore's apparatus should be taken in interpreting the text proper.

Moore's second source--rather, his alleged substitution of Enoch for the Qur'an--links *The Loves of the Angels* with the least reviewed (and apparently least known) of the angel/deluge narratives, George Croly's *The Angel of the World*, both poems earning attention in Chapter[8]. Although extensively revised for its second appearance in Croly's collected *Poetical Works*, these revisions apparently go unnoticed in the reviews. (Chapter 9, as well as the Appendix, illustrates just how extensive these changes were.) While the Qur'an may have seemed to Croly a safeguard against the unlettered orthodox, the very presence of the Qur'an itself was coming to be seen as a threat to Christianity.[9]

Chapter 10 takes up Thomas Dale's rendition of the angel/deluge theme in his *Irad and Adah*, the sole poem to derive from a New Testament redaction of Genesis 6.1-4 and its aftermath. That Dale held the first Chair in English literature at London University (as Court has recently shown) should raise no expectations about the intellectual or poetic caliber of his poem. *Irad and Adah* serves as a pretext to deliver afresh the injunction in Amos 4, "prepare to meet thy God!" In prefaces to his collections of 1822 and 1836, of which *Irad and Adah* comprises the longest entry, Dale himself identifies "that class of readers for whom the work is peculiarly designed--the young." This design is a bad idea. Dale's narrative depicts a God more relentless in His anger than even pious orthodoxy would brook in certain reviews; scenes of death luxuriate in the torture, grief, agony, necrophilia, and other, sicker manifestations of sublimity (oddly fused with Sadism by Dale's time) redolent in the age. Dale shows piety taken too far--too far, even, for the repressive decades in which he writes.

The epilogue extends observations about the genesis, and cultural implications, of "popular" literature as we have come to understand the phrase. The appendix presents for the first time since 1823 the original version of Moore's *The Loves of the Angels*, bringing back into view just what it was that all the fuss was about. An accompanying text of Croly's *The Angel of the World* illustrates what the fuss was not about. A third text closes this section, an aborted effort in this kind--Reginald Heber's posthumously printed fragment of *A Poem on the World Before the Flood* written sometime between 1813-1817, in which the Lord Bishop of Calcutta openly takes inspiration from Genesis 6.2 and from James Montgomery's epic for proposing in blank verse an engaging ethical problem about the consequences of the familial head, not the more typical prodigal offspring, using love for self-promotion.

Much more remains to be done with these works. Only Byron's has been discussed at any length. Hopefully, this study will encourage further discussion of five poems that have dropped out of view, much to the detriment of our understanding of the earlier nineteenth century. They are worth the trouble of tracking down. They prove exciting intrinsically-- especially in their informing concepts, and in their implications for individual identity. In short, I hope the angels speak to you. In doing so, they may well set me free.

Notes to the Preface

[1]Marchand, *Portrait* 387.

[2]Neither is Gilgamesh, whose obsession with his own death--perhaps a needless obsession--precludes him from entertaining the possibility that he may not be able to die. He *is* 2/3 divine.

[3]*Wordsworth Circle* 19: 67-70.

[4]*Thespis* 52.

[5]See the reassessment of "Milton" attributed to Thomas Babington Macaulay in *The Edinburgh Review* 42 (Apr. 1825-Aug. 1825): 304-346.

[6]Miriam De Ford 32.

[7]William S. Ward viii.

[8]Most of the revisions actually printed in his fifth and subsequent editions are stylistic, as Chapters 8 and 9, as well as the Appendix, make clear. Revisions in the preface and apparatus cater to those who deride his secular use of angels; detractors still detracted when he converted his angel lovers to Islam.

[9]Evidence of this compels in a review, entitled "Providential and Prophetical Histories," appearing in *The Edinburgh Review* 50 (1830): 228-344.

A Revival of Angels:
Enoch, Orientalism,
Sublimity, and Market Value

EACH AGE HAS its quirks. Popular culture records these. We embrace extraterrestrials. Scholars yet unborn will deride us and will empathize with our hopes to encounter "the other." Some in our age look to alien galaxies for sages who can supply an equilibrium, a harmony, a sense of love, or a set of technological feats that will somehow alleviate our discomfort with the world we find fashioned. Students of our popular culture will look at our articulations of these yearnings with varying degrees of amusement, bemusement, bewilderment, and, at times, kindred longings. I suspect that for these students, Erich van Daniken will rest in peace as an inexplicable monument to human confusion, his theories as dead as the wonders he would demystify. I suspect that Dean R. Koontz will touch that enduringly human something that links century to century--especially in his *Strangers*. In this admixture of sentimentality and science fiction, Koontz's female protagonist, a young physician, Dr. Weiss, willingly allows obsolescence for her years of medical training in order to accept a more promising healing power. This power--initially the gift of aliens--sets as the curative agent the touch of another:

> Soon, when Dom [a writer and friend] had passed the gift to her, as she would ask him to, she'd be able to heal with her touch. More important, with only her touch, she would be able to pass unto others the power to heal themselves. . . . Except for accidents, the specter of death would be banished to a distant horizon. No more would the Annas and Jacobs [her parents] be wrenched away from the children who loved them. No more would husbands have to sit in mourning at the deathbeds of young wives. No more, *Baruch ha-Shem*, no more. (Koontz 526)

Sentimental? Absolutely. Official culture and popular culture stand at odds. Respectable writing eschews sentimentality. Official culture would pass on the bromide that ours is an age of particularly cold, hard, reality. We are tough; we are aggressive; we write plain, utilitarian prose; the memo constitutes our high art form; calligraphy holds value only on a paycheck. Yet we leave cultural traces confirming that yes, we of the microcomputers, missiles, and meltdowns remain frail, vulnerable, human. Death and grief threaten industry. Risking grief renders love a frightening transaction. Failure to love--to risk loss and grief--threatens civilization. Koontz's characters would have it better--love without risk (save for that looming accident not even "the other" can shield us from).

Weiss' sacrifices of her training and of her professional identity prove inconsequential. What she relinquishes of the self, she bequeaths to her kind--out of a love for her kind, and out of a love for herself as a representative of her species. Weiss acknowledges that as a species, we remain interdependent; the ideal of the island self, if realized, would prove appalling and bleak. Love, sacrifice, and identity: Koontz supplies something current, namely, extraterrestrial machinery, in order to highlight dimensions of love long intriguing writers in both popular as well as serious media. The significance of love--for the self and for the species--has found treatment through far odder machinery. However explored, love--individual, physical, transcendent, corporate--unites us through the ages with its potential as a source both of joy and pain; with its power to infuse life with meaning, and to taint a lifescape too bleak to endure; with its unpredictable agency both in strengthening and debilitating the human spirit. As with Koontz's physician, through giving love we find significance in being human. We soar. We suffer.[1]

This ploy is heavy handed; it designs to engage empathy with an earlier age and with its analogously puzzling literary quirk. During the decade in England spanning 1813-1823, five long poems (and one aborted fragment) appeared, exploring sexual union between "sons of God" (usually depicted as angels) and "daughters of men" (often referring to Cain's female descendants). A lapse of nearly seven years separates the publication of James Montgomery's *The World Before the Flood* (1813) and George Croly's *The Angel of the World* (1820), although at some point in this interim, Reginald Heber conceived and aborted what he terms "a something, I know not how to call it, on the same subject with Montgomery's 'world before the flood.'"[2] Thomas Dale's *Irad and Adah, A Tale of The Flood* appeared in the year after Croly thrashed his angel (1821). Thomas Moore's *The Loves of the Angels* (1822) and Byron's *Heaven and Earth* (1823) appeared within eight days of one another.[3] The account of illicit liaisons between angels and mortal women--most familiarly rendered in Genesis 6.1-4--serves as a common backdrop for all six writers. Five of these poems (all save for Dale's) explicitly explore liaisons or attractions between embodied male angels and mortal women. (Croly's *Angel* forces us to stretch our usage of 'mortal.') Four of these poems (all save for Croly's and possibly Heber's, the latter abandoned before world-judgment) have in common the Deluge, drawn more or less directly from the account of Yahweh's world-judgment in Genesis 7. All six poems either glorify or degrade mortal love, usually the latter, the poets generally ascribing to it events leading to the Deluge, or depicting its futility against the backdrop of world-judgment--a futility most leave unmitigated by Promethean ennoblement. All anatomize love, classifying kinds of love, ordering love's hierarchies.

Reasons for this literary vogue remain uncertain, although quite likely, developments in oriental philology, mythography, and archaeology generated excitement for such ventures--excitement enhanced by explorers' accounts of Eastern voyages: scholarship influenced literature. Natural philosophy played a role, as well--particularly geology, whose practitioners debated the accuracy of the Noachian Deluge. In addition, literary theorists and reviewers encouraged this vogue; theorists (usually themselves poets), concerned with maintaining for literature its traditional status as a socially and culturally defining institution, turned to sublimity as a means of moving the masses and to Milton--including Miltonic angels--as an exemplar both of sublimity and of a poet engendering revolutionary verse of acute moral and social significance.

Reviewers (as opposed to theorists) encouraged the anti-eroticism and evangelicalistic fervor infusing the middle-classes, a fervor enhancing amiability towards angels, especially, among the range of possible biblical matters for poetry.[4] These reviewers presumed that through Milton, they knew angels and angelology--accepting what Stuart Curran calls "the twin Scriptures of the Bible and Milton" as mutually orthodox and normative (166), and assuming that both (while actually drawing upon Milton alone) delimited propriety in the poetic treatment of angels. Their readers' evangelicalistic fervor stems from a religious climate responsible for this literary vogue, a religious climate influenced by economic circumstances which poets themselves (not surprisingly) encouraged--the profits from a routinized, industrialized, England creating an audience ready to blend escapist with devotional reading, given the newly strict constraint of time imposed by the factory world; England's amorous angels supplied this dual need. These causes--scholarship, natural philosophy, literary theory and reviews, religion, and economics--created a market for the angel/deluge poems, each of the poets responsible for the works influenced more or less directly and deeply by each of these phenomena. Variations in influence render possible connections among the five completed poems difficult to trace--although above all else, hopes of success at the booksellers' stalls sustained the poets' interest in angels. Commerce became for literature an angel of a special sort; commerce--progenitor of "popular literature" in its current mass-marketing sense--attained unprecedented fecundity towards the end of the eighteenth century, fathering literature of the marketplace with a fervor increasing unto the present day.

As given first in the list of suggested causes for this vogue, several philological, mythographic, and archaeological events renewed interests in old angelologies. If Islam remained anathema to Christian Europe, Qur'anic angels intrigued; interest piqued in the Qur'an itself, Sale's English translation received hospitably upon its first appearance in 1734.[5] Abraham Hyacinthe Anquetil-Duperron's translation into French of the *Zend Avesta* in 1771 availed Europe of the long sealed classic of the East, and introduced the notion of dualism as an alternative explanation for the presence of evil--including evil angels.[6] Anquetil-Duperron stimulated European interest in oriental religious and philosophical writings--supplied to England by Calcutta's Asiatic Society of Bengal, refounded on 15 January 1784, providing English readers with the *Bhagavad Gita* and the *Hitopadesha* (translated by Charles Wilkins in 1784 and 1787, respectively), and with the *Institutes of Hindu Law*, popularly known as *The Laws of Manu* (translated by Sir William Jones and published posthumously in 1794), among others.[7] An intellectual ambience receptive to these writings may be credited to the French encyclopedists of the eighteenth century--Diderot, Bayle, Fourmont, Herbelot (Moore's apparent favorite), and other--their copious and compendious mythographic collections informed by comparatist methodologies and reflecting a syncretism tending to blur distinctions between living religions and old, dead, mythologies. New texts challenged philology--and inspired additions to mythographic compendia--when travellers with archaeological interests succeeded in antiquarian quests. James Bruce's travels in Ethiopia led to his recovery in 1783 of three manuscripts of the Book of Enoch, this pseudepigraphic text a veritable orgy of angels; one of these Bruce donated to the French National Library, and another to the Bodleian Library at Oxford. Richard Laurence's translation "from the Ethiopic MS in the Bodleian Library," appearing in 1821, afforded the first English edition of the complete text of the Book of Enoch.[8] Prior to Laurence's substantial contribution to Old Testament pseudepigrapha, J.

A. Silvestre de Sacy's brief "Notice du Livre d'Enoch," in the *Magasin Encyclopedique* of 1801, shared with the public the excitement of Bruce's discovery. Voltaire's *Dictionary* had thrashed "Les Anges" in 1772, had thrashed them generically and specifically, the very angels celebrated in the passages that Sacy oversaw.[9] The fuller account in Bruce's own *Travels* had come out in 1790 (2: 422). Enoch was all the rage. In short, a confluence of scholarly events brought to the attention of poets the angels and their amorous adventures, which these poets, in turn, adopted and infused with new life.

Uncertainty surrounds Byron's (not Moore's) firsthand familiarity with Laurence's translation; it is certainly doubtful that either had opportunities to scan the text before they wrote their poems. Moore seems to have discovered Laurence just in time--as is suggested by a journal entry from 1 October 1822, recounting a visit to Monsieur Louis Langles', during which Moore's host tells him of the new translation of Enoch. (JTM 2: 585-86)[10] Moore refers to Laurence in a note to his first four editions of the *Angels* (125)--this learning possibly superimposed after the fact of composition. Late introduction to Laurence in no way eliminates Enoch as a mine for Moore's or Byron's angel lore, or as an impetus for their efforts at capitalizing upon intellectual trends. The interested non-specialist could cull information from the French encyclopedias, into which Enoch and his angels earned entry because of their appearances in earlier discovered fragments.[11] "Concerning the Watchers"--a shorthand title attached to some fragments of Enoch--enjoyed a long, Latinate publication history once they were found in the *Chronographia* of Georgius Syncellus, an omnivorous Byzantine scholar of the eighth century A.D. The "Watchers" first came to Western Europe at the pleasure of J.J. Scaliger, who put the fragments to press in 1606; Joannes Ernestus Grabius borrowed them for the *Spicilegium S.S. Patrum*, brought out at Oxford in 1714; in 1715, one of these fragments made its debut in English, seductive under its "Englished" title, *The History of the Angels and their Gallantry with the Daughters of Men, written by Enoch the Patriarch*.[12]

Moore's notes to his first edition of *The Loves of the Angels* do evince his eventual acquaintance with both Laurence's translation and the "Watchers" fragments. In a note to his first four editions of his *Angels*, Moore finds it "lamentable to think that this absurd production [The Book of Enoch], of which we now know the whole from Dr. Laurence's translation, should ever have been considered as an inspired or authentic work" (125). As an epigraph, Moore cites and quotes Enoch 7.2, which corresponds to Genesis 6.1-2. Moore's firsthand knowledge (as opposed to his acquaintance) was possible--yet the superficiality of his discussion renders this suspect; the materials Moore collects about the "Fathers," in his note discussing problems surrounding the translation of Genesis 6.2, are, by Moore's own affirmation, available in Aquinas, and, more recently Caryl and Lightfoot (126 n). Still, Moore's knowledge of the content of (as well as the linguistic difficulties with) the writings of the Fathers led to the *Edinburgh*'s invitation to him to review a new translation of ante-Nicene treatises.[13]

His possible exposure to the "Watchers" suggests itself from his annotation to his reference in the "First Angel's Story" to "the bright Watchers near the throne" (on p. 14; in the first edition, misattributed to p. 12); Moore refers to "'The Watchers, the offspring of heaven.'--Book of Enoch," and adds that "In Daniel also the angels are called watchers:--'And behold, a watcher and an holy one came down from heaven.' iv. 13" (131). As Moore himself suggests, the vernacular Daniel places this name for angels in currency, and, as Moore seems oblivious to, this reliance upon Daniel as a support for--as secondary to--Enoch tends to devalue Daniel (and hence canonical Scripture) despite the poet's defensive concession to imagined orthodox critics.

Eimer disputes Byron's firsthand knowledge of the "Watchers" fragment (22). E. H. Coleridge argues otherwise (PW 5: 279), and evinces Byron's familiarity with the latter from the deployment in both of "the names of the delinquent seraphs (Semjaza and Azazel), and the archangelic monitor Raphael." From this he concludes that "the germ of Heaven and Earth is not in the *Book of Genesis* but in *The Book of Enoch*." This is doubtful--first, because Byron's earlier manuscript draft assigns Michael, and not Raphael, as the intervening archangel (changed at the behest of Gifford, who expressed, but failed to explain, his uneasiness with Michael's appearance, L&J 5: 93); second, because names in *Heaven and Earth* are common property of orientalists, extra-canonical writings, and the Bible itself.

For example, Azazel appears in the Bible, Leviticus 16.3 and 16.5-10, serving as a sin-receiver in the atonement ritual (James 155). This function numbers among, and conflicts with others, assigned him. In Barthelemy d'Herbelot, *Bibliotheque Orientale* (43a), the name, in its root sense of the compounded "*az*" and "*el*," signifying "strong, irresistible, impudent," only sometimes designates a demon (Jung 219). Herbelot elsewhere describes Azazel's celebration in the Talmud for extreme piety and humility (1: 305).[14] In the Talmud itself, *Tractate Yoma*, Azazel assumes a salutary role; Rabbi

Ishmael's school teaches that the joining of these roots "obtains atonement for the affair of Uza with Aza'el" (BT 3: 316). The details of this affair, reiterated in *The Zohar* (1: 99-100), derive from Genesis 6.1-4:

> And so it was, for 'When the sons of God saw the daughters of man,' they fell in love with them, and God cast them down from heaven . . . ; from them then the 'mixed multitude' derived their souls, and therefore these also are called *nefilim*, because they fell into fornication with fair women.

We are back where we started, at the Bible--with a reinterpretation of Genesis 6.1-4 designed to explain the degeneration of "the sons of God" as a result of interspeciation, or cosmic miscegenation. Impure offspring ("the 'mixed multitude'") reflect inappropriate copulation by ill-matched parents. E. H. Coleridge places too much emphasis upon Byron's choice of names in *Heaven and Earth*. Byron likely does not consider disparate reputations borne by Azaziel, Byron here as elsewhere assigning names without announcing hereby any certain exegetic or traditional affiliation.

Byron sometimes violates biblical chronology and sometimes disrupts the integrity of individual biblical stories in assigning names, as is the case with his Anah and Aholibamah, the Cainite sisters in *Heaven and Earth*. Anah finds place in the Edomite lists detailed in Genesis 36.1-43; anachronistic and relocated, the biblical Anah has a significant reason for disqualifying from the rosters of Cainite, female, antediluvians. Anah is male. In Genesis 36.2, he fathers Oholibamah (*Aholibamah* in some versions; 'of the tent of the highest'). In Genesis 36.24, Anah and Aiah are sons of Zibeon: "he is the Anah who found the hot springs in the wilderness, as he pastured the asses of Zibeon, his father." Oholobamah again appears as "the daughter of Anah," here, in Genesis 36.25. Adah in Genesis 36.2-4 is one of Esau's three Canaanite (*not* Cainite) wives, mother of Eliphaz; Genesis 4.19 names an Adah as one of Lamech's wives, mother of Jabal and Jubal. Oholibamah is also one of Esau's three Canaanite wives, mother of Jeush, Jalam, and Korah (Genesis 36.14). Byron habitually assigns names without concern for the doctrinal significance to--or even traditional or chronological accuracy of--his narrative. He similarly excises Ham from his account of the Deluge, substituting Irad, named in Genesis 4.18 as Enoch's son, and grandson of Cain. Byron applies names that defy us to tie him to any interpretation of his source. He frees himself--and us--from theological considerations, demanding that we attend to the singular world and its singular participants interacting in his original composition. (Theme, not theology, arouses interest.) In *Heaven and Earth*, carnal love becomes a means of transcending mortal limitations--at least for a while.

Byron's interest in the Noachian Deluge leads us to geology as another cause for the proliferation of the angel/deluge poems. Geologists had brought attention to the cause of the biblical deluge--sometimes determined to be the result of intercourse between angels and mortal women mentioned in Genesis 6.2 and Enoch 7.2. Geological and biblical records were beginning to conflict, according to various interpreters. James Hutton's *Theory of the Earth* appeared in 1795, asserting that "there had never been a universal flood."[15] Byron's Preface to *Cain* refers to a predecessor of Hutton's, Georges Cuvier, whose *Theory of the Earth*, appearing in English translation in 1813, posits a "series of aqueous catastrophes"--rather than the single catastrophic event of Genesis--as more plausible in accounting for the rock strata observed by geologists. Although Byron's Preface claims that Cuvier does not contradict the Noachian deluge, Moore finds disconcerting Byron's public dissemination of information which Moore feels indeed does challenge Scripture (in Moore's letter to Byron, dated 6 March 1822, LTM 2: 504-505.)

Besides the interest in concupiscent angels aroused by orientalists and geological debates, this literary vogue--flourishing concurrently with an identical vogue in France--finds critical as well as antiquarian reasons for being. Reviewers still asked for sublimity; the English, as had the French, trained themselves to marvel at dark, vast subjects--subjects that hence by reader consent (and some self-hypnosis) were empowered to trigger "the aspirations of the human mind towards the infinite." (Samuel H. Monk 31-32) Sublimity so understood inheres in many biblical subjects, not just for literature, but for exegesis, as well--some of these subjects evincing themselves in a review of the "Beauties of Emanuel Swedenborg[;] Translated from the French. . . ," in the *British Critic* NS 1 (1814): 372-76. The reviewer grants that the *Arcana Coelestia* "will impress us with the idea of grandeur and sublimity," at least "if we can for a moment overlook its temerity," for

> It is really painful to follow these rash and daring flights of a strong but a darkened imagination; it would almost appear that his unhallowed attempts to penetrate into those glories which are in mercy denied to the vision of our weak and frail understanding, had been punished with a judicious blindness, leaving to mankind an

awful example of the judgment of the Almighty upon human folly and presumption. This strange and unnatural jumble of spiritual and carnal notions, which constitutes his description of the state of future bliss, is somewhat relieved by his description of the wisdom of angels, which is a strain of a higher mood. . . . (675)

Sublimity, here, to restate the obvious, appears to equate with "rash and daring flights of a strong but a darkened imagination," involving efforts "to penetrate into those glories which are . . . denied . . . " mortal understanding, leading to futile endeavors to explain the inexplicable--as Byron has been both praised and damned for attempting. Because the angel/deluge poets turn to the heavens for their matter--to the inexplicable, some reviewers almost unthinkingly deem their products sublime (Monk 31-34). Hazlitt, generally expressing aversion to Byron's dramas, likes *Heaven and Earth*, which he finds sublime.[16] Goethe praises Byron's drama for its sublimity.[17]

Sublimity, too, manifests itself in other forms that suggest other impulses, including "the determination of English poets to revel in emotions," as Monk diagnoses this appetite (234). The Englished, Longinian treatise, "On the Sublime" (*Peri Hupsuos*), of course identifies "boldness and grandeur in the *Thoughts*" of a work and "the *Pathetic*, or the power of raising the passions to a violent and even enthusiastic degree," as "genuine constituents of the *Sublime*"; in the earlier nineteenth century, poetic endeavors with vampires and with the undead serve in "raising . . . passions" to such degrees--sublimity of a sort attempted through Keats' *Lamia*, through Byron's cursing vampire in *The Giaour*, and, in France, through the live burial in Lamartine's *La Chute d'un Ange*. Vampiric angels, as well as angels luxuriating over tortures more extreme than the burial nearly killing Lamartine's Daidha, appear throughout the Book of Enoch-- providing Moore, especially, with pseudepigraphic (as well as classical) precedents for the tortures endured by his angels. Vampirism and torture-- characteristic of sadistic, or "snuff" literature--relate the angel/deluge narratives to a reemerging kind. Poe would master the snuff genre in America; Sade ostensibly influences and perfects the kind in France. In actuality, however, Sade's ventures are far less disturbing than even the near-live burial in Lamartine. Sade's *Justine* as an instance of "the forces of terror that exist in the world," as "a sinister and strangely perverse work, in which the righteous suffer and the wicked flourish," and as a "tortured and torturing" masterpiece is grossly misrepresented. (L.T. Woodward,

Introduction, *Justine* (New York: Lancer Books, 1964) 5-11.) Sade's own sexual predilections have become confused with his literary/rhetorical *jeu d'esprit*. *Justine* exemplifies absurdist literature and dark comedy at its finest.[18] Aphorisms, abstractions,and philosophies are discussed in entirely inappropriate settings; such is the stuff out of which Ionesco would grow. Such is the source of the grim humor in Milton's *Comus*, when, after the Elder Brother discusses the degeneration of the infected soul, in descending images leading towards despair, the Second Brother pipes up with "How charming is divine philosophy!"--totally inappropriate in either the colloquial or necromancer's sense of *charming*. The Second Brother has neither been listening to the substance, nor apprehending the fact, of the decline.

In *Justine*, long philosophical discussions preceding and following instances of physical assault, a defense of murder to the announced victim, grounded upon Democritus' ancient atomic theory of matter and the universe, an absurdly inappropriate pride in "virtue" (absurd, because Justine has been raped when knocked out)--these and other patent improbabilities and *non sequiturs* render *Justine* a plethora of absurdist humor, its classification as such further justified by Justine's inordinately high pain threshold (for the woman never seems to feel the boards that bash her, nor any of the otherwise outrageous physical abuse), by her insouciance towards her plight as long as her (non-extant) virtue remains intact, as well as by her immediate readiness to forget every brutality she has endured, even engaging in conversation with its perpetrator--not out of any sick, masochistic love of abuse, but because of her abysmal incapacity to comprehend causality. Justine is one dimensional--dumb, and apparently wanting nerve endings. The violence is of the sort perpetrated against the coyote in Roadrunner cartoons. Nothing can flatten her. In the angel/deluge narratives, however, Lilis' incineration inflicts real agony--physical agony, in opposition to Rubi's enduring spiritual agony at having killed the object of his love. Tortures assail the errant angel in Croly's *The Angel of the World*. The sublimity of agony--of renewed interest in the age--inheres in materials in the Book of Enoch, as well as in related Qur'anic legends, inspiring incidents in the angel/deluge poems.

The poetic quest for innovation--leading poets towards supposedly uncharted terrains--likewise partly accounts for the angel/deluge poems' popularity. Oriental subjects had engaged the eighteenth century, an interest enhanced by sojourners' accounts of China, India, and the Middle East.[19] Byron advises Moore to "Stick to the East," in a letter of 28 August

1813, explaining that "the oracle Stael, told me it was the only poetical policy. The North, South, and West, have all been exhausted; But from the East, we have nothing but S * * * 's [Southey's] unsaleables . . . ," that is to say, *Thalaba the Destroyer* (1801), mined from legends surrounding Islam, and *The Curse of Kehama* (1810), mined from those derived of Hinduism (Letters 3: 101). The letter applauds Moore's research--largely his use of Richardson's *Persian Dictionary*--during the efforts that yielded *Lalla Rookh* (1817), although the fact that Southey's poems proved "unsaleables" hardly linked with certainty oriental subjects and commercial success. And Byron of course wrongly presumes that the Orient remained unmined by 1813. *Rasselas*--not to mention *Paradise Lost*--glare among several counter-assertions. The Oriental Tale had brought Ethiopia into familiarity in the eighteenth-century English drawing room.

Oddly enough, angels themselves were by Montgomery's time far from intrinsically attractive as subjects--exhausted, if not moribund--of no evident use for serious poetry. This becomes clear from their reduction by Pope and by their sheerly metaphoric convenience to Blake.[20] Before *The World Before the Flood* appeared, angels had come to be the dinosaurs of Christian legacy--useless, cumbersome, embarrassing, extinct; no serious poetic treatment of angels had seduced an audience for over a century. Miltonolatry--derived from an unlikely amalgam of the Bible, of select, truncated details about Milton's life, of cliches about the sublime, and of topography snatched from the Oriental Tale--resulted in critical obliviousness to the fundamentally (downright outrageously) radical and unorthodox character, ends and methods of *Paradise Lost*, eclipsing its hubristic proposition (to "assert Eternal Providence, / And justify the ways of God to men"), as well as the implications of the poet's need to so "justify" (namely, that God did not get it right the first time, bungling His theophanies and prophecies on "Horeb *or* Sinai," Milton fortuitously arriving to help God out as both ghost writer and copy editor, rewriting the Bible as it should have been inspired). Miltonolatry instead renewed interests in biblical subjects for poetry, particularly subjects Milton had treated. Angels numbered among these subjects.

By "Miltonolatry" I refer to "the other" Milton known to the age--the Milton perceived by anti-Jacobin (later ardent Tory) proponents of an anti-eroticism "fuelled by Malthusian fears of plebian overpopulation," as Taylor notes (200), recipients of the Wesleyan presence, for whom the poet enjoyed sanctification through a "process," Curran identifies, "by which Milton had been assimilated to Scripture" (163). This Milton bears no

old-style "quantitative" universe; "quantity" in the factory world meant "dollar value."

Cultural reorientation was patently utilitarian. Blake's blighted visions of industrialization became realities. Love--an outgiving, and wealth--an intaking, stem from divergent, and often incompatible, impulses. Wealth won out. Escape routes--dreams outside of a routinized universe--were wanted; England's amorous angels supplied this yearning. Lockean epistemology had given the individual some part in the verifying process; all knowledge begins with the sentient self. Lockean cognition--participatory, populist, by implication even egalitarian in its bases--became markedly effete, affordable only to an educated elite outside of the factories. Epistemology itself became undesirable. In the factory world, verification became unwanted.

Managers brooked fewer questions than God about the operations of their particular universes. From the Lockean faith in the self came the devaluation of the self concomitant with industrial reality; the self did not matter. England became foremost among European nations to encourage-- on a mass scale--the sale of hours of life; contracts replaced quantities in conferring value upon the individual; the individual was inducted into routinized monotony.

The reviewer of *The World Before the Flood* who assigns Montgome- ry's epic to the readership of novels and of "sacred classics"--if at first appalling in his elitist dismissal of the mass of readers, of Montgomery's targeted audience, as a class "below the public"--actually knows his world, and its cost accountant's world view. Hours translate into cash; this translation carries over into off-the-job activity. Reading becomes "cost effective" when it serves more than one purpose--when pleasure finds itself blended with devotional time and moral instruction. (*Quarterly Review* 11 (April 1814): 78-87)

Montgomery's--the first of the angel/deluge poems--supplies escape to two sorts of readers: those who would soar with love tales (and celebrity biography), and those who would have back an older literary world, the world of biblical epic. So suggests an anonymous biographer of "James Montgomery": "The poem had been originally intended to consist of but four cantos," but "when enlarged," at Parken's and Southey's urgings, "a love story was interwoven with it; and the ladies, in sympathising with Javan, read the story as if it was a record of James's own experience" (*Dublin University Magazine* 48 (Aug. 1856): 218). Montgomery's biblical epic, in the judgment of this biographer, attains popularity not simply because of its biblical origin, but also because of the secular emphasis--the same focus that titillates readers of the pulp love novel and that accords the poet, not the poem, the greatest speculative appeal. This answer does not wholly satisfy, either as an explanation for the popularity of Montgomery's or of the other angel/deluge poems. Personal celebrity Montgomery shared with Byron and Moore. Yet Croly and Dale did not enjoy personal celebrity, and the love tales unfolded by Byron, Moore, Croly, and Dale did not all appeal to a dual--or to a triple--audience: that is, to the working class, to the more leisured middle class, and to the educated reader.

Efforts at connecting the five completed poems draw solely from circumstantial evidence.[24] The publication histories of these works suggest more cross-fertilization than Byron, particularly, would care to acknowledge--although, again, connections among the works remain tentative, at best. The five poets do share one insight in particular---namely, that the timing was right for amorous angels. The intellectual, social, economic, religious, and literary circumstances discussed above interested the poets not so much intrinsically but rather for what they portended about the marketability of angel/deluge poems. Personal celebrity--heightened, in Moore's case, by his largely apocryphal account of his rivalry with Byron-- as well as awareness of public interests result in poems pleasing to booksellers as well as readers. The angel/deluge poems constitute "popular literature" in the sense we now use the phrase--literature composed less to expound philosophy or to illustrate poetic principles than to please (for purposes of diversion, or entertainment, rather than for didactic ends) as wide-ranging an audience as can be reached. (As popular literature, Moore's proves the most successful of the five poems.) The details that follow suggest that the poets were vaguely aware of one another's efforts (certainly and documentably aware, in the case of Byron and Moore)--an awareness inspiring imitations not intended to improve, but rather to capitalize upon earlier productions. "Popular literature" and a cost accountant's world view prove a predictable, and financially felicitous, alliance.

Dale's Spenserian heroic narrative seems to have gone unnoticed by both Moore and Byron. Chew points out that the publication of Dale's poem in 1821 corresponds roughly with the date of Byron's initial shipment of his manuscript to Murray; *Irad and Adah* for this reason alone could have had no influence upon Byron, despite what intrigues Chew as an "odd" coincidence, the "recurrence of the name Irad" (140). (The pool of antediluvian names is limited; although granted, Byron chose not to limit himself to the cast or chronology of Scripture.) Dale's pious zealotry in depicting his "JEHOVAH" and Jehovah's (along with the narrator's) luxuriations in the suffering of the doomed--not to mention Jehovah's adamancy in refusing last minute calls for mercy--result in a poem revealing a sadistic sublimity, celebrating a God as patently unacceptable to the later narrators as He would have been to Montgomery. In the sole case of Dale, no literary debt remains outstanding, although Dale himself may or may not have been influenced by Croly's Ovidian erotic epyllion in Spenserian stanzas and by Byron's use of this stanza in *Childe Harold*, at least if we accept the anonymous judgments of "Dale's Irad and Adah" in *Blackwood's* 12 (July-December 1823): 61-67.[25] The reviewer simply presumes that *Childe Harold* engenders all current attempts at the Spenserian stanza, but deems that Dale succeeds "in the management of the noblest stanza in our language," adding that "Most of the poets who write that stanza at present, give too much into imitation of the march which it assumes in Childe Harold--Lord Byron's favourite mixture of hurried apostrophe and interrogation--with lofty and long strains of declamation." Dale avoids this, he feels, unlike "Mr Croly . . . , [who] in his Angel of the World, fell into this errour; for it is always an errour, in a way not quite worthy of his high genius." Dale does better; he "has adhered much more closely to the gentle flow of Spenser himself, and Thomson in the Castle of Indolence" (12: 66-67). Obviously, this implication that Byron influences Croly and Dale has no sound biographical basis; the Spenserian stanza was ubiquitous in the age.

The other narratives intertwine, in rather complex ways.[26]

By the time Croly's and Dale's angels came into being, Montgomery's were old business--his epic owning a good part of the English literati as its copy editors. As his biographer reports (*DUM* 215-17), Southey and Parken commanded from the writer of a proposed brief epic a fullblown ten-book narrative. Without consulting with Montgomery in advance, Parken read portions of Montgomery's manuscript "to a large party, one of whom, writing to Montgomery, mentioned that Southey who had heard something of the intended poem, regretted that it was written 'in the heroic couplet'." Southey recanted upon appeal by the poet (217). (Montgomery never again discussed any of his plans for writing poetry.) Parken encouraged Montgomery's poetical treatment of Scripture, commending his respect for decorum and probability--in short, rehashing the old debate about the poet's responsibility to Biblical "Truth" that had engaged Sidney, Cowley, Milton, and, in fact, the Christian poetic world since at least the fifteenth century

(216). The fact that Southey approved of Montgomery's design would have sufficed as a cause for its neglect by Byron; Montgomery's outmoded epic design, and his narrator's celebration of divine, spiritual love as the sole love worth striving for would have likely proven too cumbersome technically and too innocuous philosophically to entice Byron into direct imitation.[27]

If Montgomery influences the others, this influence comes indirectly, a by-product of his personal celebrity--secured during his exhausting turns on the lecture circuit, and suggestive of the high esteem his age bestowed upon his putatively distinct poetic achievements, achievements encouraging his voice to resonate in his time, echoed inadvertently by contemporaries unaware of the origin of their cadences and tropes. Both his celebrity and his poetic accomplishments engage his contemporary, George Gilfillan. Because Montgomery has lapsed into obscurity, extracts from Gilfillan are worth quoting at length, offering a perspective not immediately evident to the present readers of nineteenth-century poetry. Montgomery's personal appearances were "events"--diminishing in importance in the poet's later years. Gilfillan's narrative, sharing his own excited anticipation of Montgomery's presence, illustrates what "celebrity" meant to the age. Gilfillan's "James Montgomery" in *Tait's Edinburgh Magazine* 13 (1846): 545-48 recounts Montgomery's appeal to a sadly diminished audience as a starting point for evaluating the institution of "poetic readings" by living authors. Gilfillan recalls,

> Some four or five years ago, the inhabitants of a large city in the north of Scotland were apprised, by handbills, that James Montgomery, Esq., of Sheffield, the poet, was to address a meeting on the subject of Moravian missions. This announcement, in the language of Dr. Caius, 'did bring de water into our mouth.' The thought of seeing a live poet, of European reputation, arriving at our very door, in a remote corner, was absolutely electrifying. We went early to the chapel where he was announced to speak, and ere the lion of the evening appeared, amused ourselves with watching and analyzing the audience which his celebrity had collected. It was not very numerous, and not very select. Few of the grandees of the city had condescended to honour him by their presence. . . . The church was chiefly filled with females of a certain age, one or two stray 'hero worshippers' like ourselves, a few young ladies who had read some of his minor poems, and whose eyes seemed lighted up with a gentle fire of pleasure in the prospect of seeing the author

of those 'beautiful verses on the Grave, and Prayer,' and two or three who had come from ten miles off to see and hear the celebrated poet. When he at length appeared, we continued to marvel at the aspect of the platform. Instead of being supported by the *elite* of the city, instead of forming a rallying center of attraction and unity to all who had a sympathy with piety or with genius for leagues around it, a few obscure individuals presented themselves, who seemed rather anxious to catch a little *eclat* from him, than to delight and do honour. (545)

Gilfillan wonders about the ultimate effect of celebrity upon the institution of the poet. "We left the meeting, we remember, with two wondering questions ringing in our ears": "first, Is this fame? of what value reputation, which, in a city of sixty thousand inhabitants, is so freezingly acknowledged?" "But secondly," Gilfillan recalls, "Is not this true, tender, and holy poet partly himself to blame [for his devaluation, evinced by the poor attendance]? Has he not put himself in a false position? Has he not too readily lent himself as an instrument of popular excitement?" More importantly, "Is this progress of his altogether a proper, a poet's progress?" Further, "Would Milton, or Cowper, or Wordsworth have submitted to it? And is it in good taste for him to eke out his orations by long extracts from his own poems? Homer, it is true, sang his own verse; but he did it for food. Montgomery recites them, but it is for fame."

Gilfillan doubts that familiarity has done Montgomery--or poets generally--any good. According to this estimation, the poet's frenzied life on the lecture circuit served but to debase his special status--as a poet of the first rank, Gilfillan insists, for although only "seldom, can he be called a sublime writer," (546), and although "he cannot write an epic" (547), he "has given poetic form and words, to breathings and pantings of the Christian's spirit, which himself never suspected to be poetical at all, till he saw them reflected in verse." (546) (Gilfillan echoes Shelley's pronouncement that the poet may not know when he is being poetical--by which Shelley means prophetic, legislative for a future age; Gilfillan's tolerance for this definition of the poet remains uncertain.) "Montgomery," Gilfillan determines, "is a religious lyrist, and as such, is distinguished by many peculiar merits."[28] His first "quality is a certain quiet simplicity of language, and of purpose," although "his is not the ostentatious, elaborate, and systematic simplicity of Wordsworth; it is unobtrusive, and essential to the action of his mind." Gilfillan summarizes the character of this simplicity when he notes that "in short, his is not so much the simplicity of art, nor the simplicity of nature, as it is the simplicity of faith." The principle impelling him to write ensures this poet's success. (546)

At the close of his assessment of Montgomery's writings, Gilfillan announces that

> we return to James Montgomery only to bid him farewell. He is one of the few lingering stars in a very rich constellation of poets. Byron, Coleridge, Southey, Crabbe, Campbell, Shelley, Keats, &c. are gone: some burst to shivers by their own impetuous motion; others, in the course of nature, having simply ceased to shine. Three of that cluster yet remain, in Wordsworth, Moore, and Montgomery. Let us, without absurdly and malignantly denying merit to our rising luminaries, (some of whom, such as Browning, Tennyson, and Baillie, we hope yet to see emulating the very highest of the departed,) with peculiar tenderness cherish these, both for their own sakes, and as still linking us to a period in our literary history so splendid. (548)

Montgomery here belongs clearly in the first rung of what we term "romantic writers"--Gilfillan unaware of the apportioning of the century that literary historians would achieve. He would allow audiences for new poets (not "young upstarts," but talents in their own right); he would not let Montgomery, with the contemporaries he names, be forgotten. Gilfillan, for our age, provides a useful index to the importance Montgomery held for the poet's own--an importance probably greater than Gilfillan assigns, in fact, since most reviewers trusted that Montgomery *could* "write an epic," receiving *The World Before the Flood* with warmth (if not immediately, often a decade or so after its initial appearance).

Hence Chew warrants attention when he speculates that Byron "probably obtained suggestions" from Montgomery and Croly (137). These suggestions were likely negative. Byron reacts against Croly's more certainly than Montgomery's efforts. Nothing points to Byron's active or familiar engagement with Montgomery's poem; Chew adduces as evidence for Montgomery's influence upon Byron the use by both of the name Zillah (127). (Byron's Zillah is of course in *Cain*, not *Heaven and Earth*.) We do know that Croly was in Byron's thinking well before Byron composed *Heaven and Earth*. His letter to Murray of 12 August 1820 evinces this when Byron quips,

> I say nothing against your parsons--your Smedleys--and your
> Crolys--it is all very fine--but pray dispense me from the pleasure,
> as also from Mrs. Hemans. (Letters 7: 201.)

A similar spirit prompts remarks a few weeks later, when he writes to
Murray on 9 September 1820, "Croly is superior to many--but seems to
think himself inferior to Nobody" (Letters 7: 225). *The Angel of the World*
first appeared in 1820--just in time to save the poet, according to a
Blackwood's reviewer, who laments that the favor and celebrity Croly won
for *Paris in 1815* (1817) "had begun to be forgotten" (*Blackwood's* 8-
(October-March 1820-21): 20-21). This reviewer judges that Croly among
contemporary writers comes the closest "to the burning intense rapidity of
Lord Byron's outlines" (26), a comparison all but certain to annoy Byron.

In addition, Chew outlines similarities between Croly's *Angel* and the
first tale in Moore's *Loves of the Angels* that may reflect Moore's attention
to the earlier narrative. Both tales derive from Qur'anic legends; for his fifth
edition, Moore claims to have extracted his matter from "the Eastern legend
of the two angels, Harut and Marut, as it is given by Mariti, who says, that
the author of the Taalim [commentaries upon the Qur'an] founds upon it
the Mahometan prohibition against wine" (132 n). The legend as Croly
recounts it begins after "the Angels Haruth and Maruth had spoken
arrogantly of their power to resist the temptations which made man so often
culpable." Their pride offended; Heaven commanded that they prove their
invulnerability by actually dwelling among mortals on earth. "A spirit was
sent in the shape of a woman to tempt them; they withstood her seductions,
until she had prevailed upon them to drink wine." Their judgment impaired
by drink, "they gave way to all excesses at once, and completed their crimes
by revealing the words that raise men to angels: for this they were judged,
and exiled from heaven" (Croly 179). Chew notes that both writers focus
upon a single angel rather than recalling the fates of a pair. Both angels
transgress by uttering the unutterable--words empowered to raise a lower
to a higher order of being. Female ocular dazzle proves the culpable agent.

The story is an old one, one retold with varying casts. Women are weak,
but know the secret of overpowering the stronger sex; the Achilles heel
moves up into the groin. The fact that for the earlier nineteenth century this
view of men remains acceptable--still accorded the status of "truth"--
surprises. If the personal liberation ostensibly called for after the Revolution in France proved fatuous, individual liberty became part of the

consciousness of the age--perhaps more strongly in England than in France, for only the French had to see daily and directly that the call for human liberty translated actually into the call for licensing a new ruling class to dominate; only the French intelligentsia remained culturally immersed-- and hence less able to determine that--the so-called revolutionary egalitarianism propounded in the heady 1790's amounted to mere rephrasings of the old *philosophes*, whose utopian schemes required individual adherence to strictly prescribed beliefs and modes of social interaction; a dictatorship grounded in "reason" would supplant a dictatorship backed by money and militia; dictatorship, either way, would prevail. Revolutionary calls of the 1790's or counter-revolutionary constraints at the turn of the century left this basic premise unchanged; the individual is of no consequence; corporate identity--and the power to define that identity--eventuated a bloodbath and repressive responses.

The English were free from the lifescape in France. English Owenite utopianism--if still retaining Enlightenment faith in social engineering as a beneficial and viable ideal--at least predicated itself upon concerns for individual human rights, particularly aiming to emancipate women from Pauline misogyny and Pauline stereotypical encumbrances that no longer tested true.[29] Shelley, in *Queen Mab*, calls for reform that circumvents the need for social engineers--an antiquated "emanation of the Enlightenment," their work grounded on the belief that "the rational application of knowledge could recreate society." (Dakin 23) As Curran points out, Queen Mab's "heroism is of the mind," a mind envisioning a world "free of cultural prejudice," and a future expunged of the "evils of war, empire, and entrenched power." (172) Curran adds that "the mind that contains those realities can also transform them, enacting a peaceful revolution in the public realm congruent with the paradise found within." (172)[30] The fact that Croly could get away with his vision of female beauty astounds, regardless of the general repressiveness of the counter-revolutionary decades. And yet Croly's *The Angel of the World* earns praise from a reviewer in *Ladies' Monthly Museum* S3 12 (Oct. 1820): 216, not for its own sake, but because the poet supposedly "possesses the shining imagination of Byron without his prophaneness, and all the tenderness of Moore without his licentiousness"--judgments (actually, *ad hominem* attacks against Byron and Moore) reflecting middle class sensibilities that enjoyed the backing of the Constitutional Association and its litigious power (sensibilities that, as long as unaffronted by pseudo-sensual imagery, would let pass without notice suggestions about the baseness of male and female nature degrading radically both genders).

As an instance of popular literature--and a reflection of popular culture--Croly's *Angel* bemuses; even as a poem, the underlying misogyny proves groundless; alluring women do nothing. The supposed "pilgrim" is simply within the angels' range of vision; she is where she belongs (were she really mortal), on earth, the place designed for human (and not angelic) habitation. Her being outdoors in no way suggests nascent exhibitionism, just as women in Enoch are unaware of the watchers watching. Female beauty becomes intrinsically dangerous, rendering angels (and by implication mere mortal males) weak slaves to libidinous dictates.

These stories of tainted angels suggest the survival of Judaeo-Christian-Islamic male fear of women based upon an irrational underlying fear that female sexuality looms pernicious as the sole agent through which women can overcome and dominate men. This fear was shared by men of every social and economic class; misogyny stands out grimly as one of the few concerns of the age shared by all classes. What is surprising is that men--at least the men reviewing these poems--take no offense at the implications of misogyny in Croly's *Angel* and in Moore's "orientalized" tale. By implication, both poets consign the male gender to a programmed--yet self-destructive--saga of phallocentric determinism. Male being and conduct is predetermined; a man's life is his own only at certain stages in an ongoing series of erections and detumescences. When their sensors probe and demand, men become slaves to female sexuality. Revised gender assumptions stand sorely wanting.

Moore's later claim to a Qur'anic source remains spurious--downright false. Several of his journal entries of January, 1823, reveal that Moore's revisions in no way reflect his own conviction that the first four editions threaten Christian orthodoxy. His entry of 9 January 1823 reflects his own distaste for the "strong efforts made (which I rather fear may be but too successful in some quarters) to brand it with a character of impiety and blasphemy." His entry from the previous day, 8 January 1823, agrees with the friendly critic who prefers the first two--ostensibly illicit--tales; the third story Moore concedes to be anticlimactic: "it is a falling off after the second" (JTM 2: 614). His growing uneasiness about the first four editions reflects his fear of financial failure at least as much as--probably more than--his fear of offending.

His journal entry of 21 December 1822 includes notice that he has gone "to the Longmans, where I found some copies of my book ready, and sealed up seven or eight of them for Paris." In the same entry, he recounts that he has "within this day or two (in order to enable me to get on for a little while) drawn upon Corry for £100 at three months, meaning to take up the bill myself when it becomes due." Moore's central, lifelong battle may be expressed through an old saw; he may not have robbed Peter to pay Paul, but debt was perpetually his scourge, and he borrowed to pay, and when he paid had to borrow. So it was on this day: "Out of this [£100 from Corry], I gave £40 to Mrs. Power, as a set-off against the sum Power paid for my life insurance" (JTM 2: 596-97).[31] On 26 December 1822, he reports that he is "rather fidgetty about the fate of my book," his fears exacerbated the following day, when Lady Donegal announces that "'I am both vexed and disappointed'" in his *Angels*, adding that "'I think that you will feel I am right in not allowing Barbara [her niece] to read it'."[32] About this response, Moore records, "I never remember anything that gave me much more pain than this. It seemed at once to ring the death-knell of my poem," and

> at once accounted for the dead silence of the Longmans since the publication, for the non-appearance of the second edition, which I was taught to expect would be announced the third day, for Lord Lansdowne's reserve on the subject, for everything. My book, then, (why or wherefore it was in vain to inquire) [was judged] improper ... (JTM 2: 597).

Hence he sends forth his offer to "the Longmans (who have apprised me that I must revise for a fifth edition, as they are almost half through the fourth)," to "make the 'Angels' completely *eastern*, and thus get rid of that connection with the Scriptures, which they fear will, in the long run, be a drag on the popularity of the poem" (JTM 2: 617, reported on 18 January 1823).[33] On 18 January he "received a letter"from the Longmans confirming that "'your idea is the very thing,'. . . encouraging me to follow it by all means" (JTM 2: 617).

Popularity--royalties--and not religion eventuated Moore's transformation, which his journal shows him undertaking in a workmanlike (hardly impassioned) manner. On 19 January 1823 he reports that he "turned over my 'D'Herbelot,' &c., for the project of turning the poor 'Angels' into 'Turks'." This *pro forma* revision had him "reading D'Herbelot'" the following day, 20 January; on the 22nd, he seeks out "Prideaux's 'Life of Mahomet,' and Beausobre's 'Manicheism'" from Lord Lansdowne, who could supply only the second, but who indeed provided Moore with a sort of negative vindication; Lansdowne, Moore notes, "disapproves of my idea of orientalising the 'Angels,' as it would be a sort of avowal that I was wrong in my first plan, which does not strike *him* in the least." After this encounter, Moore determines that he "shall think a little more about it" (JTM 2: 617). Reactions, although mixed, were often enough favorable for a financially solvent poet to let his original version be. As De Ford reports, Moore's poem proves at once to be "a best seller"--partly because of the revision, which drew additional attention to an already well publicized and salable poem (26). Yet Moore went ahead and revised. His awareness of the commercial auspices of a revision emerges in a letter to John Wilson Croker from 23 March 1823, Moore noting that his "corrected Edition is finished--but," he adds, "as there still remains on hand some copies of the 4th Edition (which, when sold, completes the sixth thousand since publication) they [the Longmans] mean to keep the 5th, I believe, for their Trade Sale in April" (LTM 2: 515). Were Moore, or Longman, seriously concerned about the Constitutional Association, surely the remaining copies of the fourth edition would have been pulled.

The revisions themselves aroused some ire--especially Byron's. In a letter from Genoa dated 2 April 1823, Byron deplores Moore's decision (Letters 10: 137-38). He reports that

> They give me a very good account of you, and of your nearly 'Emprisoned Angels.' But why did you change your title?--[something Moore contemplated, but did not execute.] You will regret this some day.

Byron adds that "the bigots are not to be conciliated; and, if they were--are they worth it? I suspect I am a more orthodox Christian than you are; and whenever I see a real Christian, either in practice or in theory ... , I am his disciple." He emphasizes his singular spiritual distinction by closing, "But, till then, I cannot truckle to tithe-mongers,----nor can I Imagine what has made *you* circumcize your Seraphs." Byron apparently uses stronger language when he gossips about this revision. Dr. Henry Muir gives the following report of Byron's evaluation in his *Notes on Byron's Conversations in Cephalona* (L&J 6: 429):

> To-day I rode and dined with Lord Byron. Speaking of Moore, he said he had received a letter from him, when about to publish his *Angels*, telling him that he intends to *castrate* them; that ... it was ... too warm ... : that he meant to alter his style of writing--the world was not yet ready for such luscious fruit. Lord B. added, 'I

told him he was wrong, that he would get no credit by it . . . : that mutilated Angels make Mahometans at best, and never Christian'.

White overestimates Moore's prophetic sensitivity to the temper of the time; White credits the poet with revising his *Angels* because he perceives an encroaching, thoughtless rigidity, an "intense righteousness [that] was an off-shoot of the political reaction against Jacobinism," a "change in moral tone [that] reflected the growth of the middle class"--the ever rising middle class, that with its grim morality "would soon dictate" (169).[34] To dictate, too, would be the "cash nexus" of society, as noted above. This cash-consciousness is the object of one of his reviewers (*Blackwood's* 13 (January-June 1823): 65), who quips, "his piety has a regard to the Row; in his adoration, he never loses sight of his bargain with Longman, Hurst, Rees, Orme, &c."

Salability indeed appears to have prompted Moore to fabricate his apocryphal race to publish his *Angels* before Byron's *Heaven and Earth* saw print. His comments suggest no prophetic consciousness about newly empowered repression. Instead of appealing to morality, he relies upon his own celebrity, and the popularity of celebrity biography. In his first edition, he reports that

> This Poem, somewhat different in form, and much more limited in extent, was originally designed as an episode for a work, about which I have been, at intervals, employed during the past two years. Some months since, however, I found that my friend Lord Byron had, by an accidental coincidence, chosen the same subject for a Drama; and, as I could not but feel the disadvantage of coming after so formidable a rival, I thought it best to publish my humble sketch immediately, with such alterations as I had time to make, and thus, by an earlier appearance in the literary horizon, give myself the chance of what astronomers call an *Heliacal rising*, before the luminary, in whose light I was to be lost, should appear (vii-viii).

This self-effacing apologia has some basis in truth. In his journal for 27 June 1822, Moore reports that he "began a Poem called 'the Three Angels'-- a subject on which I long ago wrote a prose story & have ever since meditated a verse one--Lord B. has now anticipated me in his 'Deluge'-- but n'importe--I'll try my hand" (JTM 2: 564). Moore seems unconcerned.

In actuality, Byron and Moore had been corresponding about the possibility of working with similar materials for nearly ten years.[35]

In the letter advising Moore to "Stick to the East," quoted above, Byron's advice tempts even Byron (who as noted listens to Stael). He adds in this message from 28 August 1813,

> I have been thinking of a story, grafted on the amours of a Peri and a mortal--something like, only more *philanthropical* than, [Jacques] Cazotte's Diable Amoureux [1772]. It would require a good deal of poesy, and tenderness is not my forte. For that, and other reasons, I have given up the idea, and merely suggest it to you, because, in intervals of your greater work, I think it a subject you might make much of (Letters 3: 101-102).

Byron had in fact sent Moore a copy of "Heaven and Earth, a lyrical kind of Drama upon the Deluge" from Pisa on 4 March 1822; Moore, in other words, had in his possession a copy of Byron's lyrical drama nine months before he published *The Loves of the Angels*--which in form, characters, and concept remains patently dissimilar to Byron's effort. Byron did not constitute the "formidable rival" Moore's Preface designates the author of *Heaven and Earth*.

Moore's letter to the Marquess of Lansdowne, from May or June of 1822, suggests Moore's eagerness for concurrent publication--hence greater publicity, hence greater sales. He notes that

> I have been employed since I came to Passy in writing a poem upon a subject which many years since occurred to me, but which was thrown by in the lumber-room of my memory, till (in consequence of Lord Byron's intention of producing something on the same theme) I have again rummaged it out, & mean to publish as soon as the Longmans think it prudent to announce me. (LTM 2: 506-7)

The Longmans thought it prudent to publish just eight days prior to the appearance of Byron's "mystery," Moore's commercial success augured by the 3,000 pre-publication subscriptions welcoming it (Jones 217). Byron's lyrical drama appeared in the second number of John and Leigh Hunts' *The Liberal* on 1 January 1823. Byron, not Croly or Dale, impels Moore to clear out the "lumber-room." Moore's letter suggests his eagerness for noteworthy competition.

Byron's correspondences suggest that Moore alone, and not Byron, thought of the poems as a likely set. Byron refers to *Heaven and Earth*-- which Marchand reports was completed in October, 1821 (Letters 9: 84 n)-- in a letter to Bryan Proctor Waller written from Pisa in 1822: "I, too, have been writing on the *Deluge*; but it is on *Noah*! I wonder if our thoughts *hit*: most probably" (Letters 3: 84).[36] (If Byron considered himself working on a project similar to anyone's, it was likely Waller's deluge, and not Moore's angels, he had in mind.) Byron again confirms that he and Moore have divergent talents, as he asserted in his suggestion in 1813 that Moore develop a tale of a Peri and a mortal lover. Moore likely banked on the differences to enhance interest--and profit.

The Longmans must have in fact kept careful attention to the problems attending publication of Byron's drama. Only close watch would have alerted Moore's publisher to the fact that, let alone the time when, *Heaven and Earth* at last found a vehicle. Byron's letters to Murray and to Kinnaird, 1822-1823, suggest something of the poet's frustration at his publisher's sloth (in Murray's case) and insolvency (in the Hunts').

Byron's letter to Murray from Genoa, 9 October 1822, registers the poet's irritation, as his brusque, direct inquiry about Murray's hesitancy suggests: "Will you say at once--do you publish Werner & the mystery or not?--You never once allude to them." (Letters 10: 13.) He calls Murray "the most timid of God's booksellers" in a letter to Kinnaird. (Yet when Byron learns of impending prosecution against Murray for the publication of *Cain*, he offers to make financial restitution (Marchand, *Portrait* 365-66).) And so Byron's publishing troubles went. Murray was sluggish. Byron made overtures towards the Hunt brothers, as his relationship with Murray soured and strained. Yet still, Byron was not enamoured of Hunt's advertising techniques, as his comments to Murray suggest. Hunt announces that in Byron's new mystery, soon to appear, "demons and the wicked descendants of Cain alone speak and argue as in character they are bound to do.[37] Byron registers contempt: "That d----d advertisement of Mr J. Hunt is out of the limits I did not lend him my name to be hawked about this way" (Letters 10: 13).

After much deliberation, Byron consigns his *Heaven and Earth* to *The Liberal*, thereby seriously curtailing his readership, as Marshall details.[38] When he decided to send to Murray for his manuscript, he learned that "Murray had already printed two thousand copies of *Werner* and *Heaven and Earth* together. Fearing that he would have another *Cain* on his hands . . . , he sacrificed the dual publication and hastily published *Werner*" (Marchand, *Portrait* 393).

Deliberations about when, and if, Byron's "mystery" would appear were clearly out of Moore's ken; solutions were beyond his control. His *Angels* had to be ready and waiting, were he to benefit from comparative reviews. And benefit he did--if not in poetic reputation, certainly in marketability. When the reviews were tallied, Byron's was clearly the favored production, earning praises from even Goethe. This did not matter. Moore's was the single poem, Ward points out, receiving the most reviews during the period between 1821-1826. (viii) Moore's poem sold well. Its literary reputation was of less interest to Moore. Of the five poems explored here, clear lines of relationship may be drawn only between *Heaven and Earth* and *The Loves of the Angels*. And this relationship is as much mercantile as literary.

All five poems share love as a concern. Only Montgomery's narrative offers a program of individual (surprisingly, not societal) salvation through love. The situations surrounding Moore's and Byron's completed poems-- resounding with frustration, ire and irritation--contrast amusingly with the poems' interest in love. England (unlike France) welcomed impotent love poems--poems without intent of explaining or prescribing how society might save itself through love.

As suggested, biblical poetry--specifically, poetic accounts of amorous angels--found encouragement through a middle class readership, touched by an Evangelical presence, maintaining misprisions about Milton, driven to an anti-eroticism by fears of working-class fecundity, looking for escape as well as devotion in their leisure reading--a goal they shared with the working class. Scholarship (antiquarianism and philology) as well as natural philosophy (geological debates) turned attention to angels. In short, a confluence of circumstances account for this literary vogue. Reviewers welcomed England's amorous angels; Milton, after all, had established ample precedents for poetic treatments of the angels. Nonetheless, reviewers in England tended to find these poems either bewildering and purposeless, or offensive--those taking offense seldom able to identify the exact cause of their ire. The cause was obvious--at least to Byron; the problem inheres in the source.

Notes to Chapter 1

[1]This is the message of Vigny's *Moise*, according to Fernande Bartfeld--namely, that it is the human lot to endure at once the grandeur of the self and servitude to another. The other is God in Vigny's narrative; in Koontz's novel, the other causing turmoil is the fragile, human, lover. See *Vigny et la figure de Moise*, Collection <<Themes et Mythes,>> 12 (Paris: Lettres Modernes Minard, 1968) 178. For Vigny, the human sense of debt--servitude--prevents grandeur from maturing. Innate human pride in human grandeur blocks willing submission to useful service. The self and the other war constantly.

[2]Heber's phrase comes from a letter to T.E.S. Hornby, dispatched from Hodnet Rectory, dated 17 May 1819. (Amelia Heber, *The Life of Reginald Heber....* (London: John Murray, 1830) 1: 504-505.) Appendix 3 reproduces the fragment, noting substantive differences between this printing of the work and its even later appearance in *The Poetical Works of Reginald Heber, Lord Bishop of Calcutta*, put out by Murray in 1845; the appendix notes only those accidental variants reflecting typographical errors in the 1830 presentation.

Amelia Heber comments that "The poem on the same subject with Montgomery's 'world before the flood,' was never completed; as a fragment it is here introduced." (1: 506-513). From Reginald Heber's remarks to Hornby, the poem seems to be the product of some point "since my Bampton lectures," collected for publication in 1815, and his appointment as "one of the select preachers" at Oxford sometime after November 1816. (1: 447). He did receive his first invitation to deliver a Bampton lecture in 1812; a composition date as early as 1813--the year Montgomery's text saw print--is not impossible. Heber, at any rate, was briefly caught up in the angel craze; his marriages to his career and to his wife (the order reflecting his time allocations) render unlikely a starting date after 1816, given Heber's augmented personal burdens and professional duties--among these R.J. Nolan's attacks on his printed Bampton lectures, involving Heber in periodical controversies in 1817, the birth in that same year of the Hebers' first child, a daughter Barbara, whose death in the next, his wife attests, he "long and severely felt" (1: 501), coupled with Heber's transfer to Wales (1817), then back to England (January 1819), along with his intensified efforts in 1818 at uniting the Society for Propagating the Gospels with the

Society for Church Missionaries, not to mention his preparation of his hymns for publication--and of his Bishop for reception of these hymns-- in 1819. (1: 442-532). Amelia inserts the fragment in Chapter 16, dated "1819," although quite likely because Heber mentions it in the letter to Hornby in that year; other compositions generated in 1819 Amelia Heber explicitly assigns to occasions and even specific months.

[3]Moore's *The Loves of the Angels* appeared on 23 December 1822; Byron's *Heaven and Earth* first appeared on 1 January 1823, in the second number of The Liberal.

These listed editions have been of the greatest use in the present study:

(1) James Montgomery (1771-1854), *The World Before the Flood*, London: Longman &c., 1813 (lines unnumbered; page numbers cited herein refer to this edition.)

(2) George Croly (1780-1860), *The Angel of the World*, London: John Warren, 1820.

(3) Thomas Dale, *Irad and Adah, A Tale of the Flood*, London: J.M. Richardson, 1822.

(4) Dale, *Irad and Adah*, from *The Poetical Workd of the Rev. Thomas Dale*, London: Charles Tilt, 1836; stanza and page citations from this edition.

(5) Byron, "*Heaven and Earth: A Mystery*," in *The Liberal* 2 (1823): 165-206.

(6) Byron, *Heaven and Earth*, in *The Works of Lord Byron*, ed. Ernest Hartley Coleridge, 7 vols., 1898-1904; rpt. New York: Octagon Books, 1966; quotations and line numbers come from Vol. 5 of this edition, hereafter PW 5: 277-321. [McGann's edition of *Heaven and Earth* has yet to appear in his multi-volume collection of Byron's *Complete Poetical Works*. Vol 5, with *Don Juan*, has recently appeared; *Heaven and Earth* should shortly follow.] Coleridge will still remain useful for the contemporary attitudes he collects and records, as well as for his own attitudes towards the poem.

(7) Byron, *Heaven and Earth*, in *Lord Byron: Selected Poems and Letters*, ed. William H. Marshall, Boston: Houghton Mifflin, 1968, pp. 403-32.

(8) Thomas Moore, *The Loves of the Angels: A Poem*, London: Longman, Hurst, Rees,Orme, and Brown (hereafter "Longmans," as Moore refers to the firm, despite shifting casts of

partners), 1822. This first edition, from which I draw my page citations, actually appeared on 23 December 1822, although the title page imprints "1823" for this and the subsequent four editions (including the revised fifth).

(9) Moore, *The Loves of the Angels: An Eastern Romance*, 5th ed., London: Longmans, 1823. (This revised edition--usually without the emended subtitle--appears in nearly all subsequent printings and editions.)

(10) Moore, *Angels*, in *The Poetical Works of Thomas Moore, Collected by Himself*, 10 Vols., London: Longmans, 1840-1841. The *Angels* appear in Vol. 8: 530-51. (This is the basis for A.D. Godley's edition of *The Poetical Works of Thomas Moore*, London: Oxford UP, 1910; rpt. 1924. Godley contributes a long introductory assessment.)

(11) *The Life of Reginald Heber, D.D., Lord Bishop of Calcutta. . . .* 2 Vols. (London: John Murray, 1830).

(12) Reginald Heber (1783-1826), a fragment of a *World Before the Flood*, drawn from *The Poetical Works of Reginald Heber, Lord Bishop of Calcutta*, London: John Murray, 1845: 97-108.

[4]So enthusiastic was this fervor by 1823, that some would proscribe for the working classes the casual reading of anything save for devotional literature. This attitude emerges in a letter entitled, "On the pernicious Tendency of Novel Reading," appearing in *The Christian Remembrancer* 5 (1823): 341. The author (signing himself "P"), would

beg leave to mention to you an instance, which has lately come within my own knowledge, of the pernicious effects resulting from the circulation of novels among the lower classes. A medical gentleman and myself were sitting one night, about eleven o'clock, engaged in a conversation, when we were suddenly alarmed by the shrieks of a person in distress. We soon found that the shrieks proceeded from a young woman, who had thrown herself into some water near the house. Having procured assistance, we succeeded in extricating her from her perilous situation; and my medical friend soon recognized her as the daughter of a poor but honest labourer in the village. He therefore insisted on accompanying her home; and, on entering the cottage, the first thing he observed on the table, lying open, was a novel, of a most pernicious tendency, which the young woman confessed she had been reading just before she went out to accomplish her desperate purpose. A slate was also lying on the table; and on this slate she had acquainted her parents with the place where they might search for her body on the following morning. It appeared, on inquiry, that the unhappy young woman had suffered some severe disappointment, which had preyed on her mind, and that the pernicious principles inculcated in the novel had a powerful influence in leading her to commit suicide, as the speediest remedy for all worldly trouble.

The young lady was right; suicide constitutes the most expeditious remedy; the author needs to examine his prejudice against suicide almost as clearly as he needs to draw explicit connections between the woman's disappointment (left too vague to link to or find parallels in any given novel) and the "pernicious principles inculcated in the [unnamed] novel" (these principles conveniently not detailed). He appeals to pity, closing with his report that

A fever, occasioned by violent agitation, and by long immersion in cold water, brought this unhappy woman, in the course of a few days, to her grave.

The woman was doubtless ill at the time she decided to die, although "P" may not be faulted for attributing her death to anguish and immersion. Not until the turn of the twentieth century has it started to become "A Vanishing Delusion" that inclement weather can impair health. (In *The Girl's Own Annual* (London, 4 Bouverie St., Fleet Street, ca. 1908) 46.) *The Christian Remembrancer*--eventually one of England's most liberal Christian magazines, by mid-century, defending redaction criticism and denouncing its detractors as nuisances and dangers to the faith--amazes here in its uncritical acceptance of "P's" narrative. The editor replies,

We make no comment on this affecting narrative; but we avail ourselves of it, to press on the Clergy the important duty of establishing parochial libraries in their several parishes, that the people now no longer ignorant, but desirous and able to gather information for themselves, may have within reach books at once interesting, instructive, and wholesome.

The working class has been admitted among England's readership. The editor assumes that these readers would avail themselves of "interesting, instructive, and wholesome" materials if at hand, rather than novels--the very novels that likely have instilled their desire to read. (For later liberal attitudes in the *Remembrancer*, see, for example, the review of "*A Plain Introduction to the Criticism of the New Testament* . . . [and] *Danger to the Bible from Licentious Criticism: Letters to the Sons in the University*. . . ," *The Christian Remembrancer* 43 (1862) 385-421. The reviewer favors textual criticism of all sorts, acknowledges that in settling a text, emendation is inevitable, finds objections to such emendation unreasonable, and finds even more unreasonable attempts to reconcile discrepancies in Scripture. In the *Remembrancer*, Graf, Wellhausen, and the other Tubingen exegetes found a friend. Early in the century, the *Remembrancer* capitulated to the neo-evangelistic masses who demanded a rigorous morality ostensibly derived from the so-called "inerrant" Scriptures, themselves sources of doubt and despair for such as Cowper, as Dale concurs in his Introduction to *Poems: by William Cowper, with A Biographical and Critical Introduction, by the Rev. Thomas Dale* 1: i-xxxv; the Bible for Cowper proved as nearly deadly as the unnamed novel supposedly was for the unnamed young woman.)

[5]There would always be those who would deplore the introduction of the Qur'an to Christendom, as was the case with a reviewer in the *Eclectic Review* 19 (1846): 375-78. In reviewing "Selections from the Kur-an, commonly called in English the Koran . . . . By C.W. Lane," the writer concedes that

> The Kur-an will no doubt remain in the libraries of the curious, as mummies will in their museums, and as the instrument of sustaining the faith of the Moslem through many centuries, as well as of keeping them in a semi-civilized state, it will always be a remarkable and interesting piece of antiquity (375).

He nonetheless finds the text "contemnable," its most positive theological contribution its denial of polytheism (376). Its very presence is a threat to Christianity, and the reviewer wishes that Lane, who derives his anthology from Sale, had gone farther than Sale in declaiming explicitly against the Qur'an (377-78).

Christian competition with Islam may well account for England's groundless assertion that the Scriptures present a coherent doctrine of angels. (If Islam has one, then Christendom must have a better one.) Sale's "Preliminary Discourse," Section 4, insists that "the existence of angels and their purity are absolutely required to be believed in the Koran." Sale adds that "he is reckoned an infidel who denies there are such beings, or hates any of them, or asserts any distinction of sexes among them." He continues that "they believe them to have pure and subtil bodies, created of fire; that they have various forms and offices, some adoring God in different postures, others singing praises to him, or interceding for mankind." In addition, "they hold that some of them are employed in writing down the actions of men; others in carrying the throne of God and other services." (Sale I: 98) This doctrine, as the following chapter suggests, comes close to the Christian doctrine of angels presumed to inhere in Scriptures. Neither the Bible nor the Qur'an makes much of angels; doctrines of angels develop through eisegesis.

George Sale's edition of *The Koran* which, as noted, first appeared in 1734 went through several editions, and was available both to Byron and to Moore. Sale's remains predominant among English translations well into the nineteenth century. Sale is not without detractors--particularly recent detractors. In his edition of *The Holy Qur'an: Text, Translation, and Commentary*, A. Yusef Ali objects to Sale's predominance:

> George Sale's translation (1734) was based on Maracci's [Moore's "Marati"] Latin version, and even his notes and his Preliminary Discourse are based on Maracci. Considering that Maracci's object was to discredit Islam in the eyes of Europe, it is remarkable that Sale's translation should be looked on as a standard translation in the English-speaking world, and should pass through edition after edition, being even included in the series called the Chandos Classics and receiving the benediction of Sir E. Denison Ross (xii-xiii).

The point is well taken. Maracci, a Confessor to Pope Innocent XI, published his Latin Qur'an in 1689, which he dedicated to Leopold I, the Holy Roman Emperor, presenting as well an accompanying volume entitled *A Refutation of the Qur'an* (xii). The only other complete text available in English to the earlier nineteenth century was A. Ross' translation of Ryer's French translation of 1674 (xii). Sale hence retains authority throughout the nineteenth century.

Those who condemn Sale's edition as a threat to Christianity seem needlessly skittish. Conversion was hardly effected by the volume. Sale himself was biased against the text. Fear of the Qur'an pointed towards fear for the status of the Bible, which, had declaimers taken note, had been thoroughly demolished well before Hume.

[6]See Moses Stuart, 152-54, for a mid-nineteenth-century account of Zoroastrian angels and their relation to their Christian counterparts. Stuart considers the notion of dualism inferior to the Christian notion of the second coming, the Messianic Kingdom promised in Revelation.

[7]Schwab 51-52.

[8]This discovery and translation are mentioned by Samuel C. Chew and Richard D. Altick in Albert C. Baugh, ed., *Literary History* 1172n. Charles Gill edits and discusses *The Book of Enoch, the Prophet, Translated from an Ethiopic Ms. in the Bodleian Library, by the Late Richard Laurence*, 1883; R.H. Charles retranslates, edits, and thoroughly annotates *The Ethiopic Version of the Book of Enoch, Edited from Twenty-Three Mss. together with the Fragmentary Greek and Latin Versions*, 1904, including a history of the discovery, loss, and rediscovery of various of these fragments and manuscripts. Charles' edition of *The Apocrypha and Pseudepigrapha of the Old Testament*, 2 vols., 1913, presents nineteenth-century attitudes towards the subject and history of non-canonical Old Testament writings. More recently, James H. Charlesworth has edited *The Old Testament Pseudepigrapha*, 2 vols., Garden City, New York: Doubleday, 1983-1984. Useful, too, are Frank Crane and Rutherford H. Platt, Jr., *The Lost Books of the Bible* [bound with] *The Forgotten Books of Eden*, 2 vols. in 1, 1926; rpt. 1973. Unless otherwise indicated, quotations from Enoch in the present study come from Charles, *Pseudepigrapha*; quotations from The Testament of the Twelve Patriarchs come from Crane and Platt.

[9]Isaac, in Charlesworth (1: 8), remarks that Bruce's introduction of the Enoch mansucripts into Europe caused no sensation until Sacy published his "notice," which contained the "first published excerpts together with Latin translations of chapters 1, 2, 5-16, and 22-32. Chapters 6-11 most directly interest students of Genesis 6.1-4; Byron and Moore would have had Sacy's translations to work with, even if neither enjoyed sufficient time to consider in great detail Laurence's 1821 translation into English. See Sacy, *Magasin Encyclopedique* 1 (1801): 382-83

Ironically, Bruce himself was unable to enjoy this excitement. Because of the extra-canonical status of Enoch, Sir William Jones dismissed the importance of Bruce's retrieval. In a letter to H. A. Schultens, dated October 1774, Jones writes of Bruce,

He is as well acquainted with the coast of the Red Sea, and the sources of the Nile, as with his own house. He has brought with him some Aethiopic manuscripts, and among them the Prophecies of Enoch, but to be ranked only with the Sybilline oracles. (From Cox 1: 389)

(Cox points out that "The far more remote sources of the White Nile were as yet hardly suspected," 1: 389.) Jones here vindicates the integrity of Bruce's account--doubted to the point that in 1800, Robert Wharton published his *Observations on the Authenticity of Bruce's Travels*, Newcastle. (Cox 1: 389) Suspicion of the account arose partly because of overpreparation by Bruce (in using navigational instruments and in medical knowledge --sources of jealousy among his peers, who would have preferred a Wiley Post's insouciance towards possible mishaps to a Howard Hughes' preparation for every conceivable contingency, Post's and Hughes' divergent attitudes towards their transcontinental flights representing the divergent attitudes of eighteenth-century explorers, some of whom decided to go and immediately and simply left port, others of whom decided then stewed and prepared before finally setting sail), partly because of underpreparation by Bruce (for he failed to note the accounts of Jesuit explorers who had discovered the same, then thought to be "source," of the Nile), and partly because of sheer jealousy on the part of Bruce's acquaintances.

Cox does not explicitly identify jealousy as a reason Bruce withheld his account. Jealousy seems indicated, however, when Cox reports that

Bruce especially prepared himself for this arduous task by acquainting himself with conditions in Africa, with instruments for taking bearings, and with some skill in medicine. This latter accomplishment proved to be very valuable, as, by saving some of the members of the royal family of Abyssinia from the smallpox, he gained needed favors.

He also was ruthlessly satirized upon his return. Horace Walpole, for example, alludes to Bruce's favorable reception by Abyssinian royalty when, in a letter to Mann dated 10 July 1772, Walpole writes that Bruce "has lived in the Court of Abyssinia, and breakfasted every morning with the maids of honor on live oxen." The live oxen were never invited.

Cox adds that "Besides he was of magnificent proportion physically and a superb horseman, both of which factors assisted him to the good graces of the Abyssinians," and, Cox should have added, both of which factors destined him to be hated by a good number of his native Englishmen. Cox reports that "Fanny Burney (*Early Diary*, Aug. 22, 1774) comments on her first meeting with Bruce: 'His figure is almost gigantic. . . . I cannot say that I was charmed with him; for he seems rather arrogant, and to have so large a share of good opinions of himself, as to have nothing left for the rest of the world but contempt.'" The novelists' remarks must be taken with some skepticism. This is the sort of thing Burney's *Evelina* writes of the noblemen upon first meeting them. This is the sort of thing that two decades earlier, Richardson's Pamela records as her first impression of Mr. B. In short, this is the sort of thing women conventionally entered in their diaries upon their first meeting handsome and accomplished men. (This initial distrust becomes predictable by the time Austen's Elizabeth Bennett scorns Darcy throughout much of *Pride and Prejudice*.) Burney later shows concern--albeit modified--when she records "how Bruce was mortified by the general doubt of his accuracy in his relation of his adventures, for which his 'Swaggering' manners were in part responsible." (Cox 1: 388-9)

Cox suggests that

He might have spared himself some attacks on his veracity had he bettered his information on what had been accomplished by the Jesuits in their better expeditions and explorations for the source of the Blue Nile. Probably he really believed at the time he stood bare-footed by the little fountain whence flows out the beginnings of the Blue Nile, that he was the first white man to gaze on and identify these waters. As it was, the doubts of the truthfulness of his narrative were numerous, occasioning several 'parodies,' best known of which are the *Travels of Baron Munchausen*. This also caused him to delay for many years the publication of his journals. The result of his travels was a very great enrichment of geography and ethnography.(Cox 1: 388-9)

His countrymen seemed willing to accept his accomplishment only of his named goal of finding the source of the Nile--a goal already accomplished (or so it was then thought), his venture hence doomed to failure in the eyes of his countrymen before Bruce ever left port. Cox adds that "Among the satires on Bruce is Peter Pindar's 'Complimentary Epistle to James Bruce, Esq.'" (1: 389) English uncharitability resulted in delayed access to the "very great enrichment" of knowledge the journals do contribute. James Bruce's *Travels (in Egypt, Arabia, Abyssinia, and Nubia), to discover the Source of the Nile, in the Years 1768-1773* appeared in 5 Vols. in London, 1790 (with a concurrent publication--Cox reporting some designating this the "better" edition--coming out in Edinburgh in the same year). Another London edition, in 8 Volumes, with a Life and Notes by A. Murray, appeared also in 1790. This was abridged by Samuel Shaw, who brought out an official second edition, in 7 Volumes, in Edinburgh, 1804. Translations into French (Paris, 1790) and into German (Leipzig, 1790-91) gave the Continent greater access to the *Travels*. Despite those who prevented Bruce from enjoying the excitement either of his journals or of the Enoch manuscripts he returned with, these journals, once published, were very popular, as this publication history suggests. Too late for Bruce to enjoy was the dissipation of the doubts about his credibility--as well as the excitement generated by the Enoch manuscripts in spite of their extra-canonical standing--by the time Laurence undertook his translation. (Cox 1: 388-9)

[10]Moore's familiarity with the Targum Onkelos (the Aramaic para-phrase of the Old Testament) came about likewise just when needed for a note to his first four editions of his *Angels*. In a journal entry from 9 October 1822, Moore remarks that he "went to the Bibliotheque du Roi in the morning: introduced by M. Langles to M. Vonpradt [both of whom supply him with references, as his journal and notes indicate], and took a hasty look at the Tarquin of Onkelos." Moore's angelological--and general Christian--learning must not be underrated, however. He has an unusually wide-ranging command of biblical commentaries, and wrote a considered review of the "Fathers," that is, of Boyd's translation of the *Fathers of the Church* for the *Edinburgh Review* 24 (1814): 58-64.

[11]Moore shows particular familiarity with Herbelot. In "the project of turning the poor 'Angels' into 'Turks,'" he finds that he "turned over my 'D'Herbelot, &c" (JTM 19 January 1823, 2: 617). The complete text of 1 Enoch 6-7.5 is very accessible to the educated of the age, appearing in full in Voltaire's *Philosophical Dictionary* (1772), see Voltaire, *Works*, trans. and ed. Morley, Smollett, et al., 42 Vols., 9: 201-202.

[12]Mentioned in PW 5: 302.

[13]See Jordan, *Upright* 237.

[14]Herbelot de Molainville, Bartheleme d'. See entry, "Azazil":

Azazil. *Anges* qui sont *les plus proches du trone de Dieu*. On les joint ordinairement avec les *Asrafil* qui sont les *Seraphins*, & avec les *Kerubiin ou Cherubins*. *Saadi* fait mention des Azazil dans la preface de son *Bostan*: cependent il les comprend tous collective- ment sous un nom singulier; car il dit que, lorsque Dieu distribue des graces, Azazil dit avec une *profonde humilite: C'est de vous seul, Signeur, que tout notre bonheur depend.*

The proximity of this order of angels to God, and their traditional commin- gling with the seraphim and cherubim, gives precedent for Byron's designating his Azaziel a "seraph" (a singular term in *Heaven and Earth*). The plural designation inhering in the name "Azazil" becomes important to Moore's argument that "Rubi" signifies an entire class, or order, of angels.

[15]According to Loren Eiseley, Hutton held that "there was observable in the buried shell-beds of the continents, which had long been taken as evidence of the Deluge, only signs of subsidence and renewed uplift which were part of the eternal youth of the world." Eiseley is quoted in James R. Moore, "Charles Lyell and the Noachian Deluge," in *The Flood Myth*, ed Alan Dundes (Berkeley: Univ. of Calif. Press, 1988), 405-25; quotation on p. 408. John Playfair simplified the "ponderous, abstruse style" of his friend's, Hutton's, prose, publishing the popularization, *Illustrations of Huttonian Theory*, in 1802. Hutton, through Playfair, rankled theologians. Georges Cuvier accommodated both Scripture and the evidence of rock strata when he "posited a series of aqueous catastrophes to account for the major rock strata" (403), and appeased at least some theologians. Debate flourished when Charles Lyell divorced geology from Genesis, thereby "draining the flood of its influence" in his *Principles of Geology*, 3 vols. (London: John Murray, 1830-34) (411). Lyell's Uniformitarianism is predated by Hume's optimistic materialism, according to Gillespie, as quoted by Moore (411 n); both Lyell and Hume insist that "fabulous tales of former ages" are not supported by "experience by more enlightened ages" (411 n).

Those expositors insisting upon the "verbal inspiration" of every "jot and tittle" of Scripture were beginning to see the threats geological and paleographical discoveries could pose. A reviewer of "Cuvier *On the Theory of the Earth*" in the *Edinburgh Review*(23: 468), although generally favoring Cuvier's discussion, accepts without question the second duration of the flood proposed in Scripture, namely, 150 years (as opposed to 40 days and 40 nights). In the "*Geology of the Deluge*," a review of William Buckland's *Reliquiae Diluvianae* in the *Edinburgh Review* (39: 202-203) asks for caution when applying scientific discoveries to biblical testimony. This reviewer insists that

> whatever may be thought of the prudence of attempting to connect the discoveries of natural science with the sacred writings, it is evident, that if the testimony of science can ever be of any value in support of Scripture history, the physical researches, by which it is intended to confirm the historical statements, should be most strikingly independent.

Evidence must not be forced to "prove" Scripture. Scientific research must freely proceed without a predetermined use for new found data. The writer of this review names Hutchinson and Catcott among those either bolstering weak evidence or presenting conclusions of scientific inquiry in language better suited to the Christian polemicist; he respects Linnaeus for presenting evidence with stylistic restraint. This reviewer insists, as a general principle, that "above all, the tone and language of such an inquiry should betray no desire to force conviction, by connecting it with extrinsic connections; or by holding up to obloquy, those who dissent from our opinions, or reject our arguments." (39: 198-199) This call for restraint quite obviously went largely unheeded.

[16]In *The Spirit of the Age*, from William Hazlitt, *Lectures on the English Poets [with] The Spirit of the Age: Or Contemporary Portraits*, Introd. Catherine Macdonald Maclean (New York: Dutton, 1967) 240. Hazlitt is not taken with Byron's dramas generally; *Heaven and Earth*, however, "is the best. We prefer it even to *Manfred* . . . : in the dramatic fragment published in *The Liberal*, the space between Heaven and Earth, the stage on which his characters have to pass to and fro, seems to fill his Lordship's imagination; and the Deluge, which he has so finely described, may be said to have drowned all his own idle humours."

[17]PW 5: 280-81.

[18]Stephen Werner would disagree with this view of *Justine*. (273-75)

[19]Raymond Schwab discusses the literary gleanings from Hinduism 354-62, and Moses Stuart offers an account of the influence upon Christian angelological thought of the *Zend-Avesta* 153-54.

[20]Just how lightly the eighteenth century intellegentsia had taken angels becomes clear from one of Pope's jestingly overlearned notes to *The Rape of the Lock*, I: 145 (Butt 233). To the line "The busy *Sylphs* surround their darling Care," Pope deliberately overburdens with his observation that

Antient Traditions of the Rabbi's *relate, that several of the fallen Angels became amorous of Women, and particularize some: among the rest* Asael, *who lay with* Naamah, *the wife of* Noah, *or of* Ham; *and who continuing impenitent, still presides over the Women's Toilets.* Bereshi Rabbi *in* Genes. 6.2.

For the origins of this tradition surrounding Naamah, see Graves and Patai 64.

[21]"Moore's Loves of the Angels," *Blackwood's Edinburgh Magazine* 13 (January-June 1823): 63-71. Quotations come from 64-65. Montgomery refers to Milton frequently in justifying his amplification of scripture in *The World Before the Flood*, as is discussed in Chapter 3, below. The pseudo-orthodox, pseudo-critical notions dashed off in awe of Milton come from a readership apparently unmoved to investigate Milton's ends in *Paradise Lost*.

This neglect of a writer so often praised moves a reviewer of "*Joannis Miltoni*, Angli, de Doctrina Christiana . . . translated by Charles Summer" in the *Edinburgh Review* 42: 304-346 to lament that "it is to be regretted that the prose writings of Milton should, in our time, be so little read" (42: 315)-- just after the reviewer has acknowledged that Milton "stood up for divorce and regicide" (42: 314), this latter conviction far from welcome in England in the 1820's, or in any age. (42: 314) This reviewer, in fact, seems unaware of the outrageousness even of Milton's poetical assertions in *Paradise Lost*. He remarks that those who recoil at Milton's "heterodoxy" in *De Doctrina*-- at Milton's "Arianism" and "notions on the subject of polygamy"-- should have anticipated these views by gleanings of both in *Paradise Lost* and in the poet's own biography. The reviewer highlights even more Miltonic heterodoxy: "The opinions which he expressed respecting the nature of the Deity, the eternity of matter, and the observations of the Sabbath, might, we think, have caused more just surprise." (42: 305) But this reviewer would move his contemporaries quickly away from these ideas, explaining that he need not discuss them because these views are outdated, adding that even if some readers are inclined to consider them, Milton's Christian doctrine surely will have no impact on contemporary active faith--Milton's views will not "edify or corrupt the present generation," for "the men of our time are not to be converted or perverted by quartos." (42: 305) In 1825, when this review was written, Milton offered a wealthy mine of ideas for rebels, not for mainstream Anglicans. The reviewer's defense of one who held himself a fit prophet to "assert eternal Providence," and "to justify the ways of God to men"--as if God had not done it quite well enough in Scriptures, warranting a new prophet, John Milton, to edit the Bible for God--fought weakly in aiming to celebrate Milton's contributions to mainstream Christianity.

[22]Douglas Dakin, "The Historical Background: Revolution and Counter-Revolution 1789-1848," in *Byron's Political and Cultural Influence on Nineteenth-Century Europe: A Symposium*, ed. Paul Graham Trueblood (Atlantic Heights, New Jersey: Humanities Press, 1981), 1-32. Dakin's discussion of the subsumption of cottage industry by the industrialized factory leads to his suggestion that with the resulting higher standard of living came the resulting lower significance of the individual (22).

Taylor documents the total disregard for the well-being of the individual during the competitions among tailors thriving in England after the Napoleonic wars. Hours became drastically longer; output--not workers--occupied managers. The sweatshop came into being. (102)

[23]This is of course the world view currently approved by official culture in the United States. Only a culture respecting the cost accountant's perspective would tolerate an article such as one appearing in *The Atlantic Monthly* in the mid-1970's, teasing with a cover question asking, if memory serves, "How Much is a Human Life Worth?"--and daring to answer, in all earnestness--with a calculated dollar amount, the mean of what an average individual can expect to earn within his or her lifetime. This is the world of the M.B.A.--the university legitimizing what the factory supervisor and the sweatshop owner have been doing since the onset of mass industry, namely, manipulating people, brainwashing (if need be bullying) them into wanting to make money for a company totally indifferent towards them, denying this indifference by overpaying professional corporate liars: M.B.A.'s bearing the exalted titles of Human Resources Development Managers, and Public Relations Officers. As in the earlier sweatshops, individuals are inter-changeable. And even universities--even small liberal arts colleges-- emulate this nightmare world view Blake excoriated in his *Songs of Experience*. College Professors are not College Professors, but rather FTE's. College Presidents are happy only if acknowledged as CEO's. College Officers seem oblivious to the fact that colleges and manufacturing plants belong on different planets. Ours is a world that discourages love--not just at the plant, but in the university. (Human Resources Development Officers insist that our workplaces--businesses or colleges--can be extensions of our families; with layoffs, tenure denials, ruthless axings, and the like, few of us can withstand the constant specter of grief that confronts us if we buy this

corporate myth.)

Antony Simpson claims that during the "period between 1789 and 1832" we can see "the creation of the first modern society." He adds that "by a modern society, I mean one whose focal point is the urban, not the rural, setting," asserting that "Economic growth centers on trade and industry, and not on agriculture." In terms of the implications of this phenomenon for the people impacted by it, Simpson suggests that

> Dominant standards of behavior in the workplace and in public reflect middle-class concerns: restraint, deferred gratification, moderation, acquisitiveness (can I say greed?), thrift, rationality, and the like. (*Wordsworth Circle* 19: 67.)

[24]All five narratives were popular--Croly's, the least popular, came out in a second edition in 1830. Undoubtedly, Byron and Moore, at least, knew of the three earlier narratives; the English romantic poets, unlike their French counterparts, stuck to their annoying belief in their abject original- ity, failing to acknowledge debts. See Chew, *Dramas*, 127-37, and PW 5: 280- 81.

Independent origins for the narratives are suggested by one of Montgomery's nineteenth-century biographers, who in his unsigned estimation of "James Montgomery" denounces other of "Montgomery's biographers [who] are anxious to shew that passages of the World before the Flood, suggested some stanzas in Byron's Childe Harold" (*Dublin University Magazine* 48 (Aug. 1856): 218-19).

[25]The writer insists that "There is nothing in this," pronouncing that

> Resemblances, no doubt, exist, but are wholly accidental; between the World before the Flood, and Moore's Veiled Prophet there are also some resemblances. It is impossible in these cases to say that such resemblance is the effect of imitation on the part of the poet whose work may have been the last published, and it is trifling with the subject of poetry to point out details of the kind (219).

This point is well taken. The time-honored tradition of literary borrowing--conscious or inadvertent--has been approved by practice, and has been documented to the point of dullness. Poets borrow from everyone everywhere, often unaware that they do so. From an historical standpoint, the resemblances still invite notice.

[26]The lives of the five poets placed them in different circles; cross-fertilization and possible direct influence seem likely only between those who banded together. Dale, as a contemporary reviewer insists, numbered among "academic," as opposed to "professional," poets; the Reverend Dale (as with the Reverend Croly) travelled in different circles and attracted different audiences than Byron and Moore. Dale had a chance to share his predilection towards religious and political conservatisim with the young intellectuals of the time by virtue of his successful application of 14 November 1827 to serve as the Chair of English Language and Literature at University College, London. (Court *PMLA* 103: 796.)

The results of the establishment of this Chair merge with the results of the establishment in 1800 of The Society for the Suppression of Vice, founded "not by middle-class Dissenters . . . . but by gentlemen of the highest rank." (Simpson 70) Simpson explains that this Society's "motivation was not religious, but political," observing that "this very sophisticated organization understood clearly that those who encouraged the rejection of the Established Church and its doctrine must next begin to question the morality of the established social order." Simpson adds that "political struggles take place over ideas," and that "to rule efficiently, a class or group must persuade the population at large to accept the rightness of its ideas--this is the Gramscian notion of hegemony--and in this was to rule by persuasion, which is more effective, and certainly less expensive, than rule by force." (70) Dale's Chair at the University College, London University, gave him an official podium from which to instill belief in the "rightness" of the status quo.

Montgomery--imprisoned during his younger years for supposedly publishing seditious material--was in his later years in demand by conservative and liberal audiences alike. His revival of the Biblical epic left him on call for communities of preachers, Sunday school societies, and a copious assortment of religious assemblies; his *Pelican Island* (1837)--based on the dubious analogy between humankind's ignorance of the birth, life, and death of generations of pelicans, and "heathen" humankind's ignorance of God and hence life--enhanced his reputation among the devout; he was still in demand for his lectures on poetry, for which he won acclaim when he worked for Parken on the *Eclectic Review*. His tact with would-be new poets--and his kindness towards unsolicited manuscripts--left him with little time for reading of his own choosing. In short, Montgomery travelled in nearly all circles, rightly complaining to Parken (in a letter Parken died before receiving) that he seldom had time to stop and comprehend what his senses would impress upon his mind; his composite acceptance of Scripture and Locke remains a bit odd, but he doubtless had no time to think about the inconsistency. Travelling in all circles left him a member of none; he died exhausted from years on the lecture circuit. Montgomery was known to and called upon by so many that he had scarcely the time to be known as a self.

[27]Obviously, Byron follows epic conventions in *Don Juan*, but in doing so mocks them as vehicles for conveying truth--which, by the time he wrote his theology of the self, remained a mere abstract fabrication; truth was no more.

[28]Beutner finds this assessment a misrepresentation 2201A.

[29]For a detailed treatment of these ideas, see Barbara Taylor, *Eve and the New Jerusalem: Socialism and Feminism in the Nineteenth Century* (New York: Pantheon Books, 1983), especially 15-18. See also Judith Scheffler, "Romantic Women Writing on Imprisonment and Prison Reform," *Wordsworth Circle* 19 (1988): 99-103. For a contrast of how Wesleyan enthusiasm worked to enforce justice and the law in the eighteenth century, see Randall McGowen, "'He Beareth Not the Sword in Vain': Religion and Criminal Law in Eighteenth-Century England," *Eighteenth-Century Studies* 21 (1987/88): 192-211; McGowen observes that the preachers in the later part of the century "provided a model of the good magistrate who was the active guardian of justice in the world, who showed mercy when he could but was not afraid to use terror when he had to." (211)

[30]In a way, these hopes recall Davenant's hope of supplying in *Gondibert* models of ideal Christian behavior for "the most necessary men"--men of the courts, colleges, and churches--who, Davenant believed, would eagerly embrace the right and virtuous alternatives to present corruption. By reforming their behavior, these leaders would become inspirations for all realms of society; all would imitate their reforms, through a sort of "trickle-down" theory eventuating the triumph of good through the collect of individuals embracing good, as manifested in their behavior. Davenant's Preface to *Gondibert* (1650) is action oriented rather than thought oriented. But in emphasizing the responsibility of the individual to reform himself or herself as a means of ultimate social reform, Davenant anticipates Shelley's notion of a peaceful revolution effected by an aggregate of individuals.

[31]Financial setbacks and security become an ongoing refrain in the autobiographical prefaces Moore prefixes to each of the 10 volumes of his own edition of *The Poetical Works of Thomas Moore*. (Here, I quote from the Preface to Vol. 8, in *The Poetical Works*, 10 vols. in 1 (Boston: Phillips,

Sampson, and Company, 1858), 527-30.) Moore includes in his Preface to Volume 8, for example, his account of having received clearance to return to London from the Longmans in a letter of September 1822, after successful "negotiation . . . with . . . [Moore's] American claimants for a reduction of their demands upon me." Moore supplies specific amounts of advances and outright gifts from friends aiding him in clearing his debt. He reports, too, that in June 1823 he "found 1000*l* placed to my credit from the sale of the Loves of the Angels, and 500*l* from the Fables of the Holy Alliance" (529). This preface is hardly "romantic" in the sense of attending to the growth of a poet's mind. It is decidedly contemporary in its obsession with capital gain. It is biographically understandable, as well. Stunned by a surprise debt of £6.000, Moore liable for the dishonest dealings of his agent in Bermuda, the poet was unable to recover financially until 1826 (JTM 3: 924), despite generous help from his friends that kept him out of prison for theft and fraud, and that eventually cleared his name for an earlier than anticipated return to England. Moore never recovered from the psychological trauma of the 1818 catastrophe, if his letters, journals, and prefaces give any indication. Many of his contemporaries were plagued by financial disasters--none so dramatic and ongoing as Moore's; few ever wrote of their financial standing in public prefaces. Moore's prefaces all but regularly assess the writings contained within each of the ten volumes according to their contribution to his solvency.

[32]If Barbara Donegal was denied the *Angels*, other daughters of Albion were not. In a journal entry dated 12 January 1823, Moore reports that he "called on Mr. Awdrey . . . , who told me how his house had been haunted by my 'Angels,' that his daughters could do nothing else but repeat verses of it." (JTM 2: 614-15)

[33]Fear of litigation and financial failure plagued both Moore and his publishers, none of whom were interested in the moral implications of charges of impiety or blasphemy. The possibility of litigation--and commercial ruin--made itself known when, as Moore reports in his journal entry for 27 January 1823, "the Longmans . . . received an anonymous letter about my poem, beginning, 'I conjure the respectable house of L.R.H.O. and Brown to pause ere they, &c.&.:' and ending, 'Beware the fate of Murray and of Cain!'" (JTM 2: 593) Perhaps to some ultra-Tories *Cain* and *The Loves of the Angels* share blasphemous inclinations; the poems differ so vastly that the former--a philosophical reflection--hardly brooks comparison with Moore's Ovidian romance.

[34]Terence de Vere White, *Tom Moore, the Irish Poet* (London: Hamish

Hamilton, 1977). By implication, Moore senses this. Yet Moore could not have. White projects a world to dominate some thirty years henceforth--a world, actually, within a world. "Intense righteousness" found its counter in free thinking, atheism, and socialist militancy. The world was becoming increasingly pluralistic. One could move on to new circles of friends. And as far as French conservatism went, Moore had no personal taste of the world of the jailed and beribboned that White alludes to when he notes that soon after the *Angels* saw print repression grew to the extent that "in Paris a girl who wore a tricolour ribbon in her dress was arrested and sent to prison" (169). In France Moore was always welcome, and his *Angels* kept French translators busy throughout the century.

[35]Moore's autobiographical Preface to Volume 8 of his *Poetical Works* less effusively expresses similar sentiments. Aware that his "Eighth Number of the Irish Melodies, and also, a Number of the National Airs," just completed, "would yield but an insufficient supply, compared with the demands hanging over me," he "called to mind a subject,--the Eastern allegory of the Loves of the Angels,--on which I had, some years before, begun a prose story, but in which, as a theme for poetry, I had now been anticipated by Lord Byron, in one of the most sublime of his poetical pieces, 'Heaven and Earth.'" He adds that

> Knowing how soon I should be lost in the shadow into which so gigantic a precursor would cast me, I endeavored, by a speed of composition which must have astonished my habitually slow pen, to get the start of my noble friend in the time of publication, and thus give myself the sole chance I could perhaps expect, under such unequal rivalry, of attracting to my work the attention of the public. In this humble speculation, however, I failed; for both works, if I recollect right, made their appearance at the same time (529).

Even in hindsight, economic concerns recur to him as an impetus for completing the narrative. The simultaneity of their appearance becomes a fact that depends upon Moore's "recollect[ing] right."

[36]Byron probably refers to Waller's *The Flood of Thessaly*, by Barry Cornwall (Waller's pseudonym), reviewed in *The Examiner* in 1823. In the review, traces of Miltonolatry inspire the writer's suggestion that "the laudable inspiration of Milton" accounts for Cornwall's reliance upon blank verse in his tale of the Deluge derived from the "mythological fable of

Deucalion"--a source Cyrus Gordon relates to the angel/deluge narratives treated here. (79) This mythological deluge becomes "a single source of pathos and description"--hinting at the sublimity inhering even in pagan accounts of world destruction. Stuart acknowledges that parallels to Scripture are ubiquitous throughout ancient mythologies, but insists that these parallels in no way suggest that the Scripture derives from these mythologies; this is evident, for example, from "the simple fact, that the Greek and Roman mythology presents us with no order of beings that corresponds to the evil spirits" in the Bible. Scripture remains unique. (119)

[37]"Announcement of 'The Liberal, No. II'," in *The Examiner* (29 December 1822): 822.

[38]*Byron, Shelley, Hunt, and 'The Liberal'* (Philadelphia: Univ. of Penn. Press, 1960) 137-39.

On the Head of a Pin: Ancient Texts and Modern Confusion

WHEN HE ASSAILS MOORE for "representing angels otherwise than as Scripture teaches us to conceive them," Theodore Hook inadvertently exposes theological negligence typical of his age. Moore cannot be faulted for failing to replicate what has not been drawn. "Scripture teaches" no particular way "to conceive" of angels, as Gustav Davidson makes clear.[1] Angel lore is largely extra-biblical. The Old Testament offers ministering and messenger angels, who sometimes impart knowledge to prophets; angels form a heavenly court (*bet din*); fiery-formed seraphim appear in Isaiah 6. Cherubim appear in Ezekiel (10.1-22, and 11.22). As George Foote Moore notes,

> There was nothing approaching a 'doctrine of angels' [in the Old Testament]. The Synoptic Gospels and the first half of Acts are the best witnesses to the popular notions . . . ; the Epistles of Paul are in the same vein; while the Revelation of John is exuberant in its use of angelic stage machinery of the Jewish apocalypse. (*Judaism* 1: 112)

Archangels make few appearances in canonical texts. Raphael ("God has healed") first finds place in Tobit 12.15, an apocryphal book. Gabriel ("God is my strength," or "man of God," or "God has shown himself mighty") makes four appearances in Scripture--two in Daniel (Daniel 8.15 and Daniel 9.21), and two in Luke (Luke 1.11 and Luke 1.26). Daniel is unusual among canonical texts, constituting the sole Old Testament apocalypse. Angels are best suited to the dream visions characterizing apocalyptic and eschatological writings, dreams providing inroads for prophecies. Apocalyptic and eschatological literature, too, introduce the greatest number of named angels--named angels bearing more authority, or credibility, than nameless ones. Michael ("who is God") serves three times in Daniel (Daniel 10.13, Daniel 10.21 and Daniel 12.1), once in the New Testament eschatology (Revelation 12.7-9), and is told of in Jude 9. He appears nowhere else in canonical Scripture. Named archangels are late additions to Judaeo-

Christian machinery.

Confusion and fluidity characterize Christian angelology. Michael, for example, usually ranks the highest among archangels. But Gustav Davidson's comparison of 9 selected hierarchies yields 30 different names, and disparate hierarchical systems (*Angels* 338-39, and 348-40). Michael and Gabriel show up in all 9 lists; Raphael appears in 6, Uriel in 5.

Moore, inadvertently, may have alerted his age to the confusion surrounding angels. In his journal entry of 29 March 1823, Moore notes that he "saw in the newspapers a work announced called 'Angelolographia,' by a clergyman, 'On the Nature and Offices of the Holy Angels,' partly occasioned by two poems, lately published, the name of the one of which, and the subject of both, is the 'Loves of the Angels'." (JTM 2: 621.) Wilfred S. Dowden identifies this treatise as Charles Spencer's "A Scriptural Account of the Nature and Employment of the Holy Angels" (1823). Spencer's numbers among several angelological treatises appearing after *The Loves of the Angels*. England's amorous angels placed angels under close scrutiny for the first time in roughly 150 years; those who would chastise Moore--or any of the angel/deluge poets--found the poets protected by diffuse, confused angelological notions surviving from antiquity.[2]

This becomes evident from contemporary efforts to malign Moore and Byron for their license in depicting angels. Objections reveal groundings in vague angelological assumptions inherited from Augustine and Aquinas, colored by Jewish and early Christian commentators--and undermined by Renaissance philosophers, seventeenth-century poets, and eighteenth-century encyclopedists. Confusion, too, stems from the fact that England's angel/deluge narratives ultimately derive from one of the most ancient and perplexing passages in Scripture, Genesis 6.1-4--a passage fraught with philological, contextual, chronological, and conceptual difficulties. Genesis 6.1-4, further, offers at least two alternative hamartigenies for the fall in Genesis 3--alternatives stressed in the revision and amplification of Genesis 6.1-4 provided by the Book of Enoch, this pseudepigraphic revision emphasizing themes of contemporary pertinence--including political oppression and economic exploitation--rendering it of particular interest to the newly industrialized England. Angelic concupiscence--as well as a third, and the most popular, hamartigeny--appear in another psedepigraphic text, *The Testament of Reuben*, obsessed with fornication, redolent of misogyny, developing themes central to Pauline Christianity, and reflecting ideas against which the Owenist exegetes reviled.

To some degree, all five completed poems and Heber's fragment call to mind Genesis 6.1-4, the passage that Enoch embellishes, that Dale's Matthew source ultimately refers to, and that even Croly's narrative--in its revival of angels as sexual beings--prompts us to think of. Enoch held more than antiquarian appeal for the age. The revisions of Genesis 6.1-4 in Enoch bore contemporary significance in their emphases upon economic and political exploitation--themes attractive to an age appalled at the outcome of industrialization, an economic development that, in its nascence, had promised boundless hopes for social good.[3]

The sexuality of angels--in Enoch and in other pseudepigraphic writings--challenged the notion of original sin, and provided an alternative hamartigeny. Humankind was relieved of culpability for the world-judgment of the flood. Divine creatures were at fault. Enoch invited nineteenth-century readers to revaluate old, theological notions about the Fall, along with newer, initially optimistic notions about the value of technological refinement. Angels in Enoch prompted both sorts of inquiries.

It is no wonder that the angel/deluge poems met with confusion. Enoch--as well as the poems partly occasioned by Laurence's translation of Enoch--challenged old attitudes towards angels when these old attitudes were patently unsettled. Some dismissed angels as superannuated Christian mythological trappings. Others felt compelled to defend them because Scripture names them. Orthodoxy was little comforted by the fact that angels remain largely divorced from canonical Scriptures. The key problems--with contemporary receptions of The Book of Enoch as well as with reactions to the angel/deluge poems--trace to a common biblical source, namely Genesis 6.1-4.

The activity, and even the presence, of angels in Genesis 6.1-4 remain difficult to monitor.

The passage obfuscates basic information. Participants as well as sequences remain uncertain; angels may or may not involve themselves. If causal links connect the sexual union mentioned in Genesis 6.2 and the birth of the giants--traditionally presumed to be the *Nephilim* of Genesis 6.4--these links derive from hermeneutic allowances, and not from the letter itself. Philological evidence marks this passage as one of the oldest in the Pentateuch. In its inception, Genesis 6.1-4 probably served as an aetiology; verses 1, 2, and 4 likely hearken back to an age of giants--no more nor no less strange than the age of Titans engendered by Greek antiquity--perhaps recounted in oral tradition. The pastiche of legends comprising the passage leaves us without clear relationships among the four verses:

*¹*When men began to multiply on the face of the ground, and daughters were born to them, *²*the sons of God saw that the daughters of men were fair: and they took to wife such of them as they chose. *³*Then the Lord said, "My spirit shall not abide in man for ever, for he is flesh, but his days shall be a hundred and twenty years." *⁴*The Nephilim were on the earth in those days, and also afterward, when the sons of God came in to the daughters of men, and they bore children to them. These were the mighty men that were of old, the men of renown.

Debate has flourished over the significance of *bene ha'elohim* in Verse 1. Often rendered "sons of God," sometimes "sons of the elohim," these entities trouble both Jewish and Christian theologians. Discussions of their ontogenic status, their potential for fleshly concupiscence, and their relationship to God have proven incendiary. Who are these "sons"? What purpose do they serve? May they be termed angels? The letter alone thwarts comprehension. Rudimentary understanding of this passage depends upon fixing upon them an order and nature of being.

Rabbis from the second century A.D. avert the problem of ontogeny by neglecting to confirm or deny *bene ha'elohim* potential for enjoying sex. These commentators do not designate the "sons of God" "angels". Instead, they equate them to earthly courtiers--explain their service, rather than identifying their essence or substance. In doing so, these exegetes create numerous theological problems. Why a "jealous God" would want attendants bewilders. Heavenly courtiers better befit an ancient Near Eastern or classical Greek pantheon--or even a monolotrous cosmogony. Their use to an omnipotent deity puzzles.

Other Rabbis, also writing in the second century A.D., bind themselves to the letter; they derive from the phrase--and court--a vision of a monarchial deity who can create sons without himself engaging in sex; these "sons of God" can, and do, take on fleshly raiments, in order to enjoy sex with mortal women.*⁴* This second notion repelled Julius Africanus, among others, and became particularly noxious when exegetes enhanced its viability by noting celestial sexuality in other places, passages in which angels--and even Yahweh himself--engage in physical sex. Among the more famous of such passages numbers Genesis 21.1-2: "And Yahweh visited [*paqad*] Sarah as He had said; and Yahweh did unto Sarah as He had spoken. And Sarah conceived and bore to Abraham a son for his old age, at the time that God had promised." The verb *paqad* is used in Judges 15.1 to designate coital visitation.

Angelic carnality is acknowledged both by Jewish and Patristic writers. Josephus (*Antiquities* 1: 3.1) equates the "sons of God" with fallen angels; Philo follows him in this (*De Gigantibus*).[5] Here, tradition follows the literal reading of *bene ha'elohim*. This reading encourages still other Rabbinical commentators in acknowledging sex among angelic enjoyments, a notion some derive from 1 Kings 7.36. Allen Edwardes reports that both Resh Laqish and Rashi (Rabbi Shelomoh ben-Yitshaq) interpret *"ki-ma'ir aysh luyut".* . . . as

"like a man embracing his companion," which describes those olivewood gold-inlaid Cherubs on the Ark in an erotic embrace. A more accurate rendering would be "like masculine nakedness entwined,"

for, he adds,

Ma'ir is both "nakedness" and "pudenda". . .; *aysh* is emphatic for *ish* (male) and *luyut*, derived from *lawweh* (to be joined closely, to stick together; to encircle, entwine), denotes a passionate embrace or physical enwreathment.

He argues that "this is substantiated by the fact that Jewish tradition tells us the Cherubim were beautiful young winged males, of the angelic type sent by Yahweh to entice the pederasts of Sodom" (63). This sexual interpretation of the Kings passage does increase the likelihood of other passages in Scripture revealing angelic sex. On the basis of Hosea 4.12, Rabbi Jochanin (BT, *Bereshith Rabba* 85) posits even an "Angel of Lust"--an angel charged with inspiring, rather than partaking in, sexual pleasure.[6] With the Angel of Lust comes hosts of problems in judging social behavior. Is concupiscence evil or inspired by God's agent? The *Sacred History of Sulpitius Severus* (A.D. 363-420) confirms, without questioning, the sexual capabilities of the angels:

When . . . the human race had increased to a great multitude, certain angels, whose habitation was heaven, were captivated by the appearance of some beautiful virgins, and cherished illicit desires after them, so much so, that falling beneath their own proper nature and origin, they left the higher regions of which they were inhabitants, and united themselves in earthly marriages. These angels gradually spreading wicked habits, corrupted the human family, and from their alliance giants are said to have sprung, for the mixture with them of beings of a different nature, as a matter of course, gave birth to monsters.[7]

Interspeciation disrupts the line of creation God designed. The heavens will not support this cosmic miscegenation.

Another problem with Genesis 6.1-4 involves coherence. An untoward jump moves attention from the "men of renown" in Genesis 6.4 to Yahweh in Genesis 6.5, who "saw that the wickedness of man was great in the earth, and that every imagination of the thoughts of his heart was only evil." The details of this wickedness remain eclipsed. Certainly the copulation in Genesis 6.1-2 has not been explicitly forbidden; Moses had not mediated any laws to this antediluvian population. Contradictory causes for the flood, supplied by Genesis 6, reflect the tension between the Yahwist and Priestly traditions responsible for the duplicates. Genesis 6.5-8 relates Yahweh's detection of "evil" in man's "heart," which leaves this J Source (Yahwist) anthropopathic deity--prototype of the artist/perfectionist--considering "blotting out" entirely from "the face of the ground" all life forms. Genesis 6.9-11 mitigates human culpability. In this later, P Source (Priestly) narrative, God sees that the earth is "corrupt" and "filled with violence."[8] Seemingly needless duplications in this account render doubtful the doctrine of inerrancy. Noah receives two sets of loading instructions. Genesis 7.2-3 prescribes that "seven pairs of all clean animals" be admitted into the ark, while Genesis 6.19 has Noah admit "two of every sort into the ark." In Genesis 7.17, the flood lasts "forty days," in Genesis 7.24, "one hundred and fifty days."[9] Anthropopathic tendencies even in the covenant of the rainbow in Genesis 9.13-15 leave us uneasy about God's omniscience:

> [13]I set my bow in the cloud, and it shall be a sign of the covenant between me and the earth. [14]When I bring clouds over the earth and the bow is seen in the clouds, [15]I will remember my covenant is between me and you and every living creature of all flesh; and the waters shall never again become a flood to destroy all flesh.

This covenant (which continues in verses 16 and 17) makes us uneasy about a God who would need to remind Himself of His own promise; the rainbow is less a miracle than a cosmic counterpart to the string around the finger. Matthew 24.37-39 (upon which Dale draws) and Luke 17.26-27 refer to ancient times, "the days of Noah," the days "before the flood" in which "they were eating and drinking, marrying and giving in marriage," until world-judgment came; the history remains sketchy. Exegetes remain uncertain about the nature of and participants in the guilt. The Book of Enoch constitutes but one of several attempts to amplify this history. (Montgomery has good reason to ignore "both the learned and the absurd hypotheses" about the panoply of individuals and incidents put forth as the causes of world-judgment.)

Genesis 6.1-4 presents yet another problem with coherence. Genesis 6.3 seems misplaced. Does Yahweh see fit to number the days of the human being because of human coitus with angels? No hint inheres in the verse. Further, the relationship between the four-verse passage and the earlier books of Genesis remains indeterminable--especially when Genesis 6.3 is compared to the expulsion of Adam and Eve in Genesis 3.22, or if Yahweh's pronouncement in Genesis 6.3 undergoes comparison with Genesis 7.6, 11.32, and elsewhere. According to F.R. Tennant, Genesis 6.1-4 "has been considered by many modern critics as parallel in meaning to Gen[esis 3], and to supply an alternative hamartigeny or explanation of the original sin and universal sin."[10] Tennant adds that in fact, "the earlier Jewish apocalyptic literature attached more importance to it [Genesis 6.1-4] in this connexion than the story of the loss of Paradise" (95). Bases for imparting Genesis 6.1-4 with this significance become clear when Yahweh's limitation of the human lifespan to 120 years (Genesis 6.3) compares with humankind's potential immortality in Genesis 6.22-24:

> [22]Then the Lord God said, "Behold, the man has become like one of us, knowing good and evil; and now, lest he put forth his hand and take also of the tree of life, and eat, and live for ever"--[23]therefore the Lord God sent him forth from the garden of Eden, to till the ground from which he was taken. [24]He drove out the man; and at the east of the garden of Eden he placed the cherubim, and a flaming sword which turned every way, to guard the way to the tree of life.

Clearly, Yahweh considers "the man" a threat to "us"--Yahweh's audience unidentified. In the text itself (rather than from exegetic accretions surrounding it), Adam's expulsion results not from disobedience, but rather from imminent danger to Yahweh's divine order. Yahweh fears that Adam and Eve will eat of the other tree, "the tree of life," and become semi-divine--in fact, "live for ever." In this light, "original sin" applies in its nominal sense of "origin," denoting the "first." The Eden transgression is parochial, its consequences particularized. The specific actions of Adam and Eve do not demarcate a pre-and post-lapsarian human species; "original sin" thus conceived is not hereditary. Rather, the actions in Eden threaten Yahweh's (and his unnamed celestial auditors') distinct identity as immortals.

Similarly, although Yahweh denies immortality to humankind, Genesis 3 does not program the species to any particular duration on earth. Genesis 6.3 does; humans will live 120 years. Yet in Genesis 7.29, Noah enjoys an active 950 years, engaging in particularly rigorous labor in Genesis 7.6-15, during his 600th year. In Genesis 11.32, Terah lives 205 years. Throughout Genesis, in fact, the 120 years assigned humans in Genesis 6.3 proves more of an exception than an edict. Neither Adam and Eve, nor even the "sons of God" coupling with the "daughters of men," engender offspring with predetermined life spans. Inconsistencies in Yahweh's decree in Genesis 6.3 and subsequent passages in Genesis, and Yahweh's ineluctable sense of danger in Genesis 3.22-24, attenuate (in their implications) Yahweh's power and credibility when Genesis 6.1-4 acquires not a literal, but rather a tropological, or moral, significance. (The letter depicts Yahweh withholding truth--overtly lying--in Genesis, as well as experiencing fear, possible only for anthropopathic deities. Yahweh here will not support the God concept embraced by later, more sophisticated theologians.) Hence Genesis 6.1-4 holds appeal as an alternative hamartigeny.

G.H. Dix suggests that a chief reason for the pseudepigraphic rendition of Genesis 6.1-4 in Enoch 7.2 proves to be exactly this--that is, the corresponding passage in Enoch supplies clearly such an alternative hamartigeny:

> The origin of evil is attributed to the fallen angels whose story is told in Genesis VI: they revealed knowledge to men, brought forth the giants whose disembodied spirits are demons, and led human beings into a sinful course of life whereby the order of nature was corrupted (29).

We are not born in sin. Adam and Eve in no way taint their legacy. Intruders of another order of being corrupt humankind. The *bene ha'elohim* have both spiritual (demonic) and corporeal (as giants) stations. Charles, as well, finds in this passage a revised, alternative hamartigeny:

> Original sin, therefore, stands not in the following of Adam, whose transgression seems limited in its effects to himself, but in the evil engendered through the fallen watchers or angels (*Pseudepigrapha* 214).

Angels and original sin are again associates in the *Clementine Homilies*, which condemn the "unhallowed intercourse" from which "spurious man sprung . . . of angels, yet less than angels as they were born of women . . . , [and who] on account of their bastard natures not being pleased with the purity of food . . . . longed after the taste of blood." Vampiric impulses drive these angels. Vampires and the Deluge share an identical originating cause.

In the Book of Enoch, the significance of Genesis 6.1-4 is reinterpreted, the Enoch account removing the burden of sin almost entirely from mankind, placing the blame for the Deluge mostly on the angels. (This attribution provides a better explanation for the predicaments of Moore's characters than do his superimposed Qur'anic and Persian legends.) In 1 Enoch 10.7, God promises to

> heal the earth which the angels have defiled, and proclaim the healing of the earth, that I will heal the earth, and that the children of men shall not perish through all the secret things that the watchers have disclosed and have taught their sons. And the whole earth has been defiled through the teaching of the works of Azazel: to him ascribe all sin.[11]

Chew suggests that from Enoch, Byron may have adapted the names Azaziel and Samiasa, although a form of the first is also available in the Bible (*Dramas* 178). The functions of the similarly named angels differ, however.[12] In Leviticus 16.8-10, Azazel plays a part in the atonement ritual; he is a demon, or evil spirit, in the desert, designated as the recipient of one of two goats. The people, in driving this goat to him, drive out their sins.[13]

1 Enoch 10, part of the oldest fragment of this theodicy, originating before 170 B.C., attributes sin to the fallen watchers in order to remove the burden from Adam. This fragment--placed among the "Watchers" fragments accessible to Moore and Byron--depicts two acts of judgment, the first occurring when the fallen angels are interred in caves under the mountains

as a temporary place of punishment (10.4-10, 12.1-2), and men's souls consigned to Sheol (10.22). These cave spirits vaguely resemble Byron's, and the spirits mocking the King of Babylon, which Montgomery quotes from Lowth in his note to Book 10, Stanza 42, of *The World Before the Flood*:

> 'The image of the state of the Dead, or the *Infernum Poeticum* of the Hebrews, is taken from the custom of burying, those at least of the highest rank, in large sepulchral vaults hewn in the rock. . . . You are to form to yourself the idea of an immense subterraneous vault, a vast gloomy cavern, all round the sides of which there are cells to receive the dead bodies: . . . . These illustrious shades rise at once from their couches, as from their thrones; and advance to the entrance to the cavern to meet the King of Babylon, and to receive him with insults on his fall.'--LOWTH'S ISAIAH, ch. XIV. v. 9, *et seq*. (220- 21)

The second judgment occurs when God choreographs the Deluge-- this plan not entirely successful, for the souls of the sons of angels and daughters of men somehow escape punishment, and are allowed to continue their evil pursuits until the final World-Judgment (16.1). (Save for Croly's, all poems treated in this study represent the Deluge as God's judgment.)

Known also through Syncellus (and hence potentially to Byron) are the Noah fragments of Enoch, 6.1-8.4:

> And it came to pass when the children of men had multiplied that in those days were born unto them beautiful and comely daughters. And the angels, the children of heaven, saw and lusted after them, and said to one another: 'Come, let us choose us wives from among the children of men and beget us children.' And Samjaza, who was their leader, said unto them: 'I fear ye will not indeed agree to do this deed, and I alone shall have to pay the penalty of a great sin.'

The themes of economic and political exploitation throughout these fragments, as well as their services as prototypes for vampiric horror tales, render them of significance to their age. Semjaza's followers bind themselves by an oath to proceed, "and they were in all two hundred; who descended in the days of Jared on the summit of Mount Hermon . . . ." "Samiaza" serves as "their leader," and "Asael" numbers among "their chiefs of tens." (Enoch 6.1-8.) In Enoch 7.1-9, they "took unto themselves wives, and each chose himself one, and they began to go in unto them and defile themselves with them." In exchange for sex, the angels "taught them [their mortal wives] charms and enchantments, and the cutting of roots, and made them acquainted with plants." An agricultural society emerges from this commune; from their sexual union, the women "became pregnant, and they bore great giants, whose height was three thousand ells: Who consumed all the acquisitions of men"--much like Penelope's suitors, who literally begin eating Penelope and Telemachos out of house and home. The giants in Enoch soon depleted the earth of food, then "turned against them [human-kind] and devoured mankind." Further, "they began to sin against birds, and beasts, and reptiles, and fish, and to devour one another's flesh, and drink the blood." The fathering angels must surely bear corporeal form. As noted, their offspring stand as prototypes for fictional vampires and cannibals. Insatiate receivers, their angelic fathers prove fatally generous givers, sharing knowledge not meant for mortals. The text prescribes that after their bloodlust, "the earth laid accusation against the lawless ones."

Accusation has a while yet to come. In Enoch 8.1, "Azazel taught men to make swords, and knives, and shields, and breastplates, and made known to them the metals of the earth and the art of working them"--first, so that they would be useful in war, devices--and a divisive consciousness--to which angels initiate humankind, and second, as means of seduction, showing them how to make "bracelets, and ornaments, and the use of antimony, and the beautifying of the eyelids, and all kinds of costly stones, and all colouring tinctures." The significant theme of this passage--the economic and political exploitation of the unlearned by the initiated--would hold obvious appeal in an age overcome by new oppressions borne of new technological knowledge. Learning--in Enoch and in the nineteenth-century factory world--proves a mixed blessing. In Enoch, from these devices, "there arose much godlessness, and they [humankind] committed fornication, and they were led astray, and became corrupt in all their ways." Mortals are not to blame. Humankind does not come upon these abomina-tions naturally.

Neither do humans unaided learn of the occult: "Semejaza taught enchantments, and root-cuttings." Other angels teach astronomy and meteorology--potentially valuable arenas of understanding, yet not in the way that humans are inducted to them; the angels show humankind learning's malevolent side. Tertullian links fallen angels with astrology in his treatise On *Idolatry*, Ch. 9: "One proposition I lay down: that those angels, the deserters from God, the lovers of women, were likewise discoverers of this curious art, on that account also condemned by God" (R&D 3: 65). This blending of fallen angels with forbidden, or occult, knowledge becomes commonplace in Jewish and Qur'anic lore. Fortunately, redeeming angels look after the newest, recently innocent, now violated species: "And as men perished, they cried, and their cry went up to heaven."

The afflicting angels find a corrective in the saviour angels in Enoch 9.1-11: "Michael, Uriel, Raphael, and Gabriel looked down from heaven and saw much blood being shed upon the earth, and all lawlessness being wrought upon the earth." They confer, and agree that the cries of men need be taken as calls for justice; humankind was formed without the innate wickedness eventuating these cries. They plead the case of humanity, entreating the "'Lord of lords, God of gods, King of kings, and God of the ages'" to look down to earth. They ask him to acknowledge "what Azazel hath done, who hath taught all unrighteousness on earth and revealed the eternal secrets which were preserved in heaven, which men were striving to learn."

Dissatisfaction with management, with the newly made officials from among the bourgeoisie--the factory managers and owners--may have come to mind when Byron's readers encountered the charges of mismanagement against Semjaza. The archangels point at "Semjaza, to whom Thou hast given authority to bear rule over his associates." Semjaza has not led well: "they have gone to the daughters of men upon earth, and have slept with the women, and have defiled themselves, and revealed to them all kinds of sins." They remark that "the women have borne giants, and the whole earth has thereby been filled with blood and unrighteousness." They acknowledge the cries of the dead which "cannot cease because of the lawless deeds which are wrought on earth." The archangels appeal to their Lord for a revolution, a course of action, which in Enoch 10.1-22 and 11.1-2, involves the usual deluge (with instructions for Noah's escape) and physical punishment for the errant angels: "And ... the Lord said to Raphael: 'Bind Azazel hand and foot, and cast him into the darkness," for "the whole earth has been corrupted through the works that were taught by Azazel: to him ascribe all sin.'" (This passage recalls the binding of Haruth and Maruth in Qur'anic legends.)

Afterwards, Michael is to "bind Semjaza and his associates who have united themselves with women so as to defile themselves with them in all their uncleanness." Humans will meet with further disasters, but God, when it is time, will restore order, "and truth and peace shall be associated together throughout all the days of the world and throughout all the generations of men" (Charles, *Pseudepigrapha* 191-95). Suffering proves neither endless nor hopeless, unlike later redactions of this tale, including some in Scripture.

Byron's angels may well derive from the angels in Enoch; the pseudepigraphic manuscripts--even the "Watchers" fragment--supply full details to draw upon, and depict the angels as characteristically carnal in their form and their desires. Yet Byron's Azaziel bears nothing of the malevolence of his counterpart in Enoch. Other Azazel/Azaziel legends enjoyed currency, available for service to pique Byron's fecund mind, and the poet's mind is here the key. Byron designed his own tradition. His Azaziel bears few if any distinguishing characteristics; his service is rhetorical: the seraph presents a point of view. If we impose upon Byron's poem inappropriate trappings from antiquity, we find ourselves unable to evaluate the angel's assertions. Byron teased with traditions of angelic concupiscence; the drama forces us to break free from tradition, and look at Azaziel as a figure in advent.

Likewise, Byron's archangel has been said to derive from Enoch. Byron's original manuscript of *Heaven and Earth* included Michael instead of Raphael. Gifford was uneasy about Michael's function in the poem, and suggests that Byron substitute Raphael. Gifford's reasons are unclear (L&J 5: 93). Michael, the highest ranking archangel, would be the most authoritative advisor for Anah and Aholibamah.[14] Raphael functions well as a substitute, however, given his equivocal appeal in pseudepigraphic literature. If Byron's Raphael is not entirely attractive, neither is he so in 1 Enoch 22 (Davidson, *Angels* 240). Raphael becomes associated with demonic spirits in traditions deriving from Enoch, not because of his suitability or credentials for the role, but because he guides the prophet through the abode of the dead--the "four hollow places," places "made for sinners when they die," their "spirits ... set apart in this great pain, till the great day of judgment" (1 Enoch 22. 1-11). This series of divided caverns is much more elaborate than the one in Byron's poem, although Byron may have borrowed the idea from this source.[15]

Moore and Croly depend more heavily than Byron upon the angels' tarnished reputations--suggested in Genesis, and amplified in extra-canonical texts. Qur'anic legends match Christian and Jewish ones, sin for sin, and punishment for punishment. A suitable tale can be drawn from any of the three traditions. *That* angels fall establishes itself in ancillary legends; *why* angels fall has a predictable explanation--although not in legends. This issue occupies Jewish and Christian commentaries. The explanation involves but one word: *women*. In effect, a third hamartigeny emerges.

Adam and Eve in Genesis 3 as well as the "sons of God" in Genesis 6.2 stand vindicated. Mortal men, helpless against their glandular urgings, take no significant part in the transgression. Women as a group bring about world-judgment--their collective guilt with the angels antedated by Eve's proclivity to sin in Eden. Moore's and Croly's narrators apparently accept this third hamartigeny as the sole and received one. Jewish, Christian, and Islamic traditions do little to dissuade acceptance. Pierre Bayle had already played his trump card and failed; Bayle's *Dictionary* judges it "inconsistent Impertinence" for "a Tempter," such as the serpent (by some called the "Spirit of Envy" or the "Spirit of Lust") to have "made the Woman eat the Apple in the absence of her husband. . . ." (2: 851)

Bayle's philosophers, in fact, offer an astute diagnosis of the psychological twists legitimized as misogyny, misogyny in Scripture deemed "Eve's fall." Male theologians--and male husbands--fail, simply, to acknowledge that they are in love. (If this remained too gentle and soft for admission by men in the France of the *philosophes*, it certainly remains too human for the "gentler, kinder America" presumably being Bush-built today; hatred and blame will prevail.) The *Dictionary* article on "Eve" includes an analysis of the judgment of the poet Sarrasin against Adam's helpmeet:

> One would think that Sarrasin wrote this [indictment against Adam's "Coquet" of a wife, who turned into the "amorous Tales of the Devil"] in a furious fit of Jealousy, when he had just had an account that his Mistress had been civil to some Sparks that admired her . . . . A Man is never more disposed to rail against the fair sex in general than when he knows, the Person who loves him and whom he loves hearkens willingly to the Courtship of others . . . . He would have the Woman . . . look down with contempt upon every Body else . . . , and become to them ill-humored, rude, cruel, and unsociable . . . . He inveigels against all Women . . . , and if at that time he should be writing a Treatise of Logic, when he comes to the Chapters of Universals, he would assign Coquetry for the *propriam quarto modo* of the female Sex . . . . If he were not in Love he would be far from this injustice, and would see nothing to be condemned in the pleasure they take in being flattered and wheedled, and in their civil and obliging way of answering a Compliment. (2: 857)

One can only mourn the fact that Bayle and his staff were born too late to advise Tertullian, to forestall Pauline Christianity, and, proleptically, to defuse Freud and Freud's advisors in the nineteenth century.

This third hamartigeny proved anathema to nineteenth-century Owenite exegetes. Fanny Wright's efforts at female emancipation from the tyrannies of Christian orthodoxy led to her call, "Fathers and husbands! Do ye not see this fact? Do ye not see how, in the mental bondage of your wives and fair companions, ye yourselves are bound?" (Taylor 147) Emma Martin refuses to allow women to take the blame for the fall, and refuses to allow male supremacy to stand unchallenged as the foundation for Christian society. Eliza Sharples in fact sees Eve as a great liberator:

> The tyrant God, Necessity, said to the subject man: 'Of the tree of the knowledge of good and evil thou shalt not eat.' Sweet and fair Liberty stepped in . . . spurned the order . . . of the tyrant, 'she took of the fruit thereof, and did eat, and gave also unto her husband with her and he did eat.' Do you not, with one voice exclaim, well done woman! LIBERTY FOR EVER! If that was a fall, sirs, it was such a glorious fall, and such a fall as is now wanted . . . . I will be such an Eve, so bright a picture of liberty! (Taylor 146)

Had the biblical account been written by a woman, another Owenite sympathizer wrote,"'we should have had a very different version of it,' for then the 'great folly' of Eve would not be eating the apple, but sharing it with Adam. 'Had she succeeded in concealing the extent of the power she possessed . . . she might have ruled by her reason, instead of becoming the slave of man's passions, and "multiplying her sorrows and her conception".'" (Taylor 146).

The early Church Fathers known to Moore and his circle vary in the degree of culpability they assign women. Athenagoras finds the angels and their mortal paramours equally guilty. In *A Plea for the Christians* (A.D. 177), Ch. 24, he accuses the amorous angels of bad management; theirs was a mandate to manage the things of the flesh; some became enamoured of those they managed, and commingled sexually, tainting their divine essences, and fathering giants. (R&D 2: 141-142) Clement of Alexandria (d. about A.D. 200) remarks in *The Instructor* (Ch. 3, R&D 3: 274) that "the angels . . . renounced the beauty of God for a beauty which fades, and so fell from heaven to earth." (Moore may well have drawn from this lore.) If women go free thus far from formal accusation of explicitly entrapping hapless angels, the predicates for this argument find articulation. With

Justin Martyr, the argument emerges; others nurture it, augmenting its strength.

Justin Martyr (A.D. 110-165) acknowledges that "the angels transgressed . . . , and were captivated by the love of women, and begat children who are those that are called demons," arguing that men wrongly attribute to God devastations brought about by these unlawful offspring. (*Second Apology*, Ch. 5, R&D 1: 190) Tertullian (A.D. 145-200) takes for granted 1) that angels can be sexually active; 2) that this activity is evil; and 3) that women take full blame for angelic degeneration into carnality. In *The Five Books Against Marcion*, Book 5, he assumes that "'spiritual wickedness' had been at work in heavenly places, when angels were entrapped into sin by the daughters of men" (R&D 3: 470); here, mortal women are wholly culpable. Misogyny proliferates in inter-testamental texts.

A particularly blighted view of women overwhelms the first of the *Testaments of the Twelve Patriarchs* (ca. 107-135 B.C.). ear of women becomes increasingly redolent throughout "The Testament of Reuben"; "hatred" applies better than "fear"--pathologically intense fears (and fear's attendant, loathing) of women's power over the male libido. Men fear their inability to control their sex drives. They fear that any association with women may undo them. They fear cuckoldry above all else. They fear ferociously the possibility of cuckolding themselves, a fear engendered by their belief in the ability of angels to invade their very corporeal bodies and enjoy through mortal senses sexual pleasures to which only a husband holds title. Husbands may be present during acts of fornication without knowing it. Their innocent participation insults; it heightens the fear and contempt of women informing this piece.

The dying Reuben issues a warning: "flee, therefore, fornication, my children, and command your wives and daughters, that they may adorn their heads and faces to deceive the mind: because every woman who uses these wiles hath been reserved for eternal punishment." He justifies his warning by explaining its cause: "For evil are women, my children; and since they have no power or strength over man, they use wiles by outward attractions, that they may draw him to themselves." (Charles, *Pseudepigrapha* 17-22)

This is a woman's sole power over men. Its results--fornication--involve a four-step process. Ocular dazzle undoes. Visual allure all but ensures damnation--not for the voyeur, who appears to have the sympathy of the narrator, but for the beautiful woman, whether or not she intends to allure. Female beauty captures the male's attention. At this point, he is helpless, however well endowed he otherwise may be in brawn, intellect, and spirituality. Eyes constitute inroads to the glands. The three ensuing stages are authorized--and commanded--by inborn, male, phallocentric determinism. Men seem incapable of applying any brake to the process once it begins. They must endure this form of entrapment by women. (Men do not condemn themselves too rigorously in this work. After all, if even angels are unable to resist, what chance has a human male?) Treacherous women transform innocent men into fornicators.

The second stage amounts to a sort of foreplay enjoyed only by the observer. This foreplay--the sex fantasy--takes place in the mind: "for thus they allured the Watchers who were before the flood; for as these continually beheld them, they lusted after them, and they conceived the act in their mind." The third stage--implanting sexual desire into the mind--is endured by both mortal and angelic victims. The final stage--coitus--invariably follows. The lust "in the mind" becomes particularly significant. At some places in Enoch, lust seems aroused by observing female beauty; the observer, not the observed, has evil designs "in the mind." In women's reckonings with angels, however, the acts as well as their results may be "in the mind" of both. Reuben explains that "the women lusting in their minds after their forms [i.e., angelic forms], gave birth to giants"; the Watchers, receiving the desires transmitted by the women's minds, accommodate them when they "changed themselves into the shape of men and appeared to them when they were with their husbands." The giant offspring become souvenirs --very bitter remembrances--of a husband's active participation in his own humiliation.

Reuben, by implication, reveals the dangers of misogyny to the idea of community. Reuben would have men always on guard against the threat women intrinsically pose: "Beware, then, of fornication; and if you wish to be pure in mind, guard your senses from every woman." In addition, "command the women likewise not to associate with men, so that they also may be pure in mind." (Charles, *Pseudepigrapha* 18) Because of this fear, men and women are separated in daily affairs. A society is ordered with institutions and customs accommodating a sexual phobia--a phobia with clear application to the earlier nineteenth century. Taylor observes that the "middle-class anxiety about working-class sexual morality . . . fuelled by Malthusian fears of plebian overpopulation . . . found concrete expression in the New Poor Law [1834], which established sex-segregated workshops for the indigent . . . ." (200) Modern Europe shares phobias with Jewish antiquity.

Fornication is the informing--as well as negating--principle of the culture responsible for "The Testament of Reuben." This culture is far from alone in generating taboos and in designing structures that transform sexual appetite from something neutral and normal into something negative; modern cultures reveal traces of taboos and other methods of discouraging sex; Reuben specializes in contempt of fornication. This impulse encouraged Owenite reformers to idealize an androgynous society.[16]

Patristic commentators prepare the way for Pauline Christianity, Christianity identifying women as a serious threat to the spiritual community. Tertullian "On Prayer" differentiates between "woman" and "virgin," while insisting on Pauline grounds that all of the female gender be "veiled" in church "'on account of the angels'" (1 Corinthians 11.10). He identifies all women as "objects of angelic concupiscence," in reference to Genesis 6.2. (R&D 3: 688) Angels retain a tarnished reputation (for those who allow them existence--as not all early Christians do).

Difficulties with this source afford insights into the liberties and strictures Byron, Moore, and even Croly assume in depicting their angels. No certain models were set. Causes for the confusion surrounding angels in the earlier nineteenth century have roots in the Restoration. Genesis 6.1-4--its letter confusing--bears potential for theological devastation, a potential (in this, and similarly difficult passages) of acute concern to seventeenth-century Anglican orthodoxy, Anglican divines responding with a defensive "doctrine of essentials," a doctrine that kept troublesome passages eclipsed. These Anglican divines, "rigorously antienthusiastic," as Gerard Reedy notes, fearing "a recurrence of privatistic and sectarian scriptural interpretation: of the apocalyptic and typological readings that characterized, for the divines, the Interregnum, and that were thought to legitimize sedition" articulated the "doctrine of essentials" that, among other things, kept angels out of view for decades. (Reedy 16) The "doctrine of essentials"--predicated upon a notion of pre-Cartesian aprioristic, or innate ideas--pronounces that "God would not reveal in Scripture something contradictory to what he had revealed of himself, in ideas innate to the human mind." (Reedy 22)

The endurance of this doctrine--and of the ambience created by it, a climate comfortable for syncretism and "rationalism"--explains why Byron and Moore had difficulty taking angels seriously, and why some of their contemporaries, in an age swept by Evangelicalism, took offense at embodied angels. Byron's freedom with angels in *Heaven and Earth* appeared licentious to those expositors for whom angels had recently reemerged as viable beings. Thomas Noon Talfourd chastises Byron and

Moore for infidelity to angelologies that had long ago been dropped by Christian orthodoxy.

As noted, the Restoration Anglican divines and their newly formulated doctrine allowed syncretism and theology to coexist companionably, and ultimately rendered passages such as Genesis 6.1-4 of clearer interest to antiquarians than to theologians. The Anglican exegetes took no offense at French encyclopedists who relegated angels--both concupiscent and chaste-- to the realm of superannuated mythological trappings; angels retired within the compendious volumes with the chimaera, the demigods, the satyrs, in short, with the full machinery of old, dead, beliefs. Typical treatment is given by Voltaire, in his *Philosophical Dictionary* (1769). In reference to Genesis 6.2 and 6.4, Voltaire asserts that

> This fancy, too, was common to all nations. China excepted, there is no nation in which some god did not have children by young women. These corporeal gods often descended to earth to visit their domains, they saw our young women and took the prettiest ones for themselves; the children born from the intercourse of these gods and mortals had to be superior to other men; so Genesis too does not neglect to mention that the gods who lay with our young women produced giants. (295)

Syncretism divests the angels of any singular intrigue. Genesis 6.2 belongs more properly to mythology than to theology. The milieu prepared by the "doctrine of essentials" would have encouraged the English to glance at Voltaire's account, grant that "yes, this is a glorious longing" (superiority through interspeciation), and dismiss Voltaire--and the original in Genesis--without experiencing any spiritual turmoil. This "doctrine of essentials"--permitting insouciance in the face of Scriptural difficulties-- finds full explanation by Reedy.

In Reedy's account, developments in Anglican exegesis resulted in an ambience allowing difficult parts of Scripture to undergo rigorous empirical scrutiny without threatening faith. The London Polyglot, finished under Walton's editorship in 1657, accorded fortuitously with a new concern among Anglican divines with the literal sense of Scripture. Efforts of Anglican divines such as Edward Stillingfleet made possible the exegetic adventures of the lay expositors associated with the "rationalistic principle of interpretation"--independent, empirical scrutiny of Scripture--practiced by Hobbes, Spinoza, Toland, and Herbert of Cherbury, among others.

(Terrien 129) Stillingfleet numbers among Anglican divines articulating the "doctrine of essentials," which presumes a "natural affinity with a theory of clear and distinct ideas" instilling as truth the assertion, quoted above, that "God would not reveal in Scripture something contradictory to what he had revealed of himself, in ideas innate to the human mind." (Reedy 17, 22)

Reason would uphold faith regardless of inconsistencies or other problems with the letter; reason would aid readers in regaining their sense of what mattered to faith--expositors until the Restoration erring by "mistaking inessentials for essentials." (Reedy 13-14) "Reason" as used by these divines "had little to do with the growing rationalism of later seventeenth-century England and Europe." (Reedy 11) Cartesian legacies-- faith in aprioristic "reason"--allowed for this distinction. As articulated by Herbert of Cherbury, Scripture, processed through "right reason"--the "reason" of *a priori*, or innate ideas--insists that "(1) there is a God, (2) to whom worship is due, (3) in acts of faith, love, and virtue, and (4) repentance for sin, which (5) will be rewarded or punished in an afterlife." "Reason"--as opposed to "rationalism"--insists upon this "universal wisdom," these "Catholic truths," imparted by the literal sense of Scripture, the only sense with which most Christians need concern themselves. (Reedy 20)

Reedy points to Herbert of Cherbury, Hobbes, Spinoza, and Toland as lay philosophers for whom "reason" (innate ideas) and "rationalism" (empirical scrutiny) remain separate matters. Spinoza is hence able to subject Scripture to close textual analysis, looking at the special history of each book--at its linguistic peculiarities, its "cultural matrix," its genre, its chronology--and, in the case of the Pentateuch, determine the impossibility of the Mosaic authorship of the whole, Spinoza's method foreshadowing the redaction criticism fostered by Graf and Wellhausen in the later nineteenth century. This tradition of Mosaic authorship he could challenge without challenging his faith; rationalism in no way held supremacy over reason. (Reedy 24-25)

Spinoza's erosion of the tradition of Mosaic authorship points to a concomitant development; "rationalistic"--that is, empirical--scrutiny of Scripture "had begun to abandon certain genres of the Bible as rationally indefensible." (Reedy 16) In response, the divines refined their "doctrine of essentials," in a manner allowing questionable texts to lapse into insignificance or obscurity. As refined, the doctrine held "that Scripture is plain and clear about matters necessary to salvation," an amendment which "cuts across, and, as it were, neutralizes critical findings of variant readings." (Reedy 103)

This solution maintained well--until Father Simon's *Critical History of the Old Testament*, available in English in 1682 through Henry Dickinson's efforts--was taken as a threat by some lay exegetes, who were overwhelmed by the mass of empirical evidence Simon collected, and who feared this evidence could undermine faith in the divine inspiration of Scriptures. (Such was not Simon's intent at all, the priest resolutely upholding the traditions evincing inspiration. Distrust of Roman Catholicism, rather than an understanding of Simon's methods and aims, accounts for much of the English outcry against the *Critical History*.) Dryden among the English laity constituted the most influential voice objecting to Simon's perceived threat. Without benefit of adequate critical tools, Dryden attempted to refute Simon's overwhelming evidence--an attempt even divines knew to avoid, realizing that the safest course was to circumvent Simon, this realization accounting for their "refus[al] to enter the empirical ground he cleared" (Reedy 113). Dryden's *Religio Laici* (November, 1682) derived from a defensive impulse--and failed miserably in discounting Simon's gleanings. Had Dryden left things alone, and retreated into Cartesian apriorism, Anglican orthodoxy would have had a chance to hold solidly. Instead, Dryden proffers the much weaker fideism, grounded upon the assertions that (1) there is a God, (2) who must be worshipped in the established church, and followed by the concomitant (imperatives), (3) so go to church and (4) do not ask any more questions about the Bible or theology. The fideistic response satisfied no one.

Locke renewed faith in the "reason" of Scripture in 1695, when he limited "reason" and "reasonableness" to the "teaching of the Gospels, Acts, and history of the New Testament." For Locke, "reason" derives from *ratio*, that is, "object in view," which he would have approached unencumbered by sectarian presuppositions. Reason implies faith, the latter for Locke constituting assent to a speaker's credibility (not necessarily to his message). By "reasonableness," Locke agrees with Stillingfleet and Tillotson in holding that "Scripture can reasonably be shown to come from God, through the argument from testimony, and that, befitting the source, the saving truth of Scripture has a decorous simplicity and plainness." In the cases of only a few doctrines--such as the existence of God and the immortality of the soul-- is "natural reason," as opposed to reason by "testimony," full proof. Yet Locke agrees with the mainstream of Anglican orthodoxy that Scripture may be verified by reason. (Reedy 140-41)

Throughout the eighteenth century, Anglicans were divided between the mainstream orthodox, whose faith was upheld by reason, and by those who followed Dryden, in finding in Simon's empirical scrutiny and its kind a source of vexation. This latter group found threatening the numerous developments in philological, form, and redaction criticism. From these seeds of doubt sprung a new solution--Evangelicalism--which, revived through Wesley, held increasing appeal for the working classes in particular, and renewed arguments for the inerrancy and verbal inspiration of all parts of Scripture. This resurgence of Christian evangelical fervor endangered cooler, more intellectual solutions posed by the Anglican divines. Wesleyanism--and sectarian offshoots--constituted a resurgence of "enthusiasm" which fomented confusion among believers about what, exactly, Christian "truth" entails. (How much of Scripture was "essential" to faith and salvation?) Angels had a chance of regaining theological pertinence. Enthusiasm worked to ruin the "doctrine of essentials." Some--such as Byron--chose to opt out of the debate altogether.

Byron adopts Hume's skepticism--which demolishes reason as a foundation for faith, denying miracles, and even, implicitly, the possibility of faith. This becomes clear from Byron's letter to Francis Hodgson from 13 September 1811. His comments--showing him at the extremity of his skepticism--are worth quoting at length, proving useful in assessing his attitudes towards his matter in *Heaven and Earth*. Byron insists that

> the basis of your religion is *injustice*; the *Son of God*, the *pure*, the *immaculate*, the *innocent*, is sacrificed for the *guilty*. This proves *His* heroism; but no more does away with *man's* guilt than by a schoolboy's volunteering to be flogged for another would exculpate the dunce from negligence, or preserve him from the rod.

Here, Byron denies the very basis for Christian redemption, finding it logically indefensible even in the face of a markedly pedestrian analogy.

Byron finds a God who would allow a single individual to suffer for the masses abhorrent. Theodicy becomes a problem plaguing the New Testament as much as the Old. "You degrade the Creator," he charges, "in the first place, by making Him a begetter of children"--a function degrading even to angels, according to some theologians who comment on Genesis 6.1-4. Byron adds that "in the next [place] you convert him into a tyrant over an immaculate and injured Being, who is sent into existence to suffer for the benefit of some millions of scoundrels, who, after all, seem as likely to be damned as ever." He follows by confirming his allegiance with Hume: "As to miracles, I agree with Hume that it is more probable men should *lie* or be *deceived*, than that things out of the course of nature should so happen," Byron naming "Mahomet," and two more recent, self-proclaimed "prophets" as a means of debunking the notion of miracles.

Byron, further, finds the notion of a chosen race indefensible, again, on grounds of common sense--here signifying "simple logic": "Besides, I trust that God is not a *Jew*, but the God of all mankind; and, as you allow that a virtuous Gentile may be saved, you do away with the necessity of being a Jew or Christian."[17] Christian doctrine renders Christianity unnecessary. Simple logic, too, tells him that the Bible reveals nothing about God or truth:

I do not believe in revealed religion, because no religion is revealed; and if it pleases the Church to damn me for not allowing a *nonentity*, I throw myself on the mercy of the "*Great First Cause, least understood*," who must do what is most proper; though I conceive He never made anything to be tortured in another life, whatever it may in this.

He is open to no further debate: "I will neither read *pro* nor *con*." Simple causality dictates that

God would have made His will known without books, considering how very few could read them when Jesus of Nazareth lived, had it been His pleasure to ratify any peculiar mode of worship.

About the afterlife, he asks, "as to your immortality, if people are to live, why die?" Once again, simple logic renders this staple of Christian doctrine ridiculous. To underscore this, he quips,

And our carcases, which are to rise again, are they worth raising? I hope, if mine is, that I shall have a better *pair of legs* than I have moved on these two-and-twenty years or I shall be sadly behind in the squeeze into Paradise. Did you ever read 'Malthus on Population?' If he be right, war and pestilence are our best friends, to save us from being eaten alive, in this "best of all possible worlds."

He closes by asserting that "I will write, read, and think no more; indeed, I do not wish to shock your prejudices by saying all I do think. Let us make the most of life, and leave the dreams to Emanuel Swedenborg" (Letters 2:

97-98). Malthusian selection becomes a better friend to humankind than Christianity as it is practiced in this world. Byron's closing reference to Swedenborg suggests that Byron remains conversant in issues in currency among Christians, his ironic comment about Swedenborg's *Arcana Coelestia* (1749-1756) suggesting his disdain for intricate anagogic readings of Scripture.

As noted, this letter to Hodgson constitutes Byron's most sustained skeptical thinking. Although at times referring to himself as an "orthodox Christian," bouts of skepticism of the sorts here expressed recur throughout his letters and poetry. "Rationalism" and "reason" become for Byron overly precise distinctions; simple logic--causality and probability--tells him that much of Christian doctrine amounts to nonsense.

Byron's comment about Hodgson's degrading his God by making Him beget children finds articulation by others in his age. Emma Martin, for example, in *The Movement: Anti-Persecution Gazette and Register of Progress* (1843) discusses the gospels in her "Christmas message to the people of London":

> Luke vaguely tells us that he [Christ] was supposed [to be] the son of Joseph; but that he 'should be called the son of God.' If HE was GOD, and there is but *one* GOD, two indisputable points, it means that he was his OWN father. Happy would it be for many a mother, could *she* and *others* believe that her child had been its own father. (Taylor 144.)

Again, the doctrine of Christ's genealogy does not withstand the tests of simple logical scrutiny.

Martin's Owenite, socialist orientation differs from Byron's systematic imperative that life is to be enjoyed (since it is all we have). Both Byron and Martin reflect a tendency of the age to deny Christian doctrine on non-scriptural and non-theological grounds. Both offer singular interpretations that oddly seem to combat a climate of renewed amenability to enthusiasm. In such a climate, unusual Scriptural passages--such as the lore about concupiscent angels--take on new and heightened significance, the old "doctrine of essentials" in danger of becoming cluttered by concern with indifferent matters. In contrast both to Anglicanism and to Enthusiasm develop wholesale dismissals of Christianity, based upon scrutiny of Scripture. Byron approaches this camp of expositors in 1811; Martin announcedly enters it in the 1840's.

Theology takes an unusual turn. The Bible has become dangerous to, rather than necessary for, faith. Emma Martin emphasizes this when she insists, "Mistake me not, then: it is not Christian differences with which I war, but the *system* itself;--not translations or commentaries, but the BOOK" (Taylor 145). "Rationalistic" exegesis, as Reedy terms textual analysis, reveals absurdities which Martin ridicules, as Byron had to Hodgson earlier. (This "rationalistic" exegesis proceeds without predication upon "right reason," that is, Cartesian, *a priori*, innate notions that God exists, and exists to be worshipped and to forgive.) Martin attributes her atheism to reading the Bible itself. *Sola Scriptura* takes on new meaning; whereas for Luther, the Bible alone was all one needed for faith, for Martin, for Martin's like-minded contemporary Robert Cooper, and, at times, for Byron and Shelley, among others, Scripture alone sufficed to inculcate skepticism, atheism, and/or nihilism. (Taylor 144.) (We need not turn to mid-century exotics such as Martin for examples of nineteenth-century doubt. Shelley and Hunt come immediately to mind--although Shelley proves himself hardly a nihilist, as his poetry, predicated on hope in a perfectible humankind, makes clear. Martin is useful, though, as an example of an outcome of readings reflecting Byron's proclivities towards subjecting Scripture to the same logical analysis one would apply to a secular text.)

In this context of Scripturally-inspired skepticism and atheism, the relative paucity of objections to the Genesis 6.1-4 narratives amazes. By enacting and amplifying this thread of folklore, Byron and others risk illustrating its conceptual extravagance. Outrage results in a wholesale reconsideration of angels by some theologians. After the publication, particularly, of Moore's and Byron's poems, systematic angelologies reappeared--expositions of the sort that had been outmoded among mainstream expositors for decades.

Anglican divines had kept angels in eclipse. Skepticism had denied their being. When England's amorous angels appeared, detractors revealed their own unfamiliarity with the legions of contending angelological notions, drawing, instead, upon notions derived vaguely from Augustine and Aquinas. These notions had been challenged by philosophers and poets in the sixteenth and seventeenth centuries, as well as by Jewish and early Christian commentators. Understanding of Genesis 6.1-4 remained unsophisticated; Enoch failed to engage efforts at understanding, this amplification of Genesis dismissed as "ridiculous."

Thomas Noon Talfourd's objections to both Moore's and Byron's angels reveal the character of the confusion marking received views about angels. "The whole machinery of angels," Talfourd writes,

> as minutely exhibited by Mr. Moore, and daringly glanced at by
> Lord Byron, has no hold on the superstitious of any age. . . . Angels
> have always been regarded as spirits, not subject to ordinary laws
> of nature, and as susceptible only of such sins and of such tempta-
> tions as mere intellect may participate. Some of them, indeed, have
> been considered as sinning and falling, but the crime, imputed to
> these, is pride, not any falling which belongs to mortal forms.

Talfourd here denies the poet license to rework biblical materials--
regardless of the thematic ends such reworkings would serve. (He would in
fact deny philosophical significance to such treatments, refusing to allow the
"superstitious" to embrace the new, poetic schemes--as if he expects that the
poets would have them substituted for Scripture, and, when, a few lines
later, he insists that "it is too late now to invent a new mythology, and
engraft it on the popular faiths"--again, as if the poets wish to register their
angel poems among apocryphal works.)[18] Talfourd's notions about angels
do not reflect the way in which "angels have always been regarded," as he
suggests, but rather constitute a rather indistinct amalgam of Augustinian-
Aquinian ideas, as the age fused--and confused--them.

For Augustine, Genesis 6.1-4 proves a source of discomfiture. *The City
of God* (15.23) devotes a section to the problems of "whether we are to
believe that angels . . . fell in love with the beauty of women, and sought
them in marriage, and that from their connection giants were born," a
discussion which Augustine refrains from answering with a definite
negative, although insisting that "I could by no means believe that God's
holy angels could have at that time so fallen," positing instead an alternative
class of "angels":--"the same holy Scripture affords the most ample
testimony that even godly men have been called angels"--this prophylaxis for
angelic reputation verging on euhemerism. Syncretism, too, provides
Augustine with another explanation here, in the form of "the *incubi*, and
other angels [as opposed to 'God's holy angels'] . . . who constantly attempt
and effect this impurity." Augustine takes recourse in the mythological
processes through which Greek antiquity bred strains of demigods and
monsters.

The issue bothers him. On the notion that "the fruit of the connection
between those who are called angels of God and the women they loved were
not men of our own breed but giants," Augustine must admit that "Giants

... might well be born, even before the sons of God ... formed a connection with the daughters of men, that is to say, before the sons of Seth formed a connection with the daughters of Cain." The acts were carnal, but the motives were originally Godly, according to his reading of Genesis 6.1-4:

> And the words 'They bare children to them,' show plainly enough that before the sons of God fell in this fashion they begat children to God, not to themselves--that is to say, [they were not] moved by the lust of sexual intercourse but discharging the duty of propagation, intending to produce not a family to gratify their own pride, but citizens to people the city of God.

Heber's misguided Patriarch orders his daughter to wed her angelic suitor out of his prideful vision of his role as head of a line of demigods; Heber may well have had Augustine in mind for his fragment recreating a "World Before the Flood". Augustine embellishes his explanation of the decline and fall of the angels with philological exegesis that he must first acknowledge, then strip of substantive significance; he refurbishes philology to suit his own theological preferences, evincing his sustained discomfort with the letter of Genesis 6.1-4. "The Septuagint indeed calls them both angels of God and sons of God, though all the copies do not show this, some having only the name 'sons of God.' And Aquila," he adds, "whom the Jews prefer to the other interpreters, has translated . . . [the phrase] 'sons of gods.'" Moore yields to this seemingly orthodox rendering in his own discussion of the phrase in a note to his preface of his first four editions of his *Loves*.[19] Moore plays it safe in following Augustine, if not as safe as he could have. Moore--among a few in his circle keenly adept at sacred philology--tacitly announces that in fact the phrase in Genesis 6.2 has, since antiquity, proven problematic; silence would have been safest, would have created no "in group/out group" distinction between those versed in the ancient texts and those relying upon vernacular ones (or at best the Vulgate). In Moore's own, earlier anonymous review of "Boyd's *Translation of the Church Fathers*," the poet makes light of angels, and takes delight in Pope's whimsical angelic fabrications for *The Rape of the Lock* (*Edinburgh Review* 24:62); Augustine, on the other hand, finds in this passage absolutely no source of delight. The letter of Genesis 6.1-4 continues to disturb Augustine well into Chapter 23 of his *City*:

> But that those angels were not angels in the sense of not being

men, as some suppose, Scripture itself decides, which unam-
biguously declares that they were men.... For by the spirit of God
they had been made angels of God and sons of God; but declining
towards lower things, they are called 'flesh,' as deserters of the
Spirit, and by their desertion deserted.

Montgomery's Enoch and Javan reverse this process of decline in *The World
Before the Flood*, both ascending spiritually. For such ascent, Renaissance
philosophers provide arguments, although with angelology so newly revived
in the earlier nineteenth century, Talfourd remains limited to Augustine
and Aquinas.

One alternative tradition--encouraging the desire for ontogenic
elevation--appears in Pico della Mirandola's "On the Dignity of Man,"
which offers a refreshingly upbeat explanation of interspeciation as a means
of ascent. There is nothing wrong--hubristic--or improper with wanting to
be close to the Godhead. Aspirations of this sort should be encouraged,
rather than damned. (Pico's treatise would support Lea's ambitions in
Moore's narrative.) Pico proposes that mortals may become seraphic, may
in fact earn entry into any of the three angelic orders "that the sacred
mysteries relate" are "nearest to the Godhead," namely, the "seraphim,
cherubim, and thrones." Pico's assertions (in Cassirer, Kristeller, and
Randall, eds. 223-56) likewise recall Aholibamah's intuited "inner ray"
ensuring her spiritual equality with her angelic lover. For Pico,

> The Seraph burns with the fire of love.... If we long with love for
> the Creator himself alone, we shall speedily flame up with His
> consuming fire into a Seraphic likeness.... Whoso is a Seraph,
> that is a lover, is in God and God in him, nay, rather, God and
> himself are one (227-28).

Of course Pico indulges in word play; of course he tantalizes with possibilities accessible solely through a mind willing to literalize metaphor and
abstractions, and to grant abstractions objective reality. Pico offers hope--
if only through word dazzle. (A reflection on Genesis 12, left in Latin notes
in Milton's commonplace book, offers evidence of Milton's sanctioning for
the subsequent century the kind of upward striving Pico applauds. Milton
writes that "A good man in some measure seeks to excel even the angels,"
and with good reason--a reason predicating Byron's quip to Hodgson about
Byron's unserviceable legs; a man will dare compete with angels, Milton

explains, "for the reason that housed in a weak and perishable body and struggling forever with desires, he nevertheless aspires to lead a life that resembles that of the heavenly host." CEWJM 18: 129) Human hopes for ascent are quashed more often than not; because of its contrasting, hopeful vision, Pico's mystic union, or becoming, appeals. Humans suspend disbelief willingly.

Talfourd is unfortunately unaware of Pico's treatise, or of any other treatise challenging the immutability of the species presumed by Aquinas perhaps more than Augustine (for Augustine does, indeed, name those odd "incubi"). Talfourd relies upon Augustinian, blended with Aquinian, lore--inadvertently and innocently disparaging Moore's and Byron's angels largely because they derive from wider ranging traditions. While for Augustine, corporeal beings of some sort--angelic rubbish (as opposed to "God's holy angels")--engage in the carnal acts described in Genesis 6.1-4, Aquinas exempts himself from troubling over the implications of the passage. He dismisses the notion of any such possible lapse as absurd. Angels do assume bodies in Aquinas's system, but "the body assumed is united to the angel not as its form, but merely as its mover, represented by the assumed movable body." Angels cannot exercise bodily functions in these assumed bodies, despite Scriptural accounts of angels eating, drinking, and copulating with mortals, for their assumed bodies "are not fashioned for the purpose of sensation through them, but to this end, that [through] such bodily organs the spiritual powers of the angels be made manifest." Aquinas (as embraced by Talfourd) would rule out the concupiscence Byron, Moore, Croly, and Montgomery ascribe to angels. In no sense are angels capable of sinning (320, Q 62.1).[20] Theirs is a "rational intellectual nature," their ontogeny inexplicable to corporeal beings (318).

Hook's understanding of angels as "Scripture teaches us to conceive them" may well translate into angels as Aquinas portrays them, Aquinas at times drawing from Scripture. For the most part, Aquinas' notion of aeveternal, acorporeal, intellection reflects scholastic creativity. About the substance of angels, Aquinas appeals with his simplicity--particularly in the fact that humans are without faculties for comprehending substance of this sort; *nescio* must serve us in attempting to apprehend particulars. Complexity surrounds his notion of angelic hierarchy.

Thomistic theory holds, even, that each individual angel is a distinct species in the hierarchy, and that hence there can be no precise "equals" in heaven. Angels approximate equality in their functions, certainly. Angels of the lowest order are messengers to humans. But assuming the function served by an angel of a lower order does not debase a substitute angel of a higher order, since their functions only, and not their taxonomic ranks, may alter. (Even an archangel will, from time to time, descend from Heaven as a messenger; Gabriel, after all, did come to Mary.) In the Thomistic scheme, however, with no "pure equals," taxonomy becomes dauntingly complex-- even moreso in its implications for an analogously complex hierarchy of mortals.[21]

The appeal of Thomistic angelology remains obvious. The incomprehensible is indescribable; things indescribable remain indisputable. Save for his complex hierarchy, Aquinas simplifies matters. Angels are never corporeal. Doctrinally sound or not, Aquinas's simplicity satisfies Talfourd and like-minded reviewers. Byron and Moore not only complicate visions of angels, but create impossibilities--if judged according to a blended Augustinian/Aquinian scheme--thereby composing theologically irrelevant poems.

The Thomistic hierarchy does not stand unopposed, although Hook and Talfourd seem unaware of the fact that the ordering of angels is fraught with confusion and undue complexity. Ficino, discussing the *Celestial Hierarchies* of the so-called Dionysius the Areopagite, reports that Dionysius posits a nine-story residence, comprised of three distinct main structures, each subdivided into a triplex. Each of the nine divisions specifically suits a particular order of angels. For example, Seraphim live in the top division of the highest compartment, called the "hierarchy of the Father." Those who find place there are commissioned to "speculate on the order and providence of God." (The highest order carries out the most cerebral, or contemplative commission, and enjoys the closest proximity to God.) "Archangels direct the divine cult and look after sacred things." Directing the cult requires attention to mortal spiritual concerns. Both the active nature of their tasks, and their proximity to--or at least their need to think about--humankind befits a lower ranking order, as Archangels indeed are in Dionysius' scheme. Archangels occupy "the hierarchy of the spirit," the second tier in the third and lowest partition (Yates 118-19). Moore approaches comic understatement when he adds a note to his fifth edition of *The Loves of the Angels* observing that

> there appears to be, among writers on the East, as well among the Orientals themselves, considerable indecision with regard to the respective claims of Seraphim and Cherubim to the highest rank (MPW 548 n).

Pico's treatise opposes Augustine's notion of fixed ontogeny, as was mentioned above. Here, Ficino adds an alternative tradition to Aquinian notions about the order of angels. Philosophical treatises of these sorts emerge during the Renaissance. In the seventeenth century, poetic depictions, rather than discussions, prove more familiar. (Angels seldom engage writers in the eighteenth century, and hence encyclopedists collect them.) During the later seventeenth century angels appear chiefly as metaphoric conveniences--implication, becoming superannuated mythological trappings; they serve poets better than philosophers.[22]

A tendency to anthropomorphize angels in seventeenth-century poetry worked to break down traditional Thomistic notions of angels as immaterial substances--a notion Hobbes finds patently absurd. Theological irrelevancy--even absurdity--had resulted from earlier efforts at poeticizing angels as sanctioned by Aquinas. In the *Davideis* (1656), Cowley's angels assume bodies that accord with Thomistic models. Angels have no physical bodies. In accommodating human limitations in envisioning beings (not simply in comprehending language), angels use external nature to fabricate what mortals will take to be bodies. By illustrating a process that Aquinas asserts (without explaining), Cowley works to show its fictional character. The narrator recalls that

> When *Gabriel* (no blest Spirit more kind or fair)
> Bodies and cloathes himself with thickned ayr.
> All like a comely *youth* in lifes fresh bloom;
> Rare workmanship, and wrought by heavenly loom:
> He took for skin a cloud most soft and bright,
> That ere the midday Sun pierc'ed through with
> light;
> Upon his cheeks a lively blush he spred;
> Washt from the morning beauties red.
> An harmless flaming *Meteor* shone for haire,
> And fell adown his shoulders with loose care.
> He cuts out a silk *Mantle* from the skies,
> Where the most sprightly azure pleas'd the eyes.
> This he with starry vapours spangles all,
> Took in their prime ere they grow *ripe* and *fall*.
> Of a new *Rainbow* ere it *fret* or *fade*,
> The choicest piece took out, a *Scarf* is made.

Small streaming clouds he does for wings display,
Not Vertuous Lovers sighes more soft then They.
Thus he gilds o're with the Suns richest rays,
Caught gliding ore pure streams on which he plays.
(2. 793-812)

In a note corresponding to this passage, Cowley acknowledges Aquinas as a precedent for his angel's literally pulling himself together for the occasion. In naming pagan precedents to Aquinas, Cowley reflects a syncretism that would tend to reduce the theological significance of Aquinas. Note 95 to Book II offers a recipe for angelic embodiment:

> *Tho. Aquinas*, upon the second of the Senten. *Distinct. 9.Art.2.* It is necessary that the Air should be *thickned*, till it come near to the propriety of earth; that is, to be capable of *Figuration*, which cannot be but in a solid body, &c. And this way of *Spirits* appearing in bodies of condensed ayr (for want of a better way, they taking it for granted that they do frequently appear) is approved of by all the *Schoolmen*, and the *Inquisitors* about Witches. But they are beholding for this Invention to the ancient *Poets*. (295-96.)

Cowley quotes the *Aeneid* 12.1125-27, and the *Iliad* 5.733-42 for credibility, this association--whether deliberate or inadvertent--adding a mythological dimension to angels that Aquinas, not to mention Augustine, would decry. Cowley's own skepticism about this process of angelic formation emerges through his phrase, "for want of a better way," and through his opposition of "Schoolmen" to "Inquisitors." His description of Gabriel's assumed body renders it difficult to accept as mimesis of anything real. Having depicted this process in verse, Cowley renders it impossible to conceive of Gabriel as "incorporeal substance."

Milton, of course, asserts that angels exist (*De Doctrina* Book 1, Chapters 3-9), although Raphael's blush at Adam's reference to angelic sex enrolls this particular angel among the casts of mythological beings generated by antiquity. "About the meaning" of Genesis 6.1-4, in particular, James Grantham Turner finds Milton "quite uncertain," Turner finding "the efforts of modern scholars to reduce him to orthodoxy . . . unsatisfactory" (268). Turner discerns the "Augustinian meaning" in *Paradise Lost* 11.580-636, which the narrative uses to "teach . . . Adam the need for sexual temperence." In *De Doctrina*, Turner judges that "Milton quotes Genesis 6.1

approvingly, as an example of sound moral judgement in love." He points to Milton's disdain for the monstrous offspring of this divine/mortal coitus in *Paradise Lost* 3.461-3, and determines that "in *Paradise Regained* [2.178-81] Milton assumes quite unequivocally that the unholy couplings in Genesis 6 were in fact done by the supernatural Belial and his 'lusty crew,' who then falsely named the perpetrators 'sons of God'." (268-69). Elsewhere in *Paradise Regained* (4.197 and 4.517), Milton suggests to Turner that "'Sons of God both Angels are and Men'." (269) What Turner designates "uncertainty" is more likely "awareness." Milton doubtless knew the range of meanings *bene ha'elohim* could bear, and doubtless chose those which best suited his given purposes--Milton no stranger to dispassionate syncretism, or to dispassionate selectivity, when confronted by multiple readings in Scripture.

Milton's belief in angels as theological realities in no way cancels out his willingness to invent mythological angels. Unlike Augustine and the host of Patristic Fathers, Milton sees no need for Christianity to fight against the mythological inventions of pagan antiquity. Inventions from the fabric of Christian doctrine will populate poetry without undermining theology. This at least seems to be the sole justification for one of his unexecuted purposes for angels--found in an outline for a tragedy about Sodom--left in his commonplace book. This outline directs attention to the fate of Lot. The poet's notes (here, kept unpunctuated, with spelling left as recorded) would have

> a Chorus of Angels concluding and the Angels relating the event of Lots journey, & of his wife. the first Chorus beginning may relate the course of the Citty each evening every one with mis-tresse, or Ganymede, glittering along the streets, or solacing on the banks of Jordan, or down the stream. at the priests inviting to Angels to the Solemnity the Angels pittying thir beauty may dispute of love & how it differs from lust seeking to win them in the last scene to the king & nobles when the firce thunders begin aloft the Angel appears all girt with flames which he saith are the flames of true love & tells the K. who falls down with terror his just suffering as also Athanes id est Gener Lots son in law for dispising the continuall admonitions of Lots their calling & the thunders Lightning & fires he bids them heare the call as command of God to come & destroy a godlesse nation he brings them down with some short warning to all other nations to take heed. (CEWJM 18:

234).

Milton's angels would have appreciated, but not succumbed to, mortal beauty. In this respect, Milton draws from a more orthodox cosmogony than Montgomery, Moore, Croly, or Byron. (The "eve of destruction" setting will find renovation--on the more usual, Noachic doomstime--in Dale's poem.) Yet the fact that Milton can use angels as commentators--and that he can ascribe to them empathy for mortal beauty--shows the poet's readiness to take liberties with angels as great as any taken by the angel/deluge poets in the earlier nineteenth century. Had this tragedy been completed, it could not have been called, strictly, biblical.

While angels did not drop entirely out of sight after the seventeenth century, their appearances diminished drastically. Much was forgotten. Emmanuel Swedenborg's *Arcana Coelestia* (1749-1756) totally disembodies the *bene ha'elohim*. In his treatment of Genesis 6.2, Swedenborg offers a wholly anagogic reading. The "sons of God" signify "doctrinal things of faith."[23] Yet after England's amorous angels made their appearances, angelology became of serious interest to nineteenth-century commentators.

Among the more interesting contemporary discussions of angels is an anonymous review of "The Congregational Lecture," specifically, James Bennett, D.D., on *The Theology of the First Ages of the Christian Church*, in *Tait's Edinburgh Magazine* N.S. 9 (1842): 261-66. The reviewer surveys "the wild opinions held by the early Christian Fathers about the nature and condition of Angels" (261). Justin and Clement of Alexandria attribute the fall of the angels to the corruption of the kind by the beauty of women (262). Clement of Alexandria as well as Athenagoras agree, concerning Genesis 6.1-4, that "the demons that sprang from angels and women are supposed, of course, to be hybrid; so that it is difficult to describe their properties"--a condition that entertained Lamb. This reviewer adds that these beings "inhabit heathen temples, animating the idols, dictating oracles, and feasting on the nidor of the sacrifices. This gave a double horror to idolatry; for, besides being an offence to God, it was almost a direct adoration of devils" (262). The writer notes that these opinions inculcated a notion that "a Millenium of sensual delights" was to follow (this notion the target of Moore's short, satirical poem on "The Millenium") adding,

It is unquestionable, that, with all the ultra-angelic spirituality of these fathers, and all their compulsory fasting, they hoped to make up for it in the New Jerusalem, as all pretences to soar above the divine rule, end in sinking far below (263).

The reviewer concludes that

> It will then be seen that the world has been imposed upon by those who appealed to the fathers, to avoid the Scriptures, aware that the people could study for themselves a single book translated into most tongues, than procure or read a library in the dead languages. But it must be shown that corruption can no more claim the fathers than the Scriptures. How the advocates for error shun the testimony of the divine Word is not sufficiently known (265).

In sum, this writer closes by explaining what he has already shown, namely, that biblical angelology is fraught with confusion. (The ideal of a sensual millenium calls to mind the Qur'anic delay of gratifications until heaven.) The reviewer apologizes for including a "long, serious extract" from Bennett's work "in a popular magazine; but its *ultra-Protestantism* was to us irresponsible." He adds that "they must have perceived that this is no commonplace theological work, as well as that it is one peculiarly adapted to the times. As such, we recommend it to all who like to investigate for themselves" (266). The reviewer reacts against the evangelicalism moving Bennett's lecture. He would likely have reacted against Hook's and Talfourd's bases for objecting to Moore's *Angels*--as antiquated as the notions put forth by the Fathers and by Bennett.

Of interest, too, is Moses Stuart, "Sketches of Angelology in the Old and New Testament," in *Bibliotheca Sacra* 1 (1843): 88-154. Stuart surveys the passages in Scripture mentioning angels, discussing various angelic functions. He closes by comparing Hebrew to Zoroastrian angelology:

> Parsee angelology looks very much as if it were made up in this way [i.e., through minings from Platonic ideals]. The Feruers must be of heathen origin. Dualism, and the total destruction of the Defs and the annihilation of Duzukah, must be of heathen (Parsee) origin. But some of the attributes of Ormuzd and Ahriman, the different orders of angels good or bad, and the like, look very much like being taken from the Jewish notions in relation to this subject (154).

However devout their intentions, discussions of angels in the nineteenth century inevitably lead to discussions of similar beings in other religions or mythologies--suggesting the difficulty the encyclopedists posed for later expositors, who found the dearth of biblical angels, as well as their extravagance in Scripture, barriers against unadulterated biblical angelology. Classical or Eastern traditions often rendered service in making sense of Christendom's angels; by themselves, the angels of Scripture made little sense as entities or as necessities tooling the universe designed by an omnipotent deity. In addition, both articles discuss materials with which Moore, particularly, proves himself conversant. Of the five angel/deluge poems, Moore's derives from the widest body of learning about angels--whether to the benefit or to the detriment of the poem remains a matter of taste.

Byron is quite correct in accepting the translation 'sons of gods' as angels, as is given as the only reading in some copies of LXX. Moore, also, is quite correct in attributing the translation "angels of God" in lieu of "sons of God" to LXX, although this rendering is not the sole property of LXX translators. Moore's conclusions about the significance of this mistranslation want validity. Because the fable was based upon a mistranslation of LXX does not make Moore's subject "non-scriptural," as Moore claims, for theologians had argued the meaning of *bene ha'elohim* for centuries, and the implications of the Genesis 6 passage belong more to theology than to pure philological analysis.

There are, of course, outstanding differences between reinterpreting Genesis 6.1-4 for the religious needs of particular communities, and using the source as a metaphoric convenience for poetry. Upon the former renderings depend the spiritual health of the cult; the latter, at best, encourage philosophical or theological discussion, and may or may not bear didactic ends. The pseudepigraphic works are rightly called cultic, not strictly imaginative, literature. Spiritual fitness and guidance for righteous conduct depend upon this latter body of works. The Enoch fragment answers a problem of theodicy for Israel, and promises a New Jerusalem--a Messianic kingdom on earth. The allied Reuben fragment is strictly didactic, enumerating laws and codes of behavior which, presumably, gain in importance because of their status as the legacies of the tribes's eponymous ancestors. These works fulfill the need of a cult, they redesign a 'truth' in Scripture to accord with the needs of a particular tribe, or they alter a passage of Scripture which a certain group finds objectionable.

Poems are exempt from this burdensome responsibility. Obviously, nineteenth-century poets asked for no "believers"--in no way proselytized--when rendering Scripture and Pseudepigrapha into poetry. (Dale may prove an exception.) The poets replicate no cosmos, past or present; each posits but one of the several cosmic structures Scripture suggests. The poets' reasons for their particular selections vary, although all share the criterion of identifying a place in which they might effectively explore human suffering--where they might postulate how it would feel to be an unelect mortal experiencing a catastrophic demolition of the universe humans take for granted. For the poets, as opposed to theologians, Gods are at the service of mortals; nineteenth-century readers care about the gods and angels only insofar as they bear pertinence to human existence. (Demolition of the universe seemed less a possibility to the previous century than to our own.) For nineteenth-century French poets and philosophers, Moore, Byron, and their angels bore crucial philosophical pertinence. For nineteenth-century British reviewers, the angels by all five poets proved bewildering, at best.

'Sublime,' 'satanic,' 'insipid,' 'prophane,' 'unengaging,' 'licentious,' 'silly': various contemporary reviewers slapped one or more of these or their kind from among a spate of labels onto England's amorous angels. Tabulating these terms yields nothing close to any consensus of opinion. Quite simply, reviewers did not know what to make of the celestials. (Reviews reflecting passion--or, often, simple authorial interest--usually take inspiration not from one of the angel/deluge poems, but rather from the opportunity to launch with impunity *ad hominem* attacks against one of the poets. Any poem by the targeted writer would have served just as well.) Theorists avoided the angels--save for the few theorists of literature on *Ponce-de-Leonic* quests for foolproof recipes for sublimity. These confused responses prove serviceable. England's divergent receptions of the angel /deluge poems reflect heterogeneous demands upon poets and poetry; they provide an index to the confusion poets faced about their responsibilities to a newly heterogeneous readership, and hint at the doubts plaguing poets about the value of imaginative literature in a world in which manufacturers and mass-marketing geniuses were amassing laurels--laurels that, if not quite of the sort once conferred upon poets, were apparently fashioned out of the raw materials once preserved for poets' laurels; poets, at least, were winning so few, and these so infrequently, suspicions inevitably arose that the poetic laurel inventory was near depletion, with no replenishment planned.

Notes to Chapter 2

[1]Gustav Davidson discusses the paucity of named angels in the Bible, and outlines the multiplicity of tasks performed by angels in the Old and New Testaments (xv-xxii). Difficulties proliferate from the phrase *bene ha'elohim* of the Masoretic text (MT). The Septuagint (LXX) manuscripts leave variant renderings of this phrase in Genesis 6.2. The Alexandrine reading, "the angels of God," earns entry into Walton's Polyglot (1657) only as a marginal variant from MS.A. (Alexandrine Manuscript), despite the fact that MS.A., "the earliest extant, complete Greek translation of the Old Testament, executed at Alexandria sometime during the third century [B.C.]," has become "so habitually known by the name of the Septuagint" that modern efforts to detach the designator LXX from this particular document have invariably failed (Brenton i-vi). Walton's text proper gives the corresponding Latin translation "filii Dei." (Walton 1: 22). Tradition has preferred the variant "sons of God" to "angels of God," the reading "sons" encouraged by the later complete Greek translations presented for comparison by Origen--namely, Aquila's (traditionally dated 120 A.D.), Symmachus' (traditionally assigned to the second century A.D.), and Theodotian's (also traditionally fixed in the second century A.D.). (Brenton i-vi) Origen's Hexaplar text, although lost, survives in fragments edited by Montfaucon in 1714. Moore's notes to his Preface to his first four editions of *The Loves of the Angels* refer to Aquila, Symmachus, Theodotian, and Montfaucon, as well as to the Alexandrine rendering. These notes refer to Philo, Hugo St. Victor, and others who accept as authoritative the reading "angels of God," on grounds that the identical Greek phrase appears in all of the early Greek translations of Job 1.6. (Brenton 665) (See also Fourmont, *Réflexions* 1: 31, *The Zohar* 1: 138, and Charles, *Pseudepigrapha* 191 for arguments in favor of this reading for Genesis 6.2.) Moore's note to this original Preface acknowledges Augustine's acceptance of "the Italic" (Vulgate, or V) reading "filii Dei," although does not concur with Augustine's philologically untenable assertion that

> among translations themselves the Italian (*Itala*) is to be preferred to the others, for it keeps closer to the words without prejudice to the clearness of expression. And to correct the Latin we must use the Greek versions, among which the authority of the Septuagint

is pre-eminent as far as the Old Testament is concerned . . . . (*CD* 2: 15).

Moore instead prefers the Aramaic paraphrase of M (The Targum Onkelos, Walton 1: 23); the accompanying Latin translation in Walton of the disputed phrase in Genesis 6.2 reads "filii principum filias hominum," and elaborates upon a related view that the sons in question are the sons of Enos, who, according to Cyril of Alexandria (also cited by Moore in his note to his original Preface), is "surnamed [son of God] because he was the guardian of righteousness and every virtue," an "appellation" his line maintained "as long as they remained righteous and avoided intercourse with the sinful race of Cain, the members of which were styled 'the children of men.'" (Kerrigan 289) Moore's familiarity with the textual and theological difficulties is comprehensive as Jordan documents. (*Upright* 261).

Charles Spencer, a contemporary of Moore's, argues against the "angels of God" reading for Genesis 6.2 on quite different grounds. Spencer predetermines a function for angels; this function involves them in various activities, excluding them from others. Copulating with mortal women remains one of the latter. An anonymous review of "*A Scriptural Account of the Nature and Employment of the Holy Angels; partly occasioned by two Poems, recently published, the Title of one and the Subject of both being the 'Loves of the Angels.'* By Charles Spencer, A.M., Vicar of Bishop's Stortford, Hertfordshire. 8 vo. 24pp. Rivingtons. 1823" appears in *The Christian Remembrancer* 5 (1823): 355-57. The review constitutes itself from lengthy excerpts from Spencer's treatise; the reviewer does contribute a footnote explaining that "The office of the Holy Angels is considered by Mr. Spencer to be twofold: their heavenly, 'to wait about the throne of God, and worship, and adore him, and celebrate, and praise;' their earthly, to execute the divine vengeance on nations and individuals, and watch over the objects of the divine mercy, as 'ministering spirits, sent forth to minister for them who shall be heirs of salvation'." [355 n] The fact that this reviewer senses the need to identify these different functions reflects the fact that Spencer did not "conceive" of angels as did either "Scripture" or the age generally; the currency of alternative views--and downright indifference--renders the note in order.

Spencer himself finds it "'painful to advert to some modern publications, which have issued from the press, in a captivating form, recommended to some by the celebrity of the authors, and engaging others, from the licentiousness of the idea'." He argues that "The subject of this double and insinuating pestilence, is a flat contradiction to the authority of the

Scriptures, though it claims to be founded on the book it insults, and is falsely described as a scriptural fact, and not as a fable of the human imagination.'" Spencer upholds the chastity of angels at the risk of assaulting the inspiration of Scriptures--a trade-off facing Augustine, Lactantius, Tertullian, Clement of Alexandria, and the full battery of ancient writers Moore discusses in his annotations to his unrevised (first four editions of his) poem. (Augustine explicitly excises as "apocrypha" both the Book of Enoch and Genesis 6.1-4, in *The City of God* 15.23). Spencer quotes Genesis 6.1-4, and at great length, argues that the "sons of God" cannot be angels, according to the principle "'that Scripture is always to be interpreted by Scripture'." Hopefully,

> 'This [Spencer's] interpretation [of "sons of God" as "angels"] having been refuted, all calumnies erected upon the base of it, are effectively overthrown. It puts to silence the ignorance of foolish, and exposes the malevolence of profane, men,--it shelters the unsullied holiness of the Deity, and the character of the sacred volume which reveals him, from the apparent design, but abortive attempt, of those who would wound the reputation of both by an indirect attack.'

Spencer closes with the imperative, "'WORSHIP GOD!!!'" (355-7) Mimetic clamor will not turn off our brains--although this vitriol against Moore's and Byron's poems seems not to bother Moore. Of far more concern to Moore is Lady Donegal's reaction. The poet expects objections from some of the professional clergy--Moore far more conversant with angelology than any of the group writing aginst him. As long as these objections do not curtail sales, they pose no problem. (They may in fact have enhanced marketability, readers eager to see what all the commotion was about.)

The same debates about the sense of *bene ha'elohim* in Moore's time still flourish. Gerhard Von Rad asserts that

> the question ... whether ... the 'sons of God' are to be understood as angelic beings or as men, i.e., as members of the 'superior human race of Seth,' can be considered finally settled. The *bene ha'elohim*, here ... clearly contrasted to the daughters of men, are beings of the upper heavenly world. The *ben* ('son') describes them, however, as sons of God, not in the physical, genealogical sense . .., but generally as belonging to the world of the Elohim.

(In *Genesis: A Commentary*, trans. John H. Marks, The Old Testament Library (Philadelphia: Westminster Press, 1961), 42.) Von Rad does not go undisputed.

Robert Davidson's commentary on Genesis 6.1-4 begins with his claim that "This section is one of the strangest passages in the whole of the Old Testament." He explains that "After noting . . . the rapid expansion in the world population (verse 1), it declares in verse 2 *the sons of the gods saw that the daughters of men were beautiful: so they took for themselves such women as they chose*: and verse 4 speaks of the time when *the sons of the gods had intercourse with the daughters of men*." Davidson continues by observing that

> From the time of the Aramaic Targums onwards, misplaced piety has led commentators to sidestep the plain meaning of the text. Attempts have been made to explain *the sons of the gods* as nobility or royalty or the true worshippers of God. By all Old Testament analogy *the sons of the gods* can mean one thing, divine beings. In Job 1:6 and 2:1 the same phrase is translated by the N.E.B. [New English Bible] *the members of the court of heaven*. This meaning was recognized in early Jewish tradition in Jubilees 5:1 and Enoch 6:2 and probably in the New Testament in 2 Peter 2:4 and Jude 6. Further, *the daughters of men* cannot mean anything other than mortal women. Such stories of sexual intercourse between gods and mortal women are common enough in religious mythology . . . . Nor is it strange that such a story should be used to explain the existence on earth of a race of supermen, the *Nephilim* (verse 4). *Nephilim* is a word of very uncertain meaning. In Num. 13:33, the only other Old Testament reference, the Nephilim are men of gigantic size who make the Hebrew incomers to Canaan feel 'no bigger than grasshoppers.' (69)

[2]Dowden JTM 2: 621 n. See my reference to Spencer above, note 1.

[3]Isaac (in Charlesworth) highlights these themes in his edition of *The Old Testament Pseudepigrapha* 1: 9. Dakin stresses the disappointment of the British with industrialization (20).

[4]The matter is complicated by the Queen of Heaven, lamented by Jeremiah (7.18, 44.16-28), sometimes taken to be a physical partner for Yahweh. In origin, this "Queen" was the "Babylonian-Assyrian goddess Ishtar, goddess of the star Venus," comparable to the "Canaanite Astarte,

Greek Aphrodite, Roman Venus," and likely the Persian Zohara. "First introduced, presumably, by Manasseh (2 Kg. 21.1-18), suppressed by Josiah (2 Kg. 23.1-14), and restored by Jehoiakim (2 Kg. 23.36-24.7), the cult was especially popular among women, who had an inferior role in the cult of the Lord." (*OAB* 972 n)

⁵Philo, *De Gigantibus*, in Colson, tr., I: 42-46. For Hebrew and other variations on this story, see Graves and Patai 100-107.

⁶G. Davidson 34:

> In Talmud *Bereshith Rabba* 85, and according to Rabbi Jochanan commenting on Genesis 38:13-26, when "Judah was about to pass by, without noticing, Tamar (Judah's daughter-in-law, squatting like a harlot at the crossroads), God caused the angel of lust to present itself to him." The angel is not named--but compare with Pharzuph (or Priapus), whom Arnobius in *Adversus Nationes III* called "the Hellespontian God of lust." [Cf. also with the "spirit of whoredom" in Hosea 14:12.] (Davidson's brackets.)

⁷From *The Sacred History of Sulpitius Severus* in Schaff, Philip, and Henry Wace, eds., *Nicene and Post-Nicene Fathers of the Christian Church*, 2nd Series, vol. 11, 1890-1900; rpt. Grand Rapids: Eerdmans, 1964: 71-72. See also "The Second Apology of Justin [Martyr]," Ch. 5 (R&D 1:190). Patristic fathers initiated many of the same arguments about the nature and function of angels--and hence the sense of Genesis 6.1-4--still flourishing today, and hinted at above in note 1. Athenagoras, in "A Plea for the Christians," holds that angels, like men, "have freedom of choice as to both virtue and vice," and that among the angels, "some . . . fell into impure love of virgins, and were subjugated by the flesh . . . ," and that through coitus with women "were begotten those who are called giants." (R&D 2: 142) Clement of Alexandria, in "The Instructor," refers to "the angels who renounced the beauty of God for a beauty which fades, and so fell from heaven to earth." (R&D 2: 274) Lactantius, in "The Divine Institutes," speaks of a time "When . . . the number of men had begun to increase," and "God . . . sent angels for the protection and improvement of the human race," angels who were by "that most deceitful ruler of the earth," that is,"the devil," "gradually enticed . . . to vices, and polluted them by intercourse with women." (R&D 7:64). See also Tertullian, "On the Veiling of Virgins" (R&D 4:32), "On the Apparel of Women" (R&D 2: 22), "Against Marcion" (R&D 3: 470, 445), and "On Idolatry" (R&D 3: 65).

Ante-Nicene and Post-Nicene commentators turn to Genesis 6.1-4 in expressing one or more of three general concerns. The writers quoted above either 1) explain the appearance of giants on the earth as a result of the intercourse described in Genesis 6.2, or 2) suggest that if angels could be corrupted by beauty, so much more likely are men to be enslaved by their passions. Other theologians turn to this passage to 3) explain the origin of idolatry, as does Tertullian, "On Idolatry" (R&D 3:64), a subject of concern to the Synod of Laodicea (A.D. 343-381), when it drafted Canon 35: "Christians must not forsake the Church of God and go away and invoke angels and gather assemblies, which things are forbidden. If, therefore, any one shall be found engaged in this covert idolatry, let him be anathema; for he has forsaken our Lord Jesus Christ, the Son of God, and has gone over to idolatry." (Schaff and Wace 14: 150) (G. Davidson discusses the fates of angel worship in his Introduction to his *Dictionary* xxiii n: "Certain early theologians like Eusebius (c. 263-c.399) and Theodoret (c.393-c.458) opposed the veneration of angels, and a Church council at Laodicea (343-381?) condemned Christians 'who gave themselves up to a masked idolatry in honor of the angels.' This, despite the fact that St. Ambrose (339?-397) exhorted the faithful in his *De Viduis*, 9, to 'pray to the angels who are given us as guardians.' In the 8th century, at the 2nd Council of Nicaea (787), there was another change of heart, for the worship of angelic beings was formally approved.") Still other writers use angels to explain the dissemination of astrology and magic, as well as technical and cosmetic knowledge, as by-products of angelic dissipation. (See, for example, Origen, "Against Celsus," R&D 4: 544, and Tertullian, "On Idolatry." R&D 3: 64-65.) Others simply explain the nature of angels as messengers from God to mortals (as does Clement of Alexandria, in the *Stromata, or Miscellanies*, R&D 2: 493, and Irenaeus, "Against Heresies." R&D 1: 361).

[8]See Norman C. Habel, "The Two Flood Stories in Genesis," in *The Flood Myth*, ed. Alan Dundes (Berkeley: Univ. of Calif. Press, 1988) 13-28.

[9]See Habel, 14, who points out that Jean Astruc had noted duplicates and contradictions of this sort in 1753--Astruc's a recent contribution to centuries of such notations beginning with the earliest Jewish and Christian commentators. (Astruc, *Conjectures sur les Mémoires originaux dont il paroît que Moyse s'est servi pour composer le Livre de Genèse*, Paris, 1753.) Prior to Astruc, H.B. Witter had in 1711 pointed to two separate creation stories in Genesis (Teeple 75). None of these observations were new; Spinoza, Hobbes --and before them, even Augustine--had pointed to duplications and discrepancies. With the eighteenth century began the tendency to use these against theories of "verbal inspiration," rather than as evidence of different divine voices accommodating different (imperfect) human ears.

[10]*The Sources of the Doctrines of the Fall and Original Sin*, 1903; rpt. New York: Schocken Books, 1968. Robert Davidson finds that "both the text and the interpretation of this verse [3] present serious difficulties." He points to "two main lines of interpretation," which he discusses in relation to the New English Bible. In the first, the phrase 'my spirit' bears ethical significance, implying "that there is a limit to God's patience"; God sees "outrageous evil," and hence "will withdraw his spirit and leave man to reap the tragic consequences." Davidson judges that "linguistically this is a very dubious reading." In the second, the phrase 'my spirit' denotes "the gift of life which comes to man from God," as in Genesis 1.2; the translation is thus "part commentary": "*My life-giving spirit. This gift of life is not man's inalienable possession; it will not remain in man forever.*" Davidson finds this "linguistically sounder," adding that it "gives a better connection with what follows." (70) Von Rad finds that the "divine penalty" in verse 3 "lacks strict relation to what precedes." Rather, "it is applied to man in general, and not only to the actual evildoers and their bastards." He concludes that "the impression here that older material could have been radically revised subsequently is now strengthened because of the remarkable position of v. 4 in the narrative context." (114-115)

[11]Charles Gill, ed., *The Book of Enoch, the Prophet, Translated from an Ethiopic Ms. in the Bodleian Library, by the Late Richard Laurence*, London: K Paul Trench & Co., 1883. See also Charles, *Pseudepigrapha*, and G. Zuntz, "Enoch on the Last Judgment," *Journal of Theological Studies*, 1st Ser., 45 (1944): 161-70.

[12]See Gustav Davidson, *Dictionary* Bernard J. Bamberger, *Fallen Angels*, Philadelphia: Jewish Publication Society of America, 1952; and Leo Jung, *Fallen Angels in Jewish, Christian, and Mohammedan Literature*, Philadelphia: Dropsie College, 1926; rpt. Ktav Publishing.

[13]He is in a very literal sense an actual scapegoat. The first goat is sacrificed to Yahweh, whose goat--the purifier--is slain. See E. O. James, *The Ancient Gods* (New York: Putnam's, 1960) 155. This function for Azazel is also mentioned in Barthelemy d'Herbelot, *Bibliothèque Orientale* 23.

[14]See Davidson, *Angels* 193-95.

[15]See G. H. Dix, who notes that in 1 Enoch, "the origin of evil is attributed to the fallen angels whose story is told in Genesis VI: they revealed knowledge to men, brought forth the giants whose disembodied spirits are demons, and led human beings into a sinful course of life whereby the order of nature was corrupted." Gill adds that these demons dwell in caves. "The Enochic Pentateuch," *Journal of Theological Studies*, 1st Ser: 27 (1926): 29-42.

[16]Taylor treats the "heresy of female messianism" shared by the Saint Simonians by 1833, and the Owenite feminists, who called for "worship [of] the female God; the goddess Nature." (Taylor 168-69)

[17]"Common sense" bears nothing of the philosophical weight the phrase carries for Shaftesbury. In this application "common sense" simply means "obvious logic." Publishing what the working-class publisher Richard Carlile took to be "common sense" of this sort resulted in Carlile's imprisonment for "blasphemous libel" from November 1819-November 1823. Carlile had published Palmer's *Principles of Nature*, which was "denigratory of the 'absurdities and contradictions' of Christianity," and which "referred to Jesus scoffingly as 'nothing more than an illegitimate Jew,'" calling the Scriptures themselves "'a vast variety of fact, fable, principle, wickedness, and error'." The Vice Society conducted the prosecution; their sentence was far severer than anyone had anticipated. (Wiener 48) Things in England were becoming more and more repressive--for the wrong people. Carlile "may be regarded as a prototypical nineteenth-century working-class re-former," according to Wiener. "At a time when the British legal system was heavily biased against the poor, he fought to bring about reform...." Indeed "He championed with deep conviction almost all of the tough issues of his day," and "Other reformers were stimulated to action by Carlile. And almost certainly, without Carlile the resistance to political change in Britain would have been more sustained and effective." Wiener quotes the "epitaph" Carlile composed for himself "a decade before his death:

> 'I have extended the freedom of the press promoted the freedom of discussion, excited public inquiry, dared the very jaws of despotism, given up my body, a sacrifice as far as its motive liberty is in question. I have lessened the conceit of kings and priests and lords--I have lessened their powers. I have given birth to mind, and if I die today, I shall leave the aggregate man better than I found him'."

(Originally printed in the *Gauntlet*, 6 August 1833; Wiener 265-6.) This record Byron would have loved claiming for himself; not Byron, and not even Shelley, went as far as Carlile and some of his fellow working-class re-formers in forcing the Vice Society into unjust actions. Carlile considered his 15 years as a tinplate worker 15 years wasted; "his hands offered him no creative satisfaction," but rather "the routine of artisan life offended Carlile." (Wiener 8) He, like others among the working class, had to fight for a voice and to fight an oppressive society. Byron and Shelley enjoyed virtual freedom of speech--their formal educations telling them instinctively when they had pushed things to the absolute limit.

[18]*Lady's Magazine*, 2nd Ser., 4 (Jan. 1823), rpt. in Donald H. Reiman, ed, *The Romantics Reviewed: Contemporary Views of British Romantic Writers; Part B: Byron and Regency Society Poets*, New York: Garland Publishing, 1972, 3: 1238-43.

The Old Testament was freely acknowledged to show human tampering, both in John Dunlop's *History of Fiction* (London, 1814), and in the anonymous review of Dunlop in the *Edinburgh Review* 24 (Nov 1814-Feb. 1815). The reviewer comments that

> the piracy of incidents may be traced from the most remote antiquity down to modern times, in the histories both of supernatural agents and of mortal men . . . . The Jewish visionaries superadded to the truth of the sacred Scripture many curious anecdotes relating to the celestial principalities,--which they learned from authentic records of their Chaldean conquerors. (24: 42)

A reviewer of "Berington's *Literature of the Middle Ages*," in the *Edinburgh Review* 23 (April 1814-Sept. 1815): 236, turns to Middleton's *Free Inquiry* and to *Whitby's remarks on Papius and Irenaeus* in order to dismiss distasteful intrusions into Scripture as "imposture" entered by "the ancient fathers" as testimony to the fact that these fathers "were extremely credulous and superstitious . . . , possessed with strong prejudices, and unenthusiastic zeal, in favor not only of Christianity in general, but of every particular doctrine which a wild imagination could engraft upon it." He finds "many instances" of this credulity in their "roundly affirming as true, things evidently false and fictitious; in order to strengthen, as they fancied, the evidence of the gospel."

[19]Moore's learned rejection of the translation "angels of God" in a note to his Preface to the first four editions of *The Loves of the Angels* numbers among Moore's essays in theological subterfuge. Comments in his anonymous review of "Boyd's *Translations from the Fathers*," *Edinburgh Review* 24 (Nov. 1814-Feb. 1815): 58-72, suggest that Moore finds the debate, not to mention the notion of angels, rather silly.

[20]As Aquinas elaborates in Question 62, Article 1, "Whether Angels Were Created in Happiness,"

> To be established or confirmed in good is of the nature of Happiness. But the angels were not confirmed in good as soon as they

were created; the fall of some of them shows this. Therefore the angels were not happy from their creation. By the name of Happiness (beatitude) is understood the ultimate perfection of rational or intellectual nature.... The first knowledge of things in the world was present to the angels from the outset of creation, while the second was not, but only when the angels became blessed by turning to the good. And this is properly termed their morning knowledge (318).

A bit of waffling mars the argument. The distinction between "blessed" and "fallen" angels slips by, without the theologian considering the problem of corporeality posed by Genesis 6.1-4. Aquinas asserts with certainty that the blessed angels cannot sin, and are in fact, incapable of taking pleasure in sensation as humans realize it.

[21]Locke likes Aquinas' comprehensiveness, but dismisses his complicated hierarchy of angels as unreal.

[22]See Arnold Williams (*The Common Expositor* 218).

[23]Swedenborg 243.

Embodying Angels:
Sources and Forms

ENGLAND'S AMOROUS ANGELS met with applause, calumniation, irritation, indifference, and neglect. Reactions by traditionally educated, native readers depended chiefly upon attitudes towards four issues, namely, the vitality of formal conventions, the limits of poetic license, the capacity of new audiences to benefit from poetry, and, for those inclined towards theory, the purpose of poetry. Issues that had been subjects of calm, printed discussions among literary theorists in England well into the seventeenth century suddenly generated vitriol and litigation. Rancor was inevitable. The newly heterogeneous audience--including the "literary public" (the privileged, educated elite), educated managerial-and other, disparately educated middle-class readers, and working-class readers dismissed as "below the public"--expected different things from poetry, especially from biblical poetry.[1] (Subgroups within each group disagreed about these matters; consensus was unheard of.) Some groups would do away with poetry altogether. Others embraced poetry, but were--for various reasons-- uneasy about the resurgence of biblical poetry. Some applauded, others deplored the fact that formal conventions encouraged varying degrees of fidelity to--or freedom from--the letter of Genesis 6.1-4, or its New Testament, Pseudepigraphic, or Qur'anic derivatives. Of no real significance were the poets' varying notions of how much liberty they were allowed in amplifying or excising their originals. In actuality, all five poets took enormous liberties with their sources--Byron alone retaining a locale identifiably biblical. Still, poets were impelled to justify their tamperings with Scripture.

In his illuminating study of *Poetic Form in British Romanticism*, Stuart Curran points out that "we have inherited the myth of a radical generic breakdown in European Romanticism that in fact never happened, but that with its own logic of cultural determinism has essentially distorted our perceptions of both Romantic literature and culture." (3) Curran's observation is apt. Generic breakdown did not take place. What did take place, however, was a proliferation of readers indifferent to (sometimes because unaware of) poetic kinds and traditions. As suggested above, the poet confronted multiple audiences, some conversant in genre theory, others oblivious to semiotic implications of formal choice, readers turning to literature for escape and devotional edification, their utilitarian needs rendering form inconsequential.[2]

Certainly, poets as well as the "literary public" remained keenly aware of formal traditions and conventions, keenly aware that no venture in a given kind ever exhibits the full possible set of formal characteristics, and keenly aware that genre theory presumes deviation conventional. Conventions, rather than constraining the poet, provide numerous channels for surprise--unanticipated renovations provocative, seducing the reader into feeling or thought. Seduction may occur, that is, for those readers cognizant of generic norms. Given England's heterogeneous readership in the 1820's, it can be said that "generic breakdown" did happen in the case of the angel/deluge poems--which, as perceived by the less educated, constituted a trans-generic class, a mode of poetry defined partly by length (all are relatively long), and mainly by matter.

The five completed poems and the fragment derive from similar--in some cases identical--sources. The poems themselves are patently dissimilar, for reasons obvious only to the "literary public"; differences result from the divergent forms the poets select, management of these forms reflecting varied operative assumptions about poetic license. Three of the works acknowledge some or all of Genesis 6.1-4 as their sources. Montgomery refers to Genesis 6.1-4 when he explains that his narrative derives from incidents after the "process of time, after the sons of God had formed connexions with the daughters of men, and there were giants in the earth" (8). Byron's poem derives from parts of Genesis 6.1-2: "And it came to pass. that the sons of God saw the daughters of men that they were fair; and they took them wives of all which they chose." Heber cites Genesis 6.2 as the source for his fragment of *A World Before the Flood*.

Dale turns to a related New Testament source for his *Irad and Adah, A Tale of the Flood*, Matthew 24.38-39: "In the days that were before the flood they were eating and drinking, marrying and giving in marriage, until that day that Noe entered into the ark, and knew not until the flood came, and took them all away" (161). These verses in Matthew (similar to Luke 17.26-27) assume a causal connection between Genesis 6.5-7 and 6.11-12 (the debauchery) and Genesis 6.8-10 and 6.13-8.22 (the Deluge). Tradition supplies Genesis 6.4 as a reason for the debauchery and the world-judgment: "The Nephilim were on the earth in those days, and also afterward, when the sons of God came into the daughters of men, and they bore children to them. These were the mighty men that were of old, the men of renown." This verse (Genesis 6.4) links naturally with Genesis 6.2, the account of the unions between "the sons of God" and "the daughters of men." Although Dale avoids concupiscent angels, his New Testament alternative, explaining world-judgment, brings to mind the causes supplied by more ancient documents.

Among these documents is the Book of Enoch, which ostensibly inspires Moore's original version of *The Loves of the Angels*, as the epigraph to the first four editions suggests: "It happened, after the sons of men had multiplied in those days, that the daughters were born to them elegant and beautiful; and when the Angels, the sons of heaven, beheld them, they became enamoured of them." This verse from Enoch (7.2) obviously derives from Genesis 6.2. Despite its alleged pseudepigraphic origin, *The Loves of the Angels* finds inspiration in the same source engendering Montgomery's, Byron's, and Heber's works. Even Dale's source is by tradition related to Genesis 6.1-4.

Croly deviates radically when he turns to the Qur'an for his *Angel of the World*, although he identifies his source as "one of those modifications of the history of the fall of Lucifer, and the temptation in Paradise, which make up so large a portion of Asiatic mythology" (Preface vi). Genesis 3 comes immediately to mind. Surprisingly his term "mythology" in describing the angel's fall and the temptation of mortals passes without controversy; the "literary public"--versed in French syncretism--would surely extend this label to the parallel biblical tales. The absence of controversy highlights the fact that his audience indeed bifurcates; those likely to extend the term to the Bible were those for whom Scripture represented a fallible, human production; those assured of scriptural infallibility would presume that "mythology" stops with the *Qur'an*, the *Zend-Avesta*, and the Pseudepigrapha. Croly shares with the five other poets concern with transgressing angels, and with the relationship of angels to mortal transgression--at least in his Preface, where Croly insists that "the author of the poem . . . has ventured to mitigate the Koran, which had undoubtedly the best right to mulct its own Angels; but he has done it in mercy to the propensities of Christendom" (vii). (Croly's phrase availing Islam of the "right to mulct its own Angels" disappears from later editions. See, for example, Croly's *Poetical Works* 1: 180.)

In his Preface, Croly identifies as his source "the story told by Mohammed, as a warning against wine," involving the angels Haruth and Maruth. Actually, Croly relies upon Qur'anic lore, and not the Qur'an itself. Harut and Marut make only one appearance in the Qur'an, Sura 2 (*Baqara*, or the Heifer) verse 102: "and Solomon was not an unbeliever; but the devils believed not, they taught men sorcery, and that which was sent down to the two angels at *Babel*, Harut and Marut; yet those two taught no man until they had said, Verily we are a temptation, therefore be not an unbeliever."[3] Croly has no use for this explicit moral ("be not an unbeliever" in Sale's translation, "so do not blaspheme" in Ali's). *The Angel of the World* relies upon the Haruth and Maruth of legend, who exchange their ontogenic stature after a draught of wine renders them vulnerable to women. In this tradition--assigning wine and women culpability for ontogenic transformation, or, in some sources, a fall--Croly's poem shows itself linked to the biblical bases of the other five works.

For their predominantly middle class readership, these sources suffice as significance. The poems chronicle the devastation that results from--reenforcing standard theological admonitions against--violating divine decrees. Some of these readers--especially those looking for "sacred classics"--took offense at the absence of devastation in Byron's lyrical drama; most of them should have taken offense at the apparent emendability of divine decree enabling Javan to change corporate affiliations--joining the "chosen"--and thereby attaining physical as well as spiritual victory in *The World Before the Flood*. The other four poems retain as predicates inflexible divine decrees, violators, and catastrophic results. The evangelistic enthusiasts objecting to Moore's sensual angels could not fault *The Loves of the Angels* for rewarding transgression. Dale's, Croly's, and--to the degree that we can tell--Heber's poems link causally transgression and catastrophe.

All save for Croly's tale ask us to consider the relationship between the incidents in Genesis 6.1-4 and the world-judgment, or Deluge, following. Two accounts of the flood appear in Genesis. In the older (Yahwist) tradition, world-judgment comes as a result of Yahweh's detection of "evil" in "man's heart" (Genesis 6.5-8). In the later (Priestly) tradition, Elohim sees "corruption" on the "earth" (Genesis 6.9-13).[4] Different poets vary in attributing world-judgment to specific, as opposed to the more general, corruptions suggested in Genesis 6.1-4.

Attention to the forms of the texts and the poetic liberties with the sources suggest how and why such similar bases result in such markedly dissimilar poems, and hint at reasons for the preference for Byron's lyrical drama among the "literary public." Despite the identical foundation for Montgomery's, Byron's, and Heber's efforts, the two completed poems (and the fragment) bear no other resemblances. Montgomery's *The World Before the Flood*--a biblical epic in ten cantos--reshapes Scripture into heroic numbers following some of the precedents set by Milton, and some (albeit without Montgomery's knowledge) set by Cowley--Miltonic practices reflecting far more liberty with Scripture than the principles for biblical epic construction articulated by Cowley in his notes to the *Davideis* and his Preface to his 1656 *Poems*; Cowley, in these places, asserts the poet's right to embellish Scripture, to supply missing details and causal connections, to reconcile discrepancies, and to add to the original anything within the limits of probability and decorum.

Montgomery's *The World Before the Flood* constitutes a renovation of the Restoration biblical epic, generally accordant more with Cowley's principled license than with Milton's conviction that the poet "ought himself to be a true poem, that is, a composition and pattern of the best and honorablest things," that for the poet "chastity" constitutes a "noble virtue"-- almost a prerequisite (Hughes 694), that the "inward promptings" to write want responding to, that the poet should be "an interpreter and relater of the best and sagest things" (668), and that "You should not despise the poet's task, divine song, which preserves some spark of the Promethean fire and is the unrivalled glory of the heaven-born human mind and an evidence of our ethereal origin and celestial descent" (83). (Milton's descriptions of the poet's calling invigorate--as do his justifications of murder, sanctioned by Scripture and executed for equally noble aims. (See Hughes 810 and 771, for example.) Cowley established principles for constructing the "divine poem" that bore authority and enjoyed widespread fame in Milton's England.

Cowley demands, above all, that scriptural accounts be probable--in their numbers, in their details, in their explanations of causal connections. Improbabilities constitute flaws in Scripture (a concession Montgomery avoids); poetic correction is indicated. These flaws become evident when Scripture fails the tests of "common sense" to which Cowley subjects it. Cowley's Book IV, n 39, provides a sample of his practices in administering such a test.

Ultimately, the note justifies the poet's deviation from the letter of 1 Samuel 13.5--specifically, Cowley's comparatively meager allocation of chariots to his Philistine invaders; he allows his band some 27,000 chariots fewer than the number assigned in the original: "the [biblical] Text," he notes, "says *Thirty Thousand Chariots*: which is too many for six thousand *Horse*." The poet will not slavishly transmit improbabilities: "I have not the confidence to say Thirty Thousand in Verse." He explains that Scripture is here corrupt: "Figures were often mistaken in old *Manuscripts*, and this may be suspected in several places in our *Bible*," of course "without any abatement of the reverence we ow to Scripture" (49-50).

Decorum remains as important to Cowley as probability. For this reason, Cowley revises Saul's expression of anger when Jonathan defends David's absence from the feast of the New Moon, 1 Samuel 20.30. In Book II, n 36, Cowley observes that the letter of the original--especially as the Vulgate renders it--amounts to Saul's condemnation of Jonathan as "*Thou Son of a whore*," an instance of name-calling Cowley rejects as simply too "ungracious" for "the mouth of a *Prince*" (51).

Scripture itself suggests to Cowley divine consent for the poet to represent apparent, over absolute reality:

> to speak according to common opinion, though it be false, is so far from being a fault in Poetry, that it is the custom even of the Scripture to do so; and that not onely in the Poetical pieces of it; as where it attributes the *members* and *passions* of mankind to *Devils, Angels*, and *God* himself; where it calls the *Sun* and *Moon* the two *Great Lights*, whereas the latter is in truth one of the smallest; but is spoken of, as it *seems*, not as it *Is*, and in too many other places to be collected here. (I, N 24: 54).

Curran determines that the biblical epic in the earlier nineteenth century "is religious in character, the legacy of a . . . formidable eighteenth-century revival, the Evangelical movement." Attempts at this mode "all revert" to Milton as a model. (163) Despite the fact that Milton remains "historically distant," he nonetheless resolves the "difficulty" confronting nineteenth-century writers of biblical epics--namely, the "definition of the subject matter." Milton's resolution involves "elaborating . . . relatively sketchy biblical texts," a confinement later comfortable to Montgomery; Curran judges that "only one religious epic during the Romantic period attempts to find room for invention in Holy Writ," namely, Montgomery's *The World Before the Flood*, although unfortunately, "if its claims to literary significance probably excel any of the others, it cannot escape the solemn piety that universally afflicts these poems" (163). Montgomery fulfills the "urge to break free of the twin scriptures of the Bible and Milton," Curran determines, "by virtually transforming . . . [his] materials into those of a romance." (166)

Problems arise when Milton's authority is sanctified. The "great Argument" of *Paradise Lost* is outrageous. Surely God needs no one besides Himself to "assert eternal Providence / And justify the ways of God to men." (25-7) Milton appropriates for the poet the priestly/prophetic role that Carlile excoriates. And Milton's assumption of this function cannot be dismissed as mere convention or narrative strategy. *Paradise Lost* may well be intended as an apocryphal work. Those "ridiculous" comparisons by which Scott and others uphold *Cain* as theologically unobjectionable may inadvertently condemn *Cain* more thoroughly than its detractors would endeavor. Certainly, authorization had been granted for the possible elevation of a "sacred" (or any) poem to the status of an apocryphal, or even canonical, writing.

A Jesuit had taken care of this. Leonhard Lessius (1554-1623) initiated a debate about the status of apocryphal writings that bore staggering implications for the status of the "sacred" poem as understood by Cowley and Milton. At Louvain in 1585, Lessius defended a notion of "subsequent inspiration," suggesting that "a book such as II Maccabees, written by human industry, without the aid of the Holy Spirit, may afterwards, if the Holy Spirit give testimony that it contains nothing false, be ranked as Holy Scripture" (translated by F.J. Crehan, in Greenslade 217). Crehan adds that "Bellarmine did not quite like the view of Lessius"--for reasons patently evident, "but," Crehan continues, Bellarmine "thought it could be defended" (217). If Maccabees enjoys "subsequent inspiration," why cannot "divine"--or any-- poems by later writers? Apparently they can, according to theories such as George Chapman's ("Preface to the Reader," ca. 1610, in Spingarn 1: 67), which insists that "divine" poems "cannot be obtained by the labor and art of man," but require "a divine infusion"--Chapman providing no means for testing whether or not a poem enjoys such "infusion." Here, Chapman antedates Shelley's confidence in the poet's service as a conduit of truth-- a service that Chapman claims comes through divine appointment, but that Shelley attributes to unknown sources. Cowley, too, seems to imply "subsequent inspiration" when he claims in the *Davideis*, Book I, note 1, that "the whole work may reasonably hope to be filled with a *Divine Spirit*, when it begins with a *Prayer* to be so" (146). Here, we have "infusion" on demand.

Montgomery would not dream of claiming for *The World Before the Flood* "divine infusion," let alone "subsequent inspiration." The fact that Montgomery does develop a romance should clearly save his work from the suspicion Milton had caused to be cast upon the biblical epic. Montgomery's source is particularly skeletal, here following Milton's precedent, and hence proves particularly amicable to additions of the sort that Cowley describes and Milton supplies. Without the urgings of Parken, editor of the *Eclectic Review*, Montgomery might well have yielded to "the old scruples against religious poetry, as adding or taking away from the Scripture," which the biographer of "James Montgomery" in the *Dublin University Magazine* (August, 1856), reports "were suggested by his own disturbed mind, when he was agitated by discussions from without and misgivings from within, on all the possibilities and impossibilities of his theme" (216). English poets considering writing biblical narratives, from at least the sixteenth century well into the nineteenth, had had to come to terms with the fact that they would inevitably be revising God's Word.

Parken assuages Montgomery's doubts about taking liberties with Scripture by absolving Montgomery from any "'intention to deceive,'" and by providing as precedent the example of *Paradise Lost*. Parken urges, "'May your poem do as much harm as Milton's in this way, [i.e., in instilling the creed of the "'fall of man, the war of the angels, and the character of Satan,'" which the masses know from Milton as much from the Scriptures], and as much good by graving religious facts on the public mind!'" (*DUM* 216) Montgomery was apparently convinced. Milton suddenly becomes Montgomery's rationale for every feature of *The World Before the Flood*. Montgomery argues in his Preface that

> There is no authentic history of the world from the Creation to the Deluge, besides that which is found in the first chapters of Genesis. He, therefore, who fixes the date of a fictitious narrative within that period, is under obligation to no other authority whatever, for conformity of manners, events, or even localities: he has full power to accommodate these to his peculiar purposes, observing only such analogy as shall consist with the brief information, contained in the sacred records, concerning mankind in the earliest ages (vii).

Here, Montgomery grants himself greater liberty with the original than had Cowley (if not Milton) before him. Cowley supplies details suggested to him by cultural comparison; Cowley does turn to other ancient cultures for "conformity of manners, events, or . . . localities." In other words, Cowley's theories mandate the poet's assuming the role of a cultural anthropologist; without cultural comparison, the poet--left to his own fancy--risks violating decorum and probability in supplying details. Montgomery maintains his "right" to "bold innovation," arguing that "success alone" will sanction it: "if he has succeeded in what he has attempted, he will need no arguments to justify it; if he has miscarried, none will avail him" (viii). Anachronisms need not be eschewed, if they arouse no ire and if they enhance the poet's didactic aims.

In justifying the manners of his own characters, Montgomery turns to Milton. Perhaps taking his suggestion from Parken, Montgomery argues that

> Those who imagine that he [Montgomery, "the present writer"] has exhibited the antediluvians, as more skilful in arts and arms than can be supposed, in their stage of society, may read the *eleventh* book of PARADISE LOST:--and those, who think he has made the religion of the Patriarchs too evangelical, may read the *twelfth* (viii).

Montgomery takes Parken a bit too seriously, perhaps. In this apologia, *Paradise Lost* takes on nearly canonical authority, rather than serving instructively as poetical precedent.

Bolder poets--those satisfied to take "no middle flight"--could well assume eventual canonicity--by virtue of "subsequent inspiration"--for their "divine" poems. Milton--ever startling in his self confidence--likely felt called to emend Holy Writ. (Milton would have doubtless agreed with Parken that *Paradise Lost* is as valuable as Scripture for teaching Christian dogma and doctrine--however unwarranted this notion may prove; Milton, after all, maintained some extremely unorthodox notions about Scripture.[5]) In addition, Milton's revisions of Scripture reflect syncretistic leanings made manifest in many places--as when the narrator allows that Moses may have stood on "Horeb" *or* on "Sinai," reflecting indifference to the accuracy of the letter. The poet values the means and content, and not the place, of this communication. No one--not Cowley, and surely not Montgomery--enjoyed the freedom with Scripture that Milton arrogated. Milton's liberty with his source in fact engages the attention of a reviewer of *The World Before the Flood* in the *British Review* S5 5 (Oct. 1813): 111-23, the writer reporting that "It appears that Paradise Lost was received by the age, on which it throws back such lustre, with far from general approbation; and that among the charges with which the author was assailed, those of profaneness and impurity were not wanting" (113). He adds that "It is not, however, to be regretted, where scripture truth is concerned, that the innovations of the poet are so suspiciously regarded," this writer relieved that "The World Before the Flood . . . is evidently the production of a pious mind, without which qualification the talents which have been engaged in it would have been perniciously employed on such a theme" (113).

The reviewer in the *Monthly Review* 73 (Feb. 1814): 144-53 bestows upon Montgomery far less charity, condemning him for any deviations whatsoever from his source--including deviations from the reviewer's highly singular understanding of the source. This writer details one of the most idiosyncratic readings of Genesis 4-7 appearing in a literary review--pious solely because of his claims to piety--and scrutinizes *The World Before the Flood* in order to fault Montgomery for failing to read into the text the same vagaries the reviewer would set forth as normative. Close attention to this review illustrates how garbled the letter, as rendered through eisegetes, had become--as well as how impossible was the task of the poet hoping to satisfy all readers naming themselves "Christians." The reviewer insists that Montgomery "should have confined himself to the intimations given in the book of Genesis . . ." (152-53). To his first particular, no objection suggests itself. The poet should have attended more carefully to biblical genealogies, for "according to the history, Zillah was one of the wives of Lamech," and hence not a fit candidate for Javan's secular lover. The critic denies the poet the right to liberate himself from biblical chronology--and hence from attendant assumptions about that chronology; as biblical criticism, however, his assertion remains tenable.

He becomes hypercritical of Montgomery, although a venerated notion--probability--accounts for the "objection [he feels] may be alleged against the outline and termination of this fable":

> If the descendants of Cain had been subdued by the 'embattled cherubim' and 'coursers winged with lightning from the sky,' no necessity would have existed for the subsequent visitation of the deluge. It appears, however, from Scripture, that this idolatrous race continued unreclaimed by divine judgments till the flood of waters swept them away: but Noah could not have been in a state of slavery to them, because they would have obstructed his building of the ark. (153)

To this reviewer, in fact, Montgomery takes wanton liberty with Scripture (the sort of abandon the reviewer in the *British Critic* recalls Milton was once charged with). For the *Monthly Review*, Montgomery "has in our judgment been too liberal to the holy sages before the flood, by representing their religious system as more perfect than it really was"--the writer countermanding Montgomery's prefatorial insistences that his account of patriarchal religion finds sufficient precedent in *Paradise Lost*.(144)[6]

Montgomery's narrative strategies reveal principles kindred to those advocated by Cowley, the most important of which is probability. Probability has directed Montgomery in delineating characters:

> With respect to the personages and incidents of his story, the Author having deliberately adopted them, under the conviction, that in the characters of the one he was not stepping out of human nature, and in the construction of the other not exceeding the limits of poetical probability (viii-ix),

the characters earn credibility. With this judgment, Curran would seemingly agree. Credibility comes from the poem's secular emphasis: the "love of the minstrel Javan for Zillah effectively humanizes the poem"; Montgomery's "hero is a minstrel whose life as an exile among the descendants of Cain has grown intolerable and who escapes to return to his threatened people, led by Enoch, the first of the post-Adamic types of Christ in *Paradise Lost*, Book XI." Curran continues, "through the central importance of this fictional hero, Javan, the power of song and its reflection of heavenly harmony become as much concerns of this epic as they are in contemporary romance." The secular emphasis persists: "until the last canto, when the venerable Enoch is translated into heaven, there are neither miraculous events (except those memorialized from the past or the revelations of dreams) nor supernatural machinery"--the latter offensive to Blackmore, particularly, in Christian epic.(166)

According to the poet, piety has motivated the whole:

> But,--here is a large web of fiction involving a small fact of scripture! Nothing could justify a work of this kind, if it were, in any way, calculated to impose on the credulity, pervert the principles, or corrupt the affections of its approvers. Here, then, the appeal lies to conscience rather than to taste, and the decision on this point is of infinitely more importance to the Poet than his name among men, or his interests on earth (ix-x).

The *British Review* would accept this argument. Strictly speaking, Montgomery's ends are thematic, rather than theological. Montgomery's piety--and the poem's status as "a sentimental epic that trades on Scott"--prove for

Curran weaknesses; the poem "lacks the dimensions customary to the genre," and, more damaging still, "the exemplification of patient endurance of one's martyrdom, while good Methodist teaching, leaves a vacuum where heroics are anticipated." This poem "cannot truly sustain epic purpose or pressure." (166)

Montgomery does not embrace "patient endurance" as a virtue, at least in his Preface. He closes his discussion of his epic with a slightly differing statement of intent: "It was . . . [the poet's] design, in this composition," Montgomery announces, "to present a similitude of events, that might be imagined to have happened in the first age of the world, in which such scripture characters as are introduced would probably have acted and spoken, as they are here made to act and speak." Here, Montgomery judges his own characters according to the criteria he applies to Wordsworth's Pedlar: "perfect and ideal existence" suffice in granting a character "poetical reality," and hence a character needs "no prototype in individual man." (*Eclectic Review* 3 N.S. (January 1815): 29) Montgomery adds that "the story is told as a Parable only, and its value in this view, must be determined by its moral, or rather by its religious influence on the mind and on the heart." The religious epic must engage the heart as well as the intellect--justifying the poem's secular emphasis. He allows that "Fiction though it be, it is the fiction that represents Truth, and that *is* Truth,--Truth in the essence though not in the name; Truth in the spirit though not in the letter" (x). ("Fiction it certainly is," answers the critic in the *Monthly Review*, "and in some parts very well managed: but, for the reasons already assigned, it is not throughout so near the essence of truth as the poet imagines." (148).) Fiction has power to extract the essence of truth, and to replicate that essence. The particulars are of no consequence.

We lose sight of the source for the greater part of Montgomery's epic. The narrator delineates lush glens and bowers, catalogues warriors, portrays heroes and villains for us to attend to. The epic begins *in medias res*, at the brink of Eden's invasion by "the Descendants of Cain" (11). The ten cantos, in heroic couplets, focus upon the life of Javan--his discovery of his lineage (for in Montgomery's version, he is found as an infant by Enoch, who leads him, and his widowed mother, to the patriarchal glen); his brooding dissatisfaction; his awareness of his physical love for Zillah; and his ultimate acknowledgment of the transforming power of love. Javan ascends from carnal love (for Zillah), to Platonic love (for Enoch, his spiritual mentor), to corporate love (for the Patriarchs), and finally to divine love; he has made himself fit to "snatch" the Prophet's mantle upon Enoch's translation to

Heaven, and has even prepared himself for visitation by the Prophetic spirit. Javan constitutes a Miltonic Christian hero as Burton O. Kurth describes the kind, exhibiting both "active" and "contemplative forms of heroism," Montgomery's conception of "heroic action" placing it both "in the arena of the world and society" (when Javan interacts and fights) and "in the mind or soul of the individual" (when Javan broods, falls in love, and enjoys platonic commingling). (118)

Love appropriates our notice. The Scriptural details get lost. The biblical Javan numbers among the sons of Japheth, and is a grandson of Noah. (Genesis 10.2-5, 1 Chronicles 1.5-10, Isaiah 66.19, and Ezekiel 27.3.) The Hebrews regarded him as the eponymous ancestor of Greece, based upon the derivation *Jawan*, Ionians, i.e. Greeks (Ezekiel 23.13). Isaiah 66.19 identifies Javan's home as the distant coastlands, which will receive some of the survivors of God's judging sword and fire (*OAB* 906 n). He is the brother of Tubal (Genesis 10.2-5, 1 Chronicles 1.5-10). Montgomery's epic rendering makes Javan Zillah's lover (although their love is never consummated). Montgomery's source makes this impossible--as the writer for the *Monthly Review* (in a rare moment of fidelity to the text) determines. Zillah appears in Genesis 4.19-23 as one of the two wives of Lamech. (Lamech's other wife, Adah, bears Jabal, the father of the nomadic cattleman: "those who dwell in tents and have cattle," Genesis 4.21, and Jubal, "father of all those who play the lyre & pipe," Genesis 4.22-23. Jubal, the Hebrew Orpheus, plays a significant role in Montgomery's epic, although Montgomery does not call upon Genesis in delineating his own Jubal.) Montgomery postpones until Canto 7 explicit references to the "monstrous love [which] combined/The sons of God and the daughters of mankind," producing Giant, blasphemous, and tyrannical offspring (145). Montgomery keeps our focus upon the hero and his spiritual journey; the narrator designs to have us contemplate the transcendence and ultimate salvation that well-directed love effects.

The World Before the Flood is subject to the question one may ask of any biblical epic? Why? What does the poet hope to do with Scripture that the text itself fails to direct us towards? In the case of Montgomery's poem, the answer stems from the poet's focus upon love as a salutary agent.

In theme as well as form, Montgomery's epic, derived from Genesis 6.1-4, bears no resemblance whatsoever to Byron's rendition of this source. *Heaven and Earth*--a lyrical drama which Byron once terms an "Oratorio"--demands and depends upon conceptual richness and rhetorical sophistication. The form of *Heaven and Earth* is somewhat unusual; Byron himself inconsistently labels this work. Compounded, his labels leave us with a permutation of lyrical drama--the lyrical drama itself a hybrid form--refined ridiculously into a "mystery/oratorio/Greek/lyrical drama." While standard in lexicons of literary terms, the mode *lyrical drama* confuses sufficiently. A drama fashioned to be read, never staged, seems better termed "gelded drama," or, more appealing, a narrative poem in dialogue. *Lyrical drama* ("closet drama" to the less lexically reverent) has become standard. Confusion begins when we focus upon Byron's Heaven and Earth as a lyrical drama, and investigate what dimensions *mystery* and *oratorio* add to our understanding of the kind.

Heaven and Earth: A Mystery appeared predesignated in the second issue of *The Liberal*. Uncertainty surrounds Byron's understanding of the term *mystery*. Is it a mode or a function? M.K. Joseph suggests that Byron had "probably picked up" the term "mystery" from Warton's *History*, but "with little sense of its meaning" (111). Dodsley's *Old Plays* would have been available to Byron, but Byron's familiarity with this volume remains in doubt (see Steffan 71, Chew, *Dramas* 121, and Bostetter 571). Anne Barton credits Byron with knowing what the label implies:

> Even *Cain* and *Heaven and Earth* reach back to the mystery cycles in more than a joking sense. They are questioning extensions, not so much of Peele's *David and Bethsabe* (1587) or Pordage's deplorable *Herod and Mariamne* (1673) as of the Wakefield Master's *Mactatio Abel* or those half-hearted murmurings against the will of God to be heard in the York and Chester versions of the Flood (155).[7]

Whether by accident or by design, Byron's "mystery" shares with the medieval mystery play a distinguishing feature--the poet's assumed right to take gross liberties with Scripture.

Albany Fonblanque, Byron's contemporary, omits references to the earliest English dramas, but does compare *Heaven and Earth* to *Samson Agonistes*, "which," Fonblanque senses, "Lord Byron has evidently borne in mind in tone, versification, and general management of subject." Fonblanque quotes extensively from Byron's lyrical drama, aiming to "prove the Miltonic character of this high-wrought and nervous production," adding that "unless 'Paradise Lost' itself is to be attacked, even the unutterably contemptible and hypocritical vermin who are prosecuting the 'Vision of Judgment' must be satisfied with the genuine scriptural tone preserved in the development of the grand incident of this dramatic mystery." Byron cannot be condemned for drawing attractive mortals, for even Milton's Dalala appeals, "as all save *auto-da-fé* people or zealots will acknowledge" (*The Examiner*, Sun. 29 Dec. 1822, 821). Fonblanque acknowledges that *Heaven and Earth* constitutes a "mystery," and that its tone is "scriptural."

Others have taken Byron to mean "mystery" in a functional sense. "Mystery" designates an effect, aiding a metaphysical end. Bernard Blackstone argues that "the Biblical plays, which Byron called 'Mysteries' in allusion to medieval drama which I think of as 'theological,' are sounding into doctrinal deeps" (25). Ernest W. Saunders' definition of "mystery" becomes suggestive: the terms "'secret' or 'mystery,'" have "characteristically referred to the selfrevelation of the hidden God" (81). If we agree with Byron himself and with William H. Marshall (154) that the three scenes constitute a thematically complete unit, we might say that Jehovah does reveal his will. He saves the Noachites, as he has promised. He has included no by-law forbidding the Cainite sisters from taking to the air instead of to the sea. (This does not render Noah a false prophet, but rather suggests that Jehovah feels free to withhold as well as to reveal particular details of his design.) As a prophet who has been briefed only sketchily, Noah shares both ignorance and insight with the other characters. Each has some truth--but only a partial truth--about what life is to mean.

The term "oratorio" Byron applies to *Heaven and Earth* in a letter to Kinnaird, from Genoa, dated 31 October 1822, discussing the advisability of finding "some other bookseller" for "the Oratorio--called 'Heaven and Earth'" (Letters 10: 24). Oratorios, marked by their tonal variations, with choral and solo contributions in opposition--including various arias, recitatives, duets, choruses, and such--may suggest the intended tonal variety Byron achieves. Certainly, distinct voices--single, in pairs, or in groups-- reflect disparate attitudes towards, and means of coping with life in the poem. Tonal shifts help us evaluate the varied characters and their articulations. Tone becomes a significant aid to understanding--and a significant narrative device for retaining interest in abstract speculation.

Oddly enough, *Heaven and Earth* does not raise the problem of theodicy. Noah is our only channel to God, and we do not always trust Noah's interpretations. Noah's God may be a grim God; such a creator may merely constitute God as Noah perceives him. The antediluvian universe has been fashioned by an anthropomorphic, anthropopathic, and personal, God-- that we never get around to meeting. Theodicy is the operative issue informing most biblical poetry; Byron refreshes with something different-- and apparently complete. This he confirms in a letter to John Murray dated

14 November 1821: "as it [*Heaven and Earth*] is longer and more lyrical & Greek than I intended at first--I have not divided it into *acts* but called what I have sent--*Part first*--as there is a suspension of the action, which may either close there without impropriety--or be continued in a way that I have in view" (Letters 9: 59). Byron's comparison of his lyrical (or closet) drama to Greek tragedy likely derives from the intellection, rather than action, characteristic of ancient Greek plays, and of course from the writer's use of a chorus to articulate consensus. (In *Samson Agonistes*, Milton has his chorus articulate collective ignorance, and I suspect that Byron's chorus of mortals so functions in *Heaven and Earth*.) While the ancient Greek dramatists work with materials known to their audiences, Byron works with a tale his readership only thinks it knows. In this, Byron proves a kindred spirit to Euripides in particular among ancient Greek dramatists; Euripides, like Byron, challenges virtually every "given" about life, society, philosophy, and, in short, all that makes up a lifescape. Aholibamah challenges the wisdom of the tribe by ignoring it; she discovers, too, that *vox populi* may be ignored with impunity. Byron's play is Greek, too, in that mortals and demigods couple.

The continuation he claims to "have in view" may be the report that Coleridge picked up from Medwin:

I once thought of conveying the lovers to the moon or one of the planets; but it is not easy for the imagination to make an unknown world more beautiful than this; besides, I did not think they would approve of the moon as a residence. I remember what Fontenelle said of its having no atmosphere, and the dark spots having caverns where the inhabitants reside. There was another objection: all the human interest would have been destroyed, which I have ever endeavored to give my angels. (PW 5:281).[8]

Byron's closing remark may be both a pun and a statement of intent. His angels do deliberate, question, and feel for their lovers's circumstances; the angels remain loyal to the mortals when chaos takes hold. Angels and mortals alike are capable of empathy, one of the rare admirable emotions humans (as well as Byron's angels) experience.

Through the successful experiments of Cainite women, *Heaven and Earth* insists that carnal love is a necessity, not a luxury. It suggests, too, that good physical love comes companioned with love of a partner's intellect, idiosyncrasies, and whole being. This is not garden variety attraction. When it comes, keep it--regardless of prejudices imposed by outsiders. In addition, the "mystery" gives each character ample time to define the reality he or she perceives; by implication, multiple perspectives account for single places, events, people, things. One can choose the blighted (Noah's) or the upgraded (Aholibamah's) vision of reality. One should not scorn those choosing the former. Gloom mongers will be gloom mongers--have a right to be gloom mongers, and even need to be gloom mongers. Life offers the greatest contentment when we are free to see a view accordant with our tastes. All characters in Byron's "mystery" apparently escape the flood unharmed.

As noted, Byron's *Heaven and Earth* derives from the same source as Montgomery's *The World Before the Flood*. As with Montgomery's epic, Byron's lyrical drama (or "mystery") focuses upon love as it affects the various personalities the poet sketches. In Byron's drama, love provides a reason for enduring in the bleak days before the Deluge. Love does not constitute Byron's chief arena of comment, in contrast with Montgomery. Rather, *Heaven and Earth* constitutes an unsettling epistemological debate. Are we to trust faith, reason, senses, intuition, or any other means of knowing "truth"? Noah argues for faith, or revelation. His sons would agree-- and, with Noah, depend upon faith as a mandate to deduce. The Cainite sisters, however, confer authority upon their senses and intuitions as sources of truth. The disparate means of knowing profoundly influence the relative joy the characters seize from life.

The grim patriarch, and his equally morose and unappealing sons, endeavor to find meaning through talking hypotheses into truths. Noah's truth derives from faith. Byron, however, leaves the patriarch with a *deus absconditas*--adequate for Locke and Voltaire, but not the kind of god suited to early inhabitants of a world just waking up and noticing itself. Since Noah's world is antediluvian, it is without benefit of God's law. Noah and his sons make their choice of life on the bases of deduction and faith. Noah claims that God has spoken to him (which we must take on faith), and he thereafter deduces God's will; God reveals no more. His sons, epistemologi- cally, show themselves to be clones. Their ark has been built. They await catastrophe by depressing one another with their gloom. (Their moods would better befit those confronting imminent death than those elected for salvation.)

The Cainite women give credence to their senses and intuitions as inroads for truth and as reasons for deeming life precious. They wish to enjoy their last days on earth. Anah, and especially Aholibamah, are prototypical

Lockean empiricists. They observe, explore, and sense; they decide from these bases how to plot their lives. They know nothing about the moral or practical implications of their affairs with angels. They are willing to proceed on the bases of what they discover. Even so, their lives do not offer incessant pleasure. At times, Anah seems a bit too fond of articulating her fears; Aholibamah will tolerate only minimal tremulant discourse--particularly when she knows and Anah knows that Anah will never give up her trysts; angelic lovers combat the tedium and austerity of patriarchal living with an unusual blend of sensitivity and pyrotechnics. Aholibamah is the boldest empiricist and adventurer. Her voyage is partly internal; she contemplates the effects of love upon her spirit. She experiments with alternative modes of being--modes far preferable to those that Noah would restrict her to-- and she meets with success.

The extant fragment of Heber's verse narrative of *A World Before the Flood* shares a common source with Montgomery and Byron, although Heber adds a new, and troubling, dimension to the concept of familial love. Heber seems to develop the theme of familial love (or duty) *versus* love of God--here, the love of God by the daughter of a Cainite king. When the king learns that an angel wishes to marry Anah, he entertains grandiose thoughts about the progeny--actually dynasty of demigods--he may anticipate. He commands Anah to wed the angel. Anah is horrified; she finds the proposal disgusting and impious. The poem breaks off before we find out what happens.

The citation of Genesis 6.2 as an epigraph suggests that Heber sees the passage as part of a causal chain leading to world-judgment, in this case, the flood. Heber sticks very closely to the idea inhering in Genesis 6.2. He explores what could happen were a patriarchal authority to abuse his power over his group, and insist that its members perform acts abhorrent to God. We have too little of Heber's work to identify its kind; it does bear likeness to the narrative debat as the mode is most commonly defined--that is, the philosophical exposition controlled by a narrator, who formulates and opposes rhetorically appealing arguments, sound and unsound, giving slightly fuller space or suasive polish to the side the writer approves. As with Montgomery's epic and with Byron's play, Heber's fleshed-out fragment turns our attention away from Scripture and towards the characters invented for the occasion. All three Genesis poems follow the Miltonic precedent of "elaborating" their "sketchy biblical texts" (Curran 163).

Montgomery's biblical epic is joined by Dale's, the latter's *Irad and Adah, a Tale of the Flood* more Spenserian than Miltonic in design. Dale in fact adopts a related biblical source, although this biblical source seldom recalls the Bible once the narrator takes charge of the matter--save, perhaps, in its expansion of Noah's prophecy. The poet directs our attention to Matthew 24.38-39, suggesting a causal link between the revelries enjoyed by the antediluvians, and the onset of the flood. Dale clearly wants us to look backward, to look at the events as past history--the history recounted in Genesis 6.5-8, in which God wipes out "evil" in the "heart" of man, and Genesis 6.9-11, in which the earth at large is "corrupt." (Here, Dale accommodates both flood stories.) Dale does not want us to look forward-- that is, to see this source as an apocalypse, or unveiling, of the coming of Christ; this becomes clear from the excised final clause of verse 39: "so will be the coming of the Son of man."[9] Dale's source and narrative involve different spots in time. In Matthew (as in the similar passage in Luke 17.26-27), Jesus recounts the flood as an event in the distant past, the ambiance before the flood proleptic of the world before the end of time. Any direct relationship to or dependence upon Genesis 6.1-4 remains unnoted. Amorous angels have no place in the New Testament histories; mankind alone seals mankind's doom.

In form, Dale's narrative recalls Giles Fletcher's four-part celebration of *Christ's Victory and Triumph*. Dale's imagery is sometimes sensuous, as is Fletcher's more often; Dale shifts his focus from the particular lovers to the widest-ranging world-judgment; Dale resembles Fletcher in attending to the individual against a cosmic backdrop. Too, Dale may well follow the Miltonic precedent of "stationing" here, as Nancy Goslee discusses the technique. "Stationing," originally referring to placement within a hierarchy, retained this meaning "well into Keats's time," yet also "gradually began to describe first the location of objects in the natural world and then the perceiver's act of composing a scene of these two related elements" (8). Dale paints tableaux of individuals, groups, incidents, and objects, against the background of disaster. This array of scenes--these frames--enhance the pathos of the end designed for creation, Dale's "stationings" emphasizing the amplitude of specific things slated for destruction. Dale's source deflects unduly from possible theological controversy. Controversy is impossible. Dale's characters belong to heroic poetry, not Scripture. In setting, *Irad and Adah* is markedly pre-Christian. Dale's New Testament source--especially with Christ delivering the message in the source--obscures the poet's ends; we look for theology, rather than heroic poetry; the theology we find is not theology at all--not if "theology" connotes considered, synthesized reflections about religion. What we find, rather, is sadistic, terrorist "enthusiasm."

Dale's three-part narrative excises explicit acts by lusty angels. In Part I, "Guilt," Dale's predominantly Spenserian stanzas denounce the "forms of angels, with the soul of Cain" (St. 34), and particularly Irad's attraction to Adah. In Part II, "Prophecy," Noah's unheeded warnings and the deluge serve as backdrops for the misery the illicit pair ensure themselves. In Part III, "Judgment," judgment is relentless. Irad cannot vanquish death; he and his lover must ultimately acknowledge their mortality. The macabre tone intensifies as Irad carries about Adah's corpse, eventually seeing her lifeless visage as a portent of "Death's darker consummation" (St. 36). Hope is offered only towards the final stanza (St. 91), when "the Creator-Spirit from above / Is moving on the waters; through the gloom / Of desolation beams superior Love, / And Mercy tempers Justice." The poet speculates that "yet may Heaven reverse the stern decree; / And yet again may cheering suns illume / The world emerging from its dungeon sea, / And beam the light of life on millions yet to be." This, even, is a pre-Christian hope. Dale's epic entails conventions of Miltonic "stationing"; its shifts in focus--rapid and wide ranging--constitute its most engaging technical feature. (Its theological appeal remains limited to millennarianists--a dwindling crowd by the 1820's.) Of most interest, however, is the fact that this biblical epic wants a hero-- active or contemplative--the narrator enticing the reader to take the hero's part, to heed the narrator's warning, the narrator parroting Amos 4.12, "Prepare to meet thy God!"

The remaining poems, Moore's and Croly's, constitute romances-- Moore's *The Loves of the Angels* formally wrought from the tradition of the Ovidian erotic epyllion, Croly's *The Angel of the World* following the less formally distinct, stanzaic romance, Croly rendering his tale in the Spenserian stanzas *Childe Harold* had made the rage. These poems link thematically, drawing from the same tradition of Ovidian metamorphosis-- a tradition effective in conveying pathos and horror. Both come with scholarly apparatus--a feature of *Lalla Rookh* which Moore credits with enhancing the poem's verisimilitude.

Taking advantage of the currency of Enoch, Moore claims to have founded his poem upon the passage of the Book of Enoch in which angels become enamored of mortal women. In a note to his poem, he insists that the corresponding passage in Genesis (Chapter 6, verse 2) has been mistranslated as a result of a scribal error in LXX. Moore argues that *bene ha'elohim* cannot be translated "angels," as some copies of LXX, "assisted by the allegorizing comments of Philo, and the rhapsodical fictions of the Book of Enoch," assert. Instead, the rendering "sons of God" must be understood to designate the "sons of Seth," an alternative offered in the Book of Enoch.[10] Moore seems unaware of the fact that this reliance upon pseudepigrapha for an authoritative reading diminishes the sanctity of Scripture. Too, the problematic phrase, when rendered "sons of Seth," assumes a euhmeristic elevation of mortals into a heavenly court. Euhemerism--mentioned without controversy in the context of Greek mythology (as in Nicolas Freret's *Mythology; or the Religion of the Greeks*, 1756)--threatens the integrity of Scripture when allowed to account for *bene ha'elohim* as a name for the "sons of Seth" (as in Samuel Shuckford's *Sacred and Profane History Connected*, 1728).[11] Humans, through euhemeristic processes, have been elevated into demigods of sorts, adopted as offspring of the Deity.

Moore's exegetic comments have absolutely no bearing on his poem. His poem bears so little resemblance to its supposed source that the notion of "poetic license" becomes irrelevant. He draws upon so many sources that they become indistinct in his collage of orientalism and invention. Moore's three-part romance constitutes a mythological, erotic, Ovidian epyllion of the sort popular among Elizabethan courtiers. As an added dimension, the first two tales are suggestive of the complaint poem of the *Mirrour for Magistrates* tradition, at least as this form is usually understood (that is, a poem in which an *ex gravis* narrator, who in life enjoyed celebrity, or power, or high esteem, laments his or her execrable fortune, and points to the cause of it, such as a character defect, another person, a situation, or an abstraction). Moore fixes our focus upon the angels; we are discouraged from considering the theological implications of the divine/mortal trysts, and the poem instead transforms into a secular love poem. (The angelic stature of the male lovers simply provides Moore with a convenient rationale for exaggerating the outcomes of ill-and well-directed love.) The first angel endures degradation and abandonment; the angel divulges a forbidden word, upon which he becomes earthbound, while his beloved, Lea, enjoys taxonomic elevation. The second angel, Rubi, accedes to Lilis's pleas to see him in his angelic splendor; upon embracing her, Lilis dissolves into ashes, and Rubi must endure eternity knowing that he has murdered his beloved. The third angel gets off easier because he marries his mortal lover; the pair will be wedded throughout eternity, not in a benign union, like Philemon and Baucis request (benign to the point of insentience), but in a typically unpredictable state of togetherness--together in anger, together in joy.

Croly differs the most obviously from the other poets in naming the Qur'an as his source. Croly, like Moore, takes such liberties with his source that the original could easily pass unnoticed had the poet not identified it. As previously noted, the Qur'an mentions nothing of Harut and Marut being themselves tempted, but rather gives them residence in Babylon to warn men against occult learning. In this sense, they were the tempters, although not volitionally; man's free will leads man to fall. (Ali 44-45)

It is not the Qur'an itself, but rather ancillary legends that provide Croly with his subject. In the Qur'an, these angels are far from proud. Ali points to a Jewish Midrash that relates a story of "two angels who asked God's permission to come down to earth but succumbed to temptation, and were hung up by their feet at Babylon for punishment" (45 n104). This tradition ascribes no particular character defect (i.e., pride) to the sinning pair. Hughes acknowledges the appearance of Harut and Marut in the Qur'an, then relates a tradition that renders their characters sympathetic: "They are said to be two angels who, in consequence for their compassion for the frailties of mankind, were sent down to earth to be tempted." Both succumbed. They were "permitted to choose whether they would be punished now or hereafter"; they "chose the former, and are still suspended by the feet at Babel in a rocky pit" (167-68). Croly emphasizes different details, as noted previously.

Croly combines traditions; in the original, Harut and Marut have nothing to do with wine, and, while possessing knowledge that God does not want humanity to share, are given this knowledge for the very purpose of tempting mortals, as a means by which God can separate the evil from the righteous.[12] Of the six angel poems, Croly's follows the simplest plot; *The Angel of the World* traces the fall of a single errant angel. Like Moore, Croly relies upon conventions of Ovidian narrative. Unlike Moore, Croly's angel undergoes a kinder transformation--total dissolution as a sentient being, rather than enduring taxonomic estrangement, or eternal misery. In a sense, however, no punishment is warranted, for Croly's angel never actually transgresses. At the moment he is about to yield, the veiled woman reveals herself in her (now his) form as Eblis, Satan's Qur'anic counterpart.

Croly follows Moore, too, in providing scholarly apparatus. He does so in part to defend his choosing a subject from the Qur'an. He follows Moore in listing analogous sources, as when in his Preface, Croly announces that

> The scholar who may turn his attention to Arabic poetry, will find some resources in our own literature;--Sir William Jones's Fourth Discourse to the Asiatic Society, Pococke's Specimen Historiae Arabum, Richardson's Dissertation on the Languages of the East,

Niebuhr, and the late Professor Carlyle's volume of specimens, are
a valuable introduction to this interesting knowledge.(x)

Croly's bibliography serves a defensive purpose, suggesting that his account
of an angel's temptation is not a fabrication of his own fancy; he likely
knows, however, that most readers will not take up his invitation to study
scholarly works on oriental lore. His notes--including long excerpts from
Bruce's *Travels*--likely serve the same end Moore's notes serve in *Lalla
Rookh*, namely, authorizing for the poem verisimilitude, and distracting the
syncretist from discovering biblical parallels.

Angels and mortals pair unhappily in the poems themselves, and in the
legends surrounding the poems. Reviewers intending to assess the
relationships among the various poems and their sources had to acknowledge the complexities of angelology. Those offended by the unions
generally, with Talfourd, held vague notions about angels extracted from
Aquinas and Augustine.

The *Blackwood's* reviewer who admonishes Croly to "devote himself
henceforth to a subject of more directly human interest" (*Blackwood's* 8
(Oct.-March 1820-21): 22) registers an objection which reviewers of all (save
for Byron's) in this group of angel/deluge poems articulate in slightly
different terms. The objection is not warranted. If some of the poems want
human interest, it is not the matter, but the mode, that is at issue. The
modes, and techniques for engaging the intellect, determine poetic appeal.
Some of these poems require readers to work to find human analogies.
Others give open and immediate access to pertinent philosophic content.

The two Ovidian narratives, Croly's and Moore's, demand that the
reader derive from the angels' fates humanly applicable situations and
allegories. Croly and Moore both warn against the deception ocular dazzle
may disguise. (The adage "appearances deceive" pertains.) The natures of
the deceptions differ; both narrators ask of their readers the willingness to
contemplate the allegorical sense each intends.

In marked contrast, Dale's narrator obviates contemplation; the moral
aim is unavoidably clear, and articulated often. Throughout, the narrator
intrudes to tell us how to interpret the incidents he relates. Didactic bombast
marks the closing imperative to the "Reader!" to "'Prepare to meet thy
God!'" The didactic intrusions are a bit heavy-handed for present-day tastes,
just as the Ovidian tales may require a bit more effort to render truth out
of allegory than we are wont to expend.

The Genesis poems likely hold the greatest appeal for current audiences.

Montgomery and Byron (and even Heber's fragment) start with stock material which we suddenly find unfamiliar. The narrators challenge us to engage our intellect, so that we may evaluate the characters and incidents; such evaluation will determine our degree of willingness to expend sympathy, to empathize, and/or to draw final distinctions between good and evil (which in our pedestrian world translate into "right and "wrong").

Poetic liberties--and confused poetic aims--stem from the fact that by the earlier nineteenth century, angelology had ceased to occupy the thoughts of the serious student of Christian theology. Bits and pieces of conflicting angelologies vied for authority--and even remembrance. After the appearance of England's amorous angels, briefer poems popularized angels, and in doing so, trivialized angelology. Treatises appeared defining the nature of angels--seldom addressing the confusion that both Scripture and tradition convey in depicting and/or discussing angels. These treatises cheapened angelology in that they pretended to be considered, theological reflections, while actually constituting mere reiterations of Scriptural passages referring to angels (some including, as well, remarks by ancient and modern commentators--the writers seldom evaluating these remarks, save for condemnatory references to the ante-Nicene fathers as "nearly pagan").

Montgomery himself plays a part in this trivializing in his "The Chronicle of Angels," which, a headnote explains, "having been suggested by the perusal of a manuscript treatise on 'The Holy Angels' by the Author's late highly esteemed friend, R. C. Brackenbury, of Raithby, ["the following Poem"] is most respectfully inscribed to Mrs. Brackenbury."[13] The poem, in three parts, merely recapitulates in verse each instance in Scripture in which an angel appears. Montgomery avoids defining the nature or substance of angels, deferring to the doctrine of accommodation, when the narrator addresses God ("Spirit made perfect, spirit of the just!"), and asserts that only God can apprehend angelic being ("--Angels, as angels stand before the throne, / By thee are without veil or symbol known"). The narrator continues with a catalogue of angels in Scripture--recalling the kind of angelological treatises the pious were putting to press during the age. Theologians, in general, avoid the issues of what, and why, the angels are, asserting merely *that* they are--that is, that Scripture deploys them. Anonymous reviewers bore far greater influence than theologians upon the public's reaction to-- and frequent disdain for--England's amorous angels.

Notes to Chapter 3

[1]This threefold division is made by a reviewer of *The World Before the Flood* in *The Quarterly Review* 11 (Apr. 1814): 78-87.

[2]"Utilitarian needs" were ascribed by an elite class to an underclass. The needs of working-class readers may well have been utilitarian--but not always for the ends the "literary public" assumed. For example, once imprisoned for publishing "blasphemous libel," Richard Carlile, a working-class radical reformer who had labored to become a publisher, would have nothing to do with poetry. Wiener remarks that "Shortly after his imprisonment began [in 1819], Carlile set out to remedy many of his educational deficiencies." (61) He studied theology assiduously so that he could combat Christianity with the right tools and the greatest force.

> 'Decorative' reading matter was eschewed by Carlile. He favored 'simple truth and plain reason,' not 'the madness of mental power,' and refused to read fiction or poetry . . . . Poetry . . . , notwithstanding a lifelong admiration that he had for Byron and Shelley . . . [,] was a 'trifling with common sense,' a 'pretty stringing together of words.' He described poets as 'the precursors of priests,--the syrens of human language, that had lured man to destruction, the general corruptors and the authors of the FALL OF MANKIND.' (Wiener 61-2)

Clearly, some working-class readers did not want devotional entertainment. They wanted reform. They wanted an end to oppression. Christianity, in Carlile's understanding, had harmed him and his fellow workers irremediably. In May 1829, he printed a circular that he proudly distributed, announcing that

> The Rev. Robert Taylor, A.B., of Carey-Street, Lincoln's Inn, and Mr. Richard Carlile of Fleet Street, London, present their compliments as Infidel missionaries, to (as it may be) and most respectfully and earnestly invite discussion of the merits of the Christian religion, which they argumentatively challenge, in the confidence of their competence to prove, that such a person as Jesus Christ, alleged to have been of Nazareth, never existed, and that the

Christian religion had no such origin as has been pretended; neither
is it in any way beneficial to mankind; but that it is nothing more
than an emanation from the ancient pagan religion.

Amazingly, Carlile remained out of prison. Taylor did not. (Wiener 61-2)

Quite different was the treatment afforded John Murray when *Cain* was
deemed blasphemous and was readily pirated, "reprinted in a cheap form by
two booksellers, under the impression that the Court of Chancery would
not protect it." (Smiles 1: 426) Never was there a question of Murray's
serving time in prison. Whether or not he would make money from *Cain* was
the overriding concern. Sir Walter Scott felt that the copyright should be
secured. Scott wrote to Murray that if *Cain* were condemned, then so must
be *Paradise Lost* (the latter an absurdity that should have been taken
seriously). Scott adds that "The fiend-like reasoning and bold blasphemy of
the fiend and of his pupil lead exactly to the point which was to be expected--
the commission of the first murder and the ruin and despair of the
perpetrator." (1: 427)

A letter to Murray from a Mr. Sharon Turner explains that

> Mr. Shadwell [an attorney], whom I have just seen, has told me that
> he had read 'Cain' some time ago, that he thinks it contains nothing
> but what a bookseller can be fairly justified in publishing, that it is
> not worse than many parts in 'Paradise Regained' and in 'Paradise
> Lost.' It is a dramatic exhibition of Lucifer speaking to Lucifer--
> often very absurdly. He [Shadwell] is King's Counsel and a religious
> man. He thinks it can hurt no reasonable mind. He will lead the
> case. If you do not apply, nothing is so likely to provoke a society
> to an indictment as letting these men go on in their printing. (1:
> 428)

"The case was presented before Lord Chancellor Eldon on 9 February 1822."
Eldon refused to issue an injunction, but implied that were Murray to
present his case before a jury, a copyright would likely be granted. Murray
followed this hint; he thereby secured his copyright to *Cain*. (1: 428)
Publishing "blasphemy" could prove an annoyance to a well-educated, well-
respected, wealthy publisher, who risked losing profits to pirates. To a
working-class publisher, printing "blasphemy" could mean the loss of liberty
for a long stretch of time. Different worlds availed themselves to the rich and
to the working-class. The rich assumed they knew what the working-class

wanted to read. People like Carlile illustrated clearly that the "literary public" had quite a stretch to go before attaining omnipotence.

[3]Sale's translation. Ali's more recent translation reads this way: "They followed what the evil ones / Gave out (falsely) / Against the power / Of Solomon: the blasphemers / Were, not Solomon, but / The evil ones, teaching men / Magic and such things / As came down to Babylon / To the angels Harut and Marut. / But neither of these taught anyone / Such things without saying: / 'We are only for trial; / So do not blaspheme'."

[4]In Norman C. Habel, "Two Flood Stories in Genesis," 13-28 in Dundes. Other differences between the Yahwist and Priestly accounts are outlined in Chapter 2, above.

[5]See Conklin, for example, 75-78 and 67-74. Among these notions are those concerning polygamy (999), regicide (810), *creatio ex nihilo* (976), the traditional dichotomy between the body and soul (980), God's expression of grief and other emotions (906), functions of the civil court (1013), heresy (843), and many, many others. He of course fulfills his own requirement that "it is only to the individual faith of each that the Deity has opened the way of eternal salvation" (900), and lives according to his belief that "Christ hath a government of his own sufficient to itself," one that "deals only with the inward man and his actions, which are all spiritual and to outward force not liable" (847). Milton's independence makes the nineteenth-century secular chiliasts seem conformist in their stance. Very Miltonic is his claim that "Lowliness of mind consists in thinking humbly of ourselves, and in abstaining from self-commendation, except where occasion requires it." (1018) Milton enjoyed more "occasions" than most. (All page numbers refer to Hughes.) It is a joke of literary history that Milton has come to be seen as the poet for Christian orthodoxy. He was not typical of the Protestant religious thinkers of his age, but rather occupied the far edges of the lunatic fringe of radical Protestantism.

[6]Montgomery's diction offends, as well--the poet's citations of Isaiah 53.1-6 and Revelation 19.12 as footnotes to Enoch's declarations suggesting that "these were the words of Isaiah and St. John," and hence "ought not to be assigned to Enoch," the reviewer adding that "without adverting to the bad taste of putting texts of Scripture into rhyme, we object to a mode by which the Patriarchal, Jewish, and Christian dispensations are confounded." (149) (One wonders if the writer objects to the melded narrative strains in Scripture itself.) Further, far from presenting the patriarchs as more skilled than seems likely (a charge against which Montgomery defends himself), in this reviewer's reckoning, the details of patriarchal life in Montgomery's

poem do injustices to their ancient civilization--"to the inventors and improvers of the arts at that early age." "Having related the death of Adam, who lived, according to the Mosaic account, 930 years," Montgomery "may be considered as placing the events which his muse records about the middle or towards the end of the tenth century from the creation." (144-45)

The detailed objections that ensue reflect the reviewer's tendencies towards grounding views of patriarchal life not on Scripture but on reckless assumptions inspired by cultural anthropology--a practice as objectionable as any poetic practices he derides. Their musical instruments--"the harp," "the pipe," and "trumpets"--suggest that "mining and the metallurgic art must have been familiar to the antediluvians," "since neither brass nor iron is found in the metallic state." (Amazingly, Christian orthodoxy has failed to commend this reviewer for reminding them of the patriarchal mining industry, which has gone neglected in most commentaries.) Similar conjectures ensue: "if they could work in brass and iron, they could not only construct trumpets to sound battle, and swords and bucklers for the combat, but also instruments and vessels of all kinds." The writer argues that "It is reasonable, therefore, to suppose that their improvements in the arts of civil life were much advanced, and that their knowle[d]ge of domestic comforts prevented the necessity of their reposing on mere beds of leaves." He provides detailed (and wholly conjectural) information about ship building that evinces to him, through "the construction of the Ark, as it is called," the advanced "practical skill of the antediluvians." Here, he goes far afield of Scripture--and of Montgomery:

> Reckoning the cubit at the medium length of 18 inches, this vessel was 450 feet long, 75 wide, and 45 deep, with a sloping deck; and the formation of such a floating machine, with its adaptation to the various uses for which it was designed, bespeaks an extensive knowle[d]ge of naval architecture. The conjecture of Dr. Geddes that it was made of osiers, or was merely a piece of basket-work, seems not to be defensible; for it is beyond the utmost ingenuity of man to make out of such materials a box or vessel of so vast a size, having, moreover, three stories or decks.

This rejection of the "osier" theory leads to his closing judgment of Montgomery's depiction of patriarchal technology: "On the face of the narrative, as it has come down to us . . . , we say that the inhabitants of the world, at the end of the first thousand years, were far more advanced in science than Mr. Montgomery has uniformly represented them"--the reviewer going so far as to compare Noah's crafting of the ark to the technology required in constructing "The Nelson first-rate ship of war, now building," which "measures from the fore-part of the figure-head to the aft-part of the taffrel 244 feet, or on the gun-deck 205: its extreme breadth, 53 feet 6 inches; and depth in hold, 21 feet." (145 and n) He judges that Montgomery's "poem would have been improved, had he more availed himself of this fact [i.e., of their technological skill] in his picture of the first patriarchs." (145)

This reviewer's conjectures rendered into "fact," he condemns Montgomery for "not [having] done sufficient justice to the inventors and improvers of the arts at that early age." If Montgomery can be charged with taking liberties with his source, the vagaries this reviewer would have him depict would have rendered the poet far more vulnerable to far more objections from the majority of (less fanciful) reviewers. This reviewer does grant that Montgomery depicts Javan as gifted musically, but still feels that patriarchal skill in the fine arts remains underrated in the epic, and judges that patriarchal skill in sepulchral architecture remains entirely unnoticed. As evidence, he claims that

> Josephus (lib. i. cap. 2. of his Antiquities) speaks of the scientific knowlege at which the human race had arrived, in the tenth age from Adam, immediately preceding the flood; and he reports that, for the purpose of transmitting a testimony of their inventions, especially in astronomy, they erected two pillars, one of brick . . . , the other of stone . . . , on which were inscriptions recording their discoveries. Now if such were their advancement in science and the arts, their burying-places must have contained other memorials than mounds of earth planted with trees and flowers. It is true that, in the author's account of the antediluvian harp, on which Javan played with such exquisite skill, the rich engraving of the shell is noticed: but still the *general* picture of the antediluvian social state, as improved and embellished by the arts, does not correspond with this hint. (147-48)

The testimony of the "rich engraving of the shell" is Montgomery's invention--on grounds of which he charges Montgomery with abasing patriarchal artistic accomplishments. This review stands out as the oddest on record.

[7]In "'A Light to Lesson Ages': Byron's Political Plays," in *Byron: A Symposium*, ed. John D. Jump (New York: Macmillan, 1975), 138-62.

[8]Coleridge refers to another Second Part sketched out according to Medwin (*Conversations* 234-34), in which the "fallen angels are suddenly called, and condemned, their destinies unknown." The waters rise.

> The scene draws up, and discovers Japhet endeavouring to persuade the Patriarch, with very strong arguments of love and pity, to receive the sisters, or at least Adah, on board . . . .

In the end, Adah perishes; Japhet despairs. (PW 5: 321.)

[9]See Charles F. Pfeiffer, *Old Testament History*, Grand Rapids, Michigan: Baker (1973), 603-606.

[10]E.A. Speiser translates the phrase "sons of God/gods," and finds the term '*elohim* "clearly differentiated from Yahweh." He notes that "the main stress is on 'immortals,' as opposed to 'mortals,'" and that they stand "in balanced contrast" to "the daughters of men." (44-45). E.G. Kraeling suggests Greek (via Phoenician) sources for the Giants, or *Nephilim*, in verse 4. ("The Significance and Origin of Gen. 6:1-4," *Journal of Near Eastern Studies*, 6 (1947): 193-205.) On the corresponding passage in Enoch, see Charles, *Pseudepigrapha*, 191. Charles attributes the myths of the "children of the heaven," and "sons of the holy angels" directly to Genesis 6.1-4, and finds support in Philo, Justin Martyr, Eusebius, Augustine, and Ambrose.

[11]See Shuckford 73-78, and Freret 96-98, in *The Rise of Modern Mythology*, 1680-1860, ed. Burton Feldman and Robert D. Richardson.

[12]See other traditions in Davidson 184.

[13]From *The Poetical Works of James Montgomery*, With a Memoir, 5 vols. in 2 (Boston: Houghton, Osgood, and Co., 1879) 2: 299-311.

Reveiwing The Angels:
in Search of Issues

MONTGOMERY DETESTED "The Periodical Press," despite his years of active service to *The Eclectic Review*. He devotes his closing section of *A View of Modern English Literature* to this blight upon contemporary poetry. *The Quarterly* and *The Edinburgh*, the two most influential reviews, offend the most, both "adopting nearly the same system of tactics in literature," by "which all authors . . . [are] liable to be transported as criminals, and there dealt with according to the laws made on the spot, and executed by those who made them." (*Lectures* 322) Yet the adjudicating essays want honesty: the writing "is fine acting," but "falls short of nature," and "since it is not nature," it "therefore cannot please, even at its best; we feel there is something wrong; we may not know exactly what it is but this we do know, that all is not right." Facade and showmanship, rather than earnest expression, constitute the ends of this kind of writing: "The contributions are got up in a masterly manner, but evidently for the purpose of producing the greatest effects upon the minds of the readers--not the unburdening of the minds of the writers themselves, glad to pour out in words the fulness of feelings long cherished in secret." Expressing things genuinely thought and felt constitutes a more promising end than that of overwhelming readers with a reviewer's facility at word dazzle; "authors write best for the public when they write for themselves." (*Lectures* 321)

All five angel/deluge poems suffered when reviewers found them. Montgomery stands far from alone among poets in deploring reviews. No poet liked them. Montgomery's diagnosis of these reviews--as efforts marred by deficits in honesty--proves apt. (The essays contrast markedly with literary theory in the romantic age, the latter reflecting an almost embarrassing candor.) Reviews of the angel/deluge poems seldom penetrate the surface; reviewers who expect devotional yields from biblical materials leave undiscerned the universally human (rather than devotional or theological) thematic statements inspiring the various performances. Few reviewers attended to any from this group of writers save for Byron's statements about the poet's social function (which Byron alone among the group determines to be negligible). Shelley's claim that "Poets are the unacknowledged legislators of the World" differs only in lexical boldness from articulations found in critical essays by Moore, Montgomery, and Dale. Wordsworth's claims that the poet enjoys "a more comprehensive soul" than other humans, as well as "an ability of conjuring up in himself passions ... without external excitement" parallels the descriptions of the poet's heightened capacity for sympathy which Montgomery deems the poet's special property, absolutely essential to any aspirants to the sublime. Reviews of the angel/deluge poems prove even less satisfactory than reviews generally; meaningful questions were not asked about the poems, significant issues went unaddressed, and the poems were hence judged according to wholly inapplicable criteria.

Of the five poets included in this study, Montgomery's theoretical comments are the most comprehensive, included in his *Lectures on General Literature, Poetry, &c.*, as well as in the roughly 35 reviews he contributed to *The Eclectic Review*. Croly's attitudes must be derived through inference from his Preface to his selections from *The Beauties of the British Poets, With A Few Introductory Observations*, as well as from scattered reviews (mentioned in Hayden). Byron's and Moore's critical remarks appear in their various prefaces, letters, reviews, and journals; Goode turns to Byron's poetry--particularly to *English Bards and Scotch Reviewers*--for remnants of criticism. (*Byron as Critic* 65-83) Dale's comments are scattered throughout his prefaces and reviews.

Croly's and Montgomery's general observations about poetry show their affiliation with their age in their appreciation of the poet's comprehensive sensibilities. Croly glances at the sublime; Montgomery offers a graphic account--an account suggesting why the angel/deluge poems would be welcomed by at least some of England's "literary public." For Croly, the sublime apparently inheres in the poet's comprehensive empathetic capacities--if we may adduce poetic theory from Croly's brief assessment of Shakespeare: "He is," Croly pronounces, "above all poets, the poet of passion; not merely of the violent and gloomy distortion into which the greater trials of life may constrain the mind, but of the whole range of the simple, the lovely, and the sublime." Further, "his knowledge of the workings of the human breast in all the varieties of passion, gives us the idea that he had either felt and registered every emotion of our being, or had attained the knowledge by some faculty restricted to himself." Sublimity is only accessible through omnivorous sensibilities such as Shakespeare holds claim to. (Preface viii)

Montgomery likewise celebrates the poet's inordinate ability to empathize with humankind--a quality tantamount to the "comprehensive soul" that for Wordsworth distinguishes the poet from other members of his species. When Montgomery designates this capacity to empathize (his "sympathy") as the inroad into the sublime, things do tend to become a bit ridiculous. Sade enters England.

"It is an affecting consideration," Montgomery tells us, "that more than half the interest of human life arises out of the sufferings of our fellow-creatures." We enjoy watching others in agony because we otherwise become downright bored: "The mind is not satisfied alone with the calm of intellectual enjoyments, nor the heart with tender and passionate emotions, nor the senses themselves with voluptuous indulgence"; rather, "the mind must be occasionally roused by powerful and mysterious events, in which the ways of Providence are so hidden, that the wisdom and goodness of God are liable to be questioned by ignorance or presumption, while faith must be silent and adore." (Secularized, Montgomery's explanation may well translate into his assertion that through the observation of others in agony, we are reminded of life's ineluctable absurdity.)

Montgomery takes Burke's notions of sublimity to the cruel ends that Burke stops short of. In his *Enquiry* (1757), Burke insists that "a mode of terror or pain is always the cause of the sublime" (1: 147). Yet in his section, "Of the Sublime" (1: 74-5), he insists that sublimity derives from pain only when pain is kept at a distance:

> When danger or pain press too nearly, they are incapable of giving any delight and are simply terrible; but at certain distances, and with certain modifications, they may be, and they are, delightful, as we every day experience.

Painting and poetry are two means of ensuring this distance. All humans are endowed with "sympathy," the passion that gives us an inroad "into the concerns of others," so that we may be "moved as they are moved, and are never suffered to be indifferent spectators of almost anything which men can suffer." (1: 79) We do not watch actual human suffering: "It is by this principle [of sympathy] that poetry, painting, and other affecting arts, transfuse their passions from one breast to another, and are often capable of grafting a delight on wretchedness, misery, and death itself." Burke shares and asserts the "common observation, that objects which in the reality would shock, are in tragical, and such like representations, the source of a very high species of pleasure." (1: 79)

If Burke's *Enquiry* fails to satisfy, it is possibly because Burke will not consign humanity to the bloodlust and innate cruelty that his theories, developed a bit further, would eventuate. (Too, Aristotle's casual reference to "catharsis," in an unfinished treatise, may well have been just that--casual, and unfinished, and not the stuff an entire aesthetic theory should grow from.) Montgomery seizes upon Burke with gusto, taking Burke's principles, as it were, to the circus, delighting in human anguish and agony. As an example of sublime pleasure, Montgomery has us envision a public execution:

> Among the crowds that follow a criminal to execution, is there one who goes, purely, for the pleasure of witnessing the violent death of a being like himself, sensible even under the gallows to the inconvenience of a shower of rain, and cowering under the clergyman's umbrella, to listen for the last word of the last prayer that shall ever be offered for him?

Montgomery responds, "No," and we expect him to continue with "there is not just one, but one hundred." His faith in the human heart amazes: "No; some may be indifferent, and a few may be hardened, but not one can rejoice; while the multitude, who are melted with genuine compassion, nevertheless gaze from the earliest glimpse of his figure on the scaffold, to the latest convulsions of his frame," deriving from this spectacle "feelings, in which the strange gratification of curiosity, too intense to be otherwise appeased, so tempers the horror of the spectacle, that it can not only be endured on the spot, but every circumstance of it recalled in cool memory, and invested with a character of romantic adventure." (Bodies, bodies, everywhere, but not a bite to eat. A few, I think, would throw up.)

For our next delight, he proposes that we meditate upon "the anguish and anxiety of a mother, watching the progress of consumption in the person of an only son, in whom her husband's image lives, though he is dead, and looks as he once looked when young, and yet a lover," embellishing this with the information that "the son [alone is the person] in whom also her present bliss, her future hopes on earth, are all bound up, as in the bundle of life . . . ." He asks, "Can any sorrow of affection exceed . . . [this]?" He does not expect an answer. Once again, we are inducted into the sublime.

His catalogue of "subjects of sublime and inspiring contemplation to the sage, and themes for the poet" includes "all that is terrible and afflictive in nature, in society, in imagination." This "is food for . . . [the] mind" of "the man of thought." Specifically, he thrives on

Earthquakes, volcanoes, lightning, tempest, famine, plague, and inundation; hard labour, penury, thirst, hunger, nakedness, disease, insanity, death; the existence of moral evil; the deceitfulness and desperate wickedness of man's heart; envy, malice, hatred, and all uncharitableness;--the commission and the punishment of crimes against society; oppression, bondage, impotent resistance of injustice; with all the wrongs and woes of a corrupt or a tyrannical government; the desolations of foreign war; the miseries of civil strife; to sum up, all the troubles to which we are born, the calamities which we bring upon ourselves, the outrages which we inflict on each other, the judgments of Divine Providence on individuals, families, nations, the whole human race,--each class, and the whole accumulation of these awakening and appalling evils, not only afford inexhaustible subjects of sublime and inspiring contemplation to the sage, and themes for the poet; but by the manner in which they affect the entire progeny of Adam, prove that more than half the interest of mortal life arises out of the sufferings of our fellow creatures. (*Lectures* 195)

(The Reign of Terror in France must have been a veritable orgy of sublime delight.) Montgomery continues this putrescence:

While the last paragraph was passing through my pen upon paper, a fly glanced through the candleflame, fell backwards into the liquid round of the wick, and lay weltering there for several seconds before the mercy of a trembling hand could inflict a speedier death than that which it was enduring. What an age of misery might have been condensed within those few moments to the poor fly is inconceivable to man; but could this be ascertained by some curious inquirer, the nightly burnings alive of flies alone would be sufficient to render his own existence miserable. (*Lectures* 196)

The sublime is sick, actually (although we get a good doses of it ourselves when dumb enough to turn on the evening news). Poets induce near-nausea at life's realities in Montgomery's age. From Montgomery's labored excretions from the mind, we get a sense of why the specter of the Deluge would appeal. One sentence summarizes Montgomery's conception of sublimity: "Death is the chief hero of poetry, though life be its perpetual theme." (*Lectures* 198) England's amorous angels come as harbingers, progenitors, or victims of death near the eve of world-judgment.

More sublimity would be hard to tolerate; Moore spares us from the sublime; he affiliates with his age in discussing an unlikely mode--political satire. As Moore conceives of the kind, it transcends time and place, aiming to effect identifiable, abstract, depersonalized social changes. Living targets become mere pretexts for assaults against bigotry and oppression. Were the satirist to come to know his victims as human beings--as opposed to representatives of offending abstractions--specific, personalized animosity would dissipate. Compassion is no stranger to the satirist's heart--satiric spleen actually vented out of compassion for humankind, and pointing to a heart capable of exchanging contempt for compassion, even for satiric targets, given time and familiarity.

The omnipresence of abstract, transcendental targets explains why Moore, self-proclaimedly "by nature so little prone to spleen or bitterness," has "frequented so much the thorny paths of satire": "By supposing the imagination ... to be ... the sole or chief prompter of the satire ... , an easy solution is found for the difficulty." Specifically, "the same readiness of fancy which, with but little help from reality, can deck out 'the Cynthia of the minute' with all the possible attractions, will likewise be able, when in vein, to shower ridicule on a political adversary, without allowing a single feeling of real bitterness to mix in with the operation."

Satire is reformative, not felt; it aims to quash oppression and bigotry, not defame ephemerae. And so satirists have always defended their vehicles; the ideas, not particulars, endure as targets. Yet Moore circumvents tradition in naming neither Horace nor Juvenal as his spiritual model, but rather finding in Dante glimpses of his satiric impulse. Moore calls Dante "the sternest of satirists," and even he, "who, not content with the penal fire of the pen, kept an Inferno ever ready to receive the victims of his wrath,-- even Dante, on becoming acquainted with some of the persons whom he had thus doomed, not only revoked their awful sentence, but even honored them with warm praise," as in his *Convivio*. Moore adds that "probably, on a little further acquaintance," Dante "would have admitted them into Paradise."

Familiarity breeds empathy, and "when thus loosely and shallowly even the sublime satire of Dante could strike its roots in his own heart and memory, it is easy to conceive how light and passing may be the feeling of hostility with which a partisan in the field of satire plies his laughing warfare." Indeed, "it may happen that even the pride of hitting his mark hardly outlives the flight of the shaft." Moore offers a theory of abstract, depersonalized political satire consonant with the revolutionary end of Shelley's, Keats', and Blake's reformative epics.[1]

Byron's attitudes towards poetry in general vacillate. (Rutherford 1-

14) Sometimes he concedes that poetry is the second best thing to action; at other times, he denies that poetry does anything at all. At still other times, Byron does seem to attribute to poetry significance of an undetermined sort, or he would not lament that "those poor idiots of the Lakes too--are diluting our literature as much as they can--in short--all of us more or less (except Campbell & Rogers) have much to answer for--and I don't see any remedy." Again, were poetry insignificant, "dilution" would not be worth reversing, nor would Byron postulate--by negating--the possibility of a "remedy." In short, the paucity of Byron's remarks about poetry make it difficult to assign Byron conceptual allegiance either with Shelley or with Johnson (through Imlac) when the fictional poet in *Rasselas* tries, but does not get away with, defining for his class a function in some ways resembling that of Shelley's description of a poet. At one point in his own reflections, in fact, Byron resembles both Shelley and Imlac when he ponders over the question, "What is Poetry?--the feeling of a Former world and Future" (Letters 8: 37). This remark Rutherford finds "not at all characteristic of him" (4); it does show his concern for key, philosophic concerns about poetry as an activity, a concern occupying Imlac as well as Shelley.[2]

Shelley's concept of the poet as an innocent reformer accords with his pronouncement that "Didactic poetry is my abhorrence," in his Preface to *Prometheus Unbound*, wherein we are to look for no "reasoned system on the theory of human life." *Prometheus*, as had *Queen Mab*, put forth the possibility of reform, although the poet withholds any system for effecting it. Byron, like Shelley, postulates, without designing, personal and social perfectibility. Byron concedes that poetry is the next best thing to acting towards reform. (Letters 8: 104-105.) Yet for Byron, the poet does not do much: "*who* has ever been altered by a poem?", he asks as a rhetorical question. (Letters 9: 53.)

Two trends, one in poetical, the other in social theory render passion commendable in Shelley and laughable in Imlac--the first of these trends involving a shift from product to process oriented poetry, the second involving the gradual abandonment of millennarianism for chiliasm. In short, the first trend--a shift towards process oriented poetry--finds illustration through Wordsworth's Lockean emphasis in his Preface to *Lyrical Ballads* (expanded in 1802); the poet begins with the self, with his own passions and observed particulars, to which he can impart general significance. Poetry can articulate particulars through which the poet hopefully leads the reader to general "truths"; such is the Wordsworthian method, or process, Lockean in its bases. Too, poetry can articulate general "truths," the poet trusting that the reader shares similar, specific preferences and life experiences and can fill in the details; such is Pope's method--in appearance Cartesian (because emphasizing conclusions, rather than the instances bolstering them), yet nonetheless grounded upon assumptions derived both from Shaftesbury and Locke. These differing modes of poetic discourse reflect no radically altered understanding of internal or external nature. The expressed ideas remain similar; differences arise from a given poet's preference for formulating truths without detailing their foundations, or for providing the particulars that have evinced general truths. (In actuality, Byron as well as Wordsworth--and Pope as well as Johnson and Swift--avail themselves of both methods at various times. Wordsworth drew attention to the formal characteristics of process-oriented poetry--his exposition, rather than the discourse mode itself, numbering among his more significant contributions.) Process-oriented poetry may or may not be best expressed in colloquial language. Conclusions, at times, may be rendered through colloquialisms--particularly in satire. Wordsworth succeeds in detailing what Imlac tries, but is unable to detail--liberation from detail allowing Shelley, but not Imlac, the freedom of rapture, grounded, presumably, in the particulars of contemporary theory.[3] Shelley's exemption from explaining how the poet gathers data determining the "truth" he formulates, proves product oriented, yet relies upon the groundwork of Wordsworth's description of the poetic process.

The second trend preparing contemporaries for Shelley's passion is the exchange of millennarianism for chiliasm--Shelley a significant exponent of chiliastic prophecy, as his age recognized. Millennarianism, anti-intellectual and anti-self-actualizing, is grounded in passivity, despite its favor among evangelicalistic "enthusiasts"; in practice, the elect wait for the eschatological overthrow of social corruption and the establishment of the Messianic Kingdom on earth promised in Revelation. Passivity proves anathema to passion, and millennarianism meets with ridicule in the age-- by none other than Moore, among others. Moore's satirical piece, "The Millennium" ("Suggested by the Late Work of the Reverend Mr. Irv-ng 'On Prophecy,'" 1826), ridicules those who stand and wait, depicting them as lower class, uneducated gullibles.[4] Because Moore's rejection of millennarianism stems from objections shared by Shelley and Byron, because his poem details these objections--and, because the piece remains largely unknown--detailed treatment seems wanting here, in order to highlight exactly why millennarianism earned disdain, and why it afforded Shelley new opportunities to express credible passion about the effects of poetry.

Moore's nine-stanza poem opens with its presumably naive (actually sardonic) speaker pleased at the prospect of "A MILLENNIUM at hand!--

I'm delighted to hear it-- / As matters, both public and private, now go, / With multitudes round us all starving, or near it, / A good rich Millennium will come *apropos*" (1-4). The new age becomes a matter of expedience ("*apropos*"), promising to fulfill economic, not spiritual ends. The lower class dialect in the second stanza matches the low, earthly visions of the speaker, who comforts an auditor with a preview:

> Only think, Master Fred, what delight to behold,
> Instead of thy bankrupt old City of Rags,
> A bran new Jerusalem built all of gold,
> Sound bullion throughout, from the roof to the
> flags--(5-8).

The heavenly city will be built of non-devaluable bullion--emphasizing the economic solvency (as opposed to the ocular dazzle, not to mention spiritual community) to be enjoyed in God's Kingdom on Earth. The poem here suggests that evangelicalism has debased Revelation, providing material visions that appeal to the working class, which embraces Wesleyanism.

The third stanza has the prophet doling out food and drugs--"wine" and "cheap corn"--as part of "a celestial *Cocaigne*" already enjoyed on this earth by "your Saints," or evangelical preachers, who "seldom fail to take care of themselves!" (9-12) For this promised abundance in a temporal world, the next two stanzas (Stanzas 4-5) constitute thanksgivings, in colloquial language, the speaker pronouncing, "Thanks, reverend expounder of raptures Elysian, / Divine Squintifobus, who, plac'd within reach / Of two opposite worlds, by a twist of your vision, / Can cast, at the same time, a sly look at each" (13-16)--the name "Squintifobus," compounding "squint," or distorted vision and salaciousness, with "fobus," an archaic term for pudendum, suggesting the salacious character of the evangelical divines, a notion which a note reenforces: "see the oration of this reverend gentleman, where he describes the connubial joys of Paradise, and paints the angels hovering round each happy fair." Paradise will be sensual, the living Divine even now a voyeur, already enjoying glimpses at the sexuality awaiting the saints. Hence the speaker is eager for this new Kingdom, eagerness prompting his next outburst of thanksgiving in Stanza 5 ("Thanks, thanks for the hope thou affordest") which, in fact, underscores his supposed gullibility, the believer willing to trust that "we / May, ev'n our own times, a Jubilee share, / Which so long has been promis'd by prophets like thee, / And so often postpon'd, we bagan to despair" (18-20). Because of his sensual and temporal promises, this latter day prophet instills faith.

Stanzas 6-8 catalogue Divines whose prophecies have proven false--among them "Whiston, who learnedly took Prince Eugene / For the man who must bring the Millennium about" (21-22), Whiston's Messiah refusing service, according to an explanatory note: "When Whiston presented to Prince Eugene the Essay in which he attempted to connect his victories over the Turks with Revelation, the Prince is said to have replied, that 'he was not aware that he had ever had the honor of being known to St. John'"; the annotator--not the speaker--determines Whiston a fraud. "Faber" is named, none of whose published prophecies came to pass (23-24), as is "Councellor Dobbs..., an Irish M.P." (25), who looked for the Millennium, or eschatological event, to take place "in the town of Armagh," an annotation explaining that "Mr. Dobbs was a member of the Irish Parliament, and, on all other subjects but the Millennium, a very sensible person," the expositor adding that "he chose Armagh as the scene of the Millennium on account of the name Armageddon, mentioned in Revelation." Stanza 8 dismisses "your Brotherses, Southcotes, and names less deserving," since all other Millenniums are hereby nullified by "the last new Millennium of Orator Irv-ng." (29-32) Stanza 9, the closing stanza, undercuts the faith that the speaker, until now, seems naively to maintain:

> Go on, mighty man--doom them all to the shelf,--
> And when next thou with Prophecy troublest
> > thy sconce,
> O forget not, I pray thee, to prove that thyself
> Art the Beast (Chapter vi.) that sees nine ways at
> > once. (33-36)

The prophet is evil ("the Beast"), his vision distorted, his prophecy untrustworthy; even the working classes are beginning to see this, as is suggested by the speaker's affiliation with this class through dialect. (MPW 566) With Shelley, Moore holds Millennarian hopes--based upon biblical prophecy--indefensible. In the earlier nineteenth century generally, the intellectual community held millennarianism in contempt. Chiliasm, depending upon the individual, was gaining adherents.

Chiliasm wants active participation in the eschatological revolution. Owenite reformers such as Goodwyn and Catherine Barmby, founders of the Communist Church in England, point to Mary Wollstonecraft and Percy Shelley as exemplars of the chiliastic ideal: "'Let the Messiah be within us'." (Taylor 180.) *Queen Mab*, with the new age beginning with an individual and an idea, constitutes a testimony to faith in the possibility of secularized, chiliastic reform. This chiliastic call, too, eventually reaches Javan in *The World Before the Flood*, whose discovery of the concept of Other People (precluded by his thorough self absorption at the onset of the narrative) begins with the senses--specifically, through neurological/glandular impulses for sexual union with Zillah, vaguely reminding him of a world outside the self. Montgomery takes Shelley's notion of the poet as a reformer a bit further than Shelley takes it, by showing how the individual may begin a personal--then ultimately social--reform.

Wordsworth again becomes important to theories of poetic language influencing Byron and his age. Like Pope, Byron remains vulnerable to external nature and its physical splendors--phenomena moving both poets to affect sublimity. Sublimity in Byron's age often is seen as a result of diction. Pope's--and Imlac's--concepts of poetic diction sound closer to Byron's than contemporary theories. Wordcrafting--particularly as espoused by Wordsworth--proves especially noxious to Byron. In the latter's review of Wordsworth's *Poems in Two Volumes* (1807), Byron charges Wordsworth with "'abandoning' his mind to the most common-place ideas, at the same time clothing them in language not simple, but puerile . . . " (*Monthly Literary Recreations* 3 (July 1807): 66 in Hayden 82). Montgomery reveals even less sympathy for Wordsworth's concepts of diction. A man "above ordinary men" will not "array the most pure, sublime, and perfect conceptions of his superior mind in its highest fervour, only with 'the real language of men in a state of excitement'" (*Eclectic Review* 4 (January 1808): 36 in Hayden 84). This shared disdain for Wordsworth's theories of poetic diction show that Byron in some respects finds kindred tastes in his own age.

Montgomery, in fact, again like Byron, recalls Pope in one of the former's praises of Wordsworth's *Poems in Two Volumes*. Montgomery finds that "in Mr. Wordsworth's poetry . . . , we frequently find images and sentiments, which we have seen and felt a thousand times, without particularly *reflecting* on them, and which, when presented by him, flash upon us with all the delight and surprize of novelty." (*Eclectic Review* 4 (January 1808): 41 in Hayden 85.) Here, we hear a rephrasing of lines from Pope's *Essay on Criticism* 2.297-300: "True wit is Nature to advantage dressed, / What oft was thought, but ne'er so well expressed; / Something whose truth convinced at sight we find, / That gives us back the image of our mind." Montgomery and Byron both find reminiscences of the former century in contemporary poetry; both espouse older as well as newer ideas. Both suggest that what we have come to accept as "romantic" poetic theory was unsettled in Byron's day--accounting, perhaps, for the unsettled remarks evoked by the angel/deluge poems published early in the nineteenth century. Still, the writers of these poems do embrace distinct and distinctly articulated theories of poetry, theories wholly neglected as operative or important by most reviewers.

The omnipresent reviews of *The World Before the Flood* do function as showcases for the reviewers' talents, rather than as vehicles for sharing felt reactions to, or considered judgments of, the poem. For this reason, the reviewers are best represented in their own words; a single, Ur-Reviewer seems to have fathered the flock of nearly identical judgments against Montgomery's epic, judgments that later reviews overturn, at least by implication, if not by fiat.

Twelve years after the fact *The World Before the Flood* "is by far Mr. Montgomery's best poem," although from the reviewer's more specific comments, we remain hard pressed to figure out why. "Mr. Montgomery's best poem," to put it mildly, is not without faults (for while "Pope has been censured severely by critics for mostly closing every couplet or two lines of his elaborate poetry with a period . . . , Montgomery "has unfortunately . . . fallen into . . . making such a pause at the end of the first line of the couplet as completely bars the progress of its natural flow into the second, and consequently ruins its best effect" (*The European Magazine, and London Review* 87 (1825): 11, 13). About its structure, "very little, indeed, . . . could cause in us any serious objections," if "we should wish, however, that the subjects of the latter Cantos [i.e., "the invasion of Eden by the descendants of Cain, . . . the foundation of the story"] had obtained a situation in some earlier part of the poem than they really have," for while "with this [impending invasion] we are made acquainted at the commencement of the first canto, . . . from that part, until so far back as the seventh Canto, we hear little or nothing of the invaders." (14) About its structure, this reviewer of *The World Before the Flood* has little positive to say--save for the concession that the poet's losing track of the invasion does not seriously mar the work. If untoward, this loss does not constitute "a material fault to this poem," nor substantiate charges "that it is not sufficiently dramatic," for the hero and his wide-ranging reflections and actions engage attention. (14-15)

The World Before the Flood in fact proves the most controversial among the three earliest English angel/deluge poems, this epic censured for "unmeaning epithets, inaccurate rhymes, and phraseology" by the reviewer in the *Theatrical Inquisitor* 3 (August 1813): 38-43, who typically judges "Mr. Montgomery . . . chiefly unfortunate in his subject," which to this writer reflects "the indications of weakness or bad taste that always tarnish the splendor of established talent when dissatisfied with its due proportion of merited praise," moving a "talent" to "undertakings to which it is *consciously* unequal." (43) Hubris here accounts for this defective work.

The writer for the *Critical Review* S4, V3 (June 1813): 618-24 shares the views of those who find Montgomery's subject daunting and Montgomery himself inadequate to his project: "we can the more readily enter into the author's sentiments . . . , because the subject is certainly not the most pleasing nor the most promising" (618). Here, however, Montgomery wins partial vindication on grounds of the impossible subject he selects. "Numerous are the difficulties which the author had to surmount, in order to treat his subject so as to interest without any offensive violation of probability" (618-19).

The subject once again offends--as does the poet for presuming talents sufficient to handling it, in *European Magazine* 64 (September 1813): 235-36, which similarly attributes the genesis of *The World Before the Flood* to the poet's defective character--to his hunger for glory:

> Mr. Montgomery has probably conceived that the more arduous and repugnant the undertaking the more glory and fame is to be attained in performing it; for it must be allowed that the subject he has chosen for his present poem is not one of the most inviting, and, on the contrary, abounding in difficulties which require more ability than the many possess to subdue. The poet's fancy must almost entirely supply the structure on which to found his chance for success; for the very scanty historical truths which relate to the antediluvian era can be at best, but secondary helps to his ideal narrative. (235)

Given this limitation, "the poet has contrived to form a very pleasing poem," or, at least, "from these scanty materials Mr. Montgomery has written no uninteresting poem" (236). (This reviewer is one whose glass is both half empty *and* half full.)

Specific infelicities are targeted by *The British Critic* N.S. 2 (July 1814): 34-45: "we feel a disappointment . . . " when "we find the sage, the minstrel, the maid, and the warrior of the antediluvian world exactly the same as the corresponding characters of our own times," this critic ignoring the fact that this is exactly what Montgomery endeavors to show--specifically, the sameness of humanity throughout the ages. Further, this writer disdains "some verbal inaccuracies," and, more specifically, objects that the application of the word 'serenade' to any music of which the Angels are performers, strikes us as particularly offensive and uncommon. Did the want of rhyme compel Mr. M. to use it?" (42) If Montgomery's diction for angelic song offends, things bode poorly for Moore and Byron, for whom attributing a "serenade" to an angel would prove too innocuous to bother with.

After the usual dismissal of Montgomery's subject and aim as far too grand for the poet to accomplish, this reviewer looks at what Montgomery does succeed in accomplishing, namely, a convincing portrayal of an abandoned lover. Zillah earns credibility--the poet's talent at characterization suggesting to the writer a possible service for Montgomery in subsequent poems. Montgomery could well compile a finishing school manual:

> Let us interest Mr. M. in this respect at least to imitate the Lake Poets, among whose highest merits is their perfect delineation of the female model. This is no slight praise; so much of the charm of society, of the grace of life, of the sum and quality of human happiness depends upon the excellence of the female character, that he may be well deemed to have fulfilled one of the most important offices of poetry, which proposes such models for their imitation, as they may please while profit the female sex. (42)

It is doubtful that this reviewer has in mind the female character" Mary Wollstonecraft would shape. Here, the epic transforms into a "courtesy" book, assuming a function previously relegated to the Richardsonian novel--that of occupying and educating women in proper subordination to male economic domination.

In light of Montgomery's theories and practices, this reviewer's suggestion bewilders by its superfluousness. Zillah admittedly represents the converse of the "female model" conventional wisdom approves; negative role models may instruct as effectively as positive ones--if these exemplars of what not to do neither triumph, nor hold intrinsic appeal. If, for example, Moll Flanders cannot credibly be presented as a negative model (the woman hearty enough to survive Newgate and repeated transatlantic crossings, her actions piquing interest, her course of life leaving her triumphant at the end, eventually secure in the economic emancipation she quests after), Zillah holds no appeal at all. We see depicted a morose and embittered woman, the narrator reporting that the past ten years for her have been fraught with misery, born of jealousy and fear; no one would volitionally follow a pattern of living ensuring an identically dismal prognosis.

Montgomery's theories of "The Influence of Poetry" (*Lectures* 207) accord with this reviewer's evaluation of poetry's beatitudes to the female gender and ultimately to society at large. "The compositions of the poets," Montgomery writes, "have also this transcendent advantage over all others, that they are the solace and delight of the most accomplished of the finer, feebler, better sex, whose morals, manners, and deportment give the tone to society." Had Eve been privy to this theory, the poor serpent would not have had to have been doomed to crawl on its belly; in flattering phrases, the gender is consigned the task of rectifying its inevitable fall and failure. Contemporary women bear the onerous responsibility for the way of the world, men securing for themselves blamelessness and absolute personal freedom, by virtue of gender roles, women "being themselves (to speak technically) its [society's] most agreeable component parts," serving as "the mothers and nurses of the rising generation, as well as the sisters, lovers, and companions most acceptable to the existing one." Montgomery's illustration is conventional--so conventional that it seldom finds articulation by his time, its underlying assumptions granted unquestioned status as "truth" (an untruth Owenites hope to set right):

> What owe we not, in Britain, at this day to Alfred?--Liberty, property, laws, literature; all that makes us a people what we are, and political society what it ought to be. And who made Alfred all that he became to his own age, all that he is to ours?--She, who was more than a parent to him. "The words that his mother taught him," the songs which his mother sang to him, were the germs of thought, genius, enterprise, action, everything to the future father of his country. We owe to poetry,--probably rude, humble, but fervent patriotic poetry,--all that we owe to Alfred, and all that he owed to his mother.

This is the sort of kindness that kills. Who is at fault when a man, or an entire society, turns cruel, brutish, and nasty?[5] When has a society ever failed to turn so? Women are clearly better off not born. Javan's childhood blighted by a mad mother, the hero ensures himself an enriching early adulthood by leaving a woman who would own him. Montgomery does not meet the reviewer's stipulations that he provide "perfect models"; far from ideal types, Montgomery's women in *The World Before the Flood* behave in ways eventuating their abandonment. His warning makes clear enough the behavior he mandates for women: perfection, as he, the arbiter of morality, defines it.

About his assessments of his own specific gifts, Montgomery remains mute. Whatever he most appreciates about his own art, he doubtless hopes he displays clearly in his epic. Conceding that "the lessons of poetic narrative may be rendered more perfect, as well as more interesting, than those of the most authentic history, because the premises from which the former is to be drawn may be exactly fitted to the purpose of exemplifying and enforcing the instruction intended," Montgomery would have us face frankly what he takes to be fact, namely, that the epic serves the poet at least as much as the reader. In short, the poet undertakes the epic kind in order to show off:

> it would be affectation to assume, that the few unrivalled epic poems have been composed, primarily, for any other reason than because the themes appeared to the authors capable of exercising their genius, and displaying their powers of invention. (*Lectures* 143-44.)

He dismisses "the conceit of Bossu, that the great masters of antiquity first fixed upon a moral, and then sought a story to illustrate it," and finds nonsensical the presentation of the *Aeneid* "in proof of this pedantic hypothesis" that "two distinct objects [are] to be kept in view in the conduct of a narrative poem, the one *poetical*, the other *moral*; the poetical being the *fictitious* action, and the moral the *real* design of the poem." Montgomery explains that "these are the notions of the republican Joel Barlow, in his preface to the strangest epic composition ever issued from the press, 'The Columbiad.'" When the opportunity arises to "serve their country or their own interest," poets have done so; yet poets will write "for the very love of the thing," and, as with all writers of epics, Virgil's "'*real* object' was to immortalize his own name"--an object one wonders if Montgomery acknowledges as his own.

If so, *The Eclectic* assents to his success, after some qualification. There, the reviewer countermands Montgomery's assertion that the poet need replicate only details actually given in Scripture; this writer--without the phantasmal eisegesis of *The Monthly Review* (quoted above, Chapter 3, n2)-- would thwart our inclination "to believe, that in the infancy of the world, there prevailed, in the human race, a simplicity, a peacefulness of character, analogous to that of childhood," such as Montgomery attributes to the Sethites in their glen. The Bible does not support this: Montgomery's "fictions . . . are absolutely irreconcilable with the scriptural representation of the older world," and we must "give up, as worthless fancies, the descriptions of the poet, so rich in beauteous imagery" (442).

(The age is awash with disparate visions of Antediluvia, Croly reasoning, for example, that "we have no certain knowledge" of "the peculiar religious corruption of mankind before the flood," but "they *must* have had a false religion," for "it is clear, that they had debased the original idea of God; and it is the natural operation of the mind to invent a substitute." (*Historical Sketches* 44) Croly, like this reviewer, displays certainty about the character of a world he claims to know nothing about. Montgomery at least admits openly that given the paucity of details in Scripture, he will invent a topography and an anthropology.)

The tone changes. Despite this writer's general condemnation of the subject, he speaks amply of places in which Montgomery succeeds in depicting "antediluvian courtship . . . as a 'similitude of events,' as a transaction of real life [which] we can contemplate . . . as neither improbable nor ludicrous." The love story wins, if the antediluvian *otium* does not (456-57). Montgomery's epic "bears the stamp" of "a work of true genius," and "the purity of its sentiments and the distinguished excellence of its tendency, will render that immortality a moral benefit to the world" (457).

The World Before the Flood, then, met with both objections and praise. A life of "James Montgomery," in the *Dublin University Magazine* (August, 1856): 216, recounts that Montgomery "found it impossible to disengage his mind from the scriptural narration of Enoch's translation, which he connected with Milton's paraphrase"; this fixation caused him to rethink "the old scruples against religious poetry, as adding or taking away from Scripture"--problems solved well before Sidney's time, but that each succeeding generation seems to have had to solve for itself. *The Quarterly Review* 11 (April 1814): 78-87, addressing "those publishers whose market lies among that portion of the people who are below what is called the public, but form a far more numerous class," a class searching for the "'sacred classics,'" places Montgomery's poem with Gessner's *The Death of Abel* (*Der Tod Abel*), which continues to mesmerize the pious, who "while they derived from it the same pleasure as from a novel, had the satisfaction of thinking they were at the same time meritoriously and even piously reading a *good book*" (78). *The World Before the Flood* promises to sweep this readership. Montgomery has chosen "the assumption of Enoch" as "the scriptural fact" serving as "the basis of his poem," this "subject possessing the religious, and susceptible to the pastoral interest of Gessner's work" (78). Given this doubly fortuitous choice, Montgomery's publisher need not worry about a hostile audience, even though "severer judges condemn all attempts at mingling fiction with sacred story." The writer acknowledges that indeed, "the principle upon which their [the severer judges'] condemnations proceeds is just, and perhaps if it were pursued would lead to a wide interdiction of historical subjects for the epopea and the drama." "But," he notes

> the people never judge severely; the book which pleases them they like because they like it:--with the why and wherefore they have no concern--*stat pro ratione voluntas*:--all they require is to be pleased--and their state is the more gracious (79).

Let the people be fooled; let them think they tend to pious matter. Independent, critical thinkers foment social upheavals. Montgomery's epic wins applause for placing a brake upon thought. (Richard Carlile would not stop thinking.)

Montgomery would doubtless reject the reviewer's consignment of his writings to a class "below the public," although the nascent heterogeneous readership and its unpredictable tastes both daunt and vex. Montgomery observes that "Books are multiplied on every subject on which any thing or nothing can be said, from the most abstruse and recondite to the most simple and puerile." The "book-jobbers," eager to sell anything to anyone, find counterparts in "genuine authors" who exercise duplicity "by disguising commonplace topics with the colouring of imagination, and adorning the most insignificant themes with all the pomp of verse." He argues that

> this degradation of the high, and exaltation of the low--this dislocation, in fact, of every thing, is one of the most striking proofs of the extraordinary diffusion of knowledge--and of its corruption too--if not a symptom of its declension by being so heterogeneously blended, till all shall be neutralized.

And while he deplores "public taste, pampered with delicacies even to loathing, and stimulated to stupidity with excessive excitement . . . , at once ravenous and mawkish--gratified with nothing but novelty, nor with novelty itself for more than an hour," he does not deplore the larger revenues afforded the poet by mass marketing--by an audience comprised of "intellects, of as many different dimensions and as many different degrees of culture . . . perpetually at work." (*Lectures* 308-309)

Poetry has a potentially large market: "there are fifty living poets . . . whose labours have proved profitable to themselves in a pecuniary way, and fame in proportion has followed the more substantial reward." Conceding that "this may appear a degrading standard by which to measure the genius of writers and the intelligence of readers," he argues that "in a commercial country, at least, it is an equitable one." (*Lectures* 312) Here, he accepts eagerly the cost accountant's gauge of poetic worth--a notion he elsewhere implicitly repudiates when he discusses Wordsworth. Montgomery notes that Wordsworth is "not a popular writer--nor one who ever can be, in the popular sense of the phrase, till the boasted march of intellect has made much more way than it is likely to do for half a century to come." Yet Wordsworth "has established a reputation of the proudest rank upon the surest basis--the most intellectual class of readers. . . ." (*Lectures* 121) Here, then, market value is not the sole measure of poetic genius, worth, or success; intelligent readers are not those who vote poets into success by casting coins as ballots; knowledgeable critics presume (with Montgomery) that faculties for discriminating worth and general human intelligence will enjoy evolutionary ascent.

Above all else, Montgomery worried about both the propriety of and techniques for reworking Scripture into epic--old concerns put to rest by Milton, as Curran points out, when Milton solved the latter problem "by elaborating in both epics what were relatively sketchy biblical texts" (163). Croly averted the problems--or supposedly did--by drawing on Qur'anic material for *The Angel of the World*: "The author of the poem," he announces, "desires to be discharged of all responsibility for the catastrophe. He has ventured to mitigate the Koran, which had undoubtedly the best right to mulct its own Angels; but he has done it in mercy to the propensities of Christendom." (Preface vii) He fails to explain his sense here, although a reviewer in the *New Monthly Magazine* 14 (October 1820) speaks for him when he claims that the angel's "doom . . . is mitigated from the austerity of the Koran, in accordance with our gentler feelings towards an indulgence in wine; and he is not consigned to the regions of torment, but condemned to be a wanderer on earth, until the hour of its destruction." (This fate contradicts the doom doled out to him in the closing stanzas of the narrative, the angel either exploding, or lapsing into a coma; Croly's syntax at the close of his *Angel* bewilders. By implication, this vindicating reviewer suggests that since Christians may get drunk, theirs is the more civilized religion.) In actuality, Croly risks renewing old objections--voiced by Blackmore (Preface to *Essays upon Several Subjects* (1716) 1: 74-75), who insists that "Epick Poetry is indeed the Theology of the Country where the Poet lives . . . ; and therefore it is as great an Absurdity for an Epick Writer to employ any other Scheme of Religion in his Poems, as if a Christian Preacher should form his Discourses upon the Plan of *Mahomet*," and asks rhetorically (Preface to *Alfred* (1723) ii), "How would a Christian Poet be received should he compile and publish an Epick Narration according to the Plan of *Mahomet* in his *Alcoran*?" (Swedenberg 281-83). *The Angel of the World* is not, strictly speaking, an epic, although Blackmore's objections to Islamic subjects in epic poetry as in sermons pertain to romance, as well, at least to romance endeavoring at moral instruction. Croly could have ensured aversion to the Qur'an had he simply developed one of its lesser known, and least favored, traditions from the apocryphal Gospel of Barnabus--an Islamic text that could pass for Christian. This tradition was disseminated by Sale, who remarks in a note to Chapter 7 ("Al Araf") that

> The Mohammedan gospel of Barnabus tells us, that the sentence which God pronounced on the serpent for introducing the devil into paradise . . . was, that he should not only be turned out of paradise, but that he should have his legs cut off by the angel Michael, with the sword of God; and that the devil himself, since he had rendered our first parents unclean, was condemned to eat the excrements of them and all their posterity; which two last circumstances I do not remember to have read elsewhere. (Sale 1: 170 n)

Enoch's cannibalistic and vampiric angels would bore in comparison to this celestial excrement-eater. Croly would have satisfied the poets' hunger for novelty.

As noted in Chapter 1, a reviewer in *Blackwood*'s 8 (October-March 1820-1821): 20-26, laments that the favor and celebrity accorded Croly's *Paris in 1815* (1817) had "been begun to be forgotten," and hence celebrates the new publication:

> it was high time that both he and it should be recalled to the public eye by some fresh and forcible demonstrations of existence as may be found abundantly in the volume now before us (20-21).

Yet the reviewer finds little to recommend the poem save for its style. *The Angel of the World* is "a beautiful paraphrase on one of the most graceful fictions of the Koran" (21). Croly,

> in order to simplify, and thereby increase the interest of the story . . . has contented himself with narrating the seduction of one angel only; but he has wisely adhered, in all other respects, to the original

of the legend.

Despite Croly's felicitous style and editing strategy, the tale disappoints: "with infinite splendour of language," the legend "has been treated in a style worthy of its beauty. Croly, however, may do well to devote himself henceforth to subjects of more directly human interest" (22-23). Croly fails to show anything vaguely useful for mortal application. (Had Croly turned to the Gospel of Barnabus, he could have at least have developed an etiological narrative, explaining why fertilizer is scarce.)

Croly himself would have disagreed. In his Preface to *The Angel of the World*, he acknowledges that "the most popular pieces of Arabian verse have had their origins in those slight events which occur in common life, and which must owe their interest to the poet's sensibility." (181) In the case of this poem, the "poet's sensibility" offers allegory applicable to human endeavors, when the "one Angel . . . fails by a succession of attempts upon his firmness, accompanied by warnings that justify the final punishment." (180) Exactly how Croly would have mortals envision a universe laden with Eblistic traps remains uncertain. Is theodicy to be an issue, or is Eblis a particular, parochial importation from the mythological framework? If the former is the case, freedom of choice is not extant. If the latter, allegorical pertinence garbles.

Dale's *Irad and Adah* proves likewise inoffensive. It likewise bores. *Blackwood's* assigns to Dale an audience similar to that presumed for Montgomery. Hence, the anonymous reviewer (*Blackwood's* 12 (July-December 1822): 61-67) condescends approval--for the right readership. Dale's narrative suits "the more strictly religious part of the community"; "those who purchase books for the benefit of their families, cannot lay before young eyes a more pure and instructive page than that of Mr. Dale." The writer adds that "It must be the fault of the person who reads that page himself, if his heart be not improved, and his taste gratified at the same time." (61) Here, Dale's value is didactic in that "finishing school" sense of the term one of Montgomery's reviewers finds Montgomery's talents suited for, the poet improving "taste" by touching the "heart."

Other responses to Dale's *Irad and Adah* were mixed. The judgment of the *Ladies' Monthly Magazine* N.S. 15 (1822): 157-61 proves of particular interest both for its singular suggestion that Byron's *Cain* influenced Dale's *Irad and Adah* (inconceivable, given Dale's rigid piety), and for its suggestion that antediluvian poems constitute a literary mode. *Irad and Adah*, according to this review, certainly does not invalidate the inspired records--on the contrary, the account it gives of the antediluvian world seems justified by the biblical narrative. The race of Cain are represented as worshipping the whole host of Heaven, particularly the Sun. Irad, one of this race, endued with every personal charm, but laden with the guilt of *murder*, feeling the curse of *Cain* upon himself, flies from his kindred, and wandering to the mountain, encounters and fell in love with Adah, a daughter of the race of Seth. In giving utterance to his love-tale, he confesses his guilt, notwithstanding which, Adah accepts his love, and departs from the worship of her God. The poetry of this first part is beautiful and very powerful. (157)

This reviewer--overstating the degree of Adah's abandonment of her God-- appreciates the "horrid imagery" at the scene of the catastrophe, and determines that "In the subject he has chosen it was not possible, consistently with the pure morality of Mr. D. to make an interesting story." (158, 160)

Dale's language receives much attention. The *Monthly Review* 99 (1822): 241-46 dislikes the "*difficult grammar*, which so strongly marks the modern metaphysic school of poetry," in which the writer includes Dale, "yet," he adds, "with this and other similar exceptions, surely both description and feeling appear in this passage that are almost worthy of the subject. ..." (244)

Byron's and Moore's poems found themselves the subjects of appreciations, and of two other sorts of reviews predominating in the age--analyses and *ad hominem* attacks.[6] Once Byron's drama saw print, Moore's narrative suffered through comparison; Moore seemed not to care. His alleged-- likely apocryphal--literary rivalry and race with Byron had served its purposes: interest had been piqued; a market had been readied. Reviewers preferring *Heaven and Earth* had to name--and keep in public view--*The Loves of the Angels* as their object of comparison, thereby increasing the public's familiarity with the work. Reviewers helped publicize the *Loves*-- whether taking it in tandem or solo; as William S. Ward points out, during the period between 1821-1826, "Thomas Moore's *Loves of the Angels* ... holds the record for the greatest number of reviews of a single work" (viii). Moore's journal entries reveal no interest in--even awareness of--his poem's literary standing when measured against Byron's lyrical drama. (His journal virtually ignores *Heaven and Earth*.) Of critical concern to Moore were judgments threatening to slow sales.

Appreciations of "beauty and sublimity" occupy an ample portion of the reviews of Moore's and Byron's poems, many reviews pairing Moore's *Loves of the Angels* with Byron's *Heaven and Earth,* and offering impressionistic judgments. Favor tends to be awarded Byron's work. One reviewer objects that "the women whom the angels love" in Moore's poem "are bluestockingish and pedantic," preferring Byron's "gentle, or . . . daring daughters of flesh and blood, dissolving in tenderness, or burning with passion for the Sons of the Morning" ("Heaven and Earth, A Mystery," in *Blackwood's* 13 (January-June, 1823): 72-77; quotation from 72). This reviewer prefers the "daring simplicity" of Byron's mystery (72). The "Review of New Publications" in *The Gentleman's Magazine* 93 (January-June, 1823): 41-44, pairs the two works, finding Moore's "language . . . soft and impassioned, and his metre . . . always regular, easy, and harmonious--though sometimes it certainly betrays too much art, and cloys by its uniformity" (41). Byron "occasionally astonishes by the gigantic scope of his mind" (41), but "we consider the piece, as a dramatic composition, a complete failure," the reviewer adding the familiar judgment that

> we certainly predict that if his Lordship continues to produce tragedies and mysteries, in such rapid succession, similar to those recently issued, he will write down his reputation much more rapidly than he acquired it (44).

For the most part, the subjects of these poems disappointed, and their artistic merits evoked impressionistic outbursts.[7] Byron's and Moore's contemporaries look for sublimity in the works, and are more often moved by Byron's. Sublimity in Byron's drama is heralded (although not defined) in an anonymous review, "Heaven and Earth; A Mystery," in the *New Monthly Magazine,* 2nd ser., 7 (1823): 354: "all over the poem there is a gloom cast suitable to the subject: an ominous fearful hue, like that which Poussin has flung ore his inimitable picture of the deluge." The review notes that "We see much evil, but we dread more. All is out of earthly keeping, as the events of time are out of the course of nature." Sublimity overwhelms. Interest does not (for Byron's drama). Neither does tolerance for Moore's poem.

Yet Moore offended the pedant perhaps more than the pious. In a review of "Arot and Marot, and Mr. Moore's New Poem," appearing in *The Edinburgh Magazine and The Literary Miscellany,* N.S. 12 (January-June 1823): 78, a reviewer (signing himself "N.J.H.O., *London,* January 9, 1823") observes that

> Every body by this time has read "The Loves of the Angels," and

every body will not yet have forgotten (whatever they may do hereafter) the story of the first Angel. Let those who bear it in mind, run their eyes over the following short passage from the celebrated French *Encyclopédie*, under the head "Arot et Marot."

This reviewer quotes the passage in French that tells of the angels' mishaps with wine and women, and shames Moore for not acknowledging his source, especially "as he has prefixed a preface, and subjoined notes, with much learning, from the Fathers, he might have inserted or at least hinted at the above-quoted passage." If Moore aims to document some of his poem, he should certainly include so fundamental a notation. This objection is not called for. Moore's first edition does include a note to line 267 explaining that "Some of the circumstances of this story were suggested to me by the Eastern legend of the two angels, Harut and Marut, as it is given in Mariti, who says, that the author of the Taalim founds upon it the Mahometan prohibition of wine." (132) Moore adds that "The Bahardanush tells the story differently." He has collected two versions of the legend; Herbelot, Fourmont, Sale, and many others treat it, as well. Two suffice. The *Encyclopédie* is unnecessary for verification, unless Moore wishes his notes to become themselves encyclopedic.

Yet eager to please (increase) his readership, Moore's revised (fifth) edition makes emends--beyond those called for. He appends to his discussion of these angels an addendum indicating that

I have since [my work was first published] found that Mariti's version of the tale (which differs from that of Dr. Prideaux, in his Life of Mahomet,) is taken from the French Encyclopédie, in which work, under the head '*Arot* et *Marot*,' the reader will find it.

Moore goes beyond Diderot, adding Prideaux' biography to his documentation.[8] This expanded apparatus was bound to annoy even further those readers derisive of scholarly annotations in poetry. But the body of readers did have the option of ignoring the apparatus, as a friendly reviewer--hostile only towards Moore's notes--authorizes. This anonymous reviewer finds Moore's pedantry alienating. His account of "'The Loves of the Angels,' a poem, By Thomas Moore . . . ," appearing in *North American Review* 16 (1823): 353-65, reflects his bewilderment:

We are at a loss to conceive the inducement under which Mr. Moore wrote the notes to this poem. The learning with which they

are overlaid, though all second hand, could not have been collected
by him with out a good deal of labor; and yet no one class of
readers will be instructed or pleased by it. The learned theologian
will smile at it; the *gentle reader* will let the leaves, which contain it,
remain uncut; while we will think that it savors too strongly of
pedantry, to become a real scholar, like Mr. Moore.

Poetry and scholarship blend awkwardly. The scholarly-minded could
turn to the French compendia for ready documentation of Moore's sources.
Moore's presentation of such data detracts--or so the reviewer says. In
actuality, Moore's notes distract, more than detract; distraction is deliberate; Moore does not simply annotate his poems because he wants a dumping
ground for biblical lore. (With Herbelot, Sale, and Fourmont at hand,
Moore could have--very easily--annotated even more heavily.) Moore wants
to divert attention from the unorthodox implications of various passages in
the text proper--such as the notion of angelic revelation of forbidden
knowledge, lines 1121-1127.

And Moore would object to the dismissal of his scholarly apparatus as
unimportant to poetry--Moore maintaining that this very sort of apparatus
accounts for the success of *Lalla Rookh* (1817). In his Preface to Volume 6
of his *Works*, Moore confesses, "I must also, in justice to my own industry,
notice the pains I took in long and laboriously *reading* for it" before
beginning to compose *Lalla Rookh*. (MPW 344)

Some reviewers took exception to Moore's matter. Outrage finds strong
articulation in an unsigned assessment in the *Eclectic Review* 2nd Ser 19
(March 1923): 211. The reviewer objects that

> these angels are, in the Poet's own showing, fallen angels; and if
> fallen, they must be impure, evil malignant intelligences. They are
> represented, however, in the poem as most amiable and interesting
> demons. The Christian reader cannot forget that these imaginary
> loves of angels are, according to the fable, the illicit amours of
> apostate spirits. The Poet, by making every angel 'tel his tale' has
> aggravated this impropriety to the utmost.

This reviewer also apparently disdains Moore's adoption of the "Rosamond
/Jane Shore ploy"--the signature of the sixteenth-century complaint poem.
This ploy offends in religious poetry, for this complaint mode generally
evokes pity for the condemned, and spite for the judge. God is the judge in
Moore's narrative; theodicy becomes the issue.

The angel poems provided welcome occasions for critics to launch *ad hominem* attacks, or to enter into political controversy. Obviously, hostile reviews of this sort are not reviews at all, in that the publication is an occasion, the poem a pretext, for a usually anonymous malcontent to slander or offer otherwise incendiary remarks. Their ammunition was potent, and ready. For example, *The North American Review* 16 (1823): 353-65, finds that

> Mr. Moore bears about with him the burthen of depraved, licentious tastes, and his genius is cramped and polluted by their foulness.

Prior to the appearance of Moore's amorous angels, this anonymous reviewer claims to have had felt optimistic about Moore's present spiritual condition; he had been certain it was in ascent, but is disheartened by what he takes as evidence that

> At present he has taken one step farther, and published the Loves of the Angels. We were almost about to say, that this was a retrograde step, but it would be perhaps rather more just to say, that he is but where he was, and the rooted vulgarity of his tastes and the sensual tendency of his imagination are made more distinctly visible by his staining such a subject with their pollution (354).

The writer notes that "the name of this poem has been long before the public, and with some seemed of itself to be quite proof enough, that the poem must be absurd and ridiculous" (355). This reviewer does not think so. He in fact had hoped that Moore "would have been borne upward by his theme from the licentiousness of his prevalent imaginations, into loftier and purer feelings" (355). The poem disappoints.

Neither did Byron escape *ad hominem* assaults. *Heaven and Earth* supplied a pretext for such. In *The Edinburgh Magazine, and the Literary Miscellany*, M.S. 12 (January-June, 1823): 9, "Oldmixon in 'The Liberal.' No. II," announces that

> Of Lord Byron's 'Heaven and Earth' I have little to say. It bears to be founded on a passage in Genesis, which his 'Satanic Majesty' has either ignorantly, or wilfully, misunderstood, and seems to be intended as an imitation of Percy Shelley's 'Queen Mab,' though

far inferior to that ill-starred performance in the higher qualities of poetry.

Heaven and Earth he determines "quite unreadable," and, savoring the infamy of *The Liberal*, Volume I, judges it "fit for no publication with which I am acquainted, except that in which it appears" (9). He concedes that

> In a moral point of view, it is certainly less exceptionable and odious than the "Vision of Judgment," and contains fewer examples of licentiousness and profanity--*tant mieux*; but still his Lordship cannot let Providence altogether escape: he is not at all satisfied with its allotments, and throws out sundry shrewd and significant hints, that had he been consulted in the distribution of good and evil in this world, things would have gone on much better. Now, this appears somewhat unreasonable on his part. Nature has made him both a peer and a poet--what would he have more? (9).

Byron himself supplies an answer later in 1823, an answer involving actions supporting earlier spent words. When he joined forces to liberate Greece from the Turks, he illustrated to his detractors as well as his supporters that he himself wanted to be a hero; writing about heroes failed to satisfy any longer. He aimed to defend, rather than need defending.

Reviewers defended him anyway. The ideologically friendly reviewer of "*The Liberal: Verse and Prose from the South* . . . ," in *The Literary Chronicle and Weekly Review* 5 (January 4, 1823): 8-11, takes the opportunity to defend the Hunts as well as Lord Byron. This reviewer, favorably predisposed towards *The Liberal*, objects that the journal has been wrongly "given . . . the notoriety of a prosecution" by "the Bridge-Street Gang," rather, "the Constitutional Society," and hence the volume "has made some noise in the world." About *Heaven and Earth* the reviewer says little, save that "It will be seen that this poem, though treating a daring subject, is less objectionable on the score of morality than Lord Byron's 'Cain,' and that it possesses much of the power and many of the beauties of his lordship's best productions" (11). He worries, however, about Byron's prolixity, articulating the familiar fear that Byron "will write down his reputation in much less time than he has gained it" (8).

Byron's poem is indeed pious, as he claimed, by virtue of the fact that one could say almost anything about the nature of angels without offending seriously serious orthodoxy. It is pious, too, because Byron leaves Jehovah alone; he never shows us a somewhat cruel and erratic God; we like Byron's

Jehovah for letting the angels and their lovers escape--if we do not understand why he allows Japhet to endure such misery. The angel/human unions do not constitute bestiality, given that fact that for the traditional angelologist, such unions remain ontogenetically impossible, and hence simply do not take place, regardless of what the poem may imply.

Byron surely realized the risks of once again associating with this journal--particularly since Shelley's death in 1822 meant for *The Liberal* the loss of a loyal moral and financial supporter, as well as an enticing contributor. Yet Byron wanted his drama read. Byron was fond of his "mystery"--as can be seen from his defensive responses to letters from Douglas Kinnaird. From Genoa, on 24 February 1823, Byron remarks

> As to popularity--Voltaire was reduced to live in a corner--and Rousseau stoned out of Switzerland--and banished in France.--I should never have thought myself good for any thing--if I had not been detested by the English.----You see I know this better than *you*--for when you wrote to me in *raptures* with the *success*!! of Heaven and Earth" I told you that your joy was premature. You can tell me nothing of hostile or oppressive from the English--which I have not contemplated--and such is my feeling towards their national meanness--that I would not wish it otherwise--except as far as it gives my friends pain.--But Courage!--I'll work them. (Letters 10: 13.)

This initial acceptance of ill fortune proves short lived. In another letter to Kinnaird, probably from April, 1823, Byron charges Kinnaird with tergiversation: "you yourself praised 'Heaven and Earth' at first and said that every body did so--*Since* you told J. Hunt it was a *failure*;--assuredly it has not been considered such from what I can hear.----"(Letters 10: 134). On 2 April 1823, Byron serves Kinnaird more of the same:

> Hunt says *you* consider the 2d. No. of the Liberal a failure. I suppose you mean in sale--for I had a letter from you three days after it's publication--in raptures with "Heaven and Earth" and it's '*success*'--as not only your own opinion--but of all those whom you knew.--You can hardly have changed yr. mind so far--without some reason--I speak as a *composition*--not with regard to it's circulation.-- (Letters 10: 136.)

He belies all disdain for British critical acclaim when he writes to John

Hunt on 5 May 1823, adding a postscript, "I see an Edinburgh Review of H[eaven] and E[arth] advertised--is it abusive?--or by Jeffrey--or by whom?--"(Letters 10: 166). He is clearly eager to know. Those reviews prove the soundest, as well, that accept--if need be, by suspending disbelief--the poetic universes depicted in the works, not confusing poetic with theological, or even mythological angels. Concern with the theological implications of the poems proves unjustified--although evangelicalistic enthusiasts worked diligently to return to the long antiquated notion of "verbal inspiration" in Scripture, a notion that would render poetic treatment of angels risky.

Heaven and Earth was spared charges of blasphemy; *The Loves of the Angels* was not--although, again, these charges were informal and relatively few. Many reviewers found the subjects of the poems without interest--testifying in part to their tendency to stop at the surface level of a biblical poem, recalling old, remembered theological significances for the informing scriptural passages, neglecting to examine poetic reworkings for any singular thematic or didactic ends.

These objections did not curtail sales. (Neither does Wilson's ethnic slur reflect the sensuality of the text. The sexual unions are far from explicit.) *The Loves of the Angels* went into its fifth edition in less than one month, its commercial success inaugurated with the 3,000 pre-publication subscriptions mentioned in Chapter 1 (Jones 217). *Heaven and Earth* failed commercially. Critical acclaim was not the problem. Circulation was. This stunning poem found only a limited readership, as its consignment to *The Liberal* all but ensured.

Moore's *Loves of the Angels* found another mode of review--namely, parody, in Lamb's "The Child Angel," first published in *London Magazine* in June, 1823. For Lamb (in his whimsical "The Child Angel: A Dream," supposedly visiting him after he finished reading *The Loves of the Angels*), Moore's poem served as a source of whimsical speculation, comedy heightened through Lamb's continuation of the biological process of divine/mortal coitus in depicting the offspring. In "The Child Angel" the speaker explains that after "I had been reading the 'Loves of the Angels,' and went to bed my head full of speculations suggested in the extraordinary legend," he gave in to sleep with the final pondering about "'what could come of it'." (Lamb 296). What came was a visionary dream, which transported him to "a kind of fairyland heaven," in which he was lucky enough to be "present at an angel's gossiping!" Their interest was in an infant. Angels hovered around its cradle, concerned that it had not yet opened its eyes. It did, "first one, then the other, with a solicitude and apprehension . . . , as if to explore its path in those its unhereditary palaces--what an inextinguishable titter that time spared not celestial visages!"

After they were through laughing at the child, somehow "were those attendants [able] to counterfeit kindly similitudes of earth, to greet with terrestrial child-rites the young *present*, which earth had made to heaven." Somehow, an illegitimate offspring of an angel and mortal tryst wound up in Heaven, rather than on earth. Upon hearing the angels play their harps--"muffled" to "accommodate" mortal ears (Lamb playing with the traditional notion of a "language of accommodation"), "the Angelet sprang forth," but was unable to ascend, as after years he still cannot, for "its white shoulders put forth buds of wings." This hybrid is deformed, and named "Ge-Urania, because its production was of earth and heaven" (this name--an obvious compound from the Greek *Ge*, "earth," *Urania*, the muse of astronomy--in its very simplicity poking fun at the complexity of some of the angelic names, as well as at the groaning puns of Moore's supposed angelic classes, specifically, RUBI, from the generic name for Che*rub*, and *ZARAPH* the Seraph). "It could not taste of death, by reason of its adoption into immortal palaces; but it was to know weakness, and reliance, and the shadow of human imbecility; and it went with a lame gait" (297-97).

This "glorious Amphibion" will remain forever a child, because "Mature Humanity is too gross to breathe the air of that super-subtile region." For all time Ge-Urania will serve as the "Tutelar Genius of Childhood upon earth," forever "lame and lovely" (perhaps a parody of Michael's revelation of his name to Mary as "Great and Wonderful"). The vision shows that the angel at times ascends, its countenance of grief when in heaven--its dimness there--"on earth an emblem of grief" (which the narrator excuses himself for not elaborating by explaining that "this correspondency is not to be understood but by dreams"). He sits alone on the "banks of the River Pison," attending "the grave of the terrestrial Adah, whom the angel Nadir loved" (299).

The closing vision plays with the stereotypical notion of parental love:

> And in the archives of heaven I had grace to read, how that once the angel Nadir, being exiled from his place for mortal passion, aspiring on the wings of parental love (such power had parental love for a moment to suspend else-irrevocable law) appeared for a brief instant in his station, and, depositing a wondrous Birth, straightway disappeared, and the palaces knew him no more . . . . And this charge was the self-same Babe, who goeth lame and lovely, but Adah sleepeth by the river Pison."

Lamb has fun with the angels. He has considered the implications of fertile interspeciation. The child's compounded name is almost as ugly to pronounce as the crossbreed's defective and stunted figure must be to envision (for "lame and lovely"--Lamb's epithet for the accidental angel--refuse credible conjunction with "and," connoting equivalence; Raphael's "Infant Angels," reproduced in G. Davidson (150) prove suitably silly looking--moreso than Titian's "Infant Angel," in Davidson (9), who is devoid of childlike grins and expressions of curiosity, the genesis of any infant angels still making the mind recoil.) The narrator almost blames Adah for child neglect by using the euphemism "sleeps" for "is dead." The father's "power" through parental love to "suspend" cosmic laws is in no way prompted by any sort of love at all. Nadir, or "the lowest possible point," his name reflecting his sense of paternal responsibility, in a burst of cosmic law-defying strength, "appeared for a brief instant" in order to get this deformed, unwanted "Amphibion" out of his purview. Genealogy gives Lamb an opportunity to amuse himself. Lamb's play with his subject, taking divine/mortal coitus to one of its two possible ends, suggests the freedom one had in treating angels; theology had silently terminated them from active service. Were they still necessary to faith, they would never be shown abandoning--let alone having--babies.

Lamb's entertainment constitutes a comment of sorts about Moore's poem. Lamb finds it a bit silly. But silliness is not to be eschewed. (The silly is part of native English poetic tradition--as *The Second Shepherd's Play* among numerous other native mystery plays illustrates.) Silliness provides pleasure--as does the idea of a literal "Child Angel." Yet in embracing silliness, Lamb takes a stand against pious utilitarianism; at various bursts in time throughout the nineteenth century, the principles of "production for pleasure" and "production for use" stand in opposition. (Somehow, the Horatian aims--to teach through delighting--were becoming dissevered; instead of both/and, poetry threatened an either/or fulfillment of these ends, "art for art's sake" constituting the maturity of an impulse felt early in the century.)

Byron's lyrical drama won the most favor among reviewers. Montgomery's biblical epic--despised when first put forth--somehow transformed into a sacred monument. Croly and Dale found buyers, as well as reviewers to recommend them to potential buyers--if these reviewers remained hard pressed to explain exactly why one should own an *Angel of the World* or an *Irad and Adah*. Moore's *The Loves of the Angels*--resoundingly maligned--found vindication in the form of booksellers' receipts, an important form of criticism in a cost accountant's world. And Moore's *Angels*, too, were vindicated as literature--by their translation, imitation, and generally warm reception in France.

Notes to Chapter 4

[1]Moore's concept of a sort of visionary satire in no way accords with Byron's notions about the kind. Byron and Pope, as Rutherford sees them, both maintain for satire a local, rather than a temporal application. Rutherford points out that Byron's satire, unlike Pope's, remains "curiously unstable, based . . . not on any firm belief or principle, but on Byron's fluctuating feelings, partly critical and hostile, partly tolerant and sympathetic, towards English aristocratic life" (201). In This, Byron differs "radically from Pope." Pope consistently identifies "with the best traditions, social, intellectual, moral, and religious, of his age, and he attacked vice, folly, and bad taste as aberrations . . . " (201). Sometimes Byron follows Pope in this; at other times, Byron shows an affinity with immorality, and rather likes the licentiousness of his class, as well as his part in fostering it. (Rutherford 201.) Much has been made of Byron's admiration for Pope, which Byron expresses unusually prolifically and effusively--perhaps pushed by polemic needs--when he engages in the Bowles controversy. This admiration does not mark Byron a throwback to some supposed "Augustan" age. (Rutherford 4, 110-11)

The Rape of the Lock accords with Byron's distaste for sham, pretense, and cant. The Dunciad reflects pain--pain of the sort that Byron, like Pope, met with in endeavoring at cultivated indifference to public scorn. In exploring Byron's admiration for Pope, it becomes particularly important that pain--and not the innocent reformer's zeal--motivates Pope's declaration of war against Theobald, a single assailant in the Dunciad in its first form, and against the Kingdom of Dullness, the formidable battalion of Pope's scorners in The New Dunciad. Pope's expansion of his Kingdom of Dullness reflects his exhaustion with attacks against his person at least as much as attacks against his art. (Attacks of this sort exhaust Byron, too--who, like Pope, does much to provoke, but seldom expects them.) The Dunciad is not written in the spirit of MacFlecknoe--although the two are often likened for a wrong reason. Dryden writes with genuine concern for the survival of poetry as a vehicle for serious instruction; he would have it worthy of the colleges, courts, and kings whose ideas, tastes, and morality he would have the poet arbitrate. For Pope--as for Byron--this hope has proven vain. (Pope has already tried to upgrade vulgar sensibilities, to reform taste, but has come to accept--with less sangfroid than his assertion conveys--that "the life of a wit is a warfare on earth." Byron would agree.)

The later Pope wishes simply to stop the sallies against him. Yet Byron admires Pope for more than his satire. Pope's complexity--in thought and mode--leads Byron to determine him "a Greek Temple, with a Gothic Cathedral on One hand, and a Turkish Mosque and all sorts of fantastic pagodas and conventicles about him" (Letters 8: 109). His linguistic virtuosity impresses; his philosophy appeals. He engages the mind in his capacity as an ethical poet. Croly also admires Pope as a philosophical poet, despite the fact that Croly's High Anglican Orthodoxy forces him to insist that the *Essay on Man* is "founded on an errouneous system"; it nonetheless "has the great preservative qualities that send down authorship to remote times." (Preface xii)

When Pope issues the judgment that "whatever is, is right," he licenses neither social stasis nor indifference towards the indigent; this tautology reflects acceptance, and marks Pope a realist, rather than a monster. *Right* as Pope here uses it does not connote "immutably good," "divinely or- dained," or even, necessarily, "unobjectionable." Rather, *right* suggests "that which has to be, given the chain of events leading to the present moment." Byron struggles to accept life, both as it is, and as it is not. Like Pope's, his efforts at acceptance meet with frustration--another circumstance leading to Byron's spiritual alliance with Pope. (See Rutherford 106.) Pope's generalizations in his moral epistles reflect the product, and not the process, of empirical investigation--Byron remaining product oriented, Wordsworth endeavoring to show processes.

Byron's defense of Pope against Bowles in fact rings with unusual compassion for the critic as well as the poet, when, in a letter to Octavius Gilchrist (5 September 1821), he remarks that "Mr. Bowles has certainly not set *you* an example of forbearance in *controversy*--but in *society* he really is what I have described him--but as we are all mad upon some subject or other--the only reason why it does not appear in *all* is that their insane chord has not been struck upon." (Letters 8: 200) Here, Byron's empathy for Bowles reflects the "romantic" proclivity towards faith in the *sensus communis*, modified from Shaftesbury to denote basic, shared, impulses that may be presumed to unify humankind. (This modification of *sensus communis* informs Wordsworth's arguments about human nature in the Preface to *Lyrical Ballads*.)

The notion flies high; Byron's example of the "insane chord" brings it closer to earth than Wordsworth's exaltation of that "knowledge . . . connecting us with our fellow beings." Bowles' "insane chord" "seems to have been touched upon the score of Pope--and for that reason it is a thousand pities that he ever meddled with him." Byron dislikes Gilchrist's suggestion that Byron is "more indecent" than Pope, although he grants that "if Pope's moral reputation can be still further elevated at the expence of mine--I will yield it as freely--as I have always admired him sincerely---- much more indeed," he insists, "than you yourself in all probability--for *I* do not think him inferior to Milton," although he recognizes that "to state such an opinion publicly in the present day--would be equivalent to saying that I do not think Shakespeare without the grossest of faults--which is another heterodox notion of my entertainment." He adds that "indeed I look upon a proper appreciation of Pope as a touchstone of taste--and the present question is not only whether Pope is or is not in the first rank of our literature--but whether *that* literature shall or shall not relapse into the Barbarism from which it has scarcely emerged for above a century and a half." Byron here raises doubts about contemporary poetry he would express in a "Detached Thought" from the following month; to Gilchrist, he asserts that "It is also a great error to suppose the *present* a *high* age of English poetry--it is equivalent to the age of *Statius* or *Silius Italicus* except that instead of imitating the Virgils of our language--they are 'trying back' (to use a hunting phrase) upon the Ennius's and Lucilius's who had better have remained in their obscurity."

Similarly, Byron's "Detached Thoughts" includes a notation recorded in Pisa on 3 November 1821 denying the present age stature as a hallmark in English poetry:

> One of my notions different from those of my contemporaries, is, that the present is not a high age of English Poetry----there are *more* poets (soi-disant) than ever there were and proportionately *less* poetry.----This *thesis* I have maintained for some years--but strange to say--it meeteth not with favor with my brethren at the Shell--even Moore shakes his head--& firmly believe[s] that it is the Grand Era of British Poesy. (Letters 9: 35.)

It is difficult to assess exactly what value Byron would place upon such a "Grand Era." (In marked contrast, Montgomery determines that "From Cowper may be deduced the third great age of English poetry," greatness stimulated by the possibilities--not the realities--of the free speech and the envisioned freedom of the French Revolution, *Lectures* 310-11.)

[2]Imlac insists that the poet "must write as the interpreter of nature and the legislator of mankind, and consider himself as presiding over the thoughts and manner of future generations, as being superior to time and place." This function derives from his "knowledge of nature," attainable

through a detailed program which Imlac outlines, and from his rendering of the self into an objective, atemporal, acultural being, able to "rise to general and transcendental truths, which will always be the same" (and which the latter modifier renders patently and absurdly obvious). Imlac goes on to explain the comprehensiveness of the poet's learning, and the poet's need to attune himself to "every delicacy of speech and grace of harmony," thereby affecting in himself an "enthusiastic fit, and proceeding to aggrandize his own profession, when the prince cried out: 'Enough! thou hast convinced me that no human being can ever be a poet'." (*Rasselas* 50-51.)

With characteristic counterpointing, Johnson has his poet, once shut up, proceed with litotes: "'to be a poet,' said Imlac, 'is indeed very difficult'." Imlac's detailed--laboriously detailed--course prescribed for the aspirant to poetry approaches Pope's supporting instructions following his assertion that "A little learning is a dangerous thing; / Drink deep, or taste not the Pierian spring," in his *Essay on Criticism* 2.215-16. Pope, in 2.217-559, provides instructions even more detailed than those Imlac attempts to impart. Both Shelley and Johnson (through Imlac) assign to the poet a legislative function--a function Shelley's poet performs in ignorance, and which Johnson's cannot be presumed to perform at all (for the constantly undercutting irony throughout *Rasselas* makes us doubt any and all speakers and assertions). Both Johnson and Pope require that the poet undertake an exhaustive course of study. Who among the three represents Byron's views, and when? This remains uncertain, although his "uncharac-teristic" entry into his *Ravenna Journal* recalls Imlac's atemporal poet, as well as Shelley's and Imlac's notion of the poet as arbiter of future ideas and morals. Poetry is serious business for Shelley; for Imlac, it is, and it is not. (*Rasselas*, characterised by its relentless irony, posits the ironist's world of both/and. Imlac aggrandizes the poet's function in a manner rendering it both feasible and improbable.)

[3]"What is a poet?" Wordsworth poses then answers this question by asserting that

> He is a man speaking to men: a man, it is true, endued with more
> lively sensibility, more enthusiasm and tenderness, who has a
> greater knowledge of human nature, and a more comprehensive
> soul, than are supposed to be common among mankind; a man
> pleased with his own passions and volitions, and who rejoices more
> than other men in the spirit of life that is in him; delighting to
> contemplate similar volitions and passions as manifested in the

> goings-on of the universe, and habitually impelled to create them
> where he does not find them. (165)

He cannot affect passions in others. He draws correspondences. He discerns
the unifying generality melding individual particulars. *Nosce teipsum* is his
starting point. The individual sentient being is the source of all truth.

Imlac reverses this process. The poet's concern is with the general. He
observes and records generalities. He does not "number the streaks of the
tulips." But he is aware that there are streaks that may be numbered--
suggesting his awareness of the particulars undergirding generalities.(51)
Only the focal points differ. Conveying truth about humankind and the
universe--grounded in nature (external and internal nature)--constitutes an
identical end.

[4]Moore and Washington Irving were close friends, but constantly
derided one another in print. See, for example, Kirby 251-2.

[5]Conceptions of this sort directly oppress women of Islam today.
Recently, a cab driver in Jordan was denouncing the disrespect his son had
shown him; he had ordered the young man to go to the store for a package
of cigarettes; the young man had refused. The driver went on to exonerate
the youth. He explained that his problems with his son were brought on by
the taint of the youth's mother's milk. The driver was convinced that his
wife had been misbehaving during pregnancy. A rotten woman brings forth
a rotten child; a rotten child means that its mother was rotten. Only the Law
of Duns Scotus can explain the logic. The incident would be laughable, were
we not forced to face the fact that this young man's mother presumably still
lives (as do many others in her circumstances), her identity and worth
deriving solely from her husband's evaluation--not of her, but of their
offspring.

[6]Montgomery met with mild *ad hominem attacks* by reviewers who
explain his choice of subject as a manifestation of his defective character, his
hubris. The peculiar analysis of Montgomery's fidelity to the Bible in the
Monthly Review constitutes one of the odder analyses of any of these poems.
Reiman collects reviews of Moore's and Byron's angel/deluge poems;
Hayden discusses them in some detail. Hoover H. Jordan remarks that
"Actually the two works do not belong in the same review," and adds that
"From a critical point of view, little that is instructive can be gained from
citing parallelisms of content, and, as so little else exists in common
between the works, the reviewers ordinarily had recourse to drawing
extravagant contrasts between the poets themselves." (439) The poems
share two highly significant similarities--their concepts, particularly their

notions of theodicy and love, and their sources. Wallace Cable Brown ("Popularity . . . Near East" 80) suggests that "the contemporary English reader's familiarity with the Near East, through the travel books, partly accounts for the instantaneous popularity of such works as Byron's *Childe Harold* (Canto II), his Turkish verse tales, Moore's *Lalla Rookh*, Thomas Hope's *Anastatius*, and James Morier's *Hajii Baba*." The angel/deluge poems move into a new mode, divorced from the oriental tale. The popularity of the angel/deluge poems remains inexplicable, save for by considering them in light of the complicated explanation of the confluence of incidents and circumstances detailed in Chapter 1.

[7]Many of these artistic judgments find record in the text of *Heaven and Earth* prepared by E. H. Coleridge, Byron's editor at the onset of the twentieth century. While Coleridge prefers Moore's narrative to Byron's mystery (PW 5: 279-282), he amply documents that contemporaries-- Goethe among them--tended to prefer *Heaven and Earth*, adding that because the two works were published within eight days of each other, the "lyric and drama were destined to run in double harness." He recalls that "critics found it convenient to review the two poems in the same article, and were at pains to draw a series of more or less pointed and pungent comparisons between the unwilling though not unwitting rivals" (PW 5: 280). Coleridge quotes from Wilson, in *Blackwood*: "'The first [the *Loves*,etc.] is all glitter and point like a piece of Derbyshire spar, and the other is dark and massy like a block of marble . . . . Moore writes with a crow-quill, . . . Byron writes with an eagle's plume;' Jeffrey, in the *Edinburgh*, likens Moore to 'an *aurora borealis*' and Byron to 'an eruption of Mount Vesuvius'!" (PW 5: 280.)

Coleridge himself finds it unfair that the *Loves of the Angels* suffered: "There is, indeed, apart from the subject, nothing in Byron's gloomy and tumultuous rhapsody, while contrast is to be sought rather in the poets than in their poems." He prefers Moore's craft. Coleridge adds that "The *Loves of the Angels* is the finished composition of an accomplished designer of Amoretti, one of the best of its kind," while "*Heaven and Earth* is the rough and unpromising sketch thrown off by a great master." (PW 5: 280.)

[8]Actually, Moore seldom refers to Diderot, preferring Herbelot and Fourmont for his oriental lore. This likely has to do with the volumes in Langlés', Vonpradt's, and Lansdowne's libraries, from which Moore borrowed the most heavily. (See, for example, JTM 2: 588.)

Angels Abroad:
Moore and Byron in France
and in Translation

ENGLAND'S AMOROUS ANGELS--at least Moore's and Byron's--
found welcome harbors in France, where in the hands of Vigny and
Lamartine they inspired oracles both of despair and of hope, oracles calling
for revisions of traditional concepts of God. England encouraged no
philosophical systems through which orthodoxy might revise assumptions
about divinity. Hence in England, the narratives amounted to instances of
an old kind--biblical narrative, and biblical drama, read by the English for
their fidelity to, and divergences from their originals. (Only Montgomery
clearly emphasizes a secular concept, and outlines a non-scriptural,
informing plan for human perfectibility in his poem.) These narratives in
England wasted away into the realm of conceptually vapid writings.

They held far greater significance on the Continent, where both kept
translators busy throughout the nineteenth century.[1] The exact philosophical significance of either poem is difficult to pinpoint. In some cases, the
poems carried the particularized symbolic significance to a specific nation
of the poets' personal celebrity. In other cases, the poems bore philosophical significance read into earlier efforts by these writers by Continental
readers. The hazy sense of the significance of the two poems in France
clarifies, a bit, from clues left in the journals and reflections of two
contemporary French poets, Vigny and Lamartine. Both acknowledge
varying degrees of debt to the two English poets. Some of this debt amounts
merely to borrowed descriptive details. The English poems were of far
greater service to Vigny and Lamartine as stimuli for philosophical
contemplation. Vigny and Lamartine find in Moore's and Byron's poems
the occasion to solve--or rather circumvent--the problem of theodicy, and
to propose systems for the perfectibility of humankind independent of
divine intervention.

Thérèse Tessier discusses the French affability towards Moore's poem,
particularly, which, for the French, provided inspiration for a notion of
religion appealing both to the heart and to the senses--a positive attraction
for Vigny, Lamartine, and Hugo. (363-65) Moore's significance to Vigny

may have come secondhand. Fernand Baldensperger ("Thomas Moore et A. De Vigny") suggests that Louise Belloc's translation, *Les Amours des Anges*, influenced Vigny far more directly than Moore's English original. (295-301) Tessier insists that Moore's influence on Lamartine was direct, and that, further, Moore accomplishes in 1900 lines what it takes Lamartine nearly 12,000 to do. (365) Claudius Grillet suggests that Byron, Moore, and Milton influence not only Vigny and Lamartine, but also Hugo (*La Fin de Satan*), Edgard Quinet (*Promethée*, 1838), and Alexandre Soumet (*La Divine Epopée*, 1838). Grillet sees in Quinet's and Soumet's writings the notion of an angel moved towards earth by pity, and in Hugo the notion of ongoing progress leading to perfection for the human species (238-39).

H. A. Taine's French perspective provides insight into why *The Loves of the Angels* and *Heaven and Earth* held far greater significance in France, and on the Continent generally, than they did in England. Taine remarks that "I prefer to see the East in Orientals from the East, rather than in Orientals in England; in Vyasa or Firdonsi, rather than in Southey and Moore." He adds that "these poems may be descriptive or historical; they are less so than the texts, notes, emendations, and justifications which they carefully print at the foot of the page." Taine argues that "beyond all general causes which have fettered this literature, there is a national one: the mind of these authors is not sufficiently flexible, and too moral. Their imitation is only literal." (2: 319) In contrast, he finds that "in Schiller, Heine, Beethoven, Victor Hugo, Lamartine, and De Musset, the poet, in his individual person, always speaks the words of the universal man . . . ." (2: 329)[2] Taine's judgments find justification in the fact that the French discerned in *The Loves of the Angels* the nuclei of systems for moral and social ascent--as well as implicit challenges to traditional theology--eluding the English. Vigny in fact finds in Moore's *Angels* possibly more systematic thinking than Moore himself would have discerned. *The Loves of the Angels* inspires Vigny to explore, and transcend, the problem of theodicy--a problem he takes up in all three of his earlier biblical poems. Vigny takes refuge, ultimately, in a secular humanism, of sorts--one that does not advocate the overthrow of the Church (for Vigny too well knows the value of structures as gauging devices for individual behavior and place within society), but that does advocate a redirection of the human impulse to worship. Humankind should turn away from God, and find solace in other humans.

Taine also charges England with a parochiality that renders its poets incapable of empathizing with other systems of belief or ways of living. This charge warrants consideration, although the English readership, rather than the poets themselves, emerge guilty. Taine urges that

> to write an Indian poem, we must be pantheistical at heart, a little mad, and pretty generally visionary: to write a Greek poem, we must be polytheistic at heart, fundamentally pagan, and a naturalist by profession. This is the reason that Heine spoke so fitly of India, and Goethe of Greece. A genuine historian is not sure that his own civilization is perfect, and lives as gladly out of his country as in it. Judge whether Englishmen can succeed in this style. In their eyes, there is only one rational civilization, which is their own; every other morality is inferior, every other religion is extravagant. Amidst such want of reason, how then can they reproduce different moralities and religions? Sympathy alone can restore extinguished or foreign manners, and sympathy here is forbidden. (2: 319-20)

Taine speaks of English oriental tales generally, rather than of the specialized mode of angel/deluge poems. In working in this latter mode, the poets do not, as Taine argues, offer "only literal imitation." Each does create a very distinct vision of the antediluvian world. The English readership, however, superimposed upon the poetic works their recollections of the literal meaning, as well as the narrative development and biblical context, of the sources. The poets deviated from the originals. Hence the poems offended. The anti-eroticism (and repressive morality) of the English middle-class partly account for negative reactions to Moore's *The Loves of the Angels,* as do the evangelicalism and conservative piety that placed the Constitutional Society on alert against supposed "blasphemy," a charge Moore's *Loves* occasionally faced informally in England.

While Byron's *Heaven and Earth* inspired Vigny--by the latter's acknowledgement, and while it retained popularity among the French "literary public," the poem enjoyed a broader, trans-continental influence than Moore's, in part because of the personality of, and legends surrounding, Byron himself. *Heaven and Earth* in translation held a special place in the hearts of the Poles--a place earned largely because of Byron's willingness to take up arms to liberate Greece. Byron's "influence in Polish literature grew after Byron's death," according to Juliusz Zuluawski. This "was a real, measurable influence," which involved not the mere appearance of translations of *Heaven and Earth*, but which also inspired action--the individual efforts to challenge tyrannical order. Through his writings and his life, Byron held special appeal for the "Polish Romantics [who] believed--quite rightly--that a writer who does not express the general feelings, who does not speak for all, is not a writer at all" (126).[3] Ironically, Byron himself did not feel that the writer does much of social significance. ("Who was ever changed by a poem?" Letters 10: 136-37. "As to defining what a poet *should* be, it is not worth while, for what are *they* worth? what have they done?" "The end of all scribblement is to amuse." "To withdraw *myself* from *myself* ... has ever been my sole, my entire, my sincere motive in scribbling at all." Letters 2: 20, and Rutherford 4-5.) His personal call is for

> 'Action--action-action' said Demosthenes: 'Action*s*--action*s*,' I say, and not writing--least of all, rhyme. Look at the querulous and monotonous lives of the 'genus';--except Cervantes, Tasso, Dante, Ariosto, Kleist (who were brave and active citizens), Aeschylus, Sophocles, and some other of the antiques also--what a worthless, idle brood it is!

(Journal for 1813 in Rutherford 3). Byron's eventual answer to his own call for action accounts for his stature in Poland--the Poles discerning revolutionary action, too, in the rebellious lovers in *Heaven and Earth*. Byron, the man, sets forth for Greece, fuelled by his indignation at political and social injustices. The contemporary poet Adam Mickiewcz, a Polish national, writing for Polish independence, marvels at the comprehensive, empathetic soul he senses in Byron's writings, yet acknowledges that "Napolean crea lord Byron; l'action de lord Byron et le bruit même de sa gloire reveillerent Pouchkine." (Jean Fabre 248)[4]

In France, Byron's personal celebrity tended to overshadow his writings, the poet's influence there at least as much biographical as literary. Edmund Estève suggests that when contemporary readers envisioned Lamartine's Cédar, they associated the angel with Byron, the living man. He points out that the day after *La Chute d'un Ange* was published, Madame de Girardin wrote to Lamartine praising the sublimity and beauty of the work, and asking, "when your angel will have achieved his ten expiations, you will, will you not, give to the entire poem this epigraph: 'Man is a fallen god who recalls the heavens'? Because is this angel not Lord Byron?" (Estève 356) Byron's personality upstages his personae.

Moore's significance to France proves more literary than biographical, although he did keep company with key figures of the Bourbon Restoration. In the Preface to Volume 7 of his *Poetical Works*, Moore recalls that during

"a short visit to Paris" made with a friend "in the autumn of the year 1817"
he "found [him]self, for the first time, in that gay capital." Paris bewildered
him:

> As the restoration of the Bourbon dynasty was still of too recent a
> date for any amalgamation to have yet taken place between the new
> and ancient order of things; all the most prominent features of
> both *régimes* were just then brought, in their fullest relief, into
> juxtaposition; and, accordingly, the result was such as to suggest to
> an unconcerned spectator quite as abundant matter for ridicule as
> for grave political consideration. It would be difficult, indeed, to
> convey to those who had not themselves seen Paris of that period,
> any clear notion of the anomalous aspect, both social and political,
> which it then presented. It was as if, in the days succeeding the
> Deluge, a small coterie of antediluvians had been suddenly evoked
> from out of the deep to take the command of a freshly-starting
> world (MPW 438-39).[5]

The "small coterie of antediluvians" became less concerned with surfaces,
and more with structures sustaining social order. The exact ties between
the Bourbon Restoration in France and the simultaneously encroaching
social, political, and religious constraints upon individual liberty in England
remain uncertain--coincidental as much as causal (Breunig 173-75). Both
cultures felt conservative impulses. The French restored--and aimed to
preserve--time honored institutions. What in France amounted to
conservatism proved in England repression.

Quite possibly, the "Third Angel's Story"--in which God rewards the
pious hearts of the Seraph and his mortal bride, sanctifying their troth
through Christian nuptial vows--appeals to monists, pantheists, and the
array of theosophical systems hoping that perfectibility is endemic to our
species, and that this process has begun taking place. The cycles of suffering, joy, tedium, and such--the fate of Zaraph and Namah, decreed by
God--will one day end, the couple presumably enjoying eternity among the
angels, Zaraph, like Lamartine's Cédar, eventually recovering his brightness, which will illuminate his bride. The couple symbolizes the theoso-
phers' visions of the ongoing process, already started.

As the conflicting notions of Tessier, Baldensperger, Estève, Guillemin,
and Bonnefoy suggest, the exact debt of Vigny and Lamartine either to
Moore or to Byron remains incalculable. Evidently, both Moore and Byron

do influence the thinking, and perhaps the practice, of Vigny and Lamartine. From their English peers Vigny and Lamartine are inspired to resolve--or dismiss--problems of theodicy by devising systems through which the individual can revalue his or her responsibility and place within society, and within the cosmic order. The diminution of the individual in these poems reflects nothing of the economic happenstance through which a kindred diminution took hold in England, but rather the conservative deliberations of the Bourbon Restoration that led poets to expound in verse political philosophy deriving from a renovation and secularization of traditional Christian theology.

Vigny and Lamartine parallel Hugo in presuming that the individual will work to foster a climate enhancing freedom of personal expression within the existing social structure. Both Vigny and Lamartine depend upon the stability of the Catholic church in order to proffer their reforms. Not even Vigny proposes toppling the Cathedrals; rather, he would redirect the object of worship; the church as an institution serves indispensable social functions. Doolittle suggests that Vigny's conservative secular humanism reveals a pattern of thought accordant with Hugo's efforts to come to peace with the Christian establishment during the Bourbon Restoration. Hugo at first argues that "'poetry in the history of mankind can be seen and judged only from the heights of monarchical ideals and religious beliefs'." (In Doolittle 16.) Hugo articulates a modified vision of the poet in the Preface to his *Odes* of 1822:

> The poet . . . sees through facts to the ideas that underlie them; these ideas are the substance of poetry, to be judged according to monarchical and Christian standards, and to be expressed in a language appropriate to monarchy and Christianity. These things are done in order that the present society may be consoled and the future societies instructed (16).

Hugo's 1824 Preface adds to the poet's task the role of prophetic leader, a legacy of Saint Martinism. Christian orthodoxy remains a means of representing the present to future ages, and not the ideal and final form of perfected Christianity. The perfectibility of religion and of society--to be effected by the poet-prophet--are goals Vigny and Lamartine share with Hugo. By 1828, as Doolittle outlines, "Hugo's progress in the third decade of the century . . . represents," with its shift from an easy royalism through increasing disillusionment to a thoughtful searching for other values and other means of expression, and also its constant faith in the high calling of the poet, the crisis of loyalties and convictions undergone by Vigny and most of his generation in the same decade (18).

Vigny's treatment of biblical materials yields a stridently secular, or at least nontheistic, humanism. Theodicy no longer poses a problem: God is not just. Man's faith must go to his own kind--leadership provided by the "poet-prophet," or "man of genius," an individual born with exceptional insight into cosmic truths and into objective reality. The human impulse towards worship should turn humans towards other humans, rather than impelling them to perform empty and unheeded rituals to an (at best) indifferent (and possibly nonexistent) God. In this fullblown humanism, Vigny espouses beliefs that Byron approaches in *Heaven and Earth* and that Moore seems to take for granted in *The Loves of the Angels*.

Vigny's earliest "mystery," *Moise*, does concern itself primarily with the individual--in this case, with the individual who, by divine calling (in his allegory) or birth (as a poet-prophet), enjoys special visionary insights and gifts that suit him for leadership, yet destine him for loneliness.[6] *Moise* most closely parallels thematic concerns expressed by Byron. In *Moise*, Vigny sets up the oxymoronic indignity upon which human existence predicates itself: the painful simultaneity of "the great grandeur and servitude of humankind," as Fernande Bartfeld phrases it.[7] *Moise*, too, establishes the estrangement of the poet-prophet. Vigny claims that his Moses

> is not the Moses of the Jews. This great name serves merely as a mask for a man of all centuries, and more modern than ancient: the man of genius, weary of his eternal widower's condition, and despairing to see his loneliness becoming ever larger and more arid as he becomes ever greater. Tired of his greatness he begs for nothingness. This despair is neither Jewish nor Christian; it is perhaps criminal; but such as it is, it seemed to me to lack neither truth nor elevation.

(Doolittle 78.) Moses' election, his unique foreknowledge of his peoples' destiny, are "expressed . . . in the laws which will one day enable those who observe them to enter into the Promised Land," in a symbolic reversal of man's expulsion from Eden, proleptic of man's ultimate anticipation of death's demise (Doolittle 79). (This interpretation of the exodus and convocation is mythic, rather than theological, reflecting the ongoing French interest in comparative mythology responsible for the great compendia of the previous century.) Yet Moses--albeit elect--must stand apart; he ascends to the mountain top, the Promised Land clearly in his purview, although yet unseen by his people; aware that he will be himself unable to participate in this triumph, he finds the state of election--and his concomitant estrangement from his kind--a form of torture: "What did I do to you, that I should be your chosen one?" (Doolittle 79.)

Nothing. The answer is nothing. Election--or, secularized, birth as a man of genius--proves capricious. Moses begs for oblivion, for death, but receives no mercy. Vigny finds the Judaeo-Christian God ineluctably powerful, but his love "imperceptible," his justice "inexplicable" (Doolittle 81). He serves man only in supplying an object for the inborn human impulse to worship--to revere something greater than the self. The collective identity of humankind proves a more appropriate, comforting, and joyous object. God, man must remember, serves at the pleasure of His worshippers. Outmoded gods are best cast out. In *Paris* (1831) Vigny promises that new god forms and new life freedoms will reward the darkness ensuing after the overthrow of the old god (Doolittle 83). The impulse to worship will find a deserving--secular, earthly--object (83). Perhaps the man of genius will then no longer need endure estrangement--particularly, according to Arnold Whitridge, since Vigny's "idea that genius is incompatible with happiness, that the artist is always lonely and misunderstood," although "recurrent," takes a turn different from the alienation plaguing Childe Harold and the like, whose defense against pain evolves into "a more or less petulant contempt for the rest of humanity." Rather, Vigny's man of genius distinguishes himself through his outpourings of empathy, his "life of solitude" developing his innate "sense of pity" (31). He eschews righteous indignation at his otherness from his kind, and instead, in endeavoring to help, finds help, or solace, in the human kind.

Moise, in conjunction with later works, solves the problem of theodicy by scrapping the informing god concept that would seduce us into expecting justice from one indifferent to our species. (If there be a God, in Vigny's system, He resembles the watchmaker God, the *deus absconditas*, made famous by Locke and English Deism.)

Theodicy wins revisitation in *Éloa, ou la soeur des anges: mystère* (1823). In *Éloa*, nothing is just. Ontogenetically, *Éloa* necessarily operates according to the dictates of pity and empathy, as would be expected of a being of her unusual origin--spawned, as she is, from one of Christ's tears spilled at Lazarus' death (an origin resembling that of the Cherubim in Persian mythology, "formed," there, "from the tears Michael shed over the sins of the faithful"--this similarity possibly reflecting Vigny's native French acceptance of, and borrowing from, the blended mythic systems of syncretism; see Davidson 194). She ascends to heaven where, admired among angels, she pities Lucifer's plight. The three parts of her chronicle--"Birth," then "Seduction," then ultimate "Fall"--are initiated by this pity (Doolittle 65). Whitridge remarks that "her downfall is the result of her own goodness"; incapable of distrusting, she cannot know that Lucifer besieges goodness, or that Lucifer enjoys knowledge she does not share--namely, "that pity leads to sympathy, and sympathy to carnal love." By acting on this knowledge, Lucifer "succeeds in dragging his unhappy mistress to the depths of Hell" (32).

In Moore's *Angels*, pity similarly undoes Moore's first two angels--male angels, in contrast to Vigny's female victim, Vigny (wrongly) presuming that his ascription of the female gender to an angel constitutes his own innovation (Doolittle 65).[8] Whitridge remarks that "the guileless innocence exhibited by Éloa," although now "one of the stock figures of comedy," found serious treatment by both Lamartine (in *La Chute d'un Ange*) and Hugo (in *La Fin de Satan*) (32). Vigny, like Moore, would engage our pity for the unanticipated fates of the well meaning angels, and would ask us to question the justness of a God who would punish the charitable heart. As an allegory for human existence, *Éloa* asks us to empathize with--and care for--those who are constitutionally unprepared for evil, and to protect the good against those who would undo innate charity. *Éloa*, if anything, would espouse social responsibility towards the guileless good.

Le Déluge: Mystère (1823) offers Vigny's most extensive foundations for the secular humanism (as opposed to Lamartine's trenchantly Christian humanitarianism, as identified by William Fortescue 103).[9] Doolittle details parallels between Vigny's *Le Déluge* and Byron's *Heaven and Earth*. Both poems derive from Genesis 6.1-2, and highlight, through the fates of the mortal women and their angelic lovers, God's indifference towards creation, animate as well as inanimate (72). Vigny's epigraph poses the problem of theodicy: "Will it be said that you will destroy the righteous along with the wicked?" The text of this poem answers "yes; what of it?" As Doolittle assesses: "God neither loves nor hates; God has no respect for human dignity" (73).

Le Déluge, as with Moore's *Angels*, opens in an innocent--almost pastoral--time, "a time when the virginal earth was itself animated with laughter, earth in her first bloom, when the day shone as brightly as the heavens" (1-3).[10] But the tone shifts rapidly: it is in this age of innocence on earth "when God felled his creatures there" (4). World-judgment reflects, apparently, mere divine "irritation," not wrath--a circumstance rendering the Deluge particularly outrageous (Doolittle 73). All elements of external nature follow God's laws; each element is satisfied with its station; earth's beauty attests to its innocence; "all is still pure--all save man." "Man was behaving wickedly." Or so it seems the creator judged.

Emmanuel, son of an angelic-mortal union, and Sara, his mortal lover, stand atop Ararat awaiting world-judgment. According to Baldensperger, in his notes to the mystery, Emmanuel and Sara must endure judgment, but do not knowingly transgress:

> The *Déluge* demonstrates the tragedy of its biblical epigraph, when two children, sole residents of an earth devastated by a decreed judgment, are themselves guilty of no fault. In addition, their deportment leads them to succeed at a sort of autonomous reparation, if not salvation. Emmanuel and Sara will celebrate love, with its physical enhancements, at the hour when obeisant nature, by order of divine decree, traverses the foreknown cycles of the inundation, the calamity, and the final return to meteorologic normalcy (1: 243).

Normalcy constitutes pre-sentient earth. When all sentient being is annihilated, a rainbow appears. This rainbow is certainly not the traditional rainbow of Yahweh's covenant with man (Yahweh casting the rainbow in the sky, somewhat amusingly, to remind himself of his vow not to annihilate mankind again); Vigny's rainbow signifies man's total subordination to and submergence in external nature, and God's indifference to animate beings, in particular. External nature, obviously, accords always with God's will, for its elements want sentience, or any enablers of independent action. In a sense, God's preferential treatment of things insentient parallels Lamartine's concept that being constitutes a "graduated, dynamic ladder" towards heaven, with "all atoms equal in the eyes of God" (Joseph Albert George 20). The ladder concept is a human fabrication; absolute egalitarianism among every particle of nature is the divine evaluation of being.

God's justice is not: "'The death of the innocent is a mystery for man . . . . The pity of mortals is not that of Heaven. God makes no treaty with the

human race. He who created without love will bring death without hatred'"
(Doolittle 73). Vigny objects, as well, to God's corporate vision of
humankind; the righteous individual suffers with--and not necessarily
because of--the wicked. Solace comes through Emmanuel's and Sara's
fidelity to one another, and in their sense that their loving is good. Their
love strengthens their ability to accept the inexplicable. Neither repents, for
repentance is not warranted.

Vigny's hope for humankind fixes fast upon humankind alone.
Superstition and dogma support fabulous notions about the requirements
of a God who is, if extant, noncommunicative. Vigny, as suggested earlier,
does not advocate mass exodus from the Catholic church. He himself
maintains nominal fidelity to the institution (as does Moore). The very
solidity of the church within the state enables him to challenge the object--
not the act--of worship. He will assume the role of the "prophet-poet," or
"man of genius." He will relate his theories of religious reform himself, and
in due time. He would assume the role of social architect--building, in this
case, appropriate foundations for what he finds to be an innate human
yearning to worship.

Vigny takes refuge in secular humanism. Lamartine finds hope in a
universal faith--a perfected religion--free from credal dissent. At times
verging upon Hinduism--in his idealized union with the Godhead, and in his
faith in upward ascent as a teleologic necessity--Lamartine rankled the
orthodox. Still other Hinduistic--sometimes mistermed 'pantheistic'--
leanings rankled even further, and suggest Lamartine's firsthand exposure
to the orient. In revamping teachings from the *Upanishads*, Lamartine
actually shares sentiments articulated by the chiliastic Christians in
England, the latter characterized by Goodwyn Barmby's call for a time when
"'all people shall have the Church of God within them and without them
and be of one heart for one work, of one possession, and of one speech; for
the time of the Millennium is at hand'."[11]

In his interest in orientalism, Lamartine clearly outclasses Moore, who,
by comparison, proves a mere armchair orientalist. Taine would judge
likewise. He disparages the fact that

> when they [Moore, Southey, and other English poets treating
> Eastern subjects] mention a custom, they put their authorities in
> a footnote; they do not present themselves before the public
> without being furnished with testimonials; they establish by
> weighty certificates that they have not made a fault in topography

or costume. Moore, like Southey, named his authorities; Sir John Malcolm, Sir William Ouseley, Mr. Carew, and others, who had returned from the East, all ocular witnesses, state that his descriptions are wonderfully faithful, that they thought Moore had travelled in the East. In this respect their minuteness is ridiculous; and their notes, lavished without stint, show that their positive public imposed on the poetical commodities the necessity of proving their origin and alloy. But the great truth, which lies in the penetration into the sentiments of characters, escaped them; these sentiments are too strange and immoral. (2: 319)

Taine, here, of course, uses "immoral" sardonically, suggesting contempt for the readiness of the English to take offense at any actions or attitudes alien to them. (As an example, Taine adds that "when Moore tried to translate and recast Anacreon, he was told that his poetry was fit for 'the stews'," by a reviewer in *The Edinburgh Review* 2: 319.) Secondary sources do not suit Lamartine. When Lamartine--as had Hugo and Chateaubriand before him--sets out to study the milieux of the Near East, Herbelot will simply not do.[12] Understanding requires observation; observation requires physical presence. (Byron would disagree. As Brown points out, in advising "Moore about oriental description in *Lalla Rookh*, he [Byron] says: 'The only advantage I have is being on the spot; and that merely amounts to saving me the trouble of turning over books which I had better read again'." "Byron and . . . the Near East" 59.) Lamartine's presumed imperatives reveal vestiges of faith in Lockean empiricism no longer affordable to industrialized England. There, shortcuts, such as Herbelot, would have to serve.

When oriental learning appealed to Lamartine, he packed up his daughter, his wife, and three friends, and boarded the *Alceste* in Marseilles on 11 July 1832, in the voyage to the Near East that would see the end of his daughter's, and the beginning of his political, life.[13] Considering Lamartine's zealous belief in what the "theosophical" leader-poet could do towards the perfection of humankind, one wonders whether Lamartine found this trade-off ultimately consumable.

The quarreling among monks in Palestine appalled him; his collected observations appeared in 1835, as *Souvenirs, impressions, pensées, et paysages pendant un voyage en orient*. Its call for the purification of Christianity, to emerge as a "universal cult" eventually "stripped of dogmas and superstition," and accommodating "truth . . . in all its forms," including the Hinduism that captured his imagination in India, won for his *Souvenirs* a place on the index (45-46).

Lamartine took his interest in the orient even further than Byron or Moore, searching for a universal religion, and a subsumption in the One, in the Creator. He may have in mind the primeval waters of Hindu creation when he meditates upon what Lombard determines a "rather pantheistic thought of becoming one with the Creator":

> Then my soul, having been merged into the great oneness, dissolved, a weak drop lost in the bosom of the seas, an insensitive load tossed by the Ocean; but where the serene or convulsive impulse which from the total abyss travels from wave to wave, throbs in the drop of water.[14]

Distinctively Lamartine's is the goal of oneness--love, a uniting principle, eventuating cessation of international and religious conflict, the "establishment of a universal cult," and "a society led by the poet-theosophist, the 'man of desire,' " an "assignment" Lamartine hoped "would be his in France" (Lombard 55). Lamartine calls for man to heed "the pure word of Cavalry, not like the one from which, in earthly tones, the distant echo of the sanctuary allowed the divine meaning to escape . . . ." (Lombard 55.) Lamartine will interpret that "pure word" through his poetic gifts. He, like Vigny, identified himself with Christ; in Lamartine's teachings, Lombard finds traces of Martinism and Saint-Simonism, and, at times, pantheism; in actuality, Christian mysticism provides ample orthodox precedent for the union of the individual with the One.[15]

La Chute d'un Ange (1838) revisits the problem of theodicy engaging Vigny, Moore, and Byron. The narrative leads to a sequence of "Visions." In the narrative, Cédar, an angel, is enamored of Daidha, with whom he fathers two children. "Daidha . . . is buried alive with them in punishment for her fornication," and Cédar must "assume human form"--fortunately, for he is able to unearth his family. This premature burial--its incumbent sadism--captures the attention of the prurient in both France and England in the middle decades of the nineteenth century, decades responsible for what our age would call "snuff" literature, literature titillating through torturing a victim to the brink of death.

The group takes refuge in the desert, where they encounter Adonai, truly wise, the true prophet of God's will. Nemphed, a wicked ruler, sends soldiers to execute Adonai, and to capture "Cédar and his family, and transport them to the tyrant's palace in a flying machine" (Lombard 51).

Here, Lamartine's interest in science fiction parallels Byron's, the latter reflected in Byron's account of Fontenelle's moon talk when Byron explains one of his early plans for a second part of *Heaven and Earth*. The influence of Moore may be detected in the just-close-to-sensual sensuality redolent throughout the narrative. (Guillemin 51-3) The angel Cédar is taken by the ocular dazzle of the mortal Daidha; Lamartine's catalogue of the physical allure of his thirteen-year-old mortal lover met with moral outrage. Even more outrage found expression when Lamartine's Cédar is tricked into infidelity by Lakmi, a royal concubine of Nemphed's, who disguises herself as Daidha. After punishing Lakmi and Asrafiel, evil successor to Nemphed following the latter's assassination, the family returns to the desert, where "Cédar and his family are abandoned by their guide," after which "Daidha and the children die, and Cédar casts himself on a funeral pyre erected for them," in a final touch drawn from Hinduism (Lombard 51-52).

The narrative proper and the "visions" interblend; the "visions" contain the philosophical and religious reflections that Lamartine insists constitute the purpose for his narrative. Philosophical credence belongs to Adonai. In "Fragment of the Primitive Book," Eighth Vision, Adonai explains that

The only divine book in which He writes His name constantly growing, man, is your spirit! It's your reason, mirror of the supreme reason where some shadow of Himself is painted in your darkness.

(Lombard 52.) The book of his works--primarily in His creation of man, is the place to find God. Lombard argues that "Man as the divine book of God's revelation is a Martinist image" (52). (It is also a rationalist image, popular among Bacon and kindred natural philosophers in England, who borrowed the image from Patristic commentators). Lombard adds that "the most apparent direct borrowing from Saint-Martin is in the title of the Eighth Vision. 'Primitive Book' was used by Saint-Martin to describe the 'man of desire' as the repository of celestial revelation in human society" (52-53). Adonai elsewhere articulates Lamartine's belief that social organization has its foundations in human nature--specifically, in the operative moral impulse leading humankind towards betterment:

The social code destined to increase, has in our nature an innate basis, the ineffable basis, this ineffable instinct of supreme justice which in us protests in secret against ourselves (Lombard 53).

La Chute d'un Ange in a sense does not bother with the problem of theodicy. Within the context of the poem, God is clearly not just. Lamartine's protagonists "are cruelly persecuted in their antediluvian world--a primitive, and primitively oriental place."[16] They do not understand why they are persecuted. They remain unaware of the nature of their transgression; interspeciation has not been forbidden, or even mentioned.

Lamartine offers hope in a secularized (neomythical) version of salvation. *La Chute* promises that the fallen angel Cédar will ultimately ascend. Lamartine--like Montgomery--refuses to divest himself of hope; life and faith will renew. Montgomery realizes hope by adapting theological convention; he uses his poem partly as a vehicle for prophecy--of another world, of a coming Messianic Kingdom on earth. Lamartine justifies chaos by turning to philosophy. He posits a renewal to be realized in the future-- not through any abrupt eschatological event, but gradually, through an ongoing process of ascent (Grillet 236).

After the fall will come Cédar's (Humanity's) rise; Lamartine's angel reascends through incessant progress, Lamartine's concept of man almost proleptic of Teilhard's *homo progressivus*, especially in its emphasis upon human ontological--with its incumbent moral--elevation.[17] (Unlike Teilhard's projection, this physical progress does not seem teleologically driven.) To Grillet's assessment of the poem as a moral and religious history of humanity, I would also add "physiological history." Cédar will regain his original ontogenic status.

Grillet argues that the poem is inspired by the evolutionary theory propounded by Lammenais, and that in poeticizing his vision of mankind, Lamartine must return to the Bible--not for specific legends or prophecies, but for a review of the kinds of supernatural traditions man should avoid (Grillet 243). Lamartine may for himself solve the problem of theodicy, but for others troubled by this issue, he asks the impossible: faith in some rather ineffable ceaseless progress designed by a poet, a seeming permutation of the supernatural. Lamartine justifies God without Scripture by superimposing an alternative mythic framework that assigns somewhat different values to specific events. (In Lamartine's solution, for example, hopelessness and eternal damnation are impossibilities; no matter how low one may lapse, imploding changes will gradually effect ascent. This theory looks forward to Darwinian evolutionary offshoots, and backwards to Hindu theories of perfectibility in the *Upanishads*.)

Moore's and Byron's angels suggest to Vigny and Lamartine opportunities for poetic prophecy--for positing a perfectible social order.

Perfection, in Vigny's system, will come when a collect of individual minds look to a poet-hero as a prophet, or harbinger of good, and embrace and act upon the prophecy this individual shares. (In this concept of a peaceful revolution beginning with an idea in the mind of the individual, Vigny recalls the "heroism . . . of the mind" that for Curran gives force to Shelley's *Queen Mab*, Curran 172.) In Lamartine's system, perfection comes to the patient--and not necessarily in the present; perfectibility comes predicated on the notion of necessity, that is, the biologically encoded, and hence inevitable ascent of external nature, of which humanity is, obviously, a part. As suggested earlier, only Montgomery's among the English angel/deluge poems suggests anything resembling a system for individual or social betterment.

Notes to Chapter 5

[1]Whether in the original English versions or in translations, Moore's and Byron's angels find gratification in France, still Europe's intellectual center in the 1820's, as well as on the Continent at large throughout the nineteenth century. Moore's *Loves of the Angels* appears in English in three separate editions brought out in Paris in 1823, by three different publishing houses ("pirates" is more exact). Several translators in France try their hands at turning the *Angels* into French verse. In his journal entry for 15 July 1823, Moore notes that he "Received another translation of the 'Loves of the Angels' by a Madame [Louise] Belloc, with a most flattering letter from herself, and a most laudatory preface to the translation . . . . " He adds that "Madame Belloc says that there are two other persons employed in translating the 'Angels' into verse" (JTM 2: 654). Two French verse translations appeared in 1823 (both published in Paris), Louise Belloc's and Davesies de Pontes'. Two more came out in 1830, Eugène Auroux's (Paris) and Lysias Moutardier's (Angoûleme). At least one more appeared within Moore's lifetime, J. K. Ostrowski's, published in Paris in 1837. (Two others appeared after the poet's death in 1852--Toussaint Cabuchet's (Paris, 1857), and Ferdinand Chimènes' (n.p. 1892).)

Translators from other European countries were taken with *The Loves of the Angels*, as well. In 1829, a German translation appeared in Berlin (*Die Liebe Der Engel; Gedicht von Thomas Moore, Aus Dem Englishche Überfest*, von Balduin). A Dutch translation by K. Sybrandi appeared in 1835; two Swedish translations, one by V. A. Alten, another anonymously rendered, appeared, respectively, in 1848 and 1864 (one prior to, the other following, Moore's death.) An edition of A. Maffei's translation into Italian verse appeared during Moore's lifetime, in 1835. (Two other editions of Maffei's appeared after Moore's death, one in 1870 and another in 1886. Also after the poet's death appeared an Italian prose translation, unassigned, in 1886; Loria Giovanni's translation into Italian ottava rima came out in 1898.) Moore's *Angels* bore no little significance for the Continent.

Along with the French efforts, Moore is also aware of at least Maffei's production. He notes in his journal for 1-3 June, 1835:

> Received a copy of an Italian translation of the Loves of the Angels, published at Milan, by a Signoir Andrea Maffei, accom-

panied by a letter from the translator, addressed, 'Per l'illustre e nobile Signore Tommaso Moore,' was full of all sorts of flattering things about my 'divine Poeme.' (JTM 4: 1689)

His success in France in the 1820's--as well as the approval of Lord Lansdowne and others at home--may account for his faith in his *Loves of the Angels*, as he pronounces in a letter to Byron from 17 July 1823: "My 'Angels' I consider a failure--I mean in the impression they made--for I agree with a 'select few' that I never wrote anything better" (LTM 2: 518). Certainly Maffei's transmission from Italy would have reenforced Moore's faith.

Byron's English *Heaven and Earth* was brought out in Paris in 1823, by the notorious pirate-publishers, A. and W. Galignani. *Heaven and Earth* held less intrigue than *The Loves of the Angels* for French translators, although Byron's mystery kept translators in other countries busy throughout the century. (All efforts were published after the poet's death in 1824.) A Danish translation appeared in 1827, *In Himmelem og Jordan: En Mysterie af Lord Byron*, trans. P. I. Wulff, Copenhagen: C. Græbe. Andrea Maffei's translation, *Cielo E Terra; Mistero*, was published in Milan (G. Gnocchi) in 1853, and Maffei's collection of translations--*Cielo E Terra; La Sposa Promessa d'Abido; Il Prigioniero di Chillon* was brought out in Milan (U. Hoepli) in 1887. Byron captured the attention of Eastern Europe, as well. A Polish translation, *Niebo i Ziemia: Drama Liryczne*, was published in Warsaw in 1874, and a Czech *Nebesa a Zemč: Sen; Mysterium*, appeared in Prague in 1891. Perhaps the most amazing of all testimonies of faith in the enduring value of *Heaven and Earth*--and of an artificial, experimental language--consists of *Cielo Kaj Tero (The Heaven and the Earth): Mistero de Lord Byron*, Nancy E. Thomas' translation of the poem into Esperanto published in 1906.

²*History of English Literature*, trans. N. Van Laun, 2 vols in 1, Chicago: M.A. Donohue & Co., n.d. Taine refreshes the reader tired of English calumniations of French tastes; the United States in the same period allied with the English, as can be seen from a review of "Lamartine's *Chute d'un Ange*" in the *North American Review* 48 (1839): 447-61. The reviewer concedes that "we know of no modern romance that can more pleasingly beguile a few hours" (459), yet discounts as foolish Lamartine's declaration that "his epic . . . is adapted not only to present time and place, but to the world, and to the future" (447). This goal remains beyond attainability:

Nature is not good enough for him. His earth is not the same earth we inhabit. His suns shine with a purer and more golden light. So his men are moral monsters, colossal in good or evil. He has not the despairing, philosophical misanthropy of Lord Byron; his views do not shut out the better things of humanity; his heart apprehends them; but his fancy colors them with strange hues. He will not paint nature as she is, in the mind of man, any more than in the external world. In short, he lacks simplicity, which he sacrifices in his morbid desire to elevate the ideal. This is the reason his creations fail to command interest, to touch the soul. They are not beings of our own brotherhood; they are creatures elaborated and refined in the furnace of M. de Lamartine's imagination, and then dressed for exhibition in his stiff vesture of embellishment.

England and the United States want people as they really are--or perhaps worse, if this critic's call for Byron's "philosophical misanthropy" represents the received view of the species. The French entertain ideals, transcending national and sectarian boundaries. Taine's charge finds support in at least this American judgment of *La Chute d'un Ange*. The French themselves occasionally strive for the word dazzle engaging the full range of senses; Taine would have Chateaubriand far shorter--as perhaps would Lamb at least jestingly, when good wishes in a letter to P.G. Patmore, dated 19 July 1827, includes a quip, "Chatty-Briant (Chateau-briand) is well, I hope." (5: 437)

[3]Zuluawski, "Byron and Poland: Byron and Polish Romantic Revolt," in *Byron's Influence in Nineteenth-Century Europe: A Symposium*, ed. Paul Graham Trueblood (Atlantic Heights, New Jersey: Humanities Press, 1981) 122-31.

[4]Byron's--and Fabre d'Olivet's--concern for the interior being was shared by Adam Mickiewicz, the Polish national, for whom poetry and politics remained inextricable. In a letter to Lelewel dated 23 May 1823, Mickiewicz finds that the politicians in France, both those who govern and those who oppose, are fundamentally alike: "ce n'est qu'une clique d'égoistes sans moralité." French poetry, as well, is without "l'âme," in particular, Lamartine's. Vigny's *Moise* merits only comparative praise; Mickiewicz points to Vigny, Fabre notes,

Mais c'était pour opposer Konrad, au sommet de sa démance créatrice et en communion fraternelle avec la misère de son peuple, à *Moise*, prophète empathètique et dolent, masque avantageux qu'usurpe l'outrecuidance du moi pour clamer son "éternel veuvage" et son pretendu désespoir. (Fabre 225)

The French poetry he encountered he judged "n'est que verbiage et mensonge.... Des 1820," Fabre reports, "guide par son instinct et non par le mode, Mickiewicz avait élu Byron comme son modèle et son maître, et de ce choix, qu'il ne réniera jamais, il resumera en une phrase la raison profonde, plus de vingt ans après: 'Lord Byron commenca l'ère de la poésie nouvelle; lui, le premièr, a fait sêntir aux hommes tout le sérieux de la poésie; on comprit qu'il fallait vivre d'après ce qu'on écrit, que le désir, la parole ne suffisent pas." (Fabre 225-226)

Through Byron, "'dira le *Cours de litterature slave*, commence l'ere de la poésie nouvelle; lui, le premier, a fait sentîr aux hommes le serieux de la poésie. On a vu qu'il fallait vivre d'après ce qu'on écrit; que le désir, que la parole--ne suffisent pas [...]. Ce besoin profondemont senti de rendre la vie poètique, de rapprocher l'idéal du réel, constitué tout le merite poètique de Byron.'" (Quoted in Fabre 248) Fabre adds, "En ce paradoxical éloge pointe l'hyperbole où tend le génie de Mickiewicz: faire de la poésie un acte, pour l'immoler ensuite à l'imperatif--ou au mirage--de l'action. Si Byron est pour lui, beaucoup plus qu'un poète, un intercesseur, s'il voit en lui 'l'anneau mystèrieux qui attache la grande litterature slave à celle de l'Occident', c'est que 'le rayon qui allumera le feu du poète partit de l'âme de Napoleon.' Il est vrai que Byron l'a depeint comme un corsaire, mais aussi comme 'une âme toujours en travail.' On ne mettra pas en question cet etonnant rapport; ni, d'avantage, le corollaire qu'en tire hardiment Mickiewicz: 'Napoleon crea lord Byron; l'action de lord Byron et le bruit même de sa gloire reveillerent Pouchkine,' et, avec lui, 'les écoles provinciales' de Pologne et toute la poésie latente au sein du monde slave." (Fabre 248)

[5]As an illustration of the "anomalous aspect" and odd "amalgamation" of old and new, Moore describes confusion over appropriate dress--especially by French acquaintances from earlier times. In Moore's "youthful days," he had "been made acquaintance with some of those personages who were now most interested in the future success of the Legitimate Cause," including, "the Comte D'Artois, or Monsieur, [whom] I had met in the year 1802-3, at Donington Park," where "a small party of French emigrants were ... staying ... when Monsieur and his suite arrived; and among those were the present King of France and his two brothers ... ," namely "the Duc de Montpensier, and the Comte de Beaujolais." When he renewed acquain-

tance with this group in 1817, "some doubt and uneasiness had, I remember, been felt by the two . . . brothers, as to the reception they were to encounter the new guest; and as, in those times, a cropped and unpowdered head was regarded generally as a symbol of Jacobinism," Beaujolais, "who, like many other young men, wore his hair in this fashion, thought it, on the present occasion, most prudent, in order to avoid all risk of offence, not only to put powder in his hair, but also to provide himself with an artificial cue." Moore recalls that "this measure of precaution . . . led to a slight incident after dinner, which, though not very royal or dignified, was at least creditable to the social good humor of the future Charles X." In short, Monsieur detected that the "cue" was "artificial," and that "having been rather carelessly put on, had a good deal straggled out of its place." Moore adds that "with a sort of scream of jocular pleasure, as if delighted at the discovery, Monsieur seized the stray appendage, and . . . , to the great amusement of the whole company, popped it into poor grinning Beaujolais' mouth." (MPW 439) He adds that at that time, he was without adequate knowledge of French politics to afford him sound insights into the social structure. (MPW 440) This admission of neglect should implicitly constitute a warning against presuming that the Bourbon Restoration had, necessarily, any direct and immediate effect on English contemporaries. (See Breunig 173-79.)

[6]Doolittle remains skeptical of the date (1822) Vigny assigns *Moise*, although he withholds the cause of his doubt (78). On Moore's influence on Vigny, see Georges Bonnefoy 112. *Moise* of course does not qualify among angel/deluge narratives. In its focus upon the isolated individual--the loneliness of the man of genius, or poet-prophet--it parallels themes developed by Byron in *Childe Harold* and later works, and points to a secular use by the French for Scripture that the English were hesitant to allow.

[7]Bartfeld, *Vigny et la figure de Moise*, Collections <<Thèmes et Mythes>> No. 12 (Paris: Lettres Modernes Minard, 1968) 178.

[8]On the gender of angels, Davidson explains that

Zoroastrianism, which was not averse to including females in its pantheon, had its Anahita, a lovely luminary characterized as "the immortal one, genius of fertilizing waters." Offsetting her was Mairya, evil harbinger of death, represented indiscriminately as male and female. She (or he) tempted Zoroaster with the kingdoms of the earth, just as, in Matthew 4, Satan tempted Jesus. Another angel of indeterminate sex was Apsu. In Babylonian-

Chaldean mythology, Apsu was the "female angel of the abyss"; but, though female, she fathered the Babylonian gods and was at the same time the husband or wife of Tamat. She (or he) was slain finally by her (his) son Ea . . . . It seems, also, according to *Genesis Rabba* and confirmed by Milton in *Paradise Lost* I. 423-24, that angels, at least some of them, were able to change their sex at will. *The Zohar* (Vayehi 232b) phrases it this way: "Angels, who are God's messengers, turn themselves into different shapes, being sometimes female and sometimes male." (xxii)

Moore's revised Preface to *The Loves of the Angels* notes that "the Arabians worshipped *female* angels, whom they called Benab Hasche, or, Daughters of God." (MPW 531)

[9]Fortescue, *Alphonse de Lamartine: A Political Biography* (New York: St. Martin's Press, 1983) 103. Fortescue challenges the old view that Lamartine's contemplations of Scripture eventuate a spiritual struggle and a loss of faith in Christianity; for this older notion, see Claudius Grillet, *La Bible dans Lamartine* (Lyon: Emmanuel Vitte, 1938) 238-39.

[10]Translated from *Oeuvres Complètes d'Alfred Vigny*, ed. F. Baldensperger (Tours: Bibliothèque de la Pléiade, 1950) 1: 31-40.

[11]Taylor 161. Barmby's "To All People, Faith, Peace, and Health," in *Some Progress of the Truth As It is In Jesus* 6 (1843): 72.

[12]In a moment of fairness to the English--at least in a backhanded fashion--Taine refers the reader to "the notes of Southey, worse than those of Chateaubriand in the *Martyrs*" (2: 319 n). The French are at times guilty of "ridiculous minuteness."

[13]Charles Lombard, *Lamartine* Twayne's World Authors Series 254 (New York: Twayne, 1973) 45: "During the voyage Julia, his daughter, died. At the same time, he received news of his election to the Chamber by the voters of Bergues."

[14]Translation by A.M. Felix Guillemardet, quoted in Charles Lombard, *Lamartine*, Twayne's World Authors Series 254 (New York: Twayne, 1973) 54.

[15]Lombard 55, 49. Lamartine's priest-hero Joycelyn proclaims that in aiming to teach tolerance to youth,

> I do not overload their senses and their mind with a sterile learning nourished by pride. I instruct their conscience rather than their reason. Nature and their eyes that's my whole technique!

Lombard finds "Rousseau's approach to religion ... evident in these lines" (49). In Joycelyn's description of the "divine principle" as "this immense, infinite, immortal soul which sees more than the star and will outlive it!", Lombard finds "a touch of Hinduism by which "the poet ... laid himself open to charges of pantheism, an accusation he always denied." Rather, "for him it was merely an appropriate image to emphasize the unity of the world" (49).

[16]From *Lamartine: Oeuvres Choisies . . . Avec une Biographie par Maurice Levailland* (Paris: Librarie A. Hatier, 1925) 716.

[17]Teilhard suggests that in the world of the middle decades of the twentieth century, there is an operative tension between the middle class, "'who simply wish to make the world a comfortable dwelling place,'" and a new visionary order of being, or "'*homo progressivus*,'" conceptualizing our world as "'a machine for progress--or, better, an organism that is progressing'." Discussed and quoted in John Passmore, *The Perfectibility of Man* (New York: Scribner's, 1970) 256-57.

The World Before The Flood:
The Glandular Route
to the Godhead

FOR THE FIVE angel/deluge poems, love supplies a thematic link--its nature, its varieties, its powers, its permissibility. Love becomes a subject as all consuming for the various narrators as melancholy becomes for Robert Burton's persona. These nineteenth-century anatomies come without the mitigating tongue-in-cheek with which Burton reduces (subsumes, or somehow transforms) all being into melancholy. Love in these poems bears no relationship to the amoral--yet essentially benign--first cause and sustaining principle that unifies elements of Empedocles' universe. The love explored in the five completed poems looms ineffably malevolent; love-- as an impulse, as an anthropomorphic and passionately anthropopathic being, or as an abstract first cause--demonstrates potential for ending the life it generates or sustains.

In all five poems, humans struggle to break down barriers blocking free and full expression of love. Some of these barriers are self-imposed, born of fear of rejection or of conditioned abstemiousness with openly expressed feelings, the victims unaware that they are depriving themselves of the sympathy with another that makes life rich and meaningful. Some of these are imposed by viciously designed laws--reflecting a temper of the times that found actual expression in vicious legislation such as the New Poor Law of 1834, which "established sex-segregated workhouses for the indigent and removed the right of unmarried mothers to claim financial support from the fathers for their children," backed by the "unity of evangelical and Mal-thusian mentalities." (In the early 1830's, "Middle-class anxiety about working-class sexual morality," when "fuelled by Malthusian fears of plebian overpopulation," found grace in the "Wesleyan presence" inspiring the "Bastardy Clause" to the New Poor Law, vindictive legislature aimed at punishing women for fornication, in the name of effecting God's law.) (Taylor 200.) Taxonomic barriers between angels and mortals also prevent spontaneous outpourings of love, these barriers finding analogies in laws against miscegenation, in taboos against homosexuality, and in less formal, social injunctions against coupling outside of one's class or "kind," prejudices anathema to Byron, Shelley, and numerous others. These poems hardly want human interest.

In many respects, Montgomery's notion of love in *The World Before the Flood* resembles Shelley's in the latter's Preface to *Alastor* (1815) and his "Essay on Love" (ca. 1814), Shelley's pieces equating love to "sympathy" with another (or others). In the Preface to *Alastor*, Shelley observes that

> They who . . . loving nothing on this earth, and cherishing no hopes beyond, yet keep aloof from sympathies with their kind, rejoicing neither in human joy nor mourning with human grief; these, and such as they, have their apportioned curse. They languish, because none feel with them their common nature. They are morally dead. (314)

Such is Javan's state at the beginning of *The World Before the Flood*. In his "Essay on Love," Shelley again equates love with "sympathy," and exclaims that love

> is that powerful attraction towards all that we conceive, or fear, or hope beyond ourselves, when we find within our own thoughts the chasm of an insufficient void and seek to awaken in all things that are a community with what we experience within ourselves. If we reason, we would be understood; . . . if we feel, we would that another's nerves should vibrate to our own, that lips of motionless ice should not reply to lips quivering and burning with the heart's best blood. This is Love. This is the bond and the sanction which connects not only man with man but with everything which exists. (170)

Montgomery's Adam and Eve attain this perfect sympathy; Javan and Zillah long for it, but their attempts to achieve it continually misfire, until Javan turns to another object for community.

David Lee Clark, in a note to the "Essay on Love" in *Shelley's Prose*, points out that Shelley's comments resemble those of Dugald Stewart's, in the latter's *Philosophy of the Active and Moral Powers of Man* (170 n). Clark argues in his headnote that it "has as its central theme the conception of love as *sympathy*, a thirsting after its likeness by the soul of man," and that "The theme had undoubtedly as its immediate inspiration the extended treatment of the idea of *sympathy* by the moral philosophers which Shelley had just read [by 1814]--Hume, Dugald Stewart, Reid, and Adam Smith." (169)

Extending this application of "sympathy" to poetry, for Montgomery, poetry is empowered to effect a sort of love. Montgomery determines that poetry succeeds when it "suggests sympathies" (*Lectures* 121), when it expands human capacities to love, by revealing for appreciation private selves (*Lectures* 37): "From poetry the reader justly expects, and from good poetry always obtains, an enlargement of his comprehension and the elevation of his fancy." (*Lectures* 153) Similarly, Shelley argues that poetry "strengthens and purifies the affections, enlarges the imagination, and adds spirit to sense." (*A Defence of Poetry* 291). Poets "can color all that they combine with the evanescent hues of this ethereal world; a word, or a trait in the representation of a scene or a passion, will touch the enchanted chord and reanimate in those who have ever experienced these emotions the sleeping, the cold, the buried image of the past." Restated, "Poetry thus makes immortal all that is best and most beautiful in the world. . . . Poetry redeems from decay the visitations of the divinity in man." (*Defence* 294-5) Restated by Montgomery, poetry "encompasses" everything "past and present," and reveals the "essence" of reality, the universally true, "truth in spirit, though not in letter." (*Lectures* 21-44)

Montgomery and Shelley converge frequently in their theories of poetry--if Montgomery would not go so far as to commend "Poets . . . [as] the unacknowledged legislators of the world." (*Defence* 297) Montgomery reflects the discomfiture of poets in a cost accountant's world in his vacillations between theories of poetry concordant with Shelley's, and his (sometimes held) belief that commercial success is a measure of poetic success (*Lectures* 312); although he decries "public taste" that "wants only novelty," he willingly accedes to public demands. *The World Before the Flood* is something of a novelty for its age--a biblical epic pursuing a philosophi-cal, predominantly secular argument. (Revivals of neglected modes may constitute novelties.) Montgomery took a risk in fashioning his *World*. As Clark points out, the equation of love with sympathy had become standard fare by the earlier nineteenth century. An epic detailing successes and failures in attaining sympathetic community could constitute overkill. And yet *The World Before the Flood* was highly popular--widely read, frequently reissued. Montgomery apparently answered the needs of the time for a coherent exposition of this standard conception of love. Of the five completed angel/deluge poems, Montgomery's won the widest acceptance; we meet the middle-class readership through this work.

Montgomery uncovers a system for overcoming death through love. In unfolding a scheme, or system, eventuating personal triumph, Montgome-ry's resembles the French, more than the English treatments of liaisons between "sons of God" and "daughters of men." Montgomery provides answers, whereas Byron and Moore raise questions and doubts--questions and doubts suited to intellectual jousts, yielding answers to abstract, metaphysical problems; Montgomery supplies practical answers to questions about the place and proper exercise of secular love in a Christian world, answers appealing to middle-class audiences. (Croly and Dale supply answers, as well, but answers appealing to a far more stringent piety than even the middle-class maintained.) Montgomery parallels French romantic writers, too, in maintaining faith in the perfectibility of humankind--perfection in *The World Before the Flood* to be effected by the individual's liberation from the bondage of the self, through successive and ascending outpourings of love. The initial, squelched impulse towards physical love for another individual diverts and breeds yearnings for spiritual, or platonic commingling. Successful platonic fusion engenders desire for subsumption by something greater than the self; individual identity melds with the group, or corporate identity (here, the Sethites). This transformation instills a longing for the ultimate subsumption by the Godhead; the individual is absorbed into the all. Indeed, in this salutary progression, Montgomery offers a theory of the evolution of, and personal salvation through, love, a theory reminiscent of Lamartine's, Hugo's, and Lammenais' faith in human regeneration through successive refinements of love--a faith the French writers derive through their ventures into Hinduism.

Montgomery's derivative, indistinct, mongrel mysticism remains surprisingly inoffensive to contemporary Christian orthodoxy--given the fact that yearning for subsumption by the Godhead is tantamount to longing for suicide. Once subsumed, the individual--as an individual--is no better off than Wordsworth's dead-as-a-doornail Lucy, who "neither hears nor sees; / Rolled round in earth's diurnal course, / With rocks, and stones, and trees." One should not be quite so successful in communing with nature--or commingling with God, unless one earnestly desires not to be (in which case mystic union will serve almost as well as a .22). Predictably, given the poem's emphasis upon love and its refinement, *The World Before the Flood* offers a hierarchy of loves, self love at the baseline, physical love a bit higher, platonic love higher still, and transcendent love the ideal.

In addition, salvation in this poem depends upon the Old Testament concept of corporate chosenness; tribal identity and chosenness appear to be partly circumstantial, and partly elective. (Apparently the Sethites will admit all who wish to belong; paternity and chosenness are not linked. The individual, however, must come to the point of choosing to be chosen.)

Montgomery's narrative, then, turns both to Judaeo-Christian tradition and to generic mysticism (with its neutered, generic godstuff). Salvation belongs to the individual who can initiate personal liberation from self-absorption, and risk the rejection always possible in expending love--in Montgomery's epic, upon an ascending range of others. The source of this poem in Genesis 6.1-4 reminds us that love may effect destruction. During the course of the poem, Montgomery calls to mind all three contending hamartigenies--the legend of Adam and Eve, the interspeciation in Genesis 6.1-4, and the Pauline calumniation of the entire female gender. Each hamartigeny emphasizes love's malevolent potential, particularized and parochial in Yahweh's expulsion of Adam and Eve from Eden, generalized in the world-judgment eventuated by offspring resulting from sexual union of "sons of God" with "daughters of men," hybrid beings traditionally assumed to be the Nephilim of Genesis 6.4, and, by context, traditionally assigned culpability for the "wickedness of man" in Genesis 6.5. So all-pervasive is this wickedness that Yahweh destroys his creation with the Deluge. The creator (as noted, prototype of the artist/perfectionist) determines to start over--saving Noah and his band as selected shards from antiquity. Something of the old world proves worth retaining in the new.

As earlier noted, this tradition of world-judgment in response to ubiquitous evil mitigates Adam's and Eve's guilt; Adam and Eve transgress, but jeopardize only their own equilibrium in Eden. Adam and Eve illustrate the ease with which unwary mortals lapse into disobedience---impelled, in their case, by native curiosity and spousal love. Montgomery diverts attention away from the theological ramifications of the Fall, forcing us to look at the pain endured by Adam and Eve--not only because of their estrangement from God, but also because of their loss of one another. The death of Adam and Eve in Canto 4 constitutes a crux, the scene, recalled by Enoch, expounding the joys and agonies inhering in love for God and in love for another human being. The pains and pleasures of both sorts of love exposed in Canto 4 prove archetypical; identical joys and agonies recur throughout the remainder of the narrative, if duly diminished in their intensity.

In Canto 4, Adam endures for the first time the pain of God's withdrawal. At his death, Adam longs for the comfort of God's voice, at least through the ministry of his angels, who had regularly conversed with him ("A soul was in his eye, and in his speech / A dialect of heaven no art could reach; / For oft of old to him, the evening breeze / Had borne the voice of God among the trees; / Angels were wont their songs with his to blend, / And talk with him as their familiar friend" 75). Things had changed after the Fall, for " ... deep remorse for that mysterious crime, / Whose dire contagion through elapsing time / Diffused the curse of death beyond controul, / Had wrought such self-abasement in his soul, / That he, whose honours were approach'd by none, / Was yet the meekest man beneath the sun" (75). Enoch, a witness to this death, recalls that "Patient of heart, though rack'd at every pore, / The righteous penalty of sin he bore; / Not his the fortitude that mocks at pains, / But that which feels them most, and yet sustains." Adam did not, with Prometheus, mock his torments or tormentors, but rather suffered deeply, yet endured. Up to the end he hoped for reunion with God. Enoch recalls that on Adam's deathbed, "''Tis just, 'tis merciful,' we heard him say; / 'Yet wherefore hath He turn'd his face away? / I see Him not; I hear Him not; I call; / My God! my God! support me, or I fall.'" (85)

Natural catastrophes ensue. (86) Adam takes these as theophanies, divine communications, and "Bright through the smouldering ashes of the man, / The saint brake forth, and Adam thus began":

"--'O ye, that shudder at this awful strife
This wrestling agony of Death and Life,
Think not that He, on whom my soul is cast,
Will leave me thus forsaken to the last;
Nature's infirmity alone you see;
My chains are breaking, I shall soon be free;
Though firm in God the Spirit holds her trust,
The flesh is frail and trembles into dust.
Horror and anguish seize me;--'tis the hour
Of darkness, and I mourn beneath its power . . . .
Rebuke the Tempter, shew thy power to save,
O let thy glory light me to the grave,
That these, who witness my departing breath,
May learn to triumph in the grasp of Death.'"
(87-88)

This is Adam's expression of "victorious faith sublimer" than the faith he had maintained when God daily gave evidence of His company and concern. Adam's attempt to impart faith to those who surrounded him was punctuated by a theophany once "He closed his eye-lids with a tranquil smile." Enoch, Seth, and Eve, his witnesses, knelt, "When suddenly a light from heaven reveal'd / A Spirit . . . / The sword of God in his right hand he bore; / His countenance was lightning, and his vest / Like snow at sunrise on the mountain's crest; / Yet so benignly beautiful his form, / His presence still'd the fury of the storm; / At once the winds retire, the waters cease; / His look was love, his salutation 'Peace!'" (89) Adam himself, reconfirmed in his faith before death, effects a theophany instilling faith in his auditors. God responds to human calls--in God's own manner and time.

God responds with love to those who maintain fixed in their faith. God's love must be accepted on faith. After the Fall, God no longer keeps regular company with mortals. He has consigned humankind to death, and His love does not preclude His executing his sentence. This is what renders Adam's faith and love at death "sublimer." It is maintained despite the "horror and anguish" Adam experiences. (Montgomery's notions of the sublime require, as we have seen, the experience of terror, terror of the sort he imagines the fly experienced before the poet's own hand abbreviated its suffering. Burke, on the other hand, would have terror kept at a distance.)

Besides depicting Adam's horror at his awareness of his own impending death, and the agony effected by his temporary estrangement from his God, this canto adds an additional crucial dimension about love, specifically, about the love of one mortal for another. For the first time, Eve realizes that she must be separated from Adam, a realization filling her with dread. Her pleas are futile, despite Adam's willingness to fulfill Eve's every wish: "--'Leave me not, Adam! leave me not below; / With thee I tarry, or with thee I go'." (82) As she realizes, death cannot be fought; death of a loved one cannot be prevented; one's own death cannot be preplanned as a prophylaxis from grief. Eve realizes this, and instinctively prepares a "grassy bed" and "Moisten'd his lips with kisses; with her breath / Vainly essay'd to quell the fire of Death, / That ran and revelled through his swollen veins / With quicker pulses, and severer pains." (82-3)

Upon the appearance of the fiery white spirit when Adam "closed his eyelids," Enoch recalls that "'Our Mother first beheld him, sore amazed, / But terror grew to transport, while she gazed: / 'Tis He, the Prince of Seraphim, who drove / Our banish'ed feet from Eden's happy grove'." (89) She must share this recognition with Adam:

'Adam, my Life, my Spouse, awake!' she cried:
'Return to Paradise; behold thy Guide!
O let me follow in this dear embrace:'
She sunk, and on his bosom hid her face.
Adam look'd up; his visage changed its hue,
Transform'd into an Angel's at the view:
I come!' he cried, with faith's full triumph
                    fired,
And in a sigh of ecstacy expired." (90)

Adam is fortunate. He was not, as all around him thought, dead. He awakens and sees the Spirit (presumably Michael, for the footnote referring to "Paradise Lost, Book ix. v. 238," likely transposes "xi" as "ix"). Death and ecstasy are simultaneous for Adam. (Montgomery likely remains unaware of the sexual innuendoes this conjunction often bore for Renaissance readers--or at least trusted that his readership would remain ignorant of such connotations; an intentional invocation of this convention would be highly out of character for Montgomery, to gravely understate an assertion.) Eve is fortunate that Adam has the life left to share this last vision she would share. Yet upon Adam's ecstatic relinquishment of the self to death, Eve is left holding the corpse: "Eve's faithful arm still clasp'd her lifeless Spouse; / Gently I shook it, from her trance to rouse; / She gave no answer; motionless and cold, / It fell like clay from my relaxing hold; . . . her soul had pass'd away; / A beauteous corse she graced her partner's side, / Love bound their lives, and Death could not divide." (90-91)

Eve is lucky. She only appears to be left with a corpse to dispose of. (Montgomery offers a tableau of the beautiful dead woman Poe reissued often.) She need not endure the agony of loss. Yet this is the first pair potentially parted by death. Those to follow will not be treated so gently. Montgomery foreshadows the grief of separation--whether by death or by circumstances--that torments secular lovers.

Canto 4 introduces the concepts of love that inform a good portion of the narrative. Secular, romantic love ("romantic love" in its casual sense of "love inspired by sexual passion") portends joy--particularly if lovers remain faithful and united. Once sexual appetites have been satisfied, a secular partnership can develop into selfless concern for the well-being of another--concern for another dampening the wanderlust and undiagnosable dissatisfaction endemic in being human, and can provide a source of joyous discovery of a cherished one's specialness. Secular, romantic love portends anguish, upon death or even geographical separation. This anguish proves often unnecessary--when separation evolves from natural human restlessness, or from suspicion and jealousy. In such cases, anguish is self-generated, and self-destructive. Divine love is rewarded by reciprocation if reciprocation is not always immediately evident. God does not respond directly or at once to every call; divine love will be lost to those unwilling to retain faith. Either sort--or preferably both sorts--of love are worth cultivating. While Javan finds salvation through an outpouring of love towards an ascending order of objects, the capacity to love--to escape enclosure within the self--humanizes, differentiates beings pleasing to God to the monstrous, tyrannical giants who, incapable of enjoying or caring for anything outside of the self, endeavor to deprive others of benevolent feelings.

A contemporary reviewing "The World Before the Flood" in the *Eclectic Review* N.S. 1 (May 1814): 441-56 fears that Montgomery's venture into love will attract the scorn of the unsophisticated reader.[1] Javan's encounter with Zillah, his "secret attachment" and "companion of childhood," ends when "the lovers separate, without Javan's disclosing to himself her suspicions":

> The first impression, however, which this 'tale of ancient constancy' will make on the minds of many readers, will be its incongruity with the solemn business of the poem (455).

Yet the "intelligent reader" will see immediately its place--and even primacy --among the themes detailed; the skilled reader will approve the place and display of love through the "simple manners of the antediluvian age." Despite the appropriateness of the love theme,

> the impression of incongruity ... is not to be wholly removed ... ; and we are disposed to attribute it to the associates insensibly attendant to the subject, as connected with the sickly sentiments of novelists, or the absurdities of real life (455).

For although the Christian poet may "rescue the name and the passion of love from the degrading or debasing associations to which we have alluded," only a Milton can properly heighten the subject (456). This reviewer returns, however, to applaud Montgomery's intention:

> A tale of antediluvian courtship may, to some persons, sound too ludicrously improbable even for romance; but as a 'similitude of events,' as a transaction of real life, we can contemplate it as neither improbable nor ludicrous (456-57).

In a sense, the reviewer defends his own defense of the love theme as the predominating merit in Montgomery's attempt to humanize Scripture. Not willing to proclaim Montgomery totally successful, the writer nonetheless aims to 1) support the poet's efforts at humanizing the Bible, and 2) remind us that the Bible remains essentially a record of human lives. These are Montgomery's aims--the poet endeavoring, as always, to illustrate the universality of human emotions. In a sense, however, the biblical locale may bother the stringently pious; the secular emphasis of the poem goes even further than Lowth's or Cowley's practices with or remarks about Scripture in inadvertently challenging the adequacy and infallibility of the sacred text.

The World Before the Flood opens "after the Sons of God had formed connexions with the Daughters of Men," and their offspring, "Giants in the Earth," are "Lords and Rulers over mankind." The king of the giants commands an army "Principally composed of the descendants of Cain." So far, this army has "subdued all the inhabited earth, except Eden," which remains an enclave for a loyal band of Sethites (8). Possibly because Montgomery stuffs away in this short introductory note his reference to Genesis 6.1-4, some commentators have assumed that the poet utilizes only the Sethite interpretation of the passage, in which "sons of God" are the human--albeit favored descendants of Seth. Admittedly, in Canto 3, the "sons of Seth" enjoy God's favor. In the introductory note, however, as well as in Canto 7, we also hear of divine/human coitus. Clearly, Montgomery uses "sons of God" in both senses of the phrase.[2]

Javan's quest informs this epic--at first a goalless quest to satisfy unknown longings--as does his return to the Sethite glen to find fulfillment in his corporate identity.[3] The mythic framework of the poem intermingles the human with the divine. The Sethites effect a synteleological overthrow of the giants, then, with the help of divine agents, establish a Messianic kingdom on earth. The tone and motifs in the poem move from secular in the first cantos (e.g., Javan's stay in the Cainite camps; his musical competition) to pastoral in the middle cantos (e.g., Zillah sleeping in her bower and freeing her sheep) to sacred in the later cantos (e.g., the prophesied Messianic kingdom to be established after the deluge). The poet's prophetic identity is established in the epigraph from Young, *Night Thoughts*, 9: "Of one departed World, / I see the mighty shadow"--Montgomery here authenticating his narrator's right to recount this spiritual journey.

Javan's relationships with women remain problematic. His mother's transforming, self-serving and consuming love leads him to retreat into himself--and presumably repress feelings of outgoing love for his youthful companion, Zillah. Javan's psychological disorders resulting from his mother's unusual demands--that he be all to her, and be whomever she please, whenever she pleases--cause Zillah's needless suffering. Bitterness results. From bitterness comes Zillah's invented conditions that she imposes upon Javan's love, once Javan is able to express it freely. These conditions would negate the sincerity of his expressions. These conditions constitute something of a defensive ploy. If Zillah can negate Javan's assertions, she can--ostensibly--protect herself from future pain. This ploy fails. She takes it too far. She allows jealously to join these conditions-- jealousy a consumptive love, not of the exact sort that Javan endured from his mother, but consumptive (and hence destructive) nonetheless, recalling Owenite objections to jealousy--a sort of superstition--as a basis for marriage. Montgomery's orthodoxy would hold little room for Owenite free thinking. Yet in targeting jealous love for attack, Montgomery parallels ideas expressed by Owenite reformers, among them Anna Wheeler's objection to conventional heterosexual union in *The Crisis*, 1833:

> Woman's love . . . is a fearful thing, because it has fixed and
> perpetuated the degradation of her sex, and arrested the moral
> progress of man himself; why should he change his unjust, cruel,
> and insulting laws for woman, when he can . . . , through woman's
> power of loving, command worship and adoration . . . ?

Love, for women is "a superstition." (In Taylor 47) In *The Crisis*, 23 November 1833, James Smith argues that

> Nothing indeed can be more binding than love while it continues
> . . . but where [it] fails . . . the case of a simple and confiding female
> is at present very hopeless. (Taylor 208)

Zillah is indeed left "hopeless" in the poem. Her consumptive love moves Javan's heart--and spirit--other varieties of love, eventually preparing him for commingling with the divine essence. A woman (his mother) turns him away from outgoing love. A woman (Zillah) frees him to love outside of himself. Javan never enjoys the more typical male/female union, however. Zillah leads him to long for other than carnal, or even companionate, union.

Canto 1 opens, typically, *in medias res*. Javan sneaks out of the Cainite camp, heading towards the patriarchal glen where, we learn, years earlier his widowed mother, "forlorn and helpless," was taken in by Enoch. About the Cainites and Sethites, the poet's headnote announces that the "land of Eden . . . , at the head of a mighty army, principally composed of the descendants of Cain," has been invaded by an offspring of the "Giants . . . , the latter assumed to be Lords and Rulers over mankind, till among themselves arose One, excelling all his brethren in knowledge and power, who became their King, and by their aid, in the course of a long life, subdued all the inhabited earth, except the land of Eden" (8). Themes of economic exploitation and political oppression--as an exchange for "knowledge and power"---bring The Book of Enoch to mind. Montgomery continues, "he has invaded and conquered ["this land"], even to the banks of the Euphrates, at the opening of the action of the poem." In closing this note, the poet remarks,

> It is only necessary to add, that for the sake of distinction, the invaders are frequently denominated from Cain, as 'the host of Cain,'--'the force of Cain,'--'the camp of Cain:'--and the remnant of the defenders of Eden are, in like manner, denominated from Eden.--The Jews have an ancient tradition, that some of the Giants, at the deluge, fled to the top of a high mountain, and escaped the ruin, that involved the rest of their kindred. In the tenth Canto of the following poem a hint is borrowed from this tradition, but it is made to yield to the superior authority of Scripture testimony.(8)

Whether this tradition--borrowed from Tractate *Nadim* in the Babylonian Talmud--actually does "yield to the superior authority of Scripture testimony"--remains equivocal. (The notion of escape that the tradition highlights predominates throughout Byron's *Heaven and Earth*.) Although Montgomery claims that his poem gives priority to Scripture, his reworkings and amplifications of Scripture prove so extensive that the supposed sacred source becomes subordinated. Such is the case in Canto I, which, introducing the time and place of the action, pauses for a non-scripturally authorized biography.

The tribal origins of Javan's mother remain unquestioned by the patriarchs, who aid her and her infant son out of an impulsive kindness towards a fellow human (not just another Sethite). As a result, Javan's genealogical ties remain obscure throughout the poem--as does much else about this hero; as noted, Montgomery takes every opportunity to embellish his source, and embellishes it so richly that the source tends to be forgotten (16-20). Certainly, Montgomery ignores it. Javan does not appear until Genesis 10.2-4, when he is named in the table of the nations (10.1-32); a son of Japheth, and a grandson of Noah, Javan ("Greece") serves as the legendary, eponymous ancestor of Greece. He has no place in the biblical antediluvian world. Enoch in Genesis 4.17-18 is Cain's eldest son, and in Genesis 5.18-24 a son of Jared and a descendent of Seth. Zillah appears as one of Lamech's wives in Genesis 4.19. Montgomery admittedly asserts that since "there is no authentic history of the world from the Creation to the Deluge, besides that which is found in the first chapters of Genesis," the poet "who fixes the date of a fictitious narrative within that period, is under obligation to no other authority whatever, for conformity of manners, events, or even localities: he has full power to accommodate these to his peculiar purposes, observing only such analogy as shall consist with the brief information, contained in the sacred records, concerning mankind in the earliest ages" (vii). He apparently need not retain the order of any of this information.

We learn a bit more "of this fugitive's past," despite the fact that the biblical Javan has a different past--or rather at least a definite, and different, genealogy--in Genesis which he loses here. His mother's "fond imagination" strangely--and positively--impacted upon the growing youth. "After her husband's death," her mind "transformed her son into his [her husband's] image in search of visual delight." She then began making other, similar transformations in perceiving. Her senses translated Javan into anyone she yearned to see: she "sought in Javan's face . . . / Her husband and parents, brethren, friends renew'd . . . ." If this woman be Cainite by birth, the transformations she forces her son to undergo by means of her percep-tions--a skilled telepathy involving a measure of telekinesis, or, more exactly, telemorphosis--constitutes his infiltration of the Sethite glen in the forms of those Cainite kindred she has left behind. Her imaging skill wards off loneliness--for her, at least, if not for Javan. Javan provides the chameleon's services; Javan only sometimes earns acknowledgement or recognition as her son.

Montgomery posits an intriguing psychological eventuality. Her demands that Javan assume the numerous identities she imposes exhaust the youth; rather than being anyone--himself included--he would be unknowable to others; he withdraws into himself, sharing his thoughts with no one. His countenance, however, gives him away, serving as "the mirror of his breast," which either "the calm or trouble of his soul express'd"-- usually trouble, for Javan grows impatient with all human encounters (21).

During years of passive brooding, Nature developed in Javan great physical strength ("the years enlarged his form, in moody hours"). The years, here, are strengthening agents, in contrast to the weak passivity of his brooding youth. In a sense, even though staying in the glen, he lives in self-imposed exile from the human community, withholding "the feelings of his heart," which are "repress'd by his tongue . . . . / Though none might rival Javan when he sung" (21). Although his "excursive fancy long'd to view / The world," and "The joys of freedom were his daily theme, / Glory the secret of his midnight dream," he remains in the glen until his mother's death, Javan's somewhat resentful sense of obligation to her rendering freedom and glory even more alluring. Not even Enoch's admonitions could restrain him from leaving for the land of Cain immediately after her death. Among the Cainites, Javan "heard the voice of Jubal's lyre, / [and] Instinctive Genius caught the ethereal fire," Javan allowing it to rage throughout his inner being until he develops musical skill including powers bordering upon Orphean necromancy. Close to Jubal, he "learn'd to wind the passions at his will, / To rule the chords with such mysterious art, / They seem'd the life-strings of his hearer's heart!" (23) Armed with this power, he "proudly trod" upon "Glory's opening field." In his proud quest for glory, he "forsook the worship and the ways of God," i.e., the God of the Sethites, pursuing "phantom Fame, / and cast away his birthright for a name" (24). He finds this goal ultimately vapid; yet the loss of his goal leaves him estranged "from any delight . . . save the tones that from his harp he drew." A human island, "Amidst the universe he sigh'd alone; / Admired, applauded, crown'd, where'er he roved, / The Bard was homeless, friendless, unbeloved"--a lonely genius, and an anointed poet-prophet (albeit not yet recognizing himself as such) resembling Byron's, Lamartine's, and Vigny's lonely "elect." Thoughts of death soon haunt him, until "remorse impell'd him, unremitting care/ Harass'd his path, and strung him to despair." Not even his harp strings could comfort him any longer.

Possibly alluding to the Saul/David story, the narrative then moves to a time further in Javan's past when "the Giant King . . . of Cain, / Delighted in the Minstrel and his vein . . . . / No hand, voice, like Javan could control/ With soothing concord, his tempestuous soul." But the power of controlling kings did not interest Javan, and could not mitigate his despair. Nor did victory satisfy him--not even victory in musical competition with Jubal, his mentor, from whom he won "a shield of tortoise" that was "exquisitely wrought / With hieroglyphics of embodied thought"--this form of epic shield appropriately decorated, perhaps described by an intentional pun, for Javan had always kept his thoughts within his body, his face a hieroglyphic of his soul (25). (The young Javan represents the embodied, cold abstraction abhorred by Blake, Keats, and Shelley.)

The first canto finally returns to the point just prior to the onset of the action. Dissatisfied, Javan finally journeys back to the forest glen. The narrative changes from past to present. The present will amaze the hero.

Perhaps the fact that it is noon inspires spiritual ascent when Javan climbs "the bordering hill, / By many an old remembrance hallow'd still"; he sees his childhood home, and

suddenly abrupt, spontaneous prayer

Burst from his lips for One who sojourn'd there;
For One, whose cottage, far appearing, drew,
Even from his Mother's grave, his transient view;
One, whose unconscious smiles were wont to dart
Ineffable emotion through his heart (26).

This first spontaneous prayer--his first attempt to reach out to another human being, foreshadows his prayers to divine beings that will mark his spiritual growth. Here, however, his emotional development begins. He suddenly remembers "a nameless sympathy" of Zillah's love that had "solaced him when she was near," without his actually realizing it, as he now discovers. He also realizes that his lust for fame "with a fiercer flame / Than untold love, had fired his soul . . . ," and that "This infant passion, cherish'd yet represt, / lived in his pulse, but died within his breast" (26). He now also realizes that he had unknowingly attempted some form of spiritual communication with Zillah:

For oft in distant lands, when hope beat high,
Westward he turn'd his eager glistening eye,
And gazed in spirit on her absent form,
Fair as the moon emerging through the storm,
Till sudden, strange, bewildering horrors cross'd
His thought . . . (26).

These attempts at spiritual union had also aroused him physically. This physical response disturbed him, however, so naive was he of any form of human intercourse, verbal or sexual. Because he had felt this disturbance when thinking of a woman, he transferred a sort of hostility to all women in general. He grew to fear women, "jealous and watchful of the Sex's wiles," and "he trembled at the light of Woman's smiles"--reminiscent of the fear of women drawn more harshly in the Testament of Reuben. Montgomery, throughout the poem, attributes love/hate relationships to repressed emotions, as we see in the case of Zillah's refusal of Javan despite the fact that she longs for him. Here, the misogyny of this male virgin comes from his repressed nascent emotions and sexual drives.

Canto 2 opens with Javan in the pastoral bower where, ten years earlier, he had left Zillah with the promise that he would return "the night / When the new moon had roll'd to full-orb'd light" (34). Unlike Javan, Zillah was then aware of her love for him. No Penelope, she has spent these ten years "without hope." She "much his death, but more his falsehood fear'd," indicative of the possessiveness of her love tainted with jealous fears, the cause of some of her hostilities towards Javan. Already Montgomery underscores weaknesses of jealous, sexual love (or at least of Zillah's kind of love), a love paralleled (with a reversal of gender roles) by Theotormon's destructive, possessive love for Oothoon in Blake's *Visions of the Daughters of Albion.*[4]

Canto 2 also explores other negative features of secular love. Lovers can be unintentionally cruel to one another. Because Javan had repressed his passions, he had not known that he longed for Zillah, and did not know how much she was tormented by waiting for him. When he finally encounters her, Javan hesitates to awaken the sleeping Zillah, instead playing his necromantic music that causes her to dream of him and call his name (40-44). Hearing his name, "Wonder and ecstasy his bosom fill'd." But at this point, he still has much to learn about successfully expressing love. Instead of awakening her as soon as he is sure she still thinks of him , and explaining to her, straightforwardly, what he has just realized, he remains mute. Zillah also fails to reach out. When she awakens, she fears asking Javan, whom she seems to recognize, if he is indeed Javan, "recoiling from the object that she sought," protecting herself from further disappointment (44). This chance to reconcile is completely blown when Javan plays the stranger and asks directions to Enoch's house.

Javan's opening soliloquy in Canto 3 reveals a temporary reversal of his intentions to pursue love, or any human interchange. He defines his role as one of

> A reprobate by birth,
> To heaven rebellious, unallied on earth . . . .
> This is the portion of my cup below,
> . . . Silent, unmingled, solitary woe;
> To bear from clime to clime the curse of Cain,
> Sin with remorse, yet find repentance vain:
> And cling, in blank despair, from breath to
> breath,
> To nought in life, except the fear of Death
> (56-57).

This, of course, he knows is rubbish. He blames fortune for what he has just realized he himself has caused by repressing his emotions. Here he indulges in a bit of masochistic, self-pitying, breast-beating--and self-aggrandizement, the latter evinced in his depiction of himself as the solitary rebel-hero. (If he still truly believed this to be his lot "by birth," he would not have continued walking towards Enoch's house.)

When Javan arrives at the patriarch's home, Enoch accepts him with unquestioning, undemanding, and unconditional love. Enoch reaffirms his sustained faith in Javan's eventual return, and claims that "This day a voice, that thrill'd my breast with fear . . . , whisper'd in my ear, / --Enoch! 'ere thrice the morning meet the sun, / Thy joy shall be fulfill'd!" This joy, he proclaims, comes from Javan's return. This reception overwhelms Javan, as does Enoch's unconditional love, a love allowing Enoch's sustained faith in the wanderer. In this environment, Javan learns to communicate:

> Ere long the guest, grown innocently bold,
> With simple eloquence his story told;
> His sins, his follies, frankly were reveal'd,
> And nothing but his nameless love conceal'd (62).

This "simple eloquence" is to become the key to his free expression of love to Zillah.

In Canto 4, as has been noted in detail, Adam's faith and Eve's faithful love are rewarded (80-82). In Canto 5, Javan learns the power of faithful love, and senses the awesomeness of divine love. Having followed Enoch to a sacrificial ceremony honoring the anniversary of Adam's death, Javan, among the other Sethites, observes Enoch entreating the "God of our Father!" to answer their sacrifice "now with fire!" When fire does not come, the pulse of the patriarchs quickens, and "Fear clipt their breath. . . , / From heart to heart a strange contagion raised." However Enoch, ever faithful in his love, be it for Javan or for God, showed "no change of hue, no cloud of care" in his "sublime, unearthly mien." He has learned that God responds in His own time. Undaunted, he exhorts the patriarchs to maintain their calm and their faith, arguing that "God is not man, who to our Father sware / All times, in every place, to answer prayer" (104). This exhortation to faith and to determined, fixed, love for divinity results in a theophany--"light from heaven" coming "with sudden beauty," "pure on the altar" (106).

Suddenly, Enoch lay prostrate, in a trance, prophesying the future: "The Saints shall suffer; righteousness shall fail, / O'er all the world inequity prevail." The giants will rule for a while, but "God the Avenger comes," with "a judgment day," and "A flood, shall sweep his enemies away." Only "One righteous family shall be saved from that wreck of Nature" (114-115). (Montgomery's "One righteous family" proves a bit more extended than the biblical family of Noah, as we shall see.) Javan witnesses the miraculous results of the sort of steadfast faith Enoch had earlier ascribed to Adam, a faith that can be transferred by tale and by enactment, Enoch's sustained faith in divine love here reciprocated, not merely a one-way outpouring of adoration.

Canto 6 returns us to secular, romantic love. We are given a new interpretation of Zillah's bower, in a sense. It is merely an enclosed garden, and not a paradise. It is a type of Javan's earlier enclosure within himself. In her bower, Zillah can isolate herself from all other humans--isolation one of Javan's earlier tricks, performed not in a garden, but within his own body (120). Enclosures of all sorts obscure, and in this sense negate, individual identity.

The narrator takes us back to the day Javan first arrived at the bower. Zillah,

> . . . from the hour, when, in a Pilgrim's guise,
> Javan returned, a stranger to her eyes,
> Not to her heart,--from anguish knew no rest,
> Love, pride, resentment, struggling in her breast.
> All day she strove to hide her misery,
> In vain . . . .

She creates her own psychological barriers against free expression of her love (121). This second meeting of the lovers proves a bit more fruitful, only because Javan has been tutored by Enoch in the "simple eloquence" needed to express love. Javan does not see Zillah walking towards him "Till, like a vision, at his side she stood. / Their eyes encounter'd; both at once exclaim'd, / 'Javan' and 'Zillah'--each other named." The power of naming, of recognizing, of potentially reaching out to her lover frightens Zillah. She turns "in terror to depart." But Javan, also shown by Enoch the power of unconditional love expressed honestly, grabs her by the hand (presumably their first physical contact), begging her not to depart. He now has courage to confess to Zillah,

> Heaven, Earth, Thyself, bear witness to my love!
> Thee have I loved from earliest infancy,
> Loved with the supreme affection only thee,
> Long in these shades my timid passion grew,
> Through every chance, in every trial true;
> I loved thee through the world in dumb despair,
> Loved *thee*, that I might no other Fair. . . .

He confesses what she, earlier, was afraid to ask--that he remains "faithful still."

At this point, however, Zillah's ten years of repressed anger and fears congeal into a barrier between her feelings of love and her abilities to express them honestly. Her instincts prove the source of both her joy and suffering. She prohibits Javan from telling her he loves her, for, she argues, one does not leave his beloved alone in a bower for ten years. Montgomery, of course, relies upon our recognition that Penelope could wait twice as long for Odysseus' return. Montgomery seems to expect his readers to accept Penelope's not as the idealized, but as the sole appropriate, behavior, the poet neglecting to suspect that she may be suigeneris, not normal. Zillah's lack of faith, of course, contrasts to Enoch's ongoing faith in his platonic love for Javan. Her hostility contrasts with the warmth expressed by Enoch at Javan's return, further underscoring the attractiveness of unconditional love compared to the harsh, restraining, possessive love of Zillah's (the latter anathema to Owenite reformers, who would nonetheless see Zillah's entrapment into this form of anxiety). Zillah claims to doubt Javan's sincerity: "Could Javan love one through the world, yet leave / Her whom he loved, for hopeless years, to grieve?" She adds that "none could love so well, / So long, so painfully--and never tell" (123).

Here, Zillah invents and imposes conditions that negate the thing she so desperately wants affirmed. Zillah denies Javan on the basis of reason and rhetoric. Javan combats this argument, claiming that "Love owns no law . . . , Except obedience to eternal truth; / Deep streams are silent, from the generous breast; / The dearest feelings are the last confest" (123). Javan then reveals that as strength came when he shed despair once he arrived back in the glen, "the path to Enoch's bower I trod; / He saw me, met me, led me back to God." During this time, he did ignore her: "O Zillah! While I sought my maker's grace . . . , / Thy tempting images from my breast I drove, / It was no season for earthly love" (125). Seemingly, divine love can only be realized by expunging from one's mind secular, sexual love.

Zillah's rejoinder--"'for earthly love it is no season now'"--is uttered "through tears of tenderness that shone, / And voice, half peace, half anger in its tone." She speaks both dishonestly--in that she hides her feelings, and honestly--in that indulgence in sex would divert significantly the Sethites' preparations for the giants' impending attack. Zillah tests Javan's loyalty by proclaiming that she resolves to die in her father's house, for "the Patriarchs never seek, nor shun a foe," while Javan, as an outsider by birth and then by choice, "may . . . from swift destruction fly." Javan affirms his loyalty to the

Sethites--a loyalty that, ironically, eventually moves him to abandon devotion to one lover in order to dedicate himself to the group. His pledge of allegiance causes "a gentle answer" to spring "to Zillah's lips," although "it died upon her tongue" (127). She frees her flocks at the end of this encounter, symbolizing her intention to release her long tendered sentiments of love.

Cantos 7 and 8 add little to the anatomy of love Montgomery offers, these cantos mainly devoted to the invasion of the Patriarchal glen, and the capture of the Sethites--instancing Javan's part as an active hero. Canto 7 does tell of the divine/human sexual unions that produced the giants. This hybrid race comes

> --Sprung from false leagues, when monstrous love
> >combined
> The sons of God and daughters of mankind . . . .
> Thence far away, beneath the rising moon,
> Or where the shadow vanishes at noon,
> The adulterous Mothers from the Sires withdrew.

In contrast to Byron, Montgomery renders divine/human sex repugnant mainly by focusing not on the lovers (attractive in *Heaven and Earth*), but on their cruel, overbearing offspring (which Anah, Aholibamah, and their angel lovers do not produce). The giants grew until "in stature o'er mankind they tower'd / And Giant strength and mortal strength o'erpower'd / To heaven the proud blasphemers raised their eyes, / And scorned the tardy vengeance of the skies" (145). (Were the skies not watching? Why was vengeance "tardy"?) Though part human, these giants abuse humans, controlling the Cainites, and attempting to conquer Eden. Here, Montgomery's narrative recalls The Book of Enoch, with its tyrannical giants depleting the earth of its abundant harvests and livestock.

Canto 9 underscores just how strong have grown the bonds of Javan's love for his adoptive family. The monarch of the giants sentences Javan to death, naming his former minstrel a traitor. Javan retorts, "To thee no traitor, here I stand. / These are my brethren." With this affirmation, Javan takes custody of his corporate identity. Later, this canto underscores the tragedy--or, rather, near tragedy--stemming from lovers' withholding their feelings. Zillah wishes to share in Javan's sentence. She admits that she has wronged him in life, and sees death as their only means of union. She hopes they can be "Espoused in death," a necrophiliac's dream, perhaps, but, hopefully, not that of an aware and sensuous lover (184-185). She then offers to die in Javan's place, and asks him to "speak the word, / Which late with feign'd indifference I heard; / Tell me, thou lovest me still" (185).

Zillah's pleas to Javan enchant and melt the hearts even of some of the giants (186), but when these pleas cease, they have proven tardy in their utterance. (The minstrel Javan--unlike Moore's and Croly's garrulous angels--intuitively remains mute, withholding powerful words which could at this point destroy her.) A "cold, shivering fear / Crept over . . . [Javan's] nerves" as he realizes that he can no longer respond to words he has for so long yearned to hear: "Thus from life's sweetest pleasures to be torn, / Just when he seem'd to new existence born." Abandoning desire for the sweet pleasure of sexual love, he experiences desire for a platonic union with his corporate group. In this canto, divine love rewards faith. Divine rewards for Enoch's corporate love come into focus. After Enoch prophesies the giants' destruction, the giants rush upon him in rage. Before the giants can catch him, a loving God intervenes, and translates Enoch to heaven.[5] The earlier metamorphosis of Javan's passions from secular to sacred prepares him spiritually to catch Enoch's mantle. As Enoch had with Adam's, so Javan "caught the Prophet's eye, / And snatched his mantle falling from the sky; / O're him the spirit of the Prophet came" (207-210).

Enoch, in exemplifying the regenerative powers of both secular and divine love, effects Javan's spiritual growth. The object of Javan's love changes from one individual woman to God and to his earthly Sethite "sons." Javan no longer desires sensual love, but, as a prophet, the new "holy man," spiritual love fulfills him. (This spiritual metamorphosis proves somewhat tragic for Zillah, who, by repressing her gentler sentiments, by for too long creating barriers to her own free expression of love, must confront a new barrier--seemingly insurmountable in this poem exalting divine love as the highest form--when her lover's passions move from earth to heaven. Javan's virginity, for obvious reasons a handicap in romantic unions, has presumably remained intact, appropriate to a newly chosen prophet.) After Enoch's prophecy realizes itself, the "ransom'd Patriarchs," protected from the deluge, somewhat ironically, by their very capture and incarceration atop the giants's mountain, fly

> Straight to their glen.
> And when they reach'd the dear sequester'd spot,
> Enoch alone of all their train 'was not.'
> With them the Bard, who from the world withdrew,
> Javan, from folly and ambition flew;
> Though poor his lot, within that narrow bound,

Friendship, and home, and faithful love he found.

Javan here learns firsthand the virtues and rewards of platonic love, of his faithful love both for God and for his platonic melding with his corporate group.

Zillah's fate remains uncertain. In a sense, since Montgomery's hierarchy upholds sacred and corporate love above sensual, the poet proves wise in dropping her from the poem in Canto 9. In that canto, we sympathize with her devotion--devotion to Javan so selfless that she offers her life for her beloved's. We are better off not to see her reaction to Javan's metamorphosis; were we to see a rather noble human (if belatedly) suffering after earnestly attempting to repent and to atone for her transgressions, we might be less likely to share the view implicit in the epic that Javan's was a desirable transformation. (In a sense, by refusing Zillah fulfillment of her love, Montgomery creates for himself artistic problems no matter how he might end the poem.) As we have learned, Zillah belongs to the Patriarchal tribe, and presumably survives with her kind. No reference is made to her, however, in this final canto.

While Byron's poem preserves the biblical tribal barriers that prohibit a totally free choice of lovers among humans (as is seen when Noah tries to prohibit his son from loving Anah, a Cainite woman, Noah condemning her more for her lineage than for anything he knows about her character), Montgomery's Old Testament world proves less orthodox. Seemingly, one can choose for oneself whether or not to join "God's chosen" earthly sons. By affirming his love for the Sethites, claiming them as his brethren, Javan transforms himself from a Cainite to a Sethite, inadvertently--and fortuitously--ensuring his survival.

The very fluidity of tribal barriers in this poem raises a problem of theodicy that I presume the poet does not intend to raise. Unlike Noah's family in Byron's drama, the family to be saved in Montgomery's epic seems not to be a numerically fixed group. Could there have been any other Cainites in the process of shifting allegiance who were not as fortunate in their timing as Javan? Self-election is possible, at least, in a world more benign than that depicted in the poem's source. In a way, Montgomery shares sympathies prompting Owenite socialist ideals in depicting the Sethite openness to strangers; Owenite exegesis finds love alone--nondoctrinal, undogmatized--sufficient for salvation; Harriet Adams, for example, renounces

the narrow-minded opinions I formerly held, that every man must have a certain creed before he could be saved; but that I believed all were right as regarded the safety of their souls, I told him Christ had taught us to love one another. (Taylor 325)

In a sense, sexual, romantic love effects the salvation of both the angel/human lovers in Byron's drama and of Javan in Montgomery's epic. The faithful romantic love of Azaziel and Samiasa for mortal women inspires them to escape to "other skies." In Montgomery's poem, Javan's repressed glandular urges towards Zillah constitute one of the two ineluctable forces stirring the psychological discontent that brings him back to the glen in time. The second force is his obsession with his meaningless existence, his failure to share sympathies with his kind leading him towards "the lasting misery and loneliness of the world" Shelley foresees for "those who attempt to exist without human sympathy," enduring "unfruitful lives," by which they only "prepare for their old age a miserable grave" (Preface . . . *Alastor*-314-15).

Notes to Chapter 6

[1]This reviewer fears that the unsophisticated reader will be taken in by popular notions of an antediluvian golden age:

> We are apt to believe, that in the infancy of the world, there prevailed, in the human race, a simplicity, a peacefulness of character, analogous to that of childhood; and the pensive fondness with which we often look back to the careless pleasures of our youth, is insensibly extended to the retrospect of man's fancied primeval happiness. It is, however, obvious, that these fictions are extremely remote from historic truth; and that the ideas which they awaken, are absolutely irreconcilable with the scriptural representation of the older world. Not only are we compelled to give up, as worthless fancies, the descriptions of the poets so rich in beauteous imagery, but we are introduced to a scene little congenial to the feelings, or, rather, wholly repulsive to the predilections of human vanity (442).

We assume for Patriarchal times an innocence comparable to--and as fictitious as--our own idealized childhoods. (In denying reality to this ideal of childhood, the reviewer reveals himself untouched by Wordsworthian predilections towards granting worth as knowledge to our recollections "from early childhood.") And, in fact, when we scrutinize Scriptures, we see a world repugnant to contemporary sensibilities. This reviewer finds no problem in the poet's revising Scripture into essential "truth," but rather finds many problems in the nature of the Biblical source. Scriptures, he finds,

> exhibit a humiliating instance of that deception which superstition induces in the human faculties, in the absence of pure religion; while they seem to shew, at the same time, the hopelessness of attempting to blend, with the simple record of eternal truth, the pitiful figments of human invention (442-43).

The Bible, "pure religion," and "eternal truth" remain independent.

[2]Montgomery's endnote to the poem recalls Enoch, the poet quoting Robert Lowth on Isaiah 19. 9, a text which leads Lowth to envision a

'vast gloomy cavern, all round the sides of which there are cells to receive the dead bodies: here the deceased monarchs lie in a distinguished sort of state, suitable to their former rank, each on his own couch, with his arms beside him, his sword at his head, and the bodies of his chiefs and companions around him . . . . These illustrious shades rise at once from their couches, as from their thrones; and advance to the entrance of the cavern to meet the King of Babylon, and to receive him with insults on his fall.'(220).

This quotation recalls Byron's cave spirits. *The World Before the Flood* appears without line numbers. Numbers in parentheses refer to pages in the first edition (1813). In Canto 7, Enoch's prophecy to Javan refers to the "Giants," who were "Sprung from false leagues, when monstrous love combined / The sons of God and daughters of mankind, / Self-styled the progeny of heaven and earth, / Eden first gave the world's oppressors birth " (145). Presumably, since these offspring are "self-styled"--not designed by God--and since they are of "heaven and earth," the prophet recalls the interspeciation of Genesis 6.2.

[3]The reviewer in *The Eclectic Review* reflects distaste for Montgomery's focus. He suggests that in Javan, the poet

has evidently bestowed elaborate pains; and has, perhaps, been seduced by a strong identification of himself with the imaginary bard, to rest too much of the interest of the poem on sympathy with his individual futures: the action of the narrative is not made to depend sufficiently upon his sufferings or exertions, to constitute him the hero of the story. In pursuing his flight, we find ourselves far from the business and action of the history, and are, at first, rather impatient at our detention in the Patriarch's glen (446-47).

[4]Gender itself suggests a sort of fall to Owenites in the nineteenth century. For Goodwyn Barmby, according to Taylor's analysis, "androgyny is divine; its realization in the individual psyche is the fulfillment of the 'Love-spirit'." (Taylor 179.) In Barmby's Communist Church, the androgynous personality was the ideal, uniting the "woman-power" and "man-power" in each--a concept proleptic of Jung's anima and animus. Barmby urges that "In the primitive paradisiacal state of the world . . . Adam and Eve was not divided, being hermaphroditically one. But when Adam

formed, as they tell us, a separate body for Eve from his rib," human dignity degenerated, effecting disintegration of the individual entity (Taylor 178-79).

Barmby's assertions find groundings in Jewish tradition. Ginsburg notes (70 n) that Jacob Ben Chajim Ibn Adonijah's reference to "the work done for Ptolemy the king" by the emending Scribes included among thirteen announced and explained alterations of the Rabbinic Bible a change in Genesis 2.21-23, "where the woman is described as having been made out of the man; as well as to introduce into the version the notion which obtained among the Jews, that man was created an hermaphrodite, thus showing the Greeks, that the Hebrew, like their philosopher, believed man to have been originally androgynous." Ginsburg refers to Plato's *Symposium* and to the *Midrash Rabba*, on Genesis 1.26. Philosophical warfare seems to have been taking place in ancient times, as well as in modern. The Greeks idealized androgyny in the period the emendation was made; the Hebrews insisted that androgyny belonged to their native tradition.

Actually, androgynous ideals--common in eighteenth-century theology--seem incompatible with hermaphroditic notions of original, embodied, humanity. Androgyny is asexual, gender-free. Hermaphroditism burdens with overt characteristics of two genders. Androgyny renders humankind closer to angelic being.

[5]On Enoch's translation, see the *Zohar* 1: 181: "Enoch was virtuous, but God saw that he would degenerate, and therefore gathered him in time, as one 'gathers lilies' because of their good scent." "Thus the good die early in order that they may not degenerate." This interpretation, attributed to Rabbi Jose, shows inordinate faith in human nature.

Heaven and Earth:
Wailing, Deluges,
and Demon Lovers

WITH *The World Before the Flood*, Byron's *Heaven and Earth* shares Genesis 6.1-2 as a source. If Montgomery obscures his source with embellishments]--lush glens, tales of secular love, genealogies, battles--Byron's "mystery" proves deceptive in its apparent fidelity to its source. Because Byron's setting is clearly antediluvian (Noah undeniably preparing for a Deluge), this lyrical drama has been taken as a reworking of the Scriptural account of the prelude to world-judgment. As has been earlier noted, much has been deleted or changed, however--Ham excised, for example, and replaced with Irad, Anah and Aholibamah pulled out of time, and Anah assigned a new sex. Further, Byron neither cites nor alludes to Genesis 6.3--Yahweh's apprehension of the "evil" penetrating the human heart; likewise unmentioned is Genesis 6.4--the birth of the Nephilim, usually taken to be the giants, the cause of world-judgment. These omissions leave Noah and his clan in a world that, at least according to the biblical record, has not quite ripened for judgment. Yet judgment is at hand--if we can trust Noah. Noah enjoys insight into the events about to transpire--although his insight, as with that of every other character, angelic or mortal, proves only partial.

Like Montgomery, Byron draws upon the Book of Enoch as a source--Enoch, in the case of the lyrical drama, inspiring the scene with the caves and their inhabiting spirits. (Montgomery, too, derives his notion of caverns from Enoch, as well as from Talmudic tradition, his epic drawing upon thematic concerns of the Book of Enoch--oppression and political exploitation--that Byron's lyrical drama leaves unexamined.) In *Heaven and Earth*, the cave spirits taunt--and inspire--Javan finally to renounce vain reminiscences of the past and to embrace the present.

Like Montgomery, too, Byron explores several varieties of love--carnal, tribal, familial, and divine. Carnal love includes the sexual union between two seraphs and two mortal women. All forms of love simultaneously allure and encumber. In *Heaven and Earth*, Byron establishes no hierarchy of love. The desirability of any given kind of love depends upon a lover's temperament and perception of the universe.

Heaven and Earth explores other themes untouched by Montgomery--themes such as the character of God, the credibility of angels, the sources and degrees of knowledge available to given individuals, the possibility of immortality, and the age (and kindred company) of the planet. These issues --particularly those related to divinity, epistemology, and astronomy--prove of concern to Byron in his Journal of 1821. Byron's source has confused some critics--in recent times as in his own day--into presuming his answers settled and orthodox (or settled and unorthodox). The dialogue leaves all matters unsettled--for all save for Goethe and like-souled readers, who find in *Cain* "beauty . . . such as we shall not see a second time in the world," Goethe judging the earlier "mystery" second only to *Heaven and Earth*, which Goethe finds "much more comprehensible and clearer than the first, which was too profound and too bitter, although sublime, bold, and impressive" (quoted by Steffan 324-325). For those whose visions of being encourage a "time that was," a time more glorious, innocent, and pure than will ever find replication, for those whose sympathies are moved by a renitent God bent on choreographing devastation catastrophic enough to warrant God's reminder to Himself never to repeat it ("I set my bow in the cloud . . . [;] When I bring clouds over the earth and the bow is seen in the clouds, I will remember my covenant which is between me and every living creature of all flesh; and the waters shall never again become a flood to destroy all flesh," Genesis 9.13-14), *Heaven and Earth* startles in its unremitting sublimity, sublimity of the sort that somehow finds Burke and Sade kindred aesthetes, Sade giving life to dictates that Burke articulates. For others, however, *Heaven and Earth* remains the most philosophically equivocal of the English angel/deluge poems.

Before *Heaven and Earth*, Byron entertained the significance of Genesis 6.1-4, the poet offering verses 2-4 as a gloss for one of his hero's contemplations in *Manfred* (1817):

> Glorious Orb! the idol
> Of early nature, and the vigorous race
> Of undiseased mankind, the giant sons
> Of the embrace of Angels, with a sex
> More beautiful than they, which did draw down
> The erring Spirits who can ne'er return.--
> (PW *Manfred* 3.2.3-8)

In Manfred's understanding, the spirits, seduced by the beauty of mortal women, eventuate their own abasement, the spirits never able to return to heaven after enjoying sexual union. Like Japhet in *Heaven and Earth*, Manfred knows that "Sorrow is Knowledge: they who know the most / Must mourn the deepest o'er the fatal truth, / The Tree of Knowledge is not that of Life" (PW *Manfred* 1.1.10-12). Like Japhet, too, Manfred encounters taunting spirits, of whom Manfred requests "Forgetfulness--" (1.1.136), as well as "Oblivion--self-oblivion! / Can ye not wring from out the hidden realms / Ye offer so profusely--what I ask?" (1.1.144-46), a spirit responding, "We are immortal, and do not forget; / We are eternal; and to us the past / Is, as the future, present. Art thou answered?" (1.1.149-51). In his response, the spirit recalls Aquinian angelology--asserting an aeveternal nature.To this response, Manfred confirms simply that "Ye mock me" (1.1.152). At one point desiring oblivion, Japhet reconciles himself to election--a resolution available to him after his encounter with the cave spirits.

Unlike *Heaven and Earth*, *Manfred*, according to Bernard Blackstone, constitutes "a Promethean play, asserting free-will and superiority over the elements to the last" (15). Unlike Manfred, neither spirit nor mortal could assert about Japhet what the First Destiny asserts about the Promethean hero of the earlier drama--namely, that

> his sufferings
> Have been of an immortal nature--like
> Our own; his knowledge, and his powers and will,
> As far as is compatible with clay,
> Which clogs the ethereal essence, have been such
> As clay hath seldom borne; his aspirations
> Have been beyond the dwellers of the earth,
> And they have only taught him what we know--
> That knowledge is not happiness, and science
> But an exchange of ignorance for that
> Which is another kind of ignorance. (2.4.53-63)

Manfred's knowledge (involving science, as does the knowledge detailed in the Book of Enoch) derives from his questioning the nature of his being. Japhet's knowledge is particularized, far more limited--pertaining solely to his own place in the oncoming Deluge. In a sense, *Manfred* proves more definite than *Heaven and Earth* in its metaphysical explorations--the participants in the latter "lyrical drama" each limited in their understandings about the universe. These limitations create difficulties in interpreting

Byron's "mystery."

Confusion surrounds Byron's purpose in *Heaven and Earth*. Is this a religious or a secular poem? Answers do not suggest themselves readily. There is almost no agreement about the thematic statement, or informing thought, of *Heaven and Earth*. John Ehrstine suggests that *Heaven and Earth* is "a parody of the impious *Cain*," and that "the whole of this [later] play forms an elaborate, often hilarious, and very serious literary joke." Ehrstine adds that "it has remained a private one," which he explains in detail (112). "By perceiving its parody," he proposes, "some understanding of the work emerges," although this does not explicitly answer the attendant question, "why would a poet of Byron's stature go to such lengths, and take such risks in comprehension, merely to parody his own work?" (122-23.) Ehrstine attempts to answer: "In the ebonized wit of the parody in *Heaven and Earth*, Japhet cannot sympathize with Jehovah, nor we with him," and "similarly, it follows by implication that man cannot have any honest sympathy with orthodoxy, or the faith it upholds, unless of course he somehow humanizes it through his own imagination. But," Ehrstine warns, "in that case he will risk heresy" (123). Byron's joke is on the orthodox reader; Byron educates orthodoxy into the impossibility of accepting with a human heart orthodox doctrine. The joke is on the elect, as well:

> it is wildly comic, and fitting, that nowhere are we given any indication that women are included on the ark; Anah cannot go, and Noah's wife is nowhere mentioned. Yet Japhet is to father a new race, Noah announced (III, 497), and Byron's darkest comedy is the implicit impossibility, sterility, and perversion of this brave new world to be (122).

Ehrstine's remains the most inventive; theological interpretations are the most common.

Robert Gleckner combines theology and philosophy in his vision of *Cain* as "a despairing prelude to the grim prophecy of *Heaven and Earth*," the latter of which signals "Byron's complete rejection of God in an almost fullblown nihilism," which "gives rise" to "despair" (128). Less grim is the *Heaven and Earth* seen through William Marshall's eyes. Marshall determines that "the central concern in the play" is "Election and human reward"; these concepts undergo no evaluation; "the principal intellectual concern of the drama, the justice of Divine Election," escapes notice because of the character of the protagonist, Japhet. Japhet remains the "one whose consciousness is most crucially affected by divine acts," and yet he accepts, rather than challenges, these acts, and hence theodicy is not a problem (*Structure* 155). Marshall's interpretation is tenable; it might be added that Japhet is ready to accept his lot only after the spiritual turmoil at the cave, resulting in self-knowledge about his inalterable status. Jerome McGann finds that through Japhet's troubles at the cave Byron "sets out . . . a redemptive program" (264).

For Murray Roston, although *Heaven and Earth* proves "by no means a theodicy," the drama still "constitutes an examination of divine justice, counterbalancing the skepticism of the earlier work [*Cain*] by the more generous appraisal of divine benevolence." As a corrective to *Cain*, *Heaven and Earth* amounts to "an almost innocuous defence" of Christianity (212-14). Neither does Michael Joseph acknowledge that the drama examines in any manner the justness of God. Rather, the drama presents "in the main, a traditional theology" which is "accepted without apparent examination" (124). For Paul West, the drama explores "the folly of brooking divine decree" (102). Ernest Lovell expands a similar notion when he finds that "the very theme of *Heaven and Earth*, of course, is destruction--destruction effected by an annihilating sea that is amoral, subject to the will of God and to universal law, which two are one, and sweeping away all but the Elect" (217). B. G. Tandon pursues the kindred claim that "*Heaven and Earth* reconsiders the theme of *Cain*," in that "both level a violent indictment against the orthodox religious tradition from the point of view of reason." He finds that "the question in *Heaven and Earth* is: Why does God punish the Cainites and reward the seed of Seth? And then, where is the badness in loving the angels?" The play's answer to these questions suggest that "good and evil are independent essences and should not be identified with any arbitrary laws, even though these may be fixed by God." A political hue colors this statement: "Byron's quarrel is with authority, even though it may be vested in God." (179)

William Fitzpatrick finds a mythic significance to *Heaven and Earth*, and a human significance as well. He argues that "Byron's vision is paradoxically dual, and although beyond human logic, ultimately honest," for "because of his devotion to the real human condition the plays defy synthesis with any abstract system, whether it be Deism, Calvinism, or Catholicism" (624). Fitzpatrick determines that *Heaven and Earth* depicts the human condition as a "paradoxical blend of Heaven and Hell" that damnation alone can resolve (615): "The paradox of *Cain* and *Heaven and Earth*," he argues, "derives from Byron's own ambivalences towards the world and the Deity" (624). Fitzpatrick adds that "the strange plight of his heroes resembles what is known as the Orpheus taboo: the breaking of an injunction not to look back, in their cases, at a lost paradise, destroyed by Eden"; unable to refrain from looking back, "the yearning for bliss that is irrecoverable brings on new agony." (624) Japhet, the hero, works with the chorus of mortals hoping to reorganize a contentious society into a new Eden. He fails, however, much in the manner that Adam and Eve fail. He listens to forbidden teachers--in Japhet's case, the spirits. In this, he disobeys, and thus "mythically duplicates" the "initial Fall, the disobedience of Adam" (623-25). Japhet provides thematic centrality for Allen Perry Whitmore, who finds *Heaven and Earth* "an interesting fragment, revolving around the theme of self-will and duty," with "Japhet as the one who follows duty" abjectly opposed to "Aholibamah as the one following her own will." This "division seriously weakens the characterization of the piece," Whitmore claims, "since little conflict within characters is the result," and absolutely no resolution of the problem of whether impulses to duty or those to self-will ultimately triumph and hence warrant our allegiance (108-109).

A philosophical significance suggests itself to Daniel Watkins. A theme recurs: "The historical tragedies (*Marino Faliero, Sardinapalus, The Two Foscari*), the metaphysical dramas (*Manfred, Cain, Heaven and Earth*), and the final personal tragedies (*Werner* and *The Deformed Transformed*) are all variations on this theme, portrayals of human crisis as social crisis" (142). Individual identity and corporate identity become inextricably entwined, to the dismay of the virtuous brought down with the vile. G. Wilson Knight removes the drama entirely out of the realm of human interest: "the power of *Heaven and Earth* derives from its extraordinary realization of the Flood's impact on animals and birds" (14). Spectacle, and pity for dumb innocence, become the drama's attractions. Most of us ask for more.

Bernard Blackstone supplies more in his singular attention to the poem's second epigraph, Byron's reference to *Kubla Khan*, "And woman wailing for her demon lover" (l. 16). Blackstone stands alone in attempting to relate Byron's epigraph from *Kubla Khan* to the fabric of the drama. In doing so, he waxes philosophical, finding unity in the concerns not only of Byron and Coleridge, but also of Byron and Blake. He asserts that *Heaven and Earth* may "be seen as a commentary on 'Kubla Khan,'" Byron's "exulting peak" (1.3 and 1.22) equivalent to Coleridge's sunlit dome, Byron's caverns equivalent to Coleridge's 'caverns measureless to man,' the "abodes of those cthonic forces which emerge from their underground labyrinths with 'shouts of laughter' to mock poor Japhet's attempts at rational discourse." For Blackstone, this drama poses a controlling question: "what happens . . . when the barrier between Heaven and Earth is lowered?" We see, in partial response, that "cthonic forces invade the sphere of the celestial-terrestrial, the sunless sea overflows the world of the shining dome and girdled garden," and we are struck by the insight that "the play is thus an assertion of the unity of being, of Blake's doctrine that the physical cannot be separated from the spiritual" (29-31). Yet why does the sea drown the garden? With the physical inextricably melded with the spiritual, and with the spiritual serving to guide the physical, the spiritual seems determined to destroy itself, through destruction of its physical manifestations.

Some insights into Byron's philosophical intent may be gleaned from his Journal for 1821, the period responsible for *Heaven and Earth*. His entries reveal an admixture of intuited faith--a sort of aprioristic faith grounded in "reason"--with his usual skepticism about revealed religion; these predispositions, articulated as early as 1811, become assumptions underlying the portrait of the universe in *Heaven and Earth*. This mixture of a desire to believe with an irremediable doubt raises specific questions about Byron's use of his biblical source in *Heaven and Earth*--namely, why does he draw from Scripture; which assumptions about the Deluge does he wish us to accept, and which discard; and what do his alterations of his source suggest about his philosophical intent? Answers to these questions begin to take shape in his Journal, particularly when Byron notes,

Of the Immortality of the Soul--it appears to me that there can be little doubt--if we attend for a moment to the action of Mind.-It is in perpetual activity;--I used to doubt of it--but reflection has taught me better.--It acts also so very independent of the body-- in dreams for instance incoherently and madly--I grant you;--but still it is *Mind* & much more *Mind*--than when we are awake.---- . . . How far our future life will be *individual*--or rather--how far it will at all resemble our *present* existence is another question--but that the *Mind* is *eternal*--seems as possible as that the body is not so.-- Of course--I have venture[d] upon the question without recurring to Revelation--which however is at least as rational a solution of it--as any other.--A *material* resurrection seems strange and even absurd except for purposes of punishment--and all punishment which is to *revenge* rather than *correct*--must be *morally wrong*-- and *when* the *World* is at and *end*--what moral or warning purpose *can* eternal tortures answer?--human passions have probably disfigured the divine doctrines here--but the whole thing is inscrutable.--It is useless to tell one *not* to *reason* but to *believe*--you might as well tell a man not to wake but *sleep*--and then to *bully* with torments!--and all that!--I cannot help thinking that the *menace* of Hell makes as many devils as the severe penal codes of inhuman humanity make villains.----Man is born *passionate* of body--but with an innate though secret tendency to the love of Good in his Main-spring of Mind.----But God help us all! --It is at present a sad jar of atoms.----

(Letters 9: 45-6) He would reject the notion of a wrathful God; in this he deviates from Scripture. In giving his reasons for rejecting Revelation, he reflects "rationalistic" principles of exegesis that kept the seventeenth-century Anglican divines away from specific, troublesome passages in Scripture, and raises many of the objections articulated in his letter to Hodgson in 1811; these he would extend to our understanding of his Genesis source in *Heaven and Earth*. Here, in his assertion that man is endowed with a "secret tendency to the love of Good," Byron echoes Shaftesbury's *Sensus Communis*. Byron in fact extends the notion of a unifying principle beyond the species to the universe:

Matter is eternal--always changing--but reproduced and as far as we can comprehend Eternity--Eternal--and why not Mind?--Why should not the Mind act with and upon the Universe?--as portions of it act upon and with the congregated dust--called Mankind?-- See--how one man acts upon himself and others--or upon multitudes?--The same Agency in a higher and purer degree may act upon the Stars &c. ad infinitum.

(Letters 9: 46) Byron rejects the notion of "Christian Materialism," however:

I have often been inclined to Materialism in philosophy--but could never bear it's introduction to *Christianity*--which appears to me essentially founded upon the *Soul*.--For this reason, Priestley's Christian Materialism--always struck me as deadly.--Believe the resurrection of the *body*--if you will--but *not without* a *Soul*--the devil's in it--if after having had a Soul--(as surely the *Mind* or what ever you call it--*is*)--in this world we must part with it in the next --even for an Immortal Materiality;--I own my partiality for *Spirit*.--

(Letters 9: 46) The immortality of the body without the soul--the notion of the undead--recalls Byron's awareness of Vampire lore in *The Giaour*, line

753, which Roy Aycock attributes to the poet's readings in Bayle's *Dictionary* (148).

In the same Journal, Byron considers "the Night ... a religious concern --and even more so--when I viewed the Moon and Stars through Herschell's telescope--and saw that they were worlds.--" (Letters 9: 46) His contemplation of a multiplicity of worlds may well reflect the projected escape of his angel/mortal lovers in *Heaven and Earth* to the moon. Despite the stations of peace and renewal these multiple worlds may or may not have offered his lovers in his projected Part II, his speculation about the "worlds" brought into his scope of reflection by Herschell's device places Byron at odds with Augustine (and much of orthodox Christianity), specifically, with Augustine's *The City of God*, Book 12, Chapter 10, "*Of those who suppose that this world indeed is not eternal, but that either there are numberless worlds, or that one and the same world is perpetually resolved into its elements, and renewed at the conclusion of fixed cycles.*" The latter belief scorned by Augustine was not held by Byron, but by Lamartine, Lammenais, Sir William Jones-- English, French, and Italians alike touched by the cyclical monism suggested by east India. The "numberless worlds" Augustine scorns appeal to Byron's need for majesty unconstrained by letter, a Byron who would likely counter Augustine's objection that

There are some, again, who, though they do not suppose that this world is eternal, are of opinion either that this is not the only world, but that there are numberless worlds, or that indeed it is the only one, but that it dies, and is born again at fixed intervals, and this times without number; but they must acknowledge that the human race existed before there were other men to beget them. For they cannot suppose that, if the whole world perish, some men would be left alive in the world, as they might survive in floods and conflagrations, which those other speculators suppose to be partial, and from which they can therefore reasonably argue that a few men survived whose posterity would renew the population; but as they believe that the world itself is renewed out of its own material, so they must believe that out of its elements the human race was produced, and then that the progeny of mortals sprang like that of other animals from their parents. (349)

Byron remains open to several theories of the time of this world's origin.[1] He does maintain that this world (and presumably all worlds) originated by the design of a First Cause--another matter of concern in *Heaven and Earth*

--when he remarks (with characteristic European chauvinism, basing the notion of a supposed hierarchy of races upon a theory of geographical determinism):

> If according to some speculations--you could prove the World many thousand years older than the Mosaic Chronology--or if you could knock up Adam & Eve and the Apple and Serpent--still what is to be put up in their stead?--or how is the difficulty removed? things must have had a beginning--and what matter is *when*--or *how*?----I sometimes think that *Man* may be the relic of some higher material being wrecked in a former world--and degenerated in the hardships and struggle through Chaos into Conformity--or something like it--as we see Laplanders--Esqimaux--&c. inferior in the present state--as the Elements become more inexorable----but even then this higher pre-Adamite Supposititious Creation must have had an Origin and a *Creator*--for a *Creator* is a more natural imagination than a fortuitous concourse of atoms--all things remount to a fountain--though they may flow to an Ocean.--

(Letters 9: 46-7) Yet, in his reflections about the creation of specific individuals, "fortuitous concourse" provides Byron with an explanation:

> What a strange thing is the propagation of life!--A bubble of Seed which may be spilt in a whore's lap--or in the Orgasm of a voluptuous dream--might (for aught we know) have formed a Caesar or a Buonaparte--there is nothing remarkable recorded of their Sires --that I know of.----

(Letters 9: 47) Individuals do not, then, reflect embodiments of souls predestined for habitation on earth.

These reflections from 1821--when Byron contemplates ideas resulting in *Heaven and Earth*--led to a consideration of the poem's significance to its own age, a concern of interest to Leslie Marchand. In his study of *Byron's Poetry* Marchand determines that *Heaven and Earth* "flew in the face of the British more directly than did *Cain*, whose speculations were generalized, whereas the illicit love with angels was both immoral and sacrilegious" (91). He seems to have modified, even dropped, this judgment in his later studies, for nowhere do his notes to the *Letters* indicate public fury. Neither was outrage expressed by Byron's contemporaries. Talfourd is "quite at a loss to understand why Mr. Murray, who published 'Cain,' should think it blasphemous," for "it seems to us quite unexceptionable on the score of religion or morals" (21). Wilson similarly concedes that "we confess that we see little or nothing objectionable in it, either as to theological orthodoxy, or general human feeling," and adds that "on the whole it is not unworthy of Byron--might have been published by Murray--and as proof against the Constitutional Association" (77). Marshall finds Wilson's reaction typical; negative reviews of *Heaven and Earth*, he notes, more often reflect disappointment than outrage (*Byron, Shelley, Hunt* 151).[2]

In some respects, Murray's fear of the Constitutional Association would have been prudent--as is suggested by Marchand's early assessment of the poem. *Heaven and Earth* does convey some potentially radical and possibly blasphemous assumptions about the character of its source, Genesis 6.1-4.[3]

The first of these appears in 3.274, when Japhet refers to the "scroll of Enoch" as the basis for the prophecy of world destruction. Byron's note claims that "the book of Enoch, preserved by the Ethiopians, is said by them to be anterior to the flood" (PW 5:302 n). By implication, the Book of Enoch is an antediluvian production--a survivor of world-destruction, and hence older than Genesis, the latter records not set down until after the flood. By imputing this transmission history, Byron suggests for Enoch a greater antiquity--and perhaps purer reproduction of God's word--than the later Scriptural text. Pseudepigrapha acquires the special authority of antiquity. Byron's borrowings from Enoch hence find full God-sanctioned precedent.[4]

In actuality, Byron borrows very little from The Book of Enoch. The names Samiasa and Azaziel may well derive from Enoch 6.1-8. In Enoch 8.1, "Azazel taught men to make swords, and knives, and shields, and breast-plates, and made known to them the metals of the earth and the art of working them, and bracelets, and ornaments, and the use of antimony, and the beautifying of the eyelids, and all kinds of costly stones, and all colouring tinctures," after which (8.2) "there arose much godlessness, and they committed fornication, and they were led astray, and became corrupt in all their ways," and (in 8.2) "Semjaza taught enchantments, and root--cuttings" (Charles 192). Byron's Samiasa and Azaziel are related to these angels in name only.[5]

In a sense, they are not the voyeurs of Enoch 6-10 (a function emphasized even more strongly in Jubilees 4.5), who come unbeckoned. Byron's Samiasa comes when called, Azaziel when entreated. The occasion of their ascent in a sense recalls a parallel ascent in The Testament of Reuben. In the latter text, the Patriarch affirms that " . . . the angel of the Lord told me, and taught me, that women are overcome by the spirit of

fornication more than men, and in their heart they ploy against men . . . ,"
adorning themselves, the means by which "they allured the Watchers who
were before the flood," and thereafter "gave birth to giants" (5.4-6.7, in
Charles 509). Yet there is nothing of the viciousness or salaciousness with
which the Testament of Reuben taints the alliances; Byron's Aholibamah
and Anah need no ornaments nor cunning to get their lovers to descend.

Byron's Raphael may acquire some of his unpleasant disposition from
associations suggested by Enoch. In Enoch 10.4 "the Lord" assigns Raphael
to "'Bind Azazel hand and foot, and cast him into the darkness: and make
an opening in the desert, which is in Dudael, and cast him therein." (Charles
emphasizes the fact that this punishment involves isolation 193 n. This
dimension would appeal particularly to many British romantic poets, who
insist that life in isolation, without sharing "sympathy" with one's kind, is in
itself torture of the most abject form.) Yet elsewhere in Enoch (Chapter
68), both Michael and Raphael are horrified at the severity of the punishment meted out to the angels. Enoch thus also gives precedent for
archangelic empathy, as well as archangelic viciousness (Byron's Raphael
coming as close as an incorporeal being can to exhibiting classic signs of the
anal retentive's gratuitous nastiness). Raphael also guides Enoch through
the underworld (22.1-14), explaining the function of the "four hollow places,
deep and wide and very smooth," created to collect "the spirits of the souls
of the dead . . . till the day of their judgment . . . ." Javan's encounters with
the cave dwellers may be a legacy of the Book of Enoch. As with all of his
sources, Byron skims off details, but ignores the theological context
justifying their appearances in the originals.

The second potentially controversial notion derives from geological
problems with the biblical account of the Deluge. At the "growing Ocean's
gloomy swell," at which the Chorus of Spirits "rejoice!", we learn of the
Spirits' contempt for the earth and its creatures, in their imperatives to

> Howl! howl! oh Earth!
> Thy death is nearer than thy recent birth;
> Tremble, ye mountains, soon to shrink below
> The Ocean's overflow!
> The wave shall break upon your cliffs; and shells,
> The little shells, of ocean's least things be
> Deposed where now the eagle's offspring dwells--
> (PW *Heaven and Earth* 1.3.234-40).

This call for a reordering of the original hierarchy of external nature reflects Byron's awareness of the geological debate over the universality and the historicity of the Noachian Deluge, a debate flourishing at least since James Hutton had insisted that "there had never been a universal flood" in 1795, participants in this debate making much of the "fossil remains of marine animals at a height above the level of the sea," (PW 5:301n). Byron's Spirits reflect a more conservative position (not necessarily Byron's) advanced by Georges Cuvier.

James R. Moore isolates the key opinions fueling contention in Byron's age.[6] James Hutton's *Theory of the Earth* (1795), Moore claims, articulates "a reasonable though unorthodox interpretation of geological phenomena," when Hutton asserts that "'there had never been a universal flood. There was observable in the buried shell beds of the continents, which had long been taken as evidence of the Deluge, only the signs of subsidence and renewed uplift which were part of the eternal youth of the world'." (408) Edward Stillingfleet, in *Origines Sacrae: or a Rational Account of the Grounds of Natural and Revealed Religion* (1697), and Bishop Robert Clayton, in *A Vindication of the Histories of the Old and New Testament in Answer to the Objections of the Late Lord Bolinbroke* (Dublin: 1752), take up the problem created by "the absence in America of some Old World animals and by the presence of new varieties (viz., how did they find their way from Mount Ararat?)," and confront "the obstacle of insufficient water for a universal Deluge," which led some geologists to "put forth a 'local flood' theory" (Moore 406). Charles Lyell advanced what have been called "Uniformitarian presuppositions" corresponding to a sort of "optimistic materialism," that led him to dismiss the catastrophic theory of the deluge; his *Principles of Geology* (1830) claimed that "'in the narrative of Moses there are no terms employed that indicate the impetuous rushing of the waters, either as they rose or when they retreated, upon the restraining of the rain and the passing of a wind over the earth'." The catastrophic notion would make "remarkable" the "fact . . . that the olive remained standing while the waters were abating'" (Moore 413). Lyell's came to be known as the "'tranquil theory'" of the Deluge (Moore 413).

Georges Cuvier "posited a series of aqueous catastrophes to account for the major rock strata. The last of these, the Noachian Deluge, was held to account for the superficial deposits of fossils in upper strata" (Moore 409). Cuvier satisfied Ussher's "received chronology" of the Old Testament, and "theologians easily found time for Cuvier's catastrophes between the original creation of the cosmos in Genesis 1:1 and the restoration described in the six-day account" (Moore 409). Philip Martin documents Byron's awareness of Cuvier's *Theory of the Earth*, available in English in 1813, and mentioned in the Preface to *Cain*, Thomas Moore worrying about the possible repercussions even of Byron's public dissemination of this conservative solution. (LTM 2: 504-505) Byron posits nothing certain about the universality of the flood in *Heaven and Earth*. Lyell's resolution comes from a close, literal scrutiny of the flood account in Genesis. Byron, too, sticks to the original--although Part I of *Heaven and Earth* does not take us through the end of the account, in which the waters recede; Byron's ostensibly conservative viewpoint goes unillustrated, Byron hence not demonstrably committed to Cuvier's over the more geologically sophisticated views of his times, which find their bases in the recession accounts. Jerome McGann, speaking of *Cain*, argues that "Cuvier provided Byron with a historical scheme for making Jehovah a sort of local deity rather than Byron's revered Almighty Lord who is the source of all Life" (260). (Byron's own reflections in his journal for 1821 prove less orthodox.)

In another, and perhaps more significant respect, Byron's conception of his antediluvian women and their angel lovers renders *Heaven and Earth* subject to controversy. Aholibamah and Anah know that their love is "right" on grounds of their feelings, or instincts; in this, they recall Owen's insistence that "Chastity is a feeling . . . mysteriously implanted in human nature" (Taylor 43). Here, Owen, with Byron, legitimizes feeling, or instinct, as an appropriate foundation for distinguishing moral "right" from moral "wrong." According to this view, Anah and Aholibamah prove justified in continuing their liaisons.

While Montgomery proposes a generic mysticism as a solution to the indignity of mortality, Byron places hope in evolution and natural philosophy. (In this, he parallels Lamartine.) In only Byron's poem does interspeciation promise an alternative to death--should the angels and their mortal lovers bear demigods, creatures endowed with the better characteristics of mortals and angels. (Suffering will come in time, however--especially for the seraphs, who will have to confront the attendant loneliness that burdens the living upon the death of their lovers. The seraphs do not quite yet understand the eternal grief they are inviting to visit them.) This response resonates with hope in natural philosophy. Drawing upon wholly human analogies, *Heaven and Earth* looks forward to a society restructured to enhance freedom of action and thought, built in exact replication of a blueprint drawn up by a refined human species. Optimism undergirds these possibilities--the hopeful assumptions that as society is perfectible so is our species, either by natural evolution (external nature, working in a manner providing Lammenais with hope) or by genetic engineering (natural philosophy).

Byron proposes interspeciation as an eventual means of humankind's overcoming mortality. In doing so, forbidden love becomes salutary. The poem hardly wants human interest. The perfectibility of humankind depends upon those bold few who will violate laws and taboos (translatable, in human terms, into those who will participate in prohibited love unions, including miscegenation--prohibitions of any form of love anathema to Byron). In terms of post-biblical human society, immortality is of course not a benefit of free participation in the heart's dictates. (Individual liberty is something at least as, and perhaps more dear to Byron than the ideal of immortality.)

Japhet's plight raises the question of how far one may pursue individual liberty under the special circumstances imposed upon this world. An answer suggests itself when we consider one of the more puzzling scenes, Japhet's confrontation of the cave dwellers, 3.124-45. In this scene, the spirits claim an identity independent of Japhet's, they may well be external, independent entities. Yet they appear only to Japhet, and only to Japhet when he is alone. These spirits may in fact be self-condemnatory projections of Japhet's tormented psyche, or they may well be "demons" suggested by the Book of Enoch--the "evil demons" John Hunt's pre-publication advertisement excitedly promises. Whatever their ontogenic status, they can claim a virtue Japhet only pretends to: they care for one another, and recognize the interdependence of their kind: "There is not one who hath not left a throne / Vacant in heaven to dwell in darkness here, / Rather than see his mates endure alone" (3.150-52).

At the caves, Japhet reaches a turning point. He must come to realize that he can no longer afford his old ideas of who he is and what he stands for; he is not the champion of egalitarianism he has prided himself for being; he has no right to patronize the masses as "my fellow-beings!" Neither does he express true kindness through the concern ostensibly leading him to ask, "Who / Shall weep above your universal grave, / Save I? Who shall be left to weep?" (3.14-16) Even if genuinely felt, expression of this concern torments its auditors more than it assuages their fears, Japhet hereby reminding them that they are scheduled for obliviation. He misrepresents himself when he addresses the masses as "My kinsmen," and, through his alleged concession of equality, reveals his underlying sense of moral superiority when he asks "what am I better than ye are, / That I must live beyond ye?" (3.17-18) Moral worth and election are not causally linked; election in Japhet's case has nothing to do with his individual worth and everything to do with his familial identity. He must face the fact that he is a "Son of the Saved!" (3.124). He is the "other" to the mass of humanity. He must stop soliciting their approval by proclaiming a love more fabricated than felt. He must affiliate. (Once he accepts his significance in terms of his clan, and stops tormenting the masses with his lament for--constituting a gratuitously cruel reminder of--their destiny, the cave spirits stop torment-ing Japhet.)

He must now bond with the elect, his designated group--a limited group--a group that will ensure his survival and save him from solitude. This option he seizes with difficulty: *festina lente*. He is not being rewarded for being; God has given him an assignment. His mission is to begin restoration once God's world judgment is completed.

His new insight leads us to revaluate Japhet's response to God's plan; our response to Japhet largely determines our understanding of *Heaven and Earth*. Some find in him a "tragic dignity," and interpret this drama as if it were a tragedy of character. We need not demand, however, that Japhet, or any character, bear the burden of "tragic hero." First, the action of the "mystery" proves tragic for no one--not even for the chorus of mortals. What West condemns as Byron's "pagan eschatology" actually promises an end to the suffering of these mortals. In Byron's antediluvian world, there is no threat (or promise, depending upon one's need for chosenness) of an afterlife--no judgment, no damnation. Once drowned, the mortals will presumably stay drowned. They will lose their identities as sentient beings. They will never know what happened; it will never matter that they lived at all. And so it is with most of us. Such futility in being is ironically only bothersome to the sentient.

There is little evidence that either angel or Cainite lovers will be punished for their unions. Presumably, the drama ends happily for them. Had Byron allowed them his allegedly planned journey to the moon in a second part, the ending would have been overtly happy. I suspect that Byron rejected this plan only partly for the reasons he supplies in his discussion of Fontenelle's moon talk. I suspect that he abandoned it for much the same reason that current soap opera writers cannot leave wedded lovers alone; "happily ever after"--impossible in life--proves at best tedious, usually deadly, in literature. (Richardson's readers admittedly welcomed a second volume detailing *Pamela in Her Exalted Condition* (1741). John Kelly and other imitators, and Fielding with other parodists, exhaust this audience into better taste.)

Second, the sense of cosmic estrangement he reveals in his closing speech (3.925-29) differs in no significant fashion from Japhet's usual discourse patterns. He describes life with an hysteric's flair. At the opening of Scene 2, we almost laugh at the self-reflexive irony in Japhet's answer to

Irad's question, "wherefore wilt thou wander thus / To add silence to the silent night, / And lift thy tearful eyes unto the stars? / They cannot aid thee" (2.1-4). The "tearful eye" replies that the stars soothe him, and, further, that

> Perhaps she looks upon them as I look.
> Methinks a being that is beautiful
> Becometh more so as it looks on beauty,
> The eternal beauty of undying things (2.5-8).

While our antediluvian swain sighs, his beloved, Anah, is indeed, at least in a sense, looking at "the eternal beauty of undying things," although Azaziel --admittedly beautiful--is hardly the kind of "undying thing" Japhet has in mind.

Japhet expresses self pity as well as pity for his brother, Irad, the latter scorned by Aholibamah, when Japhet concedes that "I feel for thee *too*" (2.8-11; emphasis mine). Irad will have nothing of this verbal nurturing of futility. Irad instead announces that he no longer loves Aholibamah, matching his with her pride as a means of coping with unrequited love:

> Let her keep her pride,
> Mine hath enabled me to bear her scorn:
> It may be, time too will avenge it . . . .
> I loved her well; I would have loved her better,
> Had love been met with love: as 'tis, I leave her
> To brighter destinies, if she so deems them
> (2.12-17).

Irad acknowledges that he has been scorned, but refuses to be bothered. Irad is well adjusted, accepts his lot without complaint, does what he is supposed to do, follows what he is told is God's will without challenge, and, when loving proves futile, simply stops loving (something even Raphael is unable to manage). Irad is easy to forget. Of all the characters in the drama, Irad is perhaps the safest from inconvenience and unhappiness. His happiness does not depend upon another, and he is safely isolated, awaiting escape. He seems neither happy nor contented, simply safe. Safe living does not constitute joyous living. If it bears any stamp of Irad's character, the Noachites' brave new world will prove a bland new world.

More attractive love relationships are explored through the experiences of Anah and Aholibamah. As the drama opens, it is unclear to whom Anah refers when she tells Aholibamah that "Our father sleeps" (1.1). As noted in Chapter 1, the biblical characters from the Esau cycle have no place in the antediluvian world, Byron redesigning biblical chronology for reasons that remain uncertain--although his alterations and deviations likely afford him freedom with his characters and themes without risking charges of impiety (or at least not as many such charges as he might otherwise incur). The opening scene reveals Anah's and Aholibamah's views of the ethical significance of their love for angels, as well as their acutely different assessments of the value and meaning of being human. In their first exchange (as well as throughout the drama) Anah seems somewhat frightened and passive. Aware that "it is the hour when they / Who love us are accustomed to descend" (1.2), she describes her physical/psychological state, exclaiming "How my heart beats!" Aholibamah, on the other hand, admits that she trembles, but not out of a superstitious reaction to nature (unlike Anah, who trembles because "the stars are hidden," 1.6, an omen that proves portentous of nothing)--Aholibamah's confession that she trembles resonating with a mild sense of lustful irony, her trembling effected by passion, her sensuality leaving her "not with fear / Of aught save their delay." (1.6-7)

From Aholibamah's invocation we learn that "there are other skies than these," that humans can perceive themselves as more than the "poor child of clay" that Anah (like Blake's Thel) dubs herself (1.23). Aholibamah, unlike Anah, lives in a world unencumbered by implications of cosmic hierarchy, the former refusing to be awed by Samiasa's status as a seraph --Samiasa in fact in seraphic ranking inferior only to "the seven" (archangels). She has no sense of inadequacy when she exhorts Samiasa to "Share the dim destiny of clay in this [world]," for her sense of self assures her that she is worth descending for, and her sense of destiny is not particularly dim. She does not beg her lover to descend; she commands him to: "I call thee, I await thee, and I love thee. ..." (1.89, 93) If her love is insufficient to draw him earthward, if he finds something in heaven more fetching or suitable, then he can just remain there: "If the skies contain / More joy than thou canst give and take [here], remain!" (1.133-34) (Her emphasis upon "give" *and* "take" suggests her awareness of the reciprocity of their attraction. In Scene 3, she endures no guilt at loving an angel, but rather enjoys a sense of ontogenic elevation through her "election": "Are *we* not the loved / Of Seraphs? and if we were not, must we / Cling to a son of Noah for our lives?" (3.444-46)

Aholibamah's sense of self does not derive from her mythic relationship to transgressing Eve--whose transgression she feels empowered to reverse. ("death and decay / Our mother Eve bequeathed us--but my heart / Defies it . . . ." 1.106-108.) Like Anah, she responds to her world--defines it, evaluates it and herself--on the basis of her intuitions and observations. Unlike Anah, however, her intuitions lead her to a positive vision of her own triumph over mortality. She claims that "There is a ray / In me, which, though forbidden yet to shine, / I feel was lighted at thy God's and thine." (1.103-105) Somehow this ray unites her with some universal essence (or substance); Aholibamah the skeptic is also Aholibamah the neoplatonic idealist. Her "heart / Defies" mortality. Simply because "this life must pass away" (1.109) does not mean that the unity of the lovers--and the oneness of the lovers with the eternal--are likewise mutable. Rather, she proclaims,

> I feel my immortality o'ersweep
> All pains, all tears, all fears, and peal,
> Like the eternal thunders of the deep,
> Into my ears that truth--'Thou liv'st for ever!' (1.111-14)

She has no assurance that her eternity will "be in joy," nor "would [she] know," she adds: "That secret rests with the Almighty giver . . . ." She posits a world designed by a god of love (as does Samiasa), a god with seemingly limited power, too, for she asserts to Samiasa that "thee and me he never can destroy; / Change us he may, but not o'erwhelm; we are / Of as eternal essence, and must war / With him if he will war with us." (1.119-22) This assertion startles--her declaration that she is ready for war emanating from a fear of God's wrath that she will not acknowledge even to herself that she entertains. Here, Byron may be entrapping us into drawing parallels with the angels' war in Heaven, and thereby enticing us to judge negatively without warrant. In the universe Byron depicts, we never see a sign of God's active agency, or even vague interest in, mundanities. God is not a character in the drama, and those who claim to speak to God are not entirely trustworthy. Of more significance here is the fact that some of Aholibamah's affirmations and certainties constitute a bravado born of hope.

It is difficult to contrast Anah's sense of her value as a being and as a lover to Aholibamah's, for we are not always certain whether Anah's utterances sincerely reflect her feelings, or reveal calculations to ensure her an image of weakness and insecurity that she strives to project without actually feeling. If we take her comments at face value, in the first scene Anah seems unable to reconcile her individual identity with her mythic identity as a mortal "made . . . of the least / Of those cast out from Eden's gate." (1.58-9) Her sense of corporate identity prevents her from greatly valuing her individual identity. She defines herself as an Adamite (1.69), a group whose "element" she identifies as "sorrow...; Delight / An Eden kept afar from sight...." (1.71-72) Her invocation to Azaziel is self-deprecatory, Anah imploring the seraph to "think of her who holds thee dear! / And though she nothing is to thee, / Yet think that thou art all to her." (1.44-46) She presumes that Azaziel cannot empathize with her "Except in love, and there thou must / Acknowledge that more loving dust / Ne'er wept beneath the skies"--wet dust far from a seductive image. (1.53-54)

She has no reason to suppose that she is "nothing" to Azaziel; he has apparently become "accustomed to" descending to her at midnight for quite some time. Furthermore, her tableau of her graveside scene that so comforts her ("death becomes / Less terrible," 1.24-25) renders her self-deprecation somewhat ritualistic, given her certainty that one day Azaziel's "immortal wings" will "hover o'er the sepulchre / Of the poor child of clay which so adored him, / As he adores the Highest." (1.21-24) Hers is a hierarchical world, her elegiast vision far from selfless, however, Anah glad that she cannot outlive her seraph lover, thereby exempt from the grief she presumes he will suffer. Also, the vision gives her a permanent relationship to Jehovah, for Azaziel is a mediator (through his dual adoration), looking downward as he hovers over her grave while projecting adoration upward. This assuredness of her future and of Azaziel's attachment to her may belie her self-deprecation, which could well be a coy byproduct of self-confidence. Lyrical drama leaves us outside of the selves of the interlocutors; lyrical drama gives us few means of judging earnestness in discourse. Taking Anah's statements at face value, hers is a vastly different universe from Aholibamah's--Anah's certain but limited in the range of events to transpire, Aholibamah's universe uncertain but free from any predetermined course of events. Both sisters may indulge in abject solipsism; both, on the other hand, may partake of truth. (Defining "truth" remains a key intellectual struggle throughout *Heaven and Earth*.) All that we do know for certain is that after Aholibamah declares essential equality with Samiasa, the seraphs descend.

It should be stressed that neither sister is necessarily "right" or "wrong" in her interpretation of the universe. Neither has any objective evidence to support her mental construction of the cosmic framework. Aholibamah proves to be wrong in totally discrediting Japhet's explanation of the purpose of his father's ark. She attempts to rally her sister to courage after Japhet's prophecy disturbs Anah; Aholibamah proclaims, "What, hath this dreamer, with his father's ark / The bugbear he hath built to scare the world, / Shaken *my* sister?" (3.442-444). Anah's reverence for her corporate identity is not intrinsically wrong--after all, such identity effects salvation for

Noah's sons. But it is not expedient in this situation, when Anah almost refuses to escape with the angels, fearing she will not enjoy the future ("What were the world, or other worlds, or all / The brightest future, without the sweet past-- / Thy love, my father's . . . ? (3.434-36).) Anah's characteristic fear, in fact, paralyzes her here, preventing her from making decisions or taking actions to ensure her survival. Luckily, she has Aholibamah to decide for her. Ethically, however, Aholibamah's *modus operandi* is no more "right" than Anah's. Aholibamah's decisions are merely more expedient given their situation. In other circumstances, her characteristic take-charge confidence could prove a liability. Noah and Raphael, the most pernicious participants in the drama, habitually try to take charge of others' affairs.

The angel lovers do not exhibit distinct personalities, but both are attractive characters. Somehow, after Raphael's admonitions to the seraphs to escape this doomed world and abandon their lovers, we expect the "demon lovers" to leave quickly, insuring their own survival. Yet the angels elect to stay, and, in the end, devise a plan to escape. The angels ignore the putative taxonomic barriers despite Raphael's threats which Raphael claims are Jehovah's decrees (although Raphael is not an entirely reliable source). Admittedly, the escape leaves us with many unanswered questions, even if we accept *Heaven and Earth* as a completed, dramatic whole. Is Aholibamah's eschatological vision well-founded, and will all dissolve into eternal essence at some indefinite time in the future? Or, will the angels be left to grieve eternally after the sisters die, if Aholibamah is not correct? Will the angels and women propagate, creating a new race to populate a new planet? The drama does not invite us to speculate about such practical details of life in outer space. The important thing thematically is that the barriers of speciation are broken down with impunity; romantic (that is, secular) love prevails.

The least attractive--and the unhappiest--characters in Byron's universe are those who claim to speak for God, and who presume a special relationship to God that licenses them to meddle into others' affairs. Noah may be right when he asks, as a rhetorical question, "Has not God made a barrier between Earth / And Heaven, and limited each, kind to kind?" (3. 475-476.) Or rather, to the best of Noah's knowledge, such barriers may indeed exist. Each character in the drama has only partial knowledge of Jehovah's will and of the cosmic structure.

Noah's limited understanding of his duties to his family almost lead him to homicide. (Familial love, as he illustrates it, proves wholly unattractive.) Noah, concerned with preserving barriers between heaven and earth, between Sethites and Cainites, is, in his wrath, almost willing to break the bonds of corporate identity. When after pleading for Anah's salvation, Japhet asks, "Can rage and justice join in the same path?" (3. 762), Noah labels his son a "Blasphemer!" Noah is at one point willing to exclude Japhet from the ark. Raphael must intervene and remind Noah of his familial obligations: "Patriarch, be still a father! smooth thy brow: / Thy son, despite his folly, shall not sink" (3. 764-765). Before Raphael intervenes, Noah would revel in his more exalted title, "Patriarch," forgetting the human transaction--that of a loving father--the title assumes. Harsh, prescriptive love repels, and never comforts. Familial love, abused, can be deadly--a notion that Heber apparently aimed to explore in his fragment of a 'World Before the Flood.'

Raphael does save Japhet, but equals Noah in bitter unattractiveness. He descends to scold, asking the seraphs, "What do ye here? / Is thus a Seraph's duty to be shown, / Now that the hour is near / When Earth must be alone?" He sternly orders them to "Return! / Adore and burn, / In glorious homage . . . . / Your place is Heaven." (3.508-16) Samiasa proves himself to be no willing rebel when he addresses and asks "Raphael! / The first and fairest of the sons of God, / How long hath this been law, / That Earth by angels must be left untrod?" (3.516-19) Samiasa reports that he just recently "saw [that] / Jehovah's footsteps [did] not disdain [earth's] her sod! / The world he loved, and made / For love; and oft have we obeyed / His frequent mission with delighted pinions: / Adoring him in his least works display'd . . . ; / And, as the latest birth of his great word, / Eager to keep it worthy of our Lord." In light of this, he asks, "Why is thy brow severe? / And wherefore speak'st thou of destruction near?" (3.517-30)

Instead of providing information that might be of use, Raphael scolds Samiasa for missing choir practice: if he and Azaziel had been "In their true place, with the angelic choir," they would have seen "Jehovah's late decree," which was "Written in fire," the usual seraphic medium. (3.531-35) His anger seems inordinate, until he begins referring to the "void / In the immortal ranks." (3.563-64) We here see his one expression of tenderness in the drama, and his unrecognized fear of additional loss and abandonment, as he recounts the fate of his "brother Satan," who fell because "his burning will / Rather than longer worship dared endure!" He exhorts the seraphs while "still . . . pure" to meditate the fate of Satan, to "Think how he was undone." (3.566-68) After this reproof, offered as an aid to correct behavior, he adds of Satan that "I loved him--beautiful he was: oh, Heaven! / Save *his* who made, what beauty and what power / was ever like to Satan's! Would the hour / In which he fell could ever be forgiven!" He seems to realize that he has gone too far in expressing a sensual attraction to his fallen brother, and quickly checks himself, asserting that "The wish is impious." (3.580-84)

Raphael scolds the seraphs almost as a pretext for speaking of Satan, naming Satan bringing him closer, somehow. (Except as an example of disobedience, he has no warrant for naming Satan.) He changes his tone, avowing to fight those who revere Satan (among whom he himself seems to number) and who condemn their lot in the creation (as he himself does, when he complains of the dimness of the righthand group of archangels). Yet neither Azaziel nor Samiasa appears guilty of either of these transgressions. In fact, Samiasa delights in what he conceives of as a world of love.

When the seraphs convince Raphael that they will not abandon their lovers, he condemns them, decreeing that "from this hour, / Shorn as ye are of all celestial power," they must be "aliens from .... God" (3. 720-722). He suddenly becomes a Maimonidean expositor, asserting that their immortality is not assured.[7] God alone, and not Raphael, has the power to excommunicate and kill, as is illustrated through the fact that they in no way change ontogenetically. Raphael has not told the truth. Their celestial powers prove intact, when they fly off with their lovers as the rains begin. If we can doubt this part of Raphael's excoriation, we might wonder how accurate a spokesman he is for divine will, or for divine love. The lovers appear more chosen by their God for salvation than abandonment. Raphael, like all other characters in the drama, knows only partial truth about the cosmos.

The poem is "very pious," as Byron claims, partly because the God choreographing turmoil never enters the action--if he indeed is to be credited with any knowledge of it at all. We do not know whether the God of *Heaven and Earth* is the wrathful Yahweh of Genesis or of enthusiast Christian sects, the loving God of John, the withdrawn God of the Deists, the indifferent God of Vigny's *Le Déluge* or Lamartine's *La Chute d'un Ange*, or a first cause of a highly different nature. Many speak for God, although their ordination to do so remains dubious. The doubts and hopes in Byron's 1821 journal go unresolved. *Heaven and Earth* is a play of possibilities. It is not, strictly speaking, biblical; *Heaven and Earth* proves the most philosophical and speculative of the five angel/deluge poems.

Notes to Chapter 7

[1]Whatever Byron's judgments may have been about the age of this planet, his certainly lacked accordance with Eusebius', the latter crediting the earth with 5611 years' duration between Creation in Genesis 1 and the Goths' conquest of Rome. Eusebius accepts the lengths of the Patriarchal ages in LXX. Augustine seems to accept Eusebius' calculations, when he argues that "they are deceived, too, by those highly mendacious documents which profess to give the history of many thousand years, though, reckoning by the sacred writings, we find that not 6000 years have yet passed." (*CG* 348 and note) Not even by Byron's age had theology or geology advanced a tenable case--or negotiated satisfactorily the age of the earth. In an article reviewing "Cuvier on the *Theory of the Earth*" in *The Edinburgh Review* 29 (1814): 463-473, the writer finds that "We have here an instance of the danger of mixing religious and philosophical opinions with one another, and a proof how readily, as Lord Bacon long ago observed, from the union of these two things the corruption of both is likely to ensue; a fantastical philosophy on the one hand, and a heterodox religion on the other." (468) The reviewer continues,

> It would be highly satisfactory, no doubt, if this pious and learned naturalist would point out any of the phenomena now existing which may fairly be called monuments of the deluge; understanding the deluge to be just what it is recorded to have been, without any such commentaries as have sometimes been applied to it. It must be the genuine deluge of the Scriptures, not that which has been so highly coloured by the eloquence of BURNET, or so nicely analyzed by the geometry of WHISTON; much less those reciprocations of the *universal water* so familiar to the followers of WERNER; nor even the torrent, or the *debacle* of PALLAS and SAUSSURE: it must be the simple and quiet ascent of the water above the tops of the mountains, and their sojourning there for 150 days, and their peaceable retreat.... (469)

A decade later, the "Geology of the Deluge" had, if anything, generated even more (and more frequent) polemic, to the detriment of both the divine and the natural philosopher--or so urges the reviewer whose article bears as a header the manageable (as opposed to the full) title in *The Edinburgh*

Review 39 (Oct. 1823-Jan. 1824): 196-204. We are warned of a forced union of geology and theology, just as we had been so warned ten years earlier (with the two centuries' backing provided by Bacon's warning, above):

> Whatever may be thought of the prudence of attempting to connect the discoveries of natural science with the sacred writings, it is evident, that if the testimony of science can ever be of any value in support of Scripture history, the physical researches, by which it is intended to confirm the historical statements, should be most strictly independent. No latent facility should incline us to accept weak evidence because of its tendency to the desired object;--but, for the sake of revelation as well as of science,--of truth in every form,--the physical part of the inquiry ought to be conducted as if the Scriptures were not in existence. (198)

Byron remained conversant with geological discoveries; his headnote to *Cain* confirms that "The reader will perceive that the author has partly adopted in this poem the notion of Cuvier, that the world had been destroyed several times before the creation of man. This speculation, derived from the different strata and the bones of enormous and unknown animals found in them, is not contrary to the Mosaic account, but rather confirms it; as no human bones have yet been discovered in those strata, although those of many known animals are found near the remains of the unknown" (*Cain*, ed. Steffan, 157). (The discovery of dinosaur teeth in England in 1822--and, where there were teeth, next came bones--stunned both divines and natural philosophers with just how giant giant could be.)

Oddly enough, Moore--who tolerated, and often encouraged, his friend's forced reviews of the status quo--urged Byron to leave Cuvier and related geological disputes for private speculation. (Martin 52; LTM 2: 504-505) Biblical subjects won Moore's approval--Moore's financial needs partly accountable for his gentling more than he would have cared to the Anglicans the Wesleyans, and, in short, high and broad churchpersons alike, whose coins, of any denomination, he needed. Yet Cuvier, blazoning as a headnote to a biblical drama, perhaps highlighted the inability of theology and science to come together graciously; otherwise, Moore's objections to this particular reference remain equivocal.

Steffan's edition of *Cain* quotes from an anonymous attack of the drama entitled "*Uriel: A Poetical Address to the Right Honorable Lord Byron, Written on the Continent: With Notes, Containing Strictures on the Spirit of Infidelity Maintained in His Works. An Examination into His Assertion, that 'If Cain is*

Blasphemous, Paradise Lost is Blasphemous', And Several Other Poems.
London: Hatchard and Son and Burton & Smith, 1822. 127pp." This
reviewer finds in Cuvier support for Scriptures:

> Cuvier states almost this remarkable fact as the result of geological
> inquiries, that strata, incumbent upon each other, exhibit fossil
> remains in gradations, corresponding to the order of creation. It is
> however to be lamented that some geologists attempt to subvert
> the truths of Revelation ... (from p. 111, quoted by Steffan 403).

This conclusion diverges patently from that of the reviewer of "Cuvier on
the *Theory of the Earth*" (quoted above), who reasons that if the waters
"raised up quietly to the great height at which they stood," and if they
"continued in that state just 150 days," then "the destruction of land animals,
and the deposition of a coat of mud over the surface of the earth, are the
only consequences which we can infer with certainty to have taken place."
He adds

> When the waters subsided, the dead carcasses would, many of
> them, be carried down into the sea, or, whey they remained, would
> soon be consumed, in the midst of the luxuriant vegetation which
> would quickly cover the earth, during the almost entire absence of
> the animals destined to feed on it. The coat of mud would be
> washed down by the ruins, or added to the general mass of vegeta-
> ble mould. It seems probable, therefore, that this great catastrophe,
> destined to cut off men and animals, would produce no other
> durable effect upon the surface of the earth; none certainly that
> could be supposed to remain distinctly visible, at the distance of
> some thousand years. We are therefore at a loss to know what the
> Editor means to speak of when he says, 'the Deluge, one of the
> grandest *natural* events described in the Bible, is equally confirmed,
> with regard to its extent and the period of its occurrence, by a
> careful study of the various phenomena observed on and near the
> earth's surface.' (*Edinburgh* 39: 469)

If Byron disturbs piety, this reviewer launches a flank attack--eight years
before Cuvier's name appears in a headnote to *Cain*. Steffan's representations from "The Major Periodicals and Pamphlets" also includes excerpts,
analyses, and summaries of John Watkins' anonymously printed *Memoirs
of the Life and Writings of the Right Honourable Lord Byron, with Anecdotes*

of Some of His Contemporaries. (London: Henry Colbern and Co., 1822, pp. 370-388), in Steffan 405-408. Steffan observes that

> Although this book . . . has been ignored as biased and unreliable, its literary opinions are representative of the era, and a few show some acumen. Watkins started his chapter on *Cain* with scornful depreciation of the old mystery plays. 'Sacred history' was not a suitable subject for secular drama. Fabrication of additional matter was necessary to fill out any play on a biblical story and no one had committed more heinous errors than Byron, for no one else had grafted upon biblical facts 'such monstrous fictions as would destroy the credit of the whole' Bible.

At any rate, Steffan continues,

> Watkins charged that Byron was insincere in associating his play with the medieval Mysteries and that, influenced by the odious Bayle, he used the term to refer to the incomprehensible and irrational aspects of religion. (Steffan 405)

Steffan notices that "One of Watkins' blunders was his supposition that Byron had never read Cuvier." (406) Steffan quotes directly from parts of Watkins' *Memoirs* intended to discredit Byron's authority to enter this geological debate:

> For {the} notion of a succession of worlds the noble author in his preface quotes the authority of Cuvier, and roundly asserts that the speculation is not contrary to the Mosaic account, but rather confirms it. Now having read the bible, he must know that the cosmogony of Moses directly maintains, and necessarily presupposes, a creation of the world in its original elements; and not the renovation of a decayed planet out of the old materials. But though Lord Byron pretends to call in the aid of Cuvier it is clear, that he never read the works of that great naturalist: and that he is indebted for this, as he is for all the rest of his machinery and sentiments, solely to Bayle, who has defended the notion at great length in various parts of his Dictionary.

(Watkins 380-381, quoted in Steffan 407-408) And had we not ample biographical testimony to Byron's firsthand familiarity with Cuvier, the contributions by *Edinburgh* and other reviewers summarize, analyze the implications of, deride, praise, and, in general, offer the interested public ample exposure to Cuvier and its real threat to the Mosaic chronology.

[2]Wilson, for example, finds it dull in places, although he justifies the "occasional stupefaction, drowsiness, and torpidity of soul [on grounds that it is] produced by the impending destruction of the antediluvians" (77).

[3]As epigraphs, Byron gives Genesis 6.1-2: "And it came to pass . . . that the sons of God saw the daughters of men that they were fair; and they took them wives of all which they chose"; as well as *Kubla Khan* (16), "And woman wailing for her demon lover" ("By" instead of "And" in Coleridge's original). The Spirits' reference to 'the glorious giants' graves" in Part 1: 3.217 derives from Genesis 6.4; Byron's lyrical drama shares with Montgomery's epic the same scriptural basis. Ernest Hartley Coleridge, in his edition of *Heaven and Earth* (PW 5:277-321) suggests that "The following extracts . . . were evidently within Byron's recollection when he planned *Heaven and Earth* . . . ." Coleridge offers 1 Enoch 6.1-3, 6.6, 8.1, and 10.1-5 (PW 5:302n).

[4]For the nature and content of these borrowings see the notes by Marshall to his edition of *Heaven and Earth* in his edition of *Lord Byron: Selected Poems and Letters* (Boston: Houghton Mifflin, 1968) 403-32 (text) and 534-35 (notes). See also PW 5: 277-321 notes.

[5]Charles notes that Chapters 6-11 in Enoch ("The Fall of the Angels: the Demoralization of Mankind: the Intercession of the Angels on behalf of Mankind. The Dooms pronounced by God on the Angels: the Messianic Kingdom") "are abruptly introduced." Enoch 6.3-8, 8.1-3, 9.7, and 10.11 "belong to a Semjaza cycle of myths." In these myths, "as in [59.2] he is chief and Azazel only tenth in command," whereas "Elsewhere in Enoch Azazel is chief and Semjaza is not mentioned." Charles concludes that "these myths . . . were already confused in their present form when [88-89.1, an account of "The Punishment of the Fallen Angels by the Archangels" and of "The Deluge"] were written." (191 n)

Charles also remarks that "The entire myth of the angels and the daughters of men in Enoch arises from Gen. vi.1-4 . . . , [which] refers not to alliances between Sethites and Cainites, but to an early Persian (?) [Charles' question mark] myth to the effect that before Zoroaster's coming demons had corrupted the earth and allied themselves with women." He notes that "the reasons for the angels' descent in the Book of Jubilees differs from those given in this chapter." In Jubilees 4 and 5 "it is said that the Watchers were sent to earth by God 'to instruct the children of men to do judgment and uprightness,' and that when so doing they began to lust after the daughters of men." (191 n) For other references to Azazel in Enoch, see

Enoch 9.6, 10.4, 10.8, 54.5, 55.5, 86.1, and 88.1. Other references to Semjaza occur in Enoch 9.7, 10.11, and 69.2.

[6]See Moore, "Charles Lyell and the Noachian Deluge," in *The Flood Myth*, ed. Alan Dundes (Berkeley: Univ. of Calif. Press, 1988) 405-25.

[7]Moses Maimonides, *The Guide for the Perplexed*, trans. M. Friedlander (New York: Dover, 1904; rpt. 1956) 161. Maimonides turns to *Bereshit Rabba*, Ch. 78, for the quotation "'Every day God creates a legion of angels; and they sing before Him, and disappear'." Maimonides adds that "When, in opposition to this, other statements were quoted to the effect that angels are eternal--and, in fact, it has repeatedly been shown that they live permanently--the reply has been given that some angels live permanently, others perish; and this is really the case . . . ." It is no wonder that Samiasa and Azaziel would want to miss choir practice.

For Paulino M. Lim, Jr., Byron, in *Heaven and Earth*, manipulates "the varying tonalities already implicit in the Psalms," and deliberately "includes moods of piety and reproach, of question and affirmation, of cursing and exultation." The drama, in essence, is informed by choral maneuvers, the tonal shifts in the Psalms responsible for the play's existential questions (76).

The Loves of the Angels:
Encountering God, the Other, and the Self
(Or, Eternal Damnation for Fun and Moore).

ANGELS, or, specifically, wavering tolerance for beliefs in embodied angels--have puzzled before--in disparate nations, and in disparate eras. Augustine's angels remained for centuries "blessed" and "holy," despite Augustine's far from blessed *or* holy end (in fact, his downright hostile one) for anatomizing angels--namely, that of thrashing, disabling, and damning the intellectual contributions of non-Christian antiquity. Thomas Moore's angels in *The Loves of the Angels* were without overt martial purposes, and yet they shocked, even met with a few charges of blasphemy, despite the fact that by 1822, angels had lost vitality in mainstream--as well as uncritical--Christian thinking. Neither does Moore's poem use angels as bait, as lures for promoting particular causes. Augustine's angels serve such ends.

Augustine made no fortune recruiting residents for *The City of God*. A bold speculator he was indeed. Today he might be charged with fraud--or, then again, might well be celebrated for innovative marketing. He promoted a development in which mortals and angels would coexist--after "this present time, while we are being healed that we may eventually be as they [the "holy angels"] are," for "it is not in locality we are distant from them, but in merit of life, caused by our miserable unlikeness to them in will, and by the weakness of our character." (*City of God* 4.8.25) Unlike many developers, tantalizing with promises of an ideal community about to be realized from off a draftsman's board, Augustine offers residency in a community already built; the residents, not the structures, want preparation. Even had he enjoyed a means of persuading that he was truly a realtor of something real, he would still surely have had to await the anxious moments brokers inescapably face before an escrow closes, moments in which brokers hope buyers will remain "sold" during the idle time the necessary paperwork eventuates; in the case of buyers into *The City of God*, surplus time could lead to speculation about just how, exactly, potential residents were to come to terms with cultural deprivation. (Jason, retrospectively, may well have decided that a community like Augustine's was indeed a safe place to settle down with Medea and the kids; yet deprived of the verve and panache of

Midtown Manhattan--its ancient counterparts, that is--safe tedium may still have driven Medea to the throats of her own, and anyone else's kids.) Those vibrant, joyous, exciting, dangerous, invigorating, life-affirming multiple worlds created by Homer, Plotinus, Apuleius, would have no place in the *City*. The payoff for residency was the promise of proximity to the blessed angels, masterworks of that very God who made two people, and then made the same two people, set them in a garden, expelled them from it, told them to bear children, drowned all of their children, and then redrowned the same children, then broiled others, turned another to salt, impregnated the elderly, terrorized a few more in a few even less credible ways, then, adolescence out of Its system, picked a shepherd to lead a tribe across a rivulet (by Nilotic standards), deciding shortly afterwards to kill the shepherd before he set foot on its banks: the wonders of Revealed Truth. (This--not Jocasta's genealogy--would indeed have been a Revelation rendering Oedipus' blinding himself wholly understandable, even rational.)

Moore proposes nothing as outrageous as Augustine. *The Loves of the Angels* remain tainted in their reputation partly because Moore has fallen through a hole in time. We hear only the calumniators of this poem, which Ward notes received more reviews than any single poem written during the period between 1821-1826 (viii), and which De Ford points out became a "best seller" (26). As has been suggested earlier, Moore's annotations constitute a counter-philosophy of angels, one highlighting their theological silliness, in contrast to the grave portrayals of the ill-fated angels offered in the text proper. Yet the notes were for Moore's crowd; their bulk, not to mention their excerpts from Latin and Greek Patristic writings, would have discouraged the less learned from contemplating what the notes are really supposed to do--or even why they appear at all. Moore's dual angelology has gone for a long time without appreciation.

Such has been the fate of Moore himself. It may indeed have been the temperament of the man, rather than the appeal of his writings, that has left him in obsolescence, his *Angels* unread.

A journal entry of 18 June 1831 records that Moore

Walk[ed] with Sydney Smith--told me his age--turned sixty--asked me how I felt about dying--answered that if my mind was but at ease about the comfort of those I left behind, I should leave the world without much regret, having passed a very happy life & enjoyed (as much perhaps as ever man did yet) all that is enjoyable in it--the only thing I have had to complain to being want of money. I could therefore die with the same words that Jostin died 'have had enough of every thing.' (JTM 4: 1414)

We have difficulty abiding the well adjusted, the content. Moore wants the existential *angst*, the prophetic call or will to restructure society so alluring in so many of his contemporaries. We need writers who take their art with Miltonic seriousness, and prefer those who suffer periods of suicidal despair, or at least thorough world-weariness. Nothing in Moore's life or his writings serves. Indeed, Sir Walter Scott's recollection of his first acquaintance with Moore does much to render any such portrait clearly inauthentic. Scott, in his journal entry from Edinburgh, 22 Tuesday, November 1825, reports that

> I was aware that Byron had often spoken both in private society and in his journal of Moore and myself in the same breath and with the same sort of regard. So I was curious to see what there could be in common betwixt us, Moore having lived so much in the gay world I in the country and with people of business and sometimes with politicians, Moore a scholar--I none--He a musician and artist--I without knowledge of a note--He a democrat--I an aristocrat--with many other points of difference besides his being an Irishman, I a Scotchman, and both tolerably national.
>
> Yet there is a point of resemblance and a strong one. We are both goodhumoured fellows who rather seek to enjoy what is going forward than to maintain our dignity as Lions. And we have both seen the world too widely and too well not to contemn in our souls the imaginary consequence of literary people who walk with their noses in the air and remind me always of the fellow whom Johnson met in an ale-house who called himself 'the great Twalmly, Inventor of the flood-gate iron for smoothing linen.' He also enjoys the *Mot pour rire* and so do I. (Anderson 5-6)

His joy with words, with word play, with his very being, remain alien to many in the present time. In Moore's age, his play with angels and with theology in general would alienate, if not seem alien. His angels met with unanticipated derision, startling to Moore's heart, one ready to share charity and laughter; but often he bestowed new pleasures for his inner circle, shaken by an omnipresent Wesleyan presence, by the uncritical piety threatening publishers and poets alike. It is for Moore's circle that the poet tailored the apparently ponderous ancilla that put off readers untutored in Latin and Greek (details that, through their accumulation, reveal that the loud, abrasive piety wasted anger without bothering to open the Scriptures, let alone theologians and Patristic commentators).

The Loves of the Angels, in its first four editions, offends English reviewers more often than any other English narrative appearing during the 1820's. Contemporaries object to Moore's irreverence and--when nothing remains to malign--to his style. Irreverence suppurates through his diction-- diction seductive in its gifts for painting facades that the unwary reader mistakes for structures; a minority in fact finds his *Loves* altogether wanting substance. (Angels are the things that for Moore want substance.) A diligent anonymous reviewer in *Blackwood's* 13 (January-June 1823): 63-71 quotes 26 excerpts from Moore's *Angels* 5 that "shew . . . by so many collected examples from one long poem, how the mind may acquire unconsciously a habit of speaking irreverently of divine things" (67). (Moore studied quite diligently to affect this habit.) Summarizing contemporary reviews, both favorable and unfavorable (*Upright* 355-58), Moore's recent biographer, Hoover H. Jordan, has difficulty understanding how this poem--which Jordan perceives as a celebration of the "holiness of human love" (355)-- could have offended. His assessment of the poem as a celebration bears consideration, especially in light of the fact that during the farewell dinner hosted by Kinnaird (11 November 1821), anticipating Moore's departure to Sloperton (on 23 November 1821), "Douglas toasted Bessy and remarked that it was altogether fitting for Moore to be writing a poem on the subject of angels since he has been living with one." (Jordan, *Upright* 346-47) Jordan appreciates Moore's erudition--both acquired during his tenure as one of the first Catholics admitted to Trinity College, Dublin (15-18), and during what Jordan quips was "a seven-year wave of morality [that swept] over England," in the aftermath of controversy surrounding the *Little* poems, a wave "which exactly fourteen years later was to inundate Byron, and [at which] Moore was, of course, stunned." (68) Sick of allegations about the "natural depravity of his] mind," he retreated "to the cottage by Cooper's Hill and plunged into extensive reading . . . ," including "Church Fathers, classical philosophers, later philosophers, especially from the eighteenth- century, literary men from classical times to modern (both continental and English), and even excursions into Cornish, Persian, and Arabic grammars, with some attempts at Gaelic . . . ." (68-69) Even Richard Cumberland, Moore's "friend," of sorts, who formulated the phrase "natural depravity of mind" that so long rode as a trailer to Moore's name, praised Moore as "a poet and a scholar of no common rank" (Jordan 86).

If Moore's contemporaries objected to the implications about God's retributive nature suggested by the first two narratives, the third tale also offended--less for its vision of God than for the vapidity of Moore's invention. The third tale depicts a gentler God--one who responds mildly to transgressors whose hearts incline towards heaven. Heavenly inclinations apparently reveal themselves on earth through gifts at anticipating (or at enacting *ersatz*) Church Sacraments. (No one in Moore's age registers bewilderment at a seraph's and an antediluvian woman's invention of sacred nuptial vows.)[1] Even Moore finds this third tale the least engaging. In his journal entry of 8 January 1823, he speaks of receiving much correspondence about *The Loves of the Angels*, including a letter which judges "the second story the best, and the *third a falling off*." Moore remarks that

> It is curious to see the difference of tastes. Lord J. here says, 'The third story is a falling off,' and just before I received his letter, I had been reading a Review, in which the wise critic says, 'The third story, which is unquestionably the best of the three.' Lord John, of course, is right; it is a falling off after the second. (JTM 2: 614.)

Another reviewer takes no theological offense, but rather finds the entire poem rather silly, all participants guiltless, no participant capable of engaging human passion (or even concern):

> The only offence of which one of these exiled angels appears to have been guilty is that of having exceeded his furlough, and tarried too long upon the earth. The second is such a foolish spirit as to enact the part of Jove towards his Semele . . . . The third spirit is, in truth, a devotional sentimentalist, a most religious demon. His crime was that of nonconformity, and his fall is an allegorical lesson to all those who are in danger of being seduced by a pretty face, good singing, or 'devotion,' from their parish Church.

This want of criminal carnality raises a question of theodicy: why would a just God punish such trivial offenses?

Today the commotion over the poem amazes--nearly. It is almost impossible to see how what De Ford diagnoses as the "vaguely allegorical, semierotic, dreamy religiosity" permeating the poem could have offended--almost. (De Ford 50) Fortunately for Moore, his readers seldom ventured into what appeared to be dauntingly learned notes; in actuality, as Moore's circle well knew, these notes show exactly where, why, and when the pious should take offense.

In supplying a Preface and notes, he verges into self-parody, as he does explicitly with *Corruption and Intolerance* (1809), opening with the observation that

> The practice which has been lately introduced into literature, of writing very long notes upon very indifferent verses, appears to me a rather happy invention; as it supplies us with a mode of turning dull poetry to account; and as horses too heavy for the saddle may yet serve well enough to draw lumber, so Poems of this kind make excellent beasts of burden, and will bear notes, though they might not bear reading.

If a poem fails, the apparatus may teach something of interest. Moore's poems come frequently with both a Preface and notes. The notes are often deflective--turning attention away from a controversial issue introduced into their given poem, forcing attention instead upon some antiquarian or other vaguely related knowledge. Yet much groundwork had been prepared for Moore's jests at uncritical piety. Bayle and Diderot constitute heavy artillery. Comparative religion and comparative literature were beginning to converge and render impossible belief in "verbal inspiration" of Scripture.

The Loves of the Angels titillated. The subject of angels cohabiting with mortals sufficed to offend, no matter how delicately treated. Fortunately for Moore, his critics engaged their glands more often than their minds; few looked beyond the veiled sexual allusions to explore the theological implications of the poem. Had they done so, the poem would have offended for good cause.

The possible theological problems attendant upon his naming his angels apparently bother Moore, although these problems were relatively small. Moore's angelological learning was so extensive that he knew that for every assertion or surrounding legend, a contradicting assertion or legend could be produced. Unfortunately, his readers were not conversant in angelology, and assumed as "scriptural" the sometimes inaccurate transmissions of the blended Aristotelian/Aquinian lore that remained in memory. Moore explains that in assigning his second angel the name "Rubi,"

> I might have chosen perhaps some better name, but it is meant (like that of Zaraph in the following story) to define the particular class of spirits to which the angel belonged. The author of the Book of Enoch who estimates at 200 the number of angels that descended upon Mount Hermon, for the purpose of making love to

the women of earth, has favoured us with the names of their leader
and chiefs--Samyaza, Urakabarameel, Akibeel, Tamiel, &c ....

He "might" have; he ventures no answer to any questions about why he
actually did not. Moore follows with what appears to be a reason: "in that
heretical worship of angels, which prevailed, to a great degree, during the
first ages of Christianity, to *name* them seems to have been one of the most
important ceremonies; for we find it expressly forbidden in one of the
Canons (35th) of the Council of Laodicea": Moore deliberately misrepresents this council (CA 343-381), which condemned those "who gave
themselves up to a masked idolatry in honor of the angels." (Idolatry, to use
Moore's phrasing, was one of the early Christian's "most important
ceremonies." He lists Josephus' inclusion "among the religious rites of the
Essenes, their swearing 'to preserve the names of the angels.'"[2] Moore's
ritual understanding of the meaning of "name" seems diversionary, Josephus
and others objecting to "name" in the sense of "invocation," or "worship";
Essenes--and Roman Church Councils--could not decree angel worship out
of practice, and, for once, conforming the Church to reality, the 2nd Council
of Nicaea (787) rewelcomed angels, assigning us "guardians" from among
their ranks, permitting us once again to "pray to the angels." (Moore
highlights haggard problems in order to subordinate fresh, new ones.)

His claim about "Rubi" signifying a class of angels simply does not
convince; Moore here deploys his learning about the significance of named
angels to deflect attention from the fact that Rubi's generic identity derives
from a pun--namely, Rubi the CheRUB. Moore has fun with his angels (if
Moore's eponomy offends). He trivializes angels. The Rubi Moore presents
cannot be annotated into kind with the Cherubim, despite Moore's appeal
to Dionysius the Areopagite in rendering them "spirits of knowledge,"
despite their frightening, winged, leonine presences rendered permanent in
Assyrian art (their root word, *karibu* in Akkadian, meaning 'one who prays,'
or 'one who intercedes'; their effect upon Theodorus, Bishop of Heraclea,
hardly that of "Angelicall powers, but rather [of] some horrible visions of
beasts," as reported by John Salkeld, *A Treatise of Angels*, London, 1613;
from G. Davidson 86). Even the name "Zaraph," for the third angel,
presents difficulties. Moore's note to his first edition suggests that the name
represents the class. Yet Moore's seraph is a decidedly distinct individual,
with a singular personality, given to particular likes and dislikes. As such,
the homophonous pun involved in the name of "Zaraph" the seraph offends
possibly even more than the singularity of the amputated pun-name "Rubi."

In addition, Moore's command of angel lore leads us to wonder whether his motives in assigning Nama as Zaraph's partner are wholly innocent. In the Cabbala (*Zohar*), which Moore refers to throughout his notes, Naamah is an angel of prostitution. Davidson adds that "Rabbi Simeon called her mother of demons," even "the 'great seducer not only of men but of spirits and demons'," according to Rabbi Hiya, and "with Lilith, she 'brought epilepsy to children'." (203) In *The Zohar, Bereshith* 55, R. Hiya explains why "Scripture particularly mention[s] Naamah," by turning to Genesis 6.4, identifying "the 'sons of God' mentioned in Scripture . . . [as] Uzza and Azael, [who] were seduced by her'." 1:175. (Her traditional association with Lilith raises questions about Moore's intention in naming his 'Lilis,' as well.) The name has other designees. Nama, of course, appears in Genesis 4.22, as Tubal-Cain's sister: "Naamah," "pleasing". Could Nama's purity in the tale be undermined by the joke inhering in her name? Undoubtedly. Moore's familiarity with Cabalistic sources becomes evident in his notes to both the original and the revised texts of the *Angels*. In *The Zohar* 1: 55a, Nama reveals her lustiest self:

> AND THE SISTER OF TUBAL CAIN WAS NAAMAH. R. Hiya said: 'Why does the Scripture particularly mention Naamah? The reason is that she was the great seducer not only of men, but also of spirits and demons.' R. Isaac said: 'The "sons of God" mentioned in Scripture (Gen VI, 4), who were Uzza and Azael, were seduced by her. R. Simeon said: 'She was the mother of demons, being of the side of Cain, and it is she who in company with Lilith brings epilepsy on children . . . . Said R. Simeon: 'Alas for the blindness of the sons of men, all unaware as they are how full the earth is of strange and invisible beings and hidden dangers, which could they but see, they would marvel how they themselves can exist on the earth. This Naamah was the mother of the demons, and from her originate all those evil spirits which mix with men and arouse them in inconcupiscence, which leads them to defilement.

Lilith--better known than Naamah--finds mention in Bayle, who Adam took as a second wife during the 130 years some commentators say he was separated from Eve. The connection between this name and *Lilis*, Rubi's beloved, is evident. Naamah comes directly from the Cabbala; this "angel of whoredom" (G. Davidson) marries the purist of Moore's not so wayward celestials. (One Jewish legend has Naamah mothering the demon Asmodeus after pairing with an angel-demon, Shamdam. (G. Davidson 203)

A related question wants asking. Could Moore be playing with the inadequacy of his readership's knowledge about angels? Yes. Even Lea, the named mortal, who replaces the nameless angel abandoned in the "First Angel's Story" may speak particularly to an audience apprised of Cabalistic explanations of the significance of the name "Leah," going well beyond the fecundity she demonstrates in Genesis 29-30. *The Zohar* 1: 49a asks that we

> Observe that throughout the Scriptures the worshippers of the sun are called servants of Baal and the worshippers of the moon servants of Asherah; hence the combination 'to Baal and Asherah.' If this is so (that Asherah is the name of the *He* [defined in 48b as "the great inscrutable called *hu* (he) [who] knows his place"], why is it not used as a sacred name? The reason is that the name brings to mind the words of Leah, 'happy am I, for the daughters will call me happy (*ishruni*)' [See Genesis 30.12-13, after Leah's maid bears Jacob a second son,'... Leah said, "Happy am I! For the women will call me happy"; so she called his name Asher," literally rendered "Happy"--uncomfortably close in form to 'Asherah.'], but this one is not 'called happy' by other nations, and another is set up in its place; nay more, it is written, 'all that honoured her despise her' (Lam. 1.8).

The Cabbalists speak not of gestation, but rather of "the breath of life . . . enclosed in the earth, which was made pregnant with it like a female impregnated by the male"; Leah's happiness in the text of departure (Genesis 30.13) compares to her happiness upon usurping the nameless angel's ontological status; the verse from Lamentations in no way fits Moore's Lea, but does reflect the thorough demoralization endured by the angel who now remains with the dust of mortals.

Moore's Qur'anic learning--particularly from Sale--gives him a backup source for his first angel's debasement. In his "Preliminary Discourse," Part 4, Sale discusses the Genii of Islamic lore, who were "corrupt," and "driven into a remote part of the earth, there to be confined." (Sale 1: 100) Sale continues,

> The Mahommedans notions concerning these Genii agree almost exactly with what the Jews write of a sort of daemons, called Shedim, whom some fancy to have been begotten by two angels named Aza and Azael, on Naamah the daughter of Lamech, before the flood.

Sale refers to the Zohar, and switches to the Shedim named there:

> ... the Shedim, they tell us, agree in three things with the minister-
> ing angels; for that like them, they have wings, and fly from one end
> of the world to the other, and have some knowledge of futurity; and
> in three things they agree with men, like whom they eat and drink,
> are propagated, and die.

Moore's angels--neither originally nor in the revision--know either
mortality (save for the nameless angel, who exchanges ontogenic status with
Lea) nor futurity (save for Rubi, who apprehends Lilis' condemnation to
hell). None eat. Had Moore wanted to convert his angels thoroughly, Sale,
with whom he is very familiar, would have been a mine for details Moore
could have superadded.

Moore's learning about angels leaves us with two poems--the poem
printed in the text proper, and the poem modified by its notes. Moore's
apparatus to his first edition bears fuller meaning for his intellectual circle
than for outsiders. This becomes particularly clear from his endnote to lines
905-907 (1), "Oh, idol of my dreams! whate'er / Thy nature be.--human,
divine, / Or but half heav'nly." (Notes, *Loves* 1, 140.) The note (excised from
his fifth and subsequent editions) remarks that

> In an article upon the Fathers, which appeared, some years since,
> in the Edinburgh Review (No. 47.), and of which I have made some
> little use in these notes, (having claim over it--as "quiddam notum
> *propriumque*"--which Lucretius gives to the cow over the calf,)
> there is the following remark:--"The belief of an intercourse
> between angels and women, founded upon a false version of a text
> in Genesis, is one of those extravagant notions of St. Justin and
> other Fathers, which show how little they had yet purified them-
> selves from the grossness of heathen mythology, and in how many
> respects their heaven was but Olympus, with other names. Yet we
> can hardly be angry with them for this one error, when we recollect
> that possibly to their enamoured angels we owe the fanciful world
> of sylphs and gnomes, and that at this moment we might have
> wanted Pope's most exquisite poem, if the version of the LXX. had
> translated the Book of Genesis correctly." (*Loves* 140-141)

Moore addresses insiders. He quotes, with very minor emendations, a
paragraph appearing on p. 61 of his own anonymous review of Hugh Stuart

"Boyd's *Translations from the Fathers*," appearing in the *Edinburgh Review* 24 (Nov. 1814-Feb. 1815): 58-72. This review was well received, by even Boyd himself, who reports,

> I have redde thee upon the Fathers, and it is excellent well. Positively, you must not leave off reviewing. You shine in it--you kill in it: and this article has been taken for Sydney Smith's (as I heard in town), which proves not only your proficiency in parsonology, but that you have all the airs of a veteran critic at your first onset.[3]

Predictably, Moore's original Preface reflects far greater caution in his efforts to free Scripture for verse than do his anonymous comments about the Bible and its expositors in his *Edinburgh* assessment of Boyd from 1814.

Moore wears his learning lightly in his "Review of Boyd's *Fathers*," which his endnote note to his first edition of the *Angels* quarries. In both, he prefers the Targum Onkelos to the LXX version of Genesis 6.2; yet in the Review, he does nothing to defend his choice, and, rather, celebrates the "abundant progeny of demons in consequence," for "Demons were much too useful a race to be so easily surrendered to reason or ridicule," dooming Chrysostom's and like endeavors to expunge them: "there was no getting up a decent miracle without them; exorcists would have been out of employ, and saints at a loss for temptation." Even "the writings of these holy Doctors abound with such stories & demoniacal possession, as make us alternately smile at their weaknesses and blush for their dishonesty." (By way of a note, he directs us not to a mainstream commentator, but to "Middleton's Free Inquiry," about which he adds "It would be difficult to add anything new to this writer upon the subject; and he is too well known to render extracts necessary.")[4] Demons entertain, too:

> from about the date of that theatrical little devil of Tertullian (so triumphantly referred to by Jeremy Collier), who claimed a right to take possession of a woman in the theatre, 'because he there found her on his own ground,' to the gallant demons commemorated by Bodin [in *De la Demonomonie des Sorciers*] and Remigius [in *Demonolatreia*], and such tragical farces as the possession of the nuns of Loudun. (24: 61-62)

Moore's review continues jesting at outrageous commentators who take themselves seriously. Context and hyperbole often constitute his weapons.

Referring to the possessions of the nuns, he remarks that

> the same features of craft and dupery are discernable through the whole from beginning to end; and when we have read of that miraculous person, Gregory Thaumaturgus, writing a familiar epistle to Satan, and then turn to the Young Nun in Bodin, in whose box was found a love-letter 'a son cher daemon,'

Moore then determines that "we need not ask more perfect specimens of the two wretched extremes of imposture and credulity, than these two very different letter-writers afford." (62)

Jesting resumes. Moore does "regret" the "loss" of the "class of demons" constituting "those 'seducing sprites, who,' as Theophilus of Antioch tells us, 'confessed themselves to be the same that had inspired the Heathen Poets.'" Indeed "we own we should like to see such cases of possession in our days," especially given a current surplus of exorcists, transformed into reviewers:

> though we Reviewers are a kind of exorcists, employed to cast out the evil demon of scribbling, and even pride ourselves upon having performed some notable cures,--from *such* demoniacs we would refrain with reverence . . . .

Having diverted attention from expositors and commentators to poetry in the present day, Moore surprises with a direct assault upon an ancient corruption (and recent enthusiasm invigorating certain Protestant sects):

> The belief of a Millennium or temporal reign of Christ, during which the faithful were to be indulged in all sorts of sensual gratifications, may be reckoned among those gross errors for which neither the Porch nor the Academy are accountable, but which grew up in the ranks of oriental fanaticism, and were nursed into doctrines of Christianity by the Fathers. (62-63)

This review, like Moore's 1823 Preface, detects corruption in the Septuagint rendering of Genesis 6.2. The Review develops this note into a discussion of the functions served by angels among early Christians living in Greece, who substituted the polytheism of the Greek poets for an elaborate angelology. It continues with a charge of widespread and ongoing corruption of the Christian faith from ancient through recent times.

The Preface of 1823 likewise defers to the Targum Onkelos's rendering of Genesis 6.2, the Aramaic paraphrase changing the LXX "angels of God" to "the sons of the nobles or great men." In this Preface, Moore uses his learning as a shield rather than a weapon. He distances us from his own poetic intention by centuries of commentators from the "allegorizing comments of Philo," through "the Fathers," the "greater number" of whom follow "Chrysostom, [who] in his twenty-second Homily upon Genesis, earnestly exposes its absurdity" (i.e., the notion of a divine/mortal tryst), through "St. Thomas to Caryl and Lightfoot," bringing us back to the text. (The Alexandrian text--the text to which tradition has affixed the designation LXX--remains undiscussed.) Moore poses as one who, only after working his way through centuries of Christian learning, can conclude that "This translation of the passage removes all difficulty; and at once relieves the Sacred History of an extravagance, which however it may suit the imagination of the poet, is inconsistent with all our notions, both philosophical and religious." In actuality, Moore uses Scripture to emancipate himself from any allegiance to it in his poem. In the 1820's, this intended emancipation is best buried in what he makes light of in the 1814 review, when he suggests that

> If we could flatter ourselves that Mr. Boyd would listen to us, we would advise him to betake himself as speedily as possible from such writers as his Gregories, Cyrils, &c.--which can never serve any other purpose than that of a vain parade of cumbrous erudition.

('Cumbrous erudition' becomes Moore's shield in 1823.) The review continues with the observation that Boyd

> will find, in a few pages of Barrow or Taylor, more rational poetry, and more true eloquence, than in all the Fathers of the Chruch together.

The review closes on the light note that

> if, as we think probable, under this better culture, his talents should bring forth fairer fruits, we shall hail such a result of our councils with pleasure,--and shall even forgive him the many personal risks he has made us run in poising down our huge folio

Saints from their shelves. (72)

The Loves of the Angels may be Moore's own contribution to this "better culture," a poem in which Jordan finds Moore celebrating "the pure love of man and woman," which to Moore was "one of the few redeeming features of life on earth." (*Upright* 266) If this be his purpose, political repressiveness of the 1820's would warrant his burying this purpose beneath some "huge folio Saints.

Minor objections could even be raised to Moore's political use of his source, the Book of Enoch 6.2 (itself derived from Genesis 6.2). From the Book of Enoch, Moore draws the theme of forbidden knowledge, specifically, its ruinously high price for both the bestower and the recipient (a theme rendering the poem amenable to Qur'anic conversion--at least to the legends surrounding Haruth and Maruth, which also explore the price exacted by induction into the occult). For Moore's age, knowledge had proven at once ruinous and liberating, technological knowledge helping the rich inherit the earth, an acquisition they hoped to maintain--and increase-- solely by making certain that there were masses of ignorant laborers who would not question the right of the bourgeoisie to circumscribe for labor appropriate behavior in the workplace, and who would be satisfied with a narrow, utilitarian arena of specialized knowledge; the masses must not ever have either the time or the chance to master enough information to be able to develop competing technologies. The theme of forbidden knowledge acutely concerns Moore's age--specifically, in its ethical implications. Have any human beings any right to keep masses in darkness? (The question is rhetorical. Yet masses, even today, particularly by large corporations and government agencies, are disabled by policed ignorance.)

In the "First Angel's Story," forbidden knowledge becomes the cause of Lea's ontogenic elevation transpiring at the same time her unnamed angel lover undergoes ontogenic debasement. In the "Second Angel's Story," likened in its age to the tale of Jove and Semele, Rubi--a cherub, "one of those bright creatures nam'd / Spirits of knowledge"--seems doomed because of an appetite endemic to his very being, an appetite he cannot help. His unending grief, and Lilis' physical dissolution and damnation, raise problems of theodicy--particularly when Rubi himself questions God's justness. The "Third Angel's Story" equalizes essences, Zaraph and Nama, by performing their own marriage rites (in a scene vaguely reminiscent of the marriage in *Romeo and Juliet*), securing their freedom to "wander here--the same, / Throughout all time" (1874-76). How and why this favorable judgment passes even the narrator does not venture; knowledge, in this tale, remains God's.[5]

Fortunately for Moore, those ready to charge blasphemy at nearly any poetic deviation from Scripture in the 1820's completely overlooked a source of serious theological controversy--namely, Moore's depiction (or rather *depictions*) of God. Each of the three stories unfolds under the provenance of a different God. A fourth God belongs to the narrator. *The Loves of the Angels* inadvertently gives assent to polytheism--or, more accurately, to serial monolatry.

A kind, loving God oversees the amours of Zaraph and Nama--an anthropopathic God who reacts to their transgression ("Yet never did that God look down / On error with a brow so mild; / Never did justice launch a frown, / That, ere it fell, so nearly smil'd," 1814-17), who actively designs "their only punishment" ("that, long / As the green earth and ocean stand, / They both shall wander here--the same, / Throughout all time, in heart and frame," 1873-75), and who determines that this punishment will be of limited (albeit long) duration. The couple intuits and thereby trusts that "their spirits shall, with freshn'd power / Rise up" at "the bright hour" when time is no more, and be "rewarded for their trust / In Him from whom all goodness springs, / And, shaking off earth's soiling dust / From their emancipated wings, / Wander for ever through those skies / Of radiance, where Love never dies!" (1415-20.) This is the good God. This God intervenes directly in earthly affairs, and, while punishing transgressions, does so lovingly, administering justice fairly, making certain that those whose lives he manages have cause to retain hope. This is the God--while not Scriptural--that uncritical Christendom found palatable. Three other Gods work in the *Loves*, and work in quite different ways.

While in the "Third Angel's Story" Zaraph and Nama need never ask God to attend to them, the "Second Angel's Story" occurs in a universe designed by a God not assuming sentryship, and certainly not into perpetuity, over earthly events. Rubi errs in presuming that through creation he may know the Creator--presuming that he can observe his works (which both narrator and angel deem wonderful, beautiful, permeated by love) and presume that these human (angelic) qualitative ascriptions apply to God, are known to God, and are valued by God. Hints that God's evaluative gauges bear no relationship to mortal (or here, angelic) gauges appear in the narrator's description of Lilis' beauty--physical, yes, initially attracting Rubi, but more significantly cerebral, for "'twas the Mind, sparkling about / Through her whole frame--the soul, brought out / To light each charm, yet independent / Of what is lighted, as the sun / That shines on flowers, would be resplendent / Were there no flowers to shine upon" (791-96). These closing two lines--suggesting that external nature consists of attributes depending upon no observer for existence--reflects Moore's oriental learning, this concept of independent attributes embraced by Vigny and Lamartine, as well. Attributes assigned by God to external nature may or may not be the attributes humans identify, describe, or value. God's scheme of attributes remains constant with or without human cognizance.

As Rubi learns, God's universe is neither qualitative (in the sense that Rubi understands quality) nor hierarchical (in the sense that Rubi assays some qualities of greater worth than others). Furthermore, God may well have withdrawn--may well have followed the pattern of Paley's watchmaker God. Withdrawn or present, He remains wholly indifferent to Rubi's entreaties, as well as to the accusation of tyranny when Rubi cries out,

> But is it thus, dread Providence--
> *Can* it, indeed, be thus, that she,
> Who, but for one, proud, fond offence,
> Had honour'd heaven itself, should be
> Now doom'd--I cannot speak it--no
> Merciful God! it *is* not so (1492-97).

Or is it? Apparently.

Lilis, "withering in agony" (1458), must in fact suffer "even worse," for, Rubi laments, "Had death, death only, been the curse / I brought upon her ..., / 'Twere not so dreadful." Yet he recalls, "In that last struggle, on my brow / Her ashy lips a kiss imprest, / So withering!--I feel it now-- / 'Twas fire--but fire, ev'n more unblest / Than was my own, and like that flame, / The angels shudder but to name, / Hell's everlasting element!" (1477-83) This, Rubi intuits; this fate, Rubi's forehead--bearing the brand that was her kiss--marks sealed. This brand carries nothing of the protective magic of the mark of Cain, Rubi, like Cain, a branded murderer. Cain's God--unlike Rubi's--protects Cain against mortal attack, and hence the mark; Rubi's mark serves to remind him--as if he needs reminding--that Rubi has murdered all in life dear to him.

Rubi rages at a "dread Provenance" who he deems unjust. He pleads with the "Great Power," to "Pardon that spirit, and on me, / On me who taught her pride to err, / Shed out each drop of agony." (1506-10) God fails to respond, either denying, ignoring--or incognizant of--this entreaty. Rubi resumes: "Again, I cry, Just God, transfer / That creature's sufferings all to me ...." (1524-25) God remains unresponsive. Rubi, the narrator reports, gives up, and "Breath'd inwardly the voiceless prayer, / Unheard by all but Mercy's ear-- / And which if Mercy did *not* hear, / Oh, God would not be what this bright, glorious universe of his, / This world of beauty, goodness, light / And endless love proclaims He *is*!" (1537-43) The narrator shares Rubi's misprisions; God's nature may not necessarily be adduced from "this . . . universe," "Mercy" may well be a human construct; "beauty, goodness, light" may be mere eisegetic intrusions into a universe indescribable according to human evaluative categories. God may well be unjust, and, furthermore, indifferent to the charge of unjustness. God in this tale bears no resemblance to God in the "Third Angel's Story." Rubi's God--at best, withdrawn, at worst vengeful--remains chillingly ineffable.

A slightly more knowable--if no more comforting--God orders the universe of the "First Angel's Story." This unnamed angel apparently knows that God *will* communicate--but only with luminescent beings dwelling in close proximity. Once the angel's disclosure removes the "vapour from this vale of tears" that "Between her [Lea] and God appears," Lea "All bright and glorified became," unfolding "Two wings magnificent as those / That sparkle round the' Eternal Throne" (366-72). Towards that throne she will rise; Lea's (not the angel's) tale ends happily. After the failure of the angel's repetition on his own behalf of "the mystic word," the angel does not even attempt to communicate with God, fully aware that God listens only to those within his celestial neighborhood. (Lea, a species climber, uses her lover to move to the right part of the cosmos.) This is an exclusive God, having no chosen people--having nothing to do with mortals at all. This the wingless angel knows far too well even to decry; despair remains his lot.

A fourth God becomes known through the narrator. This God occupies a "Throne" (51), and is attended by "those shining rows / That circle out through endless space." (52-3) God's angels, "Creatures of light," serve "through their infinite array / [to] Transmit each moment, night and day, / The echo of His luminous word!" His word translates into light, manifested not through verbal transmissions, but by angelic manifestations of their beings. God's relationship to humans remains uncertain--vaguely Scriptural, in the angel's, followed by the narrator's references to Eve's fatal hunger for knowledge (670-712). Eastern metaphors likewise account for this God, a "Fountain-head / From which all vital spirit runs, / All breath of Life, where'er 'tis shed, / Through men or angels, flowers or sun"--recalling the divine, unifying principle in the God of Hinduism, adapted by Lamartine. This God, like the Scriptural God, is an artist/creator, an intellect, and an engineer, evident when the narrator describes God's as "the Almighty Mind," who "first o'er Chaos . . . design'd / The outlines of this world; and through / That spread of darkness--like the bow, / Call'd out of rain-clouds, hue by hue-- / Saw the grand, gradual picture grow!--" His imposition of order upon chaos comes from Scripture; his gradual shaping of his design draws upon the metaphor of the artist's slow labor. Scripture--and Ovid-- suggest this God's relations to mortals:

> The covenant with human kind
> Which God hath made--the chains of Fate
> He round himself and them hath twin'd,
> Till his high task he consummate--
> Till good from evil, love from hate,
> Shall be work'd out through sin and pain,
> And Fate shall loose her iron chain,
> And all be free, be bright again!

God here becomes the experimental scientist; he himself has not determined what distinguishes good from evil, or love from hate, but will remain bound to man, observing what does and does not work well. The "sin and pain" of mortals will indicate to him failed experiments. Once a moral code has been established, God will unbind Himself from humankind, and humankind will have free will, to do or to not do what God's experiments have determined right. (Free will is a later human gift. The world is God's laboratory; he must remain bound to it until ethical norms have been fixed.) The narrator's God draws from Scripture, from the Hindu sacred writings, from Ovid and from Greek mythology, from current fashions in experimental philosophy, and from metaphors for engineering and art. So concerned were Moore's detractors with the impropriety of angelic concupiscence that they uniformly overlooked Moore's abject disregard either for Scriptural or traditional Christian God concepts, Moore assuming mythopoesis as both his right and his informing impulse, designing, ultimately, four separate cosmic structures each dominated by a different God, each God in some ways reminiscent of the Judaeo-Christian God, but none wholly acceptable to mainstream--or even evangelicalistic--Christianity. Moore's God(s) should have been the cause of serious theological objections. The sensibilities of Moore's middle class readership rendered God--four separate Gods, no less--a matter of no concern, God upstaged by the presumed sensuality of Rubi and the nameless angel.

If *The Loves of the Angels* seems structurally loose, some of this looseness stems from the Ovidian tradition Moore develops; in the *Metamorphoses* (as in Spenser's "Mutabilatie Cantos"), change is the only constant--a thematic cord yoking lightly divergent legends, loves, and horrors. If Moore's essays in this Ovidian kind fail to satisfy at times, dissatisfaction may stem from the hybrid cosmological framework projected in the poem. The eschatological vision of the third angel's tale seems property of an entirely different (and contradictory) mythic structure from the scheme in the first tale; the two mythic frameworks suffer from an uneasy grafting upon one another. The third narrative, engraved on the pillars of Cham, is undergirded by a confidence in a new--and better-- eschaton following world-judgment in the form of a flood; in the first tale, the angel is damned to be earth-bound forever (a little difficult to conceive, if there is to be an end of the earth, as the final tale prophesies). Given Moore's liberty in designing Gods, these variant cosmological systems do not surprise.

The first two tales of *The Loves of the Angels* reveal a tension between the narrator's overt condemnation of angel/mortal unions and the narrator's play for sympathy for the transgressors. The narrator abhors interspeciation, yet he entices the reader to savor it. The poet manipulates our sympathetic response by allowing the first two angels to step outside of the narrative framework, so to speak, and tell their own stories in modified forms of the complaint poem. The resulting tension between the narrator's morality and the reader's sympathy forces the reader to ask questions of theodicy, at least indirectly. We like the sensitive angel lovers; we resent their suffering as well as the harsh, unrelenting judge who sentences them. In Moore's poem as in Byron's, free expression of carnal love between angels and mortals attracts us. Unlike *Heaven and Earth*, however, such love proves far from expedient.

The narrative opens in a golden age, an age Vigny adopts for his *Le Deluge*, "when the world was in its prime," seemingly before there were any barriers restricting free communication between heaven and earth, a time

> When, in the light of Nature's dawn
> Rejoicing, men and angels met
> On the high hill and sunny lawn,--

and sat and communicated. In the antediluvian age, no sin had forced Nature to hang "'Twixt man and heaven her curtains yet!" (1-9.)

Whether or not men and angels know restrictions in the ways they can rejoice together remains unclear. In a sense, the narrator's nostalgia for those younger, brighter days "when earth lay nearer to the skies / Than in these days of crime and woe" (10-11) seems somewhat inappropriate to the ensuing tragedies. He laments,

> Alas, that Passion should profane,
> Ev'n then, that morning of the earth!
> That, sadder still, the fatal stain
> Should fall on hearts of heavenly birth--
> And oh, that stain so dark should fall
> From Woman's love, most sad of all! (15-20.)

This ascription of the source of calamity to woman's love replicates the third hamartigeny--the account of female evil freeing Adam and Eve, angels, giants, and men from guilt. This hamartigeny finds support in Judaeo-Christian and Qur'anic writings, as has been detailed. Yet as the tragedies unfold, we see that the angels themselves, and not their mortal lovers, bear most of the responsibility for their own downfalls, "responsibility" here perhaps too condemnatory in its implications. The first angel, for example, by nature observant and curious, is justified in questioning, "why have hapless angels eyes?" (238) There is never any suggestion that the angel ever had the powers to resist the visual splendors that trapped him into a self-destructive love. Allured into a territory for which he has no means of adapting, he is doomed by his own ontogenic makeup.[6]

As does *The World Before the Flood*, the "First Angel's Story" emphasizes the transforming power of love. But while Montgomery's work emphasizes its positive transformations, Moore's tale emphasizes its potential for degradation. Admittedly, Lea enjoys taxonomic elevation, but the tale focuses upon the unhappiness of the earth-trapped angel. Visual beauty first inspires love that, for the angel, develops into desire for physical union with one, he learns, who directs her goals implausibly upward. After drinking wine intended for humans (25-260), not angels, he throws away his taxonomic birthright for what amounts to one kiss "stampt upon her forehead" before Lea leaves him forever.

The first angel's susceptibility to physical beauty becomes early in the narrative quite understandable. He finds himself looking at Lea, "One of earth's fairest womankind," not just any old naked lady in a stream. (It is significant that Lea, but not the angel, bears a proper name. The angel never realizes, before relinquishing, his particular or his ontogenic identity.) The brook in which she bathes enshrines her, as if she were a goddess. Here, Lea's beauty seems to animate even external nature, the brook perhaps guilty of idolatry--if idolatry be possible in a pre-Mosaic setting. (Nature adorns humankind in Ovid and Ovid's English imitations. In a tradition fusing a classical form--the Ovidian epyllion--with Pseudepigraphic, Qur'anic, and Zoroastrian legends about stars'inhabitation by angels (see, for example, Enoch 72.4 and 75.1), this communion between mortals and nature portends ill rather than good; God's works, external nature, best glorify God, rather than framing the beauty of God's creatures.) No wonder Lea captivates the animate angel; even inanimate nature comes to life at her presence. In Lea, the angel finds a spirit, a dream-vision, a sunflower (96-104). To him, her eyes encapsulate the grandeur of all heavens and oceans: "looking into eyes where, blue, / And beautiful, like skies seen through / The sleeping wave, for me there shone / A heaven, more worshipp'd than my own" (132-35).

So fervent becomes his passion for physical union with Lea, he willingly debases himself ontogenetically, hoping this will ensure Lea's sexual love for him. He laments, however, that although

> from her eyes to gain
> One earthly look, one stray desire,
> I would have torn the wings that hung
> Furl'd at my back, and o'er that Fire
> Unnam'd in heaven their fragments flung;--
> 'Twas hopeless all--pure and unmov'd
> She stood, as lilies in the light
> Of the hot noon but look more white;--
> And though she lov'd me, deeply lov'd,
> 'Twas not as man, as mortal--no,
> Nothing of earth was in that glow--
> She lov'd me but as one, of race
> Angelic, from that radiant place
> She saw so oft in dreams (148-161).

Through their association, both human and angel become dissatisfied with their own forms of being, a hazard of breaking down barriers between human and angelic love. As noted, while he desires to be loved like a man, she exclaims, "'Oh! that it were my doom to be / The Spirit of yon beauteous star, / Dwelling up there in purity, / Alone as all such bright things are" (168-175). Lea will have no mortal lover; she will become eternal brightness.

Not only is the angel denied his celestial powers, he is also denied the mortal physical love he has desired enough to forget the heavens for. The angel arouses no passion in Lea; the woman sees him as a means of ensuring immortality. The angel is unaware that his participation in a physical encounter with a mortal signals his membership in the human community. Inadvertently, his drunken revelation of the "mystic word" forbidden to mortal ears makes Lea's wish come true, to his eventual and eternal grief. After Lea takes her place in the heavenly milieu, the angel wishes to return there, too (the first time he has desired to return since sent on his mission to earth). He recalls how he repeated the word "o'er and o'er":

> I prayed, I wept, but all in vain;
> For me the spell had power no more.
> There seemed around me some dark chain
> Which still as I essayed to soar
> Baffled, alas, each wild endeavor;
> Dead lay my wings as they have lain
> Since that sad hour and will remain--
> So wills the offended God--for ever!
> (390-398.)

In a sense, his impotency on earth as he watches Lea merge with an "immortal star" (422-423) serves as a cruel, mocking punishment for his lust. As we learn towards the beginning of this first angel's story, he originally came from "a place / Far off among those shining rows"--the realm of the stars (50-54). Moore tell us in a note,

> It is the opinion of Kircher, Ricciolus, &c. (and was, I believe, to a certain degree, that of Origen) that the stars are moved and directed by intelligences or angels who preside over them. Among other passages from Scripture in support of this notion, they cite those words of the Book of Job, 'When the morning stars sang together' (132).

Here, credibility becomes a problem. How and when did the angel assume a human form? Why did he consider doing so? Apparently, differences allure. Heavenly splendor is beautiful--but static. The angel's position in the heavens gives him an unfair advantage (as is the case with the "Watchers" in Enoch); while Lea can observe celestial beauty only infrequently, the angel is both privy and attracted to the movements and changes of embodied beauty. He will too soon learn about this sort of beauty firsthand. The angel must watch Lea merge with a star--a form of physical union symbolizing that which he has been denied; Moore's note permits our inference that this angel may well be aware that he has enabled her to unite physically with some other presiding "intelligence or angel" from his native region. The cosmos have mulcted him.

Not only do we feel sympathy with the angel, forced to watch Lea in symbolic coitus (himself doomed eternally to the pains of unrequited love), we pity him also because she rather coldly uses him to effect her own ontogenic rise. He tells her that mortals may not hear the "mystic word," and yet she pleads with him to reveal it. She shows no gratitude towards the angel whose debasement allows her elevation. He laments that she cast only one pitying look towards earth--and this, he admits, he may have merely imagined (407-410). His punishment seems excessive, for his physiological and psychological make-up render him understandably susceptible to visual allure.

The "Second Angel's Story" also warns of the potential dangers of coldly manipulating another's love. In this tale, however, both the angel, Rubi, and his mortal lover, Lilis, become victims. Rubi, originally the callous manipulator, must suffer eternally the pain of loss, a torment he would never have envisioned possible for him to need--or to be able--to endure. Further, Rubi's pride in his elevated stature helps effect his eternal devastation. Originally, Rubi chooses Lilis as a sort of laboratory rat for his research on the nature of women. Among Eve's daughters, he looks for

Some *one*, from out that shining throng,
Some abstract of the form and mind
Of the whole matchless sex, from which,
In my own arms beheld, possest,
I might learn all the powers to witch,
To warm, and (if my fate unblest
Would have it) ruin, of the rest! (743-749.)

His intentions prove jaded from the outset; Lilis does not initially attract him for her own allure, but rather promises to teach him what he need know in order to undo her sex. (He seems unaware that this goal fails to become an angel, and that his play with "Eve's daughters" would be better left to Eve's sons. Qur'anic parallels in fact condemn Rubi--parallels to Sura 2, "The Heifer," in which Alla demands that the angels "Worship Adam," upon which "they *all* worshipped *him*, except Eblis, *who* refused, and was puffed up with pride, and became of the *number* of unbelievers." (Sale 5-6) Here, the mortal, rather than the angel, undergoes the most dramatic lapse.)[7]

However, having used his celestial powers to manipulate her emotions (864-879), Rubi loses his detached objectivity. Lilis becomes more than an "abstract of the form and mind" of woman to him, and he is trapped by his emotions into a fatal love affair. Love between mortals and angels is not, per se, explicitly prohibited in this particular tale. The downfall of the lovers, as in the tragedy of the first angel, results from Rubi's revealing to a mortal that which only celestial beings may know. In this case, however, the revelation is visual, not verbal. The results for Lilis--far from the taxonomic elevation Lea enjoys--become dissolution and perdition. So intense is his love for Lilis that, despite "some dark misgivings," he realizes that he cannot deny her plea to

> 'Let me but once feel the frame
> 'Of those spread wings, the very pride
> 'Will change my nature, and this frame
> 'By the mere touch be deified' (1310-1313).

The first part of her prophecy comes to pass, but, tragically, not the second. Rubi has, of course, appeared to her in other forms. After her request, however, he recalls that

> All I could bring of heaven's array,
> Of that rich panoply of charms
> A Cherub moves in, on the day
> Of his best pomp, I now put on;
> And, proud that in her eyes I shown
> Thus glorious, glided to her arms.

In his embrace, however, she dissolves into ashes, this form of death underscoring the taxonomic incompatibility of mortal dust and angelic light. Rubi's remorse proves endless. He has killed the one he loves, and, further, knows she will suffer eternal damnation. (1477-83) In a sense, Rubi and Lilis deserve blame for pride--if we are in a particularly condemnatory mood. However, the harshness of the punishments (Lilis's eternal damnation; Rubi's eternal guilt and remorse) hardly suits the transgression. As we have seen, Rubi himself questions the justness of God in so condemning Lilis. As we have also seen, we cannot quite be certain how much, or even whether, God causes Lilis' specific transformation. If so, God's love exacts much. Once one breaks one of His rules, God strikes out in vicious and unending revenge. If not--if Lilis' metamorphosis transpires because of some laws of nature encoded into creation (laws prescribing that if "X does Y then Z happens to X")--creation is flawed; surely some failsafe mechanism is wanted so that lovers about to consign themselves to perdition will receive absolute and unequivocal warnings.

Rubi's nobility, revealed in his willingness to sacrifice himself for his lover, renders his romantic attachment to Lilis much more attractive than the so called divine love exhibited through the decreed lovers' doom. In a sense, the inalterability of Rubi's nature seals his doom. In fact, if we accept Rubi's assertion that woman is by nature driven by "(what I durst not blame, / For 'tis my own) that wish to know, / Sad, fatal zeal, so sure of woe," Lilis's similar hunger remains insatiable, both angel and mortal haunted by "the wish to know--that endless thirst," "Which ev'n by quenching is awak'd" (568-569). This appetite constitutes both the essence and substance of Rubi's being, for he is a cherub, as noted before, "one of those bright creatures nam'd / Spirits of knowledge" (465-467). (Croly's discussion of Haruth and Maruth comes to mind. In the Qur'an--as in the legends derived from it--these angels possess forbidden knowledge.)

Lilis suits as a mortal counterpart. She reveals her similar hunger when she calls out to Rubi, who has, at the time of her plea, only appeared in her dreams, that

> 'There's nothing bright above, below,
> 'In sky--earth--ocean, that this breast
> 'Dost not intensely burn to know,
> 'And thee, thee, thee, o'er all the rest!
> (921-924.)

She willingly offers to play prostitute if knowledge be her payment, or, if the still unknown being prefers, she will act the adoring suppliant and worshipper ("come, oh Spirit, from behind / The curtains of thy radiant home, / Whether thou wou'd'st as God be shrin'd, / Or lov'd and clasp'd as mortal, come!'," 925-929). Not only will she offer any form of love, she does not care what kind of being this unknown creature might be:

> 'Demon or God, who hold'st the book
> 'Of knowledge spread beneath thine eye,
> 'Give me, with thee, but one bright look
> 'Into its leaves, and let me die!' (933-936.)

The first-person complaints of the first two angels seem bound to draw more sympathy than the final tale, which "grav'd / Upon the tablets that, of old, / By Cham were from the deluge sav'd" (1642-1644). As already established above, the third tale involves a seraph, Zaraph, and Nama, his beloved mortal lover. We hardly see Zaraph at all. He responds immediately when he hears Nama call for him. On his face, "Though faded like the others, grief / Had left a gentler, holier trace; / As if, ev'n yet, through sin and ill, / Hope had not quit him" (1562-1566). In general, the imagery proves far less sensuous in this third tale, itself somewhat less engaging as a poem. Zaraph and Nama are not as well drawn as the other angels and mortals. They are generally described in abstract terms--are known for their 'humility,' 'piety,' 'faithfulness.'

We learn that Zaraph fell in heaven after forsaking divine love for his feelings for a mortal. Zaraph once numbered among the seraphs, "Spirits, of pure flame / That round the Almighty Throne abide-- / Circles of light . . . , / First and immediate near the throne, / As if peculiarly God's own" (1649-1651; 1658-1659). Among the seraphs, Zaraph's love was exemplary:

Love was to him impassioned soul
Not, as with others, a mere part
Of its existence, but the whole--
The very life-breath of his heart!
(1670-1674.)

(The neoplatonic image of a "circle of light" verges towards the Crashavian baroque when Moore implants a physical "heart".) Eventually, however, he became bored with the pure, static, all-consuming love of God, and he lapsed from "loving much," to "loving wrong" (1709-1710). From "the bright things above the moon, / Down to earth's beaming eyes" he moved (1713-1714). His "love for the Creator soon / In passion for the Creature ended!" (1715-1716.)

After hearing Nama's song, and seeing her pious devotion, he falls in love with this woman whose eyes shone radiant as if they were "rather given / To be ador'd than to adore--." He remains uncertain "when at last he fell" in love "To which attraction, to which spell, / Love, Music, or Devotion, most / His soul in that sweet hour was lost" (1791-1793).

These lovers do, however, sanctify their love "Before religion's altar," where they become, as previously noted, "Two hearts in wedlock's golden tie / Self-pledg'd, in love to live and die" (1796-1798). Presumably because they perform their own marriage, the seraph's transgression seems minor. Heaven apparently blesses those lovers who endure a bit of misery, for this couple earns more blessing because the participants feel guilty about their love. ("For gentle was their love, with awe / And trembling like a treasure kept, / That was not their by holy law, / Whose beauty with remorse they saw," 1818-21). Decreed to stay together until time's end, they will be subject to domestic quarrels, but will also have "moments rich in happiness" in earth, and, of course, throughout eternity (1896). The narrator stresses their singularity. They are the "*one* such pair below," "whose piety is love," whose love,

> Though close as 'twere their souls' embrace,
> Is not of earth, but from above--
> Like two fair mirrors, face to face,
> Whose light, from one to the'other thrown,
> Is heaven's reflection, not their own
> (1940-1945).

As in Byron's poem, divine/human unions can end happily--if statically, in Moore's case--for their participants. (Owen would not see this as a happy ending; he and his socialist reformers deem marriage enslavement-- presumably unendurable in its duration were it to last throughout all time.) Zaraph, through pious earthly love, can reascend to assume his celestial body and partake of divine love once his punishment is over, that is, when time ceases to be. (In this, he recalls Lamartine's Cedar, who will gradually reascend.) Nama conquers mortality through this union, ontogenic elevation hers to be enjoyed, too, after the end of time. In *The Loves of the Angels*, interspeciation brings on varied punishments, and the act ranges from a severe transgression to a relatively insignificant infringement of cosmic law, depending upon the attitudes of the lovers involved, and upon the lovers' observance of (or failure to observe) certain sanctifying rituals.

All three tales underscore the theme of love as a transforming power. Mortals can exchange clay for celestial nature (almost immediately in Lea's case, whose good fortune it is to be more beloved than loving); angels can be denigrated, transformed into mortals (for once Lea's angel lover is stripped of most features of celestial nature, the vestige that remains--his immortality--becomes a curse, Lea now immortal, eternally unreachable, unattainable, and not interested in the wingless angel). Love can also equalize unlike natures (especially in the case of Nama, who looks forward to the end of time with Zaraph). Physical transformations of both mortals and angels, of course, can be taken as symbols of corresponding rises or falls of individual participants in ill-or well-matched love affairs; hence an angel's fate can be directly applicable to the human situation.

The Loves of the Angels appears to forbid unauthorized unions, although whether the angels and mortals are to be taken as socially, racially, or otherwise segregated humans remains open to question. The message garbles; "one" such forbidden union alone among all such unions ever entered has earned God's sanction. If granted human applicability, Moore's tale becomes prohibitive; norms and statutes take precedence over passions. We have difficulty, however, asserting that Moore's *Loves* applies to humankind at all. French intellectual/religious tradition would sanction its applicability, however--Lammenais defining love as a unifying principle that God threads throughout all nature. Similarly, Lamartine attempts to present a systematized pattern of love, integral with the dynamic nature of creation, the whole undergoing a process of ascent, or evolution, in which he places hope--a hope conveyed through the prophecy of Cedar's ascent, a hope directly applicable to humankind. (George 42) Moore possibly had the same end in mind--or more probably, was likely to have been perceived as verging towards this end when he was met with such warmth in France. *The Loves of the Angels*, read in the context of French thought, does do more than vaguely titillate with some sensuous, if not really graphic, imagery. Moore offers hope for the redemption of humankind.

Moore's revisions for his fifth edition leave unaltered the central informing concepts of the original text. Some of the sensuality is excised-- although much remains. Rubi's passion burns with as much intensity as in the first edition. The "eastern" version (fifth edition) in actuality provides Moore with a chance to emend stylistic infelecities as much as to transfer cosmogonic settings. Although Moore's "First Angel's Story" in the revised edition has been compared to Croly's *The Angel of the World*, the similarities remain superficial, Moore unable to hide behind the Qur'an, despite its service to Croly as a protective shield against charges of blasphemy.

When Moore revises *The Loves of the Angels* by superimposing Qur'anic trappings, he fails to assuage the outraged--who too easily see the parallels, and for whom these borrowings only serve to overburden the three-part Ovidian erotic epyllion with arcane detail and cumbersome documentation. As was earlier noted, Moore revised his *Angels* quickly, relying upon Herbelot and other standard references, his transformations largely perfunctory, the dynamics and ends of the love affairs virtually unchanged. Moore's revisions are of three general sorts--textual emenda-tions, additions to (and deletions from) his notes, and revisions to his Preface.

Moore's textual emendations--emendations and excisions--aim to appease piety, rendering the poem suitable for a mass audience (including acquaintances' daughters.) Of more interest are his emendations to his notes; he deletes notes from the first edition, his substitutions sometimes establishing a clearly Qur'anic framework for his narrative, sometimes designing either to divest the text of possible Christian overtones or to detail the Islamic topography he would have newly envisioned. Finally, revisions to his preface de-emphasize the--probably apocryphal--biographical circumstances of the poem's composition and instead, at least in places, offer rare glimpses into Moore's philosophical predilections: he reflects notions consonant with Byron's beliefs in an aprioristically apprehended First Cause and in an immortality divorced from Christian materialism; at times, too, Moore's contemplations about the nature of being, when compared to similar assertions in his prose narrative, *The Epicurean*, suggest that he entertains, occasionally, neoplatonic notions about the pre-existence of the soul reminiscent of Wordsworth's neoplatonic play in the latter's Immortality Ode.

Far from enduring the castrator's hatchet as Byron dreaded, Moore's angels survive conversion barely altered. The bulk of Moore's textual emendations entail perfunctory substitutions of proper names or nominal phrases: "Alla" replaces "God" (455/439, 1095/1075, 1497/1442, 1659/1603), "Lord" (30), "th'Eternal" (372/356), and "He," pronoun for *God* (503/482); "God" becomes "Creation" (555/534), "Heaven," (1124/1104, 1315/1278, 1423/1375), or "Power" (1497/1469, 1814 /1754), lapsing at one point into passivity, when "Paradise," "which God made solely" (672) simply "sprung there solely" (651).[8] "Heaven" (152) becomes "Gehim" (156)--but only once. "Lucifer" transforms into "Eblis" (380/364). In short, the text reveals obvious, predictable exchanges, made with less than scrupulous regularity. These emendations establish the revised narrative as Qur'anic in its mythological framework.

Other changes in diction may reflect doctrinal as well as mythological considerations. God as an "Avenging Power" (1474) becomes a "Great vengeful Power" (1420); the exclamatory "Oh God!" calms down into "Such pains" (1327/1290); "damn" becomes "ruin" (740/719)--a gentler fate; "My bright twin sister" becomes less incestuous as "A bright twin sister" (813/792). Other alterations have no clear explanation--as when the "Eternal Center" becomes an "Unclouded Center" (1652/1596); when "Cham" becomes "Seth" (1644/1588); when "tender light" becomes the "mystic light's" (902/881); or when "golden clusters" become "sunny clusters" (942/921).

The first four editions unfold the three angels' tales in 1951 lines, the fifth and subsequent editions requiring only 1891. Towards the opening of the narrative, lines added to the fifth edition affiliate the "Three noble youths [who] conversing lay" (both versions) with their new, Qur'anic brotherhood of angels fallen from Alla's heaven:

> Spirits, who once, in brotherhood
> Of faith and bliss near ALLA stood,
> And o'er whose cheeks full oft had blown
> The wind that breathes from ALLA's throne" (29-33);

the three otherwise remain identical to their Judaeo-Christian predecessors:

> Creatures of light, such as still play,
> Like motes in sunshine round the Lord
> And through their infinite array
> Transmit each moment, night and day,
> The echo of His luminous word! (29-33/34-37)

Formerly, both trios served pseudo-Aquinian functions of incessantly transmitting Divinity not through words but merely through being, "being" for these angels entailing their manifestations of parts of God's nature and will.

Excised lines and passages sometimes reflect doctrinal considerations, sometimes deference to--more accurately, defense against--atrophied, conservative sensibilities.[9] An excision of the first sort--lines 1799-1802 in the first four editions--is necessitated more by the appended note than by the lines themselves. The passage appears after Zaraph and Nama have "Before religion's altar," "in wedlock's golden tie / Self-pledg'd, in love to live and die" (1796-98/1740-42). This wedding ceremony in the unrevised editions leads to the narrator's assertion that

> Then first did woman's virgin brow
> That hymeneal chaplet wear,
> Which when it dies, no second vow
> Can bid a new one bloom out there--(1799-1802).

Moore's note explains that

> In the Catholic church, when a widow is married, she is not, I believe, allowed to wear flowers on her head. The ancient Romans, honoured with a "corona pudicitiae," or crown of modesty, those who entered but once into the marriage state. (147)

This note links the passage to a specific credal affiliation--despite the fact that the narrative takes place well before Mosaic Law, let alone Church structures and creeds prevail. Further, through its reference to Roman custom, the note blurs distinctions between Christian and Roman (pagan) practices. Eliminating the note might have alone sufficed; the floral crown-- and the four lines--leave without detriment to the fifth edition.

If Moore's excisions remain largely inexplicable, this likely stems from the fact that some are prescribed by private consultants, rather than published critics. Moore seldom emends passages offending reviewers; Lady Barbara Donegal's concern for the innocence of her niece Barbara probably had at least as much to do with deletions from the first edition as had edicts by Jeffrey, Wilson, and the like. (Fortunately, the elder Barbara Donegal remains unconcerned with her own innocence, affording herself permission to read the *Loves*.) In response to the published charge that Moore's angels are men, the poet does give his celestial beings less sensuality to fall prey to. Rubi's ecstasy at the beauty of Lilis diminishes when Moore excises the angel's recollections that

> There seem'd a freshness in her breath,
> Beyond the reach, the power of death;
> And then, her voice--oh, who could doubt
> That 'twould for ever thus breathe out
> A music, like the harmony
> Of the tun'd orbs, two sweet to die!
> While in her lip's awakening touch
> There thrill'd a life ambrosial--such
> As mantles in the fruit steep'd through
> With Eden's most delicious dew--
> Till I could almost think, though known
> And lov'd as human, they had grown
> By bliss, celestial as my own! (1200-12)

Moore's Islamic Rubi never confirms that he "lov'd as human" (that is, sexually) his paramour, nor mistakes human for celestial beauty.[10] The emended Rubi is denied traces of his celestial origin marking the initial portrait, which displays

> A breathing forth of beams at will,
> Of living beams, which, though no more
> They kept their early lustre, still

Were such, when glittering out all o'er,
As mortal eye-lids wink'd before.

This "glittering" (lines 460-64) does not survive the revision. The first angel loses some of his capacity for impassioned self-condemnation and self-pity when, in the fifth edition, he no longer emphasizes that he has committed

The sin, of all, most sure to blight,
The sin, of all, that the soul's light
Is soonest lost, extinguish'd in!
That, though but frail and human, she
Should, like the half-bird of the sea,
Try with her wing sublimer air,
While I, a creature born up there,
Should meet her, in my fall from light,
From heaven and peace, and turn her flight
Downward again, with me to drink
Of the salt tide of sin, and sink! (198-211)

Emendations similarly lessen either passion and intensity, or sensuality-- as when "Suddenly, sprung within her breast-- / Like a young bird, when day-light breaking / Startles him from his dreamy nest," becomes the less evocative, "At length, as though some livelier thought / Had suddenly her fancy caught," her breast emended out of view (1253-55/1217-18); intensity decreases when "God's sublimest secrets" become merely "Alla's grandest secrets" (455/439)-- "sublime" outsoaring "grand," regardless of the Godhead's doctrinal origins.[11]

As noted already, of far more interest than his revisions to the text proper is his revised apparatus--despite the scorn accorded his notes by one reviewer for their omissions, and by another for their very presence. Through Moore's revised notes we gain some insights into Moore's infrequent ventures into philosophy--ventures about which he remains disarmingly silent even in his journals and letters. The sorts of additions Moore makes--especially viewed in light of his text and notes to his prose *Epicurean*--show him contemplating ideas about immortality and God not unlike Byron's, Moore and Byron both drawing from reason--in a sense of the term suggesting "innate ideas," pre-Cartesian (platonic) notions that impel belief in a creator, and a faith eschewing revelation. At times, Moore's reflections about faith seem predicated on a hope far too optimis-tic for Byron, namely, a hope--similar to Vigny's--in a new age, an age in which all will share one universal faith, a faith which will enhance social harmony. (In this, Moore reminds us of the Owenite chiliasts.) In addition, Moore's notes once again underscore his comfort with syncretism, his Qur'anic notes--drawn largely from Herbelot, Sale, and Prideaux--conceptually as comfortable to him as his Judaeo-Christian apparatus in the first edition. Problems arise, in fact, when he allows too much of this syncretism to eclipse the Qur'anic mythic framework. (Such is particularly the case when he imports extensive references to the *Zend-Avesta* and to Rabbinical commentaries.) Moore does succeed, for the most part, in divesting his poem of explicitly Judaeo-Christian references--although substitutions would not satisfy evangelicalism or uncritical orthodoxy, whose ignorance about angelology, and its demise as an active force in Christianity, accounts for ill-grounded objections to *The Loves of the Angels*. For these readers, any angels from any mythic scheme prove unacceptable for love poetry.

Moore's revised apparatus provides his clearest means of converting from a Judaeo-Christian to an Islamic framework. He eliminates most notes from his first edition referring explicitly and solely to the Bible or to Patristic commentators or later Christian theologians--as, for example, the note exploring Tertullian's, Clement of Alexandria's, and Chrysostom's discussion of 1 Corinthians 11.10---Paul's insistence that women remain veiled (132); he omits Suarez on Lucifer in Revelation 12.4 (133); he similarly excises Dionysious' commentary on "the manner in which God's ray is communicated, first to the Intelligences near him, and then to those more remote" (146). He does retain portions of the notes pertaining both to the Bible and the Qur'an. Such is the case with the notes appended to his "Man's" calling Eve "his Life! his Life!" (text-707/688). In the revised version, the note merely explains that "Chavah, or, as it is in Arabic, Havah (the name by which Adam called the woman after their transgression), means 'Life'." (538) In the first edition, the note begins with a different etymology: "Chavah (or, as it is in the Latin version, Eva) has the same signification for the Greek, *Zoe*," the commentary trailing into a long discussion of commentators, including "Epiphanius, among others," who are "not a little surprised at the application of such a name to Eve, so immediately too, after that awful denunciation of death, 'dust thou art, &c. &c'," Epiphanius' compared with opinions of Pererius, the Bishop of Chalon, Pierre Bayle, and Gateker (138-40). By changing his references, Moore emphasizes inadvertently that much Islamic material derives from the Bible, and that the Bible as well as the Qur'an remain subject to the syncretistic compilation through which distinctions between living religions and old, dead mythologies become blurred.

This comparison pertains only to those readers interested in comparing Moore's revision to his first edition (as some of his reviewers are). For those approaching the fifth edition unfamiliar with the first, the note places Eve firmly within a Qur'anic framework. Other of Moore's notes in his revision even more clearly direct attention towards the Qur'an. For example, that Lilis "durst not see" Rubi's form is authenticated by Moore's note reporting that "'Mohammed (says Sale), though a prophet, was not able to bear the sight of Gabriel, when he appeared in his proper form, much less would others be able to support it'." (546) "Gehim's pit" (156) in the revision is glossed by the note explaining that this is "the name given by the Mahometans to the infernal regions, over which, they say, the angel Tabhek presides." The note continues with what seems to be extraneous detail:

> By the seven gates of hell, mentioned in the Koran, the commentators understand seven different departments or wards, in which seven different sorts of sinners are to be punished. The first, called Gehennem, is for sinful Mussulmans; the second, Ladha, for Christian offenders; the third, Hothama, is appointed for Jews; and the fourth and fifth, called Sair and Sacar, are destined to receive the Sabaeans and the worshippers of fire; in the sixth, named Gehim, those pagans and idolaters who admit a plurality of gods are placed; while into the abyss of the seventh, called Derek Asfal, or the Deepest, the hypocritical canters of *all* religions are thrown. (533)

Besides its implication that the first angel would, but for a look from Lea, gladly admit himself into Gehim (the proper, sixth, realm here, for the angel does constitute an idolater when he worships a mortal), this information --vaguely recalling Dante--wants pertinence. Moore may well have included it for its ironic implications for Theodore Hook and others who charge him with blasphemy, the poet wishing to include them among the lowest of the fallen, the "hypocritical canters of *all* religions," in particular, those assailing Moore's faith.

As remarked above, Moore's first note to his revision places his poem clearly within an Islamic framework--as well as suggesting a universal faith sought by Lamartine and by the Owenite reformers--by the poet's adding a gloss to his fifth edition drawn from Herbelot:

> The Mahometans believe, says D'Herbelot, that in that early period of the world, humans had but one sole religion, and were frequent-

ly visited by angels, who gave their hands to them (aided them).[12]

This reverence for a universal faith--uncluttered by sectarian controversy (although admittedly itself controversial as soon as the Owenite chiliasts call for it)--receives Moore's benediction once again in his prose narrative, *The Epicurean*, also a product of the 1820's. In Chapter 17, the hermit prophesies the coming of a perfected, spiritually unified society on earth, after an impending eschatological event:

> 'Such,' continued the Hermit, . . 'was the last crowning dispensa-
> tion of that God of benevolence, in whose hands sin and death are
> but instruments of everlasting good, and who, through apparent
> evil and temporary retribution, bringing all things "out of the
> darkness into his marvellous light," proceeds watchfully and
> unchangingly to the great, final object of his providence--the
> restoration of the whole human race to purity and happiness!'
> (MPW 742)

As it is in the beginning of *The Loves of the Angels*--a world untainted by sin or disharmony--so it shall be in the end, according to the Hermit. Moore's note to this prophecy further idealizes the universal religion for which he maintains hope--in the *Loves*, aided by Herbelot:

> This benevolent doctrine--which not only goes far to solve the
> great problem of moral and physical evil, but which would, if
> received more generally, tend to soften the spirit of uncharitable-
> ness, so fatally prevalent among Christian sects--was maintained by
> that great light of the early Church, Origen, and has not wanted
> supporters among more modern Theologians. (MPW 742-43n)

Moore's hope for an eschatological event effecting earthly harmony provides, as well, a solution to the problem of theodicy--Moore again allied with Vigny in his thinking about an oncoming catastrophe. He names Tillotson, Paley, and Newton among others who share his "amiable doctrine" that a nonsectarian faith was to come, and adds to his notes comments suggesting that this universalism in religion constitutes a platonic, innate idea:

> See also *Magee on Atonement*, where the doctrine of the advocates
> of Universal Restoration is thus briefly, and, I believe, fairly ex-

plained:--'Beginning with the existence of an infinitely powerful, wise, and good Being, as the first and fundamental principle of rational religion, they pronounce the essence of this Being to be love, and from this infer, as a demonstrable consequence, that none of the creatures formed by such a being will ever be made eternally miserable.... Since God (they say) would act unjustly in inflicting eternal misery for temporary crimes the sufferings of the wicked can be remedial, and will terminate in a complete purification from moral disorder, and in their ultimate restoration to virtue and happiness.

(742-43 and n). (This comment--a rare glimpse at Moore's religious thinking--in its rejection of the insufferability of "eternal misery" awaiting perpetrators of "temporary crimes" recalls Byron's 1821 Journal, in which the latter doubts Revelation, determining retributive justice unworthy of a God.) Here, we see Moore attuned to the ideas propounded by Deistic faith in the idea of God, complemented by an innate idea--as opposed to a revelation--that a change is at hand. (In averting belief in revelation Moore resembles Byron.) Despite his nominal affiliation with the Roman Catholic Church, in orientation, he proves chiliast/universalist--again, in the tradition of Owenite chiliasts.[13] This note, and this hope--far more than either version of his *Loves of the Angels*--provides substance for objections by evangelical as well as Anglican orthodoxy; it is interesting that in his first note to his revised *Loves*, he leaves in French the line in Herbelot propounding that prior to corruption, universalism in religion prevailed. (While the French would not dissuade the educated reader from gleaning insight into Moore's preferences, it would at least distance that readership termed "below the public" from besieging him with emotion-wrought rejoinders spawned from evangelicalistic fervor and uncritical faith.)

In *The Loves of the Angels*, Moore divests "purgatory" of any alliance to Roman Catholicism by referring to the realm

Called by the Musselmans Al Araf--a sort of wall or partition which, according to the 7th chapter of the Koran, separates hell from paradise, and where they, who have not merits sufficient to gain them immediate admittance into heaven, are supposed to stand for a certain period, alternately tantalized and tormented by the sights that are on either side presented to them.[14] (541)

While divorcing purgatory from Roman Catholicism, another of Moore's

Islamic interpolations adds a touch of controversy to his revision, when the poet calls upon Pococke as a commentator upon Rubi's fate--"That I must still live on, when she / Would," the angel aware that he has murdered his beloved. "Pococke," Moore explains, " . . . gives it as the opinion of the Mahometan doctors, that all souls, not only of men and of animals, living either on land or in the sea, but of the angels also, must necessarily taste of death" (543). Christian mortalism--favored by Tyndale, Luther, and Milton --comes to mind in this note, despite its immediate pertinence to Islam.

    Moore's revised Preface reveals a number of philosophical inclinations reflecting Moore's awareness of discussions current in his age. (Again, the philosophical Moore proves rare.) Any direct influence by Croly upon the revised *Loves* remains conjectural, although Moore does turn for his first tale to the same source Croly claims. He names this source in his revised Preface: "the Eastern story of the angels Harut and Marut, and the Rabbinical fictions of the loves of Uzziel and Shamechazai, are the only sources to which I need refer, for the origin of the notion on which this Romance is founded" (530). (Gone is Moore's account of his supposed literary rivalry with Byron.) Immediately following this new named source is the suggested method of interpretation--allegorical--that stood without any Qur'anic references as the third and final paragraph to the original Preface:

> In addition to the fitness of the subject for poetry, it struck me also as capable of affording an allegorical medium, through which might be shadowed out (as I have endeavored to do in the following stories) the fall of the Soul from its original purity--the loss of light and happiness which it suffers, in the pursuit of this world's perishable pleasures--and the punishments, both from conscience and Divine justice, with which impurity, pride, and presumptuous inquiry into the awful secrets of Heaven God" in the first four editions] are sure to be visited. The beautiful story of Cupid and Psyche owes its chief charm to this sort of 'veiled meaning,' and it has been my wish however I may have failed in the attempt) to communicate to the following pages the same *moral* interest (MPW 530).[15]

To this notion of the descent of the soul Moore appends a reference to Macrobius--to "the account which Macrobius gives of the downward journey of the Soul, through that gate of the Zodiac which opens into the lower spheres," which Moore finds "a curious specimen of the wild fancies that passed for philosophy in ancient times." (MPW 530) (Moore's philosophy, as this revised Preface suggests, is not completely alien to Macrobius'-- save for the topographical details Macrobius assigns.) He continues by explaining that

> In the system of Manes, the luminous or spiritual principle owes its corruption not to any evil tendency of its own, but to a violent inroad of the spirits of darkness, who, finding themselves in the neighborhood of this pure light, and becoming passionately enamoured of its beauty, break the boundaries between them, and take forcible possession of it. (530)

This latter reference, attributed by Moore to the Abbe Foucher's *De La-Religion des Persees*, in *Memoires de l'Academie* 31: 456, tends to exonerate Lilis in the second tale, "enamoured" of the "beauty" of the "pure light" of her beloved. Moore's philosophical statement may provide a gloss upon the "Second Angel's Story"; the Preface may stand as a pretext for philosophical exposition. How firmly--or permanently--Moore may have held the philosophical notions expressed in the Preface remains equivocal. The significance of the essay is in its exposition of some of the philosophies popular among contemporary English and French poets.

Moore's second paragraph to his revised Preface recalls Wordsworth's discussion of the soul in the latter's *Ode:Intimations of Immortality* (1802-4, 1807), in which Wordsworth plays with--but does not promulgate, he insists--the notion of a pre-existent soul. Wordsworth deviates from Plato's *Phaedo* 73-77 in presuming that the apprehension of the glorious and eternal only gradually declines after birth. Neither does Wordsworth seem to posit the hope of the individual soul's return to its originating oneness with the divine.[16] Moore's understanding of this doctrine presumes such a return:

> Among the doctrines, or notions, derived by Plato from the East, one of the most natural and sublime is that which inculcates the pre-existence of the soul, and its gradual descent into this dark material world, from that region of spirit and light which it is supposed to have once inhabited, and to which, after a long lapse of purification and trial, it will return (MPW 530).

Because his first angel loses physical wings, the creature's plight remains hopeless (although Lamartine's Cedar retains hope for eventual regeneration after undergoing a similar metamorphosis). Again, Moore's comments may help us evaluate his angels and mortals, and/or may show us Moore's metaphysical inclinations.

With Wordsworth, Moore contradicts Plato's notion of the immediate obliviation of the originating glory upon the soul's birth; unlike Wordsworth, Moore relies on the authority of oriental doctrines, rather than the authority of the individual human heart. The Hierophant in Moore's *The Epicurean* recalls Wordsworth's reflections perhaps even more strongly than does Moore's Preface:

> this Hierophant expounded to me . . . [about] the preexistence of the soul--of its abode, from all eternity, in a place of splendor and bliss, of which whatever we have most beautiful in our conceptions here is but a dim transcript, a clouded remembrance. (MPW 708)

The priest continues with a "History of the Soul," about which Moore notes that "in the original construction of this work, there was an episode introduced here (which I have since published in a more extended form), illustrating the doctrine of the fall of the soul by the Oriental fable of the Loves of the Angels." Moore reiterates in *The Epicurean* that he intends for his *Loves* an allegorical sense. His Priest's description of the soul's hope for reascent recalls Wordsworth's "clouds of glory":

> 'To retrieve this ruin of this once blessed Soul--to clear away from around her the clouds of earth, and, restoring her lost wings, facilitate their return to Heaven--such,' said the reverend man, 'is the great task of our religion, and such the triumph of those divine Mysteries, in whose inmost depths the life and essence of that holy religion lie treasured. However sunk and changed and clouded may be the Spirit, yet as long as a single trace of her original light remains, there is still hope (MPW 709)

The perfectibility of the individual--and of humankind through the collect of individuals--again recalls the Owenite chiliast faith that each harbors the Messiah within.

At some points in the Preface, Moore's argument seems deliberately diversionary. Such is the case after his discussion of the neoplatonic ascent of the soul. Moore, for several lines, relates material taking us further and further away from this notion--and further and further away from Moore's text. Moore finds that "the mythology of the Persians has allegorized the same doctrine, in the history of those genii of light who strayed from their dwellings in the stars and obscured their original nature by mixture with this material sphere." (530) In actuality, this differs markedly from the Platonic notion of descent, verging upon the Judaeo-Christian lore surrounding Genesis 6.2, in which the commingling of unlike natures results in monstrous births and world-judgment. Moore adds still another--altogether different--myth, attempting to connect Platonism, Zoroastrianism, and ancient Egyptian beliefs: "the-Egyptians," he claims, "connecting it [the "lapse" into "this dark material world"] with the descent and ascent of the sun in the zodiac, considered Autumn as emblematic of the Soul's decline towards darkness and the reappearance of Spring as its Chief return to life and light." (530) This has absolutely nothing to do with the platonic or Zoroastrian legends, for this Egyptian notion is seasonal, cyclical, and, as such, inevitable. In the other legends, the possibility remains that the trial of purification may fail. Either Moore goes too far in his syncretism, or he would not have his reader come too close to his thinking.

The two paragraphs ensuing have absolutely no bearing on the previous discussion, and are the sole portions of the Preface devoted to the Qur'an, save for the reference to the legend of Harut and Marut, which itself actually comes from the Kalim (commentaries on the Qur'an), not from the brief reference to the angels in Islam's sacred text:

> Besides the chief spirits of the Mahometan heaven, such as Gabriel the angel of Revelation, Israfil by whom the last trumpet is to be sounded, and Azazel the angel of death, there were also a number of subaltern intelligences, of which tradition has preserved the names, appointed to preside over the different stages of ascents, into which the celestial world was supposed to be divided.

Here, Moore refers to the Koran, 41: "Then he set his mind to *the creation of heaven*; and it was smoke: and he said unto it, and to the earth, Come, either obediently, or against your will." After this, "they answered, We come obedient *to thy command*. And he formed them into seven heavens, in two days; and revealed unto every heaven its office. And he adorned the lower heaven with lights, and *placed therein a guard of angels*" (Sale 464). Clearly, by highlighting these passages, Moore risks acknowledging that the Bible, the intertestamental Book of Enoch, and biblical commentators as standard as Aquinas draw celestial maps reminiscent of this Qur'anic one. (Moore quotes an emended version of the final sentence only; "we" substitutes for "he" in Moore's reading.) Moore continues with lore surrounding this division:

> Thus Kelail governs the fifth heaven; while Sadiel, the presiding
> spirit of the third, is also employed in steadying the motions of the
> earth which would be in a constant state of agitation if this angel
> did not keep his foot planted upon its orb. (530)

In these latter assignments, Moore draws upon extra-canonical legend. He
adds that "Among the miraculous interpositions in favor of Mahomet we
find commemorated in the pages of the Koran the appearance of five
thousand angels on his side at the battle of Bedr." (530) The text Moore
refers to is the Qur'an, Chapter 3, "And God had already given you the
victory and Bedr, when ye were inferior *in number*, therefore fear God, that
ye may be thankful," for "Verily if ye persevere, and fear *God*, and *your
enemies* come upon you suddenly, your LORD will assist you with five
thousand angels, distinguished *by their horses* and attire." (Sale 1: 170). This
Qur'anic angel lore has nothing to do with the notion of the descent of the
pre-existing soul; neither has Moore's following catalogue of Persian and
Syrian angelology, occupying two long paragraphs, ultimately uniting the
"Cherubim in the sphere of the fixed stars," and "the Seraphim . . . , the most
perfect of all celestial creatures," in "the region of those stars which are so
distant as to be imperceptible." (531) The reason for this comparative
angelolgy remains uncertain; his aims seem almost diversionary, as if Moore
wishes to eclipse the legends of Harut and Marut presumably informing his
poem, not to mention the allegory of the soul's descent and regeneration
supposedly conveyed through the narrative.
If Moore does intentionally divert our attention--bombarding us with lists
of angels and their origins--this diversion may be defensive.[17]
    This later (fifth edition) preface closes with Moore's insertion about
the gender of angels:

> The Sabaeans also (as d'Herbelot tells us) had their classes of
> angels, to whom they prayed as mediators, or intercessors; and the
> Arabians worshipped *female* angels, whom they called Benab
> Hasche, or, Daughters of God (MPW 531).

Herbelot finds amplification through Sale, whose "Preliminary Discourse"
reports that "of the angels, or intelligences which they" ("the "ancient
Arabians and Indians") "worshipped," the names of "only three" appear in
"the Koran," all three of "which were worshipped under female names; Allat,

Uzza, and Manah." Sale adds that "These were by them called goddesses, and the daughters of God; an appellation they gave not only their angels, but also their images," the latter of which "they either believed to be inspired by the light of God, or else to become the tabernacles of the angels, and to be animated by them." Hence "they gave them divine worship, because they imagined they interceded for them with God." (Sale 1: 23) From this we see that Vigny's presumed originality in assigning to his angel the female gender (*Éloa*) has ample precedent--as does Éloa's means of creation; Michael, in Qur'anic lore, "formed" the cherubim "from the tears ... [he] shed over the sins of the faithful," a variant of--actually, precedent for--Vigny's creation of Éloa from one of Christ's tears shed over Lazarus' death.

Croly's influence upon Moore remains uncertain. Chew points out similarities between Croly's *Angel* and Moore's first tale in *The Loves of the Angels*. Both limit their originating legend of Haruth and Maruth to the tale of a single angel. Both depict an angel's fatal draught of wine, eventuating revelation of a forbidden word. Moore's angel is attracted by a real woman, Lea, whereas Croly's is duped by Eblis. Chew's parallels do not evince Moore's knowledge of Croly's narrative (*Dramas* 203).

Whatever influence Croly may have had, Moore's reworking of Qur'anic angelology serves different purposes. He claims in his revised Preface that his text pronounces a philosophy of the soul's degeneration and reascent--an idea somewhat more plausibly discernible because of the interpolations in the fifth edition. Through his notes, he reveals his hope for a universal religion--a hope providing hope for his angels, for, after an indefinite eschatological incident, all will be forgiven, as Moore's "reason" tells him in *The Epicurean*, and a new age will operate in the harmonious innocence of the old.

Notes to Chapter 8

[1]In this case, the sacrament of the wedding--remaining secular in Scripture, unappropriated by any Christian establishment until the Council of Trent in 1563 decreed marriage a sacrament to be performed by a priest and attended by two witnesses, Schaff *Creeds* 2: 142. Yet Moore does not adorn Zeraph's bride with any Christian marriage vestment; rather, she wears a crown of flowers adorning virgin brides in Rome.

[2]Moore's Patristic learning was extensive; Tessier points out that he wrote pseudonymous reviews of new editions of Chrysostom and others (438).

[3]Quoted in Jordan, *Upright* 240, from Prothero III: 168. Jordan remarks that "Moore did leave off for the next six years." This review of Boyd's *Fathers* was actually his second attempt at reviewing, his first evaluation appearing in the September, 1814 *Edinburgh Review*, his judgments evolving from his study of the four volumes of *Poetry by Edward, Lord Thurlow*, published in 1813-1814. (Jordan, *Upright* 239)

[4]Moore's footnote proves intrinsically incendiary. Middleton and his *Free Inquiry* appear in an anonymous review of "Berington's Literature of the Middle Ages," in the *Edinburgh Review* 23 (Apr.-Sept. 1814): 229-245. "Nothing," the writer argues, "certainly, can be conceived more wretched, than the lying stories of miracles, the fabulous lives of pretended saints, the degrading conceptions of the Divine Being, and the endless disputes about the most contemptible questions, with which the writings of the early Christians are almost universally filled." These are the "half-pagan" Fathers Moore discusses in his note to his preface to his unrevised *Angels*. The reviewer continues, "Dr. Middleton, accordingly, in the outset of his Free Inquiry, observes,

'In order to free the minds of men from an inveterate imposture, which, through a long succession of ages, has disgraced the religion of the gospel, and tyrannized over the reason and sense of the Christian world, I have shown, by many indisputable facts, that the ancient fathers, by whose authority that delusion was originally imposed . . . were extremely credulous and superstitious; possessed with strong prejudices, and enthusiastic zeal, in favour not only of Christianity in general, but of every particular doctrine which a wild imagination could engraft upon it; and scrupling no art or means by which they might propagate the same principles: in short, that they were of a character from which nothing could be expected that was candid and impartial . . . . And that this was actually the case . . . , we find them roundly affirming as true, things evidently false and fictitious; in order to strengthen, as they fancied, the evidences of gospel, or to serve a present turn of confuting an adversary, or of enforcing a particular point which they were labouring to establish.'"

The writer finds "To the same effect, Dr. Whitby, speaking of Papius, and Irenaeus, those of the Christian writers who were the nearest to the days of the Apostles, say[ing],--'It is very remarkable, that these two earliest writers of the second century, who, on the credit of idle reports, and uncertain fame, have delivered to us, things said to be done by the Apostles and their scholars . . . shamefully imposed upon us, by the forgery of fables, and false stories'." Among these the reviewer highlights "what St. Augustin relates, upon the testimony, he says, of credible persons, 'that at Ephesus, where St. John, the apostle, lay buried, he was not believed to be dead, but to be sleeping only in the grave, which he had provided for himself, till our Lord's second coming; in proof of which, they affirmed, that the earth under which he lay, was seen to heave up and down perpetually, in conformity to the motion of his body in the act of breathing'." The reviewer argues that "When the taste for fabulous legends was somewhat exhausted, that of subtle disputation succeeded." Just as bad as the fables were the manifold permutations of the "beings concerned in the scheme of redemption," the Father, Son, and Holy Spirit fuel that "engendered disputes that had no end." In short, in a review, ostensibly, of Medieval literature, this reviewer herds among the superstitious and uncritically pious not merely the Fathers surrounded by the legends of Greece and Rome, but also a number of Patristic Fathers. Middleton's *Free Inquiry*--not to mention this review--suggest that many Christian traditions and doctrines have been spawned by the conjunction of uncritical minds.

⁵Tessier's designation of *The Loves of the Angels* as a "frame tale" (354) proves apt for the first two tales. The narrator--or a narrator--advances the third tale, changing the nature of our response.

⁶Al-T abari's *Commentary on the Qur'an* (trans. and ed. J. Cooper), includes early Islamic traditions about the angels Harut and Marut linking them to the prohibition against wine and to the possibility of mortal ascent in the form of a star. Al-Tabari (A.D. 839-923) reports a tradition attributed to the Qur'anic commentator Ibn 'Abbas (ca. 617/8-687/8) that makes a

direct connection between these two angels and the prohibition against wine. J. Cooper's translation of Abu Ja-Far Muhammad B. Jarir Al-Tabari's *The Commentary on the Qur'an, Being an Abridged Translation of Jami al-bayan 'an ta'wil ay al-Qur'an* (484-5) has God rendering acleft the Heavens, permitting "His angels" to view His mortals, and their transgressions. When the angels objected to the sins they saw mortals luxuriating in, God warned the angels that were they in the place of the mortals, they would sin in kind. Upon the angels' objecting, the angels elected Harut and Marut, two of their kind, to represent them--in mortal form--upon earth. God assented to their election, permitting them any and all mortal activities, save for stealing, committing adultery, and imbibing.

Not long on earth, Harut and Marut were confronted by a women, Baidhakht by name, so beautiful in her countenance that both wanted to have sex with her immediately. She forbade liaison with either, demanding that before she submitted, both must murder a human being, get drunk, and worship a God other than Allah. The angels refused. Yet one of the angels could not give up the carnal joys he envisioned, and entreated the other to join him in murder. A drunkard walked by; the angels killed him. God was not happy. The angels did all else forbidden to them, and were offered punishment now, or for all eternity. As in all other texts of this sort, they elected present, in lieu of eternal, punishment.

Tabari, in Cooper, attributes to Al-Suddi a related tradition that accounts for mortal ascent (see Cooper 484-5).

Harut and Marut despised human legal rulings. God informed them that mortals were given "'ten carnal desires,'" and that these were the doors through which they were to obey or to disobey divine commands. Harut and Marut entreated Allah to embody them with the same impulses, the two Angels insisted that they would descend to earth, and interact with mortals without transgressing. God assented. The Angels alighted at Babil "in Dunbawand," and traversed the land until evening.

All went well until a woman, al-Zuhara (Venus) met with them; she came to sue her husband; the angels were overcome by her beauty. One of the angels wanted to copulate with her; the other--forgetting the strictures against both--asked his compatriot whether he should tell her directly, or whether he should hide his lust. At this point, he recalled Allah's prohibition, and inquired into God's likely punishment of the pair. The lustful angel did not care. His fellow agreed to care neither. Yet the two approached her with their proposition; she scorned her would-be lover.

In this case, she demanded to know the secret words that would raise her from mortal into angelic status. The angels revealed the secret words.

"She uttered them and ascended; but God made her forget what [words] she could come down with, so she stayed where she was, and God made her a star."

This tale, invoked whenever devotees referred to those wishing transformation into status higher than human, found repetition by 'Abd Allah ben Umar. His tale hardly flattered. He cursed the beauty, claiming that "'This is the one who seduced Harut and Marut!'" Harut and Marut themselves rued their lust. At eveningtime, both wished to ascend; neither could. Such was God's punishment. Humans laughed. Heaven gave them the choice of punctual over durative punishment. Both chose punishment now, rather than throughout eternity. Thus we know of their hanging in Babel, warning the people against sorcery.

Moore's interest in the authenticity of his sources--perhaps waned, but not dead--by the time he wrote *The Loves of the Angels* stands out in a note to his *Lalla Rookh*. Note 234 takes caution to assure the following: "'They suppose the Throne of the Almighty is seated in the sun, and hence their worship of that luminary.'--*Hanway*. 'As to the fire, the Gehbers place the spring-head of it in that globe of fire, the Sun, by them called Mythras, or Mihir, to which they pay the highest reverence, in gratitude for the manifold benefits flowing from its ministerial omniscience. But they are so far from confounding the subordination of the Servant with the majesty of the Creator, that they not only attribute no sort of sense or reasoning to the sun or fire, in any of its operations, but consider it as a purely passive blind instrument, directed and governed by the immediate impression on it of the will of God; but they do not even give that luminary, all-glorious as it is, more than the second rank amongst his works, reserving the first for that stupendous production of divine power, the mind of man.'--*Grose*. The false charges brought against the religion of these people by their Muselman tyrants is but one proof among many of the truth of this writer's remark, that 'calumny is often added to oppression, if but for the sake of justifying it.'" Moore's belief in none of the mythological trappings surrounding--informing--his pieces may well account for his scrupulous efforts at documenting all of them.

(Brackets are Cooper's.) Cooper notes that "Tabari records the variant reading *malikaini* (=two kings), which, he says, corresponds to the interpretation of Harut and Marut as two men." Tabari dismisses this reading "on rational grounds," namely, "on the grounds that the authoritative reciters are unanimous in rejecting it." (Cooper 485)

[7]Parallel traditions surround the falls of Satan and of Eblis. Sale reports that "this occasion of the devil's fall has some affinity with an opinion which

has been pretty much entertained among Christians (Irenaeus, Lac[tantius], Greg[orius] Nyssen, &.)," namely, "that the angels being informed of God's intention to create man after his own image, and to dignify human nature by CHRIST'S assuming it, some of them, thinking their glory to be eclipsed thereby, envied man's happiness, and so revolted." (Sale 6 n.)

Rabbinical traditions make "Lilith . . . the first woman, [formed by God] just as He had formed Adam, except that He used filth and sediment instead of pure dust." (from *yalqut Reubeni*, "kabbalistic comments on the Pentateuch compiled by R. Reuben and Hoshke Cohen (d. 1673) in Prague, ed. 2 vols, Warsaw, 1889," Graves and Patai 69). Other Lilith traditions are in *The Zohar* 1. (Patai and Graves 6-65) Contemporaries conversant with the Kabbala would doubtless make the link between Lilis and Lilith, which Moore likely intended.

[8]For a more comprehensive catalogue of substantive revisions, see the Appendix, as well as Jordan, *Bolt Upright* 354.

[9]Intolerance for even borderline sensuousness--often attributed to the middle class--actually crosses class lines in the earlier nineteenth century. Neither did prudishness nor decadence belong exclusively to any identifiable group.

[10]Sensuality is emended slightly in 1406-12/1360-64, Rubi describing in the first edition

> The curls, like tendrils that had grown
> Out of the sun--the eyes, that now
> Had love's light added to their own,
> And shed a blaze, before unknown
> Ev'n to themselves--the' unfolded wings
> From which, as from two radiant springs,
> Sparkles fell fast around, like spray

In the revision,

> The sun-bright locks, that now the eyes,
> Had love's spell added to their own,
> And pour'd a light till then unknown;
> The' unfolded wings, that, in their play,
> Shed sparkles bright as Alla's throne.

[11]Some emendations have an equivocal--or even the reverse--effect. "That splendid creature" becomes "That matchless creature"--*matchless* outsplendoring *splendid* in its connotation (538/518); desire's "range, as vague as lightnings" intensifies with an emended "range, as lawless

lightnings" (653/632); and while the deity's name is emended out, a strengthened verb intensifies the evocative power when the simile, "As though I stood on God's own ground" becomes the more adventuresome, "As though I trod celestial ground" (295/279). Moore's emendations do not all reflect defensive gestures.

[12] <<Les hommes n'eurent qu'une seule religion, et furent souvent visites des Anges, qui leur donnoient la main,>> in Moore's note.

[13] Strangely enough, Moore lives his life as if it were governed by the deity unknowable to Hume. According to Gay (*Enlightenment . . . : The Rise of Modern Paganism* 419), "without melodrama but with the sober eloquence one would expect from an accomplished classicist, Hume makes plain that since God is silent, man is his own master: he must live in a disenchanted world, submit everything to criticism, and make his own way." Moore occupies the same universe. In discussing Moore's *Travels of an Irish Gentleman in Search of a Religion* (1833), Jordan finds no declaration of Moore's "personal faith," "no mention of hell or purgatory," along with a lifetime's disdain for quarrels over minor credal articles. Jordan senses that Moore valued "love, charity, and forgiveness towards one's fellow man," and speculates that, while neither the Catholic nor Protestant orthodoxy treated one another with this decency, the poet was not such a committed Catholic that he would have refrained from converting to Protestantism had Protestantism looked more inviting. Jordan suggests two reasons for Moore's remaining a Catholic despite his marriage to a Protestant: 1) his fidelity to Ireland and its people; 2) his passion for music. (*Bolt Upright* 530) It was not until 1827 that he "took Bessy to hear mass at Wardour," her initial exposure to Roman Catholicism. With Moore's typical good nature, he was amused by his and Bessy's disparate responses, Thomas enraptured by the music, Bessy "shocked" by "the gaudy ceremonies and gesticulations of the mass . . . ." (Clifford 30) Moore reports his experiences with various churches; he does not judge, and, in fact, celebrates the fact that his wife,s Protestantism "gave me an opportunity of choosing a religion, at least for my children . . . ." (Clifford 30) Moore adds that were his marriage without any other merit, "I should think *this* quite sufficient to be thankful for." (Clifford 30) The marriage had many other advantages, as both Clifford and Jordan observe. (See *Bolt Upright* 352-354.) See also Jordan 527-29, Herbert 48-52, and Henning 114-23. Clifford finds that "Moore was not pious," and that "The trouble with Moore [for those who wish to assess his religious predilections] is that he was neither Anglo-Irish nor Catholic-nationalist. Though he admired Grattan he was not Anglo-Irish. He was undoubtedly one of the native Irish, even though he detested O'Connell." (9, 11) Further,

"He had no sense of sin, and he never considered any sacrifice worth making for the achievement of place or property." (Clifford 11) Clifford finds the "Catholicism of the Moore family" both "urbane and tolerant," although "a dying force in Ireland." (30) Moore's father's attitude towards taking his Last Rites suggests just how nominal the family's Catholicism must have been. Clifford reports Moore's journal entry for 17 December 1825, contrasting it to the "death-bed scenes" in which "Modern Irish Catholicism revels"; Moore wrote that

> . . . neither my mother nor Kate were very anxious to press upon him [Moore's father] the presence of a clergyman; but on mentioning it to him at Corry's suggestion, he himself expressed a wish for it. The subject of religion was, in deed, the only one, it seems, upon which his mind was not gone. When the priest was proceeding to take his confession, and put the necessary questions for that purpose to him, he called my mother, and said, 'Auty, my dear, you can tell this gentleman all he requires to know quite as well as I.'

(Clifford 13) His father's final Confession by proxy does surprise in the mixed signals it sends about Mr. Moore's attitude towards last rites-- namely, that they are probably a good idea, but something not to tire oneself engaging in, nonchalance in this affair wholly acceptable to the invalid Moore.

Moore's tolerance shows saliently through his marrying a Protestant, allowing his children to be baptised as Protestants, and even informing his mother in a letter of 1813 that "Little Statia went through her christening very well . . . . You have, of course, long perceived that they are both, Barbara and she *little* Protestants," news which, Clifford assesses, "his mother appears to have taken . . . in a thoroughly ecumenical spirit." He "frequently attended Protestant services, but his wife did not attend a Catholic service until sixteen years after their marriage. He recorded the event in his diary," as Clifford reports.

[14]Sale (144), *Al Araf*, reads

> And between the *blessed and the damned* there shall be a veil; and men *shall stand* on Al Araf who shall know every one *of them* by their marks; and shall call unto the inhabitants of paradise, *saying*, Peace be upon you: *yet* they shall not enter therein, although they earnestly desire *it*. And when they shall turn their eyes towards the companions of *hell* fire, they shall say, O LORD, place us not with

the ungodly people!

[15]In the first edition, the phrases "to the following pages" and "the same *moral* interest" are transposed. The arrangement in the fifth edition better serves his argumentative purpose--his ascription of a moral significance to the narrative--through the rhetorical climax. Moore generally dismisses allegorical interpretations of Scripture, as becomes salient in his note to his Preface to the first edition, ll.19-20, when he dismisses readings of Genesis 6.2 offered by Philo, Josephus, and "half-pagan" Patristic writers such as Tertullian, Lactantius, and Clement of Alexandria. (Oden's recent assessment of Genesis 6.1-4 as a tale that "corresponds to cosmogonic myths of ancient Greeks and others" (92-93) might have been well received by Moore, but not published for the unlettered interpreter of the 1820's.) Moore is no stranger to the philological exegesis in vogue in the eighteenth century largely because of efforts by Johann Albrecht Bengel (who wrote on the New Testament in 1742), and by Johann August Ernesti, who found it the "task of an interpreter . . . to attach to the text the same meaning the author himself attached." Ernesti joins philological with historical criticism of both the New and the Old Testaments. (Teeple 73) Moore would tend towards the more contemporary philological and historical exposition, rather than the traditional "moral" (or "tropological"), "mystic" (or "anagogic"), allegorical, and literal readings that had for centuries constituted the "fourfold truth" of the Bible. Philological and historical exegesis--while a form of "literal" interpretation--recognizes that biblical texts come from different times, places, sects (with sectarian needs), cultures, and the like, and come, as well, in an array of modes that determines the expositor's approach. The older "literal" sense bore nothing of this complexity and sophistication. In referring to the "moral" interest of the tale, Moore seems to hope detractors will let him "slide by" as a tropological exegete of Genesis 6.1-4.

[16]He begins his argument about the soul's pre-existence by positing an analogy to the brilliant visions of external nature apprehended by children, his certainty about children's perceptions starting with the self (his own childhood) which he assumes represents the collect of selves constituting humankind and its experience; in this, Wordsworth adapts notions popularized by such as Shaftesbury, who, in his *Sensus Communis* (1709), presumes a shared set of basic experiences and sensibilities distinctively and universally human. In this note, Wordsworth argues that

To that dreamlike vividness and splendor which invest objects of sight in childhood, everyone, I believe, if he would look back, could bear testimony, and I need not dwell upon it here.

He insists, however, that

> but having in the Poem regarded it as presumptive evidence of a prior state of existence, I think it right to protest against a conclusion, which has given pain to some good and pious persons, that I meant to inculcate such a belief.

This he denies; the notion of a pre-existent soul he finds "far too shadowy a notion to be recommended to faith, as more than an element in our instincts of immortality." He does insist that nothing in revelation contradicts the notion, granting that neither does revelation advance it, and suggests that "the fall of Man presents an analogy to its favor." He adds that "popular creeds of many nations" admit "a pre-existent state," including the literature of classical antiquity, where it derives from Plato. He justifies his own reworking of this belief by adducing the example of "Archimedes [who] said that he could move the world if he had a point whereon to rest his machine," then by asking a rhetorical question: "Who has not felt the same aspirations as regards the world of his own mind?" Again, the self is the source of general principle. Wordsworth elaborates upon the groundings for his rhetorical question (which simultaneously gives him a chance to justify his development of this notion of pre-existence): "Having to wield some of its elements when I was impelled to write this Poem on the 'Immortality of the Soul,' I took hold of the notion of pre-existence as having sufficient foundation in humanity for authorizing me to make for my purpose the best use of it I could as a Poet." He does not promulgate this belief as a creed of Christian faith; neither does he eschew it for fit material for poetry. Exactly what he does do with this belief remains uncertain; the "Intimations" Ode-- surely one of his most confusing--shifts cosmological assumptions at least three times, implying a sort of pantheism in Stanza 4, a platonic belief in pre-existence and hence immortality in Stanza 5, and a mortalism-- rendered endurable because of that unifying "primal sympathy / Which having been must ever be," uniting the dead with the living, sentient being.

[17]In actuality, he may wish to divert attention away from analogies towards conflicts between Anglicanism and Roman Catholicism inhering in discussions of conflicts between Islamic sects. For example, in *The Twopenny Post-Bag* (1813), Moore's reports of disputes about the sense of & various places in the Qur'an and the significance of various traditions

surrounding Islam intend, Clifford argues, to "make readers in those pre-Emancipation and pre-Ultramontane times feel the absurdity of the Protestant view of Catholicism." (116)

The Angel of the World
and
The Loves of the Angels Revised:
The Qur'an as Prophylaxis

THE twentieth century can stomach anything more easily than an unsophisticated angel." The judgment is Arnold Whitridge's; it is passed against Vigny's *Éloa*. Whitridge could well have been speaking for nineteenth-century England and its indifference toward--bewilderment by-- Croly's *Angel of the World*.[1] By the time Croly's *Angel* ventured to earth, England had greeted far more exotic Islamic celestials, including Moore's Peri in *Lalla Rookh* (1817).[2] One reviewer praises "some excellent descriptive passages, picturing the surrounding scenery as viewed from the mountain upon which they [the angel and the ostensibly mortal woman] stand," yet laments that Croly's poetic talent shows itself "wasted away upon beings towards whom we can feel no sympathy;--upon a demon whom we ought to hate, and an angel whom we cannot love" (*London Magazine* 2 (1820): 544). John Wilson finds in *The Angel of the World* "a beautiful paraphrase of one of the most graceful fictions of the Koran," approves of Croly's intention "to simplify, and thereby increase the interest of his story" by "narrating the seduction of one Angel only," and delights in the poem's "infinite splendour of language." Wilson, however, is also the critic who would have Croly "devote himself henceforth to subjects of more directly human interest" (*Blackwood's* 8:21-23).[3] Perhaps the English readership had had its fill of the eastern romance, characterized by "episodes" containing "elements of the strange, the exciting, and the fearful" (Brown, "English Travel Books and Minor Poetry" 268), although in focusing on an angel's passion for a woman, Croly adds to his tale a motif still very much in vogue. Had Croly drawn from Christian, rather than Qur'anic lore, his poem might well have engaged more interest.

When Croly insists that he "has ventured to mitigate the Koran, which had undoubtedly the best right to mulct its own Angels; but has done it in mercy to the propensities of Christendom," he risks disaffecting his audience--despite his claim that his account of "one Angel," who "fails by a succession of attempts upon his firmness," derives from the Qur'anic tales of Haruth and Maruth, which themselves constitute "one of those modifications of the history of the fall of Lucifer, and the temptation in Paradise, which make up so large a portion of Asiatic mythology." (vi-vii) Croly's apparent refuge in the Qur'anic fall nonetheless calls to mind the biblical parallel--the latter, by implication, also forming this body of "mythology". Coming into question, in fact, was the very wisdom of basing a serious poem on any part of the Qur'an (or upon Qur'anic legends). Croly's excision of his snipe at the Qur'an bewilders--his reference in 1820 to its right to "mulct" its "Angels". Missing from the *Poetical Works* of 1830 (1: 180), this phrase-- in 1830 even more than in 1820--appears likely as a candidate for the most universally favored expression in the entire work.

The Qur'an--at first welcomed as an addition to oriental learning when Sale's English translation appeared in November, 1734--had gradually been coming to be seen as a threat to Christianity. By the middle of the nineteenth century, a review of C.W. Lane's "Selections from the Kur'an," in the *Eclectic Review* 19 (March 1846): 375-78, reveals typical fears despite an effort to extend tolerance. The reviewer concedes that the book may be tolerated for the antiquarian (i.e., a member of the educated class): the Kur'an will no doubt remain in the library of the curious, as mummies will in their museums." Too, he assumes that "it will always be a remarkable and interesting piece of antiquity" for its service "as the instrument sustaining the faith of the Moslem through many centuries, as well as keeping them in a semi-civilized state"(375). Nonetheless the Qur'an is still "contemptible," and the best that can be said about it is that it "goes against polytheism" (376). Its very existence threatens Christianity--which Sale, from whom Lane draws, did not go far enough in warning against, and which Lane's excerpts have failed to seize the chance of correcting (376-77). If a defensive gesture, Croly's use of the Qur'an remains only partly successful.[4]

The Angel of the World derives from the same Qur'anic legend Moore names as the source of the fifth and subsequent editions of *The Loves of the Angels*, Moore superimposing Islamic trappings upon his Judaeo-Christian originals. Both Croly and Moore (in Moore's revision) avoid charges of blasphemy by turning to Islam--or would avoid such charges, in Moore's case. The ploy (if indeed so designed) succeeds in Croly's case, solely because *The Angel of the World*, as a poem, proved innocuous. *The Loves of the Angels*--disturbing when mined from Scripture--reemerged equally disturbing (to those bothered by the original) upon their conversion. Eighteenth-century syncretists had made the age so keenly aware of parallels between Islam and Christianity that Islamic angels naturally brought Judaeo-Christian counterparts to mind.[5] Other portals for possible controversy over Croly's poem readily evince themselves--ironically, in Croly's notes, presumably a means of certifying verisimilitude, the poet oblivious to their potential for affronting Scripture. His notes catch him off guard, and render him vulnerable to charges of diminishing the credibility of Scripture. Such is particularly the case with his long quotations from Bruce's *Travels*, some of which call to mind passages from Scripture, passages traditionally deemed to report miracles. What tradition acclaims as miraculous prove to be common, natural phenomena, indigenous to the Near East. (The very reverend Croly would doubtless pale were he aware that by attaching Bruce to his text, he illustrates "miracles" of the sort that abound for Voltaire and Hume, Voltaire insisting that the term be limited to its original sense of "something admirable," Hume scorning with other deists the orthodox notion that "miracles were irruptions of divine powers, the setting aside of ordinary proceedings," yet "ready to concede" the omnipresence of miracles, manifest in "the marvelous orderliness of the universe with its unbreakable laws of nature"; "to the deists," Gay notes, "the only miracle was the miracle not of irregularity but of regularity," Gay, *Modern Paganism* 148-49.) This transformation of supernatural into natural phenomena (of miracles involving "divine irruptions" into miracles of regularity) occurs, for example, when Croly appends to his poem Bruce's account of a simoom.

Croly's note introduces us to Bruce's encounter with "moving pillars of sand," a description (and a phrase) which brings to mind Exodus 13.21-22 ("And the LORD went before them by day in a pillar of cloud to lead them along the way, and by night in a pillar of fire to give them light, that they might travel by day and by night; the pillar of cloud by day and the pillar of fire by night did not depart from before the people"), Exodus 14.24-25a ("And in the morning watch the LORD in the pillar of fire and of cloud looked down upon the host of the Egyptians, and discomfited the Egyptians, clogging their chariot wheels so they drove heavily"), and the effects of Exodus 10.21-23 ("Then the LORD said to Moses, 'Stretch out your hand toward heaven that there may be darkness over the land of Egypt, a darkness to be felt'," Moses complying in verse 22, bringing "thick darkness in all the land of Egypt three days; they did not see one another, nor did any rise from his place for three days; but all the people of Israel had light where they dwelt"). In Bruce, "The same appearance of moving pillars of sand presented themselves to us this day, in form and disposition like those we had seen at Waadi Halboub, only they seemed to be more in number and less in size." Such pillars, by implication, are common enough to be compared with detached, scientific concern for measurement and number. (One wonders, too, if pillars of cloud might not be a misrepresentation for pillars of sand.) Associations with Exodus become even firmer when Bruce continues by explaining that "they came several times in a direction close upon us . . . [and] began immediately after sunrise, like a thick wood, and almost darkened the sun. His rays, shining through them for near an hour, gave them an appearance of pillars of fire."

For adherents to revealed religion, the pillars of cloud and pillars of sand in Exodus, as well as the ninth plague of thick darkness, testify to God's direct intervention in aiding Israel's passage through Egypt, the pillars of fire theophanies, comforting manifestations of the divine presence. Clearly, in the narration of Bruce, nothing miraculous (in its religious sense) associates with the pillars. Bruce, in fact, displays his companions' superstitious fear of divine involvement in these occurrences as a sort of negative proof that God had nothing to do with them: "The Greeks shrieked out, and said it was the day of judgment," while "Ismael pronounced it to be hell, and the Tucorories, that the world was on fire."

Bruce, the rational Englishman, simply "asked Idris if ever he had before seen such a sight." Bruce's guide responds that "he had often seen them as terrible, though never worse," adding that "what he feared most was that extreme redness in the air, which was a sure presage of the coming of the simoom." The sands remained at a far distance the following day--"a comfort but of short duration," and no comfort at all to Idris, who "only warned me and the servants, that, upon the coming of the simoom, we should fall upon our faces with our mouths upon the earth, so as not to partake of the outward air as long as we could hold our breath." (The disabling sandstorm in Exodus, endured by the Egyptians for three days, comes back to mind, especially its dark oppressiveness.) Eventually, Bruce recalls, the feared sandstorm comes; Idris warns the travelers to "Fall upon your faces!" Bruce then reports that he

saw from the S.E. a haze come, in colour like the purple part of the rainbow, but not so compressed or thick . . . . It was a kind of blush upon the air, and it moved very rapidly, for I scarce could turn to fall upon the ground, with my head northward, when I felt the heat of its current plainly on my face. We all lay flat on the ground as if dead, till Idris told us it was blown over. The meteor, or purple haze, which I saw, was, indeed, passed, but the light air which still blew was of heat to threaten suffocation,

and, in fact, Bruce adds that "I found distinctly in my breast that I had imbibed a part of it, nor was I free of an asthmatic sensation till I had been some months in Italy, at the baths of Poretta, about two years afterwards." (36-38)

As a gloss on the line, "The vale at once was bare," this excerpt from Bruce overwhelms and obscures the poetic text. Of intrinsic interest in the excerpt is Bruce's analytical detachment from an admittedly unpleasant natural occurrence; God has no part in forming these "pillars." The simoom disabled Bruce and his party, but not for any specified period, and not to the benefit of any contending party. Bruce's Afterward--his remarks about his pulmonary condition--tint the account with "this worldliness"; his health gradually improved, Bruce benefitting particularly from the Italian climate (as opposed to an intervening deity). This note inadvertently invites reassessment of the "miracles" in Exodus, which, in light of Bruce's account, likely reflect similar events in external nature, the divine causes and ends reflecting the editorial hands of the ancient cult scribes.

Croly's contemporaries decry both the focus and source of the poem to which Bruce's comments are appended; its "want of human interest" may derive from its uncertain aim. The notion of passion effecting an angel's fall is in no way intrinsically alienating as a subject. This concept inspires Lamartine, and, with modifications, was apparently even entertained by Milton as a sympathetic (rather than deplorable) subject for a tragedy. Milton leaves an outline for a tragedy of "Sodom," with "a chorus of Angels .... relating the event of Lots journey, & of his wife."

Milton's commonplace book leaves far too sketchy an outline of his plans to afford insight into his attitude towards the angels he envisioned, specifically, those he would have depicted "pittying this beauty," they see in the "citty each evening every one [mortal] with mistresse, or Ganymed, glittering along the streets, or solacing on the banks of Jordan." Nothing suggests that they are wanton, and certainly, none are 'indone. Yet they apparently are moved by beauty: "the Angels pittying this beauty may dispute of love & how it differs from lust seeking to win them in the last scene to the King & nobles when the Angel appears all girt with flames which he saith are the flame of true love," prior to "the thunders & fires," followed by "the call & command to God to come & destroy a godlesse nation." (CEWJM 18: 233-4) The ability of the observing angels to empathize, or feel pity, would not be out of character for a celestial being, at least if Milton's *Christian Doctrine* can be used as a gauge. In Chapter 2 ("Of God") he acknowledges that "accommodation" may account for the attributions of emotions to God. On the other hand, he allows the possibility that the alleged anthropopathic intrusions are exact representations of God, for "we may be sure that sufficient care has been taken that the Holy Scriptures should contain nothing unsuitable to the character or dignity of God, and that God should say nothing of himself which could derogate from his own majesty." For example, "if *it grieved the Lord at his heart*, Gen. vi. 6. and if *his soul were grieved for the misery of Israel*, Judges x. 16, let us believe that it did grieve him. For the affections which in a good man are good, and rank with virtues, in God are holy." Emotion is not beneath the dignity either of God or of men; presumably, "good affections" in "good angels" would be venerable. (Hughes 906)

Actually, the passion aroused in Croly's angel becomes one of the more sympathetic elements of *The Angel of the World*. The purpose of this angel's test and punishment confuses. If we are to take the narrative as an allegory, the nature, and didactic end of this allegory remains equivocal. We are apparently warned against presuming moral superiority, specifically, against boasting invulnerability to temptation--a presumption so seldom made by any humans that the warning seems needless. (If the poem has no didactic end--if it aims at art for art's sake--the narrator's moralizing intrusions obfuscate art.) Croly's angel ascends in pride, and, as a result of pride, finally dissolves as a sentient entity. The narrative adds one more to the centuries' voluminous warnings against pride. If this be its thematic end, the format alienates. If the poet aims to warn us against prohibited liaisons, this warning remains cryptic.

Like Moore's, Croly's narrative follows Ovidian patterns set in the *Metamorphoses*. Remembering this--keeping in mind that such narratives design for empathy with the victim's slow, gripping horror upon realizing that his or her metamorphosis is transpiring--we can possibly sympathize ("empathize" asks too much) with Croly's angel and his change. A frowning scorner of earth when he descends in Stanza 15, the angel changes psychologically before changing physically; he becomes a captive of a beautiful pilgrim in Stanzas 19-20, the narrator asking the moving question, "Bright Spirit was it thine that mortal woe [of love] to feel?" (Croly revises "Bright Spirit" in this stanza (21) into the more judgmental "Proud Angel" for later editions; the narrator thereby grows colder.) We are of course aware of the woes that love can bring--the woes of unrequited love, the woes of love cut short by death, the woes of lovers' misunderstandings, and the list extends. Freedom from feeling would at times be welcomed by most of us. Feelings themselves are new to the angel--and hence his plight threatens him even more than such a plight would threaten a mortal, one of a species born bound to feeling. In these early stanzas (15-21), Croly's angel becomes entrapped by his own senses--senses he had never had occasion to know he could, or to know how to, experience. Warnings against sensuality occur when the angel takes a flower--signifying his weakness to beauty, and when he asks, contemplatively, whether he could actually now be in paradise-- "the second warning in the form of the Simoom and sandstorm," suggested by Bruce's *Travels*, constituting a formidable "no" (*London Magazine* 2: 544).[6] (The Preface gives a full list of the events in external nature that convey divine displeasure with the angel's behavior.)

The angel's susceptibility to female beauty suggests for the poem foundations upon the third--and most misogynistic--of the traditional hamartigenies. The pilgrim's red cheek and undulating breast arouse warmth in the angel that he does not know how to apprehend. He is entrapped, too, by his newfound sensibilities; the angel feels pity (or something that we would understand as pity) upon hearing the woman's prayers and cries. After this odyssey into sensation and sensibility, the poem loses appeal. Croly gives us little other cause to care about the angel. Unlike Vigny--who emphasizes the goodness in his female Eloa, a goodness that eventuates her fall--Croly invites us to extract no essence of his angel's character; nothing about Croly's angel moves us to say, even, "too bad that such potential for X can end in Y."[7] All the poet offers hereafter amounts to demonic choreography, followed by an angel's pyrotechnic demise. We stand to learn nothing, save that some stronger beings, for reasons Croly never asks us to articulate or comprehend, undo weaker dupes.

A dupe this angel proves to be. Once attracted to the pilgrim, once having submitted himself to being a "Slave to her slightest word," the angel joins this presumably mortal woman in consuming a "guilty draught . . . of wine." The outcome of this drink makes sense in the context of Qur'anic lore, but has no logical explanation within the world of the poem. The poem shies away from sensual scenes, the narrator instead recapitulating the evils of intemperance (Stanzas 46-47). The woman ultimately prods him to reveal the "mighty words, / Graved on the magnet's throne where Solomon / Sits ever guarded by the genii swords" empowered to transform mortals into angels; she entreats him "To give thy servant wings, like her resplendent Lord's" (Stanza 58).

We receive instructions in the proper response to this entreaty (St. 59):

This was the sin of sins! The first, last crime,
In earth and heaven, unnamed, unnameable;
This from his throne of light, before all time,
Had smitten Eblis, brightest, first that fell.
He started back.--"What urged him to rebel?
What led that soft seducer to his bower?
Could *she* have laid upon his soul that spell,
Young, lovely, fond; yet but an earthly flower?
But for that fatal cup, he had been free that hour.

Wine, and not the woman, has effected his fall. Despite the angel's anguish at feeling himself about to utter the unutterable, the "mighty words," words potent enough to transform a lower into a higher order of being, the angel's tongue, licentious with wine, begins without volition pronouncing them (the narrator wisely refraining from revealing what these may have been). Thunder follows. Wrath from Heaven is close behind. Once again the power of the word finds demonstration.

After subjecting us to this alien anguish (for drunk or sober, mortals do not know these "mighty words"), Croly plays an unappreciated narratorial trick. The angel's seduction proves to be effected not by a mortal woman, but by a woman who is not a woman at all--this woman actually Eblis, "King of Hell's relentless sovereignties" (Stanza 64). Eblis, an archetypical shape-shifter--meeting the age's call for love with the undead that Keats supplies in *Lamia*--has predetermined the angel's fate and executes it efficiently. Women pose no viable threats, since none appear in the poem. The angel is never really given a chance to find out if he is indeed invincible. For being entrapped by a trap specifically designed for this situation--designed by an infallible engineer of such traps, Eblis punishes the angel in the poem's final stanza (Stanza 67); metamorphosis is the angel's sentence--at least apparently. Eblis has the hapless angel "burst through space, like the red comet's cone, / Leaving his track on heaven a burning, endless zone." His punishment is blatantly disproportionate to his crime (simple pride), affording nothing of the brutal didacticism endured by Ovidian victims. Metamorphoses--as their victims slowly realize the currency, and sometimes cause, of their transformations--often evoke pity or horror. An explosion is not a proper metamorphosis; it is too fast and final. The angel is spared realization--the vehicle of horror in Ovidian tales--at least if this explosion be his punishment.

The syntax of the final stanzas renders the ending of the narrative uncertain, as does the sense of the fate Eblis dooms the angel to in stanzas immediately prior to the closing action. Eblis's appearance as Eblis comes with a pronouncement of doom:

'Spirit, thou might'st have stood,
But thou hast fallen a weak and willing slave,
Now were thy feeble heart our serpent's food,
Thy bed our burning Ocean's sleepless wave,
But haughty Heaven controuls the power it gave.
Yet art thou doom'd to wander from thy sphere,
Till the last trumpet reaches to the grave;
Till the Sun rolls the grand concluding year;
The earth is Paradise; then shall thy crime be clear.'

(Hell's powers have been limited by Heaven; Eblis cannot cast the angel into Hell's "burning Ocean." Croly's expository powers have been curbed, as well, neither the poet nor Eblis identifying precisely the nature of the angel's "crime," given the mitigating circumstances under which the angel drinks wine and utters the unutterable.) The angel, "risen upon one knee, / Resolved to hear the deadliest undismay'd. / His gold starr'd plume hung round him droopingly, / His brow, like marble, on his hand was staid, / Still thro' the auburn locks, o'erhanging shade / His face shone beautiful; he heard his ban. / Then came the words of mercy, sternly said"--apparently, the words pronounced in the previous stanza, the narrator here backtracking, although the present line prepares us to hear some new, stern, merciful pronouncements. None are forthcoming; rather, "He plunged within his hands his visage wan, / And the first wild, sweet tears from his heart-pulses ran." (Stanzas 65-67)

This may be it. This may be the extent of his metamorphosis--his transformation from a cold, haughty, unfeeling entity to a wanderer of acute sensibilities, a man (or rather, angel) of feeling. There may be more. Pronouns want antecedents desperately in the ensuing stanza, when "The Giant," presumably Eblis, "grasped him as he fell to Earth, / And his black vanes upon the air were flung, / A tabernacle dark." Already, the possessor of these "black" veins remains uncertain--likely the angel, but possibly Eblis, the latter suggestion possibility reenforced by the association with a "tabernacle dark," suggestive of a black mass or a reversal of any bright totem or sacrament of Heaven. The lines following confuse even further: "--and shouts of mirth / Mingled with shriekings thro' the tempest swung"--the narrator failing to identify the source of these shouts and shrieks (nowhere clarifying whether one or both parties emit sound, Eblis shouting--Eblis the only party who could feel "mirth" at this time, the angel shrieking--"shrieking" generally associated with terror, although, again, Eblistic war shrieks may be indicated. Attempting to imagine exactly how "shriekings" may be "swung" forces the mind to recoil.)

These grammatical analyses intend not to prove *The Angel of the World* marred as a narrative--its general lucidity or obfuscation of no concern. They seem indicated by the fact that it is not at all clear, at the very end of the poem, what, exactly, happens; basic plot summaries are rendered impossible by Croly's syntax. As the remainder of this analysis will point out, two endings suggest themselves, neither particularly horrorific. The next line relieves with its clear referents: "His arm around the fainting Angel clung"--"his" recalling "the Giant" who "grasp'd him" ("grasp'd" the angel) three lines earlier, "the Giant" apparently designating "Eblis"--if this designation for "king of Hell's relentless sovereignties" proves a bit bland and uncertain. "Then on the clouds he darted with a groan," and here with this line the poet compounds confusion. The "groan" suggests the painful endeavors of someone who moves with great difficulty--such as a collapsed angel. (His rise to "the clouds" would not be prohibited by his sentence, which merely leaves him to "wander" anywhere "from thy sphere" until "Earth is Paradise"; the angel is not consigned to earth.) Next, "A moment o'er the Mount of ruin hung, / Then burst thro' space," in the manner described earlier. The actor remains uncertain. The "groan," before hovering over the "ruin," followed by a "burst," may well describe the angel's dissolution. The word "darted" suggests easier movement--and hence Eblis as the actor (yet the cause for a "groan" from Eblis remains wanting). In this case, the poem closes with Eblis "Leaving his track on heaven, a burning, endless, zone," the angel comatose. The coma is no more proper as a metamorphosis than is dissolution.

The poem predicts "the last trumpet" and earth's return to "Paradise" with apparent certainty--rendering the notion of the angel's punishment (for falling prey to an infallible set up) all the more ludicrous. Whether temporarily dissolved throughout space, or comatose on earth, the angel--once reassembled, or reawakened--has been assured that his sentenced wandering will be limited in its duration, a duration well beyond mortal comprehension, but not unendurable for an eternal being. In a sense, the angel does not suffer (because either dissolved or unconscious) a non-punishment (because his wandering, if uncomfortable or inconvenient, will end) for his non-commission (for volition has nothing to do with his acts which are effected by Eblistic design) of non-transgressions (for Eblis has set up the entire incident). *The Angel of the World* as a narrative is not fair.

The Angel of the World may well have inspired Moore's "First Angel's Tale." Moore's angel at least has a chance to escape temptation, however; Satan (later Eblis) has not programmed his demise. Croly's poem, too, maps an easy route by which Moore can convert his angel to Islam for the fifth edition. Again, even after conversion, Moore's angel finds himself clearly impelled to act because of love--a feeling Croly denies his angel. At the most, Croly's fallen angel experiences visual stimulation, and perhaps a mild form of lust. *The Angel of the World* stands alone among the five works in its limited focus; the tale recounts the cause and nature of the single angel's demise. This fall wants etiological significance; world-judgment does not result; Croly's narrative neither recalls nor demands consideration of any clearly defined, universally applicable human condition. (The French encyclopedists, popular among the English, successful particularly in their syncretism, surely suggested to contemporaries fallen Christian angels.)

Notes to Chapter 9

[1]Arnold Whitridge,*Alfred de Vigny* (London: Oxford Univ. Pr.; rpt. New York: Kraus Reprint Co., 1971) 32.

[2]See Wallace Cable Brown, "English Travel Books and Minor Poetry about the Near East, 1775-1825" 269-70, and "Thomas Moore and English Interest in the East" 584-87.

[3]Of the five completed angel poems, Croly's proved the most difficult for its own age to respond to, although according to the reviewer in the *London Magazine* 2 (1820): 542-48, the poem shows skill in mastery of the Spenserian stanza, as well as evocative power in its descriptions (many of which derive from Bruce's descriptions of the Arab world in his *Travels,* as Croly's notes quote in detail, 35-38). This reviewer condemns in Croly seductive verbal powers similar to those Jeffrey condemns in Moore-- namely, the ability to say nothing in language that deceives us into presuming sense. Croly devises "gorgeous phrases, clothing and giving apparent substance to mere shadows" (542). Style and substance remain separable--as they do for Jeffrey. The writer shares nothing of Wilson's predisposition towards Croly's matter:

> The subject . . . was, we venture to think, chosen entirely on account of facilities it offered for the *display* of the writer's powers;--for, as a story, it is without any of those qualities that are of themselves calculated to attract and fix the reader's attention. It is taken from a fiction of Mohammed's, intended to show the ill effects of wine . . . . The scene is in Arabia; the time, the first day of the first year of the Hegira . . . (542).

The verse is "at once gorgeous, picturesque, and poetical" (542). Yet once we have been taken through the angel's story, this reviewer warns us, we see poetical talent wasted. It depicts no human characters, and no situations in which humans would conceivably find themselves. "In fact, this total absence of human interest is the capital defect of the poem" (544). Croly extensively revised his first edition of *The Angel of the World* for its appearance in his *Poetical Works*. These revisions went without notice.

[4]Sale's Preface to his "Preliminary Discourse" (1:10) certainly works hard at discrediting Islam--managing to lob a grenade against Roman

Catholicism, as well. Sale argues that the missionaries of the Roman Catholic Church "are so far from having done any service in the refutations of Mohammedanism, that by endeavouring to defend the idolatry and other superstitions [i.e., their worship of saints], they have rather contributed to the increase of that aversion which the Mohammedans in general have to the Christian religion." A holy war is welcomed: "The Protestants alone are able to attack the Koran with success; and for them, I trust, Providence has reserved the glory of its overthrow." By 1820, this statement proves too weak, apparently. Fullblown attacks against the Qur'an are called for--for reasons that remain uncertain. Certainly, the availability of Sale's translation had not resulted in mass conversions. Sale himself never bothered even to venture into the Middle East. Croly's concern over the plight of Russia--which at the time he fears could be irremediably converted to Islam, forsaking Christianity forever--likely reflects contemporary fears. (*Sketches* 17) Yet Croly obviously finds nothing objectionable about Qur'anic legends for poetry. The middle-class readership was becoming even more parochial about Christianity than its more pious, orthodox, professional clergymen, among whom Croly numbered.

[5]By indirect routes, the legends of Harut and Marut relate to Genesis 6.1-4. The names of the angels derive from "Haurvatat" ("wholeness") and "Ameratat" ("longevity," later "immortality"), in Persian legend. The Vedas give "Haurvatat" as "Sarvatiti," suggesting something vaguely like "freedom from hurt" (Jung 91). They become two of the Daevas who corrupt the earth before the coming of Zarahushtra (Zoroaster):

> After 3000 years Zaratushtra . . . was sent and he spread the Religion. Before his coming the Daevas had gone into the world in human shape (in the form of man and woman fairies). And the Daevas took the women from their husbands and they met in sexual intercourse. When Zaratushtra . . . brought his religion into the world and made it evident, this band (form) of Daevas were broken up and disappeared. Henceforth if they want to commit a sin on earth they can no more appear in the shape of man, but (they do so) in the form of donkeys, cows and the like (beasts). (From *Ravayet Yasna* 915.46, quoted by Jung 91.)

This Zoroastrian legend introduces two elements ultimately entering Rabbinical writings and Pseudepigrapha--the motif of the shape-shifter (significant to Croly's poem), and the motif of interspeciation (significant to Montgomery's, Byron's, and Moore's poems). Charles (*Pseudepigrapha* 191 n) remarks that Genesis 6.14 hearkens back to Persian antiquity, in a "myth to the effect that before Zoroaster's coming demons had corrupted the earth and allied themselves with women." Jung comments that "although . . . these two spirits seem rooted in Indo-European soil, it is remarkable that Harut and Marut appear in the Koran II.96." He acknowledges that "Iran and Babylon no doubt met frequently, but in the Babylonian myth Hauvatat and Ameratat are too vague for any more definite conclusions to be drawn."

Neither Croly nor Moore use the Harut or Marut of the Koran, drawing instead from legends evolving before or after they appear in Sura 2, where God approves their service as tempters of mortals. (Throckton 342). Pertinent to the use to which Croly and Moore put the Harut and Marut legends are those involving the angels' interactions with women. These interactions begin when, in some legends, the entire body of angels in heaven deride mortals for sinning, God's rejoinder that they would likewise sin if on earth refuted by the angels (not just Harut and Marut), who claim to be "far from imperfections" that flaw the mortal character. God commands them to put their claim to a test, and to elect two representatives to descend. Harut and Marut are elected. God permits them to do anything that may be done on earth except for drinking wine, fornicating, or killing without permission. As soon as they see a woman named Bedukhut (in some versions), they want to have sex with her; she refuses unless they drink wine, kill someone (apparently at random), and worship an idol. They refuse to do the latter (the only one of her conditions that God has not forbidden them to meet). She softens a bit, demanding only that they drink wine. When drunk, they kill a beggar, at which point God lets all angels know that they are flawed. These specific angels have the choice of being punished until the end of time or throughout all eternity; they take the former sentence.

In some versions, the woman is "the star Venus," who descends in the form of a woman and seduces them. Other versions have the woman originally mortal, and have Harut and Marut the tempters, to whom the woman ultimately yields, upon the condition that they reveal "the formula, which when pronounced, would cause one to ascend to the heavens. They taught it to her. She pronounced it and consequently ascended to the heavens and was metamorphosed into a star." (Jung 132-36) This later rendition inspires Moore's first angel's story--even before he supposedly transforms it into an "eastern" tale. The shape-shifter ascending in order to tempt the angels is adopted and altered by Croly. Croly's adaptation of the shooting star as a sign that something evil has transpired may well derive from Islamic traditions articulated by Guillaume (121-22): "God created these [shooting] stars for three reasons: to be an ornament of the sky, to be used as stones against the devils, and as signs to guide people." The multiple traditions attached to these stars render them, in effect, intrinsically neutral, capable of signifying the divine guiding presence, of serving as ammunition against evil beings, or of simply providing nightime decoration; context determines their moral significance.

[6]See Byron's note to *The Giaour*, glossing l. 255 ("He came, he went, like the simoom"), as "the blast of the desert, fatal to every thing living, and often alluded to in eastern poetry."

[7]This follows Whitridge's reading of *Éloa*, who finds that "her downfall is the result of her own goodness." Éloa is capable of pity--egalitarian pity extending to those above her in the chain of being, as well as to those below her. "Satan, knowing that pity leads to sympathy and sympathy to carnal love, succeeds in dragging his unhappy mistress to the depths of Hell" (32). Wolfson points to an Islamic tradition consigning angels as well as Satan (Eblis) to a "likeness of the heart," a capacity for emotions which they may channel to good or to evil ends, according to the dictates of their free will. (639-44) Evil--incomprehensible to Éloa--disables her when confronted by deliberate and cunning evil. Croly's angel, although tempted to do ill, is matched unfairly against the master of evil.

Irad and Adah, A Tale of the Flood : Christian Guilt and Pre-Christian Perpetrators

In ASSESSING "The Social and Historical Significance of the First English Literature Professorship in England," Franklin E. Court points out that "the Reverend Thomas Dale, the first professor of English in England," has left little telling us much "about him or his courses." (*PMLA* 103: 796) His program--not to mention his status as an "author of sorts" (Court's phrase)--remain inconsequential. As Court details, the very institution of a Chair of English Language and Literature at "the new formed London University" constituted a temporary victory for Brougham and fellow campaigners for universal education. Politics, not literature, provided the impetus both for the establishment of the position, and the ultimate selection of Dale, a candidate of compromise, not choice.

Court's history, read in conjunction with documents left by Dale's contemporaries, gives rise to suspicions that perhaps "the first professor of English in England" was willing to do anything to retain the power afforded him through the podium. Dale, a Cambridge graduate already enjoying the power of the pulpit, stayed on at the then, open-admissions London University from 1827-1830, despite his displeasure "with the progress of his courses and with this prospects as a university English professor," economic constraints restricting his curricular flexibility. (Court 803) (His successor accepted a job reflecting retrenchment of the position into a composition job. See Court 806) Dale took a post at King's College, London, from 1835-1840, restricting him to an even more limited curriculum than he had undertaken at University College. (Court 807n)

Brougham, a key member of the appointment committee, had battled hard for universal education; clearly, the factory world had been locked out of the world of letters. How Dale--especially as a poet--could have been acceptable to Brougham remains unfathomable. The egalitarianism of Brougham and Brougham's supporters, when contrasted to the paternalistic, content-free poetry ("of sorts") Dale himself produced, bewilders.

Brougham's notion that all human minds were entitled to read, and to read as widely and for whatever ends they would, did not set well with those

M.P.'s who had had to swallow hard before accepting any reason for even universal functional literacy (the Old Guard overruled by the new gods, the lobbies of factory owners), and who had nearly choked before benevolating their "*id sit*" for a Votech school system tailored for the trades. Surely, conventional wisdom held, Parliament had gone as far as prudence would dare.

This becomes clear, for example, from a discussion of "High Church Opinions on Popular Education" appearing in the *Edinburgh Review* 42 (April 1825-Aug. 1825): 206-233. The writer--clearly in support of Brougham--attacks E.W. Grinfield for Grinfield's *Reply* to Brougham's *Practical Observations upon the Education of the People, addressed to the Working Classes and their Employers* (London, Rivington, 1825), huffing that Grinfield's *Reply*

> comes to a subject . . . foreign to the pamphlet he has undertaken to answer, viz. Elementary Schools for reading and writing--a topic never, we believe, once mentioned in the work of Mr. Brougham. . . . After sufficiently abusing Mr Brougham and his supporters for their 'most foolish assumption,'--'the strange notion,' which, it seems, they have, that reading and writing are tools of common use, and may very well be acquired at schools, without any peculiar use being prescribed for them while in those schools, so that religion may be taught by their parents and ministers, while their masters give them only the means of learning religion, as well as every other useful knowledge, he at once announces his opinion, that if we are really to teach reading and writing at the elementary schools, it would be far better for the common people of this country to remain *wholly illiterate*, than to be thus furnished with '*books*, by which they *would inevitably* work out their own and the public ruin!' (211)

Grinfield may have a point; the seventeenth-century English Revolution came about *after* (not because) the body of readers who could and did read Scripture had enlarged. (In the lunatic fringes, literacy was irrelevant; the Holy Spirit had sufficed; Milton, among the most lettered, numbered among the most lunatic and spirited of his age.) "Point," perhaps, misdesignates; Grinfield *does* have a fear. Yet Brougham and his camp perceived illiteracy as far more dangerous than universal literacy. The reviewer puts it more bluntly: "Now, we confess our incapacity to comprehend any thing of this," adding that "we should imagine a people who can read and write not at all more perilous to deal with, either by statesmen or churchmen, than a people sunk in the rudest ignorance, and more resembling beasts than men."(211)

The discussion closes with the reviewer's notice of a suggestion, made a few years earlier, "for improving the education of the Upper Classes in London, by the establishment of a University," a plan for which "our distinguished countryman, Mr Campbell the poet, had stood forward as an active promoter...." Further, "The last London papers announce that Mr[.] Brougham has given notice to Parliament of a bill to incorporate the new College, and we trust that the Legislature will have sanctioned it before these pages see the light." (222) This is promising, in the reviewer's judgment. Brougham's related campaigns had already yielded some benefits. As I referred to above, vocational schools, "about thirty new Mechanics' Institutions and Libraries," had been organized since Brougham's *Practical Observations* "were published late last January." And certainly the egalitarian--rather than any paternalistic--management of these schools is to the liking of the reviewer:

> Among these, the principle so strenuously recommended by Mr. Brougham has, we rejoice to find from a note to the Editors now before us, been universally adopted, of leaving the management in the hands of the men, providing that two-thirds at least of the managing committee should be workmen, and that all members, that is all who contribute, should have an equal voice in all elections. This is a principle of the most essential importance both to secure a permanent attention to the concerns of those institutions, and to keep alive the interest and confidence of the members. (222)

But access to vocational schools is not enough; the working classes deserve more. The reviewer would broaden the targeted clientele of the new University in London. All knowledge should be accessible to all, regardless of class or wealth:

> We regard this as altogether one of the most important events of our day, and the consequences of which are the most likely to prove extensive and lasting, in improving the understandings, and enlarging the views of the upper and middle classes of society in England. That the means of literary and scientific instruction should so long have been confined to a few hundred families of the highest rank and greatest wealth, and that the seats of even this

limited education should be at a day's journey from the metropolis, will in after times hardly be credited . . . . The establishment of a college in London, where every one may obtain for his children the most complete education, at the expense of ten or twelve pounds a year for each, retaining his parental superintendance, and not sacrificing the mutual pleasures of their society, is the complete and appropriate remedy for so great a defect . . . . To certain classes, the authority of Oxford and Cambridge, their power of conferring degrees, and the fellowships, and livings, and other advantages attached to them, will always prove of superior attraction; and the more general diffusion of a taste for scientific education will greatly augment the numbers of those who, being able to afford it, will prefer an university for their sons. (222-223)

As suggested earlier, Dale's appointment to the post was not a foregone conclusion. One of his chief competitors, Alexander Blair, Court tells us, "envisioned English literature as an ancillary subject to be used as a vehicle for teaching philology, his primary interest." For Blair, "whatever other values literature had were belletristic, taught in the service of taste, refinement, and a love of antiquity." (799) But as Court realizes, "Taste, refinement, and a love of antiquity . . . were not the essential objectives that Brougham and the council had in mind for the English program." Dale's program--specifically geared to the study of English literature as literature and . . . designed to appeal to a variety of reading tastes"--captured the endorsement of "Brougham and his utilitarian supporters," whose decision became final on 4 December 1827. (799) Court adds that "ironically, what sabotaged Dale's English courses was neither external political or academic pressure nor resentment over Brougham's [push for a] . . . seminary in the metropolis; instead, it was competition from his colleagues for enrollment that finally put an end to his University College career and to the first serious university effort to teach English literature in England." (805) Court's summary of the inception of a position in English literature and its inevitable decline are worth attending, particularly before we return to the qualifier of Dale's talents as a poet "of sorts." Both Court's social history, and Dale's practices as a poet, join in showing how Dale's own tinkering with poetry undermined Brougham's egalitarian hopes. But Court's history belongs first:

The founding impulse behind Dale's appointment was political reform, not social control. Popularizing literature enhanced the promotion of serious literary study. Legitimizing literary study in the university was an avenue through which the reading habit could be encouraged nationally and public sensitivity to pressing political and social reform issues subsequently increased. As long as the literary curriculum remained open-ended and primarily reader-centered, it would continue to draw on the popular appeal of the study. As the century progressed, however, that popularization came more and more under the scrutiny of those who grudgingly felt that the study of English literature, if it must have a place in the curriculum, should serve mainly to reinforce established, mainstream ideological, cultural, and social principles rather than the challenging identities of political reform, utilitarian or otherwise. (806)

Among English poets, few were more oblivious to politics than Dale; yet, in his irrationally apocalyptic poem *Irad and Adah; a Tale of the Flood* --informed by a fire-and-brimstone theology offensive even to the very Wesleyan Presence--Dale managed to interweave poetry and politics; were his readers to deviate from the norm, to challenge the status quo, their immortal souls, not simply society, stood to lose. In fact, in his Prefaces to the first edition of *Irad and Adah* (1822), as well as in the reappearances of the poem in *The Poetical Works of the Rev. Thomas Dale, M.A.* (1836), and with *The Widow of Nain, the Outlaw of Taurus, and Other Poems* (1842), Dale insists that his "Poems would, in no respect, compromise, and might possibly advance, the interests of Christian Morals and of Scriptural Religion." (From the Preface of 1842). In his added paragraphs to the later two collections, Dale argues that

> It may be objected, that, with such an end in view, the Volume ought to have consisted exclusively of SACRED POESY. In reply, it may be urged that Many of the Minor Poems, including the "Historical Sketches," were composed at a period of life when the mind does not willingly confine itself to one subject; and it was hoped that the variety, which was an agreeable relief to the writer, might not prove unacceptable to the reader, and more especially to that class of readers for whom the work is peculiarly designed--the young. (v-vi)

The minds of the young may wander--but, should they take the lead offered by Dale's poetical efforts, they would wander in an "approved" manner, contemplating mainly biblical subjects, Dale's poetic biblicity both naive and pernicious theologically. *Irad and Adah* ventures into sublimity and Sadism, yet relentlessly reminds us that attenuation of Amos 4.12 remains its informing purpose. Should the "Reader!" who follows instructions and "prepare[s] to meet thy God!" contemplate the kind of God--the heartless God--that Dale justifies, "the youth" of sound mind would be repelled or frightened away from the fold, with older, more sophisticated readers dismissing Dale's vision as pap. This poet "of sorts" turned poetry into terrorist-religious propaganda when let loose with a pen. Naturally, his University students were served a more varied menu. But the sheer approval of--by virtue of practicing--literature as a means of keeping the young Christian in line somehow clashes with not just Brougham's but with Dale's own ostensible hopes for the services literary studies might provide the masses.

Dale's *Irad and Adah, A Tale of the Flood* confused even contemporaries, one of whom ventures into discussing this narrative by lamenting the reviewer's mission:

> The delusive hope of having encouraged rising talents, or the vainer dream of having checked obtrusive ignorance, such are the visionary supports of the experienced reviewer's fancy; such the airy consolations that still direct his reluctant mind into the weary, way-worn labors of contemporary criticism.--We stop ourselves in the outset of this melancholy yet tempting career of thought, not exactly anticipating whither it would lead us; and confine ourselves "doggedly," and, as in duty bound, to our immediate business. (241 from "*Irad and Adah*, a Tale of the Flood," in *The Monthly Review* 99 (1822): 241-46).[1]

The reviewer confesses that

> Mr. Dale, in his earlier efforts, evinced very considerable poetic abilities; and we are glad to find that we were not deceived in our favorable sentiments of this youthful bard . . . . [W]e welcome some of his general and less sacred passages with a more than ordinary degree of approbation . . . . The fault which keeps him back at present, in our judgment, is an unfortunate propensity to imitate those [uncommon] personages; and especially the most imitable among them, the poet of the Giaour, the Corsair, &c. &c. [and] the unique Childe Harold . . . (241).

In handling specifics of *Irad and Adah*, the writer disdains Dale's "prosaic perplexity . . . , which so strongly marks the modern metaphysic school of poetry" (244).[2] (Dale's emphasis upon the gruesome particulars of death does provide some validation for this anonymous writer's likening *Irad and Adah* to the *Giaour*.) In the end, however, he pronounces that "the rest of the tale of 'Irad and Adah' we recommend to our readers," for the very generous reason (at least for a nineteenth-century reviewer) that "much is performed and more is promised in it" (244, 243). He all but ignores the subject of the poem. Instead, he places his faith in the promise of the poet. His obliviousness is wise. The subject is outmoded, save for riders on the lunatic fringes of evangelicalism.

As Chapter 3 suggests, the English angel/deluge poems compare most profitably according to their sources (in the case of Byron's and Montgomery's common reliance upon Genesis 6.2) or to their modes (in the cases of Moore's and Croly's Ovidian narratives). Without a direct parallel in source, Dale's Spenserian biblical epic derives from the account of world-judgment--placed in the past in his source from Matthew 24--which translates into the present in the poem; the narrator relives the horror of the flood, his tale linked by this means to the sources of the other deluge poems. Dale also shares with the others love as informing theme--divine love proving salutary, carnal love patently suicidal.

In tone, the love Dale's epic espouses differs from the love espoused in the other four poems. The narrator's ineluctable fire-and-brimstone evangelicalism obfuscates the hope the poem attempts to convey. Divine love is the only love worth reciprocating; carnal love--even with spiritual dimensions--leads inevitably to idolatry (worship of the creation rather than the creator), death, loss, grief, and despair. Dale's anomalous Spenserian rendition of antediluvian decadence recalls the Old Testament history recounted in Matthew 24. Without Christian redemption, the human state is hopeless. The narrator's sermonic bombast initially frightens us away from the God the poet hopes will entice us. The tone overwhelms the ultimate thematic implications, and their foundations in hope and promise. We get used to the narrator; we see in this poem Christian assumptions that humankind remains perfectible, through a faith prescribed in Scripture.

Dale omits direct references to angels altogether, despite a source that invites us to recall Genesis 6.1-4; his *Irad and Adah, A Tale of the Flood* stands alone in expunging angels from its activities; with Montgomery's, Byron's, and Moore's, Dale's effort shares world-judgment, in the form of the deluge. Tradition relates this world-judgment--caused by wickedness--to the Nephilim mentioned in Genesis 6.4, creatures usually depicted as giants. His cited New Testament source, Matthew 24.38-39, recalls the Priestly ascription of guilt from Genesis 6.9-13, when there was "corruption" on "earth." It hints, too, at the alternative Yahwist hamartigeny in Genesis 6.5-8, when Yahweh surveys the "evil" endemic in human hearts. This explicit condemnation of the "evil" of humankind (as opposed to creation generally) recalls Vigny's *Le Deluge*, in which all accords with Gods's will, "save for humankind", who "behaves wickedly". In their philosophies of what humans deserve for "wicked" behavior, however, Vigny and Dale differ vastly (to understate the obvious).

If we find one or all of the Genesis and/or Ovidian works garbled in their informing thought (or because of their uncertain implications for individual identity), we may object even more vehemently to the very clarity of Dale's message. Do as God wills; do not transgress as did our antediluvian forbears; world-judgment will come once again--this time for real and forever. Time will be no more. A messianic kingdom will be established on earth. We will meet, and meet the judgment of, God. The prophecies in Revelation will come to pass. *Irad and Adah* becomes a sermon in narrative form. "The last days" are its ultimate focus, despite its temporary interest in two mortal lovers, in Noah's prophecy, and in the Deluge. For like-minded contemporaries, *Irad and Adah* bears direct pertinence to evangelical Christian existence.

In short, Dale's *Irad and Adah, A Tale of the Flood* differs in focus and source from the Genesis and the Ovidian narratives, yet ends with the doom of humankind, and revels in the (sick) sublimity of the Deluge. Its source, Matthew 24.38-39, at once confuses, and mixes poorly with Spenserian heroic tradition. Spenser's Red Cross Knight remains in view--or, when off duty, finds a substitute hero to help him establish the state for the *Faerie Queene*. In Fletcher's Spenserian heroic celebration of *Christ's Victory and Triumph*, Christ participates in his own conquest. Dale's *Irad and Adah* wants a clearly identifiable hero to celebrate in its Spenserian stanzas. Irad advances his candidacy as a hero--and Shelley's Prometheus, as well as Byronic hero-rebels, provide precedents for Irad's acceptance by the age as a hero. Irad is indeed a rebel, determined to escape world-judgment on grounds of his possession of greater sentiment than ordinary men. The narrator stands in his way, so thoroughly calumniating all antediluvians--even Irad--that any heroic stature diminishes. He is doomed from the outset. No Promethean glory is allowed him by the narrator; he will have no place in establishing the new world.

Neither does Noah constitute a substitute hero. True, he will definitely have the key place in the restoration of human society. But he does not undertake this work volitionally. He numbers among those lonely elect who, like Vigny's Moise, shepherd their people only so far, never fully enjoying the community they help establish. Noah feels keenly the loneliness of election when his prophecies go unheeded. (Loneliness manifests itself in bitterness and invective. This abandoned prophet becomes an unpleasant person.) And the new world he has been chosen to forge is merely a stopgap on the way to the true state--the messianic kingdom to be established upon the second coming of Christ, as promised in Revelation.

Neither does Dale follow Fletcher in giving Christ heroic status. Eventually, Christ will triumph. The narrator apprises us of this frequently and stridently. Yet Christ is seldom mentioned (not to mention seen) in this narrative. *Irad and Adah* adds a new dimension to the Christian, Spenserian heroic poem. The reader is invited to serve as the hero; in following the narrator's directives, the reader can take on heroic leadership; the narrator enjoins us to engage in the preparatory struggle necessary before Christ can effect the eschatological overthrow of evil and establish his messianic kingdom.

Problems with chronology skew Dale's intention for his source. Dale's Matthew text recalls Genesis 4.17-20. Irad is Enoch's son--Cain's grandson --in verses 17-18. This Son of Cain fathers Mehujael, father of Methushael, father of Lamech (verses 18-19). Lamech, Irad's great, great grandson marries Adah and Zillah, neither of whom are assigned a personal ancestry, yet by marriage, Adah becomes a Cainite, and bears Jabal, "father of those who dwell in tents and have cattle," the nomads, and, presumably, Jubal, "the father of all those who play the lyre and was the forger of all instruments of bronze and iron" (verses 19-21).[3] If not by ancestry, their disparate generations render Irad and Adah improbably matched. Further, the narrator asserts that Adah is a daughter of Seth. The "sons," and not the "daughters" of Seth generally win the favor of tradition. Sethite ancestry does not creep into Genesis until Genesis 4.25-26, when

25 ... Adam knew his wife again, and she bore a son and called his name Seth, for she said, "God has appointed for me another child instead of Abel, for Cain slew him."
26 To Seth also a son was born, and he called his name Enosh. At that time men began to call upon the name of the LORD.

By that time, too, Adah's place in Cainite history was well established.

Taxonomy initially confuses. Irad is mortal. We assume this from his biblical identity as Enoch's son (and Cain's grandson) in Genesis 4.18, yet his superhuman strength and agility give us some cause for doubt until Part III, Stanza 51, when the narrator finally asserts that "he was mortal," and thereby doomed. Dale brings on a flood, but deprives us of angels.

Mortal, too, are the Sethites, the "sons of God." Dale sticks to the least controversial rendering of *bene ha'elohim*:

Long in sequestered glens and mountains wild,
Peaceful and pure, the tribes of Seth abode;
Pleased on his favored race JEHOVAH smiled,
And Seraphs hailed them as the Sons of God (St. 13).

We hear that theirs was a life of "blameless tenor," unlike that of the "Sons of Cain" (St. 14). Dale's Sethites, much like Montgomery's, "from that Apostate brood / Fled Peace, and Hope, and Joy, a lovely train! / To seek asylum in those mountains rude, / Till Eden bloomed anew in that blest solitude" (St. 14).

The poet sighs:

Ah how from such abodes of bliss serene
Could guests like these be exiled? How could Hell
Win its foul path, unheeded and unseen,
E'en to the spot where saints had loved to dwell?-Small marvel
Man should fall when Angels fell!
Ambition--Pride--the baleful lust of sway
Can pierce the peaceful Anchorite's lonely cell,
The Sage's calm seclusion: and betray
The heedless heart to cast immortal joys away (St. 15).

This moment of charity towards humankind proves rare among the poet's utterances. Who the narrator is--how he explains the presence of "saints" in a pre-Christian landscape--puzzles consistently. For this stanza, he demands from us no prior knowledge of the Bible, or even of *Paradise Lost*. The stanza brings to mind Matthew Lewis's *The Monk* (1793), still in currency when Dale's epic took shape, Lewis's ostensibly invulnerable Ambrosio, doomed to perdition for contemplating a bit wrong-mindedly a deviously placed and deviously drawn representation of the Madonna. Foreknowledge of Lewis would help make sense of Dale's otherwise absurdly anachronistic, and demeaning, explanation of the antediluvian elect in terms of the lust of a cloistered "Anchorite." This stanza makes us wonder, too, how far--and which--"Angels fell" as Dale understands them. Did they lapse into concupiscence? Perhaps. Perhaps not. We are not told. We are told only that the Sethite retreat is penetrated by "a stranger-Maid" (St. 19)--never identified; yet the narrator disdains a bit later the presence of "forms of angels with the soul of Cain" (St. 34); he withholds information about the origins of these hybrid beings. Could this penetration contribute? (Penetration by a stranger recalls Montgomery's narrative, although the results in the earlier work were not always devastating.) This one-woman invasion supports the third hamartigeny--the Pauline judgment against women, rather than angels or Adam and Eve. Yet the focus misleads. The Sethite protagonist in the poem is Adah, a woman. Irad is a Cainite. We are to beware of women, and yet the poem itself narrates the decline of Sethite good (represented by a woman) by unlawful coupling with Cainite evil (represented by a man). For a misogynist poem, alliances are skewed.

The poet condemns lavishly, but depicts sketchily, the forms of licentiousness responsible for world judgment referred to in Matthew 24. 37-39 (likewise in Luke 17.26-27), and effected in Genesis 6.5-8, and Genesis 7.6-24. Unlike Dale's predecessors in Spenserian heroic imitations, *Irad and Adah* minimizes sensuousness. We see consequences rather than causes of transgression. (We never hear--through God or narrator-- a list of clear prohibitions.) We suspect that in the world of Dale's poem, tribes may not mix. Sethites loving Cainites portend, and cause, humankind's annihilation. In the case of Irad and Adah, Irad's fatal act is his being; he is a Cainite, a threat to Seth's daughters. In Adah's case, misdirected fidelity secures her annihilation. So intense is her love for Irad that she expends her full store of love upon him, casting none of it Heaven's way. For the narrator, such constitutes idolatry--hardly befitting a descendant of "saintly Seth."

Dale's narrative, conveyed, as remarked earlier, largely in Spenserian stanzas, divides into three parts. Both his stanzas and overall structure recall Giles Fletcher's ranting, four-part history of *Christ's Victory and Triumph*. In *Irad and Adah*, Part I exhibits "Guilt"; Part II reiterates "Prophecy"; Part III belabors the "Judgment." "Judgment" consumes by far the largest space; judgment is wrathful, vicious, and complete.

The narrator's persona offends; he belongs to the lunatic fringes of millennarian fundamentalism; so pious is our poet--who so obviously savors the suppurating agonies of the dying damned--he risks engendering in the more moderate devout disdain for any deity. While we may not like the narrator, we appreciate the poet's adept control of narrative focuses. Dale masters Miltonic "stationing," as Goslee describes it--both in sketching tableaux against a cosmic backdrop, and in positioning these tableaux within a hierarchy. The poem ranges throughout the wider universe then, laser-sharp, penetrates into an individual's private, intangible being. It settles anywhere and everywhere in between; focal motion generates the excitement in this poem. The far too heavy-handed didactic intrusions annoy.

Part I opens with a rare, upbeat proclamation: "Fair art thou, Syria!" This is followed by a catalogue of beauties in a Syrian summer and autumn. We should seize each whisper of joy; we learn quite soon that this narrator seldom permits sensuous celebration. "But," the poet qualifies, "thou wert fairer in the morn of Time," and we are hereby prepared for a history of "Guilt" (Stanza 1). We next learn that "all beneath the sky was harmony and love," with one significant exception: "All save the heart of Man." (Vigny's *Éloa* comes to mind.) The poet continues with his jeremiad, lamenting that

> enthralled by woman's wanton wile
> Seth's holier offspring stoop to rites profane!
> Alas! that aught so false as Beauty's smile
> Should thus to deeds accurst the Sons of Peace
> beguile (St. 10).

The narrator condemns, but never depicts, such "rites profane"; he merely hints at sensuality: even Chapman's so-called erotic epyllion--*Ovid's Banquet of Sense*--proves more sensual and appealing, despite its total incomprehensibility. Just how degenerate were our antediluvian forebears? We never really know; we are told that they transgress; we do not get to watch. Women are at fault--yet the Cainite, tainted by tribal association --is Irad, Dale's male protagonist.

At Stanza 11, the poet stops to scold, preach, and pitch the first of many fits:

> 'Twas ever thus. A glance--a sigh--a tear--
> The downcast eye--the bosom's fluttering swell
> Can tame the mightiest--and, but Heaven were near,
> Could win the wisest--holiest to rebel.
> A world was lost by one seductive spell.
> Yet think, vain boaster, ere thou proudly dare
> Condemn or curse thy hapless Sire who fell,
> Hadst thou withstood a form so fond and fair?

If *thou* art still untried, be grateful, and beware!

This is as sensual as Dale gets--thankfully, perhaps; the thought of bosoms "fluttering" startles. The poem remains still not particularized; Stanzas 12-19 outline in general terms the course of antediluvian life. Finally, at Stanza 19, we are among the Sethites; a "stranger-Maid" appears and weeps (Stanza 20). Tears become significant focal points and symbols in the narrative. Tears portend good or ill--usually ill, usually moral degeneration. Tears prove either fatal or felt. Fatal tears are shed by women; they distract men, and thereby weaken their devotion. When the maiden weeps before "a son of Seth" she secures her observer's moral demise:

> she *wept*--
> And with her tears subduing softness crept
> Through his whole frame resistless, till he proved
> Though Passion's power had long in silence slept,
> It lived to conquer still: his soul was moved
> With specious pity first--he solaced next--then
> loved.-(St. 20)

Tears, here, soften the Sethite, and distract him from Godly matters.

The narrator contracts and expands periphery, switching from past to present, general to particular. He laments the past when "Those forms of angels, with the soul of Cain" engaged in illicit love; he laments the narrative present, his focus narrowed, fixed upon Adah, "From saintly Seth descended," and Irad, "her loved warrior [who] is a child of Cain" (St. 42). At last, our tale begins. To Irad's promise of a love that will endure after death, Adah weeps. She is the realist. Both are doomed. Tears portend fatality and at the same time are felt. The Cainite woman intuits that her love will end her life; she is torn between tribal and personal fidelity. (Sts. 47-48.) Nonetheless the pair is "entranced" in "ecstasy" (St. 49). Lest we wish them well, the narrator returns to lament the frailty of "human raptures" and to remind us of "Death's deep gloom" (St. 50)--a fitting closure to this commission of "Guilt."

Part II, "Prophecy," moves from the seductive sun--a "Symbol" inviting "idolatry" (Sts. 1-3)--to the narrative present, with Irad and Adah, then to the past, to Noah's prophecy of doom. Stanza 13 fixes focus again upon tears--felt tears, moral tears, tears that "Jesus wept." Christ's tears, unlike those of women, reflect not moral tractability, but rather compassion and empathy for the misguided tractable. From Christ's tears, the narrator widens our focus to Noah's world before the flood. He recounts Noah's prophecy, shifting focus to generalized nature: even nature's colors decline until humankind knows only black--specifically, the blackness of oblivion (St. 32). As Part II closes, Noah's prophecy begins to be realized. Transgressors see that "the festive dance is o'er." We learn that

> In vain they watched and wept and prayed,
> Hell scorned the dupes her wiles had made;
> Yea, should they to the Holiest bow,
> Their prayer would pass unheeded now! (St. 34).

The narrator shows not one iota of compassion.

This narrator revels in "Judgment," Part III, which details the fate of the doomed. Stanza 1 issues the poet's call

> for a voice of thunder! for a blast
> Of that appalling trumpet, which shall break
> Hell's shivering bolts, when Death has smote his last,
> And Time becomes Eternity.

Before this, the fun must come--fun for the poet, that is, who makes the most of his chance to depict agony and suffering.

Once again, he turns our attention to tears--fatal tears, human tears, tears for humankind's fate which humankind itself has secured. Self-pitying tears come too late, in response to mortal stupidity; the narrator finds disbelief in the fact that "Man can sleep, / Fond fool! with immortality at stake! / Sport on the wave that whirls him to the deep, / And smile when Conscience warns to tremble and to weep!" (St. 1.) Mortals weep when tears are unwarranted; mortals do not recognize occasions which should impel them to weep.

The general horror of the deluge, and the finality of the doom, occupy the narrator in Stanzas 2-15. With Stanza 16, the focus narrows; the poet examines the specific lovers' responses to impending death. Stanza 17 pronounces each guilty of his or her own demise. Stanzas 18-21 show Irad carrying Adah to the highest pinnacle, presuming that he will thereby spare his beloved. Irad's efforts double in Stanzas 22-25. Irad works; Adah ponders: "Is there no mercy for a form so fair?" She wonders, "Oh may not deepest penitence and prayer / Wing to th'Eternal's throne, and win him yet to spare?" (St. 25.) The narrator enters the tale he relates, directly answering the lovers with his "No! dream it not." He recalls that

"JEHOVAH warned," but went unheeded when he used Noah as his medium; hence "hope is now presumption. His high will / Is fixed--and cannot change--He spoke, and shall fulfil" (St. 26).

At this point, the narrator becomes more problematic than the narrative he relates, and jeopardizes the credibility of his source. He postulates a far colder "JEHOVAH" than Yahweh at his most primitive moments in Genesis. In Genesis 7, world judgment is complete. But no mortals appeal at the final hour; none believe Noah, and hence see no cause for prayer. Death comes upon them suddenly. Genesis does not leave them to agonize over the consequences of their errancy. God simply kills them; he does not torture them. The narrator transforms a jealous Yahweh into a cruel and spiteful "JEHOVAH." And to what purpose? Does Dale endeavor to teach us through history to eschew inappropriate love? Does he warn us against allowing love to replace worship, or against loving another mortal with an idolatrous fixation and intensity? Does he warn us that mortal individuals risk similar consequences should they indulge in inappropriate love? Are mortals to ignore other mortals altogether? Or does Dale merely aim to remind us to direct love towards Heaven? If so, he risks frightening believers from the fold. Dale, we fear, would want the power to pitch a thunderbolt at any who pose theodicy as a problem. Dale's "JEHOVAH" wins no hearts. Yahweh's means of testing Abraham's loyalty seems rational in comparison to any act of Dale's God.

The narrative continues detailing the lovers' demises. Tears again become focal, symbolizing the hopelessness of being. Irad "felt his spirit droop" (rather an understatement in the face of annihilation) as he viewed a tearful mother, hopelessly "bending o'er her child," the infant awakening and smiling, while "That weeping woman's marble brow o'ercast" as she became aware that death was imminent. She "strained the guiltless victim to her breast, / Kissed its fair cheek, and laid her down to die," uttering that "I dare not hope--I cannot all despair." (Sts. 28-30.) She is defeated. One wonders who the narrator worships. One rankles at his use of women. Thoroughly misogynistic throughout, he suddenly serves up a tableau of motherhood, calculating with pre-Pavlovian certainty the reaction his contemporaries have been trained to proffer. Innocence suffers because of experience. Human-kind, not God, forces injustice.

These stanzas (28-31) focus at once narrowly and broadly--we enter the very private perspective of Irad's emotional center in order to look outward at mortal despair. Stanza 32 broadens slightly; attention turns from Irad's reactions to his and Adah's actions. Irad speeds with Adah "upward still"; cataclysm erupts (St. 33); the lovers crash towards earth, Irad "a thing as lifeless," Adah "senseless by his side" (St. 34). Irad resumes his fight for life, struggling valiantly against certain defeat. (The narrator does not dignify Irad with any ennobling Promethean moral victory through certain physical defeat; the narrator relishes Irad's masochism, and not his defiance in the face of divine injustice.) Irad lasts longer than Adah; he cannot bear to discard his beloved's corpse. By Stanza 60, the battle for life is all but lost. Stanzas 61-90 become the narrator's forum; he preaches gloom, doom, guilt, hopelessness, despair, bleakness, and, in general, denounces humanity. He inserts one stanza of hope late in the narrative (St. 91):

> Yet the Creator-Spirit from above
> Is moving on the waters; through the gloom
> Of desolation beams superior Love,
> And Mercy tempers Justice. To their tomb
> Mankind have sunk in one unvaried doom;
> But yet may Heaven reverse the stern decree;
> And yet again may cheering suns illume
> The world emerging from its dungeon sea,
> And beam the light of life on millions yet to be.

Even this hope proves problematic. Who is the speaker? When does he speak? He apparently dwells in the blank space between Genesis 7 and Genesis 8. He lives after the deluge, yet before restoration has begun. He is not of Noah's crew--yet has survived. His identity remains puzzling--and annoying.

What are we to make of this tale? About this he leaves us no doubt. His closing exhortation (St. 96) implores the

> Reader! be thine the moral! If no more
> From its calmed deeps shall rise the fettered sea;
> If Heaven's fair bow proclaim *this* peril o'er;
> A wreck more fearful yet remains for thee;
> Time only bears thee to Eternity.----
> Tread then the path thy bright Exemplar trod;--
> Think on the day when this vast Earth shall be
> In bursting flames dissolved--yon skies so broad
> Shrink like a shrivelled scroll--
> "Prepare to meet thy God!"

The entire narrative builds towards this outburst from Amos 4.12. Humans are doomed, and are accountable to God. Noah may not actually serve as a "bright Exemplar" for the masses of humankind, for Noah was chosen for salvation, and was informed of this before the catastrophe. (The Deluge here becomes proleptic of the last judgment in Revelation.) The ordinary "Reader!" enjoys no tie-line to divinity (save perhaps for Dale, if the narrator reflects the poet's own attitude). Dale/the Dale narrator serves as a latter day prophet.

Among the five narratives, *Irad and Adah* stands anomalous. Certainly, none could accuse Dale of impiety. (He may well be guilty, however, of abusing God by portraying him as cruelly anthropopathic.) Dale leaves us with a "brief epic," devoid of the warmth of *Paradise Regained*, if such be its prototype, and patterned after Spenserian biblical narratives. If heroes are to come forth, the readers must assume these roles. Dale's poem invites anger at its accompanying tonal heat. As a warning to humankind, the poem fails. We simply do not see any recognizable debauchery. Yet Dale's poem held appeal for its age, as his reviewers confirm (but fail to explain). It is not without belletristic interest; the kaleidoscopic focuses--deliberate, yet unpredictable--represent considerable narrative skill. Dale's contemporary readers responded, perhaps, to its obsession with death--life-in-death, impending death, agonizing death, cataclysmic death, omnivorous death, death seasoned with necrophilia. Not even Keats could offer an inventory of deaths of such variety and amplitude. Oddly enough, Dale's *Irad and Adah* recalls the tone of the curse in Byron's *The Giaour* (1813), when the speaker pronounces,

> But thou, false Infidel! shall writhe
> Beneath avenging Monkir's scythe;
> And from its torments 'scape alone
> To wander round lost Eblis' throne;
> And fire unquenched, unquenchable,
> Around, within, thy heart shall dwell;
> Nor ear can hear nor tongue can tell
> The tortures of that inward hell!
> But first, on earth as Vampire sent,
> Thy corse shall from its tomb be rent:
> Then ghastly haunt thy native place,
> And suck the blood of all thy race;
> There from thy daughter, sister, wife,
> At midnight drain the stream of life;

Yet loathe the banquet which perforce
Must feed thy livid living corse:
Thy victims ere they yet expire
Shall know the demon for their sire,
As cursing thee, thou cursing them,
Thy flowers are wither'd on the stem.
But one that for thy crime must fall,
The youngest, most beloved of all,
Shall bless thee with a *father's* name--
That word shall wrap thy heart in flame!
Yet must thou end thy task, and mark
Her cheek's last tinge, her eye's last spark,
And the last glassy glance must view
Which freezes o'er its lifeless blue;
Then with unhallowed hand shalt tear
The tresses of her yellow hair,
Of which in life a lock when shorn
Affection's fondest pledge was worn,
But now is borne away by thee,
Memorial of thine agony!
Wet with thine own best blood shall drip
Thy gnashing tooth and haggard lip;
Then stalking to thy sullen grave,
Go--and with Gouls and Afrits rave;
Till these in horror shrink away
From Spectre more accursed than they! (PW *Giaour* 3:747-86)

Like Irad, things sensuous and dear to the auditor shall be lost in life, life to become a living hell. Dale's God enacts values Medea lives by--the accursed losing the things most cherished by him. The detail of the curse in *The Giaour* is as harsh as the detail in *Irad and Adah*--with its tableau of the innocent babe. Dale's *Irad and Adah* offers an admixture of Sadism and agony unusual in a Christian heroic poem. It is perhaps this blend that led Dale's reviewer to condemn the poet's imitation of *The Giaour*; Dale's images seem somehow out of place in a poem promising Christian re-demption (yet they do have precedents in the Old Testament prophecies, such as the bloodshed throughout Amos, the blood-drinkers in Micah 7.2, and the piles of corpses in Nahum 3; their violence has ample precedents in Revelation). Perhaps this very theme led Dale to imitate pagan, Byronic curses--in an effort to heighten the putrefaction the unelect did experience at the time of the Deluge, and will experience at the Second Coming. The horror of the unredeemed may be designed to frighten the many into the fold. And each age has its quirks. *Irad and Adah* remains both the most appalling and intriguing of the deluge narratives. At last, a poem of this kind proved too pious for some among the middle-class readership.

For others, it was not. Dale's narrator (not Dale himself) occupies the outer ranges of uncritical piety; Dale postures a spokesperson in this space because of his endeavor to edify "the young." It is difficult to accept that even Dale himself could have believed that *Irad and Adah* fortifies nascent youthful spirituality. All in this poem are damned. And while Amos 4.13 simply invokes us to "prepare," the God we meet in *Irad and Adah* renders "prepare" synonymous with "dread."

This irremediable sense of damnation Dale pinpoints as the cause of Cowper's spiritual anguish. In his "Life of William Cowper," Dale withholds until the end his

> ... remarks on the peculiar delusion under which Cowper laboured during a large portion of his life, and which caused him such pro-
> tracted, and, at times, intolerable agony: which precluded him from even attempting to apply the consolations of the Gospel, under the appalling notion that he had been, from the beginning, a vessel of wrath, fitted and destined only to destruction. This has been ascribed, by some of his biographers, to excess of religious feeling: whether it is not rather attributable to that defect of religious cultivation in his earlier years, which, when the desolation came upon him, left him unprovided with a refuge and a comforter, may be reasonably inferred from other evidence, and is altogether conclusive from his own. (*Poems* 1: lxvi-lxvii)

This biography, written long after Dale had vacated the Chair of English Language and Literature, maintains what its author had always maintained, if his brief remarks to *Irad and Adah* reflect accurately his philosophy of spiritual education--namely, that while youth will deviate in their attention from sacred poetry, they do require a fairly steady induction to the kind. (In writing Cowper's biography, Dale diagnoses Cowper's depression as an outgrowth of Cowper's youthful religious misguidance. Clearly, the guid-ance *Irad and Adah* supplies could exacerbate, rather than assuage, despair of the sort Cowper suffered.) The kind of guidance offered in *Irad and Adah*, again, surely needs no examining. The poem proves bereft of hope; any youth indulging in Dale's epic had best have a proclivity towards hope;

burgeoning Cowpers could well determine themselves "vessels of wrath" from Dale's narrative alone. Matthew may provide a source; the violence of Old Testament prophecy provides the vision of hopelessness informing Dale's narrative. One wonders how the poet could, in good conscience, direct this bleak vision of God to the body of Christian "youth."

One wonders, too, why Dale stayed on at the University of London when internal college politics redefined his function. As a preacher, a professor, and sometimes editor of the *Iris*, Dale obviously had ready ways to make himself heard--often, and loudly. Whether he had the courage, insights, or even inclination to voice anything worth listening to remains in doubt. He clearly was not "planted" at the University to preach Brougham's egalitarian notions. He liked the University setting enough to stay on and teach composition. Was it the university itself that held appeal for Dale, or did the ministry repel? Did Dale enjoy power? (If so, why did he refrain from wielding it?) Did Dale serve any cause other than his own? Were his initial impulses charitable, retrenched innocuous and placid by the University bureaucracy? Thus far, these questions remain open. This is too bad.

One would like to point to some character defects in Dale in response. One fears that University Politics then, as now, turned a moderate champion of egalitarian educational leanings into a gutless wonder; one fears that such happened then, as it happens now. One fears that Dale sold his ideals, and surrendered his idealism, once he lived through committee battles. One fears that he learned what one should not know--that Academic freedom is a sham. And that it always has been. And always will be. Free exchanges of ideas within university settings neither served (now, neither serve) the body politic nor represented (represent) a cost-effective "package" of hours of professorial lives for University budgeting committees to buy.

Brougham's victory was legislative only. Institutions characteristically remain agnostics in the face of legislation. Universities abide by constitutions, unwritten and of their own design, that serve not even inanimate objects, but rather coddle abstract ideals, such as "a university," and "excellence." Swift's flying island landed. One hopes that it is not all too clear why Dale's ideas and ideals remain unvoiced despite his multiple media for dispersing them powerfully. One fears that the reason is all too patently clear. Unfortunately, the brave new world Dale was chosen to forge was *not* merely a stopgap on the way to the true and final state. "Prepare to meet thy God!" No such luck for the professoriate. Not even Milton's personal Holy Spirit would deign identify the power source behind decisions propelling and repressing instructors at public Universities, not at Dale's, and not at its prolific offspring, both British and American. *Irad and Adah*, if sappy poetry, was politically safe. Likewise for the later biblical narratives Dale churned out while teaching English composition.

Notes to Chapter 10

[1]This reviewer maintains that poetry is important--and that the critic's task is to differentiate between poetic ventures that suit themselves to, and those that diminish from, this importance. The nature of this importance eludes. Is it a public, social occupation? Does the poet serve as arbiter of ethical, political, and social values, as Dryden, Pope, and others would have maintained (and succeeded in convincing some)? Does the poet serve as a source of philosophy? In the romantic reviews, all that remains is the "given" that poetry is important. The answer to the question why seems to have been forgotten; even the question itself stays suppressed. See Dale's conservative predilections in his various *Lectures* delivered both at University and it King's College (in References, below).

[2]In this "school," *Irad and Adah* joins Byron's "metaphysical dramas." *Metaphysic*, as applied by Romantic reviewers, apparently relates to subject more than style; anything concerned with extra-terrestrial adventures qualifies.

[3]"Presumably" qualifies here because while the text asserts that "Adah bore Jabal," it merely follows by claiming that "His brother's name was Jubal." Zillah, similarly, "bore Tubal-cain; he was the forger of all instruments of bronze and iron" (verse 22). Yet "The sister of Tubal-Cain was Na'amah" (verse 22), context, not connective, assigning Zillah as Na'amah's mother, and likewise Adah as Jubal's.

Epilogue/end

By 1830, Montgomery had discerned that literature had

. . . approached a crisis, when some considerable change for the better or worse may be anticipated; when literature in England will return to the love of nature and simplicity, or degenerate into bombast and frivolity. (*Lectures* 324)

The latter occurred. He doubtless did not anticipate how thorough going this degeneration would be. Poetry--once an arbiter of taste, ethics, and patterns of behavior--dissolved into irrelevance, not as a pastime (for, in the cost accountant's world, one must have something to do in the hours of life not bartered away), but as a mode of communication with any potential for shaping readers' views of themselves and their kind, of startling them into revaluating their institutions and means of interacting. The heterogeneous audience Montgomery identified and applauded--ensuring for poets due recompense for hard labor (or so he thought)--consigned poetry to a blandness and mediocrity that neither Sidney nor Shakespeare could have envisioned when their personae lauded, prematurely, the power and immortality of the printed word. (Sidney's and Shakespeare's texts today crumble into dust. Those not caught in time on microfilm will be totally lost in 250 years, the durability of microforms only estimable, not proven. Those not lost will go unread, save by students assigned to read them--the poets'"immortality" thus perpetuated, but under duress.)

In the repressive decade before the Reform Bill of 1832, readers were ready to take offense at anything conceivably offensive, no matter how rigorously they needed to tax their imaginations before the innocuous could be deemed objectionable. The twelve-year-old Barbara Donegal was prohibited from reading a poem telling us that love is fraught with sadness --sadness born of fear and loss--yet remains one of the few enriching parts of living. *The Loves of the Angels* warns of the dangers of love, yet recognizes that as long as individuals come together, love will be. *Heaven and Earth* tells us to go ahead and love, regardless of others' taboos, restrictions, or rules that would render some liaisons unallowable. *The World Before the Flood* shows how, from mortal love, we may ascend to divine love. *The Angel of the World* and *Irad and Adah* tell us to watch out, lest we engage in an unapproved union. The latter sentiment was the most palatable to the prudent readership of the age.

The poet-prophet, or genius associated with the "romantic" age still found publishers, if fewer readers. The Promethean individualism, the "romantic" hero (wrong in the hypocrite's valuation, "right" in the eyes of a higher morality), the problem of theodicy, the hope for social reform: these themes, commonplaces of British "romanticism," recur in the angel/deluge poems. Yet England's amorous angels--especially Byron's and Moore's-- disturbed their heterogeneous readership. Sensuality proved unacceptable when attributed to angels. (One thing must be said to the credit of these detractors: they were indeed *very careful* readers. Sensuality--not even in Moore's poem, the one most frequently faulted for licentiousness--fails to overwhelm. A bee hunts for pollen in *The Loves of the Angels*--providing one of the most lascivious metaphors we can pinpoint.) These poems affronted "theological truth," at least as theological truth was misunderstood by an audience appallingly negligent both of the Bible itself and of the histories of theology and exegesis. England illustrated the tyranny and repression inhering in judgments derived from consensus; in matters of literature, the majority was right--"right" determined by cash register receipts. No one asked that the majority be educated. The cost accountant's world flourishes, in fact, when its media direct themselves to an uninformed and uncritical majority. After all, should thinking be encouraged, human beings could well decide that their intrinsic worth far outvalues--and has absolutely nothing to do with--their liquefiable assets. (Policymakers would be deprived of some of their more cherished, simplistic ways of debasing individuals.) Should thinking be encouraged, people might decide that selling away hours of life, that deriving pleasure from making money for someone else's company, that accumulating money as a way of feeling good about oneself, that heeding policies serving the good of managers to the detriment of laborers, that placing the self second to every one of the corporate identities forced upon an individual (familial, institutional, religious, political, and the like), that accepting taboos against certain unions of individuals (responsible for irrational contempt for miscegenation and homosexuality) and that accepting unquestioned other mindless prohibitions (against suicide, against abortion, against euthanasia---by which "Cain *was* right to kill Abel," against youth and age, against, in short, all and anything human)--all prove patently absurd. Had the English readership of the 1830's demanded the time and tools for critical thought, England would have had no special legacy to corporate America, mindlessness prerequisite to the domination by large corporations currently allowed, without challenge, in the United States.

***

"I have heard the mermaids singing each to each.
"I do not think that they will sing to me."

Prufrock is luckier than he knows. One should not hear things that make no sound. This sort of thing must be halted. When I first started playing with angels, I found them intrinsically amusing. They have ceased to amuse.

I met them first in *Heaven and Earth,* which led me to Chew's study of Byron's dramas. Byron did not take angels, as angels, seriously; he used them for their metaphoric convenience. I did not expect to find them taken seriously by anyone else in his age. I was obviously wrong.

When I was working with Moore's angels, I wanted to check something in Suarez. I was in a very large research library, was pressed for time, and tried what could have been a shortcut, had it panned out--namely, the generic "Angels" section. Suarez' "Angels" do not live in the generic angels drawer, just as angels in the nineteenth century did not live undisturbed between the covers of French compendia. Under the "Angels" heading, I did find something chilling--a card, with the author, Graham, William, assigning a new role to *Angels: [as] God's Secret Agents.* The need for human secret agents is questionable. We absolutely do not need celestial ones. The angels must be set free. They are very, very tired. They have been forced to work for far too long. (The angels who, in Revelation, deafen God with their perpetual chants of "Holy, Holy, Holy," must surely annoy, and block out contending praises and prayers.) Overworking them will make them mean. This is the only explanation I can offer for the unfathomable enthusiasm (and I use the term in its eighteenth-and nineteenth-century sense) generated by the neo-evangelicalistic revival spreading hate and repression, in the name of a loving God, throughout the United States at present. Let the angels sleep, if they choose. Let them be. They are tired, and do not wish to be secret agents. They wish to find the old companions Diderot, Herbelot, and Fourmont introduced them to. They want to miscegenate with the chaemera and satyrs and nymphs they learned to live with some 250 years ago. This, they have told me personally.

(If Oral Roberts can receive bills from God for $8,000,000-, payable by a designated date, with not interest, but rather death, the penalty for delinquent payment, I can receive petitions from angels for freedom from additional duties. My angels will not kill me if I do not succeed in setting them free. Oral Roberts' God was going to kill him, had Roberts been unable to amass enough cash.

I will never understand why Roberts did not let that bill be turned over for "collection." Had I been Roberts, and had I been actually convinced that I had received God's bill, the promised death for delinquency would truly have been "Gospel," or "good news." From that point on, I would have sat in my Prayer Tower--or, in my case, on my patio--and not lifted a finger to do, or have done, anything whatsoever. Surely a believer who gets such a clear invitation to join the Creator, and to do so by such a simple means --abject passivity, has to question the wisdom of launching a fundraising campaign. Is not the goal of the Evangelist to go on home to humanity's maker? God does *not* work in mysterious ways; professional Godpeople do. I never thought I would articulate anything of this sort. This message was made clearly, and far more stridently, by the so-called Freethinkers in the later nineteenth century. I thought that this sort of work was over. From the events of the past two decades, I see that the Freethinkers have been forgotten. I have nothing against believers--who believe, and who take comfort from belief.

I am outraged at believers who try to legislate how I, or how anyone else, must behave, think, respond, or act; belief in such cases equates to tyranny. I am no friend to tyranny. I would have it expunged. It never will be. But we can try. And keep on trying.)

England's amorous angels found a welcome harbor in France in the nineteenth century, and are still kept alive by French poets, who even today write accounts of angels and mortal lovers, accounts that offend neither French Christian orthodoxy nor people in Europe and the United States offended by the recent neo-evangelicalistic revival. As with Vigny and Lamartine, and later Hugo, the French use the angels as metaphorical and allegorical figures. Perhaps Taine was right. Perhaps the literal-mindedness with which the English--and their American counterparts--confronted the Scriptures rendered the Bible useless as a source of poetic matter. The French used, and still use, the angels of Genesis 6.1-4 as starting points for expressing hope in the ultimate perfectibility of humankind.

Angels have applied for French citizenship; they do not mind French poets talking about them, as long as the French do not attempt to put them to work. God, the French apparently know, has no need for secret agents, and hence the French would allow the angels to spend their dotage where they would, in those glorious compendia of oriental learning. Meeting them there is delightful. Herbelot should be turned into English. We would have access to adventures in orientalism we have lost. We would be much closer to a European heritage that--in years, just yesterday, when compared to *Gilgamesh*--threatens otherwise to lapse into an adventure more and more impossible to reenact, more and more impossibly distant.

Appendix

This appendix presents three texts (not critical editions), intended to afford familiarity with three of the poems central to this discussion, poems often neglected because inaccessible. The first is *The Loves of the Angels* as it appeared in its first four editions, with footnotes displaying Moore's emendations for his revised (fifth) edition.[1] Since its availability in April 1823, the fifth, revised edition has been adopted by most compilers of Moore's collected poems--despite the fact that Lansdowne, Byron, and even Moore himself express preference for the original version (the text of the first four editions) which Longman brought forth with the unstoppable successive force of quadruplets coming to light.[2] Charges of blasphemy and irreverence--if relatively few--left Moore discomfited.

The present text has been appended mainly to show what all the commotion was about--to show the text that caused all the fuss, the text that, according to Ward, received more reviews between 1821-1826 than any other single poem in the period. ("Why?" remains open to debate.) Fear by the pious for the adequacy and stability of their faith may account for the onslaught of hostile responses. When we encounter the first edition--remembering that this is the text that the elder Barbara Donegal would not let her twelve-year-old niece Barbara read--we may be startled by the chokehold the compatriots in repression threatened to place upon poetry in general; doggeral and pap had the best chance of passing uncensured. (Perhaps for good reason, serious writers gradually turned to prose.)

After receiving bewildering and inordinate attention, *The Loves of the Angels* dropped through a hole in time, forgotten for nearly a century. It deserves a new appearance--for some as a poem, for most as an artifact and index of taste and sensibilities.I hope it appeals--if not poetically, at least historically, illustrating the narrow tolerance for invention in the repressive decade prior to the Reform Bill. It should help sketch a more comprehensive picture of that era in British literature designated the "romantic" period. Byron and Shelley died before experiencing the full repercussions of militant intolerances. Moore lived long, but after the 1830's, did not live well; before the 1820's, he endured with little hope for his financial security or physical comfort; by the end of the decade, he was denied even the comfort of turning concepts into verse with any certain freedom.[3]

A specific instance of repression--the fate of Byron's *Cain*--as well as the apparent endlessness of Moore's burdensome debts, prompted Moore's response to Longman's notice, sometime around 12 January, that Moore "must revise for a fifth edition, as they [the Longmans] are almost half through the fourth"; Moore offers to revise even more extensively than Longman requests. He suggests that he "could make the 'Angels' completely *eastern*, and thus get rid of that connection with the Scriptures, which they [the publishers] fear will, in the long run, be a drag on the popularity of the poem." (JTM 2: 617) By 18 January 1823, Longman had accepted, applauding heartily the wisdom of this strategy. Moore's revision, ready sometime in the middle of February 1823 (JTM 2: 619), was withheld by Longman "for their [company's] Trade Sale in April" (LTM 2: 515), by which time 6,000 copies (all copies of the first through fourth editions) had been sold.

Moore's equivocation over revising his *Angels* will render the problem of authorial intent particularly difficult for an editor of a critical edition. On the one hand, as noted, Moore himself came up with the idea of rendering his *Angels* wholly "eastern"; the fifth edition revisions may be said to reflect his intent. Yet his commitment wavered. Once he shared his proposal with Longman, he ultimately executed his idea under duress; Lansdowne's objection to the renovation prompts Moore to ask Longman to consider aborting the plans for revision. Longman's negative judgment becomes tantamount to a mandate to revise, rendering the fifth edition changes questionable as reflections of authorial intent. This issue becomes even more complicated. Lest we accept the readings in the first edition as authoritative, the present comparison reveals that the majority of Moore's revisions have absolutely nothing to do with the purported conversion of his angels into "Turks," but rather reflect stylistic decisions. Moore apparently takes his assignment to alter the poem's mythic framework as an opportunity to rectify stylistic infelicities. (Interestingly, almost none of his changes reflect reviewers' distaste for his style; many reviews object to specific passages, almost none of which Moore alters. Stylistic changes ostensibly reflect Moore's pleasure.) Moore may well prefer the design of the first edition, and particular phrases in the fifth.

As indicated earlier, the present text is not, by any means, a critical edition, in the sense that the term has come to bed used. Collation, or comparison, has been limited to copies of the first five editions of *The Loves of the Angels*, to Moore's own edition of his *Works*, to Godley's 1910 reproduction of Moore's text, and to the American edition identified in note 1, below. I have made no attempt to collate copies of all texts printed within Moore's lifetime (texts which he could possibly have emended), nor have I checked for substantive changes in any edition after the fifth--a task which seemed unnecessary for my purposes here, especially since the fifth edition is reproduced unaltered in Moore's and in Godley's editions.

(Deliberate changes by Moore himself are doubtful. Moore generally records in his journal the nature and extent of any writing he has completed on a given day--a habit evident when *The Loves of the Angels* becomes an active project for him once again, while revising the poem during January-February 1823. His subsequent references to this poem amount to reactions to reviews--both printed reviews and informal commments exchanged in conversations.) Neither have I consulted manuscripts. (Jordan reports that "one copy of the manuscript for the poem is in the manuscript collection of Trinity College, Dublin, MS Q.4.43." He adds that "a servant at Sloperton, perhaps Hannah, purportedly saved this copy to present to a Devizes watchmaker, Mr. Stratton, who wished a memento of Moore," and explains that "this servant was entrusted with burning rough drafts, usually voluminous, of Moore's poems once a final clean copy had been made for the publishers." This manuscript Jordan describes as "a draft of 67 pages, 1-19 missing, a rather clean copy having only minor changes of a word or a line," *Bolt Upright* 382.) Future editors of Moore may well find other fragments in manuscript collections.

Since Moore annotated his poem, and sometimes his notes, layers of annotations accumulate here, and want explanation. This text begins with the preface to the first edition, and is followed by the revised preface, appearing with the fifth and subsequent editions. Close proximity should provide ease in comparing the two prefaces. After the preface follows the text, presented here with its first edition readings. Footnotes indicate substantive variants, as well as potentially significant changes in punctuation.[4]

Moore's notes prove difficult to arrange; they constitute his most important device for effecting the conversion of his angels. In the first edition, Moore's text includes a few footnotes (designated by Longman's printer with asterisks), and closes with a collection of endnotes. I follow the same format here. Notes appearing as footnotes in the first edition are presented here as such. Notes gathered as endnotes to the first edition are collected as endnotes here; notes prepared new for the fifth edition appear in brackets among the endnotes to this final collection.

*****

Croly's *The Angel of the World*--the least popular of the angel/deluge poems--underwent substantial revision for its second appearance in 1830, in *The Poetical Works of the Rev. George Croly*, ten years after its initial appearance with *Sebastian; a Spanish Tale* in 1820. No one seems to have noticed. Croly's *Poetical Works* were reviewed favorably (*Eclectic Review* 51 (1830): 525-7), yet the reviewer passes by *The Angel* in order to discuss less publicized works. Retrospective reviews of Croly's writings likewise name, without exploring, *The Angel.* (See "Dr. Croly" in *Living Age* 42 (1854): 318-21), and Gilfillan's assessment of Croly's career in the *Eclectic Magazine of Foreign Literature, Science and Art* 14 (1848): 459-65.) Croly's revisions seem dictated by his own poetic sensibilities; they in no way answer reviewers' objections in 1820 that Croly's tale wants "human interest," that its outcome remains uncertain, or that its language, while enrapturing, masks the poem's lack of substance. If anything, the 1830 revisions enhance the poem's stylistic felicities, but without clarifying or humanizing the action.

This appendix presents for the first time since 1820 the original version of *The Angel of the World*, and for the first time since 1844 the 1830 text (which, bound with N. P. Willis' *Sacred Poems*, appeared in New York in 1843, and, bound with Leigh Hunt's *The Story of Rimini*, appeared again in New York, in 1844). The original has been selected instead of the revised text solely because the 1820 text was known to contemporary reviewers. The footnotes show all potentially significant variants, offered to facilitate reconstruction of the 1830 revision. The sigla here used are identical to those used for the text of *The Loves of the Angels*, as are explained below.

*****

The final text in this Appendix simply copies the *Fragment of a Poem on The World Before the Flood* as it appears in the *Poetical Works of Reginald Heber, Lord Bishop of Calcutta* (London, 1841), the first of several posthumous editions of Heber's collected poetry. Biographical and bibliographical research has yet to be completed; Heber is known best through *The Life of Reginald Heber . . . by His Widow [Amelia Heber], With Selections from His Correspondence, Unpublished Poems, and Private Papers . . . .*, 2 vols. (London: John Murray, 1830). The fragment bears intrinsic interest. Heber quotes and cites Genesis 6.2 as his epigraph His 310 completed blank verse lines (with unfinished phrases blocked out as lines 311-312), explore an unusual dimension of familial love. Jared, the King, abuses familial love; delusions of reigning as Patriarch of a race of demigods lead Jared into demanding that Ada, his daughter, yield to the propositions of an angel--propositions abhorrent to Ada, and, Ada realizes, abhorrent to God. The situation seemingly leads towards Ada's denunciation of paternal love as testimony to her allegiance to God; her emotions and allegiances are pulled in multiple directions before the close of the fragment. Montgomery's influence--save for the title--seems minimal, although both Montgomery's epic and Heber's fragment illustrate the discomfort potentially attendant upon love, particularly when love is abused. The text is reprinted here because it seldom surfaces; Heber has attracted little attention in the present century, although his writings, and writings about him, proliferated throughout the nineteenth century.

*****

Byron's *Heaven and Earth*, bound to appear quite soon in McGann's edition of Byron's poetical works, is readily available in editions by Marshall, Jump, and, of course, E.H. Coleridge. Montgomery's *The World Before the Flood* warrants a critical edition; its length, and its multiple appearances within Montgomery's lifetime, will provide an editor with a formidable challenge. Montgomery himself--particularly his *Lectures on Poetry*--reflected the taste of his age; he warrants liberation from obscurity.[5] Dale's *Irad and Adah*--also long--appeared in at least three editions during Dale's lifetime; Dale's life and writings were often heralded in the period. If he wants aesthetic or conceptual appeal for the present generations of readers, his historical importance invites us to study more fully the Dean of Rochester.

Notes to Appendix

[1]No recent text of the *Loves* reprints any variants; a nineteenth-century collection of *The Poetical Works of Thomas Moore, Complete in One Volume* (New York: Leavitt & Allen), 1858: 448-74, reproduces most of the variants in the prefaces, and many in the poem. A. D. Godley, Moore's most recent editor (1910; rpt. 1924) chose to ignore variants, giving authority to the fifth edition text.

[2]The first four editions were printed between 23 December 1822-17 January 1823.

[3]See Jordan, *Bolt Upright*, on the uncomfortable--yet coveted--congregation of Moore, Wordsworth, and Henry Crabb Robinson on 2 April 1822. According to Robinson's notes, politics offered a safer arena of discourse than poetry; neither subject was comfortably addressed directly. (359-61) Two key poets of the age--poets who wanted to meet and were able to meet--found themselves sensing constraints upon the range of permissible exchanges. In the decades following, Wordsworth would find the public acceptance that eluded the later Moore--the Wordsworth of the *Ecclesiastical Sonnets*, the Wordsworth celebrating an institution, rather than the Wordsworth who still moves us with his *Prelude*, his *Tintern Abbey*, and like ventures into the human heart. Moore turned more regularly to satire, hyperbole alone safely masking the discontent he sensed wanted articulating.

[4]I list punctuation marks that could intentionally end or suspend an idea; footnotes indicate marks that change pauses into stops, or stops into pauses. Moore--or probably the Longmans--habitually pair dashes with commas (in the revision, sometimes deleting penultimate commas from lines ending with dashes); I do not note double pauses changed to single --and single changed to double--since a pause is a pause, no matter how baroquely marked. I do note dashes turned into semicolon-dash conjunctions, since the semi marks a stop (although the function of the suspending dash *after* a stop remains equivocal.) I record added or deleted exclamation points, as well as other altered points that may influence emphasis.

[5]See the plaudits afforded "Montgomery's *Lectures on Poetry, &c*" in *The Eclectic Review* NS 10 (July 1833): 1-24.

Sigla

Symbols Used in the Present Text

I have adopted standard sigla to indicate variants. Readings appearing in the first four editions are given to the left of a terminal bracket, followed by a "1," the first four editions constituting virtual reissues of the first. A semicolon following a "1" indicates the end of a first edition reading. Revisions appearing in the fifth edition follow the semicolon, and are designated "5". No punctuation is added between the variant appearing in the fifth edition and the siglum "5" itself. (For example, should a comma, period, semicolon, dash, or other mark appear before a "5," it may be assumed that a comma (period, etc.) appears in the revised text. A swung dash (~) indicates that a corresponding word or mark appearing to the left of the bracket (the first edition reading) is retained in the fifth, the new words or points appearing before or after the swung dash. A carat (^) indicates a deletion from the first edition; everything save for the word or mark replaced with the ^ remains unaltered in the fifth edition. Variant readings are preceded by line numbers. Since lineation varies after line 28, lines to the left of a slash (/) represent numbers in the first edition, lines to the right representing corresponding lines in the fifth. Parentheses are used for editorial comments; these comments are italicized, kept to a minimum, and usually note either when and how many lines have been deleted from the first edition, or where and how many complete lines have been composed new for the fifth edition. The text of these new lines appears in the parentheses.

For readers unaccustomed to the sigla I have described, I provide three examples that will hopefully ease translation. The first example illustrates how to decode notes indicating altered punctuation. The designation "328 / 312 mine] 1 ; ~ , 5.", indicates that line 328 in the first edition corresponds to line 312 in the fifth; in the first edition "mine" appears unpunctuated. In the fifth, "mine"--indicated by a ~ (indicating an unaltered word)--is punctuated with a comma, i. e., "mine,". The second example illustrates a designation for substantive changes. The note "1302 / 1265 have I look'd doating on] 1 ; and oft I've looked upon 5." indicates that line 1302 in the first edition corresponds to line 1265 in the fifth. The first edition text reads "'Too long have I look'd doating on" and the fifth edition reads "'Too long and oft I've look'd upon". The third example highlights a less extensive substantive change. The note " 1288 / 1245 "And hold thee thus,] 1 ; "~ clasp ~ once 5.", shows that line 1288 in the first edition corresponds to line

1245 in the fifth. The first edition text reads, "'And hold thee thus, without a cloud,"; the fifth reads, "'And clasp thee once without a cloud".

Moore's endnotes for the first four editions appear as endnotes here. Moore quoted page numbers in the original. Line numbers, followed by a ".1" (for first edition) are used to indicate their corresponding lineation in the present text. (Brackets enclosing these line numbers indicate only that the original page number has been replaced by lines.) Notes that Moore composed new for the fifth edition appear also in this endnote section; bracketed line numbers followed by a ".5" indicate that a footnote has been inserted into the fifth edition. The very few notes appearing in both editions are so designated; line numbers from the first edition are indicated to the left of a slash (/); those from the fifth appear to the right. The designation ".1 and .5" indicates that the note survived the revision. A very few notes-- in their entirety, or nearly so--appear in both editions, but in such disparate places that they constitute different notes (conveying different meaning in their respective contexts). These notes are repeated in their entirety; those with line numbers alone come from the first edition; those with line numbers followed by ".5" come from the fifth.

The sigla here described also apply to the text and variant list for Croly's *The Angel of the World*. This poem, first appearing in 1820, was revised substantially for its collection into Croly's *Poetical Works* of 1830. In the present text, the designation "1" represents the 1820 reading, the designation "2" the 1830 (or second edition). Again, no attempt has been made to establish an authoritative text, or to establish authorial intent. The variants listed should help illustrate exactly how much care Croly took in emending his *Angel* for a second edition--both the new edition and the emendations remaining unnoticed.

THE

LOVES OF THE ANGELS,

A Poem.

By THOMAS MOORE.

———

It happened, after the sons of men had multiplied in those days, that daughters were born to them elegant and beautiful; and when the Angels, the sons of heaven, beheld them, they became enamoured of them.

The Book of Enoch, chap. vii. [vi] sect. 2.

———

LONDON:

Printed For

LONGMAN, HURST, REES, ORME, AND BROWN,

Paternoster-Row.
1823 [1822].

PREFACE

This Poem, somewhat different in form, and much more limited in extent, was originally designed as an episode for a work, about which I have been, at intervals, employed during the last two years. Some months since, however, I found that my friend Lord Byron had, by an accidental coincidence, chosen the same subject for a Drama; and, as I could not but feel the disadvantage of coming after so formidable a rival, I thought it best to publish my humble sketch immediately, with such alterations and additions as I had time to make, and thus, by an earlier appearance in the literary horizon, give myself the chance of what astronomers call an *Heliacal rising*, before the luminary, in whose light I was to be lost, should appear.

As objections may be made, by persons whose opinions I respect, to the selection of a subject of this nature from the Scripture, I think it right to remark, that, in point of fact, the subject is *not* scriptural--the notion upon which it is founded (that of the love of Angels for women) having originated in an erroneous translation by the LXX. of that verse in the sixth chapter of Genesis, upon which the sole authority for the fable rests.* The foundation of my story, therefore, has as little to do with Holy Writ as have the dreams of the later Platonists, or the reveries of the Jewish divines; and, in appropriating the notion thus to the uses of poetry, I have done no more than establish it in that region of fiction, to which the opinions of the most rational Fathers, and of all other Christian theologians, have long ago consigned it.

In addition to the fitness of the subject for poetry, it struck me also as capable of affording an allegorical medium, through which might be shadowed out (as I have endeavoured to do in the following stories,) the fall of the Soul from its original purity--the loss of light and happiness which it suffers, in the pursuit of this world's perishable pleasures--and the punishments, both from conscience and Divine justice, with which impurity, pride, and presumptuous inquiry into the awful secrets of God, are sure to be visited. The beautiful story of Cupid and Psyche owes its chief charm to this sort of "veiled meaning," and it has been my wish (however I may have failed in the attempt) to communicate the same *moral* interest to the following pages.

* See Note. [M.]
1-30 This Poem . . . consigned it.] 1 ; omitted in 5.

[*Below appears the Preface as Moore revised it for the fifth and subsequent editions.*]

PREFACE.

The Eastern story of the angels Harut and Marut,[1] and the Rabbinical fictions of the loves of Uzziel and Shamchazai,[2] are the only sources to which I need refer, for the origin of the notion on which this Romance is founded. In addition to the fitness of the subject for poetry, it struck me also as capable of affording an allegorical medium, through which might be shadowed out (as I have endeavored to do in the following stories) the fall of the Soul from its original purity[3]--the loss of light and happiness which it suffers, in the pursuit of this world's perishable pleasures--and the punishments, both from conscience and Divine justice, with which impurity, pride, and presumptuous inquiry into the awful secrets of Heaven are sure to be visited. The beautiful story of Cupid and Psyche owes its chief charm to this sort of "veiled meaning," and it has been my wish (however I may have failed in the attempt) to communicate to the following pages the same *moral* interest.

Among the doctrines, or notions, derived by Plato from the East, one of the most natural and sublime is that which inculcates the pre-existence of the soul, and its gradual descent into this dark material world, from that region of spirit and light which it is supposed to have once inhabited, and to which, after a long lapse of purification and trial, it will return. This belief, under various symbolical forms, may be traced through almost all the Oriental theologies. The Chaldeans represent the Soul as originally endowed with wings, which fall away when it sinks from its native element, and must be reproduced before it can hope to return. Some disciples of Zoroaster once inquired of him, "How the wings of the Soul might be made to grow again?"--"By sprinkling them," he replied, "with the Waters of Life."--"But where are those Waters to be found?" they asked.--"In the Garden of God," replied Zoroaster.

The mythology of the Persians has allegorized the same doctrine, in the history of those genii of light who strayed from their dwellings in the stars, and obscured their original nature by mixture with this material sphere; while the Egyptians, connecting it with the descent and ascent of the sun in the zodiac, considered Autumn as emblematic of the Soul's decline towards darkness, and the reappearance of Spring as its return to life and light.

Besides the chief spirits of the Mahometan heaven, such as Gabriel, the angel of Revelation, Israfil, by whom the last trumpet is to be sounded, and Azrael, the angel of death, there were also a number of subaltern intelligences, of which tradition has preserved the names, appointed to preside over the different stages, or ascents, into which the celestial world was supposed to be divided.[4] Thus Kelail governs the fifth heaven; while Sadiel, the presiding spirit of the third, is also employed in steadying the motions of the earth, which would be in a constant state of agitation, if this angel did not keep his foot planted upon its orb.[5]

Among other miraculous interpositions in favor of Mahomet, we find commemorated in the pages of the Koran the appearance of five thousand angels on his side at the battle of Bedr.

The ancient Persians supposed that Ormuzd appointed thirty angels to preside successively over the days of the month, and twelve greater ones to assume the government of the months themselves; among whom Bahman (to whom Ormuzd committed the custody of all animals, except man,) was the greatest. Mihr, the angel of the 7th month, was also the spirit that watched over the affairs of friendship and love;--Chur had the care of the disk of the sun;--Mah was agent for the concerns of the moon;--Isphandarmaz (whom Cazvin calls the Spirit of the Earth) was the tutelar genius of good and virtuous women, &. &. &. For all this the reader may consult the 19th and 20th chapters of Hyde de Relig. Vet. Persarum, where the names and attributes of these daily and monthly angels are with much minuteness and erudition explained. It appears, from the Zend-avesta, that the Persians had a certain office or prayer for every day of the month (addressed to the particular angel who presided over it), which they called the Sirouze. The celestial Hierarchy of the Syrians, as described by Kircher, appears to be the most regularly graduated of any of these systems. In the sphere of the Moon they placed the angels, in that of Mercury the archangels, Venus and the Sun contained the Principalities and the Powers;--and so on to the summit of the planetary system, where, in the sphere of Saturn, the Thrones had their station. Above this was the habitation of the Cherubim in the sphere of the fixed stars; and still higher, in the region of those stars which are so distant as to be imperceptible, the Seraphim, we are told, the most perfect of all celestial creatures, dwelt.

The Sabaeans also (as D'Herbelot tells us) had their classes of angels, to whom they prayed as mediators, or intercessors; and the Arabians worshipped *female* angels, whom they called Benab Hasche, or, Daughters of God.

---

1 See note. [M.] [page number given in text of 5].

2 Hyde, de Relig. Vet. Persarum, p. 272. [M.]

3 The account which Macrobius gives* of the downward journey of the Soul, through that gate of the zodiac which opens into the lower spheres, is a curious specimen of the wild fancies that passed for philosophy in ancient times. [M.]

In the system of Manes, the luminous or spiritual principle owes its corruption not to any evil tendency of its own, but to a violent inroad of the spirits of darkness, who, finding themselves in the neighborhood of this pure light, and becoming passionately enamoured of its beauty, break the boundaries between them, and take forcible possession of it. | [M.]

4 "We adorned the lower heaven with lights, and placed therein a guard of angels. "--*Koran*, chap. xli. [M.]

5 See D'Herbelot, *passim* [M.]

* In Somn. Scipionis, cap. 12. [M.]

| See a Treatise "De la Religion des Persees" by the Abbe Foucher, Memoires de l'Academie, tom. xxxi. p. 456. [M.]

---

9 stories,)] 1 ; ~ ^) 5.

15 God,] 1 ; Heaven ^ 5

18-19 communicate the same *moral* interest to the following pages.] 1; ~ to the following pages the same *moral* interest. 5.

The
Loves of the Angels

'Twas when the world was in its prime,
  When the fresh stars had just begun
Their race of glory, and young Time
  Told his first birth-days by the sun;
When, in the light of Nature's dawn
  Rejoicing, men and angels met
On the high hill and sunny lawn,--
Ere sorrow came, or Sin had drawn
  'Twixt man and heaven her curtain yet!
When earth lay nearer to the skies   10
  Than in these days of crime and woe,
And mortals saw, without surprise,
In the mid-air, angelic eyes
  Gazing upon this world below.

Alas, that Passion should profane,
  Ev'n then, that morning of the earth!
That, sadder still, the fatal stain
  Should fall on hearts of heavenly birth--
And oh, that stain so dark should fall
From Woman's love, most sad of all!   20

One evening, in that time of bloom,
  On a hill's side, where hung the ray
Of sunset, sleeping in perfume,
  Three noble youths conversing lay;

---

16   that] 1 ; the 5.
19   oh, that stain so dark] 1 ; that from Woman's love 5.
20   From Woman's love] 1 ; So dark a stain 5.
21   time of bloom,] 1 ; primal hour 5.
23   sleeping in perfume] 1 ; brightening rill and bower 5.

And, as they look'd, from time to time,
  To the far sky, where Daylight furl'd
His radiant wing, their brows sublime
  Bespoke them of that distant world--
Creatures of light, such as still play,
  Like motes in sunshine, round the Lord,   30
And through their infinite array
Transmit each moment, night and day,
  The echo of His luminous word!

Of Heaven they spoke, and, still more oft,
  Of the bright eyes that charm'd them thence;
Till, yielding gradual to the soft
  And balmy evening's influence--
The silent breathing of the flowers--
  The melting light that beam'd above,
As on their first, fond, erring hours,   40
  Each told the story of his love,
The history of that hour unblest,
When, like a bird, from its high nest
Won down by fascinating eyes,
For Woman's smile he lost the skies.

The First who spoke was one, with look
  The least celestial of the three--
A Spirit of light mould, that took
  The prints of earth most yieldingly;
Who, ev'n in heaven, was not of those   50
  Nearest the Throne, but held a place
Far off, among those shining rows

XX-XX / 29-32 (*Addition to 5, without corresponding lines in 1:*)
              Spirits, who once in brotherhood
              Of faith and bliss, near ALLA stood,
              And o'er whose cheeks full oft had blown
              The wind that breathes from ALLA,s throne,
              (*Hereafter, lines 30-196 in 1 correspond to*
              lines 34-200 in 5.)
29 / 34   still] 1 ; *still* 5.

That circle out through endless space,
And o'er whose wings the light from Him
In the great centre falls most dim.

Still fair and glorious, he but shone
Among those youths th'unheavenliest one--
A creature, to whom light remain'd
From Eden still, but alter'd, stain'd,
And o'er whose brow not Love alone   60
    A blight had, in his transit, sent,
But other, earthlier joys had gone,
    And left their foot-prints as they went.

Sighing, as through the shadowy Past
    Like a tomb-searcher, Memory ran,
Lifting each shroud that Time had cast
    O'er buried hopes, he thus began:--

---

55 / 59   the great] 1 ;   Heaven's 5.
57 / 61   th'] 1; the' 5.
61 / 65   sent] 1; cast 5.
63 / 67   went] 1 ; pass'd 5.
64 / 68   through the shadowy Past] 1 ; back through
          ages flown, 5.
66 / 70   cast] 1 ; thrown 5.

First Angel's Story.

'Twas in a land, that far away
    Into the golden orient lies,
Where Nature knows not night's delay,   70
But springs to meet her bridegroom, Day,
    Upon the threshold of the skies.
One morn, on earthly mission sent,
    And mid-way choosing where to light,
I saw, from the blue element--
    Oh beautiful, but fatal sight!--
One of earth's fairest womankind,
Half veil'd from view, or rather shrin'd
In the clear crystal of a brook;
    Which, while it hid no single gleam   80
Of her young beauties, made them look
    More spirit-like, as they might seem
    Through the dim shadowing of a dream.

Pausing in wonder I look'd on,
    While, playfully around her breaking
The waters, that like diamonds shone,
    She mov'd in light of her own making.
At length, as slowly I descended
    To view more near a sight so splendid,
The tremble of my wings all o'er   90
    (For through each plume I felt the thrill)
Startled her, as she reach'd the shore
    Of that small lake--her mirror still--
Above whose brink she stood, like snow
When rosy with a sunset glow.

---

68 / 72 'Twas] 1 ; '"~ 5.
88 / 92 slowly I descended] 1 ; from that airy height 5.
89 / 93 To view more near a sight so splendid] 1 ;
        I gently lower'd my breathless flight, 5.

Never shall I forget those eyes!--
The shame, the innocent surprise
Of that bright face, when in the air
Uplooking, she beheld me there.
It seem'd as if each thought, and look,   100
   And motion were that minute chain'd
Fast to the spot, such root she took,
And--like a sunflower by a brook,
   With face upturn'd--so still remain'd!

In pity to the wondering maid,
   Though loth from such a vision turning,
Downward I bent, beneath the shade
   Of my spread wings to hide the burning
Of glances, which--I well could feel--
For me, for her, too warmly shone;   110
But, ere I could again unseal
My restless eyes, or even steal
   One side-long look, the maid was gone--
Hid from me in the forest leaves,
   Sudden as when, in all her charms
Of full-blown light, some cloud receives
   The Moon into his dusky arms.

'Tis not in words to tell the power,
The despotism that, from that hour,
Passion held o'er me--day and night   120
   I sought around each neighbouring spot,
And, in the chase of this sweet light,
   My task, and heaven, and all forgot--
All, but the one, sole, haunting dream
Of her I saw in that bright stream.

Nor was it long, ere by her side
   I found myself, whole happy days,
Listening to words, whose music vied

---

120 / 124 me--day] 1 ; ~ . Day 5.
121 / 125 spot,] 1 ; ~ ; 5.

With our own Eden's seraph lays,
When seraph lays are warm'd by love,   130
But, wanting *that*, far, far above!--
And looking into eyes where, blue
And beautiful, like skies seen through
The sleeping wave, for me there shone
A heaven, more worshipp'd than my own.
Oh what, while I could hear and see
Such words and looks, was heaven to me?
Though gross the air on earth I drew,
'Twas blessed, while she breath'd it too;
Though dark the flowers, though dim the sky,   140
Love lent them light, while she was nigh.
Throughout creation I but knew
Two separate worlds--the *one*, that small,
    Belov'd, and consecrated spot
Where LEA *was*--the other, all
    The dull, wide waste, where she was *not*!

But vain my suit, my madness vain;
Though gladly, from her eyes to gain
    One earthly look, one stray desire,
I would have torn the wings, that hung   150
    Furl'd at my back, and o'er that Fire
Unnam'd in heaven their fragments flung;--
'Twas hopeless all--pure and unmov'd
    She stood, as lilies in the light
    Of the hot noon but look more white;--
And though she lov'd me, deeply lov'd,
'Twas not as man, as mortal--no,
Nothing of earth was in that glow--
She lov'd me but as one, of race
Angelic, from that radiant place   160
She saw so oft in dreams--that Heaven,
    To which her prayers at morn were sent,
And on whose light she gaz'd at even,

---

151 / 155   that] 1 ; the 5.
152 / 156   Unnam'd in heaven] 1 ; In Gehim's pit 5.

Wishing for wings, that she might go
Out of this shadowy world below,
  To that free, glorious element!

Well I remember by her side
Sitting at rosy even-tide,
When,--turning to the star, whose head
Look'd out, as from a bridal bed,   170
At that mute, blushing hour,--she said,
"Oh! that it were my doom to be
  "The Spirit of yon beauteous star,
"Dwelling up there in purity,
  "Alone, as all such bright things are;--
"My sole employ to pray and shine,
  "To light my censer at the sun,
"And fling its fire towards the shrine
  "Of Him in heaven, the Eternal One!"

So innocent the maid--so free   180
  From mortal taint in soul and frame,
Whom 'twas my crime--my destiny--
  To love, aye, burn for, with a flame,
  To which earth's wildest fires are tame.
Had you but seen her look, when first
From my mad lips the'avowal burst;
Not angry--no--the feeling had
No touch of anger, but most sad--
It was a sorrow, calm as deep,
A mournfulness that could not weep,   190
So fill'd the heart was to the brink,
So fix'd and frozen there--to think
That angel natures--even I,

---

178 / 182 fling] 1 ; cast 5.
187 / 191 had] 1 ; came 5.
188 / 192 No touch of anger, but most sad--] 1 ;
           From depths beyond mere anger's flame-- 5.
192 / 196 frozen there--] 1 ; froz'n with grief, 5.
193 / 197 even] 1 ; that ev'n 5.

Whose love she clung to, as the tie
Between her spirit and the sky--
Should fall thus headlong from the height
  Of such pure glory into sin--
The sin, of all, most sure to blight,
The sin, of all, that the soul's light
  Is soonest lost, extinguish'd in!   200
That, though but frail and human, she
Should, like the half-bird of the sea,
Try with her wing sublimer air,
While I, a creature born up there,
Should meet her, in my fall from light,
From heaven and peace, and turn her flight
Downward again, with me to drink
Of the salt tide of sin, and sink!

That very night--my heart had grown
  Impatient of its inward burning;   210
The term, too, of my stay was flown,
And the bright Watchers* near the throne,
Already, if a meteor shone
Between them and this nether zone,
  Thought 'twas their herald's wing returning;--
Oft did the potent spell-word, given
  To Envoys hither from the skies,
To be pronounc'd, when back to heaven
  It is their hour or wish to rise,
Come to my lips that fatal day;   220
  And once, too, was so nearly spoken,
That my spread plumage in the ray
   * See Note. [Moores Note.]

---

197 / 201 Of such pure glory into sin--] 1 ;
           Of all that heaven hath pure and bright! 5.
198-208 / XXX-XXX (*lines 198-208 in 1 deleted from 5. Lines*
          209-229 in 1 correspond to lines 202-222 in 5.)
215 / 208 returning;--] 1 ; ~ . 5.
219 / 212 hour] 1 ; time 5.

And breeze of heaven began to play--
  When my heart fail'd--the spell was broken--
The word unfinish'd died away,
And my check'd plumes, ready to soar,
Fell slack and lifeless as before.

How could I leave a world, which she,
  Or lost or won, made all to me,
Beyond home--glory--every thing?   230
  How fly, while yet there was a chance,
A hope--aye, even of perishing
  Utterly by that fatal glance!
No matter where my wanderings were,
  So there she look'd, mov'd, breath'd about--
Woe, ruin, death, more sweet with her,
  Than all heaven's proudest joys without!

But, to return--that very day
  A feast was held, where, full of mirth,
Came, crowding thick as flowers that play   240
In summer winds, the young and gay
  And beautiful of this bright earth.
And she was there, and 'mid the young
  And beautiful stood first, alone;
Though on her gentle brow still hung
  The shadow I that morn had thrown--
The first, that ever shame or woe
Had cast upon its vernal snow.
My heart was madden'd--in the flush
  Of the wild revel I gave way   250

---

223 / 216 play--] 1 ; ~ ;-- 5.
229 / 222 me,] 1 ; ~ ? 5.
230-233 / XXX-XXX (*Lines 230-233 in 1 deleted from 5.
    Henceforth, lines 234-280 in 1 correspond to lines
    223-269 in 5.*)
237 / 226 all heaven's proudest joys] 1 ; Paradise
       itself, 5.
249 / 238 madden'd--] 1 ; ~ ;-- 5.

To all that frantic mirth--that rush
  Of desperate gaiety, which they,
Who never felt how pain's excess
Can break out thus, think happiness--
Sad mimicry of mirth and life,
Whose flashes come but from the strife
Of inward passions--like the light
Struck out by clashing swords in fight.

Then, too, that juice of earth, the bane
And blessing of man's heart and brain--   260
That draught of sorcery, which brings
Phantoms of fair, forbidden things--
Whose drops, like those of rainbows, smile
  Upon the mists that circle man,
Bright'ning not only Earth, the while,
  But grasping Heaven, too, in their span!--
Then first the fatal wine-cup rain'd
Its dews of darkness through my lips,
Casting whate'er of light remain'd
  To my lost soul into eclipse,   270
And filling it with such wild dreams,
  Such fantasies and wrong desires,
As, in the absence of heaven's beams,
  Haunt us for ever--like wild-fires
  That walk this earth, when day retires.

Now hear the rest--our banquet done,
  I sought her in the' accustom'd bower,
Where late we oft, when day was gone,
And the world hush'd, had met alone,
  At the same silent, moonlight hour.   280
I found her--oh, so beautiful!

---

254 / 243 happiness--] 1 ; ~ ! 5.
270 / 259 eclipse,] 1 ; ~ ; 5.
276 / 265 rest--] 1 ; ~ ;-- 5.
281 / 270 I found her--oh, so beautiful!] 1 ;
           Her eyes, as usual, were upturn'd 5.

Why, why have hapless Angels eyes?
Or why are there not flowers to cull,
  As fair as Woman, in yon skies?
Still did her brow, as usual, turn
To her lov'd star, which seem'd to burn
  Purer than ever on that night;
  While she, in looking, grew more bright,
As though that planet were an urn
From which her eyes drank liquid light.   290

There was a virtue in that scene,
  A spell of holiness around,
Which would have--had my brain not been
  Thus poison'd, madden'd--held me bound,
  As though I stood on God's own ground.
Ev'n as it was, with soul all flame,
  And lips that burn'd in their own sighs,
I stood to gaze, with awe and shame--
The memory of Eden came
  Full o'er me when I saw those eyes;   300
And tho' too well each glance of mine
To the pale, shrinking maiden prov'd
How far, alas, from aught divine,

---

282 / 271 Why, why have hapless Angels eyes?] 1 ;
            To her lov'd star, whose lustre burn'd 5.
283 /   (*Lines 283-285 in 1 deleted from 5. Lines 286-288
            in 1 correspond to lines 271-273 in 5.*)
286 / 271   which seem'd to burn] 1 ; whose lustre
            burn'd 5.
289 / 274   that planet were an urn] 1 ; she borrowed
            of its light. 5.
290 /   (*Line 290 in 1 deleted from 5. Hereafter, lines
            291-459 in 1 correspond to lines 275-443 in 5.*)
293 / 277   Which would have--had my] 1 ; Which, had my
            burning 5.
294 / 278   poison'd, madden'd--held me--] 1 ; madden'd,
            would have ~ ~ , 5.
295 / 279   stood on God's own] 1 ; trod celestial 5.

Aught worthy of so pure a shrine,
  Was the wild love with which I lov'd,
Yet must she, too, have seen--oh yes,
  'Tis soothing but to *think* she saw--
The deep, true, soul-felt tenderness,
  The homage of an Angel's awe
To her, a mortal, whom pure love   310
Then plac'd above him--far above--
And all that struggle to repress
A sinful spirit's mad excess,
Which work'd within me at that hour,
  When--with a voice, where Passion shed
All the deep sadness of her power,
  Her melancholy power--I said,
"Then be it so--if back to heaven
  "I must unlov'd, unpitied fly,
"Without one blest memorial given   320
  "To soothe me in that lonely sky--
"One look, like those the young and fond
  "Give when they're parting--which would be,
"Ev'n in remembrance, far beyond
  "All heaven hath left of bliss for me!

"Oh, but to see that head recline
  "A minute on this trembling arm,
"And those mild eyes look up to mine
  "Without a dread, a thought of harm!
"To meet but once the thrilling touch   330
  "Of lips that are too fond to fear me--
"Or, if that boon be all too much,
  "Ev'n thus to bring their fragrance near me!
"Nay, shrink not so--a look--a word--
  "Give them but kindly and I fly;

---

307 / 291 saw--] 1 ; ~ ^ 5.
321 / 305 sky--] 1 ; ~ ; 5.
328 / 312 mine] 1 ; ~ , 5.
330 / 314 meet but once] 1 ; ~ , ~ ~ , 5.
331 / 315 lips that are too] 1 ; lips too purely 5.

"Already, see, my plumes have stirr'd,
"And tremble for their home on high.
"Thus be our parting--cheek to cheek--
"One minute's lapse will be forgiven,
"And thou, the next, shalt hear me speak   340
"The spell that plumes my wing for heaven!"

While thus I spoke, the fearful maid,
Of me, and of herself afraid,
Had shrinking stood, like flowers beneath
The scorching of the south-wind's breath:
But when I nam'd--alas, too well,
  I now recall, though wilder'd then,--
Instantly, when I nam'd the spell,
  Her brow, her eyes uprose again,
And, with an eagerness, that spoke   350
The sudden light that o'er her broke,
"The spell, the spell!--oh, speak it now,
  "And I will bless thee!" she exclaim'd--
Unknowing what I did, inflam'd,
And lost already, on her brow
  I stamp'd one burning kiss, and nam'd
The mystic word, till then ne'er told
To living creature of earth's mould!
Scarce was it said, when, quick as thought,
Her lips from mine, like echo, caught   360
The holy sound--her hands and eyes
Were instant lifted to the skies,
And thrice to heaven she spoke it out
  With that triumphant look Faith wears,
When not a cloud of fear or doubt,
  A vapour from this vale of tears,
  Between her and her God appears!
That very moment her whole frame
All bright and glorified became,
And at her back I saw unclose   370
Two wings, magnificent as those

That sparkle round the'Eternal Throne,
Whose plumes, as buoyantly she rose
  Above me, in the moon-beam shone
With a pure light, which--from its hue,
Unknown upon this earth--I knew
Was light from Eden, glistening through!
Most holy vision! ne'er before
  Did aught so radiant--since the day
When Lucifer, in falling, bore   380
  The third of the bright stars away *--
Rise, in earth's beauty, to repair
That loss of light and glory there!

But did I tamely view her flight?
  Did not *I*, too, proclaim out thrice
The powerful words that were, that night,--
Oh ev'n for heaven too much delight!--
  Again to bring us, eyes to eyes,
  And soul to soul, in Paradise?
I did--I spoke it o'er and o'er--   390
  I pray'd, I wept, but all in vain;
For me the spell had power no more, .
  There seem'd around me some dark chain
Which still, as I essay'd to soar,
  Baffled, alas, each wild endeavour:
Dead lay my wings, as they have lain
Since that sad hour, and will remain--
So wills the' offended God--for ever!

It was to yonder star I trac'd
Her journey up the'illumin'd waste--   400
That isle in the blue firmament,
To which so oft her fancy went
  In wishes and in dreams before,
And which was now--such, Purity,
    * See Note. [Moores Note.]

---

372 / 356 round the'Eternal] 1; around ALLA's 5.
392 / 376 more,] 1 ; ~ . 5.

Thy blest reward--ordain'd to be
  Her home of light for evermore!

Once--or did I but fancy so?--
  Ev'n in her flight to that fair sphere,
Mid all her spirit's new-felt glow,
A pitying look she turn'd below   410
  On him who stood in darkness here;
Him whom, perhaps, if vain regret
Can dwell in heaven, she pities yet;
And oft, when looking to this dim
And distant world, remembers him.

But soon that passing dream was gone;
Farther and Farther off she shone,
Till lessen'd to a point, as small
  As are those specks that yonder burn--
Those vivid drops of light, that fall   420
  The last from day's exhausted urn.
And when at length she merg'd, afar,
Into her own immortal star,
And when at length my straining sight
  Had caught her wing's last fading ray,
That minute from my soul the light
  Of heaven and love both pass'd away;
And I forgot my home, my birth,
  Profan'd my spirit, sunk my brow,
And revell'd in gross joys of earth,   430
  Till I became--what I am now!"

The Spirit bow'd his head in shame;
  A shame, that of itself would tell--
Were there not ev'n those breaks of flame,
Celestial, through his clouded frame--
  How grand the height from which he fell!
That holy Shame, which ne'er forgets
  What clear renown it us'd to wear;

---

438 / 422 What clear] 1 ; The'unblench'd 5.

Whose blush remains, when Virtue sets,
To show her sunshine *has* been there.   440

Once only, while the tale he told,
Were his eyes lifted to behold
That happy stainless star, where she
Dwelt in her bower of purity!
One minute did he look, and then--
  As though he felt some deadly pain
  From its sweet light through heart and brain--
Shrunk back, and never look'd again.

          ————————

Who was the Second Spirit?--he
  With the proud front and piercing glance--   450
  Who seem'd, when viewing heaven's expanse,
As though his far-sent eye could see
On, on into the'Immensity
Behind the veils of that blue sky,
Where God's sublimest secrets lie?--
His wings, the while, though day was gone,
  Flashing with many a various hue
Of light they from themselves alone,
  Instinct with Eden's brightness, drew--
A breathing forth of beams at will,   460
  Of living beams, which, though no more
They kept their early lustre, still
  Were such, when glittering out all o'er,
  As mortal eye-lids wink'd before.

'Twas RUBI--once among the prime

————————————————

455 / 439 God's sublimest] 1 ; ALLA's grandest 5.
459 / 443 drew--] 1 ; ~ . 5.
460 /   (*Lines 460-464 in 1 deleted from 5. Hereafter,
          lines 465-1031 in 1 correspond to lines 444-1010
          in 5.*)

And flower of those bright creatures, nam'd
Spirits of Knowledge *, who o'er Time
    And Space and Thought an empire claim'd,
Second alone to Him, whose light
Was, ev'n to theirs, as day to night--   470
'Twixt whom and them was distance far
    And wide, as would the journey be
To reach from any island star
    The vague shores of Infinity!
'Twas RUBI, in whose mournful eye
Slept the dim light of days gone by;
Whose voice, though sweet, fell on the ear
    Like echoes, in some silent place,
When first awak'd for many a year;
    And when he smil'd--if o'er his face   480
    Smile ever shone--'twas like the grace
Of moonlight rainbows, fair, but wan,
The sunny life, the glory gone.
Ev'n o'er his pride, though still the same,
A softening shade from sorrow came;
And though at times his spirit knew
    The kindlings of disdain and ire,
Short was the fitful glare they threw--
Like the last flashes, fierce but few,
    Seen through some noble pile on fire!   490

Such was the Angel, who now broke
    The silence that had come o'er all,
When he, the Spirit that last spoke,
    Clos'd the sad history of his fall;
And, while a sacred lustre, flown
    For many a day, relum'd his cheek,
And not those sky-tun'd lips alone
But his eyes, brow, and tresses, roll'd
        * The Cherubim.--See Note. [Moores Note.]

---

470 / 449 night--] 1 ; ~ ; 5.
498 / 477 But his eyes, brow, and tresses, roll'd]
           1 ; And not those eloquent lips alone 5.

Like sunset waves, all seem'd to speak--
Thus his eventful story told:--   500

---

497 / 476   And not those sky-tun'd lips alone] 1 ;
            Beautiful, as in days of old; 5.
499 / 478   Like sunset waves, all . . . --] 1 ;
            But every feature . . . ^ 5.

Second Angel's Story.

"You both remember well the day
    When unto Eden's new-made bowers,
He, whom all living things obey,
    Summon'd his chief angelic powers
To witness the one wonder yet,
    Beyond man, angel, star, or sun,
He must achieve, ere he could set
    His seal upon the world, as done--
To see that last perfection rise,
    That crowning of creation's birth,   510
When, mid the worship and surprise
Of circling angels, Woman's eyes
    First open'd upon heaven and earth;
And from their lids a thrill was sent,
That through each living spirit went
Like first light through the firmament!

Can you forget how gradual stole
The fresh-awakened breath of soul
Throughout her perfect form--which seem'd
To grow transparent, as there beam'd   520
That dawn of Mind within, and caught
New loveliness from each new thought?
Slow as o'er summer seas we trace
    The progress of the noontide air,
Dimpling its bright and silent face
Each minute into some new grace,

---

501 / 480 DAY] 1; ~ , 5.
503 / 482 He, whom all living things obey,] 1 ;
            Alla convok'd the bright array 5.
504 / 483 Summon'd his chief angelic powers] 1 ;
            Of his supreme ~ ~ , 5.

And varying heaven's reflections there--

Or, like the light of evening, stealing
  O'er some fair temple, which all day
Hath slept in shadow, slow revealing   530
  Its several beauties, ray by ray,
Till it shines out, a thing to bless,
All full of light and loveliness.

Can you forget her blush, when round
Through Eden's lone, enchanted ground
She look'd--and at the sea--the skies--
  And heard the rush of many a wing,
  By God's command then vanishing,
And saw the last few angel eyes,
  Still lingering--mine among the rest,--   540
  Reluctant leaving scene so blest?

From that miraculous hour, the fate
  Of this new, glorious Being dwelt
For ever, with a spell-like weight,
  Upon my spirit--early, late,
  Whate'er I did, or dream'd, or felt,
The thought of what might yet befall
That splendid creature mix'd with all.--
Nor she alone, but her whole race
  Through ages yet to come--whate'er   550
  Of feminine, and fond, and fair,
Should spring from that pure mind and face,
  All wak'd my soul's intensest care;
Their forms, souls, feelings, still to me
God's most disturbing mystery!

---

536 / 515   --and at the] 1 ; , ~ saw, ~ 5.
538 / 517   By God's command] 1 ; On high behests 5.
548 / 527   splendid] 1 ; matchless 5.
555 / 534   God's most disturbing] 1 ; Creation's strangest 5.

It was my doom--ev'n from the first,
   When summon'd with my cherub peers,
To witness the young vernal burst
   Of Nature through those blooming spheres,
Those flowers of light, that sprung beneath   560
The first touch of the'Eternal's breath--
It was my doom still to be haunted
   By some new wonder, some sublime
   And matchless work, that, for the time
Held all my soul, enchain'd, enchanted,
And left me not a thought, a dream,
A word, but on that only theme!

The wish to know--that endless thirst,
   Which ev'n by quenching is awak'd,
And which becomes or blest or curst,   570
   As is the fount whereat 'tis slak'd--
Still urg'd me onward, with desire
Insatiate, to explore, inquire--
Whate'er the wondrous things might be,
That wak'd each new idolatry--
   Their cause, aim, source from whence they sprung,
Their inmost powers, as though for me
   Existence on that knowledge hung.

Oh what a vision were the stars,

---

557 / 536   summon'd with my cherub peers,] 1 ;
            witnessing the primal burst 5.
558 / 537   To witness the young vernal burst] 1 ;
            Of Nature's wonders, I saw rise 5.
559 / 538   Of Nature through those blooming spheres,] 1 ;
            Those bright creations in the skies-- 5.
560 / 539   flowers of light, that sprung beneath] 1 ;
            worlds instinct with life and light, 5.
561 / 540   The first touch of the'Eternal's breath--] 1 ;
            Which Man, remote, but sees by night,-- 5.
576 / 555   source from whence they . . . ,] 1 ;
            ~ , whence-ever . . . -- 5.

When first I saw them burn on high,   580
Rolling along, like living cars
Of light, for gods to journey by!
They were my heart's first passion--days
And nights, unwearied, in their rays
Have I hung floating, till each sense
Seem'd full of their bright influence.
Innocent joy! alas, how much
Of misery had I shunn'd below,
Could I have still liv'd blest with such;
Nor, proud and restless, burn'd to know   590
The knowledge that brings guilt and woe!

Often--so much I lov'd to trace
The secrets of this starry race--
Have I at morn and evening run
Along the lines of radiance spun,
Like webs, between them and the sun,
Untwisting all the tangled ties
Of light into their different dyes--
Then fleetly wing'd I off, in quest
Of those, the farthest, loneliest,   600
That watch, like winking sentinels,
The void, beyond which Chaos dwells,
And there, with noiseless plume, pursued
Their track through that grand solitude,
Asking intently all and each
What soul within their radiance dwelt,
And wishing their sweet light were speech,
That they might tell me all they felt.

Nay, oft, so passionate my chace
Of these resplendent heirs of space,   610
Oft did I follow--lest a ray
Should 'scape me in the farthest night--

---

591 / 570   woe!] 1 ; ~ . 5.
595 / 574   spun,] 1 ; ~ ^ . 5.
602 / 581   dwells,] 1 ; ~ ; 5.

Some pilgrim Comet, on his way
  To visit distant shrines of light,
And well remember how I sung
  Exulting out, when on my sight
New worlds of stars, all fresh and young,
As if just born of darkness, sprung!

Such was my pure ambition then,
  My sinless transport, night and morn;   620
Ere this still newer world of men,
  And that most fair of stars was born
Which I, in fatal hour, saw rise
Among the flowers of Paradise!
Thenceforth my nature all was chang'd,
  My heart, soul, senses turn'd below;
And he, who but so lately rang'd
  Yon wonderful expanse, where glow
Worlds upon worlds, yet found his mind
Ev'n in that luminous range confin'd,   630
Now blest the humblest, meanest sod
Of the dark earth where Woman trod!
In vain my former idols glisten'd
  From their far thrones; in vain these ears
To the once-thrilling music listen'd,
  That hymn'd around my favourite spheres--
To earth, to earth each thought was given,
  That in this half-lost soul had birth;
Like some high mount, whose head's in heaven,
  While its whole shadow rests on earth!   640

Nor was it Love, ev'n yet, that thrall'd
  My spirit in his burning ties;
And less, still less could it be call'd
  That grosser flame, round which Love flies
Nearer and nearer, till he dies--
No, it was wonder, such as thrill'd
  At all God's works my dazzled sense;

---

621 / 600 this still] 1 ; yet this 5.

The same rapt wonder, only fill'd
  With passion, more profound, intense,--
A vehement, but wandering fire,   650
Which, though nor love, nor yet desire,
Though through all womankind it took
  Its range, as vague as lightnings run,
Yet wanted but a touch, a look,
  To fix it burning upon *One*.

Then, too, the ever-restless zeal,
  The'insatiate curiosity
To know what shapes, so fair, must feel--
To look, but once, beneath the seal
  Of so much loveliness, and see   660
What souls belong'd to those bright eyes--
  Whether, as sun-beams find their way
Into the gem that hidden lies,
  Those looks could inward turn their ray,
To make the soul as bright as they!
All this impell'd my anxious chace,
  And still the more I saw and knew
Of Woman's fond, weak, conquering race,
  The'intenser still my wonder grew.

I had beheld their First, their EVE,   670
  Born in that splendid Paradise,
Which God made solely to receive
  The first light of her waking eyes.
I had seen purest angels lean
  In worship o'er her from above;
And man--oh yes, had envying seen
  Proud man possess'd of all her love.

I saw their happiness, so brief,

---

653 / 632   vague as] 1 ; lawless 5.
665 / 644   To . . . !] 1 ; And . . . : 5.
672 / 651   God made] 1 ; sprung there 5.

So exquisite--her error, too,
That easy trust, that prompt belief   680
In what the warm heart wishes true;
That faith in words, when kindly said,
By which the whole fond sex is led--
Mingled with (what I durst not blame,
   For 'tis my own) that wish to *know*,
Sad, fatal zeal, so sure of woe;
Which, though from heaven all pure it came,
Yet stain'd, misus'd, brought sin and shame
   On her, on me, on all below!
I had seen this; had seen Man--arm'd   690
   As his soul is with strength and sense--
By her first words to ruin charm'd;
   His vaunted reason's cold defence,
Like an ice-barrier in the ray
Of melting summer, smil'd away!
Nay--stranger yet--spite of all this--
   Though by her counsels taught to err,
   Though driv'n from Paradise for her,
(And *with* her--*that*, at least, was bliss)
Had I not heard him, ere he crost   700
   The threshold of that earthly heaven,
Which by her wildering smile he lost--
   So quickly was the wrong forgiven--
Had I not heard him, as he prest
The frail, fond trembler to a breast
Which she had doom'd to sin and strife,
Call her--that what--his Life! his Life! *

* Chavah, the name by which Adam called the woman after their transgression, means "Life."--See Note.

---

679 / 658 exquisite--] 1 ; ~,-- 5.
684 / 663 with ( ] 1 ; ~ -- 5.
685 / 664 own) . . . wish] 1 ; ~ --. . . . zeal 5.
690 / 669 Man--arm'd] 1 ; ~ , ~ , 5.
691 / 670 is . . . --] 1 ; ~ , . . . , 5.
695 / 674 away!] 1 ; ~ . 5.
696 / 675 Nay-- . . . yet--] 1 ; ~ , . . . ~ , 5.
703 / 682 forgiven--] 1 ; forgiv'n!-- 5.

Yes--such the love-taught name--the first,
That ruin'd Man to Woman gave,
Ev'n in his out-cast hour, when curst,   710
By her fond witchery, with that worst
And earliest boon of love--the grave!
She, who brought death into the world,
There stepped before him, with the light
Of their lost Paradise still bright
Upon those sunny locks, that curl'd
Down her white shoulders to her feet--
So beautiful in form, so sweet
In heart and voice, as to redeem
The loss, the death of all things dear,   720
Except herself--and make it seem
Life, endless Life, while she was near!

Could I help wondering at a creature,
Enchanted round with spells so strong--
One, to whose every thought, word, feature,
In joy and woe, through right and wrong,
Such sweet omnipotence heaven gave,
To bless or ruin, curse or save?

Nor did the marvel cease with her--
New Eves in all her daughters came,   730
As strong to charm, as weak to err,
As sure of man through praise and blame,
Whate'er they brought him, pride or shame,
Their still unreasoning worshipper--
And, wheresoe'er they smil'd, the same
Enchantresses of soul and frame,

---

708 / 687 Yes-- . . . name--] 1 ; ~ , . . . ~ , 5.
712 / 691 love--] 1 ; ~ , 5.
734 / 713 Their still unreasoning . . . --] 1 ;
         He ~ the'unreasoning . . . , 5.
735 / 714 And, wheresoe'er they smil'd, . . .] 1 ;
         ~ they, throughout all time, . . . , 5.

Into whose hands, from first to last,
This world with all its destinies,
Devotedly by heaven seems cast,
To save or damn it, as they please!　　　　740

Oh, 'tis not to be told how long,
How restlessly I sigh'd to find
Some *one*, from out that shining throng,
Some abstract of the form and mind
Of the whole matchless sex, from which,
In my own arms beheld, possest,
I might learn all the powers to witch,
To warm, and (if my fate unblest
Would have it) ruin, of the rest!
Into whose inward soul and sense　　　　750
I might descend, as doth the bee
Into the flower's deep heart, and thence
Rifle, in all its purity,
The prime, the quintessence, the whole
Of wondrous Woman's frame and soul!

At length, my burning wish, my prayer,--
(For such--oh what will tongues not dare,
When hearts go wrong?--this lip preferr'd)--
At length my ominous prayer was heard--
But whether heard in heaven or hell,　　　　760
Listen--and you will know *too* well.

There was a maid, of all who move
Like visions o'er this orb, most fit
To be a bright young angel's love,
Herself so bright, so exquisite!
The pride, too, of her step, as light
Along the unconscious earth she went,
Seem'd that of one, born with a right
To walk some heavenlier element,

---

740 / 719　damn it,] 1 ; ruin, 5.
761 / 740　you will] 1 ; thou wilt 5.

And tread in places where her feet   770
A star at every step should meet
'Twas not alone that loveliness
  By which the wilder'd sense is caught--
Of lips, whose very breath could bless--
  Of playful blushes, that seem'd nought
  But luminous escapes of thought--
Of eyes that, when by anger stirr'd,
Were fire itself, but, at a word
  Of tenderness, all soft became
As though they could, like the sun's bird,   780
  Dissolve away in their own flame--
Of form, as pliant as the shoots
  Of a young tree, in vernal flower;
Yet round and glowing as the fruits
  That drop from it in summer's hour--
'Twas not alone this loveliness
  That falls to loveliest woman's share,
  Though, even here, her form could spare
From its own beauty's rich excess
  Enough to make all others fair--   790
But 'twas the Mind, sparkling about
Through her whole frame--the soul, brought out
To light each charm, yet independent
  Of what it lighted, as the sun
That shines on flowers, would be resplendent
  Were there no flowers to shine upon--
'Twas this, all this, in one combin'd,
  The'unnumber'd looks and arts that form
The glory of young woman-kind,

---

774 / 753 bless--] 1 ; ~ ; 5.
776 / 755 thought--] 1 ; ~ ; 5.
785 / 764 hour--] 1 ; ~ ;-- 5.
790 / 769 all others] 1 ; ev'n *them* 5.
791 / 770 sparkling about] 1 ; outshining clear 5.
792 / 771 brought out] 1 ; still near, 5.

Taken in their first fusion, warm,   800
Ere time had chill'd a single charm,
And stamp'd with such a seal of Mind,
  As gave to beauties, that might be
Too sensual else, too unrefin'd,
  The impress of divinity!
'Twas this--a union, which the hand
  Of Nature kept for her alone,
Of every thing most playful, bland,
Voluptuous, spiritual, grand,
  In angel-natures and her own--   810
Oh this it was that drew me nigh
One, who seem'd kin to heaven as I,
My bright twin sister of the sky--
One, in whose love, I felt, were given
  The mix'd delights of either sphere,
All that the spirit seeks in heaven,
  And all the senses burn for here!

Had we--but hold--hear every part
  Of our sad tale--spite of the pain
Remembrance gives, when the fix'd dart   820
  Is stirr'd thus in the wound again--
Hear every step, so full of bliss,
  And yet so ruinous, that led
Down to the last, dark precipice,
  Where perish'd both--the fall'n, the dead!

From the first hour she caught my sight,
I never left her--day and night
Hovering unseen around her way,
  And mid her loneliest musings near,
I soon could track each thought that lay,   830
  Gleaming within her heart, as clear

---

800 / 779 Taken . . . first fusion] 1 ;
        ~ , . . . perfection 5.
813 / 792 My . . . of the sky--] 1 ; A . . . from on high-- 5.
817 / 796 here!] 1 ; ~ . 5.

As pebbles within brooks appear;
And there, among the countless things
   That keep young hearts for ever glowing,
Vague wishes, fond imaginings,
   Love-dreams, as yet no object knowing--
Light, winged hopes, that come when bid,
   And rainbow joys that end in weeping,
And passions, among pure thoughts hid,
   Like serpents under flow'rets sleeping--   840
'Mong all these feelings--felt whate'er
Young hearts are beating--I saw there
Proud thoughts, aspirings high--beyond
Whate'er yet dwelt in soul so fond--
Glimpses of glory, far away
   Into the bright, vague future given,
And fancies, free and grand, whose play,
   Like that of eaglets, is near heaven!
With this, too--what a soul and heart
To fall beneath the tempter's art!--   850
A zeal for knowledge, such as ne'er
Enshrin'd itself in form so fair
Since that first, fatal hour, when Eve,
   With every fruit of Eden blest,
Save only *one*, rather than leave
   That one unknown, lost all the rest.

It was in dreams that first I stole
   With gentle mastery o'er her mind--
In that rich twilight of the soul,
   When Reason's beam, half hid behind   860
The clouds of sense, obscurely gilds

---

838 / 817 weeping,] 1 ; ~ ; 5.
840 / 819 sleeping--] 1 ; ~ ;-- 5.
852 / 831 fair] 1 ; ~ , 5.
855 / 834 only *one*,] 1 ; one alone-- 5.
856 / 835 one unknown] 1 ; *one* unreach'd 5.
861 / 840 sense] 1 ; sleep 5.

Each shadowy shape that Fancy builds--
'Twas then, by that soft light, I brought
　Vague, glimmering visions to her view--
Catches of radiance, lost when caught,
Bright labyrinths, that led to nought,
　And vistas, with a void seen through--
Dwellings of bliss, that opening shone,
　Then clos'd, dissolv'd, and left no trace--
All that, in short, could tempt Hope on,　　　　870
　But give her wing no resting-place;
Myself the while, with brow, as yet,
Pure as the young moon's coronet,
Through every dream *still* in her sight,
The' enchanter of each mocking scene,
Who gave the hope, then brought the blight,
Who said 'Behold yon world of light,'
　Then sudden dropt a veil between!
At length, when I perceiv'd each thought,
Waking or sleeping, fix'd on nought　　　　880
　But these illusive scenes, and me,
The phantom, who thus came and went,
In half revealments, only meant
　To madden curiosity--
When by such various arts I found
Her fancy to its utmost wound,
One night--'twas in a holy spot,
Which she for pray'r had chos'n--a grot
Of purest marble, built below
Her garden beds, through which a glow　　　　890
From lamps invisible then stole,
　Brightly pervading all the place--
Like that mysterious light the soul,
　Itself unseen, sheds through the face--
There, at her altar while she knelt,
And all that woman ever felt,

---

864 / 843　view--] 1 ; ~ ,-- 5.
867 / 846　through--] 1 ; ~ ;-- 5.
894 / 873　face--] 1 ; ~ . 5.

When God and man both claim'd her sighs--
Every warm thought, that ever dwelt,
  Like summer clouds, 'twixt earth and skies,
  Too pure to fall, too gross to rise,   900
  Spoke in her gestures, tones and eyes,--
Thus, by the tender light, which lay
Dissolving round, as if its ray
Was breath'd from her, I heard her say:--

"Oh idol of my dreams! whate'er
  "Thy nature be--human, divine,
"Or but half heav'nly--still too fair,
  "Too heavenly to be ever mine!

"Wonderful Spirit, who dost make
  "Slumber so lovely, that it seems   910
"No longer life to live awake,
  "Since heaven itself descends in dreams,
"Why do I ever lose thee? why--
  "When on thy realms and thee I gaze--
"Still drops that veil, which I could die,
  "Oh gladly, but one hour to raise?

"Long ere such miracles as thou
  "And thine came o'er my thoughts, a thirst
"For light was in this soul, which now
  "Thy looks have into passion nurs'd.   920
"There's nothing bright above, below,
  "In sky--earth--ocean, that this breast
"Doth not intensely burn to know,
  "And thee, thee, thee, o'er all the rest!

"Then come, oh Spirit, from behind
  "The curtains of thy radiant home,

---

901 / 880 tones . . . eyes,--] 1 ; ~ , . . . ~ ^ -- 5.
913 / 892 why--] 1 ; ~ ^ 5.
914 / 893 gaze--] 1 ; ~ ^ 5.

"Whether thou would'st as God be shrin'd,
"Or lov'd and clasp'd as mortal, come!

"Bring all thy dazzling wonders here,
"That I may waking know and see--   930
"Or waft me hence to thy own sphere,
"Thy heaven or--aye, even *that* with thee!

"Demon or God, who hold'st the book
"Of knowledge spread beneath thine eye,
"Give me, with thee, but one bright look
"Into its leaves, and let me die!

"By those ethereal wings, whose way
"Lies through an element, so fraught
"With floating Mind, that, as they play,
"Their every movement is a thought!   940
"By that most precious hair, between
"Whose golden clusters the sweet wind
"Of Paradise so late hath been,
"And left its fragrant soul behind!

"By those impassion'd eyes, that melt
"Their light into the inmost heart,
"Like sunset in the waters, felt
"As molten fire through every part,--

"I do implore thee, oh most bright
"And worshipp'd Spirit, shine but o'er   950
"My waking, wondering eyes this night,
"This one blest night--I ask no more!"

---

927 / 906   "Whether . . . as God be shrin'd,] 1 ;
            "If . . . be as angel shrin'd, 5.
930 / 909   may waking . . . see--] 1 ; ~ , ~ , . . . ~; 5.
941 / 920   most precious] 1 ; bright, wreathed 5.
942 / 921   golden] 1 ; sunny 5.
946 / 925   heart,] 1 ; ~ ; 5.
948 / 927   part,--] 1 ; ~ ^ ~ 5.

Exhausted, breathless, as she said
These burning words, her languid head
Upon the altar's steps she cast,
As if that brain-throb were its last--
Till, startled by the breathing, nigh,
Of lips, that echoed back her sigh,
Sudden her brow again she rais'd,
   And there, just lighted on the shrine,   960
Beheld me--not as I had blaz'd
   Around her, full of light divine,
In her late dreams, but soften'd down
Into more mortal grace--my crown
Of flowers, too radiant for this world,
   Left hanging on yon starry steep;
My wings shut up, like banners furl'd,
   When Peace hath put their pomp to sleep;
   Or like autumnal clouds, that keep
Their lightnings sheath'd, rather than mar   970
The dawning hour of some young star--
And nothing left, but what beseem'd
   The' accessible, though glorious mate
Of mortal woman--whose eyes beam'd
   Back upon hers, as passionate;
Whose ready heart brought flame for flame,
Whose sin, whose madness was the same,
And whose soul lost, in that one hour,
   For her and for her love--oh more
Of heaven's light than ev'n the power   980
   Of heav'n itself could now restore!

And yet that hour!"----

             The Spirit here

---

959 / 938   rais'd,] 1 ; ^ ; 5.
964 / 943   grace--] 1 ; ~ ;-- 5.
971 / 950   star--] 1 ; ~ ; 5.
977 / 956   same,] 1 ; ~ ; 5.

Stopp'd in his utterance, as if words
Gave way beneath the wild career
Of his then rushing thoughts--like chords,
Midway in some enthusiast's song,
Breaking beneath a touch too strong--
While the clench'd hand upon the brow
Told how remembrance throbb'd there now!
But soon 'twas o'er--that casual blaze   990
From the sun fire of other days,
That relic of a flame, whose burning
   Had been too fierce to be relum'd,
Soon pass'd away, and the youth, turning
   To his bright listeners, thus resum'd:--

"Days, months elaps'd, and, though what most
   On earth I sigh'd for was mine, all,--
Yet--was I happy? God, thou know'st,
Howe'er they smile, and feign, and boast,
   What happiness is theirs, who fall!   1000
'Twas bitterest anguish--made more keen
Ev'n by the love, the bliss, between
Whose throbs it came, like gleams of hell
   In agonizing cross-light given
Athwart the glimpses, they who dwell
   In purgatory catch of heaven!
The only feeling that to me
   Seem'd joy, or rather my sole rest
From aching misery, was to see
   My young, proud, blooming LILIS blest--   1010
She, the fair fountain of all ill
To my lost soul--whom yet its thirst
Fervidly panted after still,
   And found the charm fresh as at first!--
To see *her* happy--to reflect

---

987 / 966 strong--] 1 ; ~ ; 5.
997 / 976 all,--] 1 ; ~ ^ ~ 5.
1010 / 989 blest--] 1 ; ~ . 5.
1014 / 993 first!--] 1; ~ ^ ~ 5.

Whatever beams still round me play'd
Of former pride, of glory wreck'd,
  On her, my Moon, whose light I made,
  And whose soul worshipp'd ev'n my shade--
This was, I own, enjoyment--this   1020
My sole, last lingering glimpse of bliss.

And proud she was, bright creature!--proud,
  Beyond what ev'n most queenly stirs
In woman's heart, nor would have bow'd
  That beautiful young brow of hers
To aught beneath the First above,
So high she deem'd her Cherub's love!

Then, too, that passion, hourly growing
  Stronger and stronger--to which even
Her love, at times, gave way--of knowing   1030
  Every thing strange in earth and heaven;
Not only what God loves to show,
But all that He hath seal'd below
In darkness, for man *not* to know--
  Ev'n this desire, alas, ill-starr'd
  And fatal as it was, I sought
To feed each minute, and unbarr'd
  Such realms of wonder on her thought,
As ne'er, till then, had let their light
Escape on any mortal's sight!   1040
In the deep earth--beneath the sea--
  Through caves of fire--through wilds of air--
Wherever sleeping Mystery
  Had spread her curtain, we were there--

1022 / 1001 bright] 1 ; fair 5.
1032 / 1011 what God loves to show,] 1 ; all that, full reveal'd, 5.
XXXX / 1012 (*new line added to 5, not included in 1*):
        Th'eternal ALLA loves to show,
        (*hereafter, lines 1033-1199 in 1 correspond to lines*
        1013- 1179 in 5.)
1033 / 1013 seal'd below] 1 ; wisely seal'd 5.

Love still beside us, as we went,
At home in each new element,
  And sure of worship every where!

Then first was Nature taught to lay
  The wealth of all her kingdoms down
At woman's worshipp'd feet, and say,   1050
  "Bright creature, this is all thine own!"
Then first were diamonds caught--like eyes
Shining in darkness--by surprise,
And made to light the conquering way
Of proud young beauty with their ray.
Then, too, the pearl from out its shell
  Unsightly, in the sunless sea,
(As 'twere a spirit, forc'd to dwell
  In form unlovely) was set free,
And round the neck of woman threw   1060
A light it lent and borrow'd too.
For never did this maid--whate'er
  The' ambition of the hour--forget
Her sex's pride in being fair,
Nor that adornment, tasteful, rare,
Which makes the mighty magnet, set
In Woman's form, more mighty yet.
Nor was there aught within the range
  Of my swift wing in sea or air,
Of beautiful, or grand, or strange,   1070
That, quickly as her wish could change,
  I did not seek, with such fond care,
That when I've seen her look above
  At some bright star admiringly,
I've said "nay, look not there, my love,
  Alas, I *cannot* give it thee!"

1052 / 1032   diamonds caught--like eyes]
                1 ; ~ , from the night, 5.
1053 / 1033   Shining in darkness--by surprise,] 1 ;
                Of earth's deep centre brought to light, 5.
1054 / 1034   light] 1 ; grace 5.

But not alone the wonders found
  Through Nature's realm--the'unveil'd, material,
Visible glories, that hang round,
  Like lights, through her enchanted ground--   1080
    But whatsoe'er unseen, ethereal,
Dwells far away from human sense,
Wrapp'd in its own intelligence--
The mystery of that Fountain-head,
  From which all vital spirit runs,
All breath of Life, where'er 'tis shed,
  Through men or angels, flowers or suns--
The workings of the'Almighty Mind,
When first o'er Chaos he design'd
The outlines of this world; and through   1090
  That spread of darkness--like the bow,
Call'd out of rain-clouds, hue by hue--
  Saw the grand, gradual picture grow!--
The covenant with human kind
  Which God hath made--the chains of Fate
He round himself and them hath twin'd,
  Till his high task he consummate--
Till good from evil, love from hate,
Shall be work'd out through sin and pain,
And Fate shall loose her iron chain,   1100
And all be free, be bright again!

Such were the deep-drawn mysteries,
  And some, perhaps, ev'n more profound,
More wildering to the mind than these

1079 / 1059   hang round] 1 ; abound 5.
1080 / 1060   Like lights, through her] 1 ;
                Through all her vast, 5.
1086 / 1066   shed,] 1 ; spread ^ 5.
1093 / 1073   grow!--] 1 ; ~ ; ~ 5.
1095 / 1075   which God hath made] 1 ; By ALLA ~ 5.
1097 / 1077   consummate--] 1 ; ~ ; ~ 5.
1099 / 1079   pain,] 1 ; ~ . 5.

Which--far as woman's thought could sound,
Or a fall'n, outlaw'd spirit reach--
She dar'd to learn, and I to teach.
Till--fill'd with such unearthly lore,
And mingling the pure light it brings
With much that fancy had, before,   1110
Shed in false, tinted glimmerings--
The'enthusiast girl spoke out, as one
  Inspir'd, among her own dark race,
Who from their altars, in the sun
Left standing half adorn'd, would run
  To gaze upon her holier face.
And, though but wild the things she spoke,
Yet mid that play of error's smoke
  Into fair shapes by fancy curl'd,
Some gleams of pure religion broke--   1120
Glimpses, that have not yet awoke,
  But startled the still dreaming world!
Oh, many a truth, remote, sublime,
  Which God would from the minds of men
Have kept conceal'd, till his own time,
  Stole out in these revealments then--
Revealments dim, that have fore-run,
By ages, the bright, Saving One! *
Like that imperfect dawn, or light
  Escaping from the Zodiac's signs,   1130
Which makes the doubtful east half bright

* It is the opinion of some of the Fathers, that the knowledge which the Heathens possessed of
the Providence of God, a Future State, and other sublime doctrines of Christianity, was derived from
the premature revelations of these fallen angels to the women of earth.--See Note.

1114 / 1094 altars, in the sun] 1 ; ancient shores would run, 5.
1115 / 1095 Left standing half adorn'd, would run] 1 ;
             Leaving their holy rites undone 5.
1118 / 1098 Yet] 1 ; ~ , 5.
1124 / 1104 God] 1 ; Heav'n 5.
1125 / 1105 his] 1 ; its 5.
1128 / 1108 Saving] 1 ; Sealing 5.
1131 / 1111 bright] 1 ; ~ , 5.

Before the real morning shines!

Thus did some moons of bliss go by--
  Of bliss to her, who saw but love
And knowledge throughout earth and sky;
To whose enamour'd soul and eye,
I seem'd, as is the sun on high,
  The light of all below, above,
The spirit of sea, land, and air,
Whose influence, felt every where,   1140
Spread from its centre, her own heart,
Ev'n to the world's extremest part--
While through that world her reinless mind
  Had now career'd so fast and far,
That earth itself seem'd left behind,
And her proud fancy, unconfin'd,
  Already saw heaven's gates a-jar!
Happy enthusiast! still, oh, still
Spite of my own heart's mortal chill,
Spite of that double-fronted sorrow,   1150
  Which looks at once before and back,
Beholds the yesterday, the morrow,
  And sees both comfortless, both black--
Spite of all this, I could have still
In her delight forgot all ill;
Or, if pain *would* not be forgot,
At least have borne and murmur'd not.
When thoughts of an offended heaven,
  Of sinfulness, which I--ev'n I,
While down its steep most headlong driven,--   1160
  Well knew could never be forgiven,
  Came o'er me with an agony
Beyond all reach of mortal woe,--
A torture kept for those who know,

1137 / 1117 seem'd, . . . high,] 1 ; ~ -- . . . ~ -- 5.
1142 / 1122 part--] 1 ; ~ ; 5.
1160 / 1140 driven,--] 1 ; ~ ^ ~ 5.
1163 / 1143 woe,--] 1 ; ~ ^ ~ 5.

Know every thing, and, worst of all,
Know and love virtue while they fall!--
Ev'n then, her presence had the power
  To soothe, to warm,--nay, ev'n to bless--
If ever bliss could graft its flower
  On stem so full of bitterness--   1170
Ev'n then her glorious smile to me
  Brought warmth and radiance, if not balm,
Like moonlight on a troubled sea,
  Brightening the storm it cannot calm.

Oft, too, when that disheartening fear,
  Which all who love, beneath the sky,
Feel, when they gaze on what is dear--
  The dreadful thought that it must die!
That desolating thought, which comes
Into men's happiest hours and homes;   1180
Whose melancholy boding flings
Death's shadow o'er the brightest things,
Sicklies the infant's bloom, and spreads
The grave beneath young lovers' heads!
This fear, so sad to all--to me
  Most full of sadness, from the thought
That I must still live on, when she
  Would, like the snow that on the sea
  Fell yesterday, in vain be sought--
That heaven to me the final seal   1190
  Of all earth's sorrow would deny,
And I eternally must feel
  The death-pang, without power to die!
Ev'n this, her fond endearments--fond
As ever twisted the sweet bond
'Twixt heart and heart--could charm away;

1165 / 1145 every . . . and, . . . all,] 1 ;
             every . . . ~ -- . . . ~ -- 5.
1172 / 1152 balm,] 1 ; ~ ; 5.
1176 / 1156 the] 1 ; yon 5.
1189 / 1169 sought--] 1 ; ~ ; 5.

Before her look no clouds would stay,
Or, if they did, their gloom was gone,
Their darkness put a glory on!
There seem'd a freshness in her breath,   1200
Beyond the reach, the power of death;
And then, her voice--oh, who could doubt
That 'twould for ever thus breathe out
A music, like the harmony
Of the tun'd orbs, too sweet to die!
While in her lip's awakening touch
There thrill'd a life ambrosial--such
As mantles in the fruit steep'd through
With Eden's most delicious dew--
Till I could almost think, though known   1210
And lov'd as human, they had grown
By bliss, celestial as my own!

But 'tis not, 'tis not for the wrong,
The guilty, to be happy long;
And she, too, now, had sunk within
The shadow of her tempter's sin--
Shadow of death, whose withering frown
   Kills whatsoe'er it lights upon--
   Too deep for ev'n *her* soul to shun
The desolation it brings down!   1220

Listen, and, if a tear there be
Left in your hearts, weep it for me.

1200-1212 / XXXX (*Lines 1200-1212 in 1 deleted from 5.Hereafter,*
                    1213-1216 in 1 correspond to 1180-1183 in 5.)
1216 / 1183 sin--] 1 ; ~ , 5.
1217 / 1184 Shadow of death, whose withering frown] 1 ;
              Too deep for ev'n Omnipotence 5.
1218 / 1185 Kills whatsoe'er it lights upon--] 1 ;
              To snatch the fated victim 5.
1219-1220 / XXXX (*Omitted from 5. Hereafter, lines 1221-1252 in 1*
                  correspond to lines 1186-1217 in 5.)

'Twas on the evening of a day,
Which we in love had dream'd away;
In that same garden, where, beneath
The silent earth, stripp'd of my wreath,
And furling up those wings, whose light
For mortal gaze were else too bright,
I first had stood before her sight;
And found myself--oh, ecstasy,   1230
  Which ev'n in pain I ne'er forget--
Worshipp'd as only God should be,
  And lov'd as never man was yet!
In that same garden we were now,
  Thoughtfully side by side reclining,
Her eyes turn'd upward, and her brow
  With its own silent fancies shining.
It was an evening bright and still
  As ever blush'd on wave or bower,
Smiling from heaven, as if nought ill   1240
  Could happen in so sweet an hour.
Yet, I remember, both grew sad
  In looking at that light--ev'n she,
Of heart so fresh, and brow so glad,
  Felt the mute hour's solemnity,
And thought she saw, in that repose,
  The death-hour not alone of light,
But of this whole fair world--the close
  Of all things beautiful and bright--
The last, grand sun-set, in whose ray   1250
Nature herself died calm away!

1225 / 1190 where, beneath] 1 ; ~ -- the pride 5.
1226 / 1191 The silent earth, stripp'd of my wreath,] 1 ;
               Of seraph splendor laid aside, 5.
1227 / 1192 And furling up those wings, whose light] 1 ;
               And those wings furl'd, whose open light 5.
1228 / 1193 bright,] 1 ; ~ -- 5 .
1129 / 1194 sight;] 1 ; ~ , 5.

At length, as if some thought, awaking
  Suddenly, sprung within her breast--
Like a young bird, when day-light breaking
  Startles him from his dreamy nest--
She turn'd upon me her dark eyes,
  Dilated into that full shape
They took in joy, reproach, surprise,
  As if to let more soul escape,
And, playfully as on my head   1260
Her white hand rested, smil'd and said:--

"I had, last night, a dream of thee,
  "Resembling those divine ones, given,
"Like preludes to sweet minstrelsy,
  "Before thou cam'st, thyself, from heaven.

"The same rich wreath was on thy brow,
  "Dazzling as if of star-light made;
"And these wings, lying darkly now,
  "Like meteors round thee flash'd and play'd.

"All bright as in those happy dreams   1270
  "Thou stood'st, a creature to adore
"No less than love, breathing out beams,

1251 / 1217 if some thought, awaking] 1 ;
             though some livelier thought 5.
1253 / 1218 Suddenly, sprung within her breast--] 1 ;
             Had suddenly her fancy caught 5.
1254-1255 / XXXX (*Omitted from 5. Henceforth, lines 1256-
             1356 in 1 correspond to 1219-1319 in 5.*)
1259 / 1222 if] 1 ; 'twere 5.
1270 / 1233 "All bright as in those happy dreams] 1 ;
             "Thou stood'st, all bright, as in those dreams, 5.
1271 / 1234 "Thou stood'st, a creature to adore] 1 ;
             "As if just wafted from above; 5.
1272 / 1235 "No less than love, breathing out beams,] 1;
             "Mingling earth's warmth and heaven's ~ ,] 5.

"As flowers do fragrance, at each pore!

"Sudden I felt thee draw me near
  "To thy pure heart, where, fondly plac'd,
"I seem'd within the atmosphere
  "Of that exhaling light embrac'd;
"And, as thou heldst me there, the flame
  "Pass'd from thy heavenly soul to mine,
"Till--oh, too blissful--I became,   1280
  "Like thee, all spirit, all divine.

"Say, why did dream so bright come o'er me,
  "If, now I wake, 'tis faded, gone?
"When will my Cherub shine before me
  "Thus radiant, as in heaven he shone?

"When shall I, waking, be allow'd
  "To gaze upon those perfect charms,
"And hold thee thus, without a cloud,
  "A chill of earth, within my arms?

"Oh what a pride to say--this, this   1290
  "Is my own Angel--all divine,
"And pure, and dazzling as he is,
  "And fresh from heaven, he's mine, he's mine!

"Think'st thou, were LILIS in thy place,
  "A creature of yon lofty skies,
"She would have hid one single grace,

1273 / 1236 "As flowers do fragrance, at each pore!"] 1;
             "A creature to adore and love. 5.
1278 / 1241 "And, as thou heldst me there, the flame] 1;
             "And felt, methought, the' ethereal flame 5.
1279 / 1242 "Pass'd from thy heavenly soul to mine,] 1 ;
             "Pass from thy purer ~ ~ ~ ; 5.
1282 / 1245 bright] 1 ; blest 5.
1288 / 1251 "And hold thee thus,] 1 ; " ~ clasp ~ once 5.
1289 / 1252 my] 1 ; these 5.

"One glory from her lover's eyes?

"No, no--then, if thou lov'st like me,
  "Shine out, young Spirit, in the blaze
"Of thy most proud divinity,   1300
  "Nor think thou'lt wound this mortal gaze.

"Too long have I look'd doating on
  "Those ardent eyes, intense ev'n thus--
"Too near the stars themselves have gone,
  "To fear aught grand or luminous.
"Then doubt me not--oh, who can say
  "But that this dream may yet come true,
"And my blest spirit drink thy ray
  "Till it becomes all heavenly too?

"Let me this once but feel the flame   1310
  "Of those spread wings, the very pride
"Will change my nature, and this frame
  "By the mere touch be deified!"

Thus spoke the maid, as one, not us'd
To be by man or God refus'd--
As one, who felt her influence o'er
  All creatures, whatsoe'er they were,
And, though to heaven she could not soar,
  At least would bring down heaven to her!

Little did she, alas, or I--   1320
  Ev'n I, whose soul, but half-way yet
Immerg'd in sin's obscurity,

1302 / 1265 have I look'd doating on] 1 ;
                and oft I've looked upon 5.
1315 / 1278 man or God] 1 ; earth or heav'n 5.
1316 / 1279 felt] 1 ; knew 5.
1319 / 1282 her!] 1 ; ~ . 5 .
1322 / 1285 obscurity,] 1 ; ~ ^ 5 .

Was as the planet where we lie,
  O'er half whose disk the sun is set--
Little did we foresee the fate,
  The dreadful--how can it be told?
Oh God! such anguish to relate
  Is o'er again to feel, behold!
But, charg'd as 'tis, my heart must speak
Its sorrow out, or it will break!   1330
Some dark misgivings *had*, I own,
  Pass'd for a moment through my breast--
Fears of some danger, vague, unknown,
  To one, or both--something unblest
  To happen from this proud request.
But soon these boding fancies fled;
  Nor saw I aught that could forbid
My full revealment, save the dread
  Of that first dazzle, that unhid
  And bursting glory on a lid   1340
Untried in heaven--and ev'n this glare
She might, by love's own nursing care,
Be, like young eagles, taught to bear.
For well I know the lustre shed
From my rich wings, when proudliest spread,
Was, in its nature, lambent, pure,
  And innocent as is the light
The glow-worm hangs out to allure
  Her mate to her green bower at night.
Oft had I, in the mid-air, swept   1350
Through clouds in which the lightning slept,
As in his lair, ready to spring,

1323 / 1286 planet where] 1 ; earth whereon 5.
1327 / 1290 Oh God!] 1 ; Such pains, 5.
1339 / 1302 that] 1 ; when, 5.
1340 / 1303 And bursting glory on] 1 ;
                Such light should burst upon 5.
1341 / 1304 Untried in heaven--] 1 ; Ne'er tried ~ ~ ;~ 5.
1345 / 1308 my rich] 1 ; cherub 5.
1352 / 1315 his] 1 ; its 5.

Yet wak'd him not--though from my wing
A thousand sparks fell glittering!
Oft too when round me from above
  The feather'd snow (which, for its whiteness,
In my pure days I used to love)
Fell, like the moultings of heaven's Dove,--
  So harmless, though so full of brightness,
Was my brow's wreath, that it would shake   1360
From off its flowers each downy flake
As delicate, unmelted, fair,
And cool as they had fallen there!

Nay ev'n with LILIS--had I not
  Around her sleep in splendour come--
Hung o'er each beauty, nor forgot
  To print my radiant lips on some?
And yet, at morn, from that repose,
  Had she not wak'd, unscath'd and bright,
As doth the pure, unconscious rose,   1370
  Though by the fire-fly kiss'd all night?
Ev'n when the rays I scatter'd stole
Intensest to her dreaming soul,
No thrill disturb'd th'insensate frame--
So subtle, so refin'd that flame,
Which, rapidly as lightnings melt
  The blade within the unharm'd sheath,
Can, by the outward form unfelt,

1353 / 1316 him] 1 ; it 5.
1356 / 1319 snow (which, for] 1 ; ~ , ^ in all 5.
1357 / XXXX *(Deleted from 5. Henceforth, lines 1358-1371 in 1*
      correspond to 1320-1333 in 5.)
1363 / 1325 fallen there!] 1 ; lighted ~ . 5 .
1365 / 1327 in splendour come--] 1 ; all radiant beam'd, 5.
1366 / 1328 each beauty] 1 ; her slumbers 5.
1367 / 1329 print my radiant lips on some?] 1 ;
      kiss her eye-lids, as she dreamed? 5.
1372-1379 / XXXX *(Deleted from 5. Henceforth, lines 1380-1399 in*
      1 correspond to lines 1334-1353 in 5.)

Reach and dissolve the soul beneath!

Thus having (as, alas, deceiv'd   1380
By my sin's blindness, I believ'd)
No cause for dread, and those black eyes
    There fix'd upon me, eagerly
As if the' unlocking of the skies
    Then waited but a sign from me--
How was I to refuse? how say
    One word that in her heart could stir
A fear, a doubt, but that each ray
    I brought from heaven belong'd to her!
Slow from her side I rose, while she   1390
Stood up, too, mutely, tremblingly,
But not with fear--all hope, desire,
    She waited for the awful boon,
Like priestesses, with eyes of fire
    Watching the rise of the full moon,
Whose beams--they know, yet cannot shun--
Will madden them when look'd upon!

1380 / 1334 having (as] 1 ; ~ -- ~ 5.
1381 / 1335 believ'd)] 1 ; ~ -- 5.
1382 / 1336 black] 1 ; dark 5.
1383 / 1337 There] 1 ; Now 5.
1384 / 1338 if] 1 ; though 5.
1386 / 1340 was I to refuse? how say] 1 ;
             could I pause: how ev'n let fall 5.
1387 / 1341 word that in her heart could] 1 ;
             ~ , a whisper, that could ~ 5.
1388 / 1342 A fear, a doubt, but that each ray] 1 ;
             In her proud heart a doubt, that all 5.
1389 / 1343 her!] 1 ; ~ . 5 .
1391 / 1345 Stood up] 1 ; Arose 5.
1392 / 1346 desire] 1 ; and pride 5.
1394 / 1348 with eyes of fire] 1 ; at eventide, 5 .
1396 / 1350 beams--they know, yet cannot shun--] 1 ;
             light, when once its orb hath shone, 5.
1397 / 1351 Will] 1 ; 'Twill 5.

Of all my glories, the bright crown,
Which, when I last from heaven came down,
I left--see, where those clouds afar   1400
   Sail through the west--there hangs it yet,
Shining remote, more like a star
   Than a fall'n angel's coronet--
Of all my glories, this alone
   Was wanting--but the' illumin'd brow,
The curls, like tendrils that had grown
   Out of the sun--the eyes, that now
Had love's light added to their own,
And shed a blaze, before unknown
Ev'n to themselves--the'unfolded wings   1410
From which, as from two radiant springs,
Sparkles fell fast around, like spray--
All I could bring of heaven's array,
   Of that rich panoply of charms
A Cherub moves in, on the day
Of his best pomp, I now put on;
And, proud that in her eyes I shone

1400 / 1354   I left--see, where those clouds afar] 1 ;
                 Was left behind me in yon star 5.
1401 / 1355   Sail through the west--there hangs it yet,]
                 1 ; That shines from out those clouds afar,-- 5.
1402 / 1356   Shining remote, more like a star] 1 ;
                 Where, relic sad, 'tis treasured yet, 5.
1403 / 1357   Than a fall'n angel's coronet--] 1 ;
                 The downfall'n ~ ~ !-- 5.
1405 / 1359   wanting--] 1 ; ~ ; ~ 5.
1406-1412 / 1360-1364   (*Deleted from 5. The following*
    substitutions appear in 5 as lines 1360-1364:)
    The sun-bright locks, that now the eyes,
    Had love's spell added to their own,
    And pour'd a light till then unknown;
    The' unfolded wings, that, in their play,
    Shed sparkles bright as ALLA's throne;
    (*Henceforth, lines 1413-1448 in 1 correspond*
    to lines 1365-1400 in 5.)

Thus glorious, glided to her arms,
Which still (though at a sight so splendid
Her dazzled brow had instantly   1420
Sunk on her breast) were wide extended
To clasp the form she durst not see!

Great God! how *could* thy vengeance light
So bitterly on one so bright?
How could the hand, that gave such charms,
Blast them again, in love's own arms?
Scarce had I touch'd her shrinking frame,
When--oh most horrible!--I felt
That every spark of that pure flame--
Pure, while among the stars I dwelt--   1430
Was now by my transgression turn'd
Into gross, earthly fire, which burn'd,
Burn'd all it touch'd, as fast as eye
Could follow the fierce, ravening flashes,
Till there--oh God, I still ask why
Such doom was hers?--I saw her lie
Black'ning within my arms to ashes!
Those cheeks, a glory but to see--
Those lips, whose touch was what the first
Fresh cup of immortality   1440
Is to a new-made angel's thirst!
Those arms, within whose gentle round,
My heart's horizon, the whole bound

1418 / 1370   arms,] 1 ; ~ ; 5.
1419 / 1371   though] 1 ; ~ , 5.
1420 / 1386   had] 1 ; ~ , 5.
1421 / 1373   breast] 1 ; ~ , 5.
1423 / 1375   God] 1 ; Heaven 5.
1431 / 1386   now . . . transgression] 1 ; ~ , . . . ~ , 5.
1434 / 1386   flashes,] 1 ; ~ ; 5.
1438 / 1390   Those cheeks] 1 ; That brow 5.
1442 / 1394   arms, within whose gentle] 1 ;
              clasping ~ , ~ whose ^ mind-- 5.
1443 / 1395   horizen,] 1 ; ~ -- 5.

Of its hope, prospect, heaven was found!
Which, ev'n in this dread moment, fond
  As when they first were round me cast,
Loos'd not in death the' fatal bond,
  But, burning, held me to the last--
That hair, from under whose dark veil,
The snowy neck, like a white sail   1450
At moonlight seen 'twixt wave and wave,
Shone out by gleams--that hair, to save
But one of whose long, glossy wreaths,
I could have died ten thousand deaths!--
All, all, that seem'd, one minute since,
So full of love's own redolence,
Now, parch'd and black, before me lay,
Withering in agony away;
And mine, oh misery! mine the flame,
From which this desolation came--   1460
And I the fiend, whose foul caress
Had blasted all that loveliness!

'Twas madd'ning, 'twas--but hear even worse--
Had death, death only, been the curse
I brought upon her--had the doom
But ended here, when her young bloom

1447 / 1399 the'] 1 ; the ^ 5.
1448 / 1400 last--] 1 ; ~ ! 5.
1449-1450 / 1401-1402 (*Readings in 1 omitted.*
  Substitutions made in 5, appearing as lines 1401-1402:)
  All, all, that but that morn, had seem'd
  As if Love's self there breathed and beam'd,
  (*Lines 1451-1456 in 1 deleted. Henceforth, lines*
  1457-1489 in 1 correspond to lines 1403-1435 in 5.)
1460 / 1406 came--] 1 ; ~ ; ~ 5.
1461 / 1407 And I the fiend, whose foul caress] 1 ;
           I, the curst spirit, whose ~ 5.
1463 / 1409 'Twas madd'ning, 'twas--but hear even
           worse--] 1; ~ maddening!--but now 5.

Lay in the dust, and did the spirit
No part of that fell curse inherit,
'Twere not so dreadful--but, come near--
Too shocking 'tis for earth to hear--   1470
Just when her eyes, in fading, took
  Their last, keen, agoniz'd farewell,
And look'd in mine with--oh, that look!
  Avenging Power, whate'er the hell
Thou may'st to human souls assign,
The memory of that look is mine!--
In her last struggle, on my brow
  Her ashy lips a kiss imprest,
So withering!--I feel it now--
  'Twas fire--but fire, ev'n more unblest   1480
Than was my own, and like that flame,
The angels shudder but to name,
Hell's everlasting element!
  Deep, deep it pierc'd into my brain,
Madd'ning and torturing as it went,
  And here--see here, the mark, the stain
It left upon my front--burnt in
By that last kiss of love and sin--
A brand, which ev'n the wreathed pride
Of these bright curls, still forc'd aside   1490
By its foul contact, cannot hide!

1467 / 1413 dust,] 1 ; ~ -- 5.
1474 / 1420 Avenging] 1 ; Great vengeful 5.
1485 / 1431 went,] 1 ; ~ ; 5.
1486 / 1432 see here, the mark] 1 ;
                mark here, the brand 5.
1489 / 1435 ev'n the wreathed] 1 ;
                all the pomp and pride 5.
1490-1491 / 1436 (*Lines 1490-1491 in 1 deleted from 5.*
    The following substitution appears at line 1490
    (as line 1436 in 5):)
    Of a fallen spirit cannot hide!
    (*Hereafter, lines 1492-1549 in 1 correspond to*
    lines 1437-1494 in 5.)

But is it thus, dread Providence--
  Can it, indeed, be thus, that she,
Who, but for one proud, fond offence,
  Had honour'd heaven itself, should be
Now doom'd--I cannot speak it--no,
Merciful God! it *is* not so--
Never could lips divine have said
That fiat of a fate so dread.
And yet, that look--that look, so fraught   1500
  With more than anguish, with despair--
That new, fierce fire, resembling nought
  In heaven or earth--this scorch I bear!--
Oh,--for the first time that these knees
  Have bent before thee since my fall,
Great Power, if ever thy decrees
  Thou could'st for prayer like mine recall,
Pardon that spirit, and on me,
  On me, who taught her pride to err,
Shed out each drop of agony   1510
  Thy burning phial keeps for her!
See, too, where low beside me kneel
  Two other out-casts, who, though gone
And lost themselves, yet dare to feel
  And pray for that poor mortal one.
Alas, too well, too well they know
The pain, the penitence, the woe
That Passion brings down on the best,
The wisest and the loveliest.--
Oh, who is to be sav'd, if such   1520
  Bright, erring souls are not forgiven;
So loth they wander, and so much
Their very wanderings lean tow'rds heaven!

1494 / 1439 but . . . one . . . offence,] 1 ;
            (~ . . . *one* . . . ,) 5.
1497 / 1442 God! it *is*] 1 ; ALLA! *'tis* 5.
1500 / 1445 that look, so fraught] 1 ; so deeply ~ 5.

Again, I cry, Just God, transfer
  That creature's sufferings all to me--
Mine, mine the guilt, the torment be,
To save one minute's pain to her,
  Let mine last all eternity!"

He paus'd, and to the earth bent down
  His throbbing head; while they, who felt   1530
That agony as 'twere their own,
  Those angel youths, beside him knelt,
And, in the night's still silence there,
While mournfully each wandering air
Play'd in those plumes, that never more
To their lost home in heav'n must soar,
Breath'd inwardly the voiceless prayer,
Unheard by all but Mercy's ear--
And which if Mercy *did not* hear,
Oh, God would not be what this bright   1540
  And glorious universe of his,
This world of beauty, goodness, light
  And endless love proclaims He *is*!

Not long they knelt, when, from a wood
That crown'd that airy solitude,
They heard a low, uncertain sound,
As from a lute, that just had found
Some happy theme, and murmur'd round
The new-born fancy--with fond tone,
Like that of ring-dove o'er her brood--   1550
Scarce thinking aught so sweet its own!
Till soon a voice, that match'd as well
  That gentle instrument, as suits
The sea-air to an ocean-shell,

1524 / 1469 God] 1 ; Power 5.
1550 / XXXX (*Deleted from 5. Henceforth, lines 1551-1648*
               in 1 correspond to lines 1495-1592 in 5.)

(So kin its spirit to the lute's,)
Tremblingly follow'd the soft strain,
Interpreting its joy, its pain,
   And lending the light wings of words
To many a thought, that else had lain
   Unfledg'd and mute among the chords.   1560
All started at the sound--but chief
   The third young Angel, in whose face,
Though faded like the others, grief
   Had left a gentler, holier trace;
As if, ev'n yet, through pain and ill,
Hope had not quit him--as if still
Her precious pearl, in sorrow's cup,
   Unmelted at the bottom lay,
To shine again, when, all drunk up,
   The bitterness should pass away.   1570
Chiefly did he, though in his eyes
There shone more pleasure than surprise,
Turn to the wood, from whence that sound
   Of solitary sweetness broke,
Then, listening, look delighted round
   To his bright peers, while thus it spoke:--

"Come, pray with me, my seraph love,
   "My angel-lord, come pray with me;
"In vain to-night my lip hath strove
"To send one holy prayer above--   1580
"The knee may bend, the lip may move,
   "But pray I cannot, without thee!

"I've fed the altar in my bower
   "With droppings from the incense tree;
"I've shelter'd it from wind and shower,
"But dim it burns the livelong hour,
"As if, like me, it had no power
   "Or life or lustre, without thee!
"A boat at midnight sent alone

1555 / 1499 lute's,)] 1; ~ ^), 5.

"To drift upon the moonless sea,   1590
"A lute, whose leading chord is gone,
"A wounded bird, that hath but one
"Imperfect wing to soar upon,
    "Are like what I am, without thee!

"Then ne'er, my spirit-love, divide,
    "In life or death, thyself from me;
"But when again, in sunny pride,
"Thou walk'st through Eden, let me glide,
"A prostrate shadow, by thy side--
    "Oh happier thus than without thee!"   1600
The song had ceas'd, when, from the wood--
    Where, curving down that airy height,
It reach'd the spot on which they stood--
    There suddenly shone out a light
From a clear lamp, which, as it blaz'd
Across the brow of one, who rais'd
The flame aloft, (as if to throw
Its light upon that group below)
Display'd two eyes, sparkling between
The dusky leaves, such as are seen   1610
By fancy only, in those faces,
    That haunt a poet's walk at even,
Looking from out their leafy places
    Upon his dreams of love and heaven.
'Twas but a moment--the blush, brought
O'er all her features at the thought
    Of being seen thus, late, alone,
By any but the eyes she sought,
    Had scarcely for an instant shone
Through the dark leaves when she was gone--   1620
Gone, like a meteor that o'erhead

1601 / 1545 wood--] 1 ; ' ^ 5.
1602 / 1546 Where, curving] 1 ; Which, sweeping 5.
1603 / 1547 It reach'd the spot on which] 1 ;
             Reach'd the lone spot whereon 5.
1608 / 1552 Its . . . below)] 1 ; The . . . ~), 5.

Suddenly shines, and, ere we've said,
"Look, look, how beautiful!"--'tis fled.
Yet, ere she went, the words, "I come,
　"I come, my NAMA," reach'd her ear,
In that kind voice, familiar, dear,
Which tells of confidence, of home,--
Of habit, that hath drawn hearts near,
Till they grow *one*--of faith sincere,
And all that Love most loves to hear!　　　　　　1630
A music, breathing of the past,
　The present and the time to be,
Where Hope and Memory, to the last,
　Lengthen out life's true harmony!

Nor long did he, whom call so kind
Summon'd away, remain behind;
Nor did there need much time to tell
　What they--alas, more fall'n than he
From happiness and heaven--knew well,
　His gentler love's short history!　　　　　　1640
Thus did it run--*not* as he told
　The tale himself, but as 'tis grav'd
Upon the tablets that, of old,
　By CHAM were from the deluge sav'd,
All written over with sublime
　And saddening legends of the' unblest,
But glorious Spirits of that time,
　And this young Angel's 'mong the rest.

1623 / 1567　Look, look] 1 ; Behold 5.
1630 / 1547　hear!] 1 ; ~ ; 5.
1644 / 1588　CHAM] 1 ; SETH　5.

Third Angel's Story

Among the Spirits, of pure flame,
  That round the' Almighty Throne abide--   1650
Circles of light, that from the same
  Eternal centre sweeping wide,
  Carry its beams on every side,
(Like spheres of air that waft around
The undulations of rich sound)
Till the far-circling radiance be
Diffus'd into infinity!
First and immediate near the Throne,
As if peculiarly God's own,
The Seraphs * stand--this burning sign   1660
Trac'd on their banner, "Love Divine!"
Their rank, their honours, far above
  Ev'n those to high-brow'd Cherubs given,
Though knowing all--so much doth Love
  Transcend all Knowledge, ev'n in heaven!

'Mong these was ZARAPH once--and none
  E'er felt affection's holy fire,
Or yearn'd towards the' Eternal One,
  With half such longing, deep desire.
Love was to his impassion'd soul   1670
  Not, as with others, a mere part

  * The Seraphim are the Spirits of Divine Love.
--See Note. [M.]

1650 / 1594   round the' Almighty Throne] 1 ; in the'
                eternal heav'ns 5.
1652 / 1596   Eternal] 1 ; Unclouded 5.
1654 / 1598   (Like] 1 ; ^ ~ 5.
1655 / 1599   sound)] 1 ; ~ ^ -- 5.
1659 / 1603   As if peculiarly God's] 1 ;
                Of ALLA, as if most his 5.

Of its existence, but the whole--
The very life-breath of his heart!

Often, when from the' Almighty brow
  A lustre came, too bright to bear,
And all the seraph ranks would bow
  Their heads beneath their wings, nor dare
  To look upon the' effulgence there--
This Spirit's eyes would court the blaze,
  (Such pride he in adoring took)   1680
And rather lose, in that one gaze,
  The power of looking, than *not* look!
Then too, when angel voices sung
The mercy of their God, and strung
  Their harps to hail, with welcome sweet,
  The moment, watch'd for by all eyes,
When some repentant sinner's feet
  First touch'd the threshold of the skies,
Oh then how clearly did the voice
Of ZARAPH above all rejoice!   1690
Love was in every buoyant tone,
  Such love, as only could belong
To the blest angels, and alone
  Could, ev'n from angels, bring such song!
Alas, that it should e'er have been
  The same in heaven as it is here,
Where nothing fond or bright is seen,
  But it hath pain and peril near--
Where right and wrong so close resemble,

1674 / 1618 Often , . . . the' Almighty brow]
             1 ; Oft, . . . ALLA's
             Lifted ~ 5.
1677 / 1621 Their heads beneath their wings] 1 ;
             To shade their dazzled sight 5.
1680 / 1624 took)] 1 ; ~) , 5.
1696 / 1640 The same in heaven as it is] 1 ;
             In heav'n as 'tis too often 5.
1698 / 1642 near--] 1 ; ~ ;~ 5.

That what we take for virtue's thrill   1700
Is often the first downward tremble
Of the heart's balance into ill--
Where Love hath not a shrine so pure,
 So holy, but the serpent, Sin,
In moments, ev'n the most secure,
 Beneath his altar may glide in!

So was it with that Angel--such
 The charm, that slop'd his fall along
From good to ill, from loving much,
 Too easy lapse, to loving wrong.--   1710
Ev'n so that am'rous Spirit, bound
By beauty's spell, where'er 'twas found,
From the bright things above the moon
 Down to earth's beaming eyes descended,
Till love for the Creator soon
 In passion for the creature ended!

'Twas first at twilight, on the shore
 Of the smooth sea, he heard the lute
And voice of her he lov'd steal o'er
 The silver waters, that lay mute,   1720
As loth, by ev'n a breath, to stay
The pilgrimage of that sweet lay;
Whose echoes still went on and on,
Till lost among the light that shone
Far off, beyond the ocean's brim--
 There, where the rich cascade of day
Had, o'er the' horizon's golden rim,
 Into Elysium roll'd away!
Of God she sung, and of the mild
 Attendant Mercy, that beside   1730
His awful throne for ever smil'd,
 Ready, with her white hand, to guide
His bolts of vengeance to their prey--

1702 / 1646 ill--] 1 ; ~ ; 5.
1716 / 1660 ended!] 1 ; ! . 5.

That she might quench them on the way!
Of Peace--of that Atoning Love,
Upon whose star, shining above
This twilight world of hope and fear,
  The weeping eyes of Faith are fix'd
So fond, that with her every tear
  The light of that love-star is mix'd!--   1740
All this she sung, and such a soul
  Of piety was in that song,
That the charm'd Angel, as it stole
  Tenderly to his ear, along
Those lulling waters where he lay,
Watching the day-light's dying ray,
Thought 'twas a voice from out the wave,
An echo, that some spirit gave
To Eden's distant harmony,
Heard faint and sweet beneath the sea!   1750

Quickly, however, to its source,
Tracking that music's melting course,
He saw, upon the golden sand
Of the sea-shore a maiden stand,
Before whose feet the' expiring waves
  Flung their last tribute with a sigh--
As, in the East, exhausted slaves
  Lay down the far-brought gift, and die--
And, while her lute hung by her, hush'd,
  As if unequal to the tide   1760
Of song, that from her lips still gush'd,
  She rais'd, like one beatified,
Those eyes, whose light seem'd rather given
  To be ador'd than to adore--
Such eyes, as may have look'd *from* heaven,
  But ne'er were rais'd to it before!

Oh Love, Religion, Music--all

1748 / 1692 spirit] 1 ; sea-nymph 5.
1756 / 1700 tribute] 1 ; offering 5.

That's left of Eden upon earth--
The only blessings, since the fall
Of our weak souls, that still recall   1770
   A trace of their high, glorious birth--
How kindred are the dreams you bring!
   How Love, though unto earth so prone,
Delights to take Religion's wing,
   When time or grief hath stain'd his own!
How near to Love's beguiling brink,
   Too oft, entranc'd Religion lies!
While Music, Music is the link
   They *both* still hold by to the skies,
The language of their native sphere,   1780
Which they had else forgotten here.

How then could ZARAPH fail to feel
   That moment's witcheries?--one, so fair,
Breathing out music, that might steal
   Heaven from itself, and rapt in prayer
   That seraphs might be proud to share!
Oh, he *did* feel it--far too well--
   With warmth, that much too dearly cost--
Nor knew he, when at last he fell,
To which attraction, to which spell,   1790
Love, Music, or Devotion, most
His soul in that sweet hour was lost.

Sweet was the hour, though dearly won,
   And pure, as aught of earth could be,
For then first did the glorious sun
   Before religion's altar see
Two hearts in wedlock's golden tie
Self-pledg'd, in love to live and die--

1787 / 1731 far] 1 ; all 5.
1788 / 1732 much] 1 ; far 5.
1798 / 1742 die--] 1 ; ~ . 5.

Then first did woman's virgin brow
  That hymeneal chaplet wear,   1800
Which when it dies, no second vow
  Can bid a new one bloom out there--
Blest union! by that Angel wove,
  And worthy from such hands to come;
Safe, sole asylum, in which Love,
When fall'n or exil'd from above,
  In this dark world can find a home.

And, though the Spirit had transgress'd,
Had, from his station 'mong the blest
Won down by woman's smile, allow'd   1810
  Terrestrial passion to breathe o'er
The mirror of his heart, and cloud
  God's image, there so bright before--
Yet never did that God look down
  On error with a brow so mild;
Never did justice launch a frown,
  That, ere it fell, so nearly smil'd.
For gentle was their love, with awe
  And trembling like a treasure kept,
That was not theirs by holy law,   1820
Whose beauty with remorse they saw,
  And o'er whose preciousness they wept.
Humility, that low, sweet root,
From which all heavenly virtues shoot,
Was in the hearts of both--but most
  In NAMA's heart, by whom alone

1799-1802 / XXXX (Deleted from 1. Hereafter, lines
  1803-1951 in 1 correspond to lines 1743-1891 in 5.)
1814 / 1754 God] 1 ; Power 5.
1816 / 1756 justice launch] 1 ; Justice wear 5.
1817 / 1757 That, ere it fell, so nearly] 1;
            Through which so gently Mercy 5.
1818 / 1758 gentle . . . love,] 1 ;
            humble . . . ~ -- 5.
1819 / 1759 a] 1 ; some 5.

Those charms, for which a heaven was lost,
  Seem'd all unvalued and unknown;
And when her Seraph's eyes she caught,
  And hid hers glowing on his breast,   1830
Ev'n bliss was humbled by the thought--
  "What claim have I to be so blest?"

Still less could maid, so meek, have nurs'd
Desire of knowledge--that vain thirst,
With which the sex hath all been curs'd,
From luckless EVE to her, who near
The Tabernacle stole to hear
The secrets of the angels--no--
  To love as her own Seraph lov'd,
With Faith, the same through bliss and woe--   1840
  Faith, that, were ev'n its light remov'd,
Could, like the dial, fix'd remain,
And wait till it shone out again--
With Patience that, though often bow'd
  By the rude storm, can rise anew,
And Hope that, ev'n from Evil's cloud,
  Sees sunny Good half breaking through!
This deep, relying Love, worth more
In heaven than all a cherub's lore--
This Faith, more sure than aught beside,   1850
Was the sole joy, ambition, pride
Of her fond heart--the' unreasoning scope
  Of all its views, above, below--
So true she felt it that to *hope*,
  To *trust*, is happier than to *know*.

And thus in humbleness they trod,
Abash'd, but pure before their God;
Nor e'er did earth behold a sight

1838 / 1783   angels--] 1 ; ~ : ~ 5.
1843 / 1783   again--] 1 ; ~ : ~ 5.
1845 / 1785   anew,] 1 ; ~ ; 5.
1849 / 1789   cherub's] 1 ; Cherub's 5.

So meekly beautiful as they,
When, with the altar's holy light   1860
Full on their brows, they knelt to pray,
Hand within hand, and side by side,
Two links of love, awhile untied
From the great chain above, but fast
Holding together to the last--
Two fallen Splendors, from that tree,
Which buds with such eternally, *
Shaken to earth, yet keeping all
Their light and freshness in the fall.
Their only punishment (as wrong,   1870
However sweet, must bear its brand)
Their only doom was this--that, long
As the green earth and ocean stand,
They both shall wander here--the same,
Throughout all time, in heart and frame--
Still looking to that goal sublime,
Whose light remote, but sure, they see,
Pilgrims of Love, whose way is Time,
Whose home is in Eternity!
Subject, the while, to all the strife,   1880
True love encounters in this life--
The wishes, hopes, he breathes in vain;
The chill, that turns his warmest sighs
To earthly vapour, ere they rise;
The doubt he feeds on, and the pain
That in his very sweetness lies.
Still worse, the' illusions that betray
His footsteps to their shining brink;
That tempt him, on his desert way
Through the bleak world, to bend and drink,   1890

* An allusion to the Sephiroths or Splendors of the Jewish Cabbala,
represented as a tree, of which God is the crown or summit.--
See Note.

1865 / 1805 last--] 1 ; ~ ! ~ 5.
1871 / 1811 brand)] 1 ; ~ , ~ 5.
1886 / 1826 lies.] 1 ; ~ :-- 5.

Where nothing meets his lips, alas,
But he again must sighing pass
On to that far-off home of peace,
In which alone his thirst will cease.

All this they bear, but, not the less,
Have moments rich in happiness--
Blest meetings, after many a day
Of widowhood past far away,
When the lov'd face again is seen
Close, close, with not a tear between--   1900
Confidings frank, without control,
Pour'd mutually from soul to soul;
As free from any fear or doubt
    As is that light from chill or stain,
The sun into the stars sheds out,
    To be by them shed back again!--
That happy minglement of hearts,
    Where, chang'd as chymic compounds are,
Each with its own existence parts,
    To find a new one, happier far!   1910
Such are their joys--and, crowning all,
    That blessed hope of the bright hour,
When, happy and no more to fall,
    Their spirits shall, with freshen'd power,
Rise up rewarded for their trust
    In Him, from whom all goodness springs,
And, shaking off earth's soiling dust
    From their emancipated wings,
Wander for ever through those skies
Of radiance, where Love never dies!   1920

In what lone region of the earth
    These Pilgrims now may roam or dwell,
God and the Angels, who look forth
    To watch their steps, alone can tell.
But should we, in our wanderings,
    Meet a young pair, whose beauty wants
But the adornment of bright wings,
    To look like heaven's inhabitants--

Who shine where'er they tread, and yet
Are humble in their earthly lot,   1930
As is the way-side violet,
That shines unseen, and were it not
For its sweet breath would be forgot--
Whose hearts, in every thought, are one,
Whose voices utter the same wills,
Answering, as Echo doth some tone
Of fairy music 'mong the hills,
So like itself, we seek in vain
Which is the echo, which the strain--
Whose piety is love, whose love,   1940
Though close as 'twere their souls' embrace,
Is not of earth, but from above--
Like two fair mirrors, face to face,
Whose light, from one to the' other thrown,
Is heaven's reflection, not their own--
Should we e'er meet with aught so pure,
So perfect here, we may be sure,
There is but *one* such pair below,
And, as we bless them on their way
Through the world's wilderness, may say,   1950
"There ZARAPH and his NAMA go."

1947 / 1887   sure ,] 1 ; ~ ^ 5.
1948 / 1888   There is but *one* such pair below,] 1 ;
              'Tis ZARAPH and his bride we see; 5.
1949 / 1889   And, as we bless them on their way] 1 ;
              And call young lovers round, to view 5.
1950 / 1890   Through the world's wilderness, may say,] 1 ;
              The pilgrim pair, as they pursue 5.
1951 / 1891   "There ZARAPH and his NAMA go."] 1 ;
              Their pathway tow'rds eternity. 5.

NOTES.

PREFACE [.1, lines 19-20]

An erroneous translation by the LXX. of that verse in the sixth chapter of Genesis, &c.

The error of these interpreters (and, it is said, of the old Italic version also,) was in mistaking it οι Αγγελοι του θεου, "the *Angels* of God," instead of "the *Sons*"--a mistake, which, assisted by the allegorizing comments of Philo, and the rhapsodical fictions of the Book of Enoch * ; was more than sufficient to affect the imaginations of such half-Pagan writers as Clemens Alexandrinus, Tertullian, and Lactantius, who, chiefly, among the Fathers, have indulged themselves in fanciful reveries upon the subject. The greater number, however, have rejected the fiction with indignation. Chrysostom, in his twenty-second Homily upon Genesis, earnestly exposes its absurdity *; and Cyril accounts such a supposition as εγγυς μωριας, "bordering on folly.",+ According to these Fathers (and their opinion has been followed by all the theologians, down from St. Thomas to Caryl and Lightfoot |,) the term "Sons of God," must be understood to mean the descendants of Seth, by Enos--a family peculiarly favoured by heaven, because with them, men first began "to call upon the name of the Lord"--while, by "the daughters of men," they suppose that the corrupt race of Cain is designated. The probability, however, is, that the words in question ought to have been translated "the sons of the nobles or great men," as we find them interpreted in the Targum of Onkelos, (the most ancient and accurate of all the Chaldaic paraphrases,) and, as it appears from Cyril, the version of Symmachus also rendered them. This translation of the passage removes all difficulty, and it once relieves the Sacred History of an extravagance, which, however it may suit the imagination of the poet, is inconsistent with all our notions, both philosophical and religious.

    * It is lamentable to think that this absurd production, of which we now know the whole from Dr. Laurence's translation, should ever have been considered as an inspired or authentic work.--See the Preliminary Dissertation prefixed to the Translation. [Moore's note.]

    * One of the arguments of Chrysostom is, that Angels are no where else, in the Old Testament, called "Sons of God,"--but his commentator, Montfaucon, shows that he is mistaken, and that in the Book of Job they are so designated, (c. 1. v. 6.) both in the original Hebrew and the Vulgate, though not in the Septuagint, which alone, he says, Chrysostom read. [Moore's note.]

+ Lib. ii. Glaphyrorum. -- Philaestrius, in his enumeration of heresies, classes this story of the Angels among the number, and says it deserves only to be ranked with those fictions about gods and goddesses, to which the fancy of the Pagan poets gave birth:--"Sicuti et Paganorum et Poetarum mendacia adserunt deos deasque transformatos nefanda conjugia commisisse."--De Haeres. Edit. Basil. p. 101. [Moore's note.]

| Lightfoot says "The sons of God, or the members of the Church, and the progeny of Seth, marrying carelessly and promiscuously with the daughters of men, or brood of Cain, &c." I find in Pole that, according to the Samaritan version, the phrase may be understood as meaning "the Sons of *the Judges.*" So variously may the Hebrew word, Elohim, be interpreted. [Moore's note. This entire note to the Preface of 1, including Moore's footnotes, is deleted from 5.]

[6.5]

[The Mahometans believe, says D'Herbelot, that in that early period of the world, "les hommes n'eurent qu'une seule religion, et furent souvent visités des Anges, qui leur donnaient la main." [Added to 5].]

[32 - 33 .1.]

Transmit each moment, night and day,
The echo of His luminous word!

Dionysius (De Coelest. Hierarch.) is of opinion, that when Isaiah represents the Seraphim as crying out "one unto the other," his intention is to describe those communications of the Divine thought and will, which are continually passing from the higher orders of the angels to the lower:--διο και αυτους τους θειοτατους Σεραριμ οι θεολογοι φασιν ετερον προς τον ετερον κεκραγεναι, σαφως εν τουτω, καθαπερ οιμαι, δηλουντες, οπι των θεολογικων γνωσεων οι πρωτοι τοις δευτεροις μεταδοασι.--See also, in the Paraphrase of Pachymer upon Dionysius, cap. 2. rather a striking passage, in which he represents all living creatures, as being, in a stronger or fainter degree, "echos of God." [Omitted from 5.]

[32 .5]

["To which will be joined the sound of the bells hanging on the trees, which will be put in motion by the wind proceeding from the Throne, so often as the Blessed wish for music."--See *Sale's Koran, Prelim. Dissert.* [Added to 5].]

[55 .5]

[The ancient Persians supposed that this Throne was placed in the Sun, and that through the stars were distributed the various classes of Angels that encircled it.

The Basilidians supposed that there were three hundred and sixty-five orders of angels, "dont la perfection allait en décroissant, à mésure qu'ils s'eloignaient de la première classe d'esprits placés dans le premier ciel."-- See *Dupuis, Orig. des Cultes*, tom. ii. p. 112. [Added to 5].]

[73 . 1 / 77 . 5]

[It appears that, in most languages, the term employed for an angel means also a messenger. Firischteh, the Persian word for angel, is derived (says D'Herbelot) from the verb Firischtin, to send. The Hebrew term, too, Melak, has the same signification. [Added to 5].]

[77-79 .1]

One of earth's fairest woman-kind
Half veil'd from view, or rather shrin'd
In the clear crystal of a brook.

This is given upon the authority, or rather according to the fancy of some of the Fathers, who suppose that the women of earth were first seen by the angels in this situation; and St. Basil has even made it the serious foundation of rather a rigorous rule for the toilette of his fair disciples; adding, Ιχανον γαρ εστι παραγυμνουμενον καλλας και υιους θεου προς ηδονην γοητευσαι, και ως ανθρωπους δια ταυτην αποθνησκοντας θνητοις αποδειξαι.--De Vera Virginitat. tom. i. p. 747. Edit. Paris. 1618. [Deleted from 5.]

[156 .5]

[The name given by the Mahometans to the infernal regions, over which, they say, the angel Tabhek presides.

By the seven gates of hell, mentioned in the Koran, the commentators understand seven different departments or wards, in which seven different sorts of sinners are to be punished. The first, called Gehennem, is for sinful Mussulmans; the second, Ladha, for Christian offenders; the third, Hothama, is appointed for Jews; and the fourth and fifth, called Sair and Sacar, are destined to receive the Sabaeans and the worshippers of fire; in the sixth, named Gehim, those pagans and idolaters who admit a plurality of gods are placed; while into the abyss of the seventh, called Derk Asfal, or the Deepest, the hypocritical canters of *all* religions are thrown. [Added to 5].]

[173 .1]

The Spirit of yon beauteous star.

It is the opinion of Kircher, Ricciolus, &c. (and was, I believe, to a certain degree, that of Origen) that the stars are moved and directed by intelligences or angels who preside over them. Among other passages from Scripture in support of this notion, they cite those words of the Book of Job, "When the morning stars sang together."--Upon which Kircher remarks,

"Non de materialibus intelligitur." Itin. l. Isagog. Astronom. See also Caryl's most wordy Commentary on the same text. [Modified for 5, line 561, below, notes.]

[212. 1]

And the bright Watchers round the throne.

"The Watchers, the offspring of heaven."--Book of Enoch. In Daniel also the angels are called the watchers:--"And behold, a watcher and an holy one came down from heaven." iv. 13. [Deleted from 5.]

[259 .1]

Then first that juice of earth, &c. &c.

For all that relates to the nature and attributes of angels, the time of their creation, the extent of their knowledge, and the power which they possess, or can occasionally assume of performing such human functions as eating, drinking, &c. &c., I shall refer those who are inquisitive upon the subject to the following works:--The Treatise upon the Celestial Hierarchy, written under the name of Dionysius the Areopagate, in which, among much that is heavy and trifling, there are some sublime notions concerning the agency of these spiritual creatures--the Questions "de cognitione angelorum" of St. Thomas, where he examines most prolixly into such puzzling points as "whether angels illuminate each other," "whether they speak to each other," &c. &c.--The Thesaurus of Cocceius, containing extracts from almost every theologian that has written on the subject--the 9th, 10th and 11th chapters, sixth book, of "L'Histoire des Juifs," where all the extraordinary reveries of the Rabbins* about angels and daemons are enumerated--the Questions attributed to St. Athanasius--the Treatise of Bonaventure upon the Wings of the Seraphim *--and, lastly, the ponderous folio of Suarez "de Angelis," where the reader will find all that has ever been fancied or reasoned, upon a subject which only *such* writers could have contrived to render so dull. [Deleted from 5; misplaced in 1.]

* The following may serve as specimens:--"Les Anges ne scavent point la langue Chaldaique; c'est pourquoi ils ne portent pòint à Dieu les oraisons de ceux qui prient dans cette langue. Ils se trompent souvent; ils ont des erreurs dangereuses: car l'Ange de la mort, qui est chargé de faire mourir un homme, en prend quelquefois un autre, ce qui cause de grands désordres. .... Ils sont charges de chanter devant Dieu le Cantique, *Saint, Saint est le Dieu des armées*; mais ils ne remplissent cet office qu'une fois le jour, dans une sémaine, dans un mois, dans un an, dans un siècle, ou dans l'éternité. L'Ange qui luttoit contre Jacob le pressa de le laisser aller, lorsque l'Aurore parut, parce que c'étoit son tour de chanter le Cantique ce jour la ce qu'il n'avoit encore jamais fait." [Moore's note.]

* This work (which, notwithstanding its title, is, probably, quite as dull as the rest) I have not, myself, been able to see, having searched for it in vain through the King's Library at Paris, though assisted by the zeal and kindness of M. Langles and M. Vonpradt, whose liberal administration of that most liberal establishment, entitles them--not only for the immediate effect of such conduct, but for the useful and civilizing example it holds forth--to the most cordial gratitude of the whole literary world. [Moore's note.]

[267 .1]
Then first the fatal wine-cup rain'd, &c.

Some of the circumstances of this story were suggested to me by the Eastern legend of the two angels, Harut and Marut, as it is given by Mariti, who says, that the author of the Taalim founds upon it the Mahometan prohibition of wine. The Bahardanush tells the story differently. [See revision for 255 .5 below, note.]

[268 .1 / 255 .5]
[I have already mentioned that some of the circumstances of this story were suggested to me by the eastern legend of the two angels, Harut and Marut, as given by Mariti, who says that the author of the Taalim founds upon it the Mahometan prohibition of wine. * I have since found that Mariti's version of the tale (which differs also from that of Dr. Prideaux, in his Life of Mahomet,) is taken from the French Encyclopedie, in which work, under the head "Arot et Marot," the reader will find it. [Revised for 5, in response to reviewer.]

* The Bahardanush tells the fable differently.]
[This, Moore's footnote for 5, is taken from 1.]
[282 .1]
Why, why have hapless Angels eyes?

Tertullian imagines that the words of St. Paul, "Woman ought to have a veil on her head*, *on account of the angels*," have an evident reference to the fatal effects which the beauty of women once produced upon these spiritual beings. See the strange passage of this Father, (de Virgin. Velandis,) beginning, "Si enim propter angelos, &c.," where his editor Pamelius endeavours to save his morality at the expense of his Latinity, by substituting the word "excussat" for "excusat." Such instances of indecorum, however, are but too common throughout the Fathers, in proof of which I need only refer to some passages in the same writer's treatise, "De Anima," to the Second and Third Books of the Paedagogus of Clemens Alexandrinus, and to the instances which La Mothe le Vayer has adduced from Chrysostom in his Hexameron Rustique, Journée Seconde. [Omitted from

5.]
* 1 Corinth. xi. 10. Dr. Macknight's Translation. [Moore's note.]
[380-381 .1]
When Lucifer, in falling, bore
The third of the bright stars away.
"And his tail drew the third part of the stars of heaven, and did cast them to the earth." Revelat. xii. 4.--"Docent sancti (says Suarez) supremum angelum traxisse secum tertiam partem stellarum." Lib. 7. cap. 7. [Deleted from 5.]
[382-383 .1]
Rise, in earth's beauty, to repair
That loss of light and glory there!
The idea of the Fathers was that the vacancies, occasioned in the different orders of angels by the fall, were to be filled up from the human race. There is, however, another opinion, backed by Papal authority, that it was only the tenth order of the Celestial Hierarchy that fell, and that, therefore, the promotions which occasionally take place from earth are intended for the completion of that *grade* alone: or, as it is explained by Salonius (Dial. in Eccl.)--"Decem sunt ordines angelorum, sed unus cecidit per superbiam, et idcirco boni angeli semper laborant, ut de hominibus numerus adimpleatur, et proveniat ad perfectum numerum, id est, denarium." According to some theologians, virgins alone are admitted "ad collegium angelorum"; but the author* of the "Speculum Peregrinarum Quaestionum" rather questions this exclusive privilege:--"Hoc non videtur verum, quia multi, non virgines, ut Petrus et Magdalena, multis etiam virginibus eminentiores sunt." Decad. 2. cap. 10. [Omitted from 5.]
* F. Bartholomaeus Sibylla. [Moore's note.]
[465 .1]
'Twas RUBI
I might have chosen perhaps some better name, but it is meant (like that of Zaraph in the following story) to define the particular class of spirits to which the angel belonged. The author of the Book of Enoch, who estimates at 200 the number of angels that descended upon Mount Hermon, for the purpose of making love to the women of earth, has favoured us with the names of their leader and chiefs--Samyaza, Urakabarameel, Akibeel, Tamiel, &c. &c.
In that heretical worship of angels, which prevailed, to a great degree, during the first ages of Christianity, to *name* them seems to have been one of the most important ceremonies; for we find it expressly forbidden in one of the Canons (35th) of the Council of Laodicea: ονομαζειν τους αγγελος.

Josephus too mentions, among the religious rites of the Essenes, their swearing "to preserve the names of the angels,"--σοντηρησεν τα των αγγελων ονοματα. Bell.Jud.lib.2. cap.8.--See upon this subject, Van Dale, de Orig.et Progress.Idololat. cap. 9. [Deleted from 5.]

[466-467 .1]

..... *Those bright creatures, nam'd*
Spirits of Knowledge.

The word cherub signifies knowledge--το γνωστικον αυτων και θεοπτικον. says Dionysius. Hence it is that Ezekiel, to express the abundance of their knowledge, represents them as "full of eyes." [Deleted from 5.]

[445-446 .5 Revised for 5: "The Kerubiim, as the Mussulmans call them, are often joined indiscriminately with Asrafil or Seraphim, under one common name of Azazil, by which all spirits who approach near the throne of Alla are designated."]

[504-505 .1]

Summon'd his chief angelic powers
To witness, &c.

St. Augustin, upon Genesis, seems rather inclined to admit that the angels had some share ("aliquod ministerium") in the creation of Adam and Eve. [Deleted from 5.]

[561. 5]

["'C'est un fait indubitable que la plupart des anciens philosophes, soit Chaldéens, soit Grecs, nous ont donné les astres comme animés, et ont soutenu que les astres, qui nous éclairent n'étaient que, ou les chars, ou même les navires des Intelligences qui les conduisaient. Pour les *Chars*, cela se lit partout; on n'a qu'ouvrir Pline, St. Clément,' &c. &c.--*Mémoire Historique, sur le Sabiisme*, par M. FOURMONT.'

"A belief that the stars are either spirits or the vehicles of spirits, was common to all the religions and heresies of the East. Kircher has given the names and stations of the seven archangels, who were by the Cabala of the Jews distributed through the planets'."]

[580 .5]

[According to the cosmogony of the ancient Persians, there were four stars set as sentinels in the four quarters of the heavens, to watch over the other fixed stars, and superintend the planets in their course. The names of these four sentinel stars are, according to the Boundesh, Taschter, for the east; Satevis, for the west; Venand, for the south; and Haftorang, for the north.]

[670-671 .1]

I had beheld their First, their EVE,
Born in that splendid Paradise.

Whether Eve was created *in* Paradise or not is a question that has been productive of much doubt and controversy among the theologians. With respect to Adam, it is agreed on all sides that *he* was created *outside*; and it is accordingly asked, with some warmth, by one of the commentators, "why should woman, the ignobler creature of the two, be created *within* *?" Others, on the contrary, consider this distinction as but a fair tribute to the superior beauty and purity of women, and some, in their zeal, even seem to think that, if the scene of her creation was not already Paradise, it became so, immediately upon that event, in compliment to her. Josephus is one of those, who think that Eve was formed outside; Tertullian, too, among the Fathers--and, among the Theologians, Rupertus, who, to do him justice, never misses an opportunity of putting on record his ill-will to the sex. Pererius, however, (and his opinion seems to be considered the most orthodox) thinks it much more consistent with the order of the Mosaic narration, as well as with the sentiments of Basil and other Fathers, to conclude that Eve was created *in* Paradise. [Omitted from 5.]

* "Cur denique Evam, quae Adamo ignobilior erat, formavit *intra* Paradisum?" [Moore's note.]

[679 .1]

[Her error, too.]

The comparative extent of Eve's delinquency, and the proportion which it bears to that of Adam, is another point which has exercised the tiresome ingenuity of the Commentators; and they seem generally to agree (with the exception always of Rupertus) that, as she was not yet created when the prohibition was issued, and therefore could not have heard it, (a conclusion remarkably confirmed by the inaccurate way in which she reports it to the serpent *) her share in the crime of disobedience is considerably lighter than that of Adam. * In corroboration of this view of the matter, Pererius remarks that it is to Adam alone the Deity addresses his reproaches for having eaten of the forbidden tree, because to Adam alone the order had been originally promulgated. So far, indeed, does the gallantry of another commentator, Hugh de St. Victor, carry him, that he looks upon the words "I will put enmity between thee and the woman" as a proof that the sex was from that moment enlisted into the service of heaven, as the chief foe and obstacle which the spirit of Evil would have to contend with in his inroads on this world:--"si deinceps Eva inimica Diabolo, ergo fuit grata et amica Deo." [Omitted from 5.]

* Rupertus considers these *variantes* as intentional and prevaricatory, and as the first instance upon record of a wilful vitiation of the words of God, for the purpose of suiting the corrupt views and propensities of human nature.--De Trinitat. lib. iii. cap. 5. [Moore's note.]

 * Caietanus, indeed, pronounces it to be "minimum peccatum." [Moore's note.]

[707 .1 / 686.5]
Call her--think what--his Life! his Life! [707.1]

Chavah (or, as it is in the Latin version, Eva) has the same signification as the Greek, Zoe.

Epiphanius, among others, is not a little surprised at the application of such a name to Eve, so immediately too, after that awful denunciation of death, "dust thou art, &c. &c. * Some of the commentators think that it was meant as a sarcasm, and spoken by Adam, in the first bitterness of his heart,--in the same spirit of irony (says Pererius) as that of the Greeks in calling their Furies, Eumenides, or Gentle. + But the Bishop of Chalon, rejects this supposition:-- "Explodendi sane qui id nominis ab Adamo per ironiam inditum uxori suae putant; atque quod mortis causa esset, amaro joco vitam appellasse." +

With a similar feeling of spleen against women, some of these "distillateurs des Saintes Lettres["] (as Bayle calls them) in rendering the text "I will make him a help *meet for him,*" translate these last words "*against* or *contrary* to him" (a meaning which, it appears, the original will bear) and represent them as prophetic of those contradictions and perplexities, which men experience from women in this life.

It is rather strange that these two instances of perverse commentatorship should have escaped the researches of Bayle, in his curious article upon EVE. He would have found another subject of discussion, equally to his taste, in Gataker's whimsical dissertation upon Eve's knowledge of the τεχη ιφαντικη, and upon the notion of Epiphanius that it was taught her in a special revelation from heaven.--Miscellan. lib. ii. cap. 3. p. 200. [See abridgement and emendation for 5 in note, below.]

[686 .5 Chavah, or, as it is in Arabic, Havah (the name by which Adam called the woman after their transgression), means "Life."]

 * και μετα το ακουσαι, Γη ει και εις γην απελευση, μετα την παρα-βασιν. και ην θαυμα, οτι μετα την παραβασιν ταυτην την μεγαλην εσχεν επωνυμιαν. Haeres. 78 18, tom. i. edit. Paris,1622. [Moore's note.]

 + Lib. 6. p. 234.

 | Pontus Tyard. de recta nominum impositione, p. 14. [Moore's note.]

[905-907 .1]
Oh idol of my dreams! whate'er

Thy nature be--human, divine,
Or but half heav'nly.

In an article upon the Fathers, which appeared, some years since, in the Edinburgh Review (No. 47.), and of which I have made some little use in these notes, (having that claim over it--as "quiddam notum *propriumque*" --which Lucretius gives to the cow over the calf,) there is the following remark:--"The belief of an intercourse between angels and women, founded upon a false version of a text in Genesis, is one of those extravagant notions of St. Justin and other Fathers, which show how little they had yet purified themselves from the grossness of heathen mythology, and in how many respects their heaven was but Olympus, with other names. Yet we can hardly be angry with them for this one error, when we recollect that possibly to their enamoured angels we owe the fanciful world of sylphs and gnomes, and that at this moment we might have wanted Pope's most exquisite poem, if the version of the LXX. had translated the Book of Genesis correctly."

The following is one among many passages, which may be adduced from the Comte de Gabalis, in confirmation of this remark:--"Ces enfans du ciel engendrerent les géans fameux, s'etant fait aimer aux filles des hommes; et les mauvais cabalistes Joseph et Philo (comme tous les Juifs sont ignorans), et après eux tous les auteurs que j'ai nommé tout à l'heure, ont dit que c'etoit des anges, et n'ont pas sçû que c'etoit les sylphes et les autres peuples des élémens, qui sous le nom d'enfans d'Eloim, sont distingués des enfans des hommes."--See Entret. Second. [Deleted from 5.]

[985 .5]

[Called by the Mussulmans Al Araf--a sort of wall or partition which, according to the 7th chapter of the Koran, separates hell from paradise, and where they, who have not merits sufficient to gain them immediate admittance into heaven, are supposed to stand for a certain period, alternately tantalized and tormented by the sights that are on either side presented to them.

Manes, who borrowed in many instances from the Platonists, placed his purgatories, or places of purification, in the Sun and Moon.--*Beausobre*, liv. iii. chap. 8.]

[1027 .1]

So high she deem'd her Cherub's love!

"Nihil plus desiderare potuerint quae angelos possidebant--magno scilicet nupserant." Tertull. de Habitu Mulieb. cap. 2. [Deleted from 5.]

[1052 .1 / 1032 .5]

Then first were diamonds caught, &c. [1032 .5]

"Quelques gnomes désireux de devenir immortels, avoient voulu gagner les bonnes grâces de nos filles, et leur avoient apporté des pierreries dont ils sont gardiens naturels: et ces auteurs ont crû, s'appuyans sur le livre d'Enoch mal-entendu, que c'étoient des pièges que les anges amoureux, &c. &c." Comte de Gabalis. [In 1 and 5.]

[In 1 only:] Tertullian traces all the chief luxuries of female attire, the neck-laces, armlets, rouge, and the black powder for the eye-lashes, to the researches of these fallen angels into the inmost recesses of nature, and the discoveries they were, in consequence, enabled to make, of all that could embellish the beauty of their earthly favourites. The passage is so remarkable that I shall give it entire:--"Nam et illi qui ea constituerant, damnati in paenam mortis deputantur: illi scilicet angeli, qui ad filias hominum de coelo ruerunt, ut haec quoque ignominia foeminae accedat. Nam cum et materias quasdam bene occultas et artes plerasque non bene revelatas, seculo multo magis imperito prodidissent (siquidem et metallorum opera nudaverant, et herbarum ingenia traduxerant et incantationum vires provulgaverant, et omnem curiositatem usque ad stellarum inter-pretationem designaverant) proprie et quasi peculiariter foeminis in-strumentum istud muliebris gloriae contulerunt: lumina lapillorum quibus monilia variantur, et circulos ex auro quibus brachia arctantur; et medicam-enta ex fuco, quibus lanae colorantur, et illum ipsum nigrum pulverem, quo oculorum exordia producuntur." De Habitu Mulieb. cap. 2.--See him also "De Cultu Foem.["] cap. 10.

[in 5 only:] As the fiction of the loves of angels with women gave birth to the fanciful world of sylphs and gnomes, so we owe to it also the invention of those beautiful Genii and Peris, which embellish so much the mythology of the East; for in the fabulous histories of Caioumarath, of Thamurath, &c., these spiritual creatures are always represented as the descendants of Seth, and called the Bani Algiann, or children of Giann.]

[1066-1067.1]
The mighty magnet, set
In woman's form.

The same figure, as applied to female attractions, occurs in a singular passage of St. Basil, of which the following is the conclusion:--Διὰ τὴν ενουσαν κατα του αρρενος αυτης φυσικην δυνασειαν, ως σιδηρος, φημι, πορρωθεν μαγνετις, τουτο προς εαυτον μαγγανευι. De Vera Virginitat. tom. i. p. 727. It is but fair, however, to add, that Hermant, the biographer of Basil, has pronounced this most unsanctified treatise to be spurious. [Deleted from 5.]

[1075.1 /1055.5]
I've said, "Nay, look not there, my love," &c.

I am aware that this happy saying of Lord Albemarle's loses much of its grace and playfulness, by being put into the mouth of any but a human lover. [In 1 and 5.]

[1072 .5]

[According to Whitehurst's theory, the mention of rainbows by an antediluvian angel is an anachronism; as he says, "There was no rain before the flood, and consequently no rainbow, which accounts for the novelty of this sight after the Deluge."]

[1075 .5]

[For the terms of this compact, of which the angels were supposed to be witnesses, see the chapter of the Koran, entitled Al Araf, and the article "Adam" in D'Herbelot.]

[1128 .1]

[*Note.*]

Clemens Alexandrinus is one of those who suppose that the knowledge of such sublime doctrines was derived from the disclosure of the angels. Stromat. lib. v. p. 48. To the same source Cassianus and others trace all impious and daring sciences, such as magic, alchemy, &c. "From the fallen angels (says Zosimus) came all that miserable knowledge which is of no use to the soul." Παντα τα πανηρα και μηδεν ωρελουντα την ψυχην.--Ap.Photium. [Revised in 5 as in note.]

[1108 .5 [Revision in 5:] In acknowledging the authority of the great Prophets who had preceded him, Mahomet represented his own mission as the final "*Seal*," or consummation of them all.]

[1129-1130 .1/1109-1110 .5]

That light
Escaping from the Zodiac's signs.

[In 1:] "La lumière Zodiacale n'est autre chose que l'atmosphere du soleil." --Lalande. [[5 has only] The Zodiacal light.]

[1167 .5]

[Pococke, however, gives it as the opinion of the Mahometan doctors, that all souls, not only of men and of animals, living either on land or in the sea, but of the angels also, must necessarily taste of death.]

[1320 .5]

[The dove, or pigeon which attended Mahomet as his Familiar, and was frequently seen to whisper into his ear, was, if I recollect right, one of that select number of animals (including also the ant of Solomon, the dog of the Seven Sleepers, &c.) which were thought by the Prophet worthy of admission into Paradise.

"The Moslems have a tradition that Mahomet was saved (when he hid himself in a cave in Mount Shur) by his pursuers finding the mouth of the cave covered by a spider's web, and a nest built by two pigeons at the entrance, with two eggs unbroken in it, which made them think no one could have entered it. In consequence of this, they say, Mahomet enjoined his followers to look upon pigeons as sacred, and never to kill a spider."-- *Modern Universal History*, vol. i.]

[1374 .5]

["Mohammed (says Sale), though a prophet, was not able to bear the sight of Gabriel, when he appeared in his proper form, much less would others be able to support it."]

[1642-1644 .1 / 1586-1588.5]

As 'tis grav'd
Upon the tablets that, of old,
By Cham were from the Deluge sav'd. [Seth 5.]

The pillars of Seth are usually referred to as the depositaries of ante-diluvian knowledge; but they were inscribed with none but astronomical secrets. I have, therefore, preferred here the tablets of Cham, as being, at least, more miscellaneous in their information. The following account of them is given in Jablonski from Cassianus:--"Quantum enim anitiquae traditiones ferunt Cham filius Noae, qui superstitionibus ac profanis fuerit artibus institutus, sciens nullum se posse superbis memorialem librum in arcam inferre, in quam erat ingressurus, sacrilegas artes ac profana commenta durissimis insculpsit lapidibus." [In 1. Revision for 5 in note below.]

[1586-1588 .5 Seth is a favorite personage among the Orientals, and acts a conspicuous part in many of their most extravagant romances. The Syrians pretended to have a Testament of this Patriarch in their possession, in which was explained the whole theology of angels, their different orders, &c. &c. The Curds, too (as Hyde mentions in his Appendix), have a book, which contains all the rites of their religion, and which they call Sohuph Sheit, or the Book of Seth.

In the same manner that Seth and Cham are supposed to have preserved these memorials of antediluvian knowledge, Xixuthrus is said in Chaldaean fable to have deposited in Siparis, the city of the Sun, those monuments of science which he had saved out of the waters of a deluge. --See Jablonski's learned remarks upon these columns or tablets of Seth, which he supposes to be the same with the pillars of Mercury, or the Egyptian Thoth.--*Pantheon. Egypt.* lib. v. cap. 5. [In 5 only].]

[1648 .1]
And this young angel's 'mong the rest.

Pachymer, in his Paraphrase on the Book de Divinis Nominibus of Dionysius, speaking of the incarnation of Christ, says, that it was a mystery ineffable from all time, and "unknown even to the first and *oldest* angel," --justifying this last phrase by the authority of St. John in the Revelation. [Deleted from 5.]

[1651-1653 .1]

Circles of light that, from the same
Eternal centre sweeping wide,
Carry its beams on every side.

See the 13th chapter of Dionysius for his notions of the manner in which God's ray is communicated, first to the Intelligences near him, and then to those more remote, gradually losing its own brightness as it passes into a denser medium.--προσβαλλουσα δε ταις παχυτερας υλαις αμυδροτεραν εχει την διαδοτικην επιφανειαν. [Deleted from 5.]

[1603 .5]

[The Mussulmans, says D'Herbelot, apply the general name, Mocarreboun, to all those Spirits "qui approchent le plus près le Trône." Of this number are Mikail and Gebrail. [In 5 only].]

[1604 .5]

[The Seraphim, or Spirits of Divine Love.

There appears to be, among writers on the East, as well as among the Orientals themselves, considerable indecision with regard to the respective claims of Seraphim and Cherubim to the highest rank in the celestial hierarchy. The derivation which Hyde assigns to the word *Cherub* seems to determine the precedence in favor of that order of spirits:--"Cherubim, *i.e.* Propinqui Angeli, qui sc. Deo proprius quam alii accedunt; nam *Charab* est *i.q. Korab*, appropinquare." (P. 263.) Al Beidawi, too, one of the commentators of the Koran, on that passage, "the angels, who beat the throne, and those who stand about it," (chap. xl.) says,"These are the Cherubim, the highest order of angels." On the other hand, we have seen, in a preceding note, that the Syrians place the sphere in which the Seraphs dwell at this very summit of all the celestial systems; and even, among Mahometans, the word Azazil and Mocarreboun (which mean the spirits that stand nearest to the throne of Alla) are indiscriminately applied to both Seraphim and Cherubim. [In 5 only].]

[1799-1802 .1]

Then first did woman's virgin brow
That hymeneal chaplet wear,
Which when it dies, no second vow
Can bid a new one bloom out there.

In the Catholic church, when a widow is married, she is not, I believe, allowed to wear flowers on her head. The ancient Romans, honoured with a "corona pudicitiae," or crown of modesty, those who entered but once into the marriage state. [Lines and note deleted from 5.]

[1711 .5]

["Les Egyptiens disent que la Musique est *soeur de la Religion*."-- *Voyages de Pythagore*, tom. i. p. 422. [In 5 only].]

[1836-1838 .1 / 1776-1778 .5]

> *Her, who near*
> *The Tabernacle stole to hear*
> *The secrets of the Angel.*

Sara.

[1866 .1 / 1806 .5]

> *Two fallen Splendors.*

[In 1:] The Sephiroths are the higher orders of emanative being, in the strange and incomprehensible system of the Jewish Cabbala. They are called by various names, Pity, Beauty, &c. &c.; and their influences are supposed to act through certain canals, which communicate with each other. The reader may judge of the rationality of the system by the following explanation of part of the machinery:--"Les canaux qui sortent de la Miséricorde et de la Force, et qui vont aboutir à la Beauté, sont chargés d'un grand nombre d'Anges. Il y en a une trente-cinq sur le canal de la Miséricorde, qui recompensent et qui couronnent la vertu des Saints, &c. &c."--For a concise account of the Cabalistic Philosophy, see Enfield's very useful compendium of Brucker. [In 5, revised as in note 1806.5.]

[1806 .5 [In 5] An allusion to the Sephiroths or Splendors of the Jewish Cabbala, represented as a tree, of which God is the crown or summit.

The Sephiroths are the higher orders of emanative beings in the strange and incomprehensible system of the Jewish Cabbala. They are called by various names, Pity, Beauty, &c. &c.; and their influences are supposed to act through certain canals, which communicate with each other.]

[1866-1867 .1 / 1806-1807 .5]

> *From that tree*
> *Which buds with such eternally.*

[In 1:] "On les represente quelquefois sous la figure d'un arbre . . . . l'Ensoph qu'on met au-dessus de l'arbre Sephirotique ou des Splendeurs divins, est l'Infini."--L'Histoire des Juifs, liv, ix. ll. [Revised in 5 as in note 1806-1807.5, below.]

[1806-1807 .5 The reader may judge of the rationality of this Jewish system by the following explanation of part of the machinery:--"Les canaux qui sortent de la Miséricorde et de la Force, et qui vont aboutir à la Beauté, sont chargés d'un grand nombre d'Anges. Il y en a trente-cinq sur le canal de la Miséricorde, qui recompensent et qui couronnent la vertu des Saints," &c. &c.--For a concise account of the Cabalistic Philosophy, see Enfield's very useful compendium of Brucker.

"On les représente quelquefois sous la figure d'un arbre .... l'Ensoph qu'on met au-dessus de l'arbre Sephirotique ou des Splendeurs divins, est l'Infini."--*L'Histoire des Juifs*, liv. ix. ll.]

THE

ANGEL OF THE WORLD;

AN ARABIAN TALE:

SEBASTIAN;

A SPANISH TALE:

WITH

OTHER POEMS.

BY THE REV. GEORGE CROLY, A.M.

LONDON:

JOHN WARREN, OLD BOND-STREET.
M,DCCC,XX.

PREFACE.

The poem of the Angel of the World is founded on the story told by Mohammed, as a warning against wine. The Angels Haruth and Maruth had spoken arrogantly of their power to resist the temptations which made man so often culpable; and they were sent down to earth to give proof of their virtue. A spirit was sent in the shape of a woman to tempt them; they withstood her seductions until she had prevailed on them to drink wine; they then gave way to all excesses at once, and completed their crimes by revealing the words that raise men to angels: they were judged, and exiled from Heaven. The story is one of those modifications of the history of the fall of Lucifer, and the temptation in Paradise, which make up so large [10 a portion of Asiatic mythology. In the poem, some alterations and additions easily suggested themselves. There is but one Angel, and he fails by a succession of attempts upon his firmness, each accompanied by a warning that justifies the final punishment. Those lessons are given in some of the phenomena common to the fiery soil and exalted atmosphere of the east. The mirage, the simoom, the sand-storm, and the shooting stars, all common to the borders of Syria, are among those lessons and wonders. The Aurora Borealis though not native to the lower latitudes, has sometimes shone out in all its brilliancy on the shores of the Mediterranean.

The author of the poem desires to be discharged of all responsibility [20 for the catastrophe. He has ventured to mitigate the Koran, which had

---

6   seductions] 1 ; ~ , 2.

8   angels; they] 1 ; ~ : for this ~ 2.

9   Heaven] 1 ; heaven 2.

11   additions easily] 1 ; ~ ^ 2.

13   each accompanied] 1 ; ^ accompanied 2.

13   by a warning] 1 ; by warning 2.

14   justifies] 1 ; justify 2.

17   all common to the borders of Syria, are among those lessons and wonders] 1 ; are all frequent in Syria. 2.

18   Borealis] 1 ; ~ , 2.

18   native to] 1 ; usual in 2.

21   Koran, which had undoubtedly the best right to mulct its own Angels; but] 1 ; Koran; ^ but [phrase "which had" through "Angels" omitted in 2] 2.

undoubtedly the best right to mulct its own Angels; but he has done it in mercy to the propensities of Christendom.

Arabian literature abounds in tales of this order; and even of superior pathos, variety, and grandeur. The world have been wearied by the boundless exaggeration and figurative extravagance of the Indian and Persian poetry. The true mine is in Arabia. The barren glare of oriental fable repels the heart; the most popular pieces of Arabian verse have had their origin in those slight events which occur in common life, and which must owe their interest to the poet's sensibility. A petty chieftain had [30 been thrown into prison, at Sana, by the Imam, for plundering. A bird that alighted on the opposite roof attracted the prisoner's eye. He remembered the merit attached by the Mohammedans to letting a bird out of its cage. The chieftain was a poet, and its thoughts ran into song. The verses were of such beauty that they were learned by his guards; from the prison they spread through the town; they were like the "Cupid king of gods and men" of Abdera; an epidemic of song spread through the territory, till it reached the Imam, who was like other monarchs, at least in Asia, the last man to hear what was in the soul and lips of his lieges. The Imam was charmed, and the captive's chains fell off immediately. An incident of this rank is a [40 subject for poetry only where it meets a practised susceptibility in the people.

The scholar who may turn his attention to Arabic poetry, will find some resources in our own literature;--Sir William Jones's Fourth Discourse to the Asiatic Society, Pococke's Specimen Historiae Arabum, Richardson's

---

24 and even of superior pathos, variety, and grandeur.] 1 ;
     and has some of superior feeling and adventure. 2.
25 have] 1 ; has 2.
26 boundless exaggeration and] 1 ; [omitted from 2] 2.
27 The true mine is in Arabia.] 1 ; [omitted from 2] 2.
28 heart; the] 1 ; heart; but the 2.
30 sensibility. A] 1 ; sensibility. Of those subjects a
     single example may be given.--A 2.
34 The chieftain was a poet, and his thoughts ran into song.] 1 ;
     The chieftain's thoughts ran into song. 2.
38 was] 1 ; ~ , 2.
40 immediately. An] 1 ; immediately. The whole has been
     turned by a native bard into a popular poem. But an 2.
41 meets a] 1 ; ~ with ~ 2.

Dissertation on the Languages of the East, Niebuhr, and the late Professor Carlyle's volume of specimens, are a valuable introduction to this interesting knowledge. It would be unjust to the merits of a very able work to omit mentioning *Mr. Mill's* late History of Mohammedanism. The chapter on the Saracen literature is at once eloquent and learned. [50

---

48 a very able] 1 ; an able 2.
49 mentioning *mr. Mills's* late History of Mohammedanism.] 1 ;
    mentioning the late amiable and regretted Mr. Mills's
    History of Mohammedanism. 2.

THE ANGEL of the WORLD.

I.

There's glory on thy mountains, proud Bengal,
When on their temples bursts the morning sun!
There's glory on thy silver-tower'd wall,
Proud Ispahan, beneath his burning noon!
There's glory--when his golden course is done,
Proud Istamboul, upon thy waters blue!
But fall'n Damascus, thine was beauty's throne,
In morn, and noon, and evening's purple dew,
Of all from Ocean's marge to mighty Himmalu.

II.

East of the city stands a lofty mount,   10
Its brow with lightning delved and rent in sunder;
And thro' the fragments rolls a little fount,
Whose channel bears the blast of fire and thunder;
And there has many a pilgrim come to wonder;
For there are flowers unnumber'd blossoming,
With but the bare and calcined marble under;
Yet in all Asia no such colours spring,
No such perfumes as in that mountain's rocky ring.

III.

And some, who pray'd the night out on the hill,
Have said they heard,--unless it was their dream,   20
Or the mere murmur of the babbling rill,--
Just as the morn-star shot its first slant beam,
A sound of music, such as they might deem
The song of spirits--that would sometimes sail
Close to their ear, a deep, delicious stream,
Then sweep away, and die with a low wail;
Then come again, and thus, till LUCIFER was pale.

---

3   silver-] 1; marble- 2.
12   thro'] 1; through 2.
18   such perfumes] 1; perfumes rich 2.
19   some,] 1; ~ ^ 2.

IV.

And some, but bolder still, had dared to turn
That soil of mystery for hidden gold;
But saw strange, stifling blazes round them burn,   30
And died:--by few that venturous tale was told.
And wealth was found; yet, as the pilgrims hold,
Tho' it was glorious on the mountain's brow,
Brought to the plain it crumbled into mould,
The diamonds melted in the hand like snow;
So none molest that spot for gems or ingots now.

V.

But one, and ever after, round the hill
He stray'd:--they said a meteor scorch'd his sight;
Blind, mad, a warning of Heaven's fearful will.
'Twas on the sacred evening of "The Flight," (1)   40
His spade turned up a shaft of marble white,
Fragment of some Kiosk, the chapiter
A crystal circle, but at morn's first light
Rich forms began within it to appear,
Sceptred and winged, and then it sank in water clear.

VI.

Yet once upon that guarded mount, no foot
But of the Moslem true might press a flow'r,
And of them none, but with some solemn suit
Beyond man's help, might venture near the bow'r;
For, in its shade, in beauty and in pow'r,   50
For judgment, sat the ANGEL OF THE WORLD;
Sent by the prophet, till the destin'd hour
That saw in dust Arabia's idols hurl'd,
Then to the skies again his wing should be unfurl'd.

VII.

---

33 Tho'] 1; Though 2.
45 winged,] 1; wing'd, 2.
45 then] 1; ~ , 2.
47 flow'r,] 1; flower 2.
49 bow'r;] 1; bower: 2.
50 pow'r,] 1; power, 2.
51 judgment,] 1; judgement ^ 2.

It came at last. It came with trumpets' sounding,
It came with thunders of the Atabal,
And warriors' shouts, and Arab chargers' bounding,
The Sacred Standard crown'd Medina's wall.
From palace, mosque, and minaret's golden ball,
Ten thousand emerald banners floated free,   60
Beneath, like sun-beams, thro' the gateway tall,
The Emirs led their steel-mail'd chivalry,
And the whole city rang with sports and soldier glee.
VIII.

This was the eve of eves, the end of war,
Beginning of Dominion, first of Time!
When, swifter than the shooting of a star,
Mohammed saw the "Vision's" (2) pomps sublime;
Swept o'er the rainbowed sea--the fiery clime,
Heard from the throne its will in thunders roll'd;
Then glancing on our world of woe and crime,   70
Saw from Arabia's sands his banner's fold
Wave o'er the brighten'd orb its sacred, conquering gold.
IX.

The sun was slowly sinking to the west,
Pavilion'd with a thousand glorious dyes;
The turtle-doves were winging to the nest;
Along the mountain's soft declivities,
The fresher breath of flowers began to rise,
Like incense, to that sweet departing sun;
Low sank the city's hum, the shepherd's cries:
A moment, and the lingering disk was gone;   80

---

57 warriors'] 1; warrior 2.
58 wall.] 1; ~ ! 2.
59 palace, mosque,] 1; palace roof, 2.
61 thro'] 1; through 2.
72 orb] 1; globe 2.
75 nest;] 1; ~ ^ 2.
76 declivities,] 1; ~ ; 2.
79 Low sank the city's hum, the shepherd's] 1;
     Faint as the hum of bees the city's 2.

A moment, and th'impatient Angel's task was done.

X.

Oft had he gazed upon that lovely vale,
But never gazed with gladness such as now;
When on Damascus' roofs and turrets pale
He saw the solemn sunlight's fainter glow,
He heard the Imauns' sacred voice below
Swell like a silver trumpet on the air,
The vintagers' sweet song, the camels' low,
As home they stalk'd from pasture, pair by pair,
Flinging long giant shadows in the sunset glare.   90

XI.

He raised his sceptre, and a rush of plumes
Shook the thick dew-drops from the roses' dyes;
And as embodying of their waked perfumes,
A sudden crowd of forms, with lightning eyes,
And flower-crown'd hair, and cheeks of Paradise,
Circled the bower of beauty on the wing,
And the rich air was fill'd with symphonies
Of seeming flute, and horn, and golden string,
That slowly rose, and o'er the Mount hung hovering.

XII.

The Angel sat absorb'd in lofty thought,   100

---

81 A moment, and th'impatient Angel's task was] 1 ;
    Then were the Angel's task on earth's dim orbit 2.
86 He heard the Imauns' sacred voice below] 1;
    With joy he heard the Imauns' voices flow 2.
87 Swell like a . . . trumpet . . . ,] 1; Like breath of . . .
    trumpets . . . ; 2.
90 long giant shadows in the sunset] 1;
    their shadows tall in the steep ~ 2.
91 He raised his sceptre, and] 1; Then at his sceptre's wave, 2.
93 And] 1; ~ , 2.
94 sudden crowd of] 1; crowd of lovely 2.
96 wing,] 1; ~ ; 2.
97 the rich air was fill'd] 1; all the grove was rich 2.
100 Angel sat absorb'd in lofty thought,] 1;
    Angel's flashing eyes were on the vault, 2.

Back from his splendid brow his ringlets flung,
His broad effulgent eye on Heaven's blue vault;
Another moment, and his wing had sprung,
The evening hymn broke off.--A pilgrim clung
To the pavilion's steps. The Sun was gone;
His quivering plume upon the breeze was hung,
He heard the pilgrim's deep and struggling groan,
He paused,--and sank, half wrath, half pity, on his throne.

XIII.

Yet all was soon restor'd; this labour past
His sojourn on the cloudy earth was done.   110
His glance again upon the form was cast,
That now seem'd dying on the dazzling stone;
He bade it rise and speak. The silver tone
Of Earth's high Sovereign mingled joy with fear;

---

101 Back from his splendid brow his ringlets flung,] 1;
     That now with lamps of diamond all was hung; 2.

102 His broad effulgent eye on Heaven's blue vault;] 1;
     His mighty wings like tissues heavenly-wrought, 2.

103 Another moment, and his wing had sprung,] 1;
     Upon the bosom of the air were hung. 2.

104 The evening hymn broke off.--A pilgrim clung] 1;
     The solemn hymn's last harmonies were sung, 2.

105 To the pavilion's steps. The Sun was gone;] 1;
     The sun was couching on the distant zone. 2.

106 His quivering plume upon the breeze was hung,] 1;
     "Farewell" was breathing on the Angel's tongue;-- 2.

107 He heard the pilgrim's deep and struggling groan,] 1;
     He glanced below. There stood a suppliant one! 2.

108 He paused,--and sank, half wrath, half pity, on] 1;
     The impatient Angel sank, in wrath, upon 2.

109 soon restor'd; this . . . past] 1; quickly sooth'd,--"this
     . . . ~ , 2.

110 His sojourn on the cloudy earth was done.] 1;
     "~ coronet of tenfold light was won." 2.

113 silver] 1; solemn 2.

114 fear;] 1; ~ , 2.

As summer vales of rose by lightning shown,
As the night-fountain in the desart drear;
His voice was sudden life to that fall'n suppliant's ear.
XIV.
The form arose--the face was in a veil,
The voice was low, and often check'd with sighs;
The tale it utter'd was a simple tale;   120
A vow to close a dying parent's eyes,
Had brought its weary steps from Tripolis;
The Arab in the Syrian mountains lay,
The caravan was made the robber's prize,
The pilgrim's little wealth was swept away,
Man's help was vain. The voice here sank in soft decay.
XV.
"And this is Earth!" the Angel frowning said,
And from the ground he took a matchless gem,
And flung it to the mourner, then outspread
His mighty pinions in the parting beam;   130
The pilgrims started at the diamond's gleam,
Look'd up in pray'r, then, bending near the throne,
Shed the quick tears that from the bosom stream,
And tried to speak, but tears were there alone;
The pitying Angel said, "Be happy and be gone."
XVI.
The weeper raised the veil; a ruby lip
First dawn'd: then glow'd the young cheek's deeper hue,
Yet delicate as roses when they dip
Their odorous blossoms in the morning dew.
Then beam'd the eyes, twin stars of living blue;   140
Half shaded by the curls of glossy hair,
That turned to golden as the light wind threw

---

115   shown,] 1; ~ ; 2.
121   A] 1; " ~ 2.
126   vain. The voice here sank] 1; vain." Here sank the voice 2.
127   said,] 1; ~ ; 2.
130   mighty pinions in the parting beam;] 1; pinions,
      like the lightning's rushing ~ , 2.
132   Look'd] 1; Glanced 2.

Their clusters in the western golden glare.
Yet was her blue eye dim, for tears were standing there.

XVII.

He look'd upon her, and her hurried gaze
Was at his look dropp'd instant on the ground;
But o'er her cheek of beauty rush'd a blaze,
Her bosom heaved above its silken bound,
As if the soul had felt some sudden wound.
He looked again; the cheek was deadly pale;   150
The bosom sank with one long sigh profound;
Yet still one lily hand upheld her veil,
And one still press'd her heart--that sigh told all its tale.

XVIII.

She stoop'd and from the thicket pluck'd a flower,
Kiss'd it with eager lip, then with faint hand
Laid it upon the bright step of the bower;
Such was the ancient custom of the land.
Her sighs were richer than the rose they fann'd,
The breezes swept it to the Angel's feet;
Yet even that sweet slight boon, 'twas Heaven's command, 160
He must not touch, from her tho' doubly sweet,
No earthly gift must stain that hallow'd judgment-seat.

XIX.

---

146 Was at his look dropp'd instant] 1; Sought
     from his glance sweet refuge
147 blaze,] 1; ~ ; 2.
148 Her bosom heaved above its silken bound,] 1;
     And, as the soul had felt some sudden wound,
149 As if the soul had felt some sudden wound.] 1;
     Her bosom heaved above its silken bound.
153 one still] 1; still one 2.
154 stoop'd] 1; ~ , 2.
155 Kiss'd it with eager lip, then with faint] 1;
     And fondly kiss'd, and then with feeble 2.
156 Laid it upon the bright step] 1; She laid it on the footstool 2.
158 fann'd,] 1; ~ ; 2.
161 tho'] 1; though 2.

The flower still lay upon the splendid spot,
The Pilgrim turn'd away as smote with shame;
Her eye a glance of self-upbraiding shot,
That pierced his bosom like a shaft of flame.
The humbled one pronounced and bless'd his name,
Cross'd her white arms, and slowly bade farewell.
A sudden faintness o'er the Angel came;
The voice rose sweet and solemn as a spell,   170
She bowed her face to Earth, and o'er it dropp'd her veil.

XX.

Beauty, what art thou, that thy slightest gaze
Can make the spirit from its centre roll,
Its whole long course, a sad and shadowy maze?
Thou midnight or thou noontide of the soul;
One glorious vision lighting up the whole
Of the wide world; or one deep, wild desire,
By day and night consuming, sad and sole;
Till Hope, Pride, Genius, nay, till Love's own fire
Desert the weary heart, a cold and mouldering pyre.   180

XXI.

Enchanted sleep, yet full of deadly dreams;
Companionship divine, stern solitude;
Thou serpent, colour'd with the brightest gleams
That e'er hid poison, making hearts thy food;
Woe to the heart that lets thee once intrude,
Victim of visions that life's purpose steal,
Till the whole struggling nature lies subdued,

---

163 The flower still lay] 1; Still lay the flower 2.
164 away] 1; ~ , 2.
165 shot,] 1; ~ ; 2.
166 That pierced his bosom like a shaft of] 1;
       'Twas in his soul, a shaft of living 2.
167 The humbled one pronounced] 1;
       Then bow'd the humbled one, 2.
171 bowed] 1; bow'd 2.
171 Earth,] 1; earth, 2.
173 roll,] 1; ~ ; 2.
179 fire] 1; ~ , 2.

Bleeding with wounds the grave alone must heal;
Bright Spirit was it thine that mortal woe to feel?

XXII.

Still knelt the Suppliant cover'd with her veil,   190
But all her beauty living on his eye,
Still sunny bright the clustering ringlets fell
Around her forehead's polish'd ivory,
Her hidden cheek was still the rose-bud's dye,
He heard her parting sigh beside him swell,
He glanced around--no Spirit hover'd nigh.
He took the flow'r, and blushing, sigh'd "farewell."
What sound has stunned his ear? A sudden thunder-peal.

XXIII.

He look'd on Heaven, 'twas calm, but in the vale (3)
A creeping mist had girt the mountain round,   200
The golden minarets thro' it glimmer'd pale,
It scaled the mount,--their last faint gleam was
        drown'd.
The sky was with its livid hue embrown'd,
But what was mist swift grew a circling sea,
Reflecting lovely from its blue profound

---

188 heal;] 1; ~ . 2.
189 Bright Spirit] 1; Proud Angel, 2.
190 Suppliant] 1; pilgrim 2.
191 eye,] 1; ~ ; 2.
192 sunny bright] 1; hyacinth 2.
193 Around] 1; Wreathing 2.
193 ivory,] 1; ~ ; 2.
194 hidden cheek was still] 1; cheek unseen still wore 2.
194 dye,] 1; ~ ; 2.
195 He heard her parting] 1; She sigh'd; he heard the 2.
196 nigh.] 1; ~ -- 2.
197 He took the flow'r,] 1; Touch'd the fall'n flower, 2.
199 Heaven] 1; heaven 2.
201 The golden minarets thro' it glimmer'd pale,] 1;
      Making the golden minarets glimmer ~ ; 2.
204 what was mist swift] 1; soon the vapours 2.

Mountain, and crimson cloud, and blossomed tree,
Another Heaven and Earth in bright tranquillity.

XXIV.

And on its waters swam a small chaloupe,
That bore a woman by the mountain's side;
The silken sail that flutter'd o'er its poop,   210
Was all its canopy, too slight to hide
A form that look'd an Houri in her pride.
A hunter, as the day began to fail,
Was hastening home, he linger'd by the tide,
He listen'd to the sweet deceiver's tale,
And trusted to the wave, for beauty will prevail.

XXV.

A sudden flash illumed the vast Mirage;
The sky grew dark--the hurricane was come;
How shall the skiff with that wild sea engage?

---

206   blossomed tree,] 1; blossom'd ~ ; 2.
207   Heaven . . . Earth] 1; heaven . . . earth 2.
208   waters] 1; bosom 2.
209   bore a woman by the mountain's side;] 1;
      like a wild swan sported on the tide.
210   flutter'd o'er . . . ,] 1; canopied . . . ^ 2.
211   Was all its canopy, too slight to hide] 1;
      Show'd one that look'd an Houri in her pride; 2.
212   A form that look'd an Houri in her pride.] 1;
      Anon came spurring up the mountain's side 2.
213   hunter, as the day began to fail,] 1;
      warrior Moslem all in glittering mail, 2.
214   Was hastening home, he linger'd by the tide,] 1;
      That to his country's doubtful battle hied. 2.
215   listen'd to the sweet deceiver's] 1;
      saw the form, he heard the tempter's 2.
216   trusted to the wave,] 1; answered with his own: 2.
217   A sudden flash illumed] 1; But now in storm uprose 2.
217   Mirage] 1; mirage 2.
218   The sky grew dark--the hurricane was come;] 1;
      Where sits she now who tempted him to roam?
219   engage?] 1; ~ ! 2.

The quivering helm in vain was turn'd to home;   220
The prow sprang arrowy swift through piles of foam;
One billow chased it on with rush and roar;
It reach'd the prey, the hunter saw his doom;
Clasping his love, he sat, and strove no more;
It came and pass'd away. His corpse lay on the shore.
                    XXVI.
The Angel's heart was thrill'd--but that touch'd flow'r,
Now opening, breathed such fragrance subtly sweet,
That he still held it,--felt it overpower
His soul--he ventured not her eye to meet,
But gazed upon the small unsandal'd feet   230
That shone like silver on the floor of rose,
At length he raised his glance;--the veil's light net
Had floated backwards from her pencil'd brows,
Her eye was fix'd in melancholy, mild repose.
                    XXVII.
A simple Syrian lyre was on her breast,

---

220 The quivering helm in vain was . . . ;] 1;
     In vain the quivering helm is . . . . 2.
221 The prow sprang arrowy swift through piles of foam;] 1;
     Dark'ning above the piles of tumbling ~ , 2.
222 One billow chased it on with rush and roar;] 1;
     Rushes a shape of woe, and through the ~ ^ 2.
223 It reach'd the prey, the hunter saw his doom;] 1;
     Peals in the warrior's ear a voice of ~ .
224 Clasping his love, he sat, and strove no more;] 1;
     Down plunges the chaloupe.--The storm is o'er. 2.
225 It came and pass'd away. His corpse lay on] 1;
     Heavy and slow the corpse rolls onward to 2.
226 thrill'd . . . flow'r] 1; smote . . . flower 2.
228 That he still held it,--felt it overpower] 1;
     He felt it strangely chain him to the bower.
229 His soul--he ventured not her] 1;
     He dared not then that pilgrim's 2.
231 That shone . . . ,] 1; Shining . . . ; 2.
233 backwards] 1; backward 2.
234 in melancholy, mild] 1; on Heaven, in sad, sublime 2.

And on her lip the voice hung murmuring
An evening hymn, which from the mountain's crest
The Angel oft had heard the shepherds sing.
She paused,--her white hand floated o'er the string,
Like the Aurelia o'er the hyacinth's bell,   240
Like lilies waving in the airs of Spring.
Then woke its inmost soul's enchanting swell.
The thunder nearer roll'd:--the Angel heard no peal.
XXVIII.
He heard not even the strain, tho' it had changed

---

236 lip the voice hung] 1; crimson lip was 2.
237 An evening hymn, which from the mountain's crest] 1;
     A village strain, that in the day's sweet rest 2.
238 The Angel oft had heard the shepherds sing.] 1;
     Is heard in Araby round many a spring. 2.
239 She paused,--her white hand floated o'er the string,] 1;
     When down the twilight vales the maidens bring 2.
240 Like the Aurelia o'er the hyacinth's bell,] 1;
     The flocks to some old patriarchal well; 2.
241 Like lilies waving in the airs of Spring,] 1;
     Or where beneath the palms some desert-king 2.
242 Then woke its inmost soul's enchanting swell.] 1;
     Lies, with his tribe around him as they fell!
243 nearer roll'd:--the Angel heard no] 1;
     burst again; a long, deep, crashing 2.
244-252 (*These lines in 1 appear as lines 253-261 (i.e., St. XXIX) in*
     2). (*For Stanza XXVIII, lines 244-252, 2 has the following:*
     The Angel heard it not; as round the range
     Of the blue hill-tops roar'd the volley on,
     Uttering its voice with wild, aerial change;
     Now sinking in a deep and distant moan,
     Like the last echo of a host o'erthrown;
     Then rushing with new vengeance down again,
     Shooting the fiery flash and thunder-stone;
     Till flamed, like funeral pyres, the mountain chain.
     The Angel heard it not; its wisdom all was vain.
244/253 tho'] 1; though 2.

From the calm sweetness of the holy hymn:
His thoughts from depth to depth unconscious ranged,
Yet all within was dizzy strange, and dim;
A mist seem'd spreading between Heaven and him;
He sat absorb'd in dreams;--a searching tone
Came on his ear, oh how her dark eyes swim   250
Who breath'd that echo of a heart undone,
The song of early joys, delicious, dear, and gone!
                    XXIX.
The Angel felt his madness, waved his hand
To bid her leave the arbour--and arose;
But nearer still the Minstrel took her stand,
Impassion'd beauty on her young cheek glows;
In a sweet, tender smile her lips disclose
The pearly teeth--her form of symmetry
Bends like a rose-stem, when the zephyr blows;
And tho' her voice is trembling as a sigh   260
Love triumphs in her smile, and fond, delicious eye.
                    XXX.
At once the strain awoke--wild, potent, grand,
The praise of hearts that scorn the world's control,
Disdaining all but Love's delicious band,
The chain of gold and flow'rs, the tie of soul.
She stopp'd--strange paleness o'er her beauty stole,
She glanced above, then sank her glowing eye,
Blue as the star that glitter'd by the pole;

245/254 hymn;] 1; ~ . 2.
248/257 Heaven] 1; heaven 2.
251/260 breath'd] 1; breathed 2.
Stanza XXIX. 1. No corresponding stanza in 2.
262-297 *(for stanzas XXX-XXXIII, lines and stanza numbers in 1 and 2 correspond.)*
262 At once the strain awoke--wild, potent,] 1;
        Again it changed.--But, now 'twas wild and 2.
265 flow'rs] 1; flowers 2.
266 She stopp'd--] 1; Again ^ 2.
266 sank] 1; stopp'd 2.

One tear-drop gleam'd, her quick hand dash'd it by,
She dropp'd the lyre, and turn'd--as if she turn'd to die. 270
XXXI.
The night-breeze from its mountains had begun,
And as it wing'd among the clouds of even,
That slept along the horizon, where the Sun
Still blazed below the fiery verge of Heaven,
Their volumes in ten thousand shapes were driven,
Like flaming mountains, mighty palace halls,
Whose lights, from gold and emerald lamps were given;
Then chang'd to citadels and battled walls,
Then sank to valleys sweet with silver waterfalls.
XXXII.
The sight was glorious; but the Angel's heart   280
Was all unsettled: and a bitter sigh
Burst from his rubied lip, and with a start
He cast upon the Earth his conscious eye.
The whole horizon from that temple high
Spread out in vision from the pallid line
Where old Palmyra's pomps in ruin lie,
Gilding the Arab sands, to where supine

---

269 her quick hand dash'd it] 1; she dash'd it quickly 2.
271 its . . . ,] 1; the . . . ; 2.
273 That slept along the horizon, where the] 1;
      Where, like a routed king, the Sultan 2.
274 blazed below . . . Heaven,] 1; struggled on . . . heaven; 2.
275 driven,] 1; ~ ; 2.
276 Like flaming mountains, mighty] 1;
      Spreading away in boundless 2.
277 lights,] 1; ~ ^ 2.
278 Then chang'd to . . . ,] 1; Or airy . . . ; 2.
279 Then sank to . . . sweet] 1; Or sunk in . . . ~ , 2.
280 The sight was glorious; but] 1;
      But, for those sights of heaven 2.
282 rubied] 1; burning 2.
283 Earth] 1; earth 2.
284 temple] 1; summit 2.
285 vision] 1; ~ , 2.

The western sun flamed on thy spires, lost Palestine!

XXXIII.

But loveliest of the vision was the vale
That from the mountain sloped--the vale of bow'rs,290
Inlay of all rich hues,--the tamarisk pale
Dyed with geranium, and the Indian flow'rs
Of the spiced clove, and jessamine's white show'rs
Like shiver'd silver, and the gorgeous rose,
And, in the midst, Damascus' golden towers,
Bathed in the purple beauty of repose,
All but the central mosque that in red splendour glows.

XXXIV.

He saw the vale reclining in the shade
Of its bold mountains, like a smiling child
In its mail'd father's bosom; crag and glade   300
Festoon'd with myrtles to their summits wild,

---

288 sun flamed on] 1; lustre tinged 2.
289 But] 1; Yet, 2.
290 from the mountain sloped--the vale of bow'rs,] 1;
     sloped beneath his own imperial bowers; 2.
291 Inlay of all rich hues,--the tamarisk pale] 1;
     Sheeted with colours like an Indian mail, 2.
292 Dyed with geranium, and the Indian flow'rs] 1;
     A tapestry sweet of all sun-painted flowers,
293 Of the spiced clove, and jessamine's white show'rs] 1;
     Balsam, and clove, and jasmines scented showers, 2.
294 Like shiver'd silver, and the gorgeous] 1;
     And the red glory of the Persian 2.
295 And, in the midst, Damascus' golden] 1;
     Spreading in league on league around the 2.
296 Bathed in the purple beauty of repose,] 1;
     Where, loved of Heaven, and hated of its foes, 2.
297 All but the central mosque that in red splendour glows.] 1;
     The Queen of Cities shines, in calm and proud repose. 2.
298-306 *(Stanza 34). (No corresponding stanza in 2. From this point,*
Stanza 35 in 1 corresponds to Stanza 34 in 2, Stanza 36 in 1 to Stanza
35 in 2, through Stanza 51 in 1, which corresponds to Stanza 50 in 2.
From this point, lines 307-459 in 1 correspond to lines 298-450 in 2.)

And villages, and domes of marble piled
On rocks still towering thro' the tender mist,
That, tinged with eve, now veil'd that valley mild,
And, as the rising star their foreheads kist,
Were lustrous pearl, sweet sapphire, weeping amethyst.

XXXV.

And still he gazed--and saw not that the eve
Was fading into night. A sudden thought
Struck to his dreaming heart, that made it heave;
Was he not there in Paradise?--that spot,   310
Was it not lovely as the lofty vault
That rose above him? In his native skies,
Could he be happy till his soul forgot,
Oh! how forget, the being whom his eyes
Loved as their light of light? He heard a tempest rise--

XXXVI.

Was it a dream? the vale was wild and bare, (4)
And o'er it brooded broad a sulphurous cloud:
The soil grew red and rifted with its glare;
Down to their roots the mountain cedars bow'd;
Along the ground a rapid vapour flow'd,   320
Yellow and pale, thick seam'd with streaks of flame,
Before it sprang the vulture from the shroud;
The lion bounded from it scared and tame;
Behind it, darkening Heaven, the mighty whirlwind came.

XXXVII.

Like a long tulip bed, across the plain,
A caravan, approach'd the evening well;
A long, deep mass of turban, plume, and vane,
And lovely came its distant, solemn swell
Of song, and pilgrim-horn, and camel-bell;

---

316 / 307 was wild and] 1; at once was 2.
317 / 308 brooded broad a] 1; hung a broad and 2.
321 / 312 flame,] 1; ~ . 2.
324 / 315 darkening Heaven] 1; dark'ning heaven 2.
326 / 317 caravan, . . . well;] 1; ~ ^ . . . ~ , 2.
327 / 318 vane,] 1; ~ ; 2.
329 / 320 bell;] 1; ~ . 2.

The sandy ocean rose before their eye,   330
In thunder on their bending host it fell,
Ten thousand lips sent up one fearful cry;
The sound was still'd at once, beneath the wave they lie.
XXXVIII.
But, two escaped, that up the mountain sprung,
And those the dead men's treasure downwards drew;
One slowly, but the softer round him clung;
For now, in light, short gusts the tempest blew,
And the high tomb of sand like vapour flew.
There, naked lay the costly caravan,
A league of piles of silk and gems that threw   340
A rainbow light, and mid them stiff and wan,
Stretch'd by his camel's flank, their transient master, man.
XXXIX.
The statelier wanderer from the height was won,
And cap and sash soon gleam'd with plunder'd gold.
Again the Desart rose, in pillars dun,
Glowing with fire like iron in the mould;
With fiery speed they rush'd, recoil'd, sprang, roll'd;
Before them waned the moon's ascending phase,
The clouds above them shrank the reddening fold:
The giant columns deepen'd blaze on blaze,   350

---

331 / 322 fell,] 1; ~ ^ 2.
333 / 324 the wave] 1; its ~ 2.
336 / 327 One slowly, but the softer round him clung;] 1;
                One, with slow steps; but beautiful and young 2.
327 / 328 For now, in light, short gusts the tempest blew,] 1;
                Was she, who round his neck her white arms threw. 2.
338 / 329 And the high] 1; Away the 2.
343 / 334 wanderer] 1; wand'rer 2.
345 / 336 Again the Desart] 1; But, now the Desert 2.
346 / 337 mould;] 1; ~ , 2.
347 / 338 With fiery speed they rush'd,] 1;
                That wings with fiery speed, 2.
349 / 340 reddening] 1; redd'ning 2.

The pilgrims died, embracing in the burning haze.
XL.
The Angel sat enthroned within a dome
Of alabaster, raised on pillars slight,
Curtain'd with tissues that the earthly loom
Had never equall'd, web of blossoms bright
Of all the flowers that drank the morning light.
The roof was starr'd with buds, the flower-festoon
Waved from the columns of translucent white,
Breathing fresh odours to the mystic throne,
That in their purple shade, one glorious diamond shone.360
XLI.
And still at night, round pedestal and plinth,
Those dewy flowers were lamps before the throne,
All-colour'd radiance; there, the hyacinth
Beam'd amethyst; the broad carnation shone

---

351 / 342 The pilgrims died, embracing] 1;
           The sacrilegious died, wrapp'd 2.
353 / 344 alabaster,] 1; ~ ^ 2.
354 / 345 that the . . . loom] 1; of no . . . ~ ; 2.
355 / 346 Had never equall'd, . . . bright] 1;
           For spirits wove the . . . ~ , 2.
356 / 347 Of all the . . . .] 1; Woof of all . . . , 2.
357 / 348 The roof was starr'd with buds, the flower-festoon] 1;
           And with their beauty figured all the stone 2.
358 / 349 Waved from the columns of translucent white,] 1;
           In characters of mystery and might, 2.
359 / 350 Breathing fresh odours to the mystic] 1;
           A more than mortal guard around the 2.
361 / 352 still at night,] 1; every bud 2.
362 / 353 Those dewy flowers were lamps before the throne,] 1;
           As fell the evening, turn'd a living gem. 2.
363 / 354 All-colour'd radiance; there . . . hyacinth] 1;
           Lighted its purple lamp . . . ~ , 2.
364 / 355 Beam'd amethyst; the broad carnation shone] 1;
           The dahlia pour'd its thousand-colour'd gleam, 2.

In circling rays of pearl and ruby stone;
The myrtle buds pour'd down a diamond shower
The tulip was the opal's changeful moon;
An urn of lovely lustre every flower,
Burning before the King of that illumin'd bower.
XLII.

And nestling in that arbour's leafy twine,   370
From cedar's top to violet's perfum'd bell,
Were birds, now hush'd, of forms and plumes divine.
That, ever as the rays upon them fell,
Shot back such hues as stain the Indian shell,
Touching the deep green shades with light from eyes
Jacinth, and jet, and blazing carbuncle,
And gold dropt coronets, and wings of dyes
Touch'd by the flowers and stars of their own Paradise.
XLIII.

The Angel knew the warning of that storm;
But saw the shuddering Minstrel's step draw near, 380
And felt the whole deep witchery of her form;
Her sigh was music's echo to his ear;

---

365 / 356 In circling rays of pearl and ruby stone;] 1;
           A ruby torch the wond'ring eye might deem 2.
366 / 357 The myrtle buds pour'd down a diamond shower] 1;
           Hung on the brow of some night-watching tower, 2.
367 / 358 The tulip was the opal's changeful moon;] 1;
           Where upwards climb'd the broad magnolia's stem. 2.
369 / 360 King . . . illumin'd] 1; king illumined 2.
371 / 362 perfum'd] 1; lowly 2.
372 / 363 forms and plumes] 1; plumage all 2.
373 / 364 ever as the rays upon] 1;
           as the quivering radiance on 2.
374 / 365 Indian] 1; orient 2.
375 / 366 deep] 1; ~ , 2.
377 / 368 gold dropt] 1; gold-dropt 2.
378 / 369 Touch'd by the flowers and stars] 1;
           Bathed in the living streams 2.
381 / 372 form;] 1; ~ , 2.

He loved--and true love ever banished fear.
Now night had droop'd on earth her raven wing,
But in the arbour all was splendour clear;
And like twin spirits in its charmed ring
Shone, that sweet child of earth, and that star diadem'd King.

XLIV.

For, whether 'twas the light's unusual glow,
Or that some natural change had on her come,
Her look, tho' lovely still, was loftier now,   390
Her tender cheek was flushed with brighter bloom;
Yet in her azure eye there gathered gloom,
Like evening's clouds across its own blue star,
Then would a sudden flash its depths illume;
And wore she but the wing and gemm'd tiar,
She seemed instinct with power to make the clouds her car.

XLV.

She slowly raised her arm, that, bright as snow,
Gleam'd like a rising meteor thro' the air,
Shedding white lustre on her turban'd brow;
She gazed on Heaven, as wrapt in solemn prayer;   400
She still look'd woman, but more proudly fair;
And as she stood and pointed to the sky,
With that fixed look of loveliness and care,

---

383 / 374   true love ever banished fear.] 1;
            what has love to do with ~ ? 2.
384 / 375   wing,] 1; ~ ; 2.
386 / 377   And . . . ring] 1; ~ , . . . ~ , 2.
387 / 375   Shone, . . . earth, . . . star . . . King] 1;
            ~ ^ . . . ~ ^ . . . ~ - . . . king 2.
389 / 380   natural . . . ,] 1; dazzling . . . ; 2.
390 / 381   tho'] 1; though 2.
391 / 382   flushed] 1; flush'd 2.
392 / 383   eye there gathered] 1; eyebeam gather'd 2.
396 / 387   seemed . . . power] 1; seem'd . . . might 2.
398 / 389   thro'] 1; through 2.
400 / 391   Heaven] 1; heaven 2.
401 / 392   but] 1; yet 2.
403 / 394   fixed] 1; fix'd 2.

The Angel thought, and check'd it with a sigh,
He saw some Spirit fallen from immortality.

XLVI.

The silent prayer was done, and now she moved
Faint to his footstool, and, upon her knee,
Besought her lord, if in his Heaven they loved,
That, as she never more his face must see,
She there might pledge her heart's fidelity.   410
She turn'd, and pluck'd a cluster from the vine,
And o'er a chalice waved it, with a sigh,
Then, with bow'd forehead, rear'd before the shrine
The crystal cup.--The Angel rose in wrath--'twas wine!

XLVII.

She stood; she shrank; she totter'd. Down he sprang,
With one hand clasp'd her waist, with one upheld
The vase--his ears with giddy murmurs rang;
His eye upon her dying cheek was spell'd;
He glanced upon the brim--its bright draught swell'd
Like liquid rose, its odour touch'd his brain;   420
He knew his ruin, but his soul was quell'd;
He shudder'd--gazed upon her cheek again,
Press'd her pale lip, and to the last that cup did drain.

XLVIII.

Th'Enchantress smiled, as still in some sweet dream,
Then waken'd in a long, delicious sigh,
And on the bending Spirit fixed the beam
Of her deep, dewy, melancholy eye.
The undone Angel gave no more reply

---

406 / 397   done,] 1; ~ ; 2.
408 / 399   Heaven] 1; heaven 2.
411 / 402   She] 1; Then 2.
413 / 404   Then, with bow'd forehead, rear'd . . . shrine] 1;
            Then stoop'd the crystal cup before . . . ~ . 2.
416 / 407   With one hand clasp'd] 1; Clasp'd with one hand 2.
419 / 410   He glanced upon the brim--its bright draught] 1;
            Up to the brim the draught of evil 2.
424 / 415   Th'Enchantress] 1; Th'enchantress 2.
426 / 417   fixed] 1; fix'd 2.

Than hiding his pale forehead in the hair
That floated on her neck of ivory,   430
And breathless pressing, with her ringlets fair,
From his bright eyes the tears of passion and despair.

XLIX.

The Heaven was one blue vault, inlaid with gems (5)
Thick as the concave of a diamond mine,
But from the north now shoot quick, phosphor beams,
That o'er the mount their purple net entwine;
The smallest stars thro' that sweet lustre shine;
It shakes--it spreads, its glorious streamers die:
Again light quivers on the horizon's line,
A surge of violet lustre fills the sky,   440
Then sinks, still flashing, dancing everlastingly.

L.

But wilder wonder smote their shrinking eyes:
A vapour plunged upon the vale from Heaven,
Gloomy as night; it tower'd of mountain size;
From its high crater column'd smokes were driven;
It heaved within, as if pent flames had striven
With mighty winds to burst their prison hold,

---

433 / 424 Heaven . . . vault,] 1; heaven . . . cope, 2.
435 / 426 shoot quick,] 1; fly pale 2.
436 / 427 purple] 1; quivering 2.
437 / 428 thro'] 1; through 2.
438 / 429 It shakes--it spreads, its glorious streamers die:] 1;
           Then, like a routed host, its streamers fly: 2.
439 / 430 Again light quivers on the horizon's line,] 1;
           Then, from the moony horizontal ~ ^ 2.
440 / 431 violet lustre fills . . . .] 1;
           sudden glory floods . . . , 2.
441 / 432 Then sinks, still flashing, dancing everlastingly.] 1;
           Ocean of purple waves, and melted lazuli. 2.
443 / 434 Heaven] 1; heaven 2.
444 / 435 Gloomy as night; it] 1; Then, darkly gathering, 2.

Till from the summit to the vale 'twas riven
With angry light, that seem'd in cataracts roll'd,
Silver, and sanguine steel, and the fierce burning gold. 450
LI.
The black Volcano gave a hollow roar,
An Earthquake groan, that told convulsion near:
Out rush'd the burthen of its burning core,
Myriads of fiery globes, as day-light clear.
The sky was filled with flashing sphere on sphere,
Shooting straight upwards to the zenith's crown.
The stars were blasted in that splendour drear,
The land beneath in wild distinctness shone,
From the far billow to the Desart's pale red zone.
LII.
The globes have gone to heights above all gaze, 460
And now returning, look like moon-light rain;
But, half way down, again out flash their rays;
War floods the sky, they cross, whirl, burst in twain,
Scattering the night from mountain, vale, and main,
Or round the concave, as the storm retires,
Like mighty serpents draw the mazy train,
Gigantic sweeps of green, gold, scarlet spires,
With pearl and diamond heads instinct with living fires.
LIII.

---

448 / 439   from the summit to the vale 'twas] 1;
            all the cloud-volcano's bulk was 2.
450 / 441   the fierce burning] 1; streams of molten 2.
451 / 442   The black Volcano gave] 1;
            Then echoed on the winds 2.
452 / 443   Earthquake] 1; earthquake 2.
455 / 447   filled] 1; fill'd 2.
456 / 447   upwards] 1; upward 2.
459 / 450   the far billow to the Desart's pale red zone.] 1;
            Syria's yellow sands to Libanus' summit-stone. 2.
460-468   *(Stanza LII) in 1. (No corresponding stanza in 2. From here until the end, Stanza LIII in 1 corresponds to LI in 2, LIV in 1 to LII in 2, through LXVII in 1, which corresponds to LXV in 2. From here, lines 469-603 in 1 correspond to lines 451-585 in 2.)*

The storm of light is on the clouds receding,
The purple streamers wander pale and thin, 470
But o'er the pole an amber flame is spreading,
In shooting, starry points, and far within
Revolves a stooping splendour crystalline.
It opens, but who sits upon that throne?
The Angel knew the punisher of sin.
Check'd on his lip the self-upbraiding groan,
Strain'd with wild arms his love, and joy'd to be undone.
                    LIV.
And once, 'twas but a moment, on her cheek
He gave a glance, then sank his hurried eye,
And press'd it closer on her dazzling neck. 480
But even in that swift gaze he could espy
A look that made his heart's blood backwards fly.
Was it a dream? there echoed in his ear
A stinging tone--a laugh of mockery!
It was a dream--it must be. Oh! that fear,
When the heart longs to know, what it is death to hear.
                    LV.
He glanced again--her eye was upward still,
Fix'd on the stooping of that burning car;
But thro' his bosom shot an arrowy thrill,
To see its solemn, stern, unearthly glare; 490
She stood a statue of sublime despair,
But on her lip sat scorn.--His spirit froze,--
His footstep reel'd,--his wan lip gasp'd for air;

---

469 / 451 of light is on the] 1; is on the embattled 2.
471 / 454 an amber] 1; a fiercer 2.
472 / 454 In shooting, starry points,] 1;
           Wheel within wheel of fire, 2.
474 / 456 It opens, but who sits upon . . . ?] 1;
           A throne;--but who the sitter on . . . ! 2.
477 / 459 Strain'd with wild arms his] 1;
           And clasp'd his dying 2.
481 / 463 But] 1; Yet, 2.
481 / 463 gaze] 1; ~ , 2.
489 / 471 thro'] 1; through 2.

She felt his throb,--and o'er him stoop'd with brows
As evening sweet, and kiss'd him with a lip of rose.
LVI.
Again she was all beauty, and they stood
Still fonder clasp'd, and gazing with the eye
Of famine gazing on the poison'd food
That it must feed on, or abstaining die.
There was between them now nor tear nor sigh;   500
Theirs was the deep communion of the soul;
Passion's absorbing, bitter luxury;
What was to them or Heaven or Earth, the whole
Was in that fatal spot, where they stood sad, and sole.
LVII.
Th'Enchantress first shook off the silent trance;
And in a voice sweet as the murmuring
Of summer streams beneath the moonlight's glance,
Besought the desperate one to spread the wing
Beyond the power of his vindictive King.
Slave to her slightest word, he raised his plume,   510
A purple cloud, and stood in act to spring
Thro' that fierce upward sea of storm and gloom;
She wildly kiss'd his hand, and sank, as in a tomb.
LVIII.
The Angel cheer'd her, "No! let Justice wreak
Its wrath upon them both, or him alone."
A flush of love's pure crimson lit her cheek;
She whisper'd, and his stoop'd ear drank the tone
With mad delight; "Oh there is one way, one,
To save us both. Are there not mighty words
Graved on the magnet-throne where Solomon   520

---

503 / 485   Heaven or Earth] 1; heaven or earth 2.
505 / 487   Th'Enchantress] 1; The Minstrel 2.
509 / 491   King] 1; king 2.
510 / 492   he] 2; the 1.
511 / 493   A purple cloud, and stood in act . . .] 1;
            For life or death, he reck'd not which, . . . ; 2.
514 / 496   cheer'd] 1; sooth'd 2.
519 / 501   words] 1; ~ , 2.

Sits ever guarded by the Genii swords,
To give thy servant wings like her resplendent Lord's?"
LIX.
This was the Sin of Sins! The first, last crime,
In Earth and Heaven, unnamed, unnameable;
This from his gorgeous throne, before all time,
Had smitten Eblis, brightest, first that fell;
He started back.--"What urged him to rebel?
What led that soft seducer to his bow'r?
Could *she* have laid upon his soul that spell,
Young, lovely, fond; yet but an earthly flow'r?"   530
But for that fatal cup, he had been free that hour.
LX.
But still its draught was fever in his blood.
He caught the upward, humble, weeping gleam
Of woman's eye, by passion all subdued;
He sigh'd, and at his sigh he saw it beam;
Oh! the sweet frenzy of the lover's dream!
A moment's lingering, and they both must die.
The lightning round them shot a broader stream;
He felt her clasp his knees in agony;
He spoke the words of might,--the thunder gave reply! 540
LXI.
Away! away! the sky is one black cloud,
Shooting the lightnings down in spire on spire.
Now, round the Mount its canopy is bow'd,

---

521 / 503   Genii] 1; genii 2.
522 / 504   wings] 1; ~ , 2.
523 / 505   Sin of Sins] 1; sin of sins 2.
524 / 506   Earth and Heaven] 1; earth and heaven 2.
525 / 508   gorgeous throne,] 1; throne of light, 2.
526 / 509   fell;] 1; ~ . 2.
528 / 511   bow'r] 1; bower 2.
530 / 512   flow'r] 1; flower 2.
540 / 522   words of might,] 1; "Words of might", 2.
542 / 524   the] 1; its 2.
543 / 525   Now, round the Mount] 1; Around the mount 2.

A vault of stone on columns of red fire.
The stars like lamps along its roof expire;
But thro' its centre bursts an orb of rays;
The Angel knew the Avenger in his ire!
The hill-top smoked beneath the stooping blaze,
The culprits dared not there their guilty eye-balls raise.
LXII.
And words were utter'd from that whirling sphere, 550
That mortal sense might never hear and live.
They pierced like arrows thro' the Angel's ear;
He bow'd his head; 'twas vain to fly or strive.
Down comes the final wrath: the thunders give
The doubled peal,--the rains in cataracts sweep,
Broad fiery bars the sheeted deluge rive;
The mountain summits to the valley leap,
Pavilion, garden, grove, smoke up one ruin'd heap.
LXIII.
The storm stands still! a moment's pause of terror!
All dungeon dark!--Again the lightnings yawn, 560
Shewing the Earth as in a quivering mirror.
The prostrate Angel felt but that the one,
Whose love had lost him Paradise, was gone:
A voice burst o'er him, solemn as the tone
Of the last trump,--he glanced upon the skies,
He saw what shook his soul with terror, shame, surprise.
LXIV.
Th'Enchantress stood before him; two broad plumes
Spread from her shoulders on the burthen'd air;

---

544 / 526 A vault of stone on columns of red fire.] 1;
A fiery vault upraised on pillar'd ~ ; 2.
546 / 528 thro'] 1; through 2.
549 / 531 eye-balls] 1; glances 2.
552 / 534 thro'] 1; through 2.
556 / 538 fiery bars] 1; bars of fire 2.
560 / 542 dungeon dark] 1; dungeon-dark 2.
561 / 543 Earth] 1; earth 2.
566 / 549 saw] 1; ~ , 2.
567 / 550 Th'Enchantress] 1; The Minstrel 2.

Her face was glorious still, but love's young blooms
Had vanish'd for the hue of bold despair;   570
A fiery circle crown'd her sable hair;
And, as she look'd upon her prostrate prize,
Her eyeballs shot around a meteor glare,
Her form tower'd up at once to giant size;
'Twas EBLIS, king of Hell's relentless sovereignties.

LXV.

The tempter spoke--"Spirit, thou might'st have stood,
But thou hast fall'n a weak and willing slave.
Now were thy feeble heart our serpents' food,
Thy bed our burning ocean's sleepless wave,
But haughty Heaven controuls the power it gave.   580
Yet art thou doom'd to wander from thy sphere,
Till the last trumpet reaches to the grave;
Till the Sun rolls the grand concluding year;
"Till Earth is Paradise; then shall thy crime be clear."

LXVI.

The Angel listen'd,--risen upon one knee,
Resolved to hear the deadliest undismay'd.
His gold starr'd plume hung round him droopingly,
His brow, like marble, on his hand was staid.
Still thro' the auburn locks' o'er hanging shade
His face shone beautiful; he heard his ban;   590
Then came the words of mercy, sternly said;
He plunged within his hands his visage wan,
And the first wild, sweet tears from his heart-pulses ran.

LXVII.

The Giant grasp'd him as he fell to Earth,
And his black vanes upon the air were flung,
A tabernacle dark;--and shouts of mirth
Mingled with shriekings thro' the tempest swung;
His arm around the fainting Angel clung.

---

576 / 558 EBLIS,] 1; ~ ! 2.
587 / 570 His gold starr'd] 1; His star-dropt 2.
589 / 572 thro'] 1; through 2.
594 / 577 Earth] 1; earth 2.
597 / 580 thro'] 1; through 2.

Then on the clouds he darted with a groan;
A moment o'er the Mount of ruin hung,   600
Then burst thro' space, like the red comet's cone,
Leaving his track on heaven a burning, endless zone.

---

600 / 583   Mount] 1; mount 2.
601 / 584   thro'] 1; through 2.

NOTES
to the
ANGEL of the WORLD.

(1).--"*The sacred Evening of 'the Flight.'*"
The Hegira, the first day of our July, A.D. 622; the day of Mohammed's retreat from Mecca, the chronological standard of the Mohammedans.

(2).--"*The 'Vision's' pomps sublime.*"
The night-journey of Mohammed through the heavens, in which he saw the glories of the past and future: a fiction of great fancy and extravagance.

(3).--"*But in the vale.*"
The Mirage;--the common phenomenon of Eastern travel.

(4).--"*The vale was wild and bare.*"
"On the 15th, at a quarter past seven in the morning, we left Waadi Dimokea, keeping a little to the westward of north, as far as I could judge, just upon the line of Syene. The same ridge of hills being on our right and left as yesterday, in the centre of these appeared Del Aned. The place is called Waadi Del Aned.

"The same appearance of moving pillars of sand presented themselves to us this day, in form and disposition like those we had seen at Waadi Halboub, only they seemed to be more in number and less in size. They came several times in a direction close upon us; that is, I believe, within less than two miles. They began immediately after sun-rise, like a thick [10 wood, and almost darkened the sun. His rays, shining through them for near an hour, gave them an appearance of pillars of fire. Our people now became desperate. The Greeks shrieked out, and said it was the day of judgment. Ismael pronounced it to be hell, and the Tucorories, that the world was on fire. I asked Idris if ever he had before seen such a sight? He said, he had often seen them as terrible, though never worse; but what he feared most was that extreme redness in the air, which was a sure presage of the coming

---

(4).--"*The vale was wild and bare.*"] 1; "*The vale at once was bare.*" 2.
(*Note 4, text: quotation marks as in 2; 1 leaves*
      "*Bruce's Travels*" *without quotation marks.*)
15 sight ?] 1; ~ . 2.

of the Simoom. I begged and entreated Idris that he would not say one word of that in the hearing of the people, for they had already felt it at Imbanzara, in their way from Ras el Feel to Teawa, and again at the Acaba of Gerri, [20 before we came to Chendi, and they were already nearly distracted at the apprehension of finding it here.

"At half-past four o'clock in the afternoon we left Waadi Del Aned, our course a little more to the westward than the direction of Syene. The sands which had disappeared yesterday, scarcely showed themselves at all this day, and at a great distance in the horizon. This was, however, a comfort but of short duration. I observed Idris took no part in it, but only warned me and the servants, that, upon the coming of the Simoom, we should fall upon our faces, with our mouths upon the earth, so as not to partake of the outward air as long as we could hold our breath. We alighted, at six o'clock, [30 at a small rock in the sandy ground, without trees or herbage, so that our camels fasted all that night. This place is called Ras El Seah, or, by the Bishareen, El Mout, which signifies Death, a name of bad omen.

"On the 16th, at half-past ten in the forenoon, we left El Mout, standing in the direction close upon Syene. Our men, if not gay, were, however, in better spirits than I had seen them since we left Gooz. One of our Barbarins had even attempted a song; but Hagi Ismael very gravely reproved him, by telling him that singing in such a situation was a tempting of Providence. There is, however, nothing more different than active and passive courage. Hagi Ismael would fight, but he had not the strength to suffer. At eleven [40 o'clock, while we contemplated, with great pleasure, the rugged top of Chiggre, to which we were fast approaching, and where we were to solace ourselves with plenty of good water, Idris cried out, with a loud voice,Fall upon your faces, for here is the Simoom! I saw from the S.E. a haze come, in colour like the purple part of the rainbow, but not so compressed or thick. It did not occupy twenty yards in breadth, and was about twelve feet high from the ground. It was a kind of blush upon the air, and it moved very rapidly, for I scarce could turn to fall upon the ground, with my head to the northward, when I felt the heat of its current plainly upon my face. We all lay flat on the ground, as if dead, till Idris told us it was blown over. [50 The meteor, or purple haze, which I saw, was, indeed, passed, but the light air which still blew was of heat to threaten suffocation. For my part, I found

---

18   *Simoom] 1; simoom 2. (Upper case "S" throughout 1; lower case throughout 2.)*

25   themselves at all] 1; themselves all 2.

distinctly in my breast that I had imbibed a part of it, nor was I free of an asthmatic sensation till I had been some months in Italy, at the baths of Porretta, about two years afterwards.--*Bruce's Travels.*

(5.).--"*The Heaven was one blue vault.*"

"The night of the 11th of November was cool and extremely beautiful. Towards the morning, from half-past two, the most extraordinary luminous meteors were seen towards the East. M. Bonpland, who had risen to enjoy the freshness of the air in the gallery, perceived them first. Thousands of bolides and falling stars succeeded each other during four hours. Their direction was very regularly from north to south. They filled a space in the sky extending from the true east thirty degrees towards the south. Some of them obtained a height of forty degrees; all exceeded twenty-five or thirty. No trace of clouds was to be seen. M. Bonpland relates that, from the beginning of the phenomenon, there was not a space in the firmament [10 equal to three diameters of the moon, that was not filled at every instant with bolides or falling stars. The first were fewer in number, but as they were seen of different sizes, it was impossible to fix the limit between those two classes of phenomena. All these meteors left luminous traces from five to ten degrees in length, as often happens in the equinoctial regions. The phosphorescence of these traces, or luminous bands, lasted seven or eight seconds. Many of the falling stars had a very distinct nucleus, as large as the disk of Jupiter, from which darted sparks of vivid light. The bolides seemed to burst as by explosion; but the largest, those from one degree to one degree fifteen seconds in diameter, disappeared without scintillation, [20 leaving behind them phosphorescent bands (trabes), exceeding in breadth fifteen or twenty minutes. The light of these meteors was white, and not reddish, which must be attributed, no doubt, to the absence of vapours, and the extreme transparency of the same air. For the same reason, under the tropics, the stars of the first magnitude have, at their rising, a light evidently whiter than in Europe. Almost all the inhabitants of Cumana were witnesses of this phenomenon, because they leave their houses before four o'clock to attend the first morning mass. They did not behold these bolides with indifference; the oldest of them remembered, that the great earthqua-

---

Note 5: "*vault.*"] 1; "*cope.* 2.
Line 1: *Quotation marks as in 2. None included for*
  Humboldt's excerpt in 1.
3 East] 1; east 2.
6 regularly] 1; regular 2.

kes of 1766 were preceded by similar phenomena. The Guaiqueries in [30 the Indian suburb came out and asserted, 'that the firework had begun at one o'clock; and that, as they returned from fishing in the Gulf, they had already perceived very small falling stars toward the east.' They affirmed, at the same time, that igneous meteors were extremely rare on those coasts after two in the morning. The phenomenon ceased by degrees after four o'clock, and the bolides and falling stars became less frequent; but we still distinguished some towards the northeast by their whitish light, and the rapidity of their movement, a quarter of an hour after sun-rise. This circumstance will appear less extraordinary, when I bring to the reader's recollection, that in full daylight, in 1788, the interior of the houses in the town of [40 Popayan was brightly illuminated by an aerolite of immense magnitude. It passed over the town, when the sun was shining clearly at one o'clock. M. Bonpland and myself, during our second residence at Cumana, after having observed on the 26th of September, 1800, the immersion of the first satellite of Jupiter, succeeded in seeing the planet distinctly with the naked eye, eighteen minutes after the disk of the sun had appeared in the horizon. There was a very slight vapour in the east, but Jupiter appeared on an azure sky. These facts prove the extreme purity and transparency of the atmosphere under the torrid zone. The mass of diffused light is so much less, as the vapours are more perfectly dissolved. The same cause that weakens [50 the diffusion of the solar light, diminishes the extinction of that which emanates either from a *bolis*, Jupiter, or the moon seen on the second day after her conjunction.

"These bolides were seen at Weimar, Germany; and at Herrenhut, in Greenland. The distance from Weimar to the Rio Negro, is 1800 sea leagues; and from Rio Negro to Herrenhut, in Greenland, 1300 leagues. Admitting that the same fiery meteors were seen at points so distant from each other, we must also admit that their height was at least 411 leagues. But in the New World, between the meridians of forty-six degrees and eighty-two degrees, between the equator, and sixty-four degrees north, [60 at the same hour, an immense number of bolides and falling stars were perceived; and those meteors had every where the same brilliancy, throughout a space of 921,000 square leagues."--*Alexander de Humboldt's Personal Narrative*

---

36 but] 2; "*t*" *did not print in 1*
63 *Humboldt's*] 2; *Humbolt's* 1.

Fragment of a Poem
on
The World Before the Flood

-----+-----

The sons of God saw the daughters of men that they
were fair. *Gen*. vi. 2.

[Bp. Reginald Heber]

Fragment of a Poem
on
The World Before the Flood

----+----

There came a spirit down at eventide
To the city of Enoch, and the terrac'd height
Of Jared's palace. On his turret top
There Jared sate, the king, with lifted face
And eyes intent on Heaven, whose sober light
Slept on his ample forehead, and the locks
Of crisped silver; beautiful in age,
And (but that pride had dimm'd, and lust of war,
Those reverend features with a darker shade,)
Of saintly seeming,--yet no saintly mood,   10
No heavenward musing fix'd that stedfast eye,
God's enemy, and tyrant of mankind.
To whom that demon herald, from the wing
Alighting, spake: "Thus saith the prince of air,
Whose star flames brightest in the van of night,
Whom gods and heroes worship, all who sweep
On sounding wing the arch of nether heaven,
Or walk in mail the earth,--'Thy prayers are heard,
And the rich fragrance of thy sacrifice
Hath not been wasted on the winds in vain.   20
Have I not seen thy child, that she is fair?
Give me thine Ada, thy beloved one,

----

2 terrac'd] 1; terraced 2.
7 silver;] 1; ~ , 2.
9 shade,)] 1; ~ ^) 2.
12 mankind.] 1; ~ , 2.
20 wasted] 1; wafted 2.

And she shall be my queen; and from her womb
Shall giants spring, to rule the seed of Cain,
And sit on Jared's throne!'" Then Jared rose,
And spread his hands before the Evil Power,
And lifted up his voice and laugh'd for joy.
"Say to my Lord, Thus saith the king of men,--
Thou art my god,--thy servant I,--my child
Is as thine handmaid!--Nay, abide awhile,   30
To taste the banquet of an earthly hall,
And leave behind thy blessing!" But, in mist,
And like a vision from a waken'd man,
The cloudy messenger dissolved away,
There melting where the moonbeam brightest fell.
Then Jared turn'd, and from the turret top
Call'd on his daughter--"Haste, my beautiful!
Mine Ada, my beloved! bind with flowers
Thy coal-black hair, and heap the sacred pile
With freshest odours, and provoke the dance   40
With harp and gilded organ, for this night
We have found favour in immortal eyes,
And the great gods have bless'd us." Thus he spake,
Nor spake unheeded; in the ample hall
His daughter heard, where, by the cedar fire,
Amidst her maidens, o'er the ivory loom
She pass'd the threads of gold. They hush'd the song
Which, wafted on the fragrant breeze of night,
Swept o'er the city like the ring-dove's call;
And forth with all her damsels Ada came,   50
As mid the stars the silver-mantled moon,
In stature thus and form pre-eminent,
Fairest of mortal maids. Her father saw
That perfect comeliness, and his proud heart
In purer bliss expanded. Long he gaz'd,

---

26 Power] 1; power 2.
32 mist,] 1; ~ ^ 2.
49 ring-dove's] 1; ringdove's 2.
51 silver-mantled] 1; ~ ^ ~ 2.
55 gaz'd] 1; gazed 2.

Nor wonder deem'd that such should win the love
Of Genius or of Angel; such the cheek
Glossy with purple youth, such the large eye,
Whose broad black mirror, through its silken fringe,
Glisten'd with softer brightness, as a star   60
That nightly twinkles o'er a mountain well;
Such the long locks, whose raven mantle fell
Athwart her ivory shoulders, and o'erspread
Down to the heel her raiment's filmy fold.
She, bending first in meekness, rose to meet
Her sire's embrace, than him alone less tall,
Whom, since primoeval Cain, the sons of men
Beheld unrivalled; then, with rosy smile,
"What seeks," she said, "my father? Why remain
On thy lone tower, when from the odorous hearth   70
The sparkles rise within, and Ada's hand
Hath deck'd thy banquet?" But the king replied,--
"O fairest, happiest, best of mortal maids,
My prayer is heard, and from yon western star
Its lord hath look'd upon thee; as I sate
Watching the Heavens, a Heavenly spirit came
From him whom chiefest of the host of Heav'n
Our fathers honour'd,--whom we nightly serve
(Since first Jehovah scorn'd such sacrifice,)
With frankincense and flowers and oil and corn,   80
Our bloodless offering; him whose secret strength
Hath girded us to war, and given the world
To bow beneath our sceptre. He hath seen
My child, that she is fair, and from her womb
Shall giants spring, to rule the seed of Cain,
And sit on Jared's throne. What, silent! nay,
Kneel not to me; in loud thanksgiving kneel
To him whose choice--Now by the glorious stars
She weeps, she turns away! Unhappy child
And lingers yet thy mother's boding lore   90

---

66 tall,] 1; ~ . 2.
67 primoeval] 1; primeval 2.
68 unrivalled;] 1; unrivall'd: 2.

So deeply in thy soul? Curse on the hour
That ever Jared bore a bride away
From western Eden! Have I train'd thy youth
Untouch'd by mortal love, by mortal eyes
Seen and ador'd far off, and in the shrine
Of solemn majesty reserv'd, a flower
Of guarded paradise, whom men should praise,
But angels only gather? Have I toil'd
To swell thy greatness, till our brazen chain
From furthest Ararat to ocean's stream   100
Hath bound the nations? And when all my vows
At length are crown'd, and Heav'n with earth conspires
To yield thee worship, dost thou then rebel,
And hate thy happiness? Bethink thee, maid,
E'er yet thine answer, not to be recalled,
Hath pass'd those ivory gates--bethink thee well.
Who shall recount the blessings which our gods
Have richly lavish'd on the seed of Cain?
And who, if stung by thine ingratitude,
Can meet their vengeance?" Then the maiden rose, 110
And folding on her breast her ivory arms,
"Father," she said, "thou deem'st thy warrior gods
Are mighty,--One above is mightier:
Name Him, they tremble. Kind, thou call'st them;
Lavish of blessings. Is that blessedness
To sin with them? to hold a hideous rule,
Water'd with widows' tears and blood of men,
O'er those who curse our name? Thy bands went forth,
And brought back captives from the palmy side
Of far Euphrates. One thou gavest me,   120
A woman for mine handmaid; I have heard
Her mournful songs as, in the strangers' land
She wept and plied the loom. I question'd her:
Oh, what a tale she told! And are they good,--
The gods whose work these are! They are not good,--
And, if not good, not gods. But there is One,
I know, I feel, a good, a Holy One,
The God who fills my heart, when, with glad tears,
I think upon my mother; when I strive
To be like her, like her to soothe thy cares   130

With perfect tenderness. O father, king,
Most honour'd, most belov'd, than Him alone
Who gives us all less worshipp'd! at thy feet
I lowly cast me down; I clasp thy knees,
And, in her name whom most of womankind
Thy soul hath bless'd, by whose bed of death
In short-liv'd penitence thy sorrow vow'd
To serve her God alone,--forgive me now
If I resemble her!" But in fierce wrath
The king replied,--"And know'st thou not,weak girl,   140
Thy God hath cast us off? hath scorn'd of old
Our father's offering, driven us from His face,
And mark'd us for destruction? Can thy prayer
Pierce through the curse of Cain--thy duty please
That terrible One, whose angels are not free
From sin before Him?" Then the maiden spake:
"Alas! I know mine own unworthiness,
Our hapless race I know. Yet God is good;
Yet is He merciful: the sire of Cain
Forgiveness found, and Cain himself, though steep'd   150
In brother's blood, had found it, if his pride
Had not disdain'd the needful sacrifice,
And turn'd to other masters. One shall be,
In after times, my mother wont to tell,
Whose blood shall help the guilty. When my soul
Is sick to death, this comfort lingers here,
This hope survives within me; for His sake,
Whose name I know not, God will hear my prayer,
And, though He slay me, I will trust in Him."
Here Ada ceas'd, for from her father's eye   160
The fire flash'd fast, and on his curling lip
The white foam trembled. "Gone," he cried, "all gone!
My heart's desire, the labour of my youth,
Mine age's solace gone! Degenerate child,
Enemy of our gods, chief enemy
To thine own glory! What forbids my foot
To spurn thy life out, or this dreadful hand
To cast thee from the tower a sacrifice
To those whom thou hast scorn'd? Accursed be thou
Of Him thou seek'st in vain! accursed He,   170

Whose hated worship hath enticed thy feet
From the bright altars of the host of Heaven!
I curse Him--mark me well--I curse Him, Ada!
And, lo! He smiteth not!" But Ada bow'd
Her head to earth, and hid her face, and wept
In agony of prayer. "Yea," cried the king,
"Yea, let Him smite me now, for what hath life
Left worth the keeping? Yet, I thank the stars,
Vengeance may yet be mine! Look up and hear
Thy monarch, not thy father! Till this hour   180
I have spar'd thy mother's people; they have pray'd
And hymn'd, and have blasphemed the prince of air;
And, as thou saidest, they have curs'd my reign;
And I have spared them! But no longer--no!
Thyself hast lit the fire, nor Lucifer
Shall longer tax my sword for tardy zeal,
And thou shalt live to see it!" From his path
He spurn'd his prostrate child, and, groaning, wrapt
The mantle round his face, and pass'd away
Unheard of her whom, stretch'd in seeming death,   190
Her maidens tended. Oh that, in this hour
Her soul had fled indeed, nor wak'd again
To keener suffering! Yet shall man refuse
The bitter cup whose dregs are blessedness?
Or shall we hate the friendly hand which guides
To nobler triumph thro'ugh severer woe?
Thus Ada murmured, thus within her spake
(In answer to such impious murmurings)
A spirit not her own. Stretch'd on her couch
She silent lay. The maidens had retir'd   200
Observant of her rest. Her nurse alone,
Shaking and muttering with a parent's fear
Knelt by her side, and watch'd her painful breath,
And the wild horror of her fixed eye,
And long'd to hear her voice. "Peninnah! thou!
My mother is it thou?" the princess cried;
And that old woman kiss'd her feet and wept
In rapturous fondness. "Oh my child! my child!
The blessing of thy mother's mighty God
Rest on thine innocent head, and 'quite thy love   210

For those kind accents. All, my lovely one,
All may be well. Thy father doats on thee'
And, when his wrath is spent, his love, be sure
Will grant thee all thy will. Oh lamps of Heaven!
Can ye behold her thus nor pity her!
Is this your love, ye gods!" "Name not the gods,"
The princess cried, "the wretched gods of Cain;
My mother's God be mine; they are no gods
Whose fleshly fancy doats on mortal clay,
Whose love is ruin! Thinkest thou this night   220
I have first withstood their tempting? first have proved
Their utter weakness?" "Have the angels, then,
Visited thee of old?" the nurse enquired,
"Or hath thy father told thee of their love
And thou hast kept it from me?" As she spake
A bright and bitter glance of lofty scorn
Shot from the virgin's eyes. A mantling blush
Of hallowed courage darken'd on her cheek;
She waved her arm as one whose kingly state
Repels intrusion from his privacy,   230
And answered, with a calm but painful smile:
"They are beside us now! Nay quake not thus,
I fear them not' yet they are terrible--
But they are past, resist them and they flee,
And all is peace again; yet have I groan'd
Beneath such visitation, till my faith
In Him I serve hath almost pass'd away."
With that she rose, and wrapt in silent thought,
Gazed through the portal long,--then paced awhile
The marble pavement, now from side to side   240
Tossing her restless arms, now clasping close
Her hands in supplication, lifting now
Her eloquent eyes to Heaven,--then sought again
Her lowly couch, and, by the nurse's side,
Resum'd the wond'rous tale. "Oh friend,"she cried,
"And only mother now, yon silver moon
Has twenty times renew'd her course in Heaven,
Since, as my bosom o'er its girlish zone
With painful tightness rose, I bade thee change
Th'imprisoning cincture. Canst thou yet recal   250

Thy playful words of praise--thy prophecies
Of one to loose ere long that golden clasp,
A royal bridegroom? Strange to me, thy words
Sunk in my soul, and busy fancy strove
To picture forth that unknown visitant,
His form and bearing. Musing thus, and lost
In troubled contemplation, o'er my soul
A heavy slumber fell; I sank not down;
I saw, I heard, I moved; the spell was laid
Within me, and from forth my secret heart   260
A stranger's accents came: 'Oh! blessed maid!
Most beautiful, most honoured! not for thee
Be mortal marriage, nor the feeble love
Of those whose beauty is a mortal dream,
Whose age a shadow. What is man, whose day
In the poor circuit of a thousand years,
Reverts again to dust? Thee, maiden! thee
The Gods have seen; the never-dying stars
Gaze on thy loveliness, and thou shalt reign
A new Astarte. Bind thy flowing hair,   270
Brace on thy sandals, seek the myrtle grove
West of the city, and the cavern well,
Whose clear black waters from their silent spring
Ripple with ceaseless stir: thy lover there
Waits thee in secret, and thy soul shall learn
The raptures of a god! But cast away
That peevish bauble which thy mother gave,
Her hated talisman.' That word recall'd
My straggling senses, and her dying prayer
Passed through my soul like fire; the tempter fell   280
Abash'd before it, and a living voice
Of most true consolation o'er me came,
'Nor love nor fear them, Ada; love not them
Who hate thy mother's memory; fear not them
Who fear thy mother's God; for this she gave,
Prophetic of this hour, that graven gold,
Which bears the title of the Eternal One,
And binds thee to my service; guard it well,
And guard the faith it teaches; safer so
Than girt around by brazen walls, and gates   290

Of seven-fold cedar.' Since that hour, my heart
Hath kept its covenant, nor shrunk beneath
The spirits of evil; yet, not so repell'd,
They watch me in my walks, spy out my ways,
And still with nightly whispers vex my soul,
To seek the myrtle thicket. Bolder now,
They speak of duty--of a father's will,
Now first unkind--a father's kingly power,
Tremendous when opposed. My God, they say,
Bids me revere my parent: will He guard   300
A rebel daughter? Wiser to comply,
Ere force compels me to my happiness,
And to my lover yield that sacrifice
Which else my foe may seize. Oh God! great God!
Of whom I am, and whom I serve alone,
Be Thou my strength in weakness--Thou my guide,
And save me from this hour!" Thus, as she spake,
With naked feet and silent, in the cloud
Of a long mantle wrapt, as one who shuns
The busy eyes and babbling tongues of men,   310
A warrior enter'd; o'er his helm
The casque was drawn   *   *   *
*   *   *   *   *

Works Cited in Abbreviated Form

CEWJM-------- *The Works of John Milton*. Ed. Frank Allen Patterson, et al. 18 Vols. in 21. New York: Columbia UP, 1931-38.

Hughes--------Hughes, Thomas Patrick, ed. *A Dictionary of Islam* .... 1885. Lahore, W. Pakistan: Premier Books, n. d.

JTM-----------Dowden, Wilfred S., ed. *The Journal of Thomas Moore* 7 Vols. Newark: U of Del. PR, 1983-1988.

L&J------------Prothero, Rowland, Ed., ed. *The Works of Lord Byron: Letters and Journals*. 5 Vols. 1888-1901. New York: Octagon, 1966.

Letters---------Marchand, Leslie A., ed. *Byron's Letters and Journals*. 12 Volumes. Cambridge: Harvard UP, 1973-1982.

LTM--------------Dowden, Wilfred S., ed. *The Letters of Thomas Moore*. 2 Vols. Oxford: Clarendon PR, 1964.

MPW---------------Moore, Thomas. *The Poetical Works of Thomas Moore, Collected by Himself*. 10 Vols. London: Longmans, 1841-42.

OAB--------------May, Herbert G., and Bruce M. Metzger, eds. *The Oxford Annotated Bible with the Apocrypha*. New York: Oxford UP, 1975.

PW---------------Coleridge, Ernest Hartley, ed. *The Works of Lord Byron: Poetry.* 7 Vols. Rev. Ed. London: John Murray, 1901-1905.

R&D--------------Roberts, Alexander, and James Donaldson, eds. *The Ante-Nicene Fathers: Translations of the Writings of the Fathers Down to A.D. 325.* Rev. A. Cleveland Coxe. 10 Vols. 1899-1900. Grand Rapids: Eerdmans, 1967.

Russell----------Russell, John, ed. *Memoirs, Journal, and Correspondence of Thomas Moore*. 8 Vols. London: Longmans, 1853-1856.

Sale-------------Sale, George. *The Koran* .... 1734. London: Frederick Warne, 1890. [Page numbers refer to this edition. Where a page number is prefixed by an arabic numeral and a colon, the prefix refers to a section in the Preliminary Discourse.]

LXX-------------Benton, Charles Lee, ed. *The Septuagint Version of the Old Testament and Apocrypha*. ... 1851. Zondervan, 1978.

Zohar---------Sperling, Harry, and Maurice Simon, trans. *The Zohar* 5 Vols. London: Soncino, 1933.

[Efforts have been made elsewhere to introduce fuller citations in the body of the discussion or appendices, and only thereafter to abbreviate. Abbreviated forms should match the references in the References section, following.]

REFERENCES

[A. K. H. B., pseud.]. *The Critical Essays of A Country Parson*.
London: Longmans, Green, and Co., 1867.
Ali, A. Yusef, ed. *The Holy Qur'an: Text, Translation, and Commentary*.
1934. Brentwood, Md: Amana, 1983.
Al-Tabari, Abu Ja-Far Muhammad B. Jarir. *The Commentary on the
Qur'an, Being an Abridged Translation of Jami al-bayan 'an ta'wil ay
al-Qur'an*. Ed. J. Cooper. Oxford: UP, 1987.
Anderson, W. E. K., ed. *The Journal of Sir Walter Scott*.
Oxford: Clarendon PR, 1972.
"The Angel of the World, &c." *Blackwood's Edinburgh Magazine*
8 (Oct. 1820): 20-26.
"The Angel of the World; an Arabian Tale. . . ." *Ladies' Monthly Museum*
S3 12 (Oct. 1820): 215-16.
"The Angel of the World. . . ." *Literary Gazette*
19 (August 1820): 531-532.
[Anon., comp.] *The Poetical Works of Rogers, Campbell, J. Montgomery,
Lamb, and Kirke White; Complete in One Volume*.
Philadelphia: J. Grigg, 1834.
Anquetil-Duperron, Abraham. *Precis de l'Histoire Universelle*.
12 Vols. Paris, 1801.
Apuleius of Madauros. *The Isis-Book (Metamorphoses, Book XI)*.
Trans. J. Gwyn Griffiths. Leiden: E. J. Brill, 1975.
Aquinas, Thomas. *Summa Theologica*. Trans. Fathers of the English
Dominican Province. Rev. Daniel J. Sullivan. 2 Vols. Chicago:
Encyclopedia Britannica, 1952.
"Arot et Marot, and Mr. Moore's New Poem." *Edinburgh Magazine*
NS 12 (1823): 78.
*Asiatick Researches, or, Transactions of the Society Instituted in Bengal for
Inquiring into the History and Antiquities, the Arts, Sciences, and
Literature of Asia. . . .* Vol. 2. Calcutta, 1745.
---.Vol. 4. 4th ed. London, 1807.
Astruc, Jean. *Conjectures Sur les Memoires Originaux dont il Parait que
Moyse s'est Servi Pour Composer le Livre de Genese*. Paris, 1753.
Augustine. *The City of God*. Trans. Marcus Dods. Chicago:
Encyclopedia Britannica, 1952.

Acock, Roy E. "Lord Byron and Bayle's *Dictionary.*" *The Yearbook of English Studies* 5 (1975):142-152.

Baldensperger, Fernand. "Thomas Moore Et A. De Vigny." *Modern Language Review* 1 (1905/06): 290-301.

Bamberger, Bernard J. *Fallen Angels*. Philadelphia: The Jewish Publication Society of America, 1952.

Barber, Giles. "Galignani's and the Publication of English Books in France from 1800 to 1852." *The Library* S5 16 (1961): 267-286.

Bartfeld, Fernande. *Vigny et la Figure de Moise*. Collection < <Themes et Mythes> > 12. Paris: Lettres Modernes Minard, 1968.

Barton, Anne. "'A Light to Lesson Ages': Byron's Political Plays." In *Byron: A Symposium*. Ed. John D. Jump. New York: Macmillan, 1975: 138-162.

Basnage, Jacques-Christian. *Histoire des Juifs, depuis Jesus-Christ jusq'a Present. . . .* Paris: Louis Rouilland, 1710.

Baugh, Albert C., ed. *A Literary History of England*. 2nd ed. New York: Appleton-Century-Crofts, 1967.

Bayle, Pierre. *The Dictionary Historical and Critical of Mr. Pierre Bayle.*2nd Ed. Rev.by Des Maizeux. London: J. J. and P. Knapton and others, 1735.

---.*Dictionnaire Historique et Critique*. 4 Vols. Rotterdam, 1691.

Beausobre, Isaac. *Histoire Critique du Manicheisme*. 2 Vols. Amsterdam, 1734, 1739.

"Beauties of Emanuel Swedenborg. . . ." *British Critic* 1 (June 1814): 572-576.

Benton, Charles Lee, ed. *The Septuagint Version of the Old Testament and Apocrypha, with an English Translation; and with Various Readings and Critical Notes*. 1851. Zondervan, 1978.

"Berington's *Literature of the Middle Ages.*" *Edinburgh Review* Review 23 (Apr. 1814-Sept. 1814): 229-245.

Beutner, Harvey Fremont. "With Fraternal Feeling Fired: The Life and Work of James Montgomery." *DA* 28 (1967): 2200A-2001A.

Bevis, Richard. *Checklist of English Travel Books on the Mideast to 1914*. Boston: G. K. Hall, 1973.

Blackstone, Bernard. *Byron: Social Satire, Drama and Epic*. Writers and Their Work, 223. The British Council: Longman Group, 1973.

Bonaventure, St. *The Works of Bonaventure: Cardinal, Seraphic Doctor, and Saint*. Trans. Jose de Vinck. 5 Vols. Paterson, N.J.: St. Anthony Guild, 1966.

Observations; by the Rev. George Croly. New York: Edward Kearny, n.d.

---.*Historical Sketches, Speeches, and Characters.* London: R. B. Seeley and W. Burnside, 1842.

---.*The Holy Land, Syria, Idumea, Arabia, Egypt, & Nubia; from Drawings Made on the Spot by David Roberts...; with Historical Descriptions by the Rev. George Croly.* 3 Vols. London: F. G. Moor, 1842-49.

---.*The Poetical Works of the Rev. George Croly, Ll.D.* 2 Vols. London: Willis and Sotheran, 1830.

"Croly's Angel of the World." *London Magazine* 2 (1820): 542-548.

Curran, Stuart. *Poetic Form in British Romanticism.* New York: Oxford UP, 1986.

"*Cuvier On the Theory of the Earth.*" *Edinburgh Review* 23 (Oct. 1813-Jan. 1814): 454-475.

Dale, Thomas.*Access to God Faithfully Developed by the Church of England. 5 Discourses Preached before the Univ. of Cambridge in Jan. 1832.*2nd ed. London, *To Which is Added . . . A Spiritual Sermon* London, 1832.

---.*The Children of the World and the Children of Light* , n. p. 1836.

---.*The Duty of Associating Against the Profanation of the Sabbath Day.* [1841]

---.*English Language and Literature [An Introductory Lecture]* London, 1828.

---.*An Introductory Lecture Delivered in the University of London, Friday, Oct. 24, 1828.*4th ed. London, J. Taylor, 1828.

---.*An Introductory Lecture Upon the Study of Theology and the Greek Testament.* London, 1829.

---. *Irad and Adah, a Tale of the Flood; Poems; Specimens of a New Translation of the Psalms.* London: J. M. Richardson, 1822.

---.*National Religion Conducive to the Prosperity of the State; Two Sermons, Preached in the Parish, Church of St. Bride, in Aid of Trinity Church Endowment Fund, on Sunday, October 8, 1837.* London, 1837.

---.*The Poetical Works of the Rev. Thomas Dale, M.A.* London: Charles Tilt, 1836.

---.*The Widow of Nain, the Outlaw of Taurus, and Other Poems.* New and Enlarged Edition. London: Tilt and Bogue, 1842.

---, ed. *Poems: By William Cowper, with A Biographical and Critical*

Introduction, by the Rev. Thomas Dale. 2 Vols. London: W. Kent, 1859.

"Dale's Irad and Adah." *Blackwood's Edinburgh Magazine* 12 (July 1822): 61-67.

"Dale's Poems." *Blackwood's Edinburgh Magazine* 8 (October-March 1820-1821): 185-189.

Dalen (Dale), Antoine Van. *Dissertationes de Origine Ac Progressu Idolatriae et Superstitionum.* Amsterdam, 1696.

Darmesteter, James. *The Zend-Avesta.* 3 Vols. The Sacred Books of the East. 1898 Delhi: Motilal Banarsidass, 1965.

Davidson, Gustav. *A Dictionary of Angels Including the Fallen Angels.* New York: Free Press, 1967.

Davidson, Robert. *Genesis 1-11.* The Cambridge Bible Commentary: The New English Bible. Cambridge: UP, 1973.

De Ford, Miriam A. *Thomas Moore.* Twayne's English Authors Series, 38. New York: Twayne, 1967.

Denys L'Areopagite. *De La Hierarchie Celeste.* [With notes by Jean Pachymere.] 2 Vols. Paris, 1644.

Diderot, Denis, et al, eds. *Encyclopedie, ou Dictionnaire Raissone des Sciences, des Arts et des Metiers, Par Une Societe de Gens de Lettres.* Paris: Briasson, David, Le Breton, & Durand, 1751.

Dionysius Areopagite, [Pseudo-,]. *The Divine Names and Mystical Theology.* Tr. John D. Jones. Mediaeval Philosophical Texts in Translation, 21. Milwaukee: Marquette UP, 1980.

Dionysius the Areopagite. *The Mystical Theology and the Celestial Hierarchies of Dionysius the Areopagite.* Trans. The Editors of the Shrine of Wisdom. 2nd ed. Surrey: The Shrine of Wisdom, 1965.

Dix, G. H. "The Enochic Pentateuch." *Journal of Theological Studies* 1st Ser. 27 (1926): 29-42.

Doolittle, James. *Alfred de Vigny.* Twayne's World Authors Series 18. New York: Twayne, 1967.

Dowden, Wilfred S., ed. *The Journal of Thomas Moore.* 7 Vols. Newark: U of Delaware PR, 1983-89.

---, ed. *The Letters of Thomas Moore.* 2 Vols. Oxford: Clarendon PR, 1964.

Dundes, Alan, ed. *The Flood Myth.* Berkeley: U of Calif. PR, 1988.

"Dunlop's *History of Fiction.*" *Edinburgh Review* 24 (Nov. 1814-Feb. 1815): 38-58.

Dupuis, Charles-Francois. *Origine de Tous les Cultes ou Religion*

Universelle. 3 Vols. Paris, 1795.

Edwardes, Allen. *Erotica Judaica: A Sexual History of the Jews*. New York: Julian Press, 1967.

Ehrstine, John W. *The Metaphysics of Byron: A Reading of the Plays*. The Hague: Mouton, 1976.

Eimer, Manfred. "Das Apokryphe Buch Henoch und Byrons Mysterien." *Englische Studien* 44 (Sept. 1911): 18-31.

"The Epic and the Romantic." *London Magazine* NS 6 (1826): 309-314.

Epstein, I., ed. *The Babylonian Talmud*. 14 Vols. London: Soncino Press, 1938-48.

Erdman, David V. "Treason Trials in the Early Romantic Period." *Wordsworth Circle* 19 (1988): 67-70.

Esteve, Edmond. *Byron et le Romantisme Francais: Essai Sur la Fortune et l'Influence de l'Oeuvre de Byron en France 1812 a 1850*. 2nd ed. Paris, 1929. Geneva: Slatkine Reprints, 1973.

Fabre, Jean. *Lumieres et Romantisme: Energie et Nostalgie de Rousseau a Mickiewicz*. Paris: Librairie C. Klincksieck, 1963.

Feldman, Burton, and Robert D. Richardson, eds. *The Rise of Modern Mythology*. Bloomington: Indiana UP, 1972.

Filastrii Episcopi Brixiensis. *Diversarum Hereseon Liber*. Ed. F. Heylen. Corpus Christianorum, Series Latina. Turnholt: Typographi Brepols Editores Pontificii, 1957.

Fitzpatrick, William P. "Byron's Mysteries: The Paradoxical Drive toward Eden." *Studies in English Literature* 15 (1975): 615-625.

Fonblanque, Albany. "The Liberal No. II." *The Examiner*, 29 Dec. 1822: 818-822.

Fortescue, William. *Alphonse de Lamartine: A Political Biography*. New York: St. Martin's Press, 1987.

Fourmont, Etienne. *Memorie Istoriche Sopra il Sabiismo*. Venice, 1749.

---.*Reflexions sur l'Origine, l'Histoire et la Succession des Anciens Peuples Chaldeens, Hebreux, Pheniciens, Egyptiens, Grecs, &c., Jusqu'au Temps de Cyrus*. 2nd ed. 2 Vols. Paris: Chez de Bure l'Aine, 1747.

Gaster, Theodor H. *Thespis: Ritual, Myth, and Drama in the Ancient Near East*. 2nd ed. 1961. New York: Harper & Row, 1966.

Gataker, Thomas. *Miscellaneous Annotations Upon All the Books of The Old and New Testament*. London, 1645.

Gatje, Helmut. *The Qur'an and its Exegesis: Selected Texts with Classical and Modern Interpretations*. Trans. Alford T. Welch. Berkeley: U of Calif. PR, 1976.

Gay, Peter. *The Enlightenment: An Interpretation. Vol. I: The Rise of Modern Paganism.* New York: Norton, 1977.

---.*The Enlightenment: An Interpretation. Vol. II: The Science of Freedom.* New York: Norton, 1977.

"Geology of the Deluge." *Edinburgh Review* 39 (Oct. 1823-Jan. 1824): 196-234.

George, Albert Joseph. *Lamartine and Romantic Unanism.* 1940. New York: AMS, 1966.

Gilfillan, George. "Dr. George Croly." *The Eclectic Magazine of Foreign Literature, Science and Art* 14 (Aug. 1848): 459-65.

---."James Montgomery." *Tait's Edinburgh Magazine* NS 13 (Sept. 1846): 545-58.

Gill, Charles, ed. *The Book of Enoch, the Prophet, Translated from an Ethiopic Ms. in the Bodleian Library, by the Late Richard Laurence.* London: K. Paul Trench, 1883.

Ginsburg, Christian D., trans. and ed. *Jacob Ben Chajim Ibn Adonija's Introduction to the Rabbinic Bible... and The Massoreth Ha-Massoreth of Elias Levita, Being an Exposition of the Massoretic Notes on the Hebrew Bible,or, The Ancient Critical Apparatus of the Old Testament.* Introd. Norman H. Snaith. New York: KTAV, 1968.

Gleckner, Robert F. *Byron and the Ruins of Paradise.* Westport, Conn.: Greenwood PR, 1967.

Goetsch, Paul. "Linguistic Colonialism and Primitivism: The Discovery of Native Languages and Oral Traditions in Eighteenth-Century Travel Books and Novels." *Anglia* 106 (1988): 338-359.

Goode, Clement Tyson. *Byron as Critic.* Weimar: R. Wagner Sohn, 1923.

Gordon, Cyrus H. *The Common Background of Greek and Hebrew Civilizations.* 1962. New York: Norton, 1965.

Goslee, Nancy Moore. *Uriel's Eye: Milton's Stationing and Statuary in Blake, Keats, and Shelley.* University, Al: U of Al PR, 1985.

Graves, Robert and Raphael Patai. *Hebrew Myths: The Book of Genesis.* New York: Greenwich House, 1983.

Greenslade, S.L., ed. *The Cambridge History of the Bible: Vol.III: The West from the Reformation to the Present Day.* Cambridge: UP, 1963.

Grelot, Pierre. "La Geographie Mythique d'Henoch et Ses Sources Orientales." *Revue Biblique* 65 (1958):33-69.

Grillet, Claudius. *La Bible dans Lamartine.* Lyon: Emmanuel Vitte, 1938.

Gry, L. "Quelques Noms d'Anges et d'Etres Mysterieux en II Henoch." *Revue Biblique* 49 (1940): 447-452.

Gudde, E.G. "Traces of English Influence in Freilgrath's Political and Social Lyrics." *Journal of English and Germanic Philology* 20 (1921): 335-370.

Guillemin, Henri. *Conaissance de Lamartine.* Fribourg: Editions de la Librarie de l'Universite, 1942.

Hastings, James, ed. *Dictionary of the Bible.* Rev. Ed. New York: Scribner's, 1963.

Halevy, J. "Recherches Sur la Langue de la Redaction Primitive du Livre d'Henoch." *Journal Asiatique* 69 (1867): 352-95.

Hartshorne, Charles and William L. Reese, eds. *Philosophers Speak of God.* Chicago: U of Chicago PR, 1958.

Hayden, John O. *The Romantic Reviewers, 1802-1824.* Chicago: U of Chicago PR, 1969.

Hazlitt, William. *Lectures on the English Poets [and] The Spirit of the Age.* Introd. Catherine Macdonald Maclean. New York: Dutton, 1967.

"*Heaven and Earth.*" *Literary Chronicle* 4 (Jan. 1823): 871.

"Heaven and Earth, A Mystery." *Blackwood's Edinburgh Magazine* 13 (Jan.-June 1823): 72-77.

"Heaven and Earth: A Mystery." *New Monthly Magazine* 2nd Ser. 7 (1823): 353-358.

Heber, Amelia. *The Life of Reginald Heber . . . by His Widow, with Selections from His Correspondence, Unpublished Poems and Private Papers: Together with A Journal of His Tour in Norway, Sweden, Russia, Hungary and Germany, and A History of the Cossacks.* 2 Vols. London: John Murray, 1830.

Heber, Reginald. *Bishop Heber in Northern India: Selections from Heber's Journal.* Ed. M. A. Laird. Cambridge: UP, 1971.

---.*India A Hundred Years Ago: A Narrative of a Journey Through the Upper Provinces of India from Calcutta to Bombay 1824-1825 and Account of a Journey to Madras and the Southern Provinces, by Bishop Heber D.D.* Abriged and ed. Anthony X. Soares. Bombay: Longmans Green and Co., 1927.

---.*The Poetical Works of Reginald Heber, Lord Bishop of Calcutta.* London: John Murray, 1845.

Henning, John. "Thomas Moore as Theologian." *Irish Monthly* 75 (1947): 114-24.

Herbelot de Molainville, Barthelemy d'. *Bibliotheque Orientale, ou Dictionnaire Universel Contenant Tout ce Qui Regarde la Connaissance des Peuples de l'Orient.* 1697. Paris:

A. Maestrich, 1776.

Herbert, Beda. "Thomas Moore, Apologist." *Irish Monthly* 80 (1952): 48-52.

"High Church Opinions on Popular Education." *Edinburgh Review* 48 (Apr. 1825-Aug. 1825): 206-223.

Hobbes, Thomas. *Leviathan*. Ed. Nelle Fuller. Chicago: Encyclopedia Britannica, Inc., 1952.

Hobhouse, John Cam (1st Baron Broughton). *A Journey Through Albania and Other Provinces of Turkey in Europe and Asia, to Constantinople, During the Years 1809 and 1810*. London, 1813.

Holland, John, and James Everett, eds. *Memoirs of the Life and Writings of James Montgomery*. 2 Vols. London: Longman, 1854-56.

Hook, Theodore. "The Loves of the Angels." *John Bull* 12 (Jan. 1823): 14.

Hughes, Thomas Patrick, ed. *A Dictionary of Islam, Being, A Cyclopaedia of the Doctrines, Rites, Ceremonies, and Customs, Together with the Technical and Theological Terms, of the Muhammedan Religion*. 1885. Lahore, W. Pakistan: Premier Books, n. d.

"Humboldt, *Researches*." *Edinburgh Review* 24 (Nov. 1814-Feb. 1815): 133-137.

Hyde, Thomas. *Historia Religionis Veterum Persarum*. Oxford, 1700.

Idel, Moshe. *Kabbalah: New Perspectives*. New Haven: Yale UP, 1988.

"*Irad and Adah* . . . . " *Literary Gazette*, 301 (1822) :674-75.

"*Irad and Adah, a Tale of the Flood* . . . By Thomas Dale, of Bene't College, Cambridge . . . . " *The Monthly Review* 99 (1822): 241-46.

Jablonski, Paul Ernest. *Pantheon Aegyptiorum, Sive de Diis Eorum Commentarius, Cum Prolegomenis de Religione et Theologia Aegyptiorum*. 3 Vols. Berlin, 1750-1752.

James, E. O. *The Ancient Gods*. New York: Putnam's, 1960.

"James Montgomery." *Dublin University Magazine* 48 (Aug. 1856): 215-34.

"James Montgomery." *Littell's Living Age* 47 (Nov. 1855): 283-88.

Jeffrey, Francis. "*Loves of the Angels*--Moore *and* Byron." *The Edinburgh Review* 38 (Feb. 1823): 27-48.

"*Joannis Miltoni*, Angli, de Doctrina Christiana . . . , translated by Charles R. Sumner . . . , 1825." *Edinburgh Review* 42 (Apr. 1825-Aug. 1825): 304-346.

Johnson, Samuel. *The History of Rasselas: Prince of Abissinia*. Ed. Geoffrey Tillotson and Brian Jenkins. London: Oxford UP, 1971.

Jones, Howard Mumford. *The Harp that Once--A Chronicle of the Life of Thomas Moore.* New York: Henry Holt, 1937.

Jones, Sir William. *Poems, Consisting Chiefly of Translations from the Asiatick Languages; to which are Added Two Essays: I. On the Poetry of the Eastern Nations; II. On the Arts, Commonly Called Imitative.* Oxford, 1772.

Jordan, Hoover H. *Bolt Upright: The Life of Thomas Moore.* Romantic Reassessment, 38. Salzburg: Institut fur Englische Sprache und Literatur, 1975.

---."Byron and Moore." *Modern Language Quarterly* 9 (1948): 429-39.

Josephus. *Josephus.* Trans. H. St. J. Thackeray. 9 Vols. Cambridge: Harvard UP, 1927.

Josephus. *The Works of Flavius Josephus, Complete and Unabridged.* Trans. William Whiston. Peabody, Mass.: Hendrickson, 1982.

Joseph, M. K. *Byron the Poet.* London: Victor Gollancz, 1964.

Jung, Leo. *Fallen Angels in Jewish, Christian and Mohammedan Literature.* 1926. New York: KTAV, 1974.

Kerrigan, Alexander O.F.M. *St. Cyril of Alexandria: Interpreter of the Old Testament.* Rome: Pontificio Instituto Biblico, 1956.

Kirby, Thomas A. "Irving and Moore: A Note on Anglo-American Literary Relations." *Modern Language Notes* 62 (1947): 251-255.

Knibb, M. A. *The Ethiopic Book of Enoch.* 2 Vols. Oxford: UP, 1978.

Knight, G. Wilson. *Lord Byron: Christian Virtues.* Oxford: UP, 1943.

Koeppel, E. "Die Engel Harut und Marut in der Englischen Dichtung." *Englische Studien* 37 (Sept. 1906): 461-462.

Koontz, Dean R. *Strangers.* New York: Putnam's, 1986.

Kraeling, E. C. "The Significance and Origin of Gen. 6:1-4." *Journal of Near Eastern Studies* 6 (1947): 193-205.

Kurth, Burton O. *Milton and Christian Heroism: Biblical Epic Themes and Forms in Seventeenth-Century England.* U of Cal. Publications, English Studies: 20. Berkeley: U of Cal PR, 1959.

Lalande, Joseph-Jerome Le Francois de. *Astronomie.* 3 Vols. Paris, 1764.

Lamartine, Alphonse de. *Lamartine: Oeuvres Choisies .... Avec une Biographie par Maurice Levailland.* Paris: Librarie A. Hatier, 1925.

---.*Oeuvres Poetiques.* Ed. Marius-Francois Guyard. Bibliotheque de la Pleiade, 65. Brussels: Editions Gallimard, 1965.

---.*Oeuvres Poetiques de Lamartine.* Paris: La Societe Proprietaire des Oeuvres de Lamartine, 1921.

---.*Souvenirs, Impressions, Pensees et Paysages, Pendant un Voyage en*

Orient (1832-1833). 2 Vols. Paris, 1835.

Lamb, Charles. *The Essays of Elia*. Introd. Henry Morley and Alfred Ainger. New York: A.L. Burt, 1885.

La Mothe Le Vayer, Francois de. *Hexameron Rustique, ou Six Journees Passees a la Campagne*. Paris, 1670.

Landor, Walter Savage. *Gebir* [1798]. In *The Poetical Works of W. S. Landor*. Ed. Stephen Wheele. 3 Vols. Oxford: UP, 1937. 1: 1-55.

"Lane's Selections from the Kur'an . . . ." *Eclectic Review* 19 (March 1846): 375-378.

Langles, Louis-Matthieu. *Notices et Eclairissements Sur Le Voyage de Norden*. Paris, 1802.

Laurence, Richard. *Translation of the Book of Enoch, from the Ethiopic MS in the Bodleian Library*. Oxford, 1821.

Lavater, Lewes. *Of Ghostes and Spirites Walking by Nyght*. 1572. Ed. J. Dover Wilson and May Yardley. Oxford: UP, 1929.

Lewis, Jack P. *A Study of the Interpretations of Noah and the Flood in Jewish and Christian Literature*. Leiden: E. J. Brill, 1968.

"The Liberal: Verse and Prose from the South." *The Literary Chronicle and Weekly Review* 5 (4 Jan. 1823): 8-11.

Lightfoot, John. *The Works of John Lightfoot*. 2 Vols. London, 1684.

Lim, Paulino M., Jr. *The Style of Lord Byron's Plays*. Salzburg: Universität Salzburg, 1973.

"Literary Notices: *The Flood of Thessaly* . . . . By Barry Cornwall [Bryan Procter Waller.]" *The Examiner*, May 1823.

"Literary Review: The World Before the Flood." *Theatrical Inquisitor* 3 (Aug. 1813): 38-43.

Locke, John. *An Essay Concerning Human[e] Understanding*. Ed. Alexander Campbell Fraser. Chicago: Encyclopedia Britannica, 1952.

Lombard, Charles. *Lamartine*. Twayne's World Authors Series, 254. New York: Twayne, 1973.

"Lord Byron and Thomas Moore." *The Times* 3 Jan. 1823: 3.

Looper, Travis. *Byron and the Bible: A Compendium of Biblical Usage in the Poetry of Lord Byron*. Metuchen, N.J.: Scarecrow Press, 1978.

Lovell, Ernest J., Jr. *Byron: The Record of A Quest*. 1949. Hamden, Conn.: Archon Books, 1966.

"The Loves of the Angels." *Blackwood's Edinburgh Magazine* 13 (Jan.-June 1823): 63-71.

"*The Loves of the Angels*, a Poem, by Thomas Moore." *Eclectic Review* 2nd

Ser. 19 (March 1823): 210-217.

"'The Loves of the Angels,' a poem. By Thomas Moore." *North American Review* 16 (1823): 353-365.

Mackey, Herbert O. *The Life of Thomas Moore, Ireland's National Poet.* 4th ed. Dublin: Apollo Press, 1952.

Macknight, James. *A New Literal Translation from the Original Greek of all the Apostolical Epistles.* London, 1795.

MacManus, M.J. "A Bibliography of Thomas Moore." *Dublin Magazine* 8 (1833): 55-61.

Macrobius [,Ambrosius Aurelius Theodosius]. *Commentary on the Dream of Scipio.* Trans. William Harris Stahl. New York: Columbia UP, 1952.

MacWhite, Eoin. "Thomas Moore and Nineteenth-Century Russian Literature." *Escape* 3 (1971): 208-216.

---."Thomas Moore and Poland." *Proceedings of the Royal Irish Academy* 72 (1972): 49-62.

Manuel, Frank E. *The Eighteenth Century Confronts the Gods.* Cambridge: Harvard UP, 1959.

Marchand, Leslie A., ed. *Byron's Letters and Journals.*12 Vols. Cambridge: The Belknap Press of Harvard UP, 1973-1982.

---.*Byron: A Portrait.* Aylesbury: Futura, 1971.

---.*Byron's Poetry: A Critical Introduction.* Boston: Houghton Mifflin, 1965.

Maimonides, Moses. *The Guide for the Perplexed.* Trans. M. Friedlander. 2nd ed. 1904. New York: Dover, 1956.

Mariti, Giovanni. *Viaggi per l'Isola de Cipro e Per la Soria e Palestine* . . . . Lucca, 1769-1776.

---.*Del Vino Cipro* . . . . Firenze, 1772.

Marshall, William H. *Byron, Shelley, Hunt, and "The Liberal."* Philadelphia: U of Penn PR, 1960.

---.*The Structure of Byron's Major Poems.* Philadelphia: U of Penn PR, 1962.

Martin, Philip W. *Byron: A Poet Before His Public.* Cambridge: UP, 1982.

May, Herbert G., and Bruce M. Metzger, eds. *The Oxford Annotated Bible, with the Apocrypha.* New York: Oxford UP, 1973.

McGann, Jerome J. *Fiery Dust: Byron's Poetic Development.* Chicago: U of Chicago PR, 1968.

McGowan, Randall. "'He Beareth Not the Sword in Vain': Religion and

the Criminal Law in Eighteenth-Century England." *Eighteenth-Century Studies* 21 (1987/88):192-211.
"Memoir of James Montgomery." *The European Magazine and London Review* 87 (1825): 5-17.
Migne, J.P., ed. *Patrologiae Cursus Completus, Accurante.* Greek Series. Paris, 1859-1866.
---, ed. *Patrologiae Cursus Completus, Accurante.* Latin Series. Paris, 1844-1855.
Milik, J. T. "Fragments Grecs du Livre d'Henoch." *Chronique d'Egypte* 40 (1971): 321-343.
---. "Problemes de la Litterature Henocique a la Lumiere des Fragments Arameens de Qumran." *Harvard Theological Review* 64 (1971): 333-378.
Milton, John. *Complete Poems and Major Prose.* Ed. Merritt Y. Hughes. New York: Odyssey Pr., 1957.
---.*The Works of John Milton.* Ed. Frank Allen Patterson et al. 18 Vols in 21. New York: Columbia Univ. Pr.,1931-38.
Monk, Samuel H. *The Sublime.* 1935. Rev. Intro. Ann Arbor: U of Mich. PR, 1960.
Montfaucon de Villars, Abbe Nicolas. *Le Comte de Gabalis, ou Entretiens Sur Les Sciences Secretes.* Paris: C. Barbin, 1670.
Montgomery, James. *Lectures on General Literature, Poetry, &c.: Delivered at the Royal Institution in 1830 and 1831.* New York: Harper & Brothers, 1855.
---.The Poetical Works of James Montgomery. 4 Vols.London: Longman, Rees, Orme, Brown, & Green, 1828.
---.*The Poetical Works of James Montgomery, Collected by Himself.* 4 Vols. London: Longman, 1841.
---.*The Poetical Works of James Montgomery, With a Memorial.* 5 Vols. in 2. Boston: Houghton, Osgood, and Co., 1879.
---.*The World Before the Flood, a Poem, in Ten Cantos; With Other Occasional Pieces.* London: Longman, Hurst, Rees, Orme, and Brown, 1813.
---.*The World Before the Flood, A Poem, in Ten Cantos; With Other Occasional Pieces.* 3rd ed. London: Longman, Hurst, Rees, Orme, and Brown, 1814.
"Montgomery's *Lectures On Poetry, &c.*" *The Eclectic Review* NS 10 (July 1833): 1-21.
"Monthly Register: Poetry and the Drama [on *The Angel of the World*]."

New Monthly Magazine 14 (Oct. 1820): 454-455.

Moore, George Foote. *Judaism*. 2 Vols. Oxford: Clarendon PR, 1927.

[Moore, Thomas, auth., anon.] "Boyd's *Translations from the Fathers*." *Edinburgh Review* 24 (Nov. 1814-Feb. 1815): 58-72.

[Moore, Thomas, auth. orig.] *Die Liebe Der Engel; Gedicht von Thomas Moore, Auf Dem Englishchen Uberfest, von [Trans.] Balduin*. Berlin: Enslin'fachen Buchhandlung, 1829.

Moore, Thomas. *The Loves of the Angels, A Poem*. London: Longman, Hurst, Rees, Orme, and Brown, 1823. [1822].

---.*The Loves of the Angels, A Poem*. 2nd ed. London: Longman, Hurst, Rees, Orme, and Brown, 1823.

---.*The Loves of the Angels, A Poem*. 4th ed. London: Longman, Hurst, Rees, Orme, and Brown, 1823.

---.*The Loves of the Angels, An Eastern Romance*. 5th ed. London: Longman, Hurst, Rees, Orme, and Brown, 1823.

---.*The Poetical Works of Thomas Moore, Collected by Himself*. 10 Vols. London: Longman, Orme, Brown, Green, and Longmans, 1840-1841.

---.*The Poetical Works of Thomas Moore, Collected by Himself*. 10 vols. London: Longman, Green, and Longmans, 1852.

---.*The Poetical Works of Thomas Moore, Collected by Himself.10 Vols. in 1*. Boston: Phillips, Sampson, and Co., 1858.

---.*The Poetical Works of Thomas Moore, Collected by Himself*. 10 vols. London: Longman, Green, Longman, and Roberts, 1860.

---.*The Poetical Works of Thomas Moore*. Ed. A. D. Godley. 1910. London: Oxford UP, 1920.

---.*Travels of an Irish Gentleman in Search of A Religion*. London: Longmans, 1833.

Mulvaney, G. F. "Recollections of Moore." *Dublin University Magazine* 39 (1852): 477-496.

Murray, Patrick. *The Poetical Genius of Thomas Moore*. Cork: Mulcahy, 1856.

"News from Parnassus. No. XXII. The Loves of the Angels, a Poem; by Thomas Moore.--Heaven and Earth, A Mystery." *The Monthly Magazine* 55 (1823): 35-39.

Niebuhr, Carsten. *Beschreibung von Arabien . . . .* Engl. Trans. as *Travels Through Arabia and Other Countries in the East*. 2 Vol. Edinburgh, 1792.

"Oldmixon in 'The Liberal.' No II." *The Edinburgh Magazine, and*

Literary Miscellany NS 12 (Jan.-June 1823): 9.

Oden, Robert A., Jr. *The Bible Without Theology: The Theological Tradition and Alternatives to It.* San Francisco: Harper & Row, 1987.

Ouseley, Sir William. *Persian Miscellanies, an Essay to Facilitate the Reading of Persian Manuscripts . . . .* London, 1795.

---.*The Oriental Collections . . . .* London, 1797-1799.

---.*The Oriental Geography of Ebn Haukal . . . .*London, 1800.

---.*Travels in Various Countries of the East, More Particularly Persia.* 3 Vols. London, 1743-1745.

"P." "On the Pernicious Tendency of Novel Reading." *The Christian Remembrancer* 5 (1823): 341.

Passmore, John. *The Perfectibility of Man.* New York: Scribner's, 1970.

Pfeiffer, Charles F. *Old Testament History.* Grand Rapids: Baker, 1973.

Philo. *Philo.* Trans. F.H. Colson and G.H. Whitaker. 10 Vols. CambridgeA: Harvard UP, 1958.

---.*Philo: Supplement I: Questions and Answers on Genesis.* Trans. Ralph Marcus. Cambridge: Harvard UP, 1953.

Pico della Mirandola, Giovanni. *On the Dignity of Man.* Trans. Elizabeth Livermore Fuller. In *The Renaissance Philosophy of Man.* Ed. Ernst Cassirer, Paul Oskar Kristeller, and John Herman Randall, Jr. Chicago: U of Chicago PR, 1948.

"A Plain Introduction to the Criticism of the New Testament . . . [;reviewed with] Danger to the Bible from Licentious Criticism: Letters to Sons in the University [and other new works.]" *The Christian Remembrancer* 43 (1862): 385-421.

Plato. *The Dialogues of Plato.* Trans. Benjamin Jowett. With *The Seventh Letter.* Trans. J. Harward. Chicago: Encyclopedia Britannica, 1952.

Pliny [Gaius Plinius Secundus.] *Natural History.* Trans. H. Rackham. 10 Vols. Cambridge: Harvard UP, 1938.

Plotinus. *The Six Enneads.* Trans. Stephen McKenna and B. S. Page. Chicago: Encyclopedia Britannica, 1952.

Pococke, Richard. *A Description of the East, and Some Other Countries.* 2 Vols. London: W. Bowyer, 1743-1745.

Pope, Alexander. *The Poems of Alexander Pope.* Ed. John Butt. New Haven: Yale UP, 1963.

Prothero, Rowland E., ed. *The Works of Lord Byron: Letters and Journals.* 1898-1901. New York: Octagon, 1966.

"Providential and Prophetical Histories . . . ." *Edinburgh Review* 50

(1830): 228-334.

Purchas, Samuel. *Purchas His Pilgrimage, or Relations of the World and Religions Observed in All Ages and Places Discovered*. London, 1613.

Rad, Gerhard von. *Genesis: A Commentary*. Trans. John H. Marks. The Old Testament Library. Philadelphia: Westminster Press, 1961.

Reedy, Gerard S. *The Bible and Reason: Anglicans and Scripture in Late Seventeenth-Century England*. Philadelphia: U of Penn PR, 1984.

Reiman, Donald H., ed. *The Romantics Reviewed: Contemporary Views of the Romantic Writers*. 3 Parts in 9 Vols. New York: Garland, 1979.

"Review of New Books: The Rev. George Croly's New Poems." *Literary Gazette* 182 (July 15, 1820): 449-451.

"Review of New Publications." *The Gentleman's Magazine* 93 (Jan.-June 1823): 41-44.

"Review of New Works: Irad and Adah." *The Ladies' Monthly Museum*. NS 15 (1822): 157-161.

Reynolds, John Hamilton. "The Loves of the Angels." *London Magazine* 7 (Feb. 1823): 212-215.

Richardson, John. *A Dissertation on the Languages, Literature, and Manners of Eastern Nations[;] Originally Prefixed to a Dictionary, Persian, Arabic, and English: The Second Edition[;] to which Is Added, Part II: Containing Additional Observations[;] together with Further Remarks on A New Analysis of Ancient Mythology: In Answer to An Apology Addressed to the Aughor, by Jacob Bryant, Esq*. Oxford: Clarendon PR, 1778.

Roberts, Alexander, and James Donaldson, eds. *The Ante-Nicene Fathers: Translations of the Writings of the Fathers down to A.D. 325*. Rev. and ed. A. Cleveland Coxe. 1899-1900. Grand Rapids: Eerdmans, 1967.

Roston, Murray. *Biblical Drama in England, from the Middle Ages to the Present Day*. London: Faber and Faber, 1968.

Russell, D. S. *The Old Testament Pseudepigrapha: Patriarchs and Prophets in Early Judaism*. Philadelphia: Fortress Press, 1987.

Russell, John, Lord, ed. *Memoirs, Journal, and Correspondence of Thomas Moore*. 8 Vols. London: Longmans, 1853-56.

Rutherford, Andrew. *Byron: A Critical Study*. Stanford: UP, 1961.

Sacy, A. J. Silvestre de. "Notice du Livre d'Enoch." *Magasin Encyclopedique* 1 (1801): 382-383.

Sade, Donatien Alphonse Francois, Marquis. *Justine*. Introd. L. T. Woodward. New York: Lancer Books, 1964.

Safran, Alexandre. *The Kabbalah: Law and Mysticism in the Jewish*

Tradition. New York: Feldheim, 1975.

Sale, George, trans. *The Koran, Commonly Called the Alkoran of Mohammed, Translated into English from the Original Arabic, with Explanatory Notes Taken from the Most Approved Commentators, to which is Prefixed a Preliminary Discourse, by George Sale*. London, 1734.

---.*The Koran*. New Ed. 2 Vols. London: Thomas Tell, 1825.

---.*The Koran* . . . [with notes; without the "Preliminary Discourse"]. 5th ed. Philadelphia: J.W. Moore,1855.

---.*The Koran* . . . [with notes and Discourse.] London: Frederick Warne and Co., 1890.

Saunders, Ernest W. *Jesus in the Gospels*. Englewood Cliffs, New Jersey: Prentice-Hall, 1967.

Schaff, Philip, ed. *The Creeds of Christendom, with a History and Critical Notes*. 4th ed. 4 Vols. New York: Harper & Brothers, 1877.

Schaff, Philip and Henry Wace, eds. *Nicene and Post-Nicene Fathers of the Christian Church*. 1899. Grand Rapids: Eerdmans, 1952.

---, and ---,eds. *Nicene and Post-Nicene Fathers of the Christian Church*. 2nd Series. 15 Vols. 1890-1900. Grand Rapids: Eerdmans, 1964.

Schick, Constance Gosselin. "A Case Study of Descriptive Perversion: Theophile Gautier's Travel Literature." *Romanic Review* 78 (1988): 359-367.

Schneider, Elisabeth. "Thomas Moore and the *Edinburgh Review*." *Modern Language Notes* 61 (1946):177-179.

Schwab, Raymond. *The Oriental Renaissance: Europe's Rediscovery of India and the East, 1680-1880*. Trans. Victor Reinking and Gene Patterson-Black. New York: Columbia UP, 1984.

Scott, Jonathan. *Bahar-Danush or Garden of Knowledge, an Oriental Romance Translated from the Persic of Einaut Oolah* London, 1799.

"*A Scriptural Account of the Nature and Employment of the Holy Angels; Partly Occasioned by Two Poems, Recently Published, the Title of One and the Subject of Both Being the 'Loves of the Angels.' By Charles Spencer, A.M. Vicar of Bishop's Stortford, Hertfordshire*. 8vo. 24pp. Rivingtons. 1823." [Unsigned review.] *The Christian Remembrancer* 5 (1823): 355-57.

Sharma, Kavita A. *Byron's Plays: A Reassessment*. Salzburg: Univ. Salzburg, 1982.

Shelley, Percy Bysshe. *Shelley's Prose*. Ed. David Lee Clark. Albequerque: U of New Mexico PR, 1954.

Sibylla, Bartholomaeus, F. *Speculum Peregrinarum Quaestionum.* Rome, 1493.

Simpson, Antony E. "Social Values, Morality, and the Criminal Law in the English Romantic Era." *Wordsworth Circle* 19 (1988): 67-70.

Smiles, Samuel. *A Publisher and His Friends: Memoir and Correspondence of the Late John Murray, With an Account of the Origin and Progress of the House, 1768-1843.* 2 Vols. London: John Murray, 1891. New York: AMS, 1973.

Speiser, E. A. *Genesis.* The Anchor Bible. Garden City, N.Y.: Doubleday, 1964.

---."YDWN, Gen 6[.]3." *Journal of Biblical Literature* 75 (1956): 126-129.

Sperling, Harry, and Maurice Simon, trans. *The Zohar.* 5 Vols. London: The Soncino Press, 1933.

Spingarn, J. E., Jr. *Critical Essays of the Seventeenth Century.* 3 Vols. 1908. Bloomington: Indiana UP, 1957.

Steffan, Truman Guy, ed. *Lord Byron's Cain: Twelve Essays and a Text with Variants and Annotations.* Austin: U of Texas PR, 1968.

Stockley, W. F. P. "Moore's Satirical Verse." *Queen's Quarterly* 12 (1905): 329-346.

Strong, L. A. G. *The Mistrel Boy: A Portrait of Tom Moore.* New York: Alfred Knopf, 1937.

Strout, Alan L. "George Croly and *Blackwood's Magazine*." *Times Literary Supplement* 6 Oct. 1950: 636.

Stuart, Moses. "Sketches of Angelology in the Old and New Testament." *Bibliotheca Sacra* 1 (1843): 88-154.

Suarez, Francisco. *R.P. Francisci Suarez, E Societate Jesu, Opera Omnia*, ed. Caroli Berton. 28 Vols. Paris, 1878. Brussels: Culture et Civilisation, 1963.

---.*Theologiae R.P. Francisci Suarez.* 2 Vols. Cologne, 1732. [Part 1: *De Angelis.*]

Swedenberg, H. T., Jr. *The Theory of Epic in England, 1650-1800.* U of Cal Publications in English, 15. 1944. New York: Russell & Russell, 1972.

Swedenborg, Emanuel. *Arcana Coelestia: The Heavenly Arcana . . . Unfolded.* Trans. John Faulkner Potts. New York: American Swedenborg Printing and Publishing Society, 1919.

Taine, H. A. *History of English Literature.* Trans. N. Van Laun. 2 Vols. in 1. Chicago: M. A. Donohue, n.d.

Talfourd, Thomas Noon. "*Heaven and Earth*, and Moore, *Loves of the*

Angels." *Lady's Magazine* 2nd Ser. 4 (Jan. 1823): 19-23.

Tandon, B. G. *The Imagery of Lord Byron's Plays*. Salzburg: Universität Salzburg, 1976.

Taylor, Barbara. *Eve and the New Jerusalem: Socialism and Feminism in the Nineteenth Century*. New York: Pantheon, 1983.

Teeple, Howard M. *The Historical Approach to the Bible*. Evanston: Religion and Ethics Institute, 1982.

Terrien, Samuel. "History of the Interpretation of the Bible: III. The Modern Period." *The Interpreter's Bible*. Ed. G. A. Buttrick. New York: Abingdon Press, 1952. 1: 128-42.

Tennant, F. R. *The Sources of the Doctrines of the Fall and Original Sin*. 1903. New York: Schocken Books, 1968.

Tessier, Therese. *La Poesie Lyrique de Thomas Moore (1779-1852)*. Paris: Didier, 1976.

Thackston, W. M., Jr., trans. & ed. *Tales of the Prophets of al Kisa'i*. Boston: Twayne, 1978.

Thiard [Tyard], Pontus de. *De Recta Nominum Impositione*. Lugdunum: Jacobus Roussin, 1603.

Trueblood, Paul Graham, ed. *Byron's Political and Cultural Influence in Nineteenth-Century Europe: A Symposium*. Atlantic Heights, N.J.: Humanities Press, 1981.

Turner, James Grantham. *One Flesh: Paradisal Marriage and Sexual Relations in the Age of Milton*. Oxford: UP, 1987.

Vallat, Gustave. *Etude Sur La Vie et des Oeuvres de Thomas Moore*. Paris: Rousseau, 1886.

"A Vanishing Delusion." *The Girl's Own Annual*. London: 4 Bouvre Street, Fleet Street, ca. 1908.

Viatte, Auguste. *Les Sources Occultes du Romantisme: Illuminisme--Theosophie, 1770-1820*. 2 Vols.Paris: Librairie Honore Champion, 1965.

Vigny, Alfred de. *Oeuvres Completes*. Ed. Fernand Baldensperger. 2 Vols. Tours: Bibliotheque de la Pleiade, 1964.

Voltaire. *Philosophical Dictionary*. Trans. Peter Gay. New York: Harcourt, Brace, & World, 1962.

Walton, Brian, ed. *Biblia Sacra Polyglotta*. 6 Vols. London: Thomas Roycroft, 1653-1657. Graz, Austria: Akademische Druk.-U. Verlagsanstatt, 1963.

Ward, William S., comp. *Literary Reviews in British Periodicals, 1821-1826: A Bibliography*. New York: Garland, 1977.

Watkins, Daniel P. "Politics and Religion in Byron's *Heaven and Earth*." *The Byron Journal* 11 (1983): 30-39.

---.*Social Relations in Byron's Eastern Tales*. London and Toronto: Associated University Presses, 1987.

Weil, Karl. "Romantic Androgyny and Its Discontent: The Case of MLL De Maupin." *Romanic Review* 78 (1988): 348-358.

Wensinck, A. J. *A Handbook of early Muhammedan Traditions, Alphabetically Arranged*. Leiden: E. J. Brill, 1960.

Werner, Stephen. "Diderot, Sade, and the Gothic Novel." *Studies in Voltaire and the Eighteenth Century* 14 (1973): 273-290.

West, Paul. *Byron and the Spoiler's Art*. New York: St. Martin's Press, 1960.

Whipple, C. K. "The Claim of Infallibility for the Bible." *The Radical* 2 (1867): 359-372.

White, Terence de Vere. *Tom Moore, the Irish Poet*. London: Hamish Hamilton, 1977.

Whitehurst, John. *The Works of John Whitehurst*. London, 1792.

Whitmore, Allen Perry. *The Major Characters of Lord Byron's Dramas*. Salzburg: Universität Salzburg, 1974.

Whitridge, Arnold. *Alfred de Vigny*. 1933. New York: Kraus Reprint Co., 1973.

Wickens, G. M. "*Lallah Rookh* and the Romantic Tradition of Islamic Literature in English." *Yearbook of Comparative and General Literature* 20 (1971): 61-66.

Wiener, Joel H. *Radicalism and Freethought in Nineteenth-Century Britain: The Life of Richard Carlile*. Contributions in Labor History, 13. Westport, Conn: Greenwood PR, 1983.

Williams, Arnold. *The Common Expositor: An Account of the Commentaries on Genesis, 1527-1633*. Chapel Hill: Univ. of North Carolina Pr., 1948.

Wilson, John. "Byron's Heaven and Earth." *Blackwood's Edinburgh Magazine* 13 (Jan. 1823): 72-77.

Wilson, Joy L. C. "An Edition of Thomas Moore's *Commonplace Book*." Diss., Rice Univ., 1967.

Wolfson, Harry Austryn. *The Philosophy of the Kalam*. Cambridge: Harvard UP, 1976.

Wordsworth, William, and Samuel Taylor Coleridge. *Lyrical Ballads, 1798*. [With Preface of 1800, and "A Collation of the Enlarged Preface of 1802."] 2nd ed. Ed. W. J. B. Owen. Oxford: UP, 1969.

"*The World before the Flood*...." *British Critic* NS 2 (1814): 34-45.
"*The World before the Flood*...." *British Review* 5 (Oct. 1813): 111-123.
"*The World before the Flood*...." *Critical Review* 3 (June 1813): 618-624.
"*The World before the Flood.*" *Eclectic Review* NS 1 (May 1814): 441-456.
"*The World before the Flood; a Poem*...." *European Magazine* 64 (Sept. 1813): 235-236.
"The World before the Flood...." *Monthly Review* 73 (Feb. 1814): 144-153.
"*The World before the Flood, a Poem*...." *The Quarterly Review* 11 (Apr. 1814): 78-87.
Yates, Francis. *Giordano Bruno and the Hermetic Tradition.* New York: Random House, 1965.
Zuntz, G. "Enoch on the Last Judgment." *Journal of Theological Studies* 1st Ser. 45 (1944): 161-170.

Index

Index